ELIZABETH BACON CUSTER

AND

THE MAKING OF A MYTH

Elizabeth Bacon Custer saw herself primarily as
her husband's wife, as this self-portrait entitled *In His
Mind's Eye* indicates. Early 1870s. Courtesy of the late
John M. Carroll, of Bryan, Texas.

SHIRLEY A. LECKIE

Elizabeth Bacon Custer
and the Making
of a Myth

University of Oklahoma Press

Norman & London

BY SHIRLEY A. LECKIE

(coauthor, with William H. Leckie)
*Unlikely Warriors: General Benjamin H. Grierson
and His Family* (Norman, 1984)

(editor) *The Colonel's Lady on the Western Frontier:
The Correspondence of Alice Kirk Grierson*
(Lincoln, 1989)

Elizabeth Bacon Custer and the Making of a Myth
(Norman, 1993)

Library of Congress Cataloging-in-Publication Data

Leckie, Shirley A., 1937–
    Elizabeth Bacon Custer and the making of a myth / Shirley A.
Leckie.—1st ed.
      p. cm.
    Includes bibliographical references and index.
    ISBN 0–8061–2501–2
    1. Custer, George Armstrong, 1839–1876. 2. Custer, Elizabeth
Bacon, 1842–1933. 3. Frontier and pioneer life—West (U.S.)
4. Officers' wives—West (U.S.)—Biography. 5. United States.
Army—Military life—History—19th century. 6. Indians of North
America—Wars—1866–1895. I. Title.
E467.1.C99L4   1993
973.8'2'092—dc20
[B]   92–50717
                                        CIP

1 2 3 4 5 6 7 8 9 10

To Bill

*"Woman is a social being, created within
and by a specific society. As societies differ, so
too do women."*

Jill Julius Matthews, *Good and Mad Women*

*"Thus to argue that what happens to
women qua women is a function of what happens
to men qua men is not to postulate that women's
concerns are relative to or subsumed by those of men
but that neither can be understood without
comprehending the relationship between them."*

Marilyn Strathern, *Gender of the Gift*

*"Women have served all these centuries as
looking-glasses possessing the magic and delicious
power of reflecting the figure of man at twice
its natural size."*

Virginia Woolf, *A Room of One's Own*

Contents

Illustrations

xi

MAPS

Preface

GEORGE Armstrong Custer, during his lifetime and afterwards, inspired a wide array of responses. As Frederick Van de Water, a major biographer, notes, few men ever generated so much affection and adulation at the same time that they elicited so much hatred and loathing. There was little middle ground. More recently, Robert Utley has observed in *Cavalier in Buckskin: George Armstrong Custer and the Western Military Frontier* that the view individuals held of Custer "depended, as it still depends today, more on the beholder than the beholden."

Among Custer's major interpreters, none was more important than his wife, Elizabeth Bacon Custer. Her perception of who her husband was and what his life and death meant shaped and colored public opinion until she died. By then more than half a century had passed, and, as she intended, "tradition and history" had become "so mingled" that scholars are still untangling the skeins today.

Nonetheless, Elizabeth's unfailing devotion to commemorating her dead husband aroused my curiosity, especially since the living Custer was not the perfect husband described in her writings. I found myself wondering whether she was a masochist, a saint, or a person who had exploited her dead husband's memory in order to sell books and derive income from speeches. Preliminary research indicated that none of these judgments, taken singly or all together, sufficed. There was more to Elizabeth, but she remained strangely elusive.

Then Utley's observation renewed my hope that I might gain a greater understanding of this often baffling woman. Perhaps in Elizabeth's depiction of her dead husband one could discern her hierarchy of values and her unmet needs. If so, that would cast light on her motivation and character. To explain these, however, I had to explore her family background and the environmental influences shaping her life and thought. Finally, I wanted to know what part Elizabeth had played in the commemoration and glorification of her husband. As I delved deeper into my topic, I discovered that she had been a far greater asset to his career while he lived than scholars had previously recognized. Following his death, she played a critical role in making and sustaining the Custer myth.

I am indebted to many people. Douglas McChristian at the Little Bighorn Battlefield National Monument has assisted me with the holdings of that archive in many ways. The staff of Monroe County Historical Commission in Monroe, Michigan, especially Chris Kull and Jennifer C. Barner, gave me unfailing assistance. Students of history, such as myself, will be expressing their indebtedness to the late Sara D. Jackson of the National Archives and Records Service for decades to come. Another person who recently died is John M. Carroll of Bryan, Texas. He was a walking encyclopedia on the Custers and made available to me his hard copy of Custer Papers, which Utley had put into typescript form. George Miles, and before that, Patricia Middleton gave me a great deal of gracious assistance from the Western Americana Collection at the Beinecke Rare Book and Manuscript Library of Yale University. So too did the staff of the New York Public Library.

A work such as this builds on the efforts and skills of those who have gone before, and I am indebted to Utley, both for his scholarship, on which I have drawn heavily, and for citations he sent me. He also read a draft of this work and made valuable criticisms and suggestions. The late Sandra Myres, whose friendship I can never replace, also read a draft. So too did Glenda Riley. I have benefited greatly from their combined criticisms. Many years ago, the late Minnie Dubbs Millbrook set out to write a biography of Elizabeth Custer. While she never completed that book, I am grateful to her for her painstaking research. The late Lawrence Frost pioneered in this field, and, while he would not agree with my interpretation, his earlier study made my endeavor easier. My colleague in the Department of History at the University of Central Florida, Jerrell Shofner, read the portions of this work dealing with the Civil War and offered valuable insights.

In the Word Processing Office of the College of Arts and Sciences at the University, Karen Lynette typed the initial drafts of this manuscript many times over. The staff of the Inter-Library Loan Department, under the direction of Cheryl Walters, diligently pursued rare books, newspapers, and pamphlets with unfailing good humor. A summer fellowship awarded by the Office of Sponsored Research helped me undertake research.

Paul and Loretta Rieger of Toledo, Ohio, offered hospitality and sent me many articles and clippings. My daughter, Maria Swora, a graduate student, introduced me to a number of anthropological works on gender. Most important, my husband, William Leckie, read this manuscript over repeatedly and patiently. It was he who first suggested that I undertake this biography. Fortunately, neither of us knew at the time the difficulties involved. Finally, I want to thank John Drayton and the University of Oklahoma Press for their patience and support when the manuscript took longer to complete than anyone originally expected.

While my indebtedness is great, my mistakes are entirely my own.

SHIRLEY A. LECKIE

WINTER SPRINGS, FLORIDA

Introduction:
Myth, Gender, and
Biography

MRS. CUSTER Dead in Her 91st Year, Widow of Famous General and Indian Fighter of Post-Civil War Days," read the caption alongside Elizabeth Bacon Custer's photograph. Fifty-seven years after the Battle of the Little Bighorn, the *New York Times* of April 5, 1933, summarized the meaning of her life: "Kept His Memory Alive." As the obituary described her career, it also noted the meaning the widow had extracted from the death of George Armstrong Custer, her husband: "Perhaps it was necessary in the scheme of things, for the public clamor that rose after the battle resulted in better equipment for the soldiers everywhere, and very soon the Indian warfare came to its end."[1]

Undoubtedly most Americans who read of Elizabeth Custer's death were more concerned about the economic devastation they confronted than the passing away of a cavalryman's widow. Still, many must have shaken their heads in wonder. Had Custer's wife, born during John Tyler's presidency, survived until one month after Franklin Delano Roosevelt's inauguration initiated the New Deal? For years, doormen at the cooperative at 71 Park Avenue had greeted the tiny, shriveled old woman, hobbling along with her cane during good weather. Neighborhood policemen in the fashionable Murray Hill district had helped her cross the street so she could walk alongside the Doral Hotel before returning home.[2]

In the few years before her death, Elizabeth had received only occasional notice. Writer Frazier Hunt, in 1931, during a "New York Life Radio Hour" devoted to her husband, had touched briefly on his widow. She had put her life back together after the general's death by writing "bravely and magnificently of the west and of soldier life," and her books still inspired young boys.[3] Another writer, John B. Kennedy, after interviewing Elizabeth in

1927, had described her as a throwback to the Victorian era. When she appeared with her white hair in tendrils and wearing a lavender silk dress, she reminded him of "a benign character from Thackeray or Dickens" as she sat in her parlor.[4]

Whether forgotten or remembered, however, this throwback to another era played a continuing role in national life. More than any other person, save George Armstrong Custer himself, she had shaped the view her compatriots held of her soldier husband. When she died, most of her fellow citizens still saw him as a national hero. Throughout her long years of widowhood, she had devoted herself to perpetuating an idealized version of her husband's character. Her purpose, stated over and over, had been to transform him into a boy's hero. In that way, she had sought to inspire youth to become what she claimed he had been. She performed her self-appointed task so well that even today she remains one of her country's little-known but most successful mythmakers.

The term "myth" demands clarification. A pioneering work defines it as "an intellectual construction that fuses concept and emotion into an image."[5] Another historian, building on that insight, reminds his reader: "Myths exist only in our minds. They are, in effect, the fusion of what we see with what we want to see, the end product being that reality upon which we act, what we *believe* we see. In cultural terms, they are ingrained beliefs shared by the whole society."[6]

These explanations help to explain Elizabeth Custer's life and work. Still, one other definition of myth seems particularly applicable to this woman. One scholar uses the term "in an anthropological sense as referring to the underlying beliefs and wish-related knowledge of who we are, what the world is, and how it works and has worked.[7] Elizabeth Custer had written of her husband on the basis of her "underlying beliefs and wish-related knowledge." Because her personal needs dovetailed with the separate needs of many of her fellow countrymen and women, they received her message warmly.

Historians have noted that the Little Bighorn occurred at a time when Americans, mired in an age of unprecedented corruption and facing a severe depression, needed desperately to extract heroic lessons from that tragedy. The public identified Custer with both the recent Civil War and the westward movement. His death during a last stand in which he and his men faced overwhelming odds quickly transformed him into a martyred symbol of self-sacrificing patriotism.[8]

Nonetheless, more was needed to assure the boy general's heroic stature. From youth until death, Custer had spawned controversy and debate. His actions had won him staunch enemies and fast friends, searing criticism and accolades. In the end, questions about what happened at the Little Bighorn often turned on interpretations of his judgment and character.[9] Only a powerful force could have inflated his virtues and suppressed the doubts that persisted about him. His widow supplied that force by using her influence, based on middle-class gender roles, to magnify her husband's virtues and conceal his flaws.

In light of his controversial personality and career and his even more controversial death, Custer could not have chosen a wife better equipped to defend his life and character. Elizabeth Bacon Custer came to her marriage with excellent preparation for her role as his wife and widow. As the only surviving child of Judge Daniel Bacon and his devout wife, Eleanor Sophia Page Bacon, she had been raised in the evangelical tradition that grew out of that earlier national religious revival known as the Second Great Awakening. Her attendance at two female seminaries reinforced that upbringing.

In addition, Elizabeth's early years included another experience that reverberated throughout her life. When she was twelve her mother's death caused the disruption of her home and her father's withdrawal from her day-to-day existence. While these events were wrenching, the young woman learned a lesson that stood her in good stead later. Bereavement, while painful, evoked pity. And pity was a powerful force for manipulating people and events.[10]

Finally, all the factors in Elizabeth's early life, including her family, her education, and the books she read reinforced her attachment to the prevailing middle-class ideology, based on nineteenth-century domestic ideals.[11] As one scholar argues, most Americans "undoubtedly believed that women's chief responsibilities were homemaking and child rearing, that females represented the moral foundation of the family and society, and that," for women, "a commitment to family preceded and took precedence over a commitment to self. As a corollary, they also likely believed that women deserved respect and consideration commensurate with their high moral influence both inside and outside the home."[12]

This widespread ideology, along with Elizabeth's evangelical Christianity, shaped to a large extent her views of her responsibilities as wife and widow. She began her marriage determined to convert her husband and create a Christian home, complete with Christian children who would mature to become "cornerstone[s] in the great church of God."[13] Although her husband attended a revival in 1864, his later letters, while containing occasional references to God, convey no evidence of deep-seated religious fervor. Nor did Elizabeth ever have children.

Nonetheless, whatever her personal disappointments, Elizabeth contributed throughout her marriage to her husband's advancement. Charming, polished, and physically attractive, she cemented ties with crucial congressmen and senators and ingratiated herself with Armstrong's superiors, especially Philip H. Sheridan. To a far greater extent than historians or biographers have previously noted, George Armstrong Custer's career was based on the efforts of two people.

Later, after his death, reporters described the thirty-four-year-old widow as "prostrated." They were mistaken. Despite her anguish, she went immediately to work. Subtly but unremittingly she influenced a host of writers, especially Frederick Whittaker and later E. S. Godfrey, two men who established for decades the public's perception of George A. Custer and his role in the Battle of the Little Bighorn. When powerful men erected a West Point statue to her husband without first consulting her, Elizabeth eventually "cried it off its pedestal."[14]

She did not stop there. Nine years after her husband's death, she entered the debate herself. Although she never discussed military matters (preferring to turn these over to male friends), she described the hero's home and family life in idealized fashion. Her reputation as a "model wife" and shining example of American womanhood, along with the deference accorded female moral influence, made her, during her lifetime at least, an unassailable character witness. Equally as important, since she set her books in the West, her depiction of the relations between officers and their wives provides a contrast to her unfavorable depictions of aboriginal family life and her rendition of gender roles among Indians. In that way, her collective works served as ideological justification for the conquest of the Plains tribes.

Through her writing and later her years behind the lectern, Elizabeth transformed her domestic role as widow into a publicly sanctioned profession. While widowhood could not provide the basis for a new female profession in the way that other domestic roles such as child nurture, sick care, and benevolent activities laid the basis for schoolteaching, nursing, and settlement-house work, it was not as anomalous as it seems. Elizabeth's true occupation was author and lecturer. Her writings and speeches, which always invoked the theme of devotion to husband and home, upheld the widespread domestic ideology while permitting her to make a living.[15]

In the end, Elizabeth Custer's work, although arduous, proved profitable. The stakes were high, for she knew that the rewards, material and otherwise, were far greater for the widow of a hero than the widow of a discredited, or worse yet, disobedient soldier. Custer critics, moreover, found her influence frustrating. Col. Robert Hughes was forced to publish his article charging Custer with disobedience in an obscure military journal. Cyrus T. Brady, whose 1904 work criticized Custer, not only tendered his "*amende*" to the widow a decade later, but made Custer a hero in his novel, *Britton of the Plains*.[16]

Elizabeth's success in protecting and embellishing her husband's reputation lasted well into the 1920s. Although hero-worshipping had now become unfashionable, Custer critics still held their fire, not only out of respect for Elizabeth's conjugal loyalty, but also because of her advancing age and declining health. Not until her death did writers and historians undertake a thorough reappraisal of George Armstrong Custer.

Nonetheless, the ideology that gave Elizabeth the power to protect her husband's reputation was a double-edged sword, limiting her options from the very beginning. As a child, she had exhibited intellectual ability, but none of the professions, law, medicine, the ministry, or politics, was open to her when she graduated from the Young Ladies Seminary in 1862. Instead, only marriage to her "star" catapulted her out of a commonplace existence.[17]

Once married, Elizabeth discovered that, although her marital relationship was passionate and romantic, it was at the same time asymmetrical in terms of power. Having internalized the socially constructed gender roles of that era, she accorded her husband superiority "in judgment and in everything else" and deferred to him when disputes arose.[18] Furthermore, the double standard of morality circumscribed her behavior far more than it did Armstrong's.

In addition, as her husband's dependent, Elizabeth suffered during their marriage and afterwards from financial strain. Although her love of luxury undoubtedly pressured Armstrong to seek ways to augment his army income, most of the Custers' financial disasters arose from Armstrong's calamitous investments and his inability to give up gambling. After his death, his widow spent years extricating herself from a financial morass.

Even more frustrating, as a middle-class widow, Elizabeth had few alternatives for earning a living. To counter that situation, she aligned herself with influential women in New York City and obtained suitable, although poorly paid, employment. These contacts proved invaluable. Through these women, especially Candace Wheeler and Jeannette Gilder, she eventually met editors, journalists, and writers who helped her as she sought to commemorate her husband.

Finally, Elizabeth's life shows that while existing gender relations in the nineteenth and early twentieth centuries gave men more power over women than the reverse, men, nevertheless, were also bound by their roles. William Tecumseh Sherman answered Elizabeth's request for help in removing the hated West Point statue by noting that the secretary of war, Robert Lincoln, would assist her. He has "in his heart," the general argued, "a warm place for you, who have been so brave, so true to Custer and his memory, *that every man who is a man* [italics added] must respond to your appeal."[19] And over and over, military men refused to discuss publicly their views on Custer's character or judgment out of chivalrous regard for Elizabeth's domestic role.

Thus a study of the life and work of Elizabeth Bacon Custer sheds light on both the power women derived from the widespread middle-class ideology of domesticity and the limitations it imposed on them. It also discloses what many historians and anthropologists have long known. The worlds of private home and public affairs were not separate after all. Nor in Elizabeth's case were they dichotomous. Instead, the two worlds related to one another in dialectical fashion, events in one affecting the other.[20] Elizabeth, as a "model" wife, helped to make her husband's career. He, in turn, bequeathed her his heroic reputation at his death. She then protected that legacy by invoking her power as a model widow, her nation's equivalent to the British model widow, Queen Victoria. This last was important, since nineteenth-century Americans and British alike sentimentalized bereavement and devoted a great deal of energy and resources to commemorating the dead.[21]

Other aspects of the Victorian era must also be noted, for although Elizabeth outlived it, in some respects she never moved beyond it. If myth is a statement of "wish-related knowledge," then the Victorians as biographers were often inveterate mythmakers. They wrote of other people's lives, not to "deepen the reader's insight into human nature," but rather to give the audience "the lovely, the beautiful—the assurance of the certainty of something better than we are."[22] In fact, the desire to extract didactic lessons from past lives justified for many the production of idealized biographies rather than honest evaluations of character and motivation.[23]

Nonetheless, the disparity between Elizabeth's writings about herself and her husband and the actual historical evidence raises difficult questions for her biographer. Was she, in the end, a person whose outer life failed to conform to her inner life? Put more bluntly, was she a hypocrite? And, if so, was that not a very high price to pay for reflected glory and material rewards?

The answer is that Elizabeth herself placed the highest value, not on presenting her innermost self candidly to the world, but rather on being an unfailingly loyal wife whatever the circumstances. Furthermore, after decades of revising her husband on paper and in her speeches (and herself in the process), she lost much of her ability to separate fact from myth in the popular sense. Indeed, the person she wanted most to convince was herself, and I see the boy general she created as the fulfillment of her own unmet emotional and ideological needs.

There is no way of knowing if in the end Elizabeth succeeded in stifling all her own innermost doubts. This much, however, is certain. She suppressed a good deal of the ongoing debate. Furthermore, if she had been less successful in her chosen work, critics would have spoken out about her husband earlier and in a more forthright fashion. A truer version of his life and character would have entered the public realm, and the historical picture of Custer would be more complete and less contradictory today.

Thus an examination of the life of this nineteenth-century woman will, I hope, contribute to a better understanding of the process by which one myth was made and sustained. It will also, I believe, shed additional light on the interrelationship between private and public life and the interdependence of socially constructed male and female roles. What passed for decades as the historical Custer was an idealized figure created in large measure by a woman who derived her authority from her reputation as a model wife and her role as a loving widow.

PART ONE

LIBBIE: THE GIRL HE

LEFT BEHIND

CHAPTER I

Childhood

DANIEL Bacon said good-bye to his family in Howlett Hill, New York, on September 5, 1822. His father, Leonard Bacon, a farmer, had left Woodstock, Connecticut, twenty-five years earlier in search of more productive land in upstate New York. The property he amassed, however, would not support eight children and their future families. Despite "privations and hardships," twenty-four-year-old Daniel was moving west in search of greater opportunities.[1]

Many in Onondaga County talked excitedly about the opening of new lands farther west. The Erie Canal had reached nearby Syracuse three years earlier and now headed toward Buffalo. With increasing numbers of steamboat lines serving Lake Erie ports, the products of northwestern farmers would soon reach a national market.[2] Individuals who participated in early development might reap sizeable profits from real estate.

Daniel, unsure where he was heading, sought a promising community where land was cheap and he could rise in "politicks." His Onondaga County certificate, attesting to his competency as a teacher, provided employment along the way.[3] When asked years later how he had arrived at his final destination, he replied, "Madame (or Sir), I walked." In truth, he had traveled by stagecoach and steamboat and, after exploring small towns around Cleveland, Ohio, moved on to Michigan Territory. There he taught school in a small settlement on the banks of the River Raisin, not far from Detroit.[4]

Originally named Raisinville and later called Frenchtown by English settlers, its first white inhabitants had been Canadian traders and farmers. Their descendants spoke French and practiced Catholicism. After James Monroe toured the region in 1817, the town adopted his name. Neither that change nor the president's visit, however, loomed as large in the community's collective memory as an earlier event—the River Raisin massacre during the War of 1812. In January 1813, Indian allies of the British had slaughtered wounded Kentucky militiamen left behind by their defeated commander, Gen. James Winchester. Terrified, the settlers fled to nearby Detroit or Toledo. When they returned months later, fire had destroyed the fledgling community.[5]

Five years after the war, settlers still experienced the bleakest poverty. Monroe's fortunes improved when completion of the military road from Detroit to the Miami River rapids in 1819 transformed the village into a way station for travelers from northwestern Ohio to southeastern Michigan. When Bacon first arrived late in 1822, settlements lined the river, and a small business section had grown up on the south side. Among the town's industries were tanneries, distilleries, breweries, sawmills, and lumber yards.[6]

Increasing numbers of English-speaking settlers appeared. Like Bacon, many were from upstate New York, and others hailed from New England. Some brought with them an increasingly evangelical Protestantism. Revivalists of the Second Great Awakening, moreover, toured the new trade routes, established by the Erie Canal, and converted others. Bacon, anxious to assure his parents that he was not descending into barbarism in the wilderness, wrote in November, "This is one of the most civilized places I ever was in. There has been a verry [sic] great revival of religion this summer. Prayer-meetings are held four times a week."[7]

When a land office opened that year, Bacon purchased his first River Raisin tract. He planted apple, peach, and plum trees and sold the cleared timber as lumber. However arduous his labor, he taught school by day and read for the law at night. "I pride myself on doing more work than any other man on the Raisin," was his assessment. Later he remembered these early privations with perhaps some exaggeration. "I spent my first summer, lying on the ground, the poor man's boarding house, alternately shivering with cold and burning with fever," the bane of every "newcomer."[8]

After passing his bar examination, Bacon opened a law office. He also formed a strong friendship and partnership with Levi Humphrey, formerly of Vermont. Humphrey, Monroe's first land registrar, managed both the regional stagecoach line and the Exchange Hotel and by 1838 served as one of Michigan's commissioners of internal improvements.[9] Bacon and his partner continuously patented government land, subdividing it into city lots and selling it for a profit.[10] Once Daniel acquired sufficient property, he entered "politicks."

Monroe County elected Bacon its supervisor in 1831 and inspector of schools a year later. In 1835 and 1836, he served as his district's Whig representative in the Fifth and Sixth Territorial Legislatures. When Michigan officially entered the union in 1837, the local community held Bacon in high esteem. Almost forty, he could now marry with the assurance that he could support his family comfortably. Reflecting the new middle-class standards of his day, he wanted a wife who was also a companion and enjoyed enough leisure so that she would not be "worn out by drudgery."[11]

Eleanor Sophia Page, a devout twenty-three-year-old daughter of a prosperous Grand Rapids nursery owner, captured his attention. Her parents, recently arrived from Putney, Vermont, were already famous for marketing the "love apple." Although many dismissed the red fruit as poisonous, Abel Page and his wife sold it successfully as the tomato.[12] Bacon's courtship of Sophia, as he addressed her, was highly formal. In one letter, he wrote, "My feelings have undergone no change since I saw you. It is therefore unnecessary to give you further assurances of my friendship and affection." Despite his lack of fervor, she married him in September 1837.[14]

Shortly after their honeymoon, Bacon sustained his first political defeat as the Whig candidate for lieutenant governor. He also entered a venture destined to end disastrously. Earlier that year Michigan had enacted a free banking law, allowing residents of any county to establish local banks subject to minimum state control. While the state's auditor instructed banks to deposit securities to cover possible defaults or failures, these were often bonds and mortgages on inflated real estate.[14]

More than forty such institutions sprang up almost overnight. Free of constraints and basing their hopes on continuously rising land prices, they began doing business. Among these was the Merchant and Mechanics Bank of Monroe whose president, Daniel Bacon, was now assistant judge of the Monroe County Circuit Court. The institution placed its first notes into circulation on November 10, 1837.[15]

As a family man, judge, bank president, and property owner, Bacon stood higher in Monroe than ever. Still the earliest months of marriage proved difficult. "I have been so long a boarder in a publick house," he confided to his father, ". . . that for some time housekeeping rendered my situation lonely."[16] Perhaps his bride also felt "lonely," for she wrote her sister, Loraine Richmond of Grand Rapids, a revealing letter.

She was walking "a mile daily for my health," an oblique way of referring to her pregnancy some months after the wedding. Then, after commenting on such prosaic matters as the weather and a popular song, she entreated her sister to "make us a long visit this winter." The letter showed something else. Sophia Bacon was fond of clothes and finery, a trait she would pass on to her oldest daughter. Recently she had acquired a double shawl from New York, "the most fashionable worn," as well as "a maroon-colored merino with fluted trimmings, also a gray silk with shirred hat."[17]

Sophia's first child, Edward Augustus, was born on June 9, 1839. Shortly after, Bacon was elected to the Michigan Senate and the following spring became assessor of his ward. By November 1840, he had risen to associate judge of the circuit court. While his social position improved, a national depression, beginning in 1837 and deepening in 1839, ushered in hard times. Business failures abounded, unemployment increased, and land values plummeted. Like many similar ventures, the Merchants and Mechanics Bank of Monroe closed its doors, leaving behind trunks of worthless bank notes. In Monroe County Circuit Court judgments went against Bacon and his partner Humphrey. Given the vicissitudes of the economy, such setbacks left Bacon's reputation untarnished. These were the risks enterprising men assumed.[18] When recovery came, Bacon once more invested in real estate, taking on indebtedness always slightly more than he could comfortably handle.

Despite financial strain, Bacon built a home on South Monroe Street in the fashionable Greek revival style. Here in the center of town, now numbering 2,000 inhabitants, his second child was born on April 8, 1842.[19] Judge Bacon hoped that when the current depression lifted, harbor improvements started earlier would continue, enabling Monroe's population to surpass that of its rivals, Detroit and Toledo.[20]

The Bacons named their daughter Elizabeth Clift after Daniel's mother, revealing something of the power relationships in that marriage. Nonetheless, Sophia always called her young daughter Libbie. Once the child outgrew infancy, she played with her brother on a porch extending halfway around the green-shuttered house. Libbie was three and a half when her mother bore a second daughter. The infant, named Sophia, died within four months.[21]

Daniel placed high hopes in his seven-year-old son, whom he described as "large, destined to be as tall as myself, and one of the healthiest children I ever saw. But he requires looking after, for he is mischievous, disorderly, unmanageable." He voiced concern when Sophia took the children to visit her family in Grand Rapids, reminding her that their son was "wild, ungovernable. I fear that . . . he may fall from fences, trees, into the canal or Lake."[22]

Perhaps Daniel had a premonition. Edward plunged through a broken step and sustained a serious spinal injury. After a year in bed he recovered, only to contract an unidentified but deadly disease, most likely cholera or diphtheria. He died on April 11, 1848, three days after Libbie's sixth birthday. Before the year ended, Sophia gave birth to her fourth child, whom she named Harriet after her sister. This infant died at six months, leaving Libbie an only child.[23]

Before Elizabeth turned eight, her parents had lost three of their four children. While not uncommon in that era, these events undoubtedly left her mother depressed during much of Libbie's early childhood. Sophia, a quiet woman whose life centered on her home and the Presbyterian church, where she taught Sunday school, found consolation in religion.[24] Given their losses, however, she and Daniel became very protective of their remaining child.

Libbie, headstrong like her brother before her, delighted in eluding her mother's watchful eye. Escaping outside, she frequently played with neighborhood children until Sophia frantically retrieved her. As punishment, her mother shut her in a closet, but, rather than protesting, Libbie slept in a clothes basket. This unexpected response showed that, from earliest years, Libbie's even temperament and "wonderful disposition" predisposed her to adapt to any situation.[25]

From her earliest age, Libbie was also eager to please others. This trait helped Sophia as she sought to subdue her daughter's will, "the keystone to the evangelical method of child-rearing."[26] When confinement to the closet proved ineffective, Sophia put her to bed in midday. Instead of contesting her fate, Libbie napped. Later she awoke to the sound of an anguished voice praying over her. Sophia was invoking the newer, less punitive methods of child-rearing, described in *Mother's Magazine* and increasingly favored by the middle class. The goal was to produce a child whose sense of right and wrong sprang from within, rather than from fear of punishment. Sophia's tactics were so successful that Libbie remembered that day the rest of her life. Tearfully she promised never to disobey again.[27]

At nine, Libbie received a diary with her name and the inscription, "to be kept and preserved by her as the wish of her Father Daniel S. Bacon." Since Daniel admonished her to write neatly, a year passed before she overcame her fear that she could not "write well enough."[28] On her tenth birthday she began her entries.

On weekdays, after attending the Boyd Seminary's primary school, Libbie played with other children in her backyard, where her father had constructed a swing. She devoted Saturdays to Sabbath study in the mornings and singing lessons in the afternoon. On Sundays, she often attended church twice. Despite her youth, Libbie frequently commented on the sermon, noting the text selected and often complimenting the preacher. And since she and her friends were curious about other faiths, they visited Catholic and Methodist churches. In short, religious fervor dominated her childhood.[29]

At ten Libbie displayed another trait—a penchant for writing brief vignettes based on close attention to details. One entry displays her youthful reporting skills while showing a hint of nativism: "It has been more like Spring today than any we have had this month. A dissipated german by the name of Mr. Aulwringden living near the depot committed suicide by hanging himself this after-noon near tea time."[30]

The summer of 1852 proved exciting for a young girl. An organ grinder came to town with his monkey, and later, P. T. Barnum arrived with his traveling museum, which included Tom Thumb. So many people attended the show that the stand collapsed. Libbie, recording the event as if she were a journalist, noted that one woman suffered a broken leg and another a crushed jaw.[31]

By September some who had succumbed to California fever were returning home disappointed. Libbie, despite her youth, sensed this movement's historical importance. She listened intently as a neighbor told her father that California was not the promised land after all. The gold had "been all dug over by the thousands and thousands of people," and "the plains were . . . a burying place for the dead, that the emigrants feel so burdened with baggage they throw it away, so that the plains are covered with clothes."[32]

The coming election loomed large when her father attended a Whig convention in Hillsdale. The party's candidate, Gen. Winfield Scott, hero of the recent Mexican war, excited Bacon. Some of Libbie's earliest and most enduring memories concerned Scott's portrait in her family's parlor. It showed "a colossal figure on a fiery steed, whose prancing forefeet never touched the earth." Around his horse's feet "was the smoke of battle, in which I supposed the hero lived perpetually." From her earliest days, Libbie revered military figures, and Daniel's annual commemoration of Commodore Oliver Perry's victory over the British naval fleet in 1813 reinforced that attitude.[33]

When Bacon returned from Hillsdale, he reported that cholera had struck nearby Toledo. Thankfully, while the dread disease made its inevitable appearance in Monroe, claiming the life of their minister, the Bacon family escaped unscathed. Libbie's awareness of death, nonetheless, increased. In mid-September she wrote of her household and religious activities. "This morning I hope was profitably employed in doing what—if I am permitted to live to become a woman—will make me more useful and happy." Among her duties she listed "reading one chapter in the Bible, learning a verse of my Sabbath School lesson, reading a part of my Sabbath School book, writing in my Diary." By afternoon, she had darned her first stocking.³⁴ Weeks later, the Democratic candidate Franklin Pierce's victory over "Old Fuss and Feathers," as Scott was affectionately known to his soldiers, disappointed Bacon. But the coming of Christmas had already diverted Libbie's attention. All her life, this holiday never lost its appeal.³⁵

Shortly before her eleventh birthday Libbie received a piano from her mother. She also began copying lines of poetry or aphorisms in her journal, a practice she followed intermittently the rest of her days. Among the lines she selected were, "Trifles make the sum of human things and half our misery from one's foibles spring." Earlier she had started, at her mother's insistence, committing whole portions of the Bible to memory. Libbie began with the twelfth chapter of Romans but made no comment on the admonition, "Be not wise in your own conceits." Such counsel, however, reinforced her mother's advice that females were to be modest and humble.³⁶

The few remaining entries for 1853 and early 1854 are sparse but revealing. Libbie, for example, accompanied her mother as Sophia visited a poor family and dispensed food and clothing as Christian charity. Later, a new teacher of Italian descent arrived in the city, indicating that Monroe's population, numbering many Irish and German immigrants, was becoming more diverse. More important, the onset of smallpox closed school for several weeks until the epidemic subsided.³⁷

On March 19, 1854, after a lapse of several days, Libbie asked "the most humble pardon of my diary for being so negligent in not writing." She recorded a quiet scene of domesticity. "Mother sits by the fire warming her feet and reading Mothers Magazine," while Daniel was studying a dispute among New York Quaker abolitionists.³⁸

The next entry, dated August 27, 1854, explained Libbie's latest omission. "When last I wrote you my Mother sat comfortably in her dear rocking chair by the fire. . . . Two weeks ago my mother was laid in the cold ground,

& as I stood by that open grave & felt—oh! God only knows what anguish filled my heart. O! Why," the twelve-year-old asked, "did they put my mother in that great black cofin [*sic*] & screw the lid down so tight?" Sophia had died from the "bloody disentary [*sic*], the second case in town." During her last hours, she had gazed at her daughter's portrait. "I hope," the young girl continued, "the Lord will spare me to my father for I am his only comfort left."[39]

After his wife's death, Daniel followed common custom when he sent Libbie to Sophia's sister, Loraine Richmond. The young girl remained in Grand Rapids for several months, deriving comfort from her aunt and two cousins, Rebecca and Mary. Daniel in the meantime vacated the Bacon home. From now on he would live at the Exchange Hotel, while Libbie would board at the Boyd Seminary. Young Elizabeth hid her turbulent emotions so skillfully that when Bacon arrived at Grand Rapids to escort her back to Monroe, her apparent equanimity startled him. He wrote a sister that his daughter was "without gloom, without a murmur at her sad fate—and even happy!"[40] He was wrong; although she gave little outward sign, Libbie grieved inwardly for her mother.

By November Elizabeth had settled into her new life at the seminary. The principal, Rev. Erasmus Boyd, sympathizing with her bereavement, gave her special privileges. Only Libbie enjoyed a parlor and a bedroom on the third floor, which she shared with a beloved teacher. Their rooms boasted three windows with splendid views of Lake Erie and the city and a rose bush on one of the sills.[41] Now twelve, Libbie had advanced to the Academic Department, where she prepared for secondary studies. Once completed, her education, more extensive than that of most women of her era, would end.

Prominent Monroe citizens had established the Young Ladies' Seminary and Collegiate Institute (the school's official name) in 1849. A year later it offered its first classes. Despite its name, its founders had never envisioned giving young women the same education available in men's colleges. As the catalogue stated, men and women performed distinct but complementary functions. Women would never "fill the learned professions." Nor would they ever be "marshaled in the battle-field . . . nor [found] mingling in political strife at the ballot box, nor gathering legal honors in the Court House or Congressional Hall." Such public activities were closed since God had made them "for other scenes of usefulness and honor."[42]

What were these "scenes of usefulness and honor" ? And why did they require a four-year course of study "equal to that of a college, yet very materially modified" ? Woman, whose mind was "immortal," would fill many different roles. She would reign as "the presiding genius of love in the charmed circle of social and literary life." More important, once married, she would become the companion of "an educated man" and impart to her children "a correct and elevated literary taste." Finally, she would undertake charity and good works. Thus, her seminary training should "cultivate, not only the mind, but the taste and heart—to make Woman what she should be, not *masculine*, coarse and unlovely, but *educated*, and at the same time refined, and ready for every good work that becomes her."[43]

After noting the various responsibilities females held and the most-sought-after characteristics of future wives and mothers, the catalogue specified the program. Unlike their male counterparts, these young women would not study Hebrew, Greek, or higher mathematics. Instead, they would learn French, literature, and the "Fine Arts."[44] In designing the curriculum and the extracurricular activities for boarders, Reverend Boyd relied heavily on his wife, Sarah, an alumna of Emma Willard's Troy Seminary in New York State.[45]

As Libbie accommodated to her new surroundings, an undercurrent of sadness filled her diary during the first year after her mother's death. Her father had left for New York and Vermont, leaving her "quite lonely all alone."[46] Nonetheless, Libbie was already adept at exploiting the sympathy she derived from being "poor motherless Libbie Bacon." Years later she confessed, "how shamelessly I traded on this. What an excuse I made of it for not doing anything I didn't want to do! And what excuses were made for me on that score."[47] Sympathy, she had learned, was an emotion she could exploit. It was a lesson she never forgot.

Whatever her situation, the young girl performed splendidly in her classes. "Although some times I give up in despair and say I can't," she confided to her journal, "when I think how my sweet mother used to love to have me be diligent I am inspired with new hope." Boyd continued to give her advantages, including a small garden where she tended her flowers. She also started drawing lessons and, appreciative of her teacher C. C. Zens's patience, always brought him a bouquet. Resilient, she took her comforts and compensations wherever she found them and eagerly awaited her father's weekly visits.[48]

As she entered her teens, Libbie, who had always been plump, grew taller and slimmer. She was changing into a young woman, and in an era when curves were considered comely, she worried about becoming too thin to attract males. Nor did she like her "milkmaid" cheeks.[49] Although she never commented on her hair, photographs show an abundance of thick, brown locks, easily coaxed into elaborate styles. Her deep-set gray eyes were her most striking feature. In many photographs they gaze out with a soft, often luminous expression.

In photographs of Elizabeth taken even in youth, one catches the slightest hint of sardonic humor or cynicism lurking behind her brow. In posing, she sometimes tilted her head to one side, as if seeking to ingratiate herself with her audience. These were not her best pictures. She was more attractive when she held her head straight and gazed ahead, meeting her observer with a discerning look and a slight smile.

On Christmas Day, 1855, several Monroe youths called at the Boyd Seminary. Anticipating their arrival, Libbie gave her appearance careful thought. All the girls had agreed to dress in white. Still in half-mourning, Elizabeth seized the opportunity to set herself off from the others by tying her long hair in two black ribbons. The many compliments she received proved her strategy's effectiveness. C. C. Zens thought she resembled a Swiss girl.[50]

When families called on New Year's Day, several married men became too attentive. Despite her protestations, a physician kissed Libbie. When the thirteen-year-old slapped him, "he did not care." Elizabeth was becoming aware of both the power and danger of her burgeoning sexuality.[51]

Libbie had other interests besides the growing impact she was having on men. A bright student, she performed better in literature and mythology than mathematics or French. And she loved books. Although she had not yet read Shakespeare, Byron, or Milton, she had "beguiled many an hour by reading an interesting story and Fannie [sic] Fern and Grace Greenwood are my favorites now." She had read "two series of Fern Leaves over several times" and looked forward to *Rose Clark*. As for Greenwood, Libbie appreciated her "warm heart" and concern for children. "If I ever am privileged to write for newspapers or even a little book," she confided to her journal, "I *won't* forget children. No I *won't*. Oh! How I wish to write for some paper. I love to compose & I can too."[52]

The two books Libbie had read "several times" by Fanny Fern (Sara Payson Willis) were *Fern Leaves from Fanny's Portfolio* and *Fern Leaves . . . Second Series*. Published in 1854, both contained ambiguous messages for a young reader.[53] In the first half of *Fern Leaves from Fanny's Portfolio*, the author presented conventional heroines who endured without reproach or complaint the injustices heaped on them by unkind employers, alcoholic husbands, or penurious widowhood. In the end, as literary formula dictated, domestic virtue and female chastity triumphed over evil, and wrongs righted themselves. Fern approached similar material in part two differently. By derisively mocking widows or mistreated wives as accomplices in their own victimization, she stirred her readers' rebelliousness.[54]

Whatever her ambiguity in portraying women, Fern often presented men in an unfavorable light. In *Rose Clark*, one of Fern's characters described males as "so gross and unspiritual . . . so wedded to making money and promiscuous love, so selfish and unchivalric."[55] A character in *Fresh Leaves* (which Libbie undoubtedly read later) warned against trusting any man, since "variety is as necessary to his existence, as a looking-glass and a cigar; and . . . his vows are made, like women's hearts, to break."[56]

Such ideas could leave an impressionable adolescent, especially one whose mother was dead and whose father was often absent, wary of men. It could also predispose her to expect that, in the end, males would often prove unreliable. One fact is certain. When Libbie reached adulthood, the men who sustained her interest were those who exhibited rakish and unpredictable behavior.

Equally important were the views of Greenwood (Sara Lippincott), a more conventional writer.[57] Like Fern, Greenwood thought that women should be self-reliant and adaptable, never trusting too much in the promises of others. Nor should they ever surrender their pride and dignity, even when faced with deception or desertion. Greenwood's gentle heroines always proved capable of outwitting the men in their lives, although if they cared for them, they left male pride intact.[58]

Thus two of Libbie's favorite authors presented ideas that proved influential as she formulated her view of the larger world. On the one hand, Fern warned against placing too much trust in often "gross" and materialistic men. On the other, Greenwood argued that, although men held power, women might still triumph provided they used their wits and maintained their pride and virtue.

Greenwood conveyed other messages as well. Unlike Fern, she accepted conventional restrictions on female authors. Women could write for a public audience when their work served purposes other than self-aggrandizement. Their literary labors should help others solve the moral or practical problems arising from friendships, courtship, and family life and relationships.[59]

When an aspiring female poet wrote Greenwood, expressing a longing for "a share of public admiration," however, the noted writer instructed her to "fling away ambition." Reputation could be won only at the expense of love and domestic bliss, and while she "might joy over it with a dizzy exultation for a while . . . you would soon hunger for the simplest home-pleasures, and pant for affection as the hart panteth after the water-brook.'"[60]

Whatever her gifts or abilities, Greenwood cautioned the disappointed poet to remember, "True feminine genius is ever timid, doubtful, and clingingly dependent; a perpetual childhood. A true woman shrinks instinctively from greatness. . . . The fact of your having grown up to womanhood without your genius being recognized, amounts to nothing; or rather, it is better as it is." Then Greenwood warned, "Never *unsex* yourself for greatness. The worship of one true heart is better than the wonder of the world."[61]

These ideas influenced Libbie as she formed her views of female identity. One day she would attain a reputation as a writer and a lecturer. But she would justify her work as serving didactic and inspirational purposes. To the end of her long life, she functioned publicly as the wife or widow of the man whose fame she extolled. Some women nourished on similar precepts moved beyond these restrictions, but Elizabeth was not one of them. For her, femininity and fame remained irreconcilable unless she performed her public work as service to a person or cause beyond herself.

During the Christmas break of 1855–1856, many pupils left the seminary until the second week in January. Libbie experienced intense loneliness and contrasted in her diary the "vast difference" between life in a boarding school and a home. She also fantasized about moving back with her father and keeping house for him. Since she spent Saturday mornings cleaning stairs and windows and sweeping and dusting, routine tasks at female seminaries, she thought she could manage a home.[62]

Increasingly, Libbie's diary revealed religious turmoil as she constantly berated herself for her inadequacies as a Christian. "Oh! I am very wicked. I feel it," was a typical lament.[63] In part her intense guilt stemmed from adolescent moodiness. But on another level it arose from her preparations for conversion, an experience that would signify, as an evangelical Protestant, her religious coming of age. Conversion, however, came only after she had submitted herself to God's will and sincerely acknowledged her sinfulness. Only then could she feel certain that God's grace had bestowed salvation.[64] For a few days Libbie wrote only perfunctory remarks in her diary before stopping for two years.

When Elizabeth resumed journal-keeping, she was a young woman of fifteen who had not yet undergone conversion. Early in January 1858, as she sat with her father in the seminary parlor during their weekly visit, he broached the subject of remarriage. Earlier, she had objected, but now she struggled to respond more maturely. If he had found someone, she assured him, she would adapt. In her diary, however, she noted that she would be "deprived of keeping house for him for I think of it often."[65]

Her moods varied, but frequently she was irritable as she constantly examined her character to identify her faults and failures. She attributed her lack of progress in French and piano to her lazy and sporadic practice. And fearing she was not a reliable friend, she redoubled her efforts to be considerate to other young women.[66]

Finally there remained the troubling matter of conversion. The pressures mounted as the sermons alerted her to a coming revival. "God grant that if I am ever converted it may be in my own closet before God for I think so many false conversions are made hastily at revivals." Still, she saw little chance of escaping, for Reverend Boyd was holding conversations with a friend "on religious subject[s]." Libbie knew he would soon approach her.[67]

Given the new uncertainties regarding her father and the religious pressures confronting her, Libbie wanted school to end. She longed to visit her aunt, Mary Case, at Howlett Hill and feel a part of a family again. "No one knows how much I lost but myself, when mother died," the young woman confided to her diary. To make matters worse, the guilt, the sense of shame and sin she had carried for two years were now more burdensome. "How wild I am getting. Oh! how discouraged I am with regard to doing right. God help me for I know I do wrong every day."[68]

Sensing her turmoil, her father removed her from the seminary before the semester ended. After allowing Libbie a summer given over to horseback riding and exploring the countryside at a sister's Onondaga County farm, Daniel enrolled his daughter in the Young Ladies Institute in Auburn, New York. Founded by Winthrop Tappan, a relative of the wealthy and devout benefactors Lewis and Arthur Tappan, it brought Elizabeth under the influence of Tappan's co-principal, Rev. Mortimer L. Browne.[69]

Both Browne and his wife diverted the adolescent's attention away from herself. Wisely, they placed her with two homesick younger girls and told her to set a good example. The new responsibility brought to the surface all the uncertainty Libbie felt towards entering adulthood, and her letters to Daniel expressed her agitation. She was sure her father would approve: "You wish me to become womanly do you not. I don't want to though—I like being a *little* girl," she admitted, adding, "I dread being a young lady *so* much." In the same vein, she explained, "I like acting *free* and *girl like* Not being so *prim* and *particular* about what I say and do!" Now, however, challenged by the responsibility for two younger charges, she struggled to master her feelings. For she feared her father was sometimes "*ashamed*" of her.[70]

Her turmoil had increased recently given Daniel's engagement to Rhoda Wells Pitts. In time, Libbie learned that her father's fiancée was the widow of Samuel Pitts. The Pittses had managed a thriving Canandaigua, New York, inn until a revival conducted by the Presbyterian minister Charles Grandison Finney had convinced them to take the temperance oath. Once their establishment offered a dry menu, business declined. But Pitts, having experienced conversion, interpreted his misfortune as a call to the ministry. He moved to New York City and trained in Finney's Tabernacle Church. Afterwards he served the poor in a city mission, an early forerunner of the later settlement-house movement.[71]

The arduous work sapped Pitts's strength and, after developing tuberculosis, he moved to Tecumseh, Michigan. He died in 1855, leaving a forty-six-year-old widow with a small amount of property and a reputation as an excellent housekeeper.[72] Bacon's friend, Judge Stillman Blanchard, introduced Daniel to Rhoda. After a year-long courtship the two married on February 23, 1859, in Orange, New Jersey. When the newlyweds returned to Monroe, they boarded in a private home until repairs were completed on Bacon's South Monroe Street residence.[73]

In May 1859, Libbie left the Auburn Young Ladies Institute and moved to Howlett Hill, where she awaited her summons to join her father and stepmother. During this transition, she reflected on the changes in her life and her indebtedness to Mortimer Browne and his wife. When she had arrived at their home, she had been "steeped in *sin* and *guilt*." Their confidence in her ability to guide younger children had given her faith in herself. For the first time in a long while, she had felt useful and needed.

Having undergone conversion, she was now determined "to serve God." Browne's wise counsel had brought her to "the feet of the Savior," and his "Christian example" would continue to "guide and save and keep me." As for Mrs. Browne: "She lingers in my mind as does the breath of fragrant flowers. She was a mother to me, and *God* will repay her for her kindness for I never can."[74]

Thus Libbie closed this chapter of her life by concluding that after all the loneliness and uncertainties, she had turned out well. The Brownes' parental affection had provided the turning point: "I went there an entire stranger—

they took me into their hearts as if I were their child and ever *ever* will I thank them for it. . . . Although there is yet *much* to do to make me what I should be, yet I cannot but feel that I have improved much. I went there a *child*, but came away a *woman*. God be praised!"[75]

CHAPTER 2

Libbie Bacon Chooses
a Husband

WHEN LIBBIE returned to Monroe in 1859, she adapted easily to her stepmother. Rhoda made no demands on her, insisting that her "Young Responsibility" devote attention to school-work. Later that winter, Libbie fell ill, and her parents removed her from classes the rest of the year. The young woman flourished under Rhoda's conscientious care and returned to school in the fall. On New Year's Day, 1861, Daniel Bacon wrote relatives, "Libbie was never so well and fleshy and full of fun and wit." The new arrangements permitted them to "live well, but not extravagantly, have company enough to keep us cheerful, and the *neatest house you ever saw*."[1]

Libbie wanted to graduate as valedictorian of her class in 1862. One of her rivals, academically and socially, was Fanny Fifield. The daughter of a wealthy Monroe steamboating entrepreneur, Fanny was a fashionable young woman and a notorious flirt.[2] She and Libbie competed for grades, approba-tion, and beaux. At times, Libbie felt disadvantaged since her father forbade card playing, dancing, and ice-skating, activities allowed Fanny. Libbie's home, nonetheless, was open to friends who congregated in good weather on the porch outside.[3]

While Libbie's concerns usually centered around religion, school, young men, and clothes, she thought increasingly about her country's fate. Since the Whig party's demise, her father had become a Republican. Southern response to Abraham Lincoln's November victory, on a platform pledging the nonextension of slavery into the territories, however, surprised him. Distressed to learn that a convention in South Carolina had voted unani-mously on December 20 to secede from the Union, Daniel worried that other states might follow. If so, he feared the onset of war.

When the Boyd Seminary reopened on January 3, Libbie found the blackboard edged in black "because of the fearful state of our country." The next day, Monroe churches honored President James Buchanan's request for a day of prayer. As Libbie listened to Rev. A. K. Strong speak from the text, "God is our refuge, a very present help in the time of trouble," she beseeched the Almighty to spare the nation "fearful" violence.[4]

By mid-January, Mississippi, Florida, and Alabama had joined South Carolina in secession. Two weeks later, Georgia, Tennessee, and Texas had followed. Libbie's attention, however, was diverted by her new responsibility. Like her mother before her, she now conducted Sunday School for Monroe's poorer children. She noted proudly that the Catholic priest considered *"those girls who taught"* more threatening to his parishioners than itinerant spiritualists. When lessons went well, she was elated, but when her students were bored and restless, she bemoaned her "ragged class."[5]

February brought bitter cold. With the river and ponds frozen, Libbie, having worn down her father's resistance, tried out her new skates. As she struggled to stay upright, she wondered what lay ahead now that seven seceded states had formed the Confederacy. In truth, sentiment was hardening on both sides. Faced with secession, many Northerners feared the unraveling of the entire Union. But although some called for preserving the Union at all cost, few wanted war. Everyone anxiously awaited Lincoln's inauguration.[6]

By early April, tension was high in Monroe. Men gathered at the train station and the Humphrey House (which had replaced the Exchange Hotel) and debated whether South Carolina would allow Lincoln to resupply Fort Sumter, the federal garrison off the coast. On April 8, Libbie noted that Laura Noble's father was pessimistic. Days later the news arrived. Following thirty-three hours of Confederate bombardment, Maj. Robert Anderson had fired a fifty-gun salute to his tattered flag before surrendering the fort on April 13.

The report stunned Monroe citizens. Unable to believe that Southerners had fired on Old Glory, they put up flags everywhere. Civic leaders gathered at the courthouse the following Wednesday and affirmed their support for the Union cause. Even a Quaker called for military action against "the rebellion at whatever cost and whatever sacrifice." Rapidly, local boys answered Lincoln's call for ninety-day volunteers, and many joined the Fourth Michigan Volunteer Infantry, organized in Monroe.[7] Some young women experienced a swift decline in beaux, but Elizabeth Clift Bacon was not among them.

While Libbie studied diligently, practiced her elocution, and read vora-ciously, nothing delighted her more than attracting men. When her art instructor made advances during lessons, compelling her to twist and turn to escape his embraces, she exultantly judged him "*licentious* beaucoup." He was not the only one. Others who frequented the Bacon home included John Rauch, a young attorney, and Elliot Bates, recently appointed to West Point.[8]

Initially the war went well for Union forces. Ohio volunteers, led by Maj. Gen. George B. McClellan, invaded western Virginia. On June 3 their victory assured Yankee control in the region and West Virginia's eventual statehood. Whatever euphoria Monroe citizens felt, however, disappeared following Bull Run. On July 21, Confederate forces routed Union troops under Gen. Irvin McDowell in northern Virginia. The defeat revealed the Union Army's deficiencies in training and leadership and destroyed all hopes for a quick victory.[9] By early September Daniel Bacon wrote relatives that both Rhoda and Libbie were "busy sewing and baking for the officers and soldiers." Surely the war would end by spring since he could stand no further taxation.[10]

Shortly after, a scene occurred that mattered little at the time but left a lasting impression. A young lieutenant from the Fifth Cavalry, home on leave because of a minor injury, was visiting his sister in Monroe. One evening, after drinking heavily with his friends at a local tavern, he staggered down South Monroe Street as Bacon entered his home. The judge turned and watched the spectacle. Two years later he remembered vividly that the young man was George Armstrong Custer.[11]

The holiday season of 1861 was festive despite the war. Libbie accom-panied a group of young people to a Toledo exhibition. Free of constraints imposed by Monroe gossips, she "laughed and elevated my foot high in the sky and cut up generally." By evening's end a high school principal, introduced himself. Libbie recorded afterwards, "He talked and looked me through! I guess he knew I had ruffles on my drawers. . . . The exhibition was fine but the Principal finer."[12]

Days later, Libbie gave John Bulkley, another young attorney, "in sport my locket and chain." When he returned them with his photograph inside, Libbie was embarrassed. He misunderstood, she explained, but the disap-pointed suitor reproached her for leading him on.[13] Not yet twenty, Libbie had no idea why she vacillated between frivolity and high-minded serious-ness. When classes resumed she turned her attention to Shakespeare's *King Lear* and *Macbeth*. She enjoyed them so much that she concluded, "If I don't get the valedictory I am amply repaid for going in the pleasure I feel in studying and . . . how much interest Mr. Boyd takes in our class."[14]

Bulkley, Rauch, Bates, the Toledo principal, and several others faced a new rival. While attending church, Libbie, bored by a "dry as a stick" sermon, drew a satirical picture of the preacher. Later, Reverend Dutton, a substitute for Pastor Strong (now an army chaplain), chided Libbie for ridiculing people. Shortly after, under the pretense of tuning the piano or conversing with Daniel, Dutton visited the Bacon household.

Libbie, discerning his true purpose, found the attentions of a brilliant sermonizer flattering. He had one unattractive trait, however; he sometimes had the "vapors." Rhoda, undaunted, advised her, "She could bear it or some other disagreeable trait once in a while if a person was so fascinating at other times."[15] Doubtlessly, the psalm-singing, piano-thumping Dutton was Rhoda's choice for a son-in-law.

Increasingly the war intruded on life in Monroe. Among Libbie's friends, young men entered the Fifteenth Michigan Regiment and headed for duty in the western theater. A few, who had joined earlier regiments such as the Fourth or the Seventh, had been wounded or maimed. Some had arrived home in caskets. At parties or socials young lieutenants or captains on leave discussed army life and their experiences in combat.[16]

By Washington's birthday, Monroe citizens were celebrating. Union forces under Gen. Ulysses S. Grant had penetrated the heart of the Confederacy in the western theater by taking forts Henry and Donelson on the Tennessee and Cumberland rivers. From her bedroom window Libbie gazed at houses lit up in celebration while the Presbyterian church's cupola illuminated the sky.[17]

Several nights later Libbie dreamed she had married a soldier in the army. "We were obliged to hide from rebels in a pond of water and go through many perils all of which I was willing to do for my spouse." The next night her dream continued. Forced to kill someone in self defense, she became "terribly agitated." Still, her dream "ended so beautifully, my cares and sorrows had vanished and I was walking with my arm in that of the dear man who forms the subject of my journal often." Since she immediately recorded Dutton's visit, he was probably the subject of her dream.[18]

Throughout March and early April the minister's calls were more frequent. Libbie knew his intentions were serious when he gave her a book containing his late wife's reminiscences of their dead child. But as his ardor increased, hers diminished. Soon she again darted around a room to escape an older man's embraces. Neither Dutton nor any other suitor had won her affection.[19]

As the school year drew to a close, Libbie prepared her graduation speech and her brief valedictorian's farewell. Shunning ambitious themes, she chose the topic "Crumbs" since she saw "as much essential greatness in little things as in larger ones." When the day arrived, she curtsied to the trustees (including her father), the teachers, ministers, townspeople, and newspaper men and delivered her address.

Libbie had calculated correctly that "the oddity of the subject attracted attention." Although she read without airs, "for I do so hate them in anybody," her voice quivered. From the audience, her cousin Rebecca watched intently. Afterwards, she noted there was "scarcely a dry eye, so many were there who had watched her through her motherless girlhood." Daniel, sitting on stage, was "greatly affected."[20]

Later, the *Detroit Free Press* judged Libbie's speech "one of the best." By contrast, Fanny's "Majesty of Intellect," while well delivered, lacked "originality."[21] Libbie attributed her success to "simplicity and originality." More important, she had discovered a useful formula for the future. She could earn praise by extrapolating wisdom from everyday events.

Libbie spent a pleasant summer, enjoying the companionship of Rebecca and her younger sister, Mary. In September, she visited their home in Grand Rapids, where she attracted a new admirer, a railroad clerk looking for a wife. He sustained her interest no longer than the others, and, exasperated, Libbie sought advice from the twenty-three-year-old Rebecca, "a model girl who acts from principle." By contrast, the younger Mary struck her as a flirt who might one day marry a "crooked stick."[22]

After long talks with her older cousin, Libbie concluded that as long as she felt "supremely indifferent" about the men she knew, she would cease worrying about marriage. Earlier she had decided, "If no one ever comes that I love then I shall be a 'spinster' but," she thought, "to be one from necessity and one from pleasure are different things." Besides, she knew she would never find herself in the first category.[23]

Libbie met Capt. George Armstrong Custer at a party hosted by the Boyds late in November 1862. She knew him by reputation, since he had achieved some distinction as an aide to General McClellan. Given his family's modest circumstances, Democratic party affiliation, and Methodist church membership, Custer did not usually travel in Libbie's social circles. The war, however, had opened new opportunities for men of military achievement. Extending her hand, Libbie gazed up at a youth of medium height with reddish blond hair and penetrating blue eyes. When she observed that his advancement had been "very rapid," he replied, "I have been very fortunate."[24]

Daniel, who kept abreast of military matters, could have told Libbie much about this young man. Armstrong was the first surviving child of Emmanuel Custer and his wife, Maria Kirkpatrick Custer. Both had been widowed earlier and had brought children to their marriage. At fourteen, Autie, as his family called him, had resided in Monroe with his maternal half-sister, Lydia Ann Reed, the wife of David Reed, farmer and drayman. After attending Stebbins Academy, he returned to Harrison County, Ohio, to finish his education and enter school teaching. In 1856 he sought appointment to West Point Military Academy from Rep. John Bingham. Since Emmanuel Custer was an outspoken Democrat, Armstrong's chances had appeared remote.[25]

Custer may have owed his appointment in 1857 to the intercession of his father's friend, John Wirt, a wealthy New Rumley merchant and a leading Republican.[26] Some historians, however, find the explanation in the vexations of a local citizen, Alexander Holland. While teaching school, Custer boarded in his house and fell in love with Holland's daughter, Mollie (Mary). When her father, the story goes, intercepted a note asking her to meet Custer "at the trundle bed," he evicted the young man from his house. Holland's troubles continued, however, for the persistent suitor moved next door and besieged Mollie with letters and poems. In desperation, Holland prevailed upon Bingham to send the young man to the academy.[27]

Whatever the reasons (and perhaps both were at work), Bingham won Custer the appointment. At the academy, Custer narrowly avoided dismissal for his numerous demerits and graduated in 1861, last in a class of thirty-four.[28] Three days later, assigned to the Second Cavalry, he watched as enemy forces routed the federal army at Bull Run. Unlike the Confederates, who used their cavalry as a separate, hard-striking military arm, Union commanders confined theirs to courier, scouting, and picket duty. Gaining distinction would not prove easy for an aspiring cavalry officer.[29]

Despite the obstacles, Custer made the most of opportunities. Military expansion brought reorganization, and the Second Cavalry became the Fifth when it returned to Washington following Bull Run. Custer, assigned as aide to Brig. Gen. Philip Kearny, learned to apply strict military discipline to enlisted men.[30] He also acquired some inner discipline of his own.

Following his drunken spree in Monroe in the winter of 1862–1863, his sister, Lydia Ann, delivered a lecture so effective that Armstrong abstained from alcohol the rest of his life.[31]

During the Peninsula campaign, Custer's scouting activities won him appointment as McClellan's aide-de-camp and promotion to captain.[32] The campaign itself had failed a few miles short of Richmond. McClellan proved too cautious in the face of smaller Confederate forces and by summer 1862 had retreated down the James River. Shortly after, Lincoln relieved him of his command.

After Gen. John Pope's disastrous defeat at the Second Battle of Bull Run on September 1, Lincoln reluctantly recalled McClellan. Three weeks later, on the blood-soaked fields of Antietam, Union forces fought Gen. Robert E. Lee to a standstill. Instead of seizing the initiative, McClellan allowed Lee's Army of Northern Virginia to escape across the Potomac. When Lincoln again removed his overly cautious commander, Custer returned to Monroe, still loyal to McClellan and awaiting further developments.[33]

The day following the Boyd party, Libbie glanced down the street as she delivered clothes to a seamstress and saw Captain Custer coming towards her. Ever alert to male reaction, she knew she attracted him. By December, he had mastered her routine, joining her as she left church on Sunday or singing school in the evening. One chilly day he escorted her home and "in spite of rain and sleet went soldierlike without an umbrella, for which I admire him."[34] But when Custer called at her home, Libbie refused to see him. Nor would she attend a seminary concert with him, accompanying her father instead. Later, as she left the grounds, the gate stuck until a hand reached over and swung it wide. "Thank you sir," she responded, as the captain stepped aside.[35]

The following evening, her father returned from a visit to the Humphrey house with news of the war. In passing, he noted Custer would return to the Chickahominy at midnight. "I could almost have given way to the melting mood. I feel so sorry for him," Libbie wrote in her diary. "I think I had something to do with his going. . . . I wish him success and hope he'll come back a 'Gigodeer Brindle.'" Although she would miss his "daily walk up and down our street," he had been "in too much haste tho' I admire his perseverance."[36]

On Christmas Day, Custer was back. Within a week he resumed his vigil, passing the Bacon home "forty times a day." Forecasting "a renewal of the attack soon," Libbie left nothing to chance. While gathering her cloak, following Sunday evening choir practice, she threw Armstrong a package of candy.[37]

By New Year's the captain talked of marriage. He also revealed the attraction Libbie held for him. "Nobody," Elizabeth noted, "could entertain him but me over an hour without his being lonely. . . . He tells me he would sacrifice every earthly hope to gain my love and I tell him if I could I would give it to him."[38] Suddenly, Custer began appearing in public with Fanny. Years later, Libbie insisted she had instigated this relationship to divert gossip. At the time, however, she wrote in her diary, "Fan is trying to get him to be her devoted and all the time I know how he feels towards me."[39]

In February, Annie Colten, a visitor from Toledo, invited Libbie to return home with her. The idea delighted Bacon since rumors had reached him that his daughter was keeping company with the fair-haired army officer. When Custer appeared at the train station to see Libbie off, however, Daniel was dumbfounded. And when the captain helped her with her bags and touched her elbow as she ascended the steps, Bacon's anger rose. Libbie knew the officer far better than her father had imagined. Thankfully, Custer did not accompany the young women to Toledo.[40]

The larger city afforded Libbie a chance to attend lectures, concerts, and other outings. When she was invited to a grand ball at the Oliver house, she sent home for a formal dress. It arrived with an irate note from her father. He disapproved of the ball and the dancing involved. More important, Elizabeth had become too friendly with Captain Custer.

Libbie fired off a reply. Despite her fondness for the young man, she had dispelled his hopes. "I did it *all for you*. I like him very well, and it is pleasant always to have an escort to depend on." Still, she would never appear publicly with him again. "But," she warned, asserting herself, "I did not promise *never* to see him again. . . . You have never been a girl, Father, and you cannot tell how hard a trial this was for me."[41]

When she returned home, Elizabeth surreptitiously pursued Armstrong while he courted her and Fanny. Nettie Humphrey played the role of go-between, delivering Libbie's notes and her ambrotype. Furthermore, since Nettie lived at the Humphrey House, Libbie visited her more frequently, knowing that she would often find Armstrong in the hotel parlor.[42]

One Friday night, while attending a supper, Libbie wandered off with Custer to a small room where the two sat facing each other on a tête-à-tête. Looking up, she saw their reflection in a mirror and blurted out that it reminded her of "books and pictures I've seen." As she leaned forward,

Armstrong tried to embrace her. Libbie drew back, reminding him that she was no Fanny Fifield or Helen W. either, another young woman of questionable virtue with whom his name was linked. Never, he assured her, would he place her in their category.[43]

Armstrong continued escorting Fanny around town. After the two appeared at Sunday night church service, Libbie analyzed her feelings. She felt "little jealousy" and instead chafed at the restrictions governing her behavior. "But I think my reputation is of more account and so I am content tho' the chain frets me often." Nonetheless, her anxiety rose as she realized Custer's leave would soon expire. He might not survive his next assignment.

Increasingly, as the time drew near for his departure, Libbie worried about the notes she had sent him and her ambrotype. If these items remained on his person when he went into battle, they could fall into strange hands. Then her father might learn the true extent of her involvement. Equally as disturbing, one of Armstrong's nieces had recently told an acquaintance that Fanny's picture "isn't nearly as good as *A*'s picture of me." Later, when Libbie questioned Custer about his niece's comment, he swore that no one had seen her picture.[44]

Early in April, Libbie encountered a different Armstrong. While she and Nettie were visiting the Fifield residence, Custer began upbraiding Libbie for drinking a small amount of beer at the Humphrey house. After his lecture, Elizabeth flared back in anger. Later, when Armstrong joined a game of euchre, he directed sarcastic remarks at her during the evening.

The next day Libbie reevaluated his character. "I think I should not like C—— so well after I had become acquainted with him. I am glad I saw him last night as I did for to me he only showed one side and I saw him always in the light of a lover." Moreover, it struck her that he was "far too much interested in his game of euchre." And she admitted, "I know he fibs, for the matter of the ambrotype shows it"[45] Yet, while his flaws disturbed her, "some traits he has are splendid and I have never seen them so fully developed in any other." Besides, before leaving Fanny's house, Libbie had told Armstrong to write her through Nettie. In the end Libbie was convinced that Armstrong was not a man of "transient love." Whatever his faults, he would not desert her.[46]

Soon after, Custer joined McClellan in New York City before returning to his regiment. The officer helped his former commander prepare a defense against the criticisms leveled by Lincoln and others. Custer also learned that McClellan might seek the Democratic nomination for the presidency in 1864[47]

"I don't have near as much fun now C is gone," Libbie lamented, "but I know very well now that it is best he has gone. I am doing my duty and away from temptation." He still corresponded with Fanny, and her rival hinted at an engagement. Libbie thought it absurd, if "C—— knowing the low-minded girl as he does, should wish to *marry* her. He, like others," she surmised, "takes all she gives which I sometimes think is *everything*, but when a man has all he desires in one he rarely desires the girl for his wife. And he has," Libbie knew, "as exalted ideas about what a woman should be as anyone."[48]

Whatever the outcome, Libbie understood the rules governing court-ship. Given the double standard of morality for male and female behavior, she had played the game correctly. "I *know* the reason he loved me [was] because I wouldn't let him kiss me and treat me as if we were engaged. Yes, indeed, for on that memorable Friday night he said, Libbie, you are so different from other girls, I know girls better than you [do]." Then Armstrong had related the story of one young woman he had met in the afternoon. By evening she had initiated lovemaking by sitting on his lap, and "he kissed her as he liked. Then, from his remarks I know he knows Fan. He told me I haven't read her wrong. She little knows," Libbie added, "he made her a convenient tool to carry out his plans."[49]

With Custer gone, former suitors reappeared, including Bulkley, Rauch, Bates, and the railroad clerk from Grand Rapids, France Chandler. New ones came on the scene as well, including Maj. Frank Earle, a recent widower. Libbie found all wanting. "I like a man who is so pleased with what I say as to listen and treasure my words but the Frank or France is either too conceited to wish to listen or isn't interested." Never would her husband interrupt her as France did constantly. "C—— has quite spoiled me. Everything I said or did was remembered and treasured by him. He was," she thought, "more devoted than I ought to expect in any other man."[50]

By June, Libbie was determined to forget Custer. Each time her "violent fancy" subsided, however, Nettie received a letter from the officer. With McClellan gone, Custer's rank had reverted to first lieutenant in the Fifth Cavalry. Still, with changes occurring in the army, his correspondence contained exciting news.

McClellan's replacement, Ambrose Burnside, had sustained a humiliat-ing and costly defeat at Fredericksburg, Virginia, in December. Afterwards, Gen. Joseph Hooker proved no more capable against Robert E. Lee and his lieutenants than his predecessors. Hooker did, however, institute badly needed reforms, including a more aggressive role for the cavalry. To infuse new life, he appointed Brig. Gen. Alfred Pleasonton head of the two cavalry divisions.

Custer was assigned to Pleasonton's staff and soon won his new chief's respect by his talent for gathering accurate information and his fearlessness in combat.[51] Early in May 1863, Hooker attacked Lee at Chancellorsville, but the badly outnumbered Confederates outfought, outflanked, and routed the Union Army. Pleasonton's cavalry performance was one of the few bright spots in an otherwise dismal federal effort.[52]

After Chancellorsville, Lee again invaded the North. He sought a victory on enemy soil, resounding enough to win an alliance with Great Britain and France and assure the Confederacy's independence. As Lee's legions poured through gaps in the Blue Ridge Mountains and pushed north up the Shenandoah Valley, Jeb (James Ewell Brown) Stuart and his "Invincibles" screened his movement. Pleasonton bore responsibility for breaching the mountain passes to determine the strength and direction of the fast-moving Confederates. The result was almost constant cavalry action.

On June 9 at Brandy Station, after a full day of fighting, Stuart forced Pleasonton to retreat.[53] Nonetheless, that day marked a turning point. The Federals had fought well. Infused with pride, they never again saw the Confederate cavalry as invulnerable, even under Jeb Stuart. Among those earning commendation were Capt. Wesley Merritt and Lieutenant Custer, who arrived at Pleasonton's headquarters with a captured Confederate flag.[54]

While these events were occurring in the eastern theater of the war, Libbie enjoyed a new conquest. Fluent in French, he claimed to be a scholar, and, as always, she analyzed her latest triumph. She attributed her success to her unaffected behavior and her "lively & unversed & talkative" manner. Beguiling men was easy, requiring her only to be herself, rather than putting on airs like Fanny.[55]

In the end, however, her success left her bored. As spring gave way to summer, Libbie sank into ennui. When a friend married a captain, Libbie felt pressured to announce an engagement. She wanted none of the men now courting her. Furthermore, when she visited her married friends, she saw that they had traded in their carefree existence for the myriad and confining duties of running a household. With luck she might delay matrimony another two years or maybe forever.[56]

Still, if she never married, then what? There were no positions for young women of her background except teaching, and her experience in Sunday school left her unenthusiastic about that possibility. Years later, she claimed she would have attended the New York School of Design. If so, she never voiced that ambition in her diary, although drawing and painting were favorite pastimes.[57]

Increasingly as she feared that she was useless and idle, she turned her frustration and pent-up energy inward. She described herself as "nothing in particular" or "little beginnings of what a woman ought to be."[58] Moreover, she was irritated by the limitations of her environment. Monroe offered all the solid comforts and constrictions of small-town America.[59] In some ill-defined but deeply felt way, Libbie Bacon, attractive, bright, and ambitious, wanted more.

In Virginia, Armstrong had no time for boredom. After the engagement at Brandy Station, the cavalry entered weeks of unremitting activity, and Custer's career began a meteoric ascent. On June 22, Pleasonton was promoted to major general, and his young aide became a captain again. Custer initially was disappointed. He had sought appointment as colonel in the Fifth or Seventh Michigan Cavalry regiments. Others had received those commands instead.

On June 28, Custer received a stunning surprise—promotion to brigadier general. Pleasonton, busily reorganizing his cavalry and seeking young and aggressive leadership, believed his aide's ability warranted the new rank. Captains Wesley Merritt and E. J. Farnsworth also received brigadier commissions. Nonetheless, Custer, at twenty-three, was the youngest general in the Union Army.[60]

In addition to promoting youthful officers, Pleasonton added the Third Division to the First and Second divisions, under two brigadier generals, John Buford and David Gregg. Commanded by Brig. Gen. Judson Kilpatrick, the third consisted of two brigades under Farnsworth and Custer. Ironically, Custer's brigade included the First, Fifth, Sixth, and Seventh Michigan Cavalry regiments—two of which he had sought in vain to command only a few months earlier. The "Boy General" now led the entire Michigan brigade.[61]

By the evening of July 4, Monroe citizens were celebrating Independence Day and twin victories. The telegraph wires relayed the news that General Grant had accepted Gen. John C. Pemberton's surrender of the Southern fortress of Vicksburg that day. Following months of siege the major barrier to full federal control of the Mississippi River had been removed. Monroe citizens also learned that Lee's invasion onto Northern soil had been turned aside after a three-day battle in Pennsylvania. Moreover, the town's own boy general had played a vital role in the victory.

Lee's Army of Northern Virginia, 75,000 strong, had continued its march up the Shenandoah, roughly paralleled by Union forces under Hooker's replacement, Maj. Gen. George G. Meade. On July 1, the two armies collided at and around the little town of Gettysburg. For two days heavy fighting raged. Confederates sought to dislodge the Federals from positions along Cemetery Ridge, south of the town. On July 3, Lee, having ordered an assault on the Union center, commanded his cavalry, under Stuart, to attack the Union's right and rear.

After a heavy bombardment, some 14,000 gray infantry led by Maj. Gen. George E. Pickett advanced on the Union center. Simultaneously, Stuart, who had formed his Invincibles three miles away, moved to attack Union cavalry under Gen. David Gregg. Custer's brigade from Kilpatrick's division reinforced Gregg's two brigades.[62]

In a three-hour fight, Stuart came no closer than two and a half miles from the Union rear. Largely, this was due to the headlong charges of the Michigan brigade, led by Custer, shouting, "Come on you Wolverines."[63] Meanwhile, Pickett had suffered a bloody and disastrous repulse in his attack on the Union center. The high tide of the Confederacy was over, and Lee retreated as best he could.

The cavalry battle at Gettysburg gave the Union a new national hero, George Armstrong Custer. Lost among the accolades heaped on the boy general was the realization that his Michigan Brigade had suffered more than 25-percent casualties. An almost prohibitive loss, it would exemplify his impetuous charges.[64]

When Libbie learned about Armstrong's most recent promotion from Fanny, she hid her elation. Her rival also suggested that Libbie and Nettie might serve as bridesmaids when Fanny married Custer in the fall. Libbie wondered if Armstrong was "in earnest" or simply "flirting *desperately*" in order "to jilt such a renowned flirt." For whatever Fanny maintained, Custer's letters to Nettie declared his love for Libbie. He also wondered how Bacon had responded to his promotion and achievements.[65]

Recently Libbie had learned that Custer had shown her ambrotype to Fanny. "You look so careless like, to the plaid Garibaldi, the little bow on your head and the curl," was Fanny's detailed description. Once more Elizabeth felt ambivalent. "He had no business to write the passionate messages he has about me & to me when he has been writing so constantly

& lovelike to Fan. He is nothing to me. He never will be," she concluded. Still, her feelings were mixed as she acknowledged, "I like him much."[66]

On July 5, David Reed, Armstrong's brother-in-law, appeared at the Bacon home, carrying a "huge envelope like the affairs of state!" Inside was a large drawing of Custer, bearing the signature of Al Waud, an artist for *Harper's*. Libbie stared incredulously at Armstrong's beardless face, framed by long locks and "an old slouch *reb* hat, a brigand jacket & shirt & scarf on his shoulder—old forlorn pants & boots over them." The "brigand jacket" was of black velveteen with swirls of gold braid from wrists to elbows. Underneath he wore a sailor's shirt with wide collar on which his orderly had sewn a star. Around his neck was a bright red tie.

As Libbie gave the sketch back to Reed, he handed her a letter from Custer. Despite her embarrassment and confusion, she read that Armstrong had narrowly escaped death and capture, largely because he had been wearing his rebel hat.[67] Reed explained that Custer had commissioned him to show this packet to Fanny and his friends, and most especially—and this was important—to make certain she saw it. Libbie thanked him, noting that she was grateful to Custer for "a great many pleasant times last winter as he was so gallant & polite." Then she remarked casually as Reed was leaving that she expected Armstrong to return in the fall and marry Fanny. Was that what Libbie thought, Reed inquired, turning round. If she did not know Custer's intentions, no one did. "By his manner his words & all," the young woman concluded, "he knew C—— loved me."

Since Custer had confided in his family, Libbie's doubts now receded. "C—— loves me devotedly & then honest people know it." Still, fearful of her father's reaction if he learned about Reed's visit, she begged Rhoda, who was recovering from a prolonged illness, to say nothing to Daniel.[68] That evening Laura Noble gave Libbie additional verification that, among the women in Custer's life, she stood first. While visiting a mutual friend in Maryland, Armstrong had shown her the ambrotype he carried on his person—Libbie's. Fanny's was in his trunk. Elizabeth's spirits, high since Reed's visit, now soared.[69]

Several days later, Armstrong's letter to Nettie contained additional assurances. He regretted Libbie's statement that he had "violated my promise to her in regard to her ambrotype. I never showed it, nor even described it, to Fanny." He had no idea where Fanny had obtained her information unless she had inquired at the gallery. Whatever, "Fanny *has nothing in her power to bestow what wd. induce me to show her that ambrotype*. I know nothing of what representations of our intimacy she has made to Libbie," he added. "It is no different from what I told her. I would write more, but must mount on my good horse and away."[70]

Whatever Armstrong's assurances, he had not broken off with Fanny. Earlier he had shown Pleasonton the young woman's picture. His commander was so taken with her that he now offered Custer a leave, provided he returned home to marry her. On July 26, Armstrong wrote his sister, Lydia Ann Reed, asking, "Shall I come?"[71]

Following Gettysburg, Custer's Second Brigade pressed hard on the heels of the retreating Confederates. Had Mead pursued with all his force, he might have cornered Lee's battered army. Unfortunately, he exhibited too much of McClellan's earlier caution.[72]

Whatever the deficiencies of high command, Custer's flamboyant leadership captivated his troopers. Always in front, urging them, "Come on, you Wolverines," he shared their dangers as he directed their movements. Soon red ties abounded throughout the brigade, and newspapers reported on the American Murat, the newest hero—the boy general.[73]

By mid-August Custer wrote Nettie, giving her information on Capt. Jacob Greene, now his assistant adjutant general and Nettie's sweetheart. The young hero also wondered how Judge Bacon had responded to his latest triumphs. Surely by emerging a brigadier general, Custer was becoming more acceptable. Nettie's response was not encouraging: Bacon still held "strong prejudices," but, she wrote, "If the time ever comes when I find myself able to assist in removing any of those prejudices, you know I will enter the work most heartily."[74]

By late September, Custer had suffered a minor leg wound in a second battle at Brandy Station and returned home for fifteen days. After her frequent meetings with the general, Libbie wrote of her love for "Dear C——," although increasingly she called him "Autie." "True a thousand doubts come into my mind like tormenting devils and I doubt if I love him," she wrote, still displaying some equivocation. "I do tho," she told herself, "and I shall sometime be his 'little wife.'"[75]

During their courtship, Libbie had received conflicting signals from Armstrong. Although he had sent messages of devotion through Nettie, she knew that he still wooed Fanny. Faced with such contradictions, Libbie resolved her confusion by interpreting any uncertainties in Custer's favor. Even his flamboyant appearance, almost repelling earlier, now magnified his appeal. She saw him as if he were a literary hero. "I read him in all my books.

When I take in the book heroes there comes dashing in with them my life hero my dear boy general."[76] Late in October she summarized her feelings: "Every other man seems so ordinary beside my own particular *star*."[77]

While Libbie had not yet obtained her father's consent to their courtship, Custer's rising fame made it likely. Already Daniel listened to her "because he feels how much harm has often been done by parents utterly refusing." In fact, "Father is to my surprise on my side." Instead, Rhoda proved recalcitrant, convinced that Armstrong would make a poor husband.[78] The opinions of others, save Daniel's, no longer counted. Custer's rising career could rescue Libbie from a staid, conventional life.

And so Elizabeth had made up her mind. When Armstrong left for the front on October 5, Daniel came to the train station to see him off. Since Bacon deliberately surrounded himself with a crowd, Armstrong had no chance to ask permission to correspond with his daughter. Libbie knew, however, that, at the earliest moment, he would write her father.[79] Although anxious until permission was given, she expected Daniel's consent. After all, one day strangers would ask him if he knew General Custer's father-in-law. Then, straightening himself up to show his full height, his eyes would fasten on theirs and he would respond, "Look upon my face."[80]

Libbie Bacon had chosen her husband.[81]

CHAPTER 3

The Bride

DANIEL responded equivocally to Armstrong's request to correspond with Libbie. "Your ability, energy and force of character I have always admired and no one can feel more gratified than myself at your well-earned reputation and your high & honorable position." A decision, however, might take "weeks or even months."[1] Custer wrote again, thanking Bacon for the compliments and acknowledging past faults, but surely two years of abstinence alleviated concerns. Finally, Armstrong had been out in the world since sixteen and "surrounded with temptation," but he had "always had a purpose in life."[2] Satisfied by these statements, Bacon consented to Custer's request. Soon Armstrong received Libbie's letter addressed to "my more than friend—at last."[3]

Fanny, angry over her rejection, spread stories "prejudicial" to Custer. Although the gossip distressed her, Libbie concluded, "I love him though notwithstanding all."[4] Bacon, nonetheless, worried. How would she respond should Armstrong "play the hypocrite." Libbie assured her father that, while Armstrong's death "would almost kill me," if he deceived her, "my pride would support me and all my love would vanish."[5] Relieved, Daniel raised no further objections. "When I say anything that would seem an impediment to my marrying Armstrong Father is the one to explain it all away," Libbie recorded in her diary. He now judged the Custer daughters "as good as ours or your mother's." As for the various young women Autie had courted earlier, she wrote, "Why he was a boy then & never had been in society & etc."[6]

By Thanksgiving Armstrong pressed for a winter wedding. Libbie, however, pleaded for time. As a judge's daughter, she probably knew better than most young women the legal disabilities wives assumed in marriage.

Certainly she regretted losing her identity as a single woman, for in one letter, she wrote: "How I love my name Libbie BACON. Libbie B-A-C-O-N. Bacon. Libbie Bacon." Aware that wedlock "means trouble," she also lamented the loss of youthful pleasures.[7]

On a more prosaic level, Libbie needed time to prepare for a wedding. More important, she may have wondered if the gift too readily given would be fully appreciated, for she asked, "If I am worth having am I not worth waiting for?"[8] Armstrong assured her she would always remain Libbie Bacon, merely adding Custer to her name. As for her pleasures, he personally guaranteed her happiness. Finally, better to marry soon before spring campaigns precluded a honeymoon.[9]

Libbie hesitated, afraid that by giving in on this last point, she would establish a precedent for resolving other matters. Rhoda, now captivated by the eager suitor, counseled otherwise. When she had capitulated to Mr. Pitts's wish for an early wedding, "I always had my own way afterwards, in Everything!"[10] Nonetheless, Rhoda also counseled Libbie that if she were ever unhappy, she should tell her parents. "But that," Elizabeth informed her fiancé, "I could never do."[11] As she now planned for a February wedding, Libbie reminded Autie of the valuable prize he had won. He would never know how many rivals he had overcome, although few had actually proposed.[12]

On December 12, Daniel wrote Armstrong. While the character references Armstrong had solicited from Monroe's prominent citizens were reassuring, he wished his future son-in-law were a devout Christian. Still, at Armstrong's age, "My morals and my future were far short of what you are now."[13] Seeking to dispel any misunderstandings, Bacon noted he was "not a wealthy man." Most of his holdings were in real estate, with "sale and price depending on unseen contingencies." Libbie would inherit his homestead, and he had set aside several hundred dollars for a trousseau befitting her status "as the wife of a General. Beyond this," she might inherit nothing, "but circumstances occurring ever so favorable, she would not have a patrimony at my death exceeding $10,000."[14]

Whatever the tensions between Daniel and Armstrong, Libbie's relations with her father improved. As she informed Armstrong, "We have become so intimate." In the past Daniel had dismissed her attempts to "tell him some joke," by "walk[ing] away downtown, leaving me to finish a sentence to the wall." Now he laughed at her humor, and she was discovering "what a splendid old gentleman he really is."[15]

Libbie, however, still had faults. She often satirized people, said "the most *withering* things," loved flattery, and enjoyed the stares of strange men. While she had not allowed other men to kiss her, her virtue rose "more from principle than from inclination."[16] Despite professed flaws, the ideals of Victorian womanhood, to which both Libbie and Autie subscribed, envisioned a wife uplifting her spouse.

As soon as the engagement was official, Libbie began attempting to improve Autie. Laura Noble's mother had advised her, "General Custer has elements of character which will develop . . . and, dear girl, some of that development rests with you. Oh, Autie," Libbie continued, "I tremble at the responsibility. I am but a little girl — not of course in years, but being an only child. . . . It is a solemn thought to become a wife."[17]

Elizabeth never doubted that her fiancé needed reformation. While he no longer drank, she knew of "a stain" on his character. She had heard that "Genl. Kilpatrick used an oath with every sentence he uttered, and that General Custer was not much better. I know this is exaggerated. But . . . God cure you of it." More troubling was Autie's lack of faith, for "religion is part of my life."[18]

Armstrong, acknowledging his faults in turn, noted that while he had overcome intemperance, he found profanity a minor vice, too satisfying to give up. Gambling was more serious, and given his impending marriage, he now made a solemn pledge. Never again would he "engage in any game of chance with any intention of staking money or . . . participate in any game played for stakes of any kind."[19] It was a promise he never kept.

The holidays arrived, bringing Libbie, not Autie, but his large photograph. At Christmas parties she saw Fanny, bedecked in furs and displaying a large diamond on her hand. In time Miss Fifield's marriage to Charles Thomas, "wholesale merchant prince," gave her a fashionable address on Boston's Newbury Street.[20]

Although Libbie had originally favored a simple afternoon ceremony in her home, she decided upon the more fashionable "ostentation" of an evening church wedding. After instructing Autie to wear his "full-dress uniform," she selected an elaborate gown and train and ordered a bouquet of roses, tied with yellow ribbon, the cavalry's color. "After all, you are not marrying a girl *entirely* unknown in this State and elsewhere." She chose Erasmus Boyd to officiate and the Rev. C. N. Mattoon to assist.[21]

A month before the wedding, an alarmed Bacon wrote his future son-in-law. Some members of Congress had objected to Custer's confirmation as brigadier general. Autie assured him that Senator Zachariah Chandler and Rep. F. W. Kellogg saw no cause for concern. Enemies, including Michigan's governor, Austin Blair, had tried to obstruct his promotion to colonel of the Seventh Michigan Cavalry by calling him a "Copperhead." That epithet implied that, as a Democrat, Custer could not be relied upon to support the Lincoln Administration's war aims, which now included the end of slavery. The allegations were baseless. (He did not note that they had grown out of hot-tempered remarks from McClellan's staff, to which he may have contributed, following the general's second removal.) Custer believed all charges against him "completely refuted" and had "no anxiety whatever in regard to my confirmation." He had said nothing earlier to spare Libbie "unnecessary anxiety and discomfort."[22]

On her wedding day, Libbie told her father, "I have proved my admiration for your belief in selfmade men by marrying one."[23] That evening an overflow crowd assembled at the First Presbyterian Church. Shortly before eight, the bridal party arrived. When Custer escorted Rhoda to her pew, many were disappointed that he had cut off his locks.[24]

Then Libbie appeared on her father's arm. Her full, stiff silk dress seemed to "walk into church alone," while a long veil, fashionable since the 1840s, floated from the wreath of orange blossoms around her head.[25] Weddings had recently become solemn affairs, eliciting tears rather than laughter, but Daniel prided himself on "not acting the babe." Later he wrote his sister Charity: "It was said to be the most splendid wedding ever seen in the State. From one to two hundred more in the church than ever before and as many unable to enter for want of room." Afterwards, three hundred attended the reception and admired the expensive silver serving set and other costly gifts.[26]

With Libbie gone, Daniel wrote her cousin in Grand Rapids. "We want to adopt you, Rebecca, for our girl. . . . True, we cannot promise you a General. But—it might be better in some ways—we can promise you a lawyer or a minister. Mark that."[27] One of Custer's biographers believes that Libbie's father "was not quite reconciled to her choice of a boisterous soldier. Someday, when he felt better satisfied, he must write Armstrong's name in the family Bible, but not now." And he notes: "He never did."[28]

In 1864, attendants often accompanied newlyweds part way as they left for their wedding tour, a whirlwind of visiting before settling down to married life.[29] At Cleveland, the bridesmaids and groomsmen said good-bye and returned to their homes, leaving Libbie and Autie to continue by train alone. In Rochester, New York, Libbie saw her first play, *Uncle Tom's Cabin,* before stopping in Onondaga, where she introduced her husband to her Aunt Charity's family. Then they called on Libbie's Aunt Eliza Sabin of Howlett Hill, who had invited relatives to bring their fiddles for dancing. All were excited about meeting Armstrong, the general they had read about in the *New York Herald.* Initially his short hair disappointed them. Bacon was relieved to learn later, however, that "acquaintance with him changed everybody's views. Everywhere, without exception, he made *a most favorable impression.*"[30]

After leaving Onondaga, Libbie and Autie went on to West Point Academy. When she arrived, Elizabeth's first impressions confirmed all her husband had told her. She had never seen "so lovely a place in the United States," and she understood why he wanted to be buried there. Proudly he introduced her to his former professors. Everyone, including the dogs, remembered Armstrong.[31]

When he left Elizabeth alone, several cadets escorted her down the shaded bower known as Lovers' Walk. Later a professor kissed the bride. When Autie returned, Libbie related these events. After they boarded the train for New York City, she noticed her husband's silence and his expression, which resembled an "incarnated thundercloud." "But," she argued, the professor had been "a veritable Methuselah. And the cadets who showed me Lovers' Walk were like school-boys with their shy ways and nice, clean, friendly faces." Explanations availed her nothing. Eventually she blurted out, "Well, you left me with them, Autie!"[32]

The silence continued. In rising consternation and fearful of rejection, Libbie sought an explanation. Armstrong explained that he had incurred many demerits at the academy. As a result, "these long lonely beats that he walked [and] the many solitary confinements of the guard house where he served his time for misdemeanors had established a habit of long silences," and he asked her "not to mind them."[33] Libbie had experienced the first of her husband's "many silent seasons."[34]

After a brief stay in New York, the couple traveled on to Washington, where for the first time, Libbie met politicians, diplomats, dignitaries, and their families. In a city where "some one attempted to throw a stone across Pennsylvania Avenue and" instead "hit five brigadiers," the boy general and his attractive bride received more attention than most.[35] Military duty, however, cut their honeymoon short. Within days after their arrival, Custer received orders to rejoin his brigade.[36]

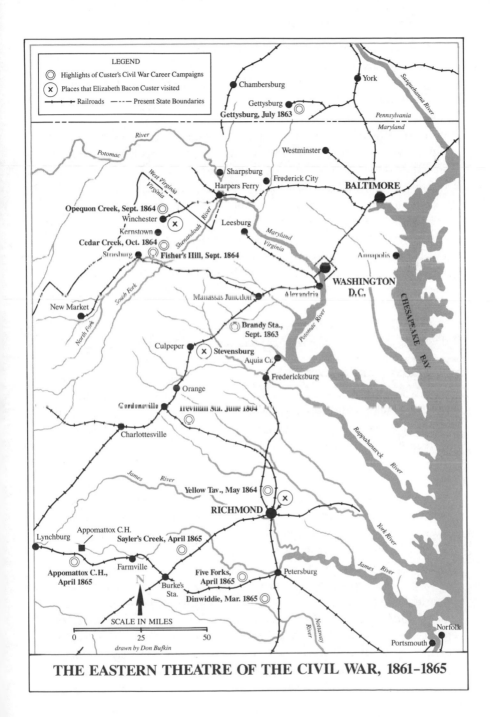

LEGEND

◎ Highlights of Custer's Civil War Career Campaigns
⊗ Places that Elizabeth Bacon Custer visited
┼┼┼┼ Railroads   ┄┄┄ Present State Boundaries

Chambersburg

York

Susquehanna River

Gettysburg
Gettysburg, July 1863 ◎

Pennsylvania
Maryland

Potomac River

Westminster

Sharpsburg
Harpers Ferry   Frederick City

BALTIMORE

Opequon Creek, Sept. 1864 ◎
Winchester ⊗
Kernstown
Cedar Creek, Oct. 1864 ◎
Strasburg
Fisher's Hill, Sept. 1864 ◎

Leesburg

Shenandoah River

West Virginia
Virginia

Annapolis

Maryland
Virginia

New Market

South Fork

North Fork

Manassas Junction   Alexandria

WASHINGTON D.C.

CHESAPEAKE BAY

Potomac River

◎ **Brandy Sta., Sept. 1863**

Culpeper   ⊗ **Stevensburg**
Aquia Ct.

Orange   Fredericksburg

Gordonsville   **Trevilian Sta. June 1864** ◎

Charlottesville

James River

Rappahannock River

Yellow Tav., May 1864 ◎ ◎
⊗

RICHMOND ●

York River

Appomattox C.H.
Lynchburg   **Sayler's Creek, April 1865** ◎

Farmville   James River

Appomattox C.H., April 1865 ◎

N

Burke's Sta.
Five Forks, April 1865 ◎   Petersburg

Dinwiddie, Mar. 1865 ◎

Nottoway River

Norfolk

SCALE IN MILES

0   25   50   Portsmouth

drawn by Don Bufkin

THE EASTERN THEATRE OF THE CIVIL WAR, 1861–1865

Libbie had no intention of enduring unnecessary separation. She accompanied her husband when he returned to his command at Stevensburg, Virginia, south of Brandy Station on the extreme right flank of the Army of the Potomac. Their quarters consisted of three upstairs rooms in a farmhouse serving as headquarters. Furnishings came from odds and ends provided by a destitute couple living downstairs and camping equipment supplied by the army. Outside, staff members lived in tents, and farther away was the brigade camp.[37]

Here Libbie met her husband's two black servants, a twelve-year-old named Johnny and another "contraband" about twenty-five or twenty-six named Eliza.[38] The short, stocky woman had walked away from her impoverished master's plantation after she had heard about the Emancipation Proclamation. She met Custer at Amosville, in Rappahannock County, Virginia, in August 1863. When the newly minted general asked her to join him in exchange for serving as his cook and maid, she had evaluated him carefully before responding, "I reckon I would."[39]

Eager for female companionship, Eliza welcomed the young bride, and the two fashioned an arrangement that lasted for five years. In return for mothering Libbie and serving the couple, Eliza brooked no interference. "Day by day Eliza tactfully & quietly took us all in hand. It was tacitly understood that I was not to know anything about the 'mess,'" Libbie recalled. "I felt no [discernible] aspirations to housekeeping . . . and I knew that I was not foisted upon anyone without a perfect understanding of my ignorance of housework."[40]

From the beginning of their marriage, Autie instructed Libbie to avoid housekeeping so that she could always join him in some activity at a moment's notice.[41] Thus Eliza remained cook, laundress, and domestic overseer—areas in which she was expert. She added tasty bits to the army mess "by wheedling, some scolding that was not dangerous, and by as delicate diplomacy as many a subtle, deep-thinking person could have exercised," Libbie remembered fondly.[42]

Despite the comfort Eliza provided, Libbie experienced a "violent transition" in adapting to army life. Each day demanded new adjustments. To Elizabeth, Autie was her exuberant young husband. To the men, often middle-aged or gray-haired, he was the general, barking out gruff and often harsh commands. Moreover, she sometimes unwittingly violated military protocol. As she wrote her parents six weeks after her wedding, "One day I was expatiating over the pleasant gentlemanly air an officer in the regular army has. After the company left I was informed that by such remarks I would produce hard feeling, and so I am improving."[43]

But marriage to a general also had its compensations. The young couple enjoyed Pleasonton's six-course meals and reveled in the perquisites of rank. Not many young women could have written their parents, "Such style as we go in!" Although most officers and wives relied on army ambulances, "my General has a carriage with silver harness that he captured last summer, and two magnificent matched horses (not captures). We have an escort of four or six soldiers riding behind."[44]

Whatever the pleasures, war loomed in the background. During their Washington stay, Autie had received word of an impending raid. Kilpatrick, as commander of the Second Division of the Cavalry Corps, and Col. Ulric Dahlgren, his assistant, planned to strike Richmond and free imprisoned soldiers. Meanwhile, Custer would lead 2,000 men into Albemarle County, Virginia. Swinging around Lee's left flank, he would tear up the Virginia Central railroad and move to Charlottesville, thereby drawing troops away from the Confederate capital.[45] Late in February Libbie maintained a brave front as she said good-bye to her husband. Afterwards, she felt "overwhelmed." Stevensburg seemed "desolate," and she distrusted the Southern family who owned the property. Reluctantly she returned to Washington.[46]

The raid proved disastrous. Kilpatrick and Dahlgren were driven back, and lives were lost, including Dahlgren's. Custer made it almost to Charlottesville, burning a mill and a bridge on the Rivanna River but barely escaping a Confederate ambush. Nothing was accomplished other than "disabl[ing] for the time being 3,000 or 4,000 of the very flower of our cavalry," according to one account.[47] Libbie's anxiety was not relieved until she received Pleasonton's telegram informing her of Autie's safe arrival at Madison Court House.[48]

Soon after the abortive Kilpatrick-Dahlgren raid, Autie appeared in person. The couple resumed their pleasurable round of activities, visiting dignitaries, friends, theaters, and restaurants while continuing their honeymoon. Later, when again separated, their letters indicate that they had become passionate, eager, and imaginative lovers.[49]

The Custers stayed in Washington briefly before returning to Stevensburg. Libbie immersed herself in her husband's career, often traveling with him to Signal Station to observe the tent city that was the Army of the Potomac. Periodically, Armstrong undertook small scouting expeditions or reconnaissance missions around Ely's Ford and Blair Mountain in Madison

County, Virginia. These Libbie dreaded.[50] She waited fearfully until she heard an "unforgettable" sound, "the clank of a sabre rattling on stairs. . . . In the middle of a wakeful night of suspense, the door burst open to welcome a mud besplattered but perfectly fresh and buoyant warrior, whooping with joy, having eluded with an inferior force, the pursuing foe."[51]

They had not been at the farmhouse long before disturbing news arrived. Meade's headquarters requested information on a young woman's visit to Custer's brigade the previous fall. Incarcerated in the Old Capitol prison on charges of spying, Annie Eleanor Jones was seeking a pardon and asked Custer to verify her statements.

After joining the troops at eighteen, Jones, an orphan, had lived with several officers, including Gen. Franz Sigel. Later Gen. Julius Stahl's staff had arrested her for crossing enemy lines at Fairfax Court House although they had later released her. Jones then joined Kilpatrick's command "and went to the front as the friend and companion of Gen. Custer." Kilpatrick, "jealous of Gen. Custer's attention," accused her of spying for the Confederates. Tried, sentenced, and paroled on condition she leave Virginia, she rejoined the soldiers. Her second arrest brought a long sentence. She was not a spy, however, and ill from her "long confinement and other causes," wished to return to her home in Massachusetts.[52]

Custer responded that Annie Jones had served as a nurse before he had ordered her out of the Third Division. Shortly after, she had reappeared at Hartwood Church and, given the late hour and her fatigue, Custer had allowed her to spend the night. He had not seen her since, but he believed her innocent of spying. Instead, her almost mad determination "to distinguish herself by some deed or daring" was the source of her troubles. "So far as her statement in relation to General Kilpatrick and myself goes," he added, "it is simply untrue."[53]

During this period, Autie suffered a severe concussion in a carriage accident and received twenty days sick leave.[54] The Custers boarded a train for Washington, specially outfitted to transport Ulysses S. Grant to the capital. On March 1, Grant had been promoted to lieutenant general and general-in-chief, following his most recent victories at Chattanooga, Lookout Mountain, and Missionary Ridge. The train "swayed like a boat," over newly repaired and rickety tracks, but Libbie wrote her parents, "If the country could afford to lose so valuable a man as Grant it could afford to lose us."[55]

Libbie found the general-in-chief "very ordinary-looking." Where others saw him as quiet or shy, however, she described him as talkative and "funny" and laughed at his joke that "small army men invariably ride horses 17 hands high." He was also considerate and, rather than smoke in her presence, retired to the platform. Armstrong brought him back by assuring him that Libbie had no objections to cigars.[56]

In Washington the couple were pleasantly surprised. On the cover of the March 19 issue of *Harper's Weekly* was an Al Waud sketch of Autie leading the Charlottesville raid. A week later, the same magazine devoted its centerfold to Custer's raid.[57] When they arrived at the Capitol, congressmen invited Armstrong to the House floor. Libbie watched from the balcony as a gathering of politicians introduced themselves. "None of the other generals," she wrote her parents, "received half the attention, and their arrivals are scarcely noticed in the papers. I am so amazed at his reputation I cannot but write you about it. I wonder his head is not turned. Tho not disposed to put on airs," she continued, "I find it very agreeable to be the wife of a man so generally known and respected."[58]

Shortly after, Libbie rented a room in Hyatt's Sixth Street Washington boardinghouse while her husband returned to the front.[59] Under Grant, changes were affecting Autie's career. Though General Meade remained in nominal command of the Army of the Potomac, the general-in-chief assumed control in the field. He transferred Pleasonton and Kilpatrick to the western theater and replaced them with Maj. Gen. Philip H. Sheridan and Brig. Gen. James H. Wilson. Initially Custer was upset. While he knew of Sheridan's victories at Chattanooga and Missionary Ridge, he had no idea "Little Phil" was eager to engage Jeb Stuart's Invincibles in Northern Virginia. First, however, Sheridan had to overcome Meade, who still relegated cavalry to escort and picket duty.[60]

More immediate, Custer thought he deserved command of Kilpatrick's Third Division. Instead, James Harrison Wilson, "a friend of Grant's," had no command experience whatsoever and "since assuming command of the Division, he has made himself ridiculous by the ignorance he displays in regard to cavalry." Armstrong consoled himself that at least his brigade, now part of the First Division, occupied the place of honor under Maj. Gen. Alfred A. Torbert.[61]

By April, Libbie was socializing with government officials and other dignitaries. Attractive, a good conversationalist, and always fashionably attired, she had no trouble obtaining invitations in her husband's absence. Michigan Sens. Zachariah Chandler and Morton Wilkinson and Rep. F. W. Kellogg eagerly sought her company and filled her dance books at "hops."[62]

Elizabeth's association with these powerful men would pay dividends when Autie again sought promotion. For the present, however, she faced delicate problems. Chandler and Kellogg often became lecherous after consuming alcohol, but despite her youth and inexperience, Libbie evaded their advances without bruising their egos. At the same time she always informed her husband of their attempts to kiss her. In part she was being honest, but in part, she may have been reminding him that other men found her attractive.[63]

Whatever her motivation, Libbie was as dedicated as her husband to advancing his career. In addition to the strong physical attraction binding them together, they had formed a partnership, committed to moving the boy general up the ladder of success. Since his youth, Autie had read works by Sir Walter Scott and Charles Lever glorifying knights of old and the escapades of Napoleonic-era cavaliers. Many of his closest friends at West Point, moreover, had been Southerners who viewed the cavalier as the epitome of manhood.[64]

Given these influences and an intuitive sense that Northerners yearned for their own version of a cavalier, similar to the South's Jeb Stuart, both Custers contributed to that image. Armstrong recalled devil-may-care cavaliers of days gone by, his long, golden curls, flamboyant gold-braided costume, and scarlet cravat taunting Confederate sharpshooters in battle. Libbie, by contrast, a doll-like figure, supplied the female attractiveness, well-bred decorum, and social skills of a polished lady. The combination was magical.[65]

Among Washington notables important to impress, none surpassed Lincoln. Libbie had already seen his "careworn" face at the theater, but she met him for the first time when Representative and Mrs. Kellogg took her to a scheduled levee. When they arrived at the White House at 10 A.M., Elizabeth found herself in a huge throng. The press of the crowd propelled everyone through the porch and into "the Holy of Holies, the Blue Room." There the tall, gaunt, and rapidly aging man stood beside his "short, squatty, and plain" little wife.

When Libbie was introduced, Lincoln shook her hand, but no sooner had she moved away than the significance of her name struck him. Reclaiming her hand, Lincoln remarked, "So this is the young woman whose husband goes into a charge with a whoop and a shout. Well, I'm told he won't do so any more," he noted, implying that marriage had made Custer more careful. When Libbie disagreed, Lincoln replied, "Oh, then you want to be a widow, I see," and both laughed. As she was leaving, Libbie instructed one of Lincoln's secretaries "to tell Mr. Lincoln he would have gained a vote, if soldiers' wives were allowed one."[66]

Autie had good news of his own. His first meeting with Sheridan had gone well, for the new chief of cavalry appreciated his bravery. Libbie's participation in Washington society, especially her attendance at Lincoln's levee, also delighted him. "You certainly were honored by his Highness—as you should be. You know how proud I am of my darling." As for attending hops with Senator Chandler: "You did perfectly right in accepting; it is just what I urged you to do. Do not heed the idle opinions of those whose time is occupied with other people's business."[67] If such socializing led to unwelcome advances, Autie obviously believed she could extricate herself.

Besides, Libbie's relationship with the Kelloggs was paying dividends. True, Autie had not yet obtained command of the Third Division, but the Michigan congressman counseled hope. "No true man like you can be killed by such gross favoritism on the part of the Chief of the Army."[68]

The Custers, married a short time, were still working out their respective roles. Armstrong appointed Libbie family treasurer and asked her to "practice economy and avoid extravagance" while obtaining "anything needful for your comfort or happiness." He also cautioned her to remember that they were "just entering on life's journey with all its cares, and, I hope, in a short time its *responsibilities*."[69] Of the $500 Autie deposited with her that summer, Libbie spent $300 on clothes and other items "apart from board."[70] Time was required before she would learn to "practice economy and avoid extravagance."

Armstrong, like most nineteenth-century men, believed his wife his moral superior. Through her influence he was becoming a better man. "Loving so fine a being truly and devotedly as I do, it seems impossible that I ever should or could be very wicked."[71] Several weeks later, he returned to the same theme. "I suppose my little one has been to church to-day. Among the traits of her character I first learned to love was her religious earnestness. . . . It may seem strange to you, dear girl, that I, a non-professing (tho not an unbeliever) Christian, should so ardently desire you to remain so." Very likely his statement did not strike Libbie as strange at all, since her upbringing had stressed piety as the primary virtue for women.[72]

Although Autie did not pray in the usual sense, before each battle he "never omitted to pray inwardly, devoutly. Never have I failed to commend myself to God's keeping, asking Him to forgive my past sins, and to watch over me in danger." Afterward, he felt confident "that my destiny is in the hands of the Almighty. This belief, more than any other fact or reason, makes me brave and fearless as I am." Nonetheless, he could not explain in a letter why he resisted formal religion. "You are the first to whom I ever made this explanation. . . . I want you to know me as I am."[73]

While Libbie still hoped to convert her husband one day, his statement alleviated some of her anxieties. Inwardly she felt a sense of foreboding. "The silence in the papers," she wrote her parents, "shows that a great battle is expected." She saw signs everywhere. "Long trains of army wagons rumble over the pavement. On an average three regiments of Potomac veterans back from furlough and some new ones pass through a day. Mrs. Wooster and I hang from my windows watching them, as, just a block from here, they turn to cross the bridge—'into the jaws of death' it seems. The bands—they have fine ones—always play."[74]

Elizabeth was correct. Grant had assigned the highest priority to destroying Confederate armies, as opposed to occupying territories and cities. Thus he had laid plans to wage unremitting warfare against Lee's army before taking Richmond. He hoped to avoid a war of siege and attrition since it would endanger Lincoln's administration. Nonetheless, if one came, Grant could replace his losses; Lee could not. In the end that promised Northern victory, provided Union will did not falter.[75]

As Grant began his offensive, Autie wrote Libbie on May 4. "This is probably the last letter you will get before the coming fight. The entire army moves to-night and begins crossing the Rapidan at Germania and lower fords. Communication with Washington will probably be abandoned for several days but do not borrow trouble."[76]

The next day the 118,000 men making up the Army of the Potomac clashed with 64,000 graybacks in a heavily wooded region. After two days of fighting, Union forces had sustained 17,500 casualties to the Confederates' 7,000. Instead of retreating across the river, as Hooker had done a year earlier after Chancellorsville, Grant ordered an advance. As the weary men realized they would not withdraw, "our spirits rose." One participant remembered, "We marched free. The men began to sing."[77]

At Spotsylvania Courthouse on Lee's right, they renewed the struggle. Again at Cold Harbor in early June, Union casualties were staggering, totaling more than 44,000 men to the Confederates' 25,000. But Grant had promised Lincoln he would not turn back. And Lincoln, despite cries of "Butcher" Grant, never wavered in his support for a general who would fight. With each move, Grant, always driving southeastward, came closer and closer to Richmond.[78]

That spring, Grant's intervention had freed Sheridan from General Meade's directives. The cavalry now received orders to break off Lee's communication lines and destroy supplies bound for his forces. Above all, they were to go after Jeb Stuart.[79]

Stuart met the Federals at Yellow Tavern, six miles north of Richmond. The Union forces outnumbered the Invincibles two to one and, equipped with rapid-fire carbines, advanced against heavy fire. Custer led his brigade in a "brilliantly executed" charge, according to Sheridan, that started as a walk, accelerated to "a trot, then, at full speed, rushed on the enemy." Seeing the Michigan brigade charging on his left, Stuart dashed to the front to rally his troops. In the onslaught, he was mortally wounded, and the gray cavalry was driven across the Chickahominy River.[80]

Elated, Custer wrote his bride. "The Michigan Brigade has covered itself with undying glory. . . . Genl. Sheridan sent an aide on the battlefield with his congratulations. So did Genl. Merritt: 'The Michigan Brigade is at the top of the ladder.'" He enclosed honeysuckle from "inside the fortifications of Richmond."[81]

Two days later, he wrote that a captain would bring Libbie messages, giving her "a full account of our late battles." Already she had changed him for the better, for in recent engagements, he had "sworn far less . . . than ever before." Even "with the bullets whistling by me and shells bursting all around me I thought of you. You are in my thoughts, always, day and night."[82]

The next day, Autie devoted an entire letter, except for brief comments on Stuart's death, to his tender feelings and his wish to be with "the idol of my heart. I never loved my Gipsie as I do now my love *almost* makes me wish I was out of the Army so that nothing could separate me from my more than life dear girl." Noting her influence, he assured Libbie, "You control nearly every action of my life you shape my conduct." If he sought glory in battle, it was only to leave her a name "which will be a source of pride to you in after life." Had he fallen, her name would have been the last word he uttered and her "memory the last I cherished and my last wish would have been for my little one."[83]

On June 11 and 12, at Trevillian Station, sixty miles northwest of Richmond, Sheridan faced Stuart's successor, Wade Hampton. Custer's Michigan brigade found itself in the thick of fighting as the two opposing forces fought in dense underbrush and trees, and casualties totaled 20 percent, the highest for the cavalry in the entire war. At one point the boy general, nearly surrounded, fought his way out of an entrapment. He left behind Eliza and Johnny, three horses, and all of Libbie's letters.[84] By late evening on the twelfth, Sheridan retraced his steps to the Union base at Cold Harbor. He had not won at Trevilian Station, but he had exacted a heavy toll from his adversaries.[85]

Eliza escaped the Confederates and rejoined Autie. She failed, however, to retrieve his valise with Libbie's ambrotype and other personal material. "I regret the loss of your letters more than all else. I enjoyed every word you wrote," Autie confided, "but do not relish the idea of others amusing themselves with them, particularly as some of the expressions employed. . . . Somebody must be more careful hereafter in the use of *double entendu*."[86]

Libbie was not concerned. "Let me unburden my mind about the matter, since your letter implies chiding, tho the slightest and the kindliest. No Southerner could say, if they are *gentlemen* that I lacked refinement. There can be nothing low between man and wife if they love each other." In her view, their correspondence was "holy and sacred. Only cruel people would not understand the spirit in which I wrote it."[87]

The Bacons read the reports of mounting carnage with rising alarm. "Do not fail to telegraph if anything happens to Armstrong, Greene or [Frederick] Nims," Daniel admonished his daughter. "Be calm, submissive and composed is the wish and prayer of your Father."[88] Libbie was afraid, but she dwelt on the future. "I think of the day of peace when little children's voices will call to us. I can hardly wait for my little boy and girl," she confided in one letter. In it she included drawings of two imagined offspring and a sketch of an older, parental Autie. "Dear *Father*, do you think you will look that way?" War or no war, Libbie wanted children.[89]

By mid-June, the Army of the Potomac was before the Confederate entrenchments at Petersburg, and Lee's plight was becoming desperate. Nonetheless, Union forces had sustained casualties totaling more than 65,000 in six weeks. Jim Christiancy, the son of Judge Isaac Christiancy, a founder of Michigan's Republican party, had been wounded at Harris's Shop, Virginia, on May 29. Libbie deterred him from entering a crowded hospital, "unbearable on account of the horrible odor." Instead she nursed him at her boarding house, thereby satisfying her need to perform good works. She also sought the heavy drinking rake's "reformation." Libbie told young Christiancy he needed "a wife who would save him from wrong" and preached to him "of a God Who came to save sinners, not righteous men."[90] Simultaneously, by placing Jim's father in her debt, she stored up capital for Autie among Michigan Republicans.[91]

The arrangement provided another benefit as well. It gave Elizabeth another chance to remind her husband of her attractiveness to men. Young Christiancy venerated her as a genuine lady, sympathizing when she pricked her finger and expressing gratitude for her solicitude. "I shall never give up my friendship for Jim," Libbie informed her husband. "He has a fine pliable nature but has been without the influence of good Christian women." And, "I hope, my dear, you do not think I did wrong because when he came he had much fever and was very sick and I in my sympathy kissed the poor boy as I should have done had I been unmarried."[92]

While generating some insecurity, Libbie also showered her husband with flattery. She would act coquettishly were she not married, but "I have no desire to do so. Tho still enjoying gentlemen's society nobody should misconstrue my laughing and talking as flirting. I know that tho I have a pretty face it is my husband's reputation brings me so much attention." Autie had no reason to fear. In a city where so many wives were "wives in name only, idling around with other men," Libbie was entirely loyal.[93] One day Autie's response would change. For now, whatever his past experience with women, he would "as soon harbor a doubt of my Creator as of my darling little wife."[94]

While she nursed Christiancy, Elizabeth continued associating with important men. She and a friend visited the Capitol, accompanied by the Radical Republican senator from New Hampshire, John Hale. Entering the House they met Speaker Schuyler Colfax, who praised Custer enthusiastically. "I like him best of all here," Libbie confided to her husband. "He is so polite but not a bit of a flirt."[95]

Later in the House garden, Kellogg told her that Armstrong would soon become a major general. Libbie's landlady repeated a similar prophecy, based on her conversation with Sen. Benjamin Wade, also a Radical Republican. It mattered little that a recent report issued by Gen. Wesley Merritt, briefly commanding the Second Division, failed to give Custer sufficient credit in recent engagements. Merritt was "jealous."[96]

When Isaac Christiancy arrived in Washington to escort his ailing son home, Elizabeth learned that Jacob Greene languished in a Confederate prison. Her friend Frederick Nims was recovering from a wound. Libbie's anxiety rose further as she read her husband's letter of June 21. Autie had been "struck twice by spent balls, on the shoulder and arm." When one of the Fifth Michigan had been "shot in the heart by a sharp-shooter," Custer had "rushed forward" to move him to a safer place. "As I turned a sharpshooter fired at me—the ball glanced, stunning me for a few moments."[97]

Autie's letter deepened Libbie's apprehension as she witnessed the results of unrelenting warfare. Washington was grim that spring and summer. Daily from late May through June, steamers, wagons, and trains brought large numbers of the dead and wounded. As the heat intensified, the capital, unable to cope with the mangled and dead bodies, seemed like a "charnel house." Overnight, Libbie wrote her parents, a host of embalming establishments had arisen, and funerals were held continuously. Military escorts accompanied the hearses bearing the flag-wrapped coffins to their graves.[98]

Medical personnel, faced with unprecedented demands, called for volunteers to attend the dying and wounded. Libbie visited Mount Pleasant Hospital, where her presence as General Custer's wife comforted the wounded. She no longer criticized the overburdened hospitals, but the number of "cripples, soldiers all bandaged up for wounds, men with one arm, one limb" appalled her.[99] Briefly, she considered becoming a nurse until she learned that her duties would prevent her from joining her husband at a moment's notice.[100]

By June's end, Sheridan's cavalry was camped on the north bank of the James River, ten miles below City Point. When Libbie learned that officials had chartered the presidential yacht the *River Queen* to visit the troops, she sought Kellogg's permission to accompany them. Once more she fended off his too "cordial" advances, "moving aside and offering him a chair" when he attempted to kiss her.[101]

Early June found her at City Point, reunited with Autie and meeting Sheridan for the first time. The latter brought a band, and although he struck her as a novice dancer, Libbie welcomed the opportunity to waltz with him. As the short, ungainly man bobbed up and down to the strains of music, neither melody nor conversation drowned out the siege guns in the distance bombarding Petersburg.[102] The booming was incessant because Grant had promised Lincoln he would fight it out on this line "if it takes all summer." So was the bloodshed. Increasingly, Northerners asked the purpose of all this carnage, while Democratic papers railed against Grant.[103]

Still, Libbie had seen Autie briefly. On July 9, she said good-bye to her husband aboard the *River Queen* as it returned to Washington. In parting, the young couple had two desires. They hoped Armstrong would survive the war, and, almost as important, both wanted him to win his second star.

Events would soon bring the longed-for promotion within Custer's grasp. To relieve some of the pressure Grant exerted on Petersburg, Lee had ordered Gen. Jubal Early to move into the Shenandoah Valley and raid northward through that highway. By June 18, Early and his 13,000 veterans had easily brushed aside Gen. David Hunter's timid resistance at Lynchburg, Virginia. On July 9, the day Libbie and Autie said good-bye after their brief reunion, Early was within forty miles of Washington, D.C. Only a hurriedly assembled force under Maj. Gen. Lew Wallace, a mediocre soldier, stood between him and its capture.[104]

Grant, however, planned to counter Early's threat with one of his own, which would include a more important role for Sheridan's cavalry. Custer would soon face new dangers and opportunities, while Libbie would experience new anxieties and elation. For both, the second star was nearer realization.

CHAPTER 4

Mrs. Major General

WHEN ARMSTRONG rejoined his brigade on July 9, Libbie steeled herself for loneliness and anxiety. A few days later she heard on the stairs "a bounding step as no one else has," and the door flew open. The news that General Early had appeared on the capital's outskirts brought Autie back to assure his wife's safety.[1] Some panicky citizens thought Washington's fall more likely than Richmond's. Grant, however, quickly dispatched the Sixth Corps to man the sturdy fortifications ringing the District of Columbia. On July 12, Early, facing seasoned veterans in front and a federal column in his rear, withdrew into the Shenandoah Valley.[2] The alarm had, nonetheless, given the Custers time together.

Armstrong soon returned to his command, and Libbie struggled to adapt to the heat and apprehension of wartime Washington. For diversion she and another officer's wife ventured out for ice cream or listened to the Marine Band on the nearby White House grounds. Occasionally they enjoyed the scenery in a nearby park. "Washington's surroundings," Libbie wrote her friend, Laura Noble, "are so pleasant, thickly wooded, with the old Potomac like a silver band, seen from the heights."[3] Still, if she strolled too far on major avenues, someone might accost her as "one of the 'ten thousand.'"[4]

Elizabeth saw other women on the streets, namely the growing number of female clerks employed by the government. They were an "army of black [clad?][5] and weary creatures who had lost their husbands or sons in the war and were working for daily bread for themselves or their children." Seeing them "hurrying home to cook dinner for their children," Libbie felt grateful she spent her days drawing, painting, reading, and sewing.[6] In the evenings, she visited in the boarding house parlor with other officers' wives. Sometimes she entertained them by playing her favorite song on the piano, "Then You'll Remember Me," or the popular tune, "When This Cruel War Is Over."[7]

When bedtime arrived, summer's oppressive heat and humidity continued unabated. Lying close to her window to catch the slightest breeze, Libbie often heard "the groans of sufferers as long trains of ambulances trailed through the city after a battle." Many nights she slept fitfully, wondering what morning would bring. The news was distressing for the Union throughout July and August.[8]

Despite Grant's success in establishing his divisions along a twenty-five-mile front above and below Petersburg, Lee's forces remained entrenched around the city. The siege that Grant had hoped to avoid had become a horrifying war of attrition with high casualties on both sides. Libbie never forgot the scores of women who haunted the War Department's office, searching the casualty lists, hoping their husbands' names would not appear.[9]

Although Early no longer threatened the District of Columbia, his raids continued. After extorting money from Hagerstown and Frederick, Maryland, two of his brigades demanded half a million dollars from Chambersburg, Pennsylvania. When citizens refused, the raiders burned the town. Faced with these humiliations, newspapers noted that Petersburg withstood Grant, and Atlanta resisted Sherman's best efforts to capture the nerve center of the lower South.[10]

On July 30, the day Early's brigades torched Chambersburg, Union efforts to destroy a Confederate stronghold on Petersburg's defensive ring ended in disaster. After exploding a mine to create a huge crater, poorly led soldiers marched into the pit and became easy targets for enemy guns. Northern casualties totaled twice those of Lee's army. Small wonder that many newspapers declared the Union cause lost, while the price of gold, always an accurate inverse barometer of Northern hopes, rose dramatically.[11]

Grant was not discouraged. He instructed Sheridan to pursue Early's army, destroy it, and render the Shenandoah Valley useless for future gray cavalry operations. If this meant destroying or seizing everything of possible military value—all forage, livestock, and provisions in a corridor 150 miles long and 10 to 20 miles wide—then so be it.[12]

During the first week of August, Sheridan assumed command of the newly created Army of the Shenandoah. His forces numbered about 40,000 infantry and cavalry. The latter included three divisions commanded by Torbet. Brig. Wesley Merritt led the First; Maj. Gen. William Averell, the Second; and Brig. Gen. James H. Wilson, the Third. Custer and his Michigan brigade formed part of Merritt's division. Sheridan now prepared to take on Early, and preliminary skirmishes were under way.[13]

Faced with discouraging news from the front, Libbie intensified her efforts to convert Autie. Two allies assisted her, Lydia Ann and Father Custer. Their combined assaults and the hardships and terror of warfare weakened Armstrong's defenses. He not only curbed his profanity but became more receptive to their views.[14] He also shared with Libbie his daily successes.

Late in August, after a "successful fight near Front Royal," some "stoical and undemonstrative" regulars in Autie's brigade took off their hats and waved "Three Cheers for General Custer!" No one, save McClellan, Autie noted, had inspired such a demonstration. "The commander is a graduate of West Point long before my time, and yet as enthusiastic over your boy as if he were a youth of eighteen." Merritt had given no "order or suggestion, even."[15]

That same month the Democrats met in Chicago and nominated Autie's old mentor. Allied with the Democratic party's war faction, McClellan declared himself at West Point in favor of Union through victory. On August 24, however, he issued another statement. If elected, he would "recommend an immediate armistice and a call for a convention of all the states and insist upon exhausting all and every means to secure peace without further bloodshed."[16]

Although Libbie could not vote, she found the "great excitement over the political campaign" contagious, especially since banners of the opposing parties hung on each side of her boarding house. "The soldiers make demonstrations as they pass, some cheering for McClellan, and groaning for Lincoln and the reverse." Shrewdly she predicted that George Pendleton, the Democrats' vice presidential candidate, backed by the Copperhead Clement Vallandingham, had already cost McClellan "many votes by this association."[17]

Lincoln himself believed that Northern war weariness and military stalemate assured McClellan's victory, an opinion Libbie shared despite her assessment of McClellan's running mate. The election would bring "peace — perhaps dishonorable." She confided to Autie, "It is treasonable and un-womanly but way down in my heart I want peace on any terms, for much as I love my country I love you more." Nonetheless, if anyone wondered about her politics, "I am for Abraham."[18]

Libbie awoke on September 3 to the sound of cannon, signaling Atlanta's fall. That news followed word that Adm. David Farragut had captured Mobile. "These victories," Libbie wrote her parents, "have caused a great tumble in gold."[19] Still, Petersburg withstood its siege, and Sheridan had enjoyed no demonstrable success in the Shenandoah Valley.

Early was biding his time, waiting for Southern farmers to reap their bountiful harvest. As for Sheridan, his sources inflated Early's numbers and left him cautious. His critics, impatient for decisive action, referred to his army, headquartered at Harper's Ferry, as the "Harper's Weekly."[20] By mid-September, Libbie resided at Sandy Hook, not far from Little Phil's headquarters, and Armstrong visited her frequently. He found it hard, he wrote his sister Lydia Ann, to keep her away from camp, for "she likes the army about as well as I do."[21]

During their hours together, Libbie tutored her husband in literature and poetry. Since she loved Alfred Lord Tennyson's works, especially "Enoch Arden," a lengthy poem of self-sacrificing love, Autie gave her a complete volume of the British poet. Discovering that she had named herself "Philopena" in her collection of Nathaniel Parker Willis's verses, he inscribed the volume, "Philopena from Autie, August 5, 1864." On one level, the word means a loving forfeit made on the basis of a pledge, and in another sense, it is a diminutive, meaning little sweetheart. It also refers to a two-kerneled nut. The young woman, who loved language, probably applied all these meanings to herself.[22]

After one of these visits, Autie wrote from the front. "My dear little Army Crow—following me around everywhere. . . . Not even the supposed proximity of Mosby's gang could drive away my happy thoughts of you." He referred to guerrilla raiders led by Virginia lawyer John Singleton Mosby. Their persistent harassment reduced the cavalry's effectiveness so much that Grant ordered Sheridan: "Where any of Mosby's men are caught hang them without trial."[23]

By mid-September attrition was costing the Confederates more than they could afford. When Sheridan learned that some of Early's troops had been dispatched southward to assist Lee in defending Petersburg, he decided to strike. Before dawn on September 19, Little Phil launched a full-scale assault on Early's depleted forces near Opequon Creek, ten miles outside Winchester, Virginia. A day of savage fighting ended when Merritt's division charged Early's left flank and shattered it. The entire Confederate line collapsed, and Early saved his army only by taking up new positions at Fisher's Hill.[24]

Custer and his Michigan brigade were in the forefront of the cavalry charge, which routed Early's army and resulted in the capture of almost 800 men and two pieces of artillery. In his report Armstrong took credit for most of the captures and received a brevet as a colonel in the regular army.[25]

The northern press now described Custer in heroic terms. Reporters loved the young man in the "D'Artagnan boots, and a plumed piratical sombrero." E. A. Paul, of the *New York Times*, portrayed his favorite soldier as a cavalier of "coolness," whose strategy and skill under fire were "worthy of a NAPO-LEON."[26] Still another correspondent from the *New York Tribune* prohesized, "Future writers of fiction will find in Brig. Gen. Custer most of the qualities which go to make up a first-class hero, and stories of his daring will be told around many a hearthstone after the old flag again kisses the breeze from Maine to the Gulf." While some accused Custer of impetuosity, this journalist judged the Michigan general as "always circumspect, never rash."[27]

Small wonder that others, lacking such accolades, felt underrated. After Winchester, the rivalry between Custer and Merritt intensified. Although Merritt praised his brigade commander, Custer thought it insufficient. Merritt, on the other hand, a gallant and able officer, was no match when it came to winning national publicity. He remained in the shadow of his more flamboyant competitor.[28]

Armstrong's letter of September 30, 1864, contained news that delighted Libbie. "My Rosebud—Before this 'She' will have learned that her Boy General has been assigned to permanent command of a Division." Libbie already knew from newspaper reports that three days after Winchester, Sheridan had driven Early's threadbare and hungry troops from Fisher's Hill. Disappointed that some of his commanders had not been aggressive enough to follow and destroy the Confederate army, Sheridan decided upon yet another reorganization. He transferred Wilson to the western theater, where he performed admirably for the rest of the war, and gave Custer his heart's desire, command of the Third Division.[29]

Saying good-bye to his Michigan brigade saddened Autie. His soldiers, railing against the separation, demanded a transfer to his division. "Some of the officers said they would resign if the exchange were not made. . . . Some of the band threatened to break their horns," Armstrong noted.[30] The hard-fighting Custer and his Wolverines had endured together, and with the interest he had shown in their equipment and supplies, they had established a remarkable esprit de corps. Although they were parting, the élan he had infused would inspire them in future combat. Unfortunately, before the end of the war, 525 would be either dead or mortally wounded, a higher number than any other Union cavalry brigade.[31]

There was a joyous side to the separation. Surely Custer would win a second star. And sooner or later he believed (mistakenly as it turned out) the Wolverines would become part of the Third Division. Meanwhile, Libbie would enjoy his huge "circus" tent when she visited his camp.[32]

With the Confederates unable at present to oppose him, Sheridan began carrying out Grant's instructions. He was transforming the Great Valley into "a barren waste." In a few days more than ninety miles lay devastated, and Little Phil reported the people had nothing left "but their eyes to weep with over the war.[33] The smoke lingered for days after Sheridan's troops departed, leaving a heavy gray haze over the blue October sky.[34]

Libbie made no reference to such destruction and instead imagined her father's pride over Autie's new honors. "Now I can see you hold the letter down as you are reading it, and look over your spectacles at Mother and say, 'I knew it!' and then beg her not to interrupt." Kellogg wished to visit Monroe and deliver a speech in Custer's honor, and Libbie urged her father to ask his friends to invite him. "But don't let anybody know you did so. For when he praises Autie they might think us proud. We have a right to be, but not to be 'set up.'" In closing, she entreated, "Do write often, Father. Your letters comfort me."[35]

As Sheridan torched the valley, Early, reinforced by the Laurel brigade, under Autie's old West Point classmate, Brig. Gen. Thomas Rosser, was not idle. An audacious fighter, Rosser, hailed as the "Savior of the Valley," soon harassed Sheridan's rear. "Darling little one," Libbie read as she opened her letter dated October 10. "Yesterday, the 9th, was a glorious day for your Boy. . . . I attacked Genl. Rosser's Division of 3 Brigades with my Division of 2, and gained The most glorious victory." Not only had he driven Rosser "in confusion," but in the Battle of Tom's Brook, Custer had taken "6 cannon, all his advance trains, ambulance train, all Genls. Rosser's, Lomax's & Wickham's headquarters wagons containing all their baggage, private & official papers." Best of all, he had recovered Libbie's ambrotype, missing since Trevilian Station.[36]

Armstrong had also found letters written by Gen. Thomas Mumford's wife. No one would read them, since the relationship between spouses was "too sacred to be violated, even in war."[37] Libbie knew that Armstrong regretted the loss of her letters. Although she believed there could "be nothing low between husband and wife," the thought that someone might be extracting amusement from her frank expressions of affection disturbed him. Thus Libbie, somewhat chagrined, gave her pledge. "I shall not again offend my dear boy's sense of nicety by departing from that delicate propriety which, I believe, was born in me—the lady in me inherited from my mother. . . . Trust me, my dear," she assured him. "I am glad you are so particular with me. With my much loved and honored parents I felt indignant at reproof, but when you express yourself as ever so slightly displeased I feel grieved and try to do better."[38]

While marriage to her "star" was exhilarating, it also called for self-abnegation on Libbie's part. Everything in her religious and cultural upbringing had prepared her to submit to her husband, although she did not necessarily welcome the experience.[39] Still, Armstrong's renown compensated her. As an intelligent and perceptive woman, with no theater of her own in which to express her ambition, her husband's career was vicariously hers.

Echoing sentiments similar to those expressed by Grace Greenwood in a *Greenwood Leaves* short story, Libbie wrote her husband in another letter, "Remember, I cannot love as I do without my life blending with yours. I would not lose my individuality, but would be, as a wife should be, part of her husband, a life within a life."[40] Her next statement revealed some unresolved conflict within herself. "I never was an admirer of a submissive wife, but I wish to look to my husband as superior in judgment and experience and to be guided by him in all things."[41]

Libbie also noted her concern over reports that Confederate sharpshooters were after Armstrong. The wife who wished "to be guided" by her husband "in all things" now expressed her goals for Armstrong after the war. "Autie darling, your arm has been raised often enough in defence of your country. You can make yourself more useful in directing and planning for others."[42]

Nonetheless, Libbie delighted in Autie's triumphs. "Oh, that last battle was a magnificent affair," she wrote her parents in one letter. She took up her husband's rivalries as if they were her own. Was it not "splendid, that his first move with his Division was to recapture what Genl. Wilson had lost?" Unlike his predecessor, Autie had won his command "by merit, not by hinting and begging."[43]

While Libbie reveled in her husband's glory, she also maintained her contacts with the right people. True, Autie now commanded a division, but his second star required congressional confirmation. When Chandler visited her, "tight as usual, and disgusting when he has taken too much," she found it hard "to keep him from kissing me." Whatever the hazards, however, she stayed on good terms with the powerful senator, a member of the Committee on the Conduct of the War. As a Radical Republican, his support could overcome lingering doubts regarding Autie's affiliation with McClellan and other Democrats.[44]

Sheridan meanwhile had positioned his army at Cedar Creek. Believing Early no longer a significant threat, he left to confer with Grant. At dawn on October 19, as thick fog shrouded the valley, the Confederate leader threw five divisions of infantry against the Union left. Caught off guard, Federal defenders fled in panic despite the efforts of Custer and Merritt to stem the rout.[45] Informed of a possible Union debacle, Sheridan returned at breakneck speed, rallied his men, and reorganized his lines. As dark closed in after a day of bitter fighting, Custer led a charge into the Confederate left flank. Driven back, the exhausted rebels fled to new positions down the valley. Cedar Creek won Sheridan promotion to major general in the regular army, and he requested brevet major generals for the "brave boys," Custer and Merritt.[46]

Libbie had gone to visit Rhoda's relatives, Mr. and Mrs. William Russell, in Newark, New Jersey. No sooner had she arrived, than she threw herself into shopping, despite her stepmother's warnings that she spent too much on clothes. After all, thirty-five dollars for a "purple poplin, worsted and silk" was a bargain compared to Washington prices. And, despite her husband's admonishments to forego long-distance lovemaking, she wrote: "I don't care if fifty rebels read this letter. I miss your kisses."[47]

On Sunday morning, October 23, William Russell told Libbie that Custer was in Washington presenting the Confederate flags captured at Cedar Creek to Secretary of War Edwin Stanton. Incredulous, Libbie read the newspaper over Russell's shoulder and saw that her trip had cost her the chance to see her husband. As she flew upstairs to weep in private, children's voices screamed that Armstrong stood at the front door. When Stanton's unexpected illness had delayed the presentation ceremony, he had caught the first train for Newark.[48]

The next day the Custers returned to Washington on a train that flew at the unheard-of speed of forty miles an hour. An omnibus with a captured Confederate flag hanging from each window met them at the station and drove them up Pennsylvania Avenue to the roar of cheering crowds.[49] On Tuesday, Libbie watched the presentation ceremony in Stanton's office. As the delegates accompanying Custer brought forth each flag, the secretary asked for details. After the men had related their stories, Stanton gave them a furlough while he commissioned their medals. Then he announced, "To show you how good Generals and good men work together I have appointed your commander, Custer, Major-General." Clasping Armstrong's hand, he added, "General, a gallant officer always makes gallant soldiers." Everyone cheered, and one soldier blurted out, "The 3rd Division wouldn't be worth a cent if it wasn't for him!"[50]

As the Custers were leaving, the secretary asked Armstrong if he were related to Emmanuel Custer, one of his law firm's Ohio clients. When the young general answered that Emmanuel was his father, Stanton asked why he had not visited earlier. "Because I never had any business to bring to your office, Sir," Armstrong replied. Libbie proudly wrote her parents, "People are beginning to call me Mrs. Major-General. But I have been too well-trained by you to be 'stuck up.'"[51]

Following the ceremony, Autie returned to cavalry headquarters at Martinsburg. Shortly after, Libbie received a visit from a tired General Torbert. Thank goodness her husband was not exhausted, for she could never stand a man without "life and animation." She continued, "Oh Aut, give me men for action who have the enthusiasm, energy and ardent temperament of my warrior brave. . . . I cannot help but compare other men with my hero and how far, far they come from being like him!"[52]

A young private on his way to Monroe also called. Regrettably, during his incarceration in Richmond's Libby Prison, he had heard a doctor discussing "General Custer's wife's letters. I felt deepest chagrin," Libbie admitted, but she would not allow it to bother her "when I have everything to make me happy."[53] Or, almost everything. She still desired children.

Recently, while attending church, she had prayed for "a child that I might try and make it a cornerstone in the great church of God—and Autie, if God gives me children I shall say to them: 'Emulate your Father! I can give you no higher earthly example.' But *then* I can say to them: 'Emulate him in his Christian as well as his moral character,' can I not?"[54] Before she could create a Christian home, however, her husband must be converted, an end towards which she was working.

Shortly after returning to Martinsburg, Autie asked Libbie to join him. "You will lead a real soldier's life," he noted, advising her to leave her good clothing behind. Libbie immediately replied, "I love luxury, dress, comfort. But, oh, how gladly I will give them up. I can be ready in a day or two. I can hardly wait."[55]

Autie met her at the station early in November, disguised in Confederate clothing and "looking every inch a rebel." After lodging with a Union sympathizer, the couple set out for camp next day. They took with them an escort of 150 cavalrymen since Mosby's guerrillas controlled the area.[56] Along the way, Libbie learned that Tom Custer, her brother-in-law and a corporal in the Twenty-first Ohio Volunteers, would soon transfer to the Sixth Michigan Cavalry. Autie, having used his influence to win him a commission as second lieutenant, planned to make Tom his aide-de-camp. Others who practiced similar nepotism included Philip Sheridan, whose brother Michael had served as his aide since June.[57]

On arriving at camp, forty miles from Martinsburg, Libbie found her two large tents, in the midst of evergreens, delightful. Daniel had warned her that military life meant "gypsying, no better than riding on the plains in a covered wagon." Now she wrote her parents, proudly, "In this age of delicate females none is better adapted to army life than your daughter."[58] True, she rose before dawn and took breakfast by candlelight when the army moved to Winchester. Still, what pleasure when she "rode in my Virginia carriage, just in the rear of Autie, his staff and color-bearers. The escort rode behind. I had the honor of moving with the army."[59]

Lincoln emerged victorious in November, largely because of recent Union victories, including those in the Shenandoah Valley. Early in December, Little Phil, dissatisfied with his subalterns' performance and convinced that their wives "often interfered with official duties," ordered the women to leave headquarters. Only Libbie, whose husband "still charged the enemy with the same impetuosity after as before marriage," was allowed to stay.[60]

Autie's continuing raids into the Virginia countryside in December destroyed Libbie's hope of spending Christmas in Monroe. When bitter cold prevented further forays, two court martials demanded his presence. Finally, in mid-January, as the Custers prepared to leave for Michigan, Sheridan gave them a surprise party. Fortunately, Libbie learned about it in time to decorate their quarters with "crossed sabres, regimental flags and evergreens," while local ladies provided delicacies. Elizabeth, now finding Sheridan "a beautiful dancer," noticed how much he relished "such entertainments."[61]

In Monroe, Autie fulfilled his wife's long-sought wish when he attended a Presbyterian Week of Prayer. On Sunday night, February 5, Autie told

Reverend Mattoon, one of the clergymen who had officiated at his wedding, that he "accepted Christ as my Saviour."[62] Later when Rhoda and Rebecca accompanied Autie and Libbie, as they returned to Custer's command at Winchester, Daniel remained in Monroe. He wrote his son-in-law, expressing his satisfaction with his daughter's choice of a husband. While Armstrong's character and reputation was everything he "could desire or wish," more important was Armstrong's "acceptance of the terms of salvation" and his decision "to lead a Christian life."[63]

Late in February, Bacon arrived in Winchester and escorted the women to Lincoln's second inauguration. Libbie and Rebecca listened to the addresses from the Senate balcony, where they noted with disgust that Vice President Andrew Johnson "was drunk unfortunately." By contrast, Libbie thought Lincoln "appeared with great dignity." His words, however, in which he spoke of the war as perhaps continuing "until all the wealth piled by the bond-man's two hundred and fifty years of unrequited toil shall be sunk, and until every drop of blood drawn with the lash, shall be paid with another drawn with the sword," was almost inaudible to the two women.[64]

Afterwards Libbie attended the inaugural ball with Senator Chandler. "I went solely as a spectator, and danced with him simply out of etiquette," she assured her husband. More important, Chandler introduced her to a host of celebrities, including Adm. David Farragut, who was "right jolly and unaffected." As for the ladies, their "costumes were superb;—velvets, silks, diamonds dazzled my eyes." The food was "a miracle of confectionary and substantials were not wanting." If only Autie could have tasted the turkey, but he was involved in fierce campaigning.[65]

After Cedar Creek, Early had retreated with the pitiful remnant of a once proud army to the vicinity of Waynesboro near Brown's Gap in the Blue Ridge. Before Sheridan could move east to join Grant in the all-out struggle to overwhelm Lee's army, he had to destroy what remained of his adversary's forces. Disappointed with Torbert's recent performance, he replaced him with Merritt and gave Custer free rein.

On March 2, two days before the inauguration, in a sea of mud and rain, the boy general, in typical fashion, charged and shattered Early's defenses at Waynesboro. Early barely escaped capture, and his army ceased to exist.[66] The next day Custer moved unopposed into Charlottesville. E. A. Paul, having devoted much of his coverage to the golden-haired general, decided to chronicle the war's closing days from the vantage point of Custer's Third Division.[67]

Libbie, who remained in Washington with Rebecca after the Bacons had returned to Monroe, shared with her cousin Autie's triumphant letter of March 11. After sixteen days of marching through rain and drizzle over muddy roads, he reported, "Your Bo is safe and well. We will probably cross [the Pamunkey] to-morrow."[68] Waiting for him were supplies from General Grant since his division was now part of the Army of the Potomac. Custer's task was to destroy the railroads, thereby cutting off Lee's supply lines and compelling him to leave Petersburg's fortifications.[69]

Exuberantly, Armstrong proclaimed his most recent accomplishments. "Our raid has been a chain of successes, and the 3rd Division has done all the fighting." If Libbie visited his headquarters now she would see the sixteen battle flags his division had recently captured with no help from either Sheridan or Merritt. Paul's report in the *New York Times*, which she should send their fathers, would tell her everything. "The 3rd stands higher than ever, in advance all the time . . . 3,000 prisoners and our own loss not exceeding 30. Your bo has won new laurels."[70]

Libbie was equally ecstatic. "Oh Autie How delighted I was to hear of your success. O, you dear glorious warrior—my warrior. . . . What wonders you have accomplished in two weeks . . . and in such unpleasant weather." Maternally she reminded him to wear his raincoat.[71]

Luck had been with him in his most recent engagements. Unlike many commanders, Custer routinely positioned himself in front of his lines, where he observed the enemy and assessed their strength and location. With his golden locks and red tie, he made an excellent target for sharpshooters, except that he constantly kept moving. Eleven mounts had been shot from under him, and, most recently, Jack Rucker had stepped into a hole and somersaulted, falling on his rider. When his staff lifted the steed, Custer called for another and returned to battle.[72]

Libbie read with relief Autie's letter of March 20, telling her that his division was resting at White House Landing. Officers had gathered round the fire to sing "It's a Way We Have in the Army" and "Let Every Old Bachelor Fill Up His Glass" before concluding with "Auld Lang Syne" and "Home, Sweet Home." "Oh," he confessed, "how lonely I felt for my little one," whose influence he felt across the miles. Recently, he assured her, he had not "uttered a single oath, nor blasphemed, even in thought, since I saw you, so strictly have I kept my resolution." She would soon receive a chess set, captured from Early's private wagon. After the war, they would play the game together.[73]

The news that Autie no longer took God's name in vain lifted Libbie's spirits. Even more exhilarating was a letter Autie had received from Theodore Holmes, formerly the Third Division's chaplain. After congratulating Custer on his military valor, the clergyman praised him for committing his life to Christian principles. He prayed that Custer would "be safely kept by the Power that has so strangely shielded you in the past."[74]

Libbie saw in this correspondence evidence of her success in the most important role a wife assumed—that of saving her husband's soul. Following Autie's instructions she sent the letter to their parents and the two clergymen who had married them. Emmanuel Custer responded immediately, urging his daughter-in-law to "counsel Thomas."[75]

As always Libbie combined loving flattery with exhortations in her letters to Autie. She was learning chess but told Rebecca that Autie would always win. When her cousin responded, "Well, wouldn't you rather have it that way?" Libbie replied, "Yes, I wouldn't want a husband who wasn't my superior."[76]

Libbie also searched for a new, more suitable boarding house. One location proved unacceptable since Autie thought a resident, identified as "Major P," was enamored of Libbie. "But, my dear, I should only see him at table in the presence of his wife." Besides, Autie had no competitors. One observer thought Libbie would "drive a whole brigade of officers wild because of my indifference to mankind. I compare them all with you."[77] Then the young wife entreated her husband to be more careful. "Don't expose yourself so much in battle. Just do your duty, and don't ride out so daringly. Oh, Autie, we must die together. Better the humblest life together than the loftiest, divided." If he made his wild charges for her, she wrote, "My hopes and ambitions are more than a hundred times already realized in you."[78]

Mrs. Major General could not have been more elated. Recently, as she and Rebecca were shopping, they had discovered that the flags captured at Waynesboro were about to be presented. Although Autie could not be spared, members of his division were present. Without hesitation, Elizabeth brought her cousin into Stanton's chambers in the War Department to witness the ceremony. The secretary of war, recognizing her immediately, introduced her as "the wife of the gallant General." As each banner was presented, the words "Brevet Major-General Custer commanding" were called out, and Libbie "could hardly keep from crying out my praise of my boy."[79] Afterwards she told Stanton that the event consoled her since she had not heard from Autie lately. "General Custer," he replied, "is writing lasting letters on the pages of his country's history." As Libbie and Rebecca left the War Department, a crowd outside called out, "Custer's wife. . . . That's the wife of Custer!"[80]

Shortly after, Autie's letter of March 24 informed her that Sheridan's army was joining Grant's. Together they would administer the final blow to the Confederacy by capturing Richmond and, more important, destroying Lee's Army of Northern Virginia.[81] On March 30, Autie described the almost continuous rain he had faced since starting toward Dinwiddie Court House. That morning, he had woken "in a puddle of water about two inches deep." His first thought, he had told Eliza, had been of Libbie. "Oh, of course. You would think of Miss Libbie the first thought and I expect you wanted her there with you," Eliza had responded. "And Miss Libbie is just willing to come if she had been there last night and found herself in the water she would have said Eliza can't you give me something just to keep my feet out of water, but I'm very comfortable, this is nice."[82]

Actually, Autie looked forward to seeing Libbie under more congenial circumstances. In her new boarding house, she had mentioned a variety of comforts, and Armstrong had been "glad to hear that there is a soft place upon somebodys carpet because as that lady remarked in reference to piercing ears &c there are a great many ways of *doing things* some of which I believe are not generally known."[83] Libbie and her husband enjoyed an imaginative love life.

Before they could be reunited, however, Armstrong faced the final days of the war. He sensed that "the great battle is probably near at hand" and yearned for its aftermath. Whatever Libbie had read, he was not "rash and reckless. At Waynesboro I acted with caution—more for the sake of Her than from any other motive."[84] Libbie had made a flag for her husband's "last raid" described as "red and blue silk with white crossed sabres on both sides, and edged with heavy white cord." Lt. Peter Boehm carried it to Custer by wearing it under his uniform as he returned to the division.[85]

At Dinwiddie Court House, Sheridan fought General Pickett. The daylong fight brought heavy casualties to both sides and inconclusive results. Custer and his Third Division, nonetheless, once more distinguished themselves. When they arrived to reinforce Merritt and Gen. George Crook, late in the afternoon, Libbie's flag was unfurled. During the battle, her name, embroidered on the corner of the flag, was shot off, and the young soldier carrying it was killed.[86]

During the evening, Pickett retired north to Five Forks and entrenched. Sheridan followed, and hard fighting began on the morning of April 1, continuing to mid-afternoon, when Union forces breached the Confederate defenses and routed the gray defenders. Among the first over Pickett's barricades were Sheridan and Custer.

Five Forks was a disaster for Lee's army. Pickett's division was destroyed, with losses in killed and captured of nearly 6,000 men. Lee, realizing he could not hold his positions around Richmond and Petersburg, notified President Jefferson Davis on Sunday, April 2, that he planned to evacuate the defenses. Davis made immediate plans to move the Confederate government to another location.[87]

Two days later Lincoln visited Richmond, a city largely consumed by flames. Grant and Sheridan pursued Lee's retreating army westward, as Lee headed towards the Lynchburg railhead, where he hoped to move south and join Gen. Joseph Johnston in North Carolina. Sheridan's cavalry and Grant's infantry paralleled his march. On April 6, at Sayler's Creek, Custer mounted a thundering charge into a gap in Lee's long and straggling column. Sheridan dispatched infantry and cavalry, and by that evening, Union forces had taken between 7,000 and 8,000 Confederate prisoners.[88]

In a single day, Lee lost a third of what remained of his once magnificent army. During the fighting, Lt. Tom Custer, struggling to obtain an enemy flag, took a bullet through his right cheek that exited through his neck. His effort earned him the second of his two Medals of Honor for gallantry in action. Four days earlier, his capture of a flag and fourteen prisoners in a skirmish at Namozine Church had won him his first medal and a captain's brevet.[89]

Lee's chances of joining forces with General Johnston ended at Sayler's Creek. Still he resisted surrender, maintaining a forlorn hope of reaching supplies and ammunition at Appomattox Station. Meanwhile, Grant sent his adversary a message on April 7, urging the end of bloodshed and the arrangement of surrender terms. Lee's reply hedged on terms. Then on April 8, he discovered that Custer, having reached Appomattox Station, had captured four trains carrying sorely needed supplies.

The next day, April 9, Palm Sunday, Lee's desperate, hungry, poorly clad and armed troops broke through Sheridan's cavalry in one great burst of energy. In the opening created, they saw Federal infantry massing for action. To Lee's rear were additional blue-clad divisions. It was hopeless. Lee sent Grant a note, stating his willingness to discuss surrender.[90] They agreed to meet at Appomattox Court House.

Custer's role in the surrender of Lee's forces became the subject of controversy. Confederates, including Gens. James Longstreet and E. P. Alexander, Col. J. C. Haskell, and Adj. O. M. Owen, maintained that the boy general violated military protocol by demanding surrender while a truce was in effect.[91] Custer's defenders, however, recalled a different version. While preparing to lead a charge against Gen. John B. Gordon's cavalry, Custer suddenly saw a Confederate officer galloping across the field, waving a white towel tied to a stick. After dispatching one aide to receive the makeshift flag of truce, he sent another to inform Sheridan. When the first aide failed to return shortly, Custer investigated. Braving bullets, he waved a borrowed white handkerchief around his head. Later he came back from Confederate lines, crying: "It's all right, boys. Lee has surrendered."[92]

As one historian notes, in Wilmer McLean's parlor at Appomattox Court House, "the son of an Ohio tanner dictated surrender to the scion of a First Family of Virginia." Grant gave Lee generous terms. He allowed the defeated Confederate soldiers to lay down their arms and return home for spring planting, on promise of observing their parole. After Grant and Lee signed the papers, Lee shook hands with Grant's staff, and the two men saluted and went their separate ways.[93]

Those present in McLean's parlor wanted mementos. As officers purchased various items in the room, Sheridan paid twenty dollars in gold for a small, dark pine table with spool-shaped legs on which Grant had written the surrender terms and signed the peace document.[94] Little Phil gave the table to Custer as a present for Libbie. He also included a note which read: "My Dear Madam, — I respectfully present to you the small writing-table on which the conditions for the surrender of the Confederate Army of Northern Virginia was written by Lt. General Grant, and permit me to say, Madam, that there is scarcely an individual in our service who has contributed more to bring about this desirable result than your very gallant husband."[95] Exuberantly, Custer bounded down the steps of the McLean home with the surrender table on his head.

On April 10, Libbie awoke to the sound of booming cannon signaling Lee's surrender. Shortly after, Senator Chandler invited her to join the Committee on the Conduct of the War and their wives as they departed for Richmond. At Fortress Monroe the group boarded the president's gunboat, the *Baltimore*. "Admiral [David] Porter," she wrote her father, "sent a pilot, and we ran through the blockade safely, and were guided through the torpedoes after dark." At City Point, Porter sent Armstrong a telegram, informing him that Libbie would be in Richmond the next day.[96]

Libbie stayed with Gen. Godfrey Weitzel and his wife at Jefferson Davis's former White House. Curious about the furnishings, Elizabeth wandered from room to room under the housekeeper's watchful eye. The first night she slept in Jefferson Davis's bedroom and the second in his wife Varina's, where Autie found her in the morning. "He is tanned, but thin and worn," she wrote her friend, Laura Noble, but he was not alone. "Genl. Sheridan is very tired after all those battles."[97]

After leaving Richmond, the couple returned to Armstrong's command and moved with the army towards Petersburg. Libbie and the wife of Col. A. C. Pennington rode in a spring wagon at the head of the Third Division.[98] When the column stopped at Nottaway Court House, soldiers heard of Lincoln's assassination. Since the story was garbled, Sheridan dismissed it as wild rumor, but at Petersburg they learned the truth.[99] They also discovered that General Sherman and his Army of the West had forced Joseph Johnston's Army of Tennessee to surrender. The war was over. True, Jefferson Davis was still at large, but Union Cavalry under James Wilson captured him at Irwinsville, Georgia, on May 10.[100]

During Libbie's brief stay at Petersburg, Autie presented her with a bay pacer acquired at Five Forks. He had named the horse Custis Lee after Robert E. Lee's oldest son, a general commanding a regiment of Confederate mechanics at that battle.[101] Both gentle and responsive, Custis Lee became Libbie's favorite mount. Autie also gave his wife the surrender table, which she sent her parents, advising them, "Don't give away a splinter even. They tell me I might sell it for a million dollars." Libbie enclosed a copy of Sheridan's letter, which she treasured even more. Her other prized possessions included the white towel used as the Confederate surrender flag and the handkerchief Autie had waved when he had moved into Confederate lines on April 9.[102]

To celebrate Union victory, thousands of spectators gathered on May 23 to watch the Army of the Potomac, 80,000 strong, and almost as professional as European armies after four years of war.[103] One of the heroes was not present. Sheridan had been transferred to the Department of the Gulf. In Texas, Confederate general Edmund Kirby Smith had not surrendered, and across the border, the French-installed puppet, the Archduke Maximilian of Austria, remained in power.[104]

Merritt, now responsible for Sheridan's command, placed Custer's division in the forefront of the cavalry. Libbie watched as her husband led the

Third Division, clad in scarlet neckties, along the parade route. Just before reaching the reviewing stand, a young girl, amidst a group of cheering, waving, and singing schoolchildren, tossed a flower wreath at Autie's horse. The animal bolted, carrying its rider past the reviewing stand. As Custer drew his saber to salute President Johnson and General Grant, the sword caught his hat, leaving his head bare and his curls unfurled, while the saber fell to the ground. Reining in his horse, Custer retrieved his hat and sword from a nearby soldier before returning to the head of his division. The crowd went wild.

Once more there was controversy. Some watching the event concluded they had witnessed the calculated ploy of a master showman, since his horse had known combat. Others, including Libbie, believed that Custer's steed, Don Juan, had shied away from the wreath.[105]

That afternoon Libbie appeared with her husband as he said good-bye to his troops. She wore a black velvet riding cap adorned with a red feather, signaling her identification with Armstrong's career and personality. The soldiers applauded the couple enthusiastically, and Custer read his farewell. Despite the flowery language, with reference to the "God of Battles," he credited victory to the men themselves.[106]

On this glorious day, Libbie looked out over the soldiers and exulted in her choice of a husband. He was a national hero, but, more important, under her guidance he had become a devout Christian. Even her father celebrated the wisdom of her choice.[107] She needed only the arrival of children to complete her happiness.

The following day Sherman's 65,000 men of the armies of Georgia and Tennessee climaxed the victory celebration as they, in turn, moved down Pennsylvania Avenue. They were thinner than the eastern forces and wore dusty, often threadbare uniforms after returning from 2,000 miles of campaigning. Within their ranks were many volunteer units who had fought well but remained citizens first and soldiers second. Armstrong would soon command troops like these.

Sherman held his breath, fearful that after the Army of the Potomac's polished performance, his men would look more like a "mob" than a company of disciplined soldiers. To his relief, they closed ranks in good formation and, with "glittering muskets . . . moving with the regularity of a pendulum," marched proudly as the bands played and the crowd sang "John Brown's Body."[108]

CHAPTER 5

Adjusting to Hard Times

S OON AFTER the grand review, the Custers, Eliza, and Custer's staff left for New Orleans so that Armstrong could rejoin his old commander, Philip Sheridan. Since Kirby Smith had not yet surrendered, Elizabeth knew that further military action might be required in Texas. Armstrong said nothing, however, about the possibility of serving as a cavalry commander for an expedition into Mexico. "He preferred transportation by steamer, rather than to be floated southward by floods of feminine tears," she later recalled.[1]

Upon their arrival, the Custers registered at the St. Charles Hotel. Gen. Winfield Scott resided there, but when Libbie met her father's hero, she saw little resemblance between the handsome soldier portrayed in her parents' parlor and the "decrepit, tottering man" barely able to rise. More pleasurable were their dinners with an uncharacteristically "gay" Sheridan, headquartered in a nearby manor house.

During Autie's leisure hours the couple sampled French cuisine, strolled along Canal Street, and browsed through small shops. During one outing they visited the New Orleans painter Randolph Lux and commissioned their portraits on vases.[2] Their New Orleans stay ended when Sheridan ordered Autie to Alexandria to organize and march a cavalry unit to Texas to threaten the French-supported puppet government in Mexico. "Don't feel badly for us as we are quite pleased," Libbie wrote Rebecca. "You know it might have been to Indian Territory or Arizona."[3]

In Alexandria, the Custers moved into the mansion recently vacated by Gen. Nathaniel Banks. Although the countryside was beautiful, much of the town, burned during the war, lay in ruins. As she visited homes, Elizabeth concluded that even in its prime, Alexandria had been backward and desperately needed Yankee inventions.[4] During their stay, a young man who had attended school in Monroe introduced himself. Libbie, remembering that he had invited Michigan belles to join him in "the halls of his ancestors," was surprised when she visited his home and found it a modest cottage. Discreetly, she made no mention of his "poetic license."[5]

Custer's command at Alexandria consisted of volunteer units from the western theater. While many had fought bravely in the recent war, they traditionally exhibited impatience with spit-and-polish regulations of the regular army and West Pointers. Their officers, moreover, had risen through the ranks and frequently questioned orders they considered unreasonable. Additionally, all were resentful since the war was over and they wanted to go home. Some had already deserted. Nothing in Custer's background, training, or youthful experience had prepared him for dealing with such troops.[6]

In addition to commanding sullen men, Custer faced another problem. Southerners resented the soldiers' presence, and Sheridan insisted that under no circumstances should troops antagonize civilians. One day after arriving at Alexandria, Armstrong announced that, given the "numerous complaints" against the command, he was issuing General Order No. 2. Wisely he forbade foraging from the civilian population, but he went further. Since the command was "unsettled," court-martials were suspended. Instead, any soldier who violated orders would *"have his head shaved and in addition will receive twenty-five lashes upon his back, well laid on."* Furthermore, any officer who failed to report violations would be cashiered. Custer invited local citizens to inform his headquarters of any derelictions.[7]

The results were disastrous. The soldiers had only recently arrived in Alexandria, and, according to one account (disputed by Custer), "no acts of lawlessness had been committed, and no unsoldierly conduct had taken place." Congress, furthermore, had banned flogging of troops in 1861, and head-shaving was considered demeaning. Finally, many were bitter that the word of former rebels was accepted over that of Union soldiers.[8]

The volunteer units assembled under Custer's command were the First Iowa Cavalry, the Third, Fifth, and Twelfth Illinois, the Seventh Indiana, and the Second Wisconsin. Despite its proud fighting record, the lieutenant colonel of the Second Wisconsin, Nicholas Dale, had been court-martialed for allegedly rejoicing over Lincoln's assassination. While the hearsay evidence brought only official reprimand, it cost the officer his regiment's respect.[9] The other units, while less troubled, seethed at Custer's orders. The colonel of an Illinois regiment called on the young commander and suggested that, in his experience, volunteer units obeyed more readily when they understood the reasons behind regulations. Custer, after listening politely, ignored his advice.[10]

Desertions mounted, totaling seventeen by July 3. When men of the Second Wisconsin petitioned for Dale's removal, Custer, interpreting their action as mutiny, ordered them arrested, imprisoned, and their seventy-six noncommissioned officers reduced to privates. Those who apologized were released. Sgt. Leonard Lancaster, a soldier with a proud war record, had spearheaded the action. He refused and remained in jail.[11]

Discontent increased, and since some companies had lost all noncommissioned officers, desertions rose again. Lifting the ban on court-martials, Custer ordered trials for Lancaster and William A. Wilson, a deserter from the Twelfth Illinois Cavalry. Both were sentenced to death by firing squad.[12]

Libbie had heard rumors of mutiny and rebellion and, concerned for her husband's safety, begged him to arm himself. To allay her fears, Armstrong slept with a pistol under his pillow. Later she learned it had never been loaded. When execution day arrived, she cowered in her quarters with Eliza, terrified someone would kill her husband.

The soldiers assembled on the parade ground and waited. At last Custer appeared at the head of his staff, followed by the wagon bearing the condemned men. When it stopped at the fresh graves in the middle of the square the two men alighted, received their blindfolds, and sat on their caskets. As Libbie heard the chaplain's voice calling down God's mercy upon their souls, she buried her head in her pillow. The sound of a shot would signal their death or Autie's.

When the word "ready" rang out, carbines were raised, but in the split second between "aim" and "fire," Leonard Lancaster was pushed aside. Armstrong spared the startled man, who served time in Florida's Dry Tortugas prison. Eventually he won exoneration and an honorable discharge with back pay.[13] The death of the other condemned soldier, a "vagabond and criminal" who had deserted several times, excited little sympathy, according to Libbie.[14] She was mistaken. Wilson, a farm boy from Illinois, had enlisted in 1863, at age sixteen. His service record mentioned no desertions or criminal behavior[15]

Custer had, nonetheless, outwitted his detractors. After exposing himself to their bullets, he had displayed compassion by sparing Lancaster's life and toughness by carrying out Wilson's sentence.[16] Unfortunately, he had also laid the basis for a charge that darkened the rest of his career—he mistreated enlisted men.

In late June, Libbie startled her husband by inquiring when they were leaving for Texas. When Armstrong asked how she had learned about the move, she explained that she had heard him conversing with the quartermaster and had seen him studying Texas maps.[17] Though most officers believed an army march too arduous for wives, the Custers decided that Libbie would accompany the troops. Daniel Bacon, while not enthusiastic about the idea, was not surprised. He knew his daughter preferred marching with the army to standing "over a cook-stove or a wash tub."[18]

Armstrong ordered an ambulance converted for Libbie's use. By the time soldiers completed their assignment, the vehicle, driven by four gray horses, boasted curtains, a "rain-proof" roof, and movable seats. In addition, the saddler covered a canteen with black leather and inscribed the name "Libbie" on one side and "Lady Custer" on the other.[19]

Although General Smith's forces in Texas had disbanded, some ex-Confederates, lured by promises of land, had crossed the Rio Grande to join Maximilian. Thus both Grant and Sheridan saw the situation in Mexico as a continuation of the Civil War. Sheridan also considered the Union Army the world's best fighting force and yearned to prove it in further warfare.[20] Late in June, he promised Grant that "two of the handsomest columns of cavalry, one under Custer, the other under Wesley Merritt" would arrive in Texas, ready for action.[21]

The moon cast a soft light on Alexandria's ruins as 3,000 cavalrymen assembled at four A.M. on August 8. Suddenly there was a loud shout as Custer and his staff rode to the front and the march began.[22] Afterwards, each day's march began before dawn and continued until the heat became unbearable. The division then halted and, later in the afternoon, started again, stopping about ten at night.

Supplies were meager, for the quartermaster had requisitioned only 1,000 shirts and pants for 3,000 men.[23] Custer, fearing additional desertions and hoping to prevent foraging on the civilian population, ordered the soldiers to wear their woolen uniforms and march in close units.[24] Besides increasing the incidence of heat stroke, the men, their throats parched from marching in dust, found the water insufficient for themselves and their horses when they arrived at the region's few and often brackish streams.[25]

By omitting the midday meal and serving the men freshly killed and often poorly cooked meat at night, the division averaged fifteen miles a day. Not

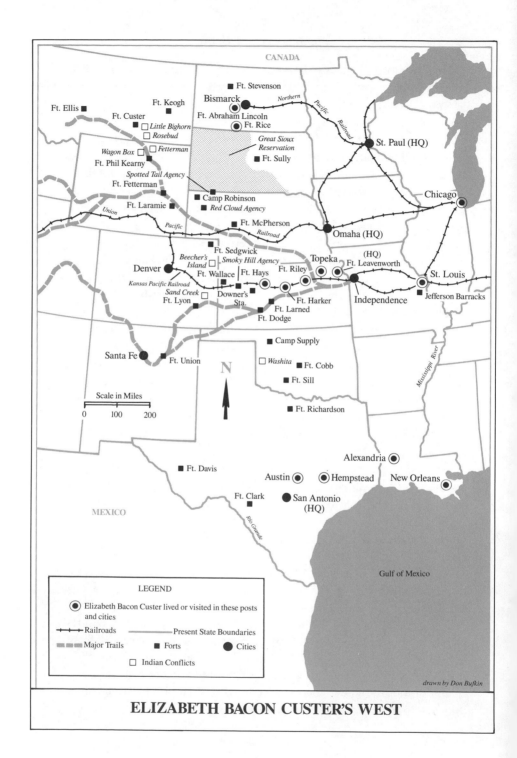

CANADA

■ Ft. Stevenson

Bismarck
◉ Ft. Abraham Lincoln
Ft. Keogh
Ft. Ellis ■
Ft. Custer
☐ *Little Bighorn*
☐ *Rosebud*
Northern
Pacific
Railroad
St. Paul (HQ)
◉ Ft. Rice
Great Sioux Reservation
■ Ft. Sully
Wagon Box ☐
Ft. Phil Kearny
☐ *Fetterman*
Spotted Tail Agency
Ft. Fetterman
Chicago
Ft. Laramie ■
■ Camp Robinson
Red Cloud Agency
Union
Pacific
Railroad
■ Ft. McPherson
Omaha (HQ)
Ft. Sedgwick
Beecher's Island ☐
Smoky Hill Agency
Topeka
(HQ)
Ft. Leavenworth
Denver
Ft. Wallace
Ft. Hays
Ft. Riley
St. Louis
Kansas Pacific Railroad
Sand Creek ☐
Ft. Lyon
Downer's Sta.
Ft. Harker
Independence
Jefferson Barracks
Ft. Larned
Ft. Dodge

■ Camp Supply

Santa Fe ● Ft. Union

☐ *Washita* ■ Ft. Cobb

N

■ Ft. Sill

Scale in Miles

0   100   200

■ Ft. Richardson

Mississippi River

Alexandria ◉

■ Ft. Davis

Austin ◉   ◉ Hempstead   New Orleans ◉

Ft. Clark ■ ● San Antonio
(HQ)

MEXICO

Rio Grande

Gulf of Mexico

LEGEND

◉ Elizabeth Bacon Custer lived or visited in these posts and cities

+—+—+ Railroads   —— Present State Boundaries

▬▬▬ Major Trails   ■ Forts   ● Cities

☐ Indian Conflicts

drawn by Don Bufkin

ELIZABETH BACON CUSTER'S WEST

surprisingly, many soldiers fell ill with dysentery. Out of seventeen ambulances accompanying the 240-mile march from Alexandria to Hempstead, Texas, ten carried the sick. Headquarters appropriated the other seven and assigned five to equipment, one to Libbie, and the other to Custer's hounds. Some now concluded that Custer valued his dogs more than his soldiers.[26]

Libbie found the nineteen-day march a grueling ordeal. For 150 miles, the column traveled over a rough trail through a pine forest. "For exasperating heat," the young woman wrote her Aunt Eliza, "recommend me to a pine forest."[27] Most of the time, she tried to be unobtrusive. Sensitive to the feelings of others, she knew that many of the men resented her presence. Not only did she take away a badly needed vehicle, but Armstrong, in violation of regulations, ordered soldiers to wait on her.[28]

Since the small wagon was stifling by midday, Libbie often rode horseback. During the Civil War, she had learned to ford rivers, but she found the steep-banked streams along the way frightening. Anxiously, she "wound" her fingers through Custis Lee's mane until she had reached the other side. Sometimes the surgeon ordered her to remain in the wagon. Then she called out "be careful" to the men easing her conveyance down difficult embankments and onto the pontoon bridges. Later Libbie told Eliza she admired their skills, knowing that her compliments would make their way back to the soldiers. Nonetheless, compliments or no compliments, many in the division considered her a nuisance.[29]

In addition to poor water and intense heat, all encountered countless insects, among them centipedes, scorpions, tarantulas, and the less dangerous but more troublesome chiggers and ticks. On the thirteenth day, the division arrived at "Camp Rattlesnake," so named because soldiers killed several large specimens there. Libbie's terror of the place proved well founded when a stick turned out to be a "pine-tree rattlesnake." Afterwards the Custers slept in the wagon rather than a tent.[30]

Each morning when reveille sounded at two, Armstrong lifted his wife from the wagon. Then Libbie washed, dressed in her drawers, corset, and multiple petticoats, drew on a skirt, and frantically buttoned her blouse. She then combed her hair without parting it. The whole enterprise, conducted by candlelight, took seven minutes when Armstrong timed her. Once she left her gold-braided riding habit behind in the forest.[31]

Libbie did not escape the scourge of the march, backbone fever. For several days, she lay in her wagon, taking quinine by the spoonful, a medicine the officers carried and ingested whenever they suffered a chill.

Quinine for the men, however, was in short supply, and most suffered their agonies without relief.[32]

As long as the cavalry remained in the pine forest, Libbie was appalled at living conditions in the sparsely settled region. She wrote her aunt Eliza, "almost every house" was "too poor" for her family's pigs and "only about as large as your sitting room with the father and mother and eight children and six dogs all living in them." Later, she recalled the "vacant faces of the filthy children of poor white trash and negroes. The men and women slouched and skulked around the cabins out of sight, and every sign of abject, loathsome poverty was visible, even in the gaunt and famished pigs that rooted around the doorway." Elizabeth preferred her tent or wagon to such hovels.[33]

Once the column crossed the Sabine river into Texas, "the country improved" as the column entered a region of cotton plantations. Libbie saw freedmen and freedwomen working in the fields, which stretched "for miles and miles." For the first time the Custers could purchase butter and milk from the more prosperous farmhouses.[34] But while Libbie and Autie enjoyed a more varied diet, rations for the men were reduced by half since supplies were running low and a wide prairie stretched ahead.

Shortly before reaching their destination, some soldiers inadvertently incurred their commander's wrath. They met Custer on the trail, dressed for hunting in a linen duster, a broad-rimmed hat, and a shotgun across his saddle. Several men approached and, mistaking him for a cowboy, offered to exchange hats. When Armstrong ordered them to headquarters for punishment, however, Libbie intervened, telling him to wear his "proper" uniform in the future. One veteran wrote nothing about the incident for two decades because of "my respect for her, for I am satisfied she was the best General of the two."[35]

At last, on August 26, the column entered a land of giant cacti with red blossoms and fragrant wildflowers. Reaching Hempstead, Custer awaited Sheridan's further orders. He also picked up his mail and discovered his brevets of major, lieutenant colonel, and brigadier general in the regular army.[36]

Autie was still celebrating when Sheridan arrived, accompanied by Emmanuel Custer. Armstrong, who always took good care of relatives, had arranged for his father to become the division's new forage master. Little Phil brought news as well. Secretary of State William Seward was unwilling to involve the United States in another war, hence action against Maximilian was out of the question. Instead, he ordered Custer to proceed to Austin to assume Reconstruction duties as chief of cavalry of the state of Texas after first resting his command.[37]

Since Tom was still a member of Armstrong's staff, the two brothers and their father passed many hours playing practical jokes on one another. Often Autie and Tom took Emmanuel horseback riding. While one engaged him in conversation, usually about politics, the other often slapped his horse's backside, causing Emmanuel's mount to plunge forward, with his heels high in the air. Fortunately for his bones, fifty-nine year old Emmanuel was never unseated.[38]

Libbie meanwhile recovered from the recent march. Later, looking in a mirror for the first time in months, she discovered to her horror that the sun had tanned her face and streaked her hair. Whatever the cost, the march had been worth it. She was the only army wife to have accompanied the cavalry.[39]

The ordeal, Libbie believed, had also benefitted the men. Under her husband's direction, the soldiers had learned discipline. "It was hard to realize," she noted later, "that the column marching in a methodical and orderly manner was, so short a time before a lawless and mutinous command." No wonder Sheridan had been pleased at "how few horses had perished from the heat, and how seldom sunstroke had occurred."[40]

Not everyone agreed. One officer, who accompanied Col. John P. C. Shanks of the Seventh Indiana to Texas by sea rather than overland, was shocked when he arrived. The troops were, he thought, "in the most destitute situation of any soldiers I had ever seen." Visiting the regimental hospital tent, he found thirteen men "sick, mostly with the flux," and lying in filthy, lice-ridden clothes on ragged blankets. Despite the clean garments and bedding, which he readily obtained from the town two miles away, "every evening at sun down. . . we buried one of these poor fellows, whose constitution had broken down from this long fatiguing march."[41]

Others also complained. The regimental and company returns of the Second Wisconsin, late in August, noted that in Co. G, twenty-six out of eighty-three men were ill. In general, the report attributed the deplorable conditions to the absence of soap and the dispensing of "fresh meat issued with less than ¼ ration of salt which rendered it impossible to use. No beans, vinegar or rice was issued and much of the hard bread was damaged and spoiled."[42]

Nor did the food improve greatly while the division rested. "Beef cattle were plenty," wrote one officer, "but our rations was hog jowls and flour and mouldy hard tack." The hog jowls sported tusks, and worms and bugs inhabited the hardtack.[43] Small wonder that some men, largely from the First Brigade, stole beef and a turkey from a neighboring farmer. Those charged had their heads shaved, their ranks reduced, and received twenty-five lashes. Afterwards Custer paraded them before their regiment.[44]

Some soldiers wrote their families, alleging poor rations and urging an investigation. Stories soon appeared in midwestern newspapers, and Governor William Stone of Iowa and the Wisconsin legislature complained to Stanton and Sheridan.[45] The latter, however, gave his junior officer strong support and told Custer, "Your acts are my acts on any question of discipline." He also assured Stanton that Custer no longer flogged his men.[46] To Grant, who still had questions, Sheridan responded, "Custer had not done anything not fully warranted by the insubordination of his command. If anything he has been too lenient."[47]

Libbie, knowing of her husband's problems, attributed his difficulties to his situation rather than his character. "A boy of twenty-five was then expected to act the subtle part of statesman and patriot, and conciliate and soothe the citizen; the part of stern and unrelenting soldier, punishing evidences of unsuppressed rebellion on the part of the conquered." At the same time, he was also to function as "the vigilant commanding officer, exacting obedience from his own disaffected soldiery."[48] In the end, she wrote, the volunteer troops "hated us, I suppose. That is the penalty the commanding officer generally pays for what still seems to me the questionable privilege of rank and power."[49]

The encampment at Hempstead lay along the banks of Clear Creek near Leonard Groce's Liendo plantation. Although four sons had served in Lee's Army of Northern Virginia, the Groces offered Libbie a room in their house. She refused, preferring to live in a tent. Besides, her old friend Nettie Humphrey Greene had recently arrived in camp, and the two women spent hours visiting. Elizabeth did not, however, refuse the easy chair and delicacies such as mutton roasts, jams, jellies, and desserts sent to her quarters. Later, when she fell ill with malaria, the family moved her to their home and nursed her back to health. "No country in the world can equal the South for hospitality," Elizabeth wrote her parents.[50]

During this period Libbie honed her riding skills. Autie wrote her father, "She thinks nothing of mounting upon a girthless saddle upon a strange horse and setting off at such a gait that even some of the staff officers are left behind." This was remarkable achievement since she rode sidesaddle. Tom considered his sister-in-law ("the old lady," as he and Armstrong referred to her when the three were together) the best female rider he knew.[51]

Daniel Bacon, more affectionate with his daughter now that she was married, assured her that her letters were "more than acceptable in our lonely moments." He judged her "descriptive powers" as "extra," and urged her to keep a journal. At the same time he lauded her spirit and stamina. Elizabeth, he boasted to a sister, "makes as much of a woman as we could have expected, & best of all she is married to her satisfaction & as such so with us." Libbie, who took increasing pride in her stamina, learned with pleasure that her relatives wondered "how a girl brought up as you had been could endure so much."[52]

The march to Austin began in November. Unlike the earlier trek, it started later in the day, and cold, rather than heat, was the problem. Libbie suggested that her husband let her stay in bed. With the mules pulling the tent, she could "go straight on to camp, warm all the way." Autie threatened to call her a "feather-bed soldier."[53] On the way they met rain and mud, but the varied menu, given the abundance of dairy products from Texas farmhouses, mitigated their hardships. They also enjoyed rabbit and game caught with the help of Byron, one of the five hounds Texas planters had presented Autie.

The dog's devotion to Libbie's husband meant that Libbie competed with Byron at night for bed space. Eliza, disgusted that Armstrong allowed the dog to intimidate his mistress, threatened to inform mother Custer of his delinquencies as a husband. One night, however, Byron received his comeuppance. When he growled at Libbie as she nudged him to make room, Armstrong kicked him, sending him yipping through space. Eliza was not placated. "No matter whether it's right or wrong, Miss Libbie's sho' to side with the Ginnel."[54]

In Austin, the Custers moved into the Blind Asylum quarters. Its amenities included a good-sized dining room, an ample parlor, and two pianos. Each evening, the staff and their wives assembled to play and sing. On special occasions, the couple hosted dances, and Eliza once gave a ball for her acquaintances. From the window of their second floor quarters, Libbie looked out on the state capital and the Colorado River. Across the river stood the Deaf and Dumb Asylum, where Autie learned the rudiments of sign language, a skill that would soon prove useful.[55]

Libbie found Texas both fascinating and repelling. While she perceived wide opportunities for land speculation and business investments, she expressed surprise at the crude, often unfinished homes of even the well-to-do. Manners and mores, moreover, left much to be desired as well-armed and trigger-happy men readily resorted to duels and gunfights. Worst of all, Texans branded their mounts to prevent horse stealing.[56]

Although Texas had escaped the wartime devastation suffered by Virginia or Mississippi, many residents openly declared their hatred of Yankees. Some threatened Reconstruction troops and any who befriended them. Nor were all whites ready to acknowledge the new status of blacks. Libbie noted with disbelief that slave-trading still persisted in some parts of the state.[57]

Despite the tensions of duty, the Custers found time for favorite pastimes. They raised hounds and, to Eliza's annoyance, took the offspring of Jennie, Libbie's favorite dog, to bed with them. They also bought and raced horses. Custer wrote his sister that they owned fourteen, but Libbie mentioned only three plus "a fast pony" to her father. Whatever the number, they built a small race track where Armstrong, despite his earlier pledge, placed bets.[58]

Libbie remembered fondly in later years the picnics at nearby Mount Bonnell, where the band serenaded the surrounding countryside with the Anvil Chorus. She also entered into the practical jokes the Custer men waged against one another. When Autie offered Libbie a pony if she could select the best horses in their stable, she enlisted Emmanuel as her ally. Surreptitiously he gave her the answers. With the forty dollars she made from selling her prize, she bought a silk frock, which became known as "Libbie's horse-dress."[59]

Elizabeth was "enjoying life so thoroughly." With no spring campaign in sight, she relaxed, "free from fear of a coming separation."[60] Autie, however, worried about the impending decline in his income. In all likelihood, he would soon be mustered out of the volunteer army. Then his pay would decline from $8,000 a year, paid major generals, to less than $2,000, earned by captains in the regular army. Looking for ways to augment his income, Armstrong tried to interest his father-in-law in buying plantation acreage, now that prices had dropped following the war. Daniel, having invested too much in Michigan real estate, had neither the cash nor the interest.[61]

As Custer faced the prospect of leaving Texas, he asked his aide, Capt. Jacob Greene, to investigate conditions in the state. Greene's report predicted racial warfare and "indiscriminate murder and destruction of property—every outrage" when the army left.[62] It was no use; congressional cutbacks mandated the troops' removal. Sheridan, moreover, had failed to win a promotion for his protégé, perhaps in part because of the complaints about Custer's handling of volunteer troops.[63]

Earlier, Custer had written his father-in-law, expressing horror at the harsh treatment accorded blacks around Alexandria. One young woman's back bore the scars of 500 lashings received at one time. "If the War has attained nothing else," he maintained, "it has placed America under a debt of gratitude for all time for removal of this evil."[64]

A few months later, as portions of his command were being mustered out, Custer suggested mustering out black soldiers even faster so they could "lay down musket for shovel and hoe. There are white men, veterans, anxious to fill up the Army, to whom preference should be given."[65] He then indicated his true stand on race relations. Although he supported raising blacks "morally and mentally as well as physically, also socially," he was "opposed to making this advance by correspondingly debasing any portion of the white race."[66] As for black suffrage, it made as much sense as "elevating an Indian Chief to the Popedom of Rome."[67]

On January 31, Custer received orders informing him his rank now reverted to captain in the Fifth Cavalry. Regretfully he and Libbie gave away their dogs, sold off their "embryo blue-grass farm," and said good-bye to the planters with whom they felt such affinity.[68] At Brenham, the Custer men, Libbie, Eliza, and a young black jockey named Johnny caught a rickety train, a relic of the late war. Arriving at Galveston they boarded a converted blockade-runner for New Orleans. As they crossed the Gulf of Mexico, a fierce gale arose, leaving them terrified and seasick. Reaching New Orleans on February 20, they traveled by steamboat and train to Michigan, arriving in Monroe on March 3.[69]

Libbie and Autie moved in with Daniel and Rhoda on South Monroe Street. Soon after, Autie left for the east, seeking advancement in the military or opportunities elsewhere. Given their slim purse, Libbie remained at home awaiting Armstrong's daily letters.

On March 10, the day after arriving in Washington, Custer appeared before the Joint Committee on Reconstruction. His testimony expressed strong reservations regarding Texas loyalty and described the former slaves as eager for education and capable of hard work when properly motivated.[70] Shortly after, Custer visited Stanton, who greeted him effusively. Autie left the meeting elated, convinced he had advanced his career and gained Tom an army commission. "Dear Old Sweetness," he instructed Libbie, "tell Tom he must study Tactics all the time now."[71]

Then Armstrong revealed the tenuousness of his commitment to radical Reconstruction. "I think if I stay here much longer and Andy Johnson remains firm, the Constitution will be able to stand alone." Very likely Armstrong referred to the Civil Rights Bill of 1866, designed to protect blacks by giving them "the full and equal benefits of all laws," enjoyed by whites. Shortly after, the president vetoed the measure, calling it an unwarranted encroachment of federal power on states rights that benefited blacks at the expense of whites.[72]

Everywhere in Washington that spring Armstrong received attention. Photographers and artists, including young Vinnie Ream, Lincoln's sculptor, wanted to create his likeness, and hosts and hostesses sought his presence at dinners. Inside one letter, Libbie found a photograph taken at a party given by Chief Justice Salmon P. Chase. Among those present were Chase's daughters, including the "queenly" Kate Chase Sprague and Maj. Gen. James A. Garfield, like Armstrong, a fair-haired soldier from Ohio. As Armstrong thanked his host that night, the chief justice prophesied that one day he would be lieutenant general.[73]

When Armstrong wrote that he might soon be offered a foreign minister's position paying between $7,000 and $10,000 a year, Libbie's hopes soared. While she hoped he would "accept it," she left the matter in his hands. "I am quite willing to have you decide on everything as your judgment in everything is beyond criticism." And she thanked her creator "for the gift of a husband who is so far superior to me in judgment and in everything else."[74]

By March 28, Custer was in New York City, attending operas and plays and taking in the sights. At Ole Balling's Eighth Street studio, he enjoyed seeing himself as one of thirteen Civil War generals depicted in the large mural, "Heroes of the Republic." He also dined with brokers and financiers of Wall Street, including Levi Morton, August Belmont, and John Jacob Astor.[75]

Armstrong's letters also recorded his socializing with a variety of women. He took Cora and Fannie Bean, two of Libbie's friends, to dinner and shopping. Later the three attended Maggie Mitchell's performance in *Little Barefoot*. The blond actress had become one of the most popular figures on stage, following her role in *Fanchon, the Cricket*, a play she now owned.[76]

During curtain calls, Custer and the two young women threw a bouquet with a card: "from an admiring trio." Later Armstrong attended Mitchell's rehearsal for *A Child of Fortune* and afterwards escorted her to her next appointment. Before long he visited the actress and her mother at their home on 54th Street. "I wish you could meet her," Libbie read in one of his letters, a sentiment she undoubtedly seconded. "I am sure you would like and admire her, her character is so excellent, there is nothing of the flirt about her."[77]

During his New York stay, Custer saw Pleasonton and dined with old friends from West Point. One evening he accompanied them to the theater and then a shooting gallery. Before the night ended they found themselves in a "pretty-girl-waitress saloon" and afterwards wandered onto the streets, where they flirted with prostitutes. "'Nymphes du Pave' they are called. Sport alone was our object. At no time," Autie assured his wife, "did I forget you."[78]

Several weeks later, he instructed Libbie to look at a recent issue of *Harper's Weekly,* where she would see drawings by Thomas Nast, depicting her husband attending the Bal Masque with Cora and Fannie. He was "the Devil, the only one." Present also was Clara Louise Kellogg, a prima donna, appearing as Marguerite in Gonoud's *Faust.* In time, Autie formed a close friendship with the opera singer that lasted many years.[79]

Libbie wrote later in *Tenting on the Plains* that she and Autie enjoyed watching the beautiful women in New York City. Perhaps in that context, Armstrong's descriptions of females did not surprise her. At a party given by Mr. and Mrs. Levi Morton, Armstrong sat beside Mrs. John Jacob Astor, who introduced him to Jessie Benton Fremont. Among the other guests was a baroness who "wore a very handsome satin, and oh so low. I sat beside her on a sofa and 'I have not seen such sights since I was weaned' and yet," he told his wife, "it did not make my angry passions rise, nor *nuthin* else. But what I saw went far to convince me that a Baroness is formed very much like all other persons of the *same sex.*"[80]

The letters Armstrong wrote Libbie that spring bore some similarity to those he had sent his first serious sweetheart years earlier. As a young schoolteacher at Beach Point, Ohio, he had told Mollie Holland, "You occupy the first place in my affections and the only place as far as love is concerned. . . . If any power which I possess or control can aid in or in any way hasten our marriage it shall be exerted for that object."[81]

From West Point, Armstrong had continued corresponding with Mollie. One letter included startling information on intimacies he had enjoyed with a mutual friend: "I think I know more about her than any other person and have done more with her or *rather to* her and she to me than any other one . . . and if she had a husband he could not have done but one thing more than I did." Then, having conveyed that news, Armstrong begged Mollie to see him when he came home. "At your house what room do you have as your own and tell what plan you can make up so that we can have the great 'Sleep.'" He signed his letter "your true and devoted H——––d GAC."[82]

Such a letter, taking Mollie, of all people, into his confidence as he described his sexual encounter with another woman is hard to explain, unless he believed this information enhanced his attractiveness. Perhaps it did, but it also told her that her relations with Custer were not exclusive. And yet, despite this strange confession, Armstrong expected to enjoy all the benefits of a committed, loving, and intimate attachment.

As he had in his earlier letters to Mollie, Autie often told Libbie she occupied the first place in his affections. At the same time he often referred to his social activities with other women. That and the talk of "sport" with prostitutes and gazing down a baroness's dress suggest a more subtle variation of the pattern established earlier with Mollie.

Armstrong's behavior also suggests a high degree of personal insecurity. At this point in his life, he had reason to feel uncertain. Two years earlier, he had married a young woman of higher social status than his own. By rising to national prominence, he had put to rest many of her family's earlier misgivings. More recently, however, he had failed to win the respect of volunteer troops and instead had incurred widespread enmity. To make matters worse, his current rank was not general but captain.

Finally, Libbie wanted children, and, as yet, their marriage had produced none. Whether or not Armstrong shared that desire, his failure to father a child after two years of wedlock must have raised disturbing questions for a man of that era, especially one from a large family. Emmanuel had fathered ten children during his two marriages, and six were still living.[83]

But Armstrong's letters were also full of flattery and loving messages. No matter how many beautiful or charming women he saw, Armstrong missed his wife. "People think, and correctly too, that I am having a magnificent time, but how much more my enjoyment would be increased if my other and better self was with me." Although he constantly came in contact with "the fairest of our land," none of them matched Libbie's "loveliness" or "purity of mind and character." And because their relationship was at heart erotic, he wrote in thinly veiled code: "I suppose you will have a great many nice *things* for me when I return. I will be in good condition to appreciate them."[84]

Still Autie procrastinated, apologizing that their separation lasted longer than expected. Missing her greatly, on April 21 he conjured up their shared memories. A carriage ride through Central Park reminded him of one they had enjoyed in Texas. "I never will comprehend the manner in which the window of that carriage was broken. Can you?" He was, he confessed, "nearly starved for just such a *ride* as that was. You know I am a great advocate of exercise as a promoter of health. Well I *firmly* believe that I require a ride every morning before breakfast but you know that being in New York and having left my horses saddles and all my *things* in Monroe I cannot without great expense and *much danger* enjoy the luxury of such a ride as that I refer to. I never did enjoy riding strange horses," he added, denying infidelity despite his many female friends. "It is a great risk."[85]

In concluding that letter, he noted that a mutual friend of theirs, a black-haired, balding politician and a "constitutional supporter" was staying at the hotel. When the politician returned to Monroe, Custer wrote, "For *my* sake I hope you will show him marked attention. I am sure he will appreciate and reciprocate it. You will find that he is fond of a great many *things*."[86]

The trip east, despite the pleasurable whirl of activities, provided no suitable civilian employment. Sheridan's recent letter to Stanton on Custer's behalf, however, provided some hope. On the basis of a record "so conspicuous as to render its recital by me unnecessary," Little Phil asked the secretary to give "one of the most gallant officers that ever served under me" a colonel's rank in the postwar army.[87]

Nonetheless, Armstrong remained "very anxious to leave the army provided I can enter some business or employment which is certain to bring me an increased income."[88] Until then he would not resign. "For you and you alone," he wrote his wife, "I long to become wealthy, not for wealth alone but for the power it brings." To that end, he would make "any honorable sacrifice. Once acquired we will enjoy it together with no more separations. My cup of happiness will then be full." Armstrong planned to start for home on April 24 or 25.[89]

With her husband away, Libbie visited friends and family. Anna Darrah, an attendant at her wedding, moved into the Bacon home to provide additional companionship. Neither Daniel nor Rhoda were well, however, and Libbie was preoccupied with their care. Moreover, since her clothes were out-of-date and Autie's income was reduced, she spent hours making new dresses. She had read Armstrong's descriptions of fashionable women in their "water-green silk trimmed with velvet a darker shade" and wanted to compare favorably when he returned. On her birthday, she wrote her Aunt Eliza: "I am twenty-four. Would you believe it? But people do not think my looks changed in spite of all I have been through. Autie is too necessary to my happiness for me not to miss him every hour he is away."[90]

In May, Daniel's health took a turn for the worse. As he lay dying, he told his daughter of his happiness with her marriage. "No man could wish for a son-in-law more highly thought of!" He also advised her "to ignore self" and accept Armstrong's military career. "In that life he had made a name, and there, where he was so eminently fitted to succeed, he should remain."[91]

Father Custer was with Libbie when Daniel died on May 18, but Autie was not beside her. He may have returned earlier to Monroe and then left again for New York City. Or perhaps he had not yet returned from his March trip. Whatever the situation, Libbie and her stepmother arranged the funeral. They chose the hymn, "Cast thy burdens on the Lord," for the choir and prepared Bacon's obituary. In another letter to Eliza Sabin, Libbie dismissed her husband's absence with brief remarks. Her father had "seemed stronger, and as Autie had to be in New York for a few days when he returned it was too late."[92]

Libbie had experienced a trying year full of hard realities. Resilient and adaptive, she presented a smiling face to the world, whatever her thoughts on her current state. She counted her blessings that her husband did not face a spring campaign and remembered with pride how well she had endured the march from Louisiana to Texas. Nonetheless, Armstrong's career remained unsettled, and his letters, full of frequent references to other women, must have antagonized her at times. She was, after all, human.

But Libbie lived in an era in which the good wife was unfailingly loyal, and had she been angry or disappointed the world would never have known. Instead the person who spoke candidly was Eliza. As she had noted earlier, "No matter whether it's right or wrong, Miss Libbie's sho' to side with the Ginnel."[93]

CHAPTER 6

Paradise Regained

DANIEL left his daughter his homestead, personal possessions, and a few vacant city lots and Armstrong inherited real estate valued at $800. Aside from a generous donation to the American Bible Society, Bacon's will directed that $5,000 be invested in securities to provide Rhoda an annual income. After her death, the fund would revert to Libbie.[1] With no windfall imminent, Autie's plans for making a living assumed greater importance.

Attracted by a salary of $16,000—twice his Civil War pay—Armstrong considered becoming an adjutant general in Benito Juarez's Mexican army. Libbie opposed the idea but planned to accompany him if he accepted.[2] When Armstrong discovered that Secretary of State Seward insisted he resign from the army first, he reconsidered. The Mexican position was temporary, and afterwards he might not regain his commission.[3]

Armstrong was also unsuccessful when he sought the newly created position of inspector general of the United States Cavalry. At last he received an appointment, dated July 28, as lieutenant colonel in the Seventh Cavalry, one of the new regiments authorized by the Army Act of 1866. As one biographer notes, it was "quite a comedown for a major general who had been feted everywhere by great men, though better than the captaincy he now held."[4]

He also joined President Johnson's "Swing around the Circle." Promoted as a unifying tour for Democrats and Republicans, it served another purpose. Johnson, at odds with Congress over recent passage of the Fourteenth Amendment, hoped to sway voters in the fall elections.[5] Since Custer had attended the president-sponsored Philadelphia National Union Convention earlier, his break with the Radical Republicans was now public.[6]

Custer's new stance brought vilification from Radical newspapers. Even the *Monroe Commercial* accused him of "fawning" on Johnson to gain a colonelcy.[7] Libbie attributed her husband's recent fluctuations to his fear of renewed warfare if congressional power went uncurbed. On the bright side, she wrote Rebecca, the uproar had dissuaded Autie from running for Congress. Libbie refused, despite the blistering editorials, to "give way to settled melancholy over such abuse."[8] Besides, Autie had been unusually attentive since her father's death. "He is growing so much dearer and dearer every day I am at loss to know how he can get any better. He is so indulgent and far more devoted than when we first were married."[9]

On September 4, Libbie joined her husband, already aboard the presidential train as it arrived in Monroe. The entourage sped through Indiana and on to Illinois. At Springfield, Libbie and the other ladies joined the ceremonies at Oak Ridge Cemetery, where all paid their respects at Lincoln's tomb. After the president's party returned to the St. Nicholas Hotel, however, Johnson spoke from a balcony to a jeering mob. Later, as the train traveled through Indiana, the crowds became even more unruly.[10]

Libbie was embarrassed for the president and disappointed that he seemed distant and preoccupied. Secretary of State Seward, however, struck her as "calm and bright," despite his scars from injuries administered by an accomplice in Lincoln's assassination. Libbie found his luncheon invitation flattering. Her father had spoken so highly of him that she "was almost surprised to see him eat and drink like other mortals, and enjoy the good things our car supplied."[11]

Shortly after, Armstrong announced that, given the disrespectful crowds, they were leaving the train at Steubenville, Ohio.[12] Disappointed, Libbie returned to Monroe as her husband started for Washington, stopping first in Cleveland to attend the Soldiers and Sailors Convention. The meeting, called to rally veterans supportive of the president's Reconstruction policies, was poorly attended. When someone circulated a petition against Stanton, Custer left very likely to avoid damaging his military career.[13]

Arriving in the capital, Armstrong went directly to the secretary of war and requested Tom's transfer from the First Infantry to his regiment. Stanton not only consented but raised Tom's rank to first lieutenant. Then, noting Libbie's absence, the secretary asked if she were "as pretty as ever." Armstrong replied that his wife was "still improving." As Custer left the War Office, a clerk assured him he would soon win promotion.[14]

Armstrong returned home to help Libbie pack. On October 8, the Custers, Eliza, Johnny (the young jockey), and Libbie's friend, Anna Darrah, set off for Fort Riley, Kansas. The first of many young women the Custers brought west, Anna would keep Libbie company while making the Custer quarters more attractive to unmarried officers. Autie's good friend, Kirkland C. Barker, a wealthy tobacco magnate and mayor of Detroit, requisitioned a separate car for their dogs and horses. Missing was Don Juan, who had recently died.[15]

On the way the entourage stopped at Saint Louis. After registering at the newly built and impressive Southern Hotel, they visited the Southern Relief Fair, designed to raise funds for families of Confederate veterans. They also toured the botanical gardens and the art museum where Libbie stood entranced before Albert Bierstadt's *Storm in the Rocky Mountains.*[16]

At the theater the group saw the popular play *Rosedale.* Lawrence Barrett's performance as a wily lover so affected them that Armstrong went backstage. When he talked Barrett into accompanying them to the fair's climax, a ball honoring the newly crowned Queen of Love and Beauty, he inaugurated a close friendship. Always awed by "self-made men," Libbie wrote Rebecca that Barrett had started out "as a bell boy at the Russell House in Detroit."[17]

On October 16, the Custers arrived at Fort Riley. Libbie had expected something "like Fortress Monroe, with stone walls, turrets for the sentinels, and a deep moat." Instead she saw a few limestone buildings, surrounding a parade ground on the left bank of the Kansas River. Nearby stood the sutler, quartermaster, and commissary's storehouses, along with stables. Beyond in all directions rolled "soft undulations of green turf," reminding her of the "surface of a vast ocean," and unbroken by trees except for cottonwoods along the rivers.[18] What she saw as remote and isolated, delighted her husband, Libbie later claimed. Armstrong always gloried in his new environment, rejoicing in "the exquisite haze that covered the land with a faint purple light," so reminiscent of Bierstadt's paintings. Besides, boyish and enthusiastic, he adapted easily, given his attitude that, wherever he was, "nothing could exceed his surroundings."[19]

Libbie's statements reflect her carefully crafted mythology. Beneath the surface, as events would soon prove, her husband was a troubled young man, and with good reason. Although he was relieved to have won a lieutenant colonelcy, it was a far cry from being a major general. Not long ago, moreover, he and Libbie had consorted with powerful individuals. Now he faced an indeterminate exile in the "American Siberia"—a lonely outpost on the Kansas plains. These broad fluctuations had occurred before he turned twenty-seven and would have taxed the equanimity of an older and more seasoned individual.[20]

The day the Custers and their entourage arrived, General Sherman, now commander of the Division of the Missouri, visited Riley. Since the commanding officer's quarters were unfinished, all moved into Maj. Andrew Gibbs's small quarters, with Libbie and Autie occupying the master bedroom. When Libbie apologized for the intrusion, she learned that post commanders' wives routinely provided such hospitality.[21]

The next day the Custers, Eliza, and Anna moved into their new home, a double house, which they furnished with six chairs. A few weeks later, when the Seventh's colonel, Andrew J. Smith, arrived with his wife, Libbie for the first time experienced "ranking out." Forced to vacate her spacious quarters to a higher-ranking family, she and Autie, in turn, chose the smaller dwelling of a lower-ranking officer. They set in motion a reshuffling that eventually forced some families to double up. The War Department had designed the six buildings housing officers as accommodations for eleven families, with the commanding officer's household enjoying double quarters. Since officers from other regiments were also at Riley, neither that post nor any other had sufficient housing.[22]

When Autie left for Washington to take the test required in the postwar army, Libbie became acquainted with the Seventh's officers as they arrived at the post. Most passed through quickly before moving on with their companies to various forts and substations along the Santa Fe Trail and the Smoky Hill River. Libbie had already formed a close friendship with the punctilious and often intemperate Gibbs and his wife.[23] The other two majors, Wyckliffe Cooper and Joel Elliott, formed a study in contrasts. Cooper was a hard-drinking and seasoned Indian fighter and the youthful Elliott, a former Toledo school superintendent.[24]

The captains ranged from fifty-four-year-old William Thompson to Louis McLane Hamilton, Alexander Hamilton's grandson and the army's youngest captain. Irish immigrant Myles Keogh had served as a papal Zouave, while Edward Myers, a martinet, came from Prussia. George Yates hailed from Monroe, and Albert Barnitz, a veteran of Armstrong's Third Division, had enlisted to serve again under his hero. By contrast, hard-drinking Robert West hated Armstrong from their first meeting.[25]

So too did Frederick Benteen, a Virginia-born soldier with an outstanding record in the Union Army. After Custer returned to Riley, Benteen paid his first courtesy call. Armstrong dominated the conversation, and at one point read his farewell address, which Benteen dismissed as "bluster, brag and gush." In turn, the captain read the farewell by his wartime commander, James Harrison Wilson. Always attuned to emotional undercurrents, Libbie sensed the captain's growing hostility. Attempting to make peace, she assured him that his commander "wrote beautifully." The damage was irreparable. Earlier that evening, Armstrong had made disparaging comments about his old rival.[26]

Among the lieutenants, William W. Cooke, a Canadian, eventually became Custer's adjutant. E. G. Mathey had emigrated from France, and Myles Moylan had risen from the ranks. The officer Libbie later described as an "educated Indian" was Lt. Donald McIntosh, part Scotch and part "Six Nations." His wife, Mollie, became one of Libbie's closest friends, as did Nettie Smith, wife of Lt. Algernon E. Smith.

Thomas Weir, a University of Michigan graduate, achieved popularity with the ladies, including Libbie, despite his attachment to the bottle. Another individual who never overcame his fondness for alcohol was Tom, although his sister-in-law tried hard to reform him. "The scamp," as Libbie fondly called him, reached Riley shortly before Christmas. Subdued by rheumatism at first, his spirits and the frequency of practical jokes against the "old lady" rose as his health improved.[27]

Molding such "incongruous elements" into a cohesive regiment was hard work. Colonel Smith had served on the frontier before distinguishing himself as major general of volunteers at Tupelo, Nashville, and Atlanta. Now past fifty, he left much of the drilling to his lieutenant colonel. On February 27, 1867, he turned it over entirely to Armstrong when he assumed command of the District of the Upper Arkansas.[28]

Low morale, arising from many factors, added to Custer's difficulties. Enlisted men received thirteen dollars a month, poor pay by standards of the day. Instead of the fervent Custer admirers Libbie remembered from wartime, their ranks contained many Irish or German immigrants, prodded into service by limited opportunities in civilian life. Among the native born, many were fleeing poverty or a disreputable past and were poor candidates for military discipline.[29]

The Seventh's company commanders provided most of the actual training, but numerous frustrations impeded their effectiveness. Regular army ranks were lower than wartime brevets, and so was the pay. Since protocol gave officers the right to use their brevet titles, confusion abounded, confounding some army wives entirely. Promotion, moreover, occurred only when resignations, deaths, or retirements created vacancies in individual regiments. The loneliness and boredom on isolated western posts invited excessive drinking, and quarrels in crowded quarters often turned into festering feuds.[30]

As Libbie struggled to adapt to regular army life, the divisions among officers disturbed her. She attributed much of the dissension to divergent backgrounds, jealousy or uneasiness over serving under a youthful commander, and tension between West Pointers and those from the volunteer ranks. Her husband, she maintained, understood these problems and sought to win his officers' trust through fairness and impartiality.[31]

In truth, Armstrong was himself a major source of conflict within the regiment. He elicited either "infatuated praise or vindictive condemnation" from others, never indifference.[32] Two cliques formed immediately. Hamilton, Keogh, Cooke, and Yates supported him, while Cooper, West, and Benteen opposed him.[33] Nonetheless, Armstrong assured Libbie that the divisions were temporary. Problems would disappear once the regiment experienced combat, for "it was on the battle-field, when all faced death together, where the truest affection was formed among soldiers."[34] Such statements hardly alleviated Libbie's fears. Although she also wanted a unified regiment, she was not enthusiastic about the prospect of seeing her husband face combat again.

Whatever their problems, the Custers found time for individual and mutual enjoyments. Libbie spent hours drawing and once made her husband a sketch of a bulldog smoking a pipe. Sometimes Tom joined them in a "wild game of romps," as they and their barking dogs chased each other through their quarters, banging doors and breaking through barricades of furniture. Most often, however, the young couple spurred their horses, Custis Lee and Phil Sheridan, across the prairies. Then, while both animals raced neck to neck, Autie reached out and lifted Elizabeth from her saddle, holding her "poised in the air for a moment." In those seconds she found herself "suspended between heaven and earth" as she struggled to "cling to my bridle and keep control of my flying horse, and trust to good fortune whether I alighted on his ear or his tail." Discovering that no disaster befell, she learned "to prepare for sudden raids of the commanding officer after that."[35]

The Seventh had been organized and sent west to protect the growing number of farms and towns rapidly appearing along the Saline, Solomon, and Republican rivers. Moreover, increasing numbers now traveled the old

Santa Fe Trail and the newer one between Kansas City and Denver. Simultaneously, work proceeded on the Union Pacific, Eastern Division, the forerunner of the Kansas Pacific, and construction crews needed protection. Additional tasks assigned the regiment included exploration, mapping, and laying out new roads and communication systems.[36]

This population movement with its accompanying growth in transportation and commercial lines ran headlong into the Plains Indians' determination to prevent further encroachment on the vast area they called home. These nomadic tribes included the Southern Cheyennes and Arapahoes, who roamed the Great Plains between the Platte and Arkansas rivers to the Rocky Mountain foothills. At times the Oglala and Brulé Sioux, who ranged largely along the Platte and Republican rivers, joined them as allies. South of the Arkansas, Kiowas and Comanches claimed dominion.[37]

The inexorable intrusion of miners on Indian lands and the removal of frontier regulars from western posts during the Civil War had ignited new Plains warfare. In October, 1865, the signing of the Little Arkansas Treaties with the Southern Plains tribes had brought an uneasy peace to the region south of the Platte River. But in December 1866, Sioux, led by Chief Red Cloud, wiped out Capt. William J. Fetterman and his eighty men not far from Fort Phil Kearny in Wyoming Territory.

Sherman, as commander of the Division of the Missouri, feared a resurgence of hostilities elsewhere. To prevent outbreaks on the Central or Southern Plains, he instructed Gen. Winfield Scott Hancock, commander of the Department of the Missouri, to intimidate or whip potential hostiles. Above all, westward settlement and railroad construction must continue unabated.[38]

Chiefs often desired peace. Certainly Black Kettle of the Southern Cheyennes wanted no warfare, despite the suffering his people had endured from the Sand Creek massacre in Colorado Territory in November 1864. Many younger braves, however, among them the Cheyenne Dog Soldiers, had not signed the Little Arkansas treaties. Eager to reclaim their Smoky Hill hunting grounds, they often urged war.[39]

Given these developments, the Seventh prepared for a spring campaign under General Hancock. Fourteen hundred infantry, cavalry, and artillery were concentrated to overawe the Indians. Armstrong assured Libbie that, despite extensive preparations, war was unlikely. "The Indians would be so impressed with the magnitude of the expedition, that . . . they would accept terms and abandon the war-path."[40]

By late March, the entire Seventh had encamped at Fort Harker, and Armstrong instructed Libbie to prepare to join him on twenty-four hours notice. Given the rumors of fights and skirmishes that drifted back to Riley, however, Libbie doubted Hancock would allow wives on the campaign. Tense and unhappy, she entreated her husband to "put an end to it, and desert."[41]

By April 8, Hancock's forces had assembled at Fort Larned. Hancock planned to meet with chiefs from the Cheyennes and the Brulé and Oglala Sioux, who had migrated south following the Fetterman massacre and were encamped on Pawnee Creek.[42] A snowstorm delayed the council set for April 9 and gave Autie time for reflection. In his youth, Custer remembered, "My every thought was ambitious—not to be wealthy, not to be learned, but to be great. I desired to link my name with acts and men, and in such a manner as to be a mark of honor, not only to the present, but to future generations." Since the war, however, "patriotism" had replaced "ambition," and he wanted to become "worthy of the blessings heaped upon me."[43]

Three days later only two chiefs and a few tribesmen showed up for the council. Convinced that the Indians were avoiding talks, Hancock marched to Pawnee Creek and instructed Custer to throw a cordon around the village. Libbie discovered, in her next letter, that when her husband arrived at the village, dog meat was simmering over the fires, but the lodges held only a blind old man and a young girl. Hancock ordered Custer to pursue the Indians.[44]

Armstrong never doubted he could overtake them, "their horses being in very poor condition." Instead, after a rapid chase northwestward, he found tracks running in all directions. He had lost their trail, but he had learned an important lesson. Once Indians eluded an enemy, intercepting them was almost impossible.[45]

Several days later, Libbie heard from her husband what she had already learned from Delaware scouts. Custis Lee was dead. While chasing Indians, Armstrong had left his command to pursue a buffalo. When the beast had unexpectedly charged, he had accidentally fired a bullet into the horse's brain. Alone and unmounted on the Plains and easy prey for an Indian war party, Armstrong had trudged across the prairie until the appearance of a guidon signaled his rescue[46]

While Libbie lamented her loss, grief over a horse paled in comparison to her anxiety over the perils Armstrong faced during the campaign.[47] For in the same letter telling of the horse's death, Armstrong had disclosed a terrible discovery. He had come upon the charred bodies of three station-keepers, killed by Indians at Lookout Station. Wolves had ravaged the remains, making it "one of the most horrible sights imaginable."[48]

And yet, despite the possibility that warfare was likely, Autie, now at Fort Hays, wanted his wife with him. If he were "sent off independently during the summer, as I am at present, I believe you can go with me." After all, "the fatigues of the march will be all that you will have to contend against, and these will not be greater than those encountered in going through Texas."[49]

Although he still hoped hostilities could be avoided, inadvertently he had set them off. On April 16, Armstrong had telegraphed Hancock, blaming the Lookout Station depredations on the Pawnee Creek Indians. Later, learning that the killings had occurred on April 15, he knew that these Indians could not have traveled fifty miles in twenty-four hours on heavily laden ponies. His realization came too late. Shortly after receiving Custer's telegraph on April 18, Hancock had ordered the deserted village on Pawnee Creek burned. In the process, he ignited war from the Platte to the Red River.[50]

At Riley, Libbie awaited her mail, fought back depression, and struggled with the uncertainty of joining her husband. She also faced new problems. The warmer weather brought prairie fires, and one threatened to engulf the fort before soldiers extinguished it. Moreover, Libbie, subscribing to the common racial prejudices of her day, feared the black soldiers from the Thirty-eighth Infantry at Riley.[51] Characterizing their time at the post as "a reign of terror to us women, in our lonely, unprotected homes," she remained overwrought until Major Gibbs returned to assume command.[52] Eventually, these soldiers won her grudging respect when they proved their mettle by bravely guarding the supply wagons "through the worst of the Indian country." Elizabeth concluded that blacks made useful soldiers, provided the army relegated them to "certain duty to which they were fitted."[53]

The irritation, confusion, and despondency that surfaced in her husband's letters added to her distress that spring, as did the erratic mail delivery. Forced to remain at Fort Hays until rivers subsided and supplies and forage arrived, Autie described his "inaction" as "almost unendurable." Even when the necessary provisions appeared, he saw little chance of overtaking the Indians. He had no idea of their whereabouts, and he now knew that army horses "cannot endure the marching that their ponies can, fed upon nothing but prairie-grass." Autie described himself as "extremely homesick."[54]

At Riley, wild rumors circulated, leaving Libbie in "a perfect whirlwind of anxiety." Not even an earthquake distracted her from her fears. Yet, whatever the dangers, if Autie sent an army wagon to the railroad's end, she would try to meet it[55] In response, Armstrong directed her to await Colonel Smith's arrival at Riley so that she could return with him to Hays. "We have a beautiful camp," he promised, "and you will be delighted with the country."[56] Two days later he was even more insistent. "You remember how eager I was to have you for my little wife. I was not as impatient then as now. I almost feel tempted to desert and fly to you. I would come if the cars were running, this far."[57]

Despite the fervent and frantic messages the couple sent each other that spring, Armstrong's letters disclose that dissension had come between them. The two exchanged poetry, but Autie's selections were preoccupied with reconciliation. On April 25 he included these lines:

> Blest, indeed, is he who never fell,
> But blest much more, who from the verge of hell
> Climbs up to Paradise; for sin is sweet,
> Strong is temptation, willing are the feet
> That follow pleasure; manifold her snares
> And pitfalls lurk beneath our very prayers.
> Yet God, the clement, the compassionate,
> In pity of our weakness, keeps the gate
> of pardon open.[58]

Several weeks later, he enclosed other lines, adding his own emphasis. "Man's best possession is a *loving wife* / She *tempers anger* and *diverts* all *strife*."[59]

Separation intensified his desire. Earlier, he had instructed Libbie to bring fresh vegetables, lard, and a croquet set when she came. As May progressed, he became explicit. He wanted "*something* much, very much better and be sure you bring *it* along. *I am entirely out at present* and have been so long as to almost forget how it tastes."[60]

On May 10, he wrote Libbie twice. In the morning his disclosure that he was reading Robert Burton's *Anatomy of Melancholy* hinted at his sadness.[61] Later that day, a backlog of Libbie's letters arrived. While all were affectionate, none referred to his earlier instructions to accompany Smith to Hays. He pleaded, "*Do* hurry and come to your boy."[62]

After emphasizing his wish never to leave her side, Autie made a revealing digression. His relations with other women had created problems in the

Custer marriage, for he wished Libbie could "read my innermost heart and see the disgust even with which the remembrance of other girls of our acquaintance fills me." Then, vowing there was not a single female that he would "go outside of my tent to see but you except to be polite," he reemphasized an earlier pledge.[63]

He wrote, "You know I promised never to give you fresh cause for regret by attentions paid to other girls, so firmly has this become my creed and my resolve, thus my determination, carried forward by my love for you." That love in fact had "driven all thoughts even of them from my mind from the moment I left you until now. I have never thought of a single girl," he added, "to whom I ever paid the slightest attention with any feeling but that of supreme indifference, and without wishing to see them, have cared nothing if I never met either of them again." Significantly, he signed this letter, "Yours and yours only I would not be another's if I could."[64]

By May 12, Autie was in despair. Libbie's most recent letter indicated she had left for Fort Leavenworth, which meant she would not accompany Smith to Hays. Very likely they would not see each other "until fall or winter as I do not intend to leave my command while there is anything to do." Disappointed and impatient, Armstrong complained bitterly. With both Hancock and Smith prodding him, he would, if he heard nothing soon, "try to kill time by killing Indians and will set out on the contemplated march." In the meantime, he consoled himself by sleeping with Libbie's gown beneath his pillow.[65]

Theodore Davis, an artist from *Harper's Weekly*, accompanied the Seventh that spring and summer and described Custer as "depressed" and "moody."[66] Captain Barnitz went further. In letters to his wife, Jennie, he described his commander as "obnoxious" and "the most complete example of a petty tyrant" and charged him with "cruelty to the men, and discourtesy to the officers."[67] One incident proved especially disillusioning. Lacking adequate provisions, the soldiers suffered from scurvy. When Custer learned that six men had left their command without permission to buy canned goods from the Fort Hays sutler, he ordered them marched through camp with half their heads shaved. Facing such treatment, ninety men deserted in six weeks.[68]

In mid-May General Sherman arrived at Fort Riley. By now fellow officers knew that Custer pined for Libbie. The long epistles he wrote her daily amused them, as did his habit of carrying her letters in his shirt pocket. Sherman, feeling compassionate, brought Libbie, Anna, and Eliza to Harker. From there Colonel Smith transported the women to Hays.[69]

Libbie, Anna, and Eliza arrived on May 18, and the following day, Barnitz wrote his wife that the women now resided in tents on "a pleasant place on the stream two or three hundred yards in rear of camp." Custer had decorated their home by ordering "bowers and screens of evergreens erected, and triumphal arches, and I know not what all else." When Jennie joined him, Albert promised her a "rival bower."[70]

On June 1, necessary supplies had arrived, and six companies of the Seventh set out again in search of marauding Indians. Autie stayed behind an extra day to oversee the transfer of Libbie's tents to higher ground along Big Creek. Assured of her safety, he hurried off to join his command.[71]

While Custer had remained at Hays, the hostiles had moved northward to a region along the Platte River. There they threatened emigrant trains traveling to California and Colorado and the Union Pacific's construction crews. Custer's orders were to march towards Fort McPherson and then westward, clearing hostiles from the plains between the Platte and Republican rivers.[72] After a ten-day march through heavy rains and swollen streams, Custer arrived at McPherson. He had sustained one casualty when Major Cooper shot himself, along the way, in a fit of delirium tremens. His suicide left his pregnant wife ineligible for a pension.[73]

While Custer awaited General Sherman's arrival, a Sioux chief, Pawnee Killer, arrived unexpectedly at the post. Blaming Cheyennes for the recent depredations, he promised to move his people close to the fort. Custer issued him bread, sugar, and coffee and wrote Libbie that with peace impending, they would soon be reunited.[74]

Unfortunately, when Sherman arrived next day he disagreed since Custer had taken no hostages to enforce compliance. Instead, the general instructed Armstrong to march south to the forks of the Republic, ordering any Indians along the way to move to forts McPherson or Sedgwick. Afterwards, Custer was to move northwest to Fort Sedgwick in Colorado Territory for supplies and additional orders before scouting the source of the Republican River.[75]

During the conference Sherman mentioned that Libbie could soon join her husband. He assumed she would come by train to Omaha, but Armstrong had other plans. In his letter of June 17, he told Libbie to go to Fort Wallace, where he would send a squadron for her. That same day, however, Libbie had left Fort Hays.[76] Although she had intended remaining along Big Creek come the proverbial "hell or high water," in the end, high water had driven her away.

Libbie's troubles had started on June 5, when she and Anna had persuaded Lieutenant Weir, Colonel Smith's acting assistant adjutant general, to take them for a stroll outside the post. When they returned at dusk, sentries, mistaking them for Indians, fired in their direction. Weir told the women to lie flat on the ground while he crawled slowly toward the post to identify himself. At ten o'clock, an alarm sounded, signaling that the two women and Weir had not yet returned. Suddenly bugles blew, and the panicky sentries discharged bullets in all directions. Luckily Weir established contact and explained the situation. The uproar ceased, and Libbie and Anna returned to their tent greatly embarrassed.[77]

Two nights later, torrential rains fell. Awakened by shouts from the guard, Libbie looked outside. Persons new to the Plains were unprepared for the rapidity with which heavy rains brought flooding. The stream above had overflowed, and "the water on either side of us, seen in the lightning's glare, appeared like two boundless seas." She saw only the tree tops, "as the current swayed the branches in its onward sweep."[78]

Suddenly Libbie heard the screams of soldiers, swept along by the swift current and in danger of drowning. Eliza saw a soldier clinging to a branch and threw him a clothesline. She, Libbie, and Anna towed him and other men to shore. Despite their strenuous efforts, however, seven other men perished that night.[79]

Rain fell again the next evening. As Big Creek rose once more, the camp was evacuated, although three days passed before ambulances, mired in mud, moved to the next divide. General Hancock was at Hays and explained to the army wives that an escort would take them to Harker. When Libbie expressed concern about moving farther from her husband, Hancock told her Custer now scouted in the Division of the Platte. Very likely she would not see him the rest of the summer.[80]

Arriving at Harker, the women discovered there was no room for them. Rather than intrude on crowded families, Libbie slept in the wagon with Anna and Eliza. That night another storm arose, and, as the wind whipped their conveyance back and forth, the rope to the moorings broke. As the screaming women careened downhill at accelerating speed, soldiers arrived barely in time to prevent a crash landing. "Fished out of their watery camp-bed," Libbie, Anna, and Eliza were taken inside for the night.[81] On June 21, they and the other officers' wives from the encampment at Big Creek left by train for Riley.[82]

Armstrong, knowing nothing of these misadventures, reached the forks of the Republican River on June 21. He decided that, since Sedgwick and

Wallace were equidistant, the road to Wallace was better for wagons than the rougher terrain to Sedgwick. Never mind that by marching to Sedgwick, as Sherman had instructed, the cavalry provided greater safety to the Union Pacific's Platte River construction crews. And never mind that Sedgwick was more easily provisioned. When Lieutenant Cooke returned from Wallace, he would bring what was important—Libbie. To ensure her safety, Custer ordered Captain West and Company D to provide additional escort.[83]

Custer still sent a detachment under Major Elliott to Sedgwick for orders on June 23. With a third of his column dispersed elsewhere, he met a party of fifty warriors the next day. After they almost stampeded the cavalry's horses, Custer parleyed with seven chiefs, including Pawnee Killer. Later, correspondent Davis concluded, "Our little party escaped, and the affair ended without a sanguinary conclusion, mainly by the peculiar influence of Custer's presence." Even so, the Indians lured one company into ambush, and only Captain Hamilton's able leadership extricated the soldiers from peril.[84]

Custer, increasingly worried about Libbie's safety now that she was supposedly aboard the returning supply wagon, dispatched Company E under Captain Myers as additional protection. When the reinforced supply train returned to the camp on the Republican on June 27, Armstrong was both disappointed and relieved that Libbie was not aboard. The Seventh's officers had orders to shoot wives entrusted to their care when Indians attacked. As Custer learned, only the arrival of West and Myers had saved Cooke from an earlier Indian ambush thirty miles west of Wallace. Moreover, the troopers had discovered at Wallace that Cheyennes had recently raided the Smoky Hill stations and on June 21 had attacked the post itself, leaving two men dead.[85]

Libbie did not receive her husband's letter calling her to Wallace until after her arrival at Riley. In her response, of June 27, she described herself as willing to brave Indians "or anything else, if you are at the end of the trip."[86] Still, she held out little hope since "General Sherman sent word to me that I had best remain quietly at Riley, as my husband will be on the march all summer." Angrily, she flared, "Quietly! He may talk about living quietly, but I cannot." She also noted that, given the increased attacks between Hays and Harker, she and the other ladies had left camp "just in time."[87]

Custer's summer campaign deteriorated quickly. Elliott, finding no orders at Sedgwick, returned safely to the Republican on June 28. When the orders arrived next day, Lt. Lyman Kidder left Sedgwick with a ten-man detachment to carry them to Custer. Meanwhile, Armstrong belatedly decided to follow Sherman's earlier instructions. He began marching westward towards the South Platte in Colorado Territory despite an experienced scout's conviction that hostiles were encamped on Beaver Creek, between the Smoky Hill and the Republican.[88] As the troopers rode sixty-five miles through rugged country, the column approached the trails leading to western mines. Desertions, which had occurred all along, now increased.[89]

At Riverside Station, Armstrong learned that Kidder's detachment was out on the Plains looking for him. When he telegraphed for a duplicate set of orders, he discovered that Sherman now instructed him to march to Wallace. With Kidder's detachment exposed to war parties, Custer announced another forced march. That night another thirty to forty men deserted.[90]

Determined to halt such derelictions, Custer ordered his officers to pursue fifteen men deserting during the noon rest and "bring none in alive." Three were shot, but when the surgeon approached the wagon carrying the wounded, Custer ordered him away as a warning to others. Afterwards, the lieutenant colonel reversed himself, telling the doctor to tend the men secretly. Nonetheless, the doctor, lacking water, neither dressed the wounds nor removed the men from the wagon.[91]

Custer, low on supplies, realized that, in addition to overtaking Kidder, he must march farther than expected to reach Wallace before forage gave out. As the column approached Beaver Creek en route, they found the mutilated remains of Kidder and his party, very likely the work of Pawnee Killer's band.[92]

On July 13, Custer arrived at Wallace. Original plans had called for him to join Hancock, but the general had gone without him, leaving Captain Keogh in charge of the post. Armstrong was disappointed that neither Libbie nor her letters awaited him. Still, if he contacted Smith at Harker, he might obtain a brief leave and reunite with his wife. Perhaps he could bring her back while his men and horses recuperated.

Hancock's unfortunate campaign now faced another problem. Companies of the Thirty-eighth Infantry, on their way from Jefferson Barracks in Missouri to New Mexico, had stopped at Fort Harker. There, on June 28, one week after Libbie had left the post, a physician had diagnosed a soldier's illness as cholera. Six days earlier, a civilian employee at Fort Riley had died of the disease the same day his symptoms appeared. On July 11, Riley suffered its second and last case of cholera until November, 1867.[93]

Later Custer claimed that he reached Fort Wallace on July 13, just in time. As he told the story in *My Life on the Plains*, "Stages had been taken off the

route . . . No dispatches or mail had been received at the fort for a considerable period, so that the occupants might well have been considered as
undergoing a state of siege." Worse yet, "The reserve of stores at the post
were well-nigh exhausted, and the commanding officer reported that he
knew of no fresh supplies being on the way. . . . Cholera made its appearance among the men, and deaths occurred daily." Libbie, in her book
Tenting on the Plains, later told the same story[94]

As one scholar has noted, these statements were false. The post was not
under "siege," for additional companies had arrived at Wallace, and the
Indian attacks were less frequent.[95] Moreover, mail stages were coming
through about once a week. Finally, while forage remained scarce and
Custer lacked enough horseshoes to refit his mounts, the post was supplied.[96]

Nor had cholera yet arrived at the post. Not until July 22 did the Seventh
Cavalry experience this scourge, and then, given the troop's weakened
condition, it exacted a heavy toll.[97] On July 13, those stationed at Wallace
probably had not heard about the cholera at Harker.[98] Thus Custer's later
argument that he left Wallace with an escort of four officers and twenty-two
men to obtain badly needed supplies and medicine for men dying of the
dread disease was false.[99]

According to another source, however, Custer received a disturbing
message at Wallace. Frederick Benteen maintained years later that Lt.
Charles Brewster, urged on by Eliza, had written Custer anonymously. He
called on him to come home and "look after his wife a little closer." Libbie
and Lieutenant Weir were becoming too attached.[100]

While Benteen's antipathy to Custer must always be noted when evaluat-
ing his statements, Lieutenant Mathey (by then a colonel) told an interviewer virtually the same story. According to his testimony, "Some officer in
the regiment wrote an anonymous letter to some newspaper accusing
Captain [sic] Weir, who was at Fort Riley, of paying too much attention to
Mrs. Custer. Custer's attention was brought to this, and he became furious
and very impatient to get to Fort Riley. This is the reason why Custer left his
command without permission" and hurried to rejoin his wife.[101]

Weir, Libbie, and Anna Darrah had been together frequently during the
past six weeks. Not only had Weir escorted the two women outside Fort
Hays on June 6, but, as Colonel Smith's aide, he had assisted Libbie, Anna,
and Eliza during the flooding at Big Creek. Later he and Smith had
accompanied the officers' wives as they traveled to Fort Harker.[102] Possibly

such proximity generated unfounded gossip, or perhaps some Seventh officers seized upon unfounded rumor to exact revenge upon Custer.

There is another strong possibility. The memoirs of officers' wives indicate that ladies of the frontier army considered flirtations one of the benefits of post life.[103] As an accomplished charmer in her youth, Libbie had undoubtedly honed her skills to a high level since marriage. Beyond that, the young woman, who had sought to make her husband aware of her attractiveness to other men shortly after their wedding, may have been playing that game again with expert skill.

Libbie had read many letters in the spring of 1866 in which Autie had described at length his outings with various women in Washington and New York while she remained in Monroe. Custer's recent letter of May 10, in which he had pledged never again to give her "fresh cause" for jealousy, reveals, moreover, that the two had discussed his relationships with other females. Thus Elizabeth may well have decided to reignite jealousy as a way of settling old scores.

The hard-drinking but college-educated Weir would have made a likely candidate. Libbie had always been intrigued by men who needed reformation, as demonstrated by her earlier interest in Jim Christiancy and her continuing fondness for Tom. Furthermore, she could always justify her interest, even to herself, as arising from her desire to save souls. Thus, while it is improbable that a physical relationship existed between Elizabeth and the alcoholic lieutenant, she may well have encouraged his attentions.[104]

If that was the game she was playing (and she had played it before), then she succeeded admirably in making her husband jealous. Armstrong became so concerned about rumors of Libbie and Lieutenant Weir that his career became of secondary importance. The fear that his wife had become interested in another man, rather than the absence of supplies or the existence of cholera, accounted for Armstrong's subsequent actions.

Armstrong turned Fort Wallace over to Major Elliott, explaining that he had to check with his commanding officer from the nearest telegraph office. Had he taken the stage, few would have questioned his actions, but instead he selected an escort of seventy-six officers and men, mounted on most of the command's best horses.

On July 15, Custer set out, beginning a 150-mile trek of fifty-five hours of nonstop marching. Arriving at Monument Station in the morning, he met a supply train under Captain Benteen, which had left Fort Hays on July 12.

Undoubtedly, Custer inquired about Libbie and others and learned that, as far as Benteen knew, all were well. Earlier, on June 18, after the ordeal at Big Creek, Smith had telegraphed Custer on military matters. He had included the message, "The people are here with me and all [are] well." Thus it is unlikely, as Libbie later maintained, that her husband had been "assailed by false reports of my illness" or feared that she had been injured in the flooding at Big Creek.[105]

On the second day, the column came upon mail stages two miles east of Castle Rock station. After searching the mail bags for letters or orders, Custer noticed that his mare, Fanchon, was missing. Before resuming the march, he told Sgt. James Connelly and six men to retrieve the horse and the soldier responsible for her care.

After locating the trooper and mare at Castle Rock, the detachment hurried to rejoin the main column. Suddenly Indians attacked, wounding two troopers. As the mare, frightened by gunfire, tried to pull Connelly off the trail, warriors moved in to encircle him. Precious time was lost in recapturing the horse and rescuing Connelly. The detachment, seeing the Indians upon them, left the injured men behind. Even so, the hostiles pursued the small party almost to Downer Station, where Custer had halted.[106]

When Connelly and his men rejoined the column and breathlessly told their tale of wounded men and pursuing Indians, the command waited for Custer's response. When he ordered no rescue attempt, Captain Hamilton informed his commander that the men were becoming "demoralized." Armstrong ordered the column to move on.[107]

Questioned later, Custer gave his version: "A sergeant and six men had been sent back to bring up a man who had halted at the last ranch; when returning, this party was attacked by between forty and fifty Indians, and two of them killed. Had they offered any defense this would not have occurred, instead however they put spurs to their horses and endeavored to escape by flight."[108] Later, he wrote that the men had "without authority halted some distance behind."[109]

Custer's column came into Big Creek station near Fort Hays early on the morning of July 18. Waiting for him were letters from Libbie.[110] Nonetheless, Armstrong, along with his brother Tom; Lieutenant Cooke; the journalist, Davis; and an orderly, attached fresh mules to two ambulances and set out for Harker. Along the way, they met Capt. Charles C. Cox of the Tenth Cavalry. He carried Custer's orders instructing him to retain his base at Fort Wallace and scout between the Platte and the Arkansas rivers while keeping his cavalry "constantly employed."[111]

Orders were now of secondary importance. Armstrong, obsessed with seeing his wife, knew that if he made it to Riley, he could bring her back before resuming the campaign. He went on to Harker and, arriving about 2 or 2:30 on the morning of July 19, roused Colonel Smith from a deep slumber.

Without asking permission, Armstrong informed the drowsy colonel he was going to Riley. Still confused, Smith dispatched Weir to accompany Custer and his party to the train station. Returning to bed, he called out his respects to the ladies. Then, according to Benteen (and confirmed by Mathey), Custer "'tackled Weir' at Harker making him beg for his life on his knees."[112]

Next morning, in the clear light of day, Smith had second thoughts. When he learned that Custer had traveled part way with an escort and the rest of the way in an ambulance, he "immediately ordered him back to his command."[113]

Elizabeth awoke one morning to hear "the clank of a sabre on our gallery and with it the quick, springing steps of feet, unlike the quiet infantry around us. The door behind which I paced uneasily, opened, and with a flood of sunshine that poured in, came a vision far brighter than even the brilliant Kansas sun. There before me, blithe and buoyant, stood my husband!"[114]

Libbie began packing to return with Autie to his command.[115] Shortly after his arrival, Armstrong received Smith's telegram ordering him back to Harker immediately. The couple caught the first train, and when they appeared at the post, Custer was arrested. Given the cholera at Harker, Smith, concerned for Libbie's well-being, sent the couple back to Riley to await Armstrong's court-martial.[116]

Custer's unexpected appearance at Riley had, nonetheless, proved his willingness to risk his career to be with his wife. Thus Libbie never forgot that grand, romantic gesture: "There was in that summer of 1867 one long, perfect day. It was mine, and—blessed be our memory, which preserves to us the joys as well as the sadness of life!—it is still mine, for time and for eternity."[117]

And so it was; but the days ahead would bring their share of new troubles and, eventually, new triumphs as well. First, however, the Custers were compelled to attend to the more immediate matter before them—Autie's impending court-martial.

CHAPTER 7

"Woe be unto Mr. Lo to say nothing of Mrs. Lo and the little Lo's"

ARMSTRONG faced charges of "absence without leave from his command" and "conduct to the prejudice of good order and military discipline." Among the specifications, he had over-marched men and government horses and mules and used public vehicles for private business. More serious, he had failed to care for the two men shot near Downer's Station. Unexpectedly, Captain West lodged additional charges. Custer had ordered deserters shot "without trial" and afterwards withheld medical care from the wounded. As a result, Charles K. Johnson, the most seriously injured, had since died.[1]

Libbie threw all her energies into helping her husband, spending long hours copying "foolscap . . . a labor of love" for his defense. Putting up a brave front, she assured relatives that neither she nor Autie worried about the court-martial's outcome. Besides, when he had left Wallace, Armstrong had known the possible "consequences . . . and we are quite determined not to live apart again, even if he leaves the army otherwise so delightful to us."[2]

Weir, eager to assist the Custers, wrote Armstrong on August 14: "Will any little favor I may be able to give be kindly received? I am anxious in the affair to go on your side."[3] Although Weir later testified for both the prosecution and the defense, his answers, indicating that Smith had apparently given Custer permission to travel from Harker to Riley, were helpful to Custer.[4]

The court-martial, which convened on September 15 and concluded on October 11, resulted in a verdict of guilty on all counts. Custer's sentence deprived him of rank, command, and pay for one year. The court, however, attached no criminality to any charges. Very likely the officers hearing the trial thought that Custer's command had been close to mutiny when he had ordered deserters shot.[5] Grant, as commanding general, however, judged the

sentence "lenient," adding that the court "must have taken into consideration his previous services."[6]

Libbie dismissed the outcome as "nothing but a plan of persecution for
Autie."[7] According to Armstrong, Sheridan saw it as "an attempt by
Hancock to cover up the failure of the Indian expedition," and many
historians have since agreed.[8] Whatever the interpretation, the court-martial
tarnished Custer's reputation. It also deepened divisiveness in the Seventh
and jeopardized further Autie and Libbie's hopes for a unified regiment.[9]

Sheridan's actions spoke louder than words. Now commander of the
Department of the Missouri, he was in Washington serving on a board to
revise the Articles of War. He turned his comfortable Leavenworth quarters
over to the Custers and that, added to the "emoluments" Armstrong would
still receive, saved the Custers from hardship. "Autie and I, " Libbie wrote
Rebecca, "are the wonder of the garrison, we are in such spirits."[10]

Whatever the couple's outward demeanor, the verdict bothered Armstrong. In his letter to the *Sandusky* [Ohio] *Daily Register*, he portrayed the
outcome of the court-martial as unfair. The court had included members of
Hancock's staff, others lacking in command experience, and officers below
Custer in rank. Another member had served in the commissary, the department Custer blamed for the 156 desertions his command had suffered
between April 19 and July 13.[11]

West, unhappy over the court-martial's verdict, filed charges against
Custer in civil court. Hearings began on January 8 in the town of Leavenworth. Ten days later, to Libbie's immense relief, Judge Moses S. Adams
dismissed the case as unsubstantiated.[12]

While the Custers contended with these problems, changes were occurring in Indian affairs. Late in October 1867, the government signed treaties
at Medicine Lodge Creek in Kansas with the Kiowas, Comanches, Southern
Cheyennes, and Arapahoes. The Indians agreed to live on reservations away
from the Kansas Pacific Railroad. In return they were promised the right to
hunt buffalo south of the Arkansas River and collect government annuities
for thirty years. Neither Major Elliott nor Captain Barnitz, both of whom
observed the ceremonies, invested much hope in the proceedings, a perception shared by journalist Henry Stanley. The signatory chiefs had little
understanding they were expected to become settled Christian farmers
whose children would attend schools established by whites.[13]

Under the circumstances, Elizabeth and Armstrong passed their time
agreeably at Fort Leavenworth. Both Rebecca and Anna Darrah were with

them, and Rebecca's sister, Mary Richmond Kendall, and her husband, Charles Kendall, visited. They were en route to Topeka, where as newlyweds they were establishing their Kansas home. Moreover, the Custers entertained frequently, and, in turn, were invited to post dinners, hops, and mule and horse races. Only complaints about their numerous dogs marred their pleasure.[14]

In June, Libbie and Autie returned to Monroe. Elizabeth renewed old acquaintances, while Armstrong hunted and fished and visited Barker in Detroit.[15] That same month, Cheyennes raided a Kaw Indian village. As punishment, Superintendent of Indian Affairs Thomas Murphy withheld arms and ammunition from their annuities. In retaliation a party of young warriors raided along the Saline and Solomon rivers. Within days they raped five women, killed fifteen men, and left behind devastated farms and fields. They also disrupted work on the transcontinental railroad.[16]

Sheridan, determined to succeed where Hancock had failed, planned to drive the Southern Plains Indians from the region between the Platte and Arkansas rivers and force them onto reservations. The expedition's commander, the Third Infantry's Lt. Col. Alfred Sully (brevet brigadier general) took the field with a strong force but showed little enthusiasm for the assignment. After a week of chasing Indians from an army ambulance, Sully returned to his base at Fort Dodge, complaining, "These sand hills are interminable."[17]

Pursuing elusive hostiles was futile. Sheridan needed someone who would tenaciously follow the Indians into their villages and employ the same methods that had proved effective in the Shenandoah Valley—the scorched-earth policies of total war. The man to carry out such a campaign was his old friend and trusted subaltern, George Armstrong Custer.[18]

The Custers were visiting friends when Sheridan's telegram arrived. Libbie felt ambivalent as her husband, whooping with delight, read: "General Sherman, Sully and myself and nearly all the officers of your regiment, have asked for you, and I hope the application will be successful. Can you come at once?"[19] Without waiting to learn whether his old commander had obtained remission of his sentence, Armstrong left immediately for Fort Hays, Sheridan's headquarters for the impending campaign.[20] Over breakfast on October 4, Little Phil explained his strategy to Custer. Three strong columns would take the field. The first from Fort Lyon, Colorado, would push southeastward, while a second would drive east from Fort Bascom, New Mexico. They would propel the Indians directly into the path of the third and strongest column, moving south from Fort Dodge and led by Custer. In the dead of winter, when the tribes were most vulnerable and least expected attack, the Seventh would strike their villages.[21] Armstrong could use whatever means were necessary to subdue them. As Sheridan explained: "I rely upon you in everything, and shall send you on this expedition without giving you any orders, leaving you to act entirely upon your judgment."[22]

To many, launching a winter campaign on the Plains appeared fool-hardy. Jim Bridger, the old mountain man, hastened to Fort Hays to convince Sheridan of the folly of trying to supply horses and men amidst blizzards.[23] Late in October, Libbie learned from her husband that his commander remained undaunted. "If we cannot find the Indians and inflict considerable damage upon them, we will be on the wing all winter. If however we are fortunate enough to strike a decisive and telling blow against any one of the many hostile tribes, we will then obtain a respite." A resounding victory would "practically end the Indian war." Reading on, she discovered that the Seventh would move southward "into the heart of the Indian country where," her husband maintained, "white troops have never been before."[24]

In Monroe, Libbie packed for Leavenworth, where she and her friend, Nellie Bates, would await Autie's return.[25] While Elizabeth wondered when she would see her husband again, his steady stream of fervent letters provided comfort. Recently she had chided him for being more demonstra-tive in correspondence than in person. "I do not like to hear her say that it is only when I am away that I appreciate her," Armstrong had protested several weeks earlier. "I will admit that I express more then, but when with her I feel and know how dear she is, feeling as much as when absent."[26]

Autie's letters that fall stressed the misbehavior of some officers at nearby Fort Dodge, thereby contrasting the Custer marriage favorably with other unions. Some men were carrying on illicit affairs with laundresses, and one had recently accused an officer of fathering her child. Nor were all wives above reproach. One woman's infidelities had transformed her husband into an alcoholic, while a second had recently spent a night with another officer.[27]

Earlier, Libbie had expressed her desire for children. Armstrong now suggested they adopt a boy, referred to as Autie Kirk. Here "your wishes will be my guide. I will do nothing which in the future might interfere with or mar our happiness."[28] Since nothing came of the idea, Libbie probably dismissed it as unwise.

Still, Elizabeth's thoughts turned to children from time to time. While visiting the Barkers in Detroit, she noted (perhaps in part to console herself) the care infants demanded. Armstrong was delighted "that my little darling bride is having an opportunity of really seeing and determining how troublesome and embarrassing babies would be to us. Our pleasure would be continually marred and circumscribed. You will not find in all our travels a married couple possessing and enjoying so many means of pleasure and mutual happiness as you and your boy. Our married life to me has been one unbroken sea of pleasure."[29]

Husband and wife may have agreed, especially since each made a child of the other. Libbie remained her husband's "little Durl," and Autie was her "bo," meaning both boy and beau. Years later, however, Libbie identified two regrets in her life—her husband's death and the son she never bore.[30]

By late October, Armstrong waited impatiently to set off, "not for glory or fame," he explained, but to end "this trying separation." With five tribes located in the region southward, he expected to find an "abundance of Indians in the country to which we are going. If so," he noted, summarizing the meaning of total war, "woe be unto Mr. Lo to say nothing of Mrs. Lo and the little Lo's. One good effective blow . . . will intimidate the others." Then the Southern Plains tribes would seek peace, "and a peace made after giving them a sound drubbing will be of more permanent character than those concluded with them of late year." If Custer's luck held, and he found the village quickly, Libbie could expect him at Leavenworth in three weeks.[31]

Necessary supplies for the expedition had not appeared when Libbie, Nellie Bates, and Eliza left Monroe on November 4. Several days later they arrived at Leavenworth. Finally, on the 12th, the Seventh Cavalry, along with five companies of the Third Infantry, 400 wagons, and guides and scouts crossed the Arkansas River. A week later the long column reached the North Canadian River and constructed a stockade, named Camp Supply, to hold provisions.[32]

By November 21, the Nineteenth Kansas, a volunteer cavalry regiment formed especially for the campaign had not appeared. Meanwhile Custer had learned of "a fresh trail of a large war party," which his guides told him came from a village "located within fifty miles of us in a southerly direction." Custer wanted to pursue it immediately, but Lieutenant Colonel Sully, claiming to rank him as district commander, ordered him to wait for the Kansas militia.[33]

The next day, shortly before midnight, Armstrong wrote Elizabeth. Sheridan's arrival had resolved the dispute in Custer's favor. "I move tomorrow morning at daylight with my eleven companies taking thirty days rations." He would head "south from here to the Canadian River then down the river to Fort Cobb then southwest toward the Wichita Mts. then northwest, then back to this point my whole march not exceeding 250 miles." He would be back, he assured her, in three weeks.[34]

Outside his tent the snow, already five or six inches deep, was "still falling. It is to our advantage," he believed, since if forewarned, the Indians could easily be tracked.[35] After the column had forded the icy Canadian River, Armstrong wrote again. Major Elliott, dispatched downriver to scout, had sent back a courier informing his commander of "the fresh trail of a war party, 150 strong, leading nearly due south."[36] Moving as rapidly as possible, Custer force-marched his men through the melting snow, while the lightly guarded wagon train followed more slowly. By nine the night of November 26, the column caught up with Elliott and his detachment in the Washita River Valley. On they continued, despite plunging temperatures and crusting snow.[37]

About 1 A.M. the command halted when the scouts found the last dying embers of a fire. The men, cold, hungry, and exhausted, sat silently on their mounts in the frigid air, while Custer and an Osage scout ascended a hill overlooking the valley. From that ridge, the scout announced, "Heap Injuns down there."[38] That was the last Libbie heard from Armstrong until she pieced together the events of the battle from her husband's writings and other accounts.

Later she learned that Armstrong heard a dog's bark, the sound of a bell, and an infant's cry.[39] No one told her, however, that before dawn, while the Seventh huddled together on the frozen snow, Osage scouts questioned the wisdom of charging into an unknown number of Indians. Earlier, Captain Thompson, harboring similar concerns, had asked, "Suppose we find more Indians there than we can handle?" "Huh," his commander had replied, "all I am afraid of is we won't find half enough. There are not Indians enough in the country to whip the Seventh Cavalry."[40]

As the moon set and the morning star rose, Custer split his command into four battalions, thereby encircling the sleeping Indians.[41] At daylight, as the battalions closed, a single shot came from the village. Custer signaled the charge, and the first few notes of "Garry Owen" sounded and then died as lips froze to instruments. As the Seventh assailed the village, the confused warriors, bounding out of their tents, were no match for the soldiers. Within ten minutes Custer had taken the village. Among those killed were Black

Kettle and his wife. The Seventh's few losses included one of Libbie's favorites, Captain Hamilton.[42]

At midday, while rounding up grazing ponies outside the village, Lt. Edward Godfrey scaled a small embankment. Looking out over the valley he saw "tepees—tepees. Not only could I see tepees," he recalled, "but mounted warriors scurrying in our direction." From across the river came the sound of heavy firing where Major Elliott had led a small detachment earlier.[43]

When Godfrey informed his commander that Elliott might be under attack, Custer dismissed his fears. "Captain Myers had been fighting down there all morning and probably would have reported it." By now, increasing numbers of mounted braves appeared on the hills surrounding the village. They had driven off the guard protecting the men's overcoats and haversacks, and although the ammunition wagon had made its way through attacking Indians, the Seventh's supply train was still out on the trail.[44]

Custer hastened the destruction of the village. Everything of possible value—food, clothing, utensils, and ponies—was either burned or shot. He then sent Captain Myers down the valley to scout for Elliott and the eighteen men accompanying him. After traveling two miles and seeing no sign of the missing detachment, Myers returned.

The growing number of warriors on the hillsides required quick withdrawal, but any sign of timidity invited attack. Resorting to a feint, Custer marched downriver toward the villages. The braves, believing he threatened their families, retreated. After dark, Custer marched his troops back through the destroyed village to the next divide and north towards Camp Supply.[45]

Shortly after, Elizabeth received a message from Sheridan dated November 29. "I have only time to tell you of your husbands grand success in killing 103 Indians & capturing nearly 1000 horses & much other property."[46]

While Libbie rejoiced over her husband's newest victory, she anxiously awaited further news. At last Autie's letter of December 6 arrived. Although Sheridan praised the Washita as "the most complete and successful of all our Indian battles," another expedition was necessary.[47] Despite the widespread terror among the Southern Plains Indians, many bands remained out. As Custer set off to force them onto reservations, both Sheridan and the Nineteenth Kansas would accompany him. (The militia, after losing its way in a blizzard, had finally arrived at Camp Supply.)[48] On her map at Leavenworth, Elizabeth located her husband's destination, Fort Cobb, downriver from the Washita battlefield.

Armstrong's letter, dated December 19, contained shocking news. Marching southward back through the battleground, the column had come upon the "horribly mutilated" bodies of Major Elliott and eighteen men. Perhaps to soften the blow, Armstrong raised his earlier estimate of warriors killed in the recent battle from 103 to 133. Either figure was inflated, although Indian estimates of 9 to 20 men and 18 to 40 women and children were too low.[49]

Downstream, the force of some 1,700 men came upon the corpse of a mother and child. Custer described Clara Blinn as a "young, beautiful white woman," who with her baby had been "killed and mutilated by the Indians."[50] Outrage over such incidents justified military action for many. Among the volunteers, Daniel Brewster had joined the Kansas militia to search for his sister, Anna Brewster Morgan. The Indians, probably hoping to win concessions from white authorities, held her captive with another woman, Sarah White.[51]

On December 17, about twenty miles from their destination, the column met an Indian envoy under a flag of truce. He carried a message from William Hazen, commander of the Southern Military District, attesting to the peaceful conduct of the Kiowas under his jurisdiction. One of the Kiowa chiefs, Satanta, moreover, wanted a parley.[52] Sheridan sent Custer, along with his aide, Lt. J. Schuyler Crosby, and several other officers to meet with Satanta, now accompanied by Lone Wolf, another Kiowa chief.[53] The Seventh's commander informed the chiefs that he and Sheridan would accept Hazen's judgment as valid—provided the Kiowas moved to Fort Cobb. The chiefs agreed.

Shortly after, when the Kiowas failed to arrive, Sheridan concluded that Satanta and Lone Wolf had misled them and ordered them seized until Custer's demand was met.[54] As Libbie read of these incidents, she felt frustration, for, despite the recent victory, the campaign dragged on.[55] Beyond that, Autie warned her to steel herself against criticisms "by all papers that do not believe in punishing hostile Indians."[56]

Eastern humanitarians objected strenuously. Samuel Tappan, one of the Medicine Lodge peace commissioners, saw the recent outbreaks among Indians as resulting from congressional failure to supply promised annuities. Calling for the "immediate and unconditional abandonment of the present war party," he denounced any resort to military force unless it was used impartially against Indians or whites who had violated the law. Tappan was not alone. Indian agent Edward Wynkoop resigned his position, protesting that Black Kettle had been a man of "great moral dignity and lofty bearing." Twice the white man had deceived him, repaying his trust with the Sand Creek massacre four years earlier and now the Washita battle.[57]

Wynkoop's condemnation underscored Black Kettle's role as a peace chief. Shortly before the battle, the chief, fearful of military reprisals against his people because of the depredations of Cheyenne braves, had met with Hazen at Fort Cobb. When he had asked permission to move his people to Cobb, however, the colonel had instructed the chief to return to his camp and seek peace with Sheridan. Within hours after Black Kettle's return, the Seventh had struck. That fact, added to the earlier Sand Creek massacre, predisposed many to see Custer's attack on Black Kettle's village as the slaughter of innocent people.[58]

On the other side, western frontiersmen and railroad interests argued that since the band had harbored violent Dog Soldiers, the attack was justified. At the Washita, soldiers had discovered mail and household articles taken from Kansas homes.[59] Elizabeth was learning that, while Armstrong could achieve victory in battle, the divisions within American society on Indian policy precluded anything but a mixed reaction to his success. How different from Civil War days, when an adoring Northern public had heaped praise on its boy general! Fighting Indians was a more frustrating and less rewarding enterprise than fighting Confederates.[60]

Moreover, whatever Armstrong thought about the criticism, Libbie was defensive. In a later letter to her aunt Eliza, she wrote: "Surely you do not believe the current rumors that Autie and others are cruel in their treatment of the Indians? Autie and others only do what they are ordered to do." She noted the "degradations unspeakable" suffered by captive women and other "brutalities." "People in civilized conditions cannot imagine it. But we who have seen it know."[61]

At Fort Leavenworth Libbie faced problems besides inuring herself to public criticism and the loss of her husband's companionship. Lacking fuel, she, Nellie, and Eliza struggled to stay warm.[62] She also tried to extract comfort from her husband's assurances that the remaining Cheyennes, Arapahoes, Kiowas, and Comanches would soon come on the reservation. Then the Indians wars would end, and "a permanent peace is almost sure to follow." Afterwards they would enjoy "a long uninterrupted period of happiness to compensate for this long separation."[63]

As Libbie awaited her husband's return, she transformed their quarters into a home. After soldiers constructed crude wooden frames for her, she covered them with mattresses and her Mexican blankets from Texas. Then she made calico curtains for her windows and pressed dried ferns to the pane as "a bit of fairy-land." Afterwards she stitched together four old gray blankets as a rug for her floor. Finally, she hung her own paintings and drawings on the walls and noted with satisfaction that her quarters were cheerful and attractive.[64] When weather permitted, Libbie, Nellie, and Eliza visited her cousin Mary Kendall in Topeka.

By early January, the steadily arriving Indians at Fort Cobb had stripped the region of available forage for horses and ponies. Sheridan ordered the assembled forces, along with the bands that had surrendered, to relocate some thirty-six miles south to Medicine Bluff Creek, at the foot of the Wichita Mountains. Originally called Camp Wichita, the site became Fort Sill on July 1, 1869.[65]

While Kiowas were now on their reservation, many Cheyenne bands and some Arapahoes moved slowly because of the muddy trails and rain-swollen rivers. "I am as impatient as a crazed animal to have them come in, so that I can start on my homeward journey rejoicing," Autie assured his wife.[66] He had other news. "Tell Eliza I have just the thing for her. One of the squaws among the prisoners had a little pappoose a few nights since, and I intend to bring it home to add to the orphan asylum she always keeps."[67] The infant was the child of Monahsetah, the daughter of Chief Little Rock. Next to Black Kettle he had been the most influential member of the band before perishing at the Washita.[68]

Despite the obstacles, Armstrong planned on returning to Leavenworth in time to escort Libbie to Grant's presidential inauguration on March 4. With Sherman's impending promotion to commanding general of the army, changes were inevitable. Obviously Armstrong felt that his recent victory placed him in a good position to win promotion or a more desirable assignment. But to leave nothing to chance, he instructed Libbie to make reservations at the National Hotel on the same floor as the Chandlers. The exact nature of his hopes and plans remained so secret he dared not write them out. If only Libbie were near. "I feel so much at a loss," she read, "without having you to make suggestions. Although I generally make my own plans, this latter are generally made with reference to you as you no doubt are aware of."[69]

Earlier, while still at Fort Dodge, Autie had been expounding on the infidelities among officers and wives. In one of those letters, he had let slip a brief but revealing comment. "I know you are in earnest when you say you mean never again to give me an uneasy moment. I have the sublimest confidence that you never will."[70]

Now in the same letter, in which he acknowledged his dependence on his wife, Armstrong turned peevish when the subject of one officer arose. "Weir I reprimanded sharply in writing and as you prophesied when speaking to him, he has been *huffy* ever since. . . . I think he will soon grow ashamed of his childish conduct and act differently. The more I see of him Little one," Autie continued, "the more I am surprised that a woman of your perceptive faculties and moral training could have entertained the opinion of him you have, but enough upon this subject." Still, Armstrong wondered about someone else. "In speaking of a certain mutual friend against whom I warned you, you refer to my remark and place yourself upon guard, but you did not ask who I referred to from this infer that you knew to whom reference was made. N'est ce pas?"[71]

Both husband and wife attracted admirers. Libbie, if she saw it, must have wondered about a letter Armstrong received that winter from Detroit, signed by "Anna." "My dear Gen.," it began. "Fannie is at the piano singing 'Goodby, sweetheart goodby' and I am so forcibly reminded of you that I cannot resist the temptation of telling you how I wish you were here."[72] Although Anna Darrah is the likely author of this letter, the writer may have been using a pseudonym.[73] Earlier, Armstrong had asked Hattie Mitchell of Richmond, Virginia, to correspond with him, disguising herself as "Gloria."[74] Whatever Anna's actual identity, the young woman had read of his recent victory and wanted "very much to see you and hear you talk." She also wanted her picture back.[75]

Late in January, Custer mounted an expedition with Lieutenant Cooke's corps of elite sharpshooters to bring in the Arapahoes and remaining Cheyennes. When he returned to Camp Wichita, he wrote Libbie, explaining that he and his men had traveled without wagons and lived "on parched corn and horse-flesh," but they were back safely.[76] Although he had brought in the Arapahoes, terrified Cheyenne bands had fled into Texas.[77] Custer faced yet another campaign and, unfortunately, would not return in time for Grant's inaugural.

On March 2, Custer left Camp Wichita with the Seventh and the Kansas militia. "I am almost as nomadic in my proclivities as the Indians themselves," he had written Libbie a day earlier.[78] He had also enclosed a photograph "which it may not occur to you is the picture of your husband. How do you like the beard?" His costume was "a very fine one, made of dressed buckskin and fringed. The cap is the one without a visor, that I have worn all winter."[79]

Three captives accompanied the expedition: a sister of Black Kettle, named Mawisa; Mawisa's friend (an unnamed Sioux woman); and Monahsetah, the mother of the newborn. In Cheyenne her name meant "The young grass that shoots in the spring." She was, according to Armstrong, "an exceedingly comely squaw" in her late teens. All served as intermediaries between Custer and their people.[80]

Captain Benteen alleged in later correspondence that his commander "lived with" Monahsetah and was seen "many times in the very act of copulating with her!"[81] Although Benteen's hatred diminishes the value of his testimony, another witness, Ben Clark, Custer's chief of scouts, verified that story in a confidential interview.[82] Scholars working with the Cheyenne Indians, including Thomas B. Marquis, Mari Sandoz, and Charles Brill, recorded similar and separate accounts. According to Cheyenne tradition, Monahsetah, after leaving her first husband, considered herself Custer's wife. She may also have borne him a child, her second, before the end of the year.[83]

Benteen and Clark made another statement. Both maintained that some Seventh Cavalry officers sexually coerced Cheyenne women captives at Camp Supply.[84] Since Indian accounts substantiate their claims, such action demonstrated a tragic double standard. These men were engaged in a campaign devoted in part to rescuing white women from similar atrocities.[85]

After days of slogging through rain and mud and eating nothing but mules, Custer's persistence paid off. A trace he followed widened into a trail leading to the eastern edge of the Texas Panhandle. On March 15, Custer and Cooke, moving ahead of the column, found themselves on the banks of the Sweetwater, overlooking the Cheyenne villages of Medicine Arrows and Little Robe.

When Armstrong learned that this band held Anna Morgan and Sarah White, he seized Little Robe and three of his party. Three days later the Cheyennes released the captives. That task accomplished, Custer now turned towards Camp Supply. He knew that hunger would compel the destitute Cheyennes to move to the reservations as soon as their ponies had fed on spring grass. To assure compliance, however, Custer took three hostages. He emphasized that until they came in, the women and children captured at the Washita remained prisoners. With his duties in this long campaign ended, Armstrong looked forward to seeing Libbie after an absence of over five months.[86]

One hope cherished by both husband and wife would not be realized. Armstrong had seen in combat the means of forging strong regimental bonds. Instead, the Battle of the Washita had deepened divisions within the Seventh. When the regiment had revisited the battleground the first time, the stripped and mutilated bodies of Elliott and his detachment and the numerous spent cartridges attested to a prolonged fight in which hoped-for aid had never arrived. Undoubtedly some officers concurred with the sentiments expressed by Benteen in a bitter diatribe in the St. Louis *Missouri Democrat* of February 8. His depiction of besieged and despairing men left many officers fearful that one day, facing similar straits, they would endure the same fate[87]

The Washita's significance for the Seventh, however, did not derive from Elliott's fate. Rather it stemmed from the lessons Armstrong extracted from his victory. He had defied conventional military wisdom by failing to conduct the usual reconnaissance. With no prior knowledge of either the strength or position of his adversaries, he had gone into battle. Had he followed textbook rules, the Indians would probably have detected him. Then, as his experience in the Hancock campaign had taught him, they would have fled. Armstrong now concluded that standard tactics did not apply when waging war against Indians. The real task was to cut off any avenues of escape before launching an all-out assault.[88]

On April 7, an elated Libbie greeted her husband on his return to Leavenworth.[89] How different their circumstances were now compared to eighteen months earlier. Then the loving wife had seen Autie as the object of persecution. Now he had proven himself a diligent follower of trails and a shrewd negotiator with Indian leaders. More important, he had won the only "pitched battle" on the Plains since the onset of the Civil War.[90] Surely such accomplishments entitled him to a furlough or at least a more restful assignment. For Libbie a joyous summer loomed ahead. She had her husband home safely and reveled in his newly won glory.

CHAPTER 8

Mixed Messages

THE FIFTH Infantry band played "Garry Owen" as the Seventh marched into Fort Hays on April 18, 1869. On hand to welcome the Custers were Col. Nelson Miles and his wife, Mary, General Sherman's niece. Miles immediately put the Custers at ease when he announced that he planned to use Armstrong's tactics when he fought Indians. Although Miles was transferred to Fort Harker on May 18, he had inaugurated a warm friendship between the two couples. Libbie was especially fond of him, since he insisted on taking her and Mary on buffalo hunts. The women could not safely ride sidesaddle over the plains, pitted with gopher holes and buffalo wallows. Instead they accompanied their husbands in an ambulance outfitted for their comfort and safety.[1]

The regiment, needing additional forage and water, returned to its previous camp on Big Creek. After Autie erected a hospital tent for Libbie's parlor, he attached an overhanging tarpaulin for dining and relaxing with friends. A second canvas served as a bedroom. Since its floor extended to the trunk of a cottonwood alongside the creek, soldiers constructed a railing around the unenclosed portion. There Libbie, Autie, and Tom spent their evenings, enjoying their "beer-garden" and pretending Big Creek was the Hudson and their cottonwood a "graceful maple, or stately, branching elm."[2] During the day, Libbie sewed and visited with Nettie Smith and Mollie McIntosh, whose husbands, lieutenants Smith and McIntosh, erected tents nearby.

Libbie remembered vividly her introduction to the captive women and children housed in a stockade beside Fort Hays. Undoubtedly the stories she had heard since childhood of the River Raisin massacre, along with the often unflattering portrayal of Indian women by popular writers such as

James Fenimore Cooper, predisposed her to expect treachery.[3] She entered the stockade fearful that one of them would stab her with a concealed weapon. Instead they examined her closely, comparing her shoes, clothing, and hair with theirs. She must have struck them as exotic with her kid gloves, her cloak with military buttons, and her hat adorned with a bird. When the Cheyenne women learned that Libbie was her husband's only wife, they expressed sympathy, probably wondering how anyone so attired performed the tasks they associated with womanhood.[4] Libbie, in turn, felt sorry for them. She never questioned the commonly held view that married Indian women were exploited chattel who performed unremitting "work of the most exhausting kind."[5]

But while Libbie viewed most Indian women as degraded squaws, she saw Monahsetah as "the Princess," another stereotype.[6] Cheyenne women were not, in Libbie's opinion, attractive since their features were "rarely delicate, high cheek-bones and square jaw being the prevailing type."[7] Thus, although Armstrong later extolled Monahsetah's beauty, Libbie's comments, while laudatory, were more restrained[8] She judged Monahsetah's face as "not pretty in repose, except with the beauty of youth, whose dimples and curves and rounded outlines are always charming." When the young woman smiled, however, "the expression transfigured her, and made us forget her features."[9]

When Libbie discovered that Monahsetah had shot her former husband in the knee rather than submit to his authority, her anxiety increased. The Cheyenne woman's willingness to deprive the warrior of his most prized attribute—his prowess as a hunter and fighter—indicated a ruthlessness she might direct at her conquerors. The best way to retaliate against Armstrong, Libbie thought, was to kill his wife.[10]

Concerns for her own safety receded, however, when Monahsetah offered to let Libbie keep her infant during her captivity. This was more than Libbie had bargained for, but fortunately Armstrong came forward and declined the offer.[11] Nonetheless, Elizabeth studied the children intently. Later, when an Indian woman brought her sons to Armstrong and tearfully informed him that their father had perished at the Washita, Elizabeth set aside her stereotypes long enough to see the woman in human terms. She wished "with all my soul that instead of these embryo warriors she might have had daughters, who would never be reared to go to war."[12]

When the Cheyenne bands under Medicine Arrows and Little Robe arrived at their reservation, the hostages at Fort Hays were allowed to rejoin their people. Monahsetah, whom Tom had named "Sallie Ann," regretfully waved good-bye to the Custers as she and the others set off for their new home.[13]

By late June, Armstrong knew that Sheridan's promotion would bring no immediate advancement. Samuel Sturgis had replaced A. J. Smith as the Seventh's colonel. Custer also applied to become West Point commandant, but that went instead to Emory Upton. Nonetheless, Armstrong and Libbie extracted the maximum enjoyment from Big Creek.[14]

After Armstrong dispersed unfriendly officers to substations and other posts, the admirers left behind formed a convivial group. That summer Custer supporters and their wives helped create an "animated zoo" along the river banks. Autie and Libbie supplied blooded dogs and a wolf, Tom provided boxed rattlesnakes in his tent, and Eliza raised chickens. Other officers contributed "prairie dogs, raccoons, porcupines, wildcats, badgers, young antelopes, buffalo calves, and any number of mongrel dogs."[15]

Given the recent victory over the Southern Plains Indians, the Kansas Pacific tracks now headed swiftly towards Denver. The railroad, eager to generate traffic and land sales, offered rates as low as ten dollars for special excursions and free passes to politicians and dignitaries.[16] Rich and not-so-rich, famous and obscure, Americans and Europeans (including two members of the British House of Lords) arrived that summer, along with the occasional reporter.[17] The notables the Custers met at the Fort Hays depot came to hunt buffalo with the West's famous Indian fighter.

Although the Miles were no longer at Hays, Libbie still accompanied the hunters in her carriage. Henry, the Custers' coachman, was so anxious to see the kill that he drove her carriage at breakneck speed over the gutted prairies. While she always arrived flustered and unnerved, she nonetheless joined the group in time to witness the deathblow and share in the camaraderie.[18] One young participant wrote in her diary: "What a party it was! General Custer was the hero of all who knew him, and Mrs. Custer, who attended in a carriage, was like a queen, surrounded by her court."[19]

Custer became so proficient at the sport that he once killed seven buffalo "without leaving the saddle." He was only one of many hunters. His activities, along with those of others who arrived on the proliferating railroad lines, meant that the herds on the Southern Plains would be gone by 1878. Five years later, they would disappear from the Northern Plains, taking with them the mainstay of the Indian way of life.[20] Even in his recreational activities, Armstrong contributed to the Red Man's defeat.

Libbie had wanted the summer to go on forever. Despite a siege of malaria, the "bedouin life" appealed to her with its freedom from social constraints. "We don't see much of Mrs. Grundy out here and we dress as we like and live with no approach to style," she wrote her old schoolmate, Laura Noble Stoddard. She welcomed freedom from the "everlasting 'they say,'" so common in Monroe.[21]

When the Custers returned to Fort Leavenworth in November, Eliza was not with them. Earlier, Libbie had sensed increasing unhappiness as her maid sat for hours staring into space. When Elizabeth had asked why, Eliza had replied, "Miss Libbie, you's always got the ginnel, but I hain't got nobody, and there ain't no picnics nor church sociables nor no buyings out here."[22] Shortly after, the break had occurred. "We had to send her away, as she got on a spree & was insolent," was Libbie's explanation. Although she missed Eliza as a friend, Susan Mundy now served as Libbie's maid. Despite the demands of a year-old son, she proved more efficient and more economical as a cook.[23]

Late in November, Armstrong traveled east to visit Sheridan's headquarters in Chicago before stopping in Monroe to investigate problems concerning Daniel Bacon's estate. Libbie remained at Leavenworth since her cousin, Anne Northrop Bingham planned to visit her. Formerly a resident of Howlett Hill, Anne and her husband hoped to purchase a farm near Junction City.[24] In mid-December, Libbie learned that Autie planned to extend his "leave" until January. Sheridan's illness had delayed their meeting in Chicago, and when he belatedly arrived in Michigan, he found Bacon's estate a tangled mess.

Walter Bacon, the estate's executor, had spent three years putting together $5,000 to invest for Rhoda's income. In the end, he had refinanced real estate he could not sell.[25] Rhoda, objecting to the delay, had asked Libbie at one point to sign a statement that Daniel had discriminated against his widow. Libbie, fiercely loyal, had refused, but the matter left her disturbed.[26]

To make matters worse, the federal government in 1869 seized $3,000 from Daniel Bacon's estate. More than two decades earlier, Bacon had cosigned (along with five others) Levi Humphrey's surety bond as Michigan's federal marshal. Belatedly, long after the deceased Humphrey's travel accounts and other funds had shown a deficit, the government demanded repayment.[27] Adding to problems, the Old Homestead needed expensive repairs. Autie advised Libbie to sell it to obtain capital for other investments. Despite a slow market, he was disposing of the lots Bacon had bequeathed him in Milan, Michigan, so he could buy Kansas land.[28]

Whatever her disappointment in Autie's absence during the holidays, Libbie celebrated a merry Christmas.[29] Anne Bingham visited Leavenworth, and Captain Yates escorted them to a turkey dinner in the enlisted men's barracks. Bingham noted that Elizabeth "seemed greatly beloved by all, and I had to notice that each officer appeared to feel that he was being especially entertained by her; such was her charm."[30]

Early in 1870, Armstrong's younger sister Maggie, Libbie's old school-mate Julie Thurber, and Cousin Rebecca arrived at the post.[31] Late in March the women visited Mary Kendall in Topeka, where they filled out question-naires composed by relatives. The answers Libbie gave are revealing. Rose was her choice in color, autumn her best-loved season, and horses and dogs her favorite creatures. For perfume she preferred English violet, and her best-loved poet was Tennyson. Aside from the Bible, the book she would "part with last" was her photograph album.

The masculine traits she admired were "unselfishness—willingness to let it be sure he loves wisely & well." In females, "absence of vanity, Refine-ment—culturation [*sic*]" seemed most important. When asked, "If not yourself, who would you rather be," Libbie replied, "I don't know I am sure." When her relatives inquired about her most "distinguishing charac-teristics," she noted thoughtfully, "'Know thyself' is too hard for me to accomplish." Asked the same question about Armstrong, she responded, "unselfishness, courage, energy."

She considered "to love, with heart and soul," the "sublimist passion." The "sweetest words" remained, "Would I were with thee every day & hour." Asked for her definition of happiness, she offered "No separation from my other self." Finally, her life's goal was "to be an honor to my sex." Her greatest fear, by contrast, was "having to take care of myself."[32]

That summer, the Seventh's headquarters again moved to the encamp-ment near Fort Hays and set up tents along Big Creek. The previous July, the Fifth Cavalry under Maj. Eugene A. Carr had decisively defeated Cheyenne Dog Soldiers at Summit Springs in northeastern Colorado.[33] With most Southern Plains Indians now on reservations, Kansas was more peaceful, and the Seventh's duties consisted largely of patrolling, scouting, and providing escort service.

This left the Custers more time to entertain the steadily increasing excursion and hunting parties arriving at Hays City. Although such groups had brought pleasure and excitement a year earlier, those who came west in 1870 often proved burdensome. Some thought that as taxpayers they owned the forts. A few even entered the officers' quarters at Fort Hays without knocking and left without apology.[34] Some of the dignitaries arriving at Hays, moreover, questioned the frequent hunting parties leaving the fort. When Gen. John Pope, commander of the Department of the Missouri, visited briefly, he dismissed these activities with "a scathing rebuke." Libbie, on the other hand, took issue. Disregarding the parties of enlisted men who were dispatched frequently to bring in game, she argued that buffalo meat added variety to an otherwise monotonous diet of army beef.[35]

While the summer of 1870 was not as pleasant as 1869, Libbie and Autie still created an environment at Big Creek conducive to regimental romance. Maggie Custer, who remained behind after Julie Thurber returned to Monroe, fell in love with James Calhoun, a second lieutenant with the Twenty-first Infantry. By August, the couple were pressuring Armstrong to obtain Jimmi's transfer to the Seventh Cavalry.[36]

Annie Roberts was the dark-haired niece of Col. George Gibson, Miles's replacement at Fort Hays. Her father, W. Milnor Roberts, a noted railroad engineer, had built the railroad from Rio de Janeiro to Brazil's interior. Thus Annie had experienced life in jungles, in the Organ Mountains, and various South American cities. She had emerged from this upbringing fluent in several languages and an expert equestrienne and markswoman.[37]

Libbie noticed that whenever Annie was expected at Camp Sturgis, a freshly groomed Captain Yates appeared at her tent with a magazine. "Don't mind me, Mrs. Custer, I'll take care of myself," he assured her. When the ambulance arrived, Yates always stepped forward to "assist the ladies in alighting." Later, Libbie learned that the captain paid her maid's young son a quarter each time he warned him of Annie's pending visit.[38]

Yates also received aid from Libbie and Armstrong, whom Annie saw as the ideal romantic couple. One afternoon on the creek left a strong impression on the twenty-one-year-old. Libbie, her eyes reflecting the blue trim on her white dress, lay in a hammock rocked by her husband. Occasionally when he bent over and whispered in her ear, her face flushed. Watching them intently, Annie wondered, "Will it ever come to me like this."[39] Inspired by what she saw of the Custer marriage, Miss Roberts appeared more frequently at Big Creek. She often accompanied the hunts, and her skill in bringing down the beasts netted her the sobriquet "Buffalo Annie." By summer's end, she was seriously considering marrying Yates despite her family's objection to his earlier divorce.[40]

Before the second hunting season ended, the Custers had entertained, among others, P. T. Barnum. While the circus magnate's party of ten killed only twenty buffalo to avoid "wanton butchery," Barnum never forgot his enjoyment. Five years later, in appreciation for their kind hospitality, he sent Libbie and Armstrong three English hounds.[41]

The relative calm on the Southern Plains that year permitted the Custers to make several side trips. In September they attended the Denver celebration of the Kansas Pacific Railroad's completion. The following month they visited the Saint Louis Fair. As usual, they stayed in the Southern Hotel and attended the newest plays.[42] By mid-October Libbie wrote Cousin Rebecca that buffalo hunts had become "such a bore to us." She had entertained more than 200 guests that season. Now she looked forward to returning to Leavenworth so they could "go east as soon as we can and spend the holidays. . . . I am anticipating a great deal of pleasure."[43]

The rains were heavy that fall, swelling the rivers and turning the roads into quagmires. "Tenting on the Plains" dragged on interminably, and the "rag houses" provided little protection against autumn's damp, cold winds. After a delay of several days, the Seventh started for Leavenworth without the Custers. Instead the couple boarded a train for Topeka, where they visited the Kendalls until the regiment arrived in the city, bringing along Armstrong's new pet, "a young cinnamon bear." Described as an "amusing little cuss," by the *Topeka Commonwealth*, it had "already bitten off one man's finger. Parties desiring to play with him," the newspaper noted, "are invited to call at camp today."[44]

By mid-November the Custers were back at Leavenworth. Shortly after, despite Libbie's earlier anticipation of traveling east, Armstrong left alone. After stops in Monroe and Detroit, he appeared before the "Benzine Board," a commission designed to weed out incompetent officers. Lieutenant McIntosh's only offense, he told the commission, consisted of antagonizing Sturgis. As for Weir, although his alcoholism was worse, he never drank on duty.[45]

Shortly after his thirty-first birthday, Armstrong wrote Libbie a letter that revealed serious problems in the Custer marriage. Some of their troubles stemmed from his gambling. Although Libbie believed him incapable of stopping, he promised that, beginning January 1, "henceforth and forever I cease to risk at faro any money or its equivalent." Since he expected to return to Big Creek next summer, he pledged that even on the Plains, "I cease so long as I am a married man to play cards or any other game of chance or its equivalent."[46]

While Libbie disapproved of gambling, Autie's inability to stop was not the major problem. True, his broken promises extended all the way back to their engagement, but she had in the past tolerated the habit. Benteen remembered her presence during poker games at the Custer residence, and on occasion, she had been interested in their outcome.[47] Something more serious than Autie's addiction lay behind this letter.

Armstrong could not forget Elizabeth's "distressing words" at the Southern Hotel, "the culmination of thoughts which had long filled your mind against me." More important, he had detected recently "the absence of that fervor that enthusiasm and joy which once caracterized the manner with which you gave or accepted little attentions to and from me." Instead, Libbie had become "more or less mechanical," depriving him of her "accustomed warmth." Patiently he had waited, hoping time would convince her "that however errattic [sic] or unseemly my conduct with others may have been you were still to me as you always have been the one great all absorbing [sic] object of my love."[48]

Regarding his behavior, Armstrong admitted that "measured by the strict law of propriety or public opinion I was wrong. I knew it then as plainly as I know it now," and he added, "I might extenuate but not defend it."[49] And as he contemplated their future, he feared that never again would Libbie love him "as of old. . . . While I am absent you may perhaps think kindly of me and remember much that is good of me but when I return that spark of distrust which I alone am responsible for first placing in your mind but which others have fanned into a flame, will be rekindled and little burning words will be the result. But they will not come from me . . . I think you have seen me in anger for the last time."[50]

Continuing his lament, Armstrong noted that "most men in my situation, feeling that the greatest disappointment of their lives had overtaken them, that the love of the one person whose love alone was desirable was surely but slowly departing from them, would endeavor to hide or drown their troubles by drink or dissipation." He was "not so inclined" and instead pledged himself to "live such a life that I at least may have no further reproach to answer for. . . . My love for you," he assured her, "is as unquenchable as my life. . . . No woman has nor ever can share my love with you. As there is to me but one God Supreme and alone, there is also but one woman who in my heart reigns as supreme as does that God over the universe."[51]

Years before, Autie had written his former sweetheart, Mollie Holland, "You occupy the first place in my affections and the only place as far as love is concerned." In a strikingly similar phrase, he now told Libbie, "You are and ever will be that one single object of my love."[52]

Other than Autie's long, contrite letter, only one other source sheds light on what may have occurred between the Custers. That source is Benteen.[53] Although his hatred for his commander means that his testimony must always be carefully scrutinized it may, nonetheless provide a missing piece in a puzzle. This much is certain. Serious problems had arisen in the Custer marriage, and the most likely explanation is that they sprang from Armstrong's infidelity.[54]

While the couple were at Leavenworth, the captain alleged, "It was notorious that Custer was criminally intimate with a married woman, wife of an officer of the garrison, besides, he was an habitue of demimonde dives, and a persistent bucker of Jayhawker Jenison's faro game. These facts," he maintained, "all being known to Mrs. Custer, rendered her—if she had any heart (?) a broken-hearted woman." Benteen gave Libbie little sympathy. "From knowing her as well as I do, I only remark that she was about as cold-blooded a woman as I ever knew, in which respect the pair were admirably mated."[55]

Armstrong's letters to Libbie, subdued in tone during this separation, made no references to escorting other women to the theater or opera. Libbie received none of the teasing messages he had sent a year earlier, telling Tom and Cooke to "come quick" and help him fend off ardent female admirers or follow a "warm trail."[56] Instead Armstrong related to Libbie the many compliments she received from others. Sen. Jacob Howard had recently stopped by Fort Hays while Armstrong was absent and "made several flattering allusions and desired to be remembered to you."[57] Afterwards the senator remembered Libbie as "one of America's model wives," who "unites in her charming personality all that goes to make a woman attractive to a manly, chivalric man."[58]

Meanwhile Armstrong's energies sagged, leaving him "quite tired & exhausted" and filled with "anxiety. I feel little like writing physically," began one letter. He had, however, just read Libbie's "nice warm loving letter of Sat last," the first after a long silence. Greatly relieved, he dashed off his second letter that day, hoping it would leave in the evening mail.[59]

Two days after Christmas, Armstrong was in Detroit, writing Libbie from Barker's. It mattered little that his letter would arrive after his return to Leavenworth. Libbie's recent letter had comforted him. "I cannot help but think that 'notwithstanding all, [words she had written],' you too may derive some pleasure from hearing from me when *absent*."[60] Autie had identified an important phrase. Years earlier, Libbie had recorded in her diary that, whatever statements the jilted Fanny Fifield had made about Autie, she loved him, "notwithstanding all."[61]

On January 1, 1871, the Custers welcomed in the New Year at Leavenworth. What it would bring was again in question. Rumors circulated that the Seventh would be transferred from the Department of the Missouri and assigned to various posts. Facing this uncertainty, Autie applied for a leave to explore alternatives to the military.[62] When her husband left the post on January 11, Libbie again remained behind, setting a pattern for much of 1871. By March, Libbie was visiting her cousin, Mary Kendall, in Topeka.[63]

In addition to exploring new employment opportunities, Armstrong hoped to sell shares in the Stevens Mine in Clear Creek County, Colorado. The company's brochure listed him as having subscribed $35,000 of the $100,000 the company was seeking to raise for operations by selling shares. Although he and Libbie had recently mortgaged the Bacon homestead, that sum was beyond them. Instead, if Armstrong owned stock at all, it was very likely, as one historian notes, a "broker's share," subscribed for him or due him as a commission for successful sales.[64]

Custer, nonetheless, enjoyed some success in his new venture. After August Belmont purchased $15,000 worth of stock, fellow capitalists Levi Morton and John Jacob Astor invested $10,000 each. Charles J. Osborn, banker and stockbroker, followed suit.[65] Another of Custer's endeavors included selling the bonds of a woman identified only as Mrs. Hough. If he succeeded, he expected to earn $30,000 in commission. "Can it be," he wrote Libbie, optimistically, "that my little standby and I who have long wished to possess a small fortune, are about to have our hopes and wishes realized?" Surely this represented "the stepping stone to larger and more profitable undertakings."[66]

Armstrong mixed pleasure with business as he appeared in fashionable circles, wearing a "light stove top." He dined at Delmonico's and afterwards applauded Lawrence Barrett's rendition of Iago in *Othello*. One evening he attended the opera with George and Ellen McClellan; Orvil Grant, the president's brother; and Governor Ito of Japan.[67]

He also passed time with Clara Kellogg, visiting her home, escorting her to the Academy of Music, and watching her performances. When she played Gilda in *Rigoletto*, he was in the audience with Osborn. Between breaks, Clara asked him to come backstage and tell "how it passed off." At first

Armstrong declined, noting she would be changing clothes. When she insisted, he relented, "although," he explained to Libbie, "I could only open the door a few inches and tell her, as she was dishabille." Nonetheless, he caught "occasional glimpses of a beautifully turned leg encased in purple tights."[68]

Earlier in 1866, when Armstrong had faced a similar period of uncertainty, his letters to Libbie had described at length his outings with various women. Now, he again gave her the details. This time, however, he placed the emphasis upon his attractiveness to the opposite sex.

The pattern unfolded as Armstrong began a series of letters. "Darling Standby . . . The old Irish servant who takes care of my room looks at me with suspicion when I return, sometimes not till morning, the bed not having been touched. I think," he added, "she believes I do not pass my nights in the most reputable manner. In fact, circumstances, as she sees them, are against me." Later in the same letter, Armstrong extolled the happiness of their union. "Only think, little one, how much pleasure we have, planning to procure this or that article, make this or that journey. I have yet to find husband and wife here who enjoy life as we do."[69]

Libbie also read of the various females who sought her husband's affection. Autie described a certain "beautiful girl eighteen or nineteen, blond, who has walked past the hotel several times trying to attract my attention. Twice for sport," he confided, "I followed her. She lives about opposite Mr. Belmont's. She turns and looks me square in the face, to give me a chance to speak to her. I have not done so yet." Upon reaching her home, "she enters, then appears at a window, raising this for any attention I may offer."[70] Still another young woman, Armstrong noted, "has evidently taken a strong fancy to your Bo. She makes no effort at concealment." Assuring Libbie he had not encouraged her, he explained she "cannot control herself." His "Darling Standby," however, need feel "no uneasiness, no regret. . . . Girls needn't try to get her dear Bo away from her, because he loves only her, and her always."[71]

So many women pursued Custer that Libbie became confused. "In referring to *the* young lady you ask if I told her about you. If you will look over my letters," Autie responded impatiently, "you will find I told her I love you and you alone. She frankly said she would only ask me to love her next to you, which I did not consent to do." Later, in the same letter, he advised Libbie to free herself of any anxiety about another admirer. As for "*that* young lady—Her dear Bo don't care if She did tear up the photograph he sent her. He never could care for a woman who so far forgot herself as to make the advances."[72] Nonetheless, Libbie could hardly have been relieved when her husband continued, "I care for no one in town but Miss Kellogg, and I respect her and she respects me. My girl should be grateful that, seeing so many people as I do, to me she stands all the higher by contrast, in bright relief, true womanhood."[73]

At some point, Libbie complained that her husband wrote less faithfully than usual. Soon after, she received six letters in one day with the message, "You shall never hereafter accuse me of indolence in correspondence." Armstrong sent no one else such frequent and lengthy letters. If Libbie doubted she was foremost, this proved "what a different estimate I place upon you and upon the entire world," since he seldom wrote "even duty letters to others."[74]

In the end, only Libbie inspired love. "Last night the thought flashed through my brain that if I ever lost you, no other woman could or ever should reawaken it [love]. You are irrevocably my first, my present and my last love. All the women are," he added, in a revealing statement, which told his wife exactly where she stood—first among many—"but as mere toys compared to you."[75]

Despite that acknowledgement, the double standard persisted in their marriage. Although Autie thought his outings with Clara Kellogg entirely appropriate, he became irritated when Libbie corresponded with two officers of the Seventh. Recently he had learned that the regiment would be transferred to Reconstruction duty in the South. Despite his earlier hopes for an assignment to Lexington, Kentucky, in the heart of bluegrass country, headquarters would be located at Louisville instead. He had instructed Libbie to tell no one, but Captain Keogh knew.

"How did it reach him? If I was of a suspicious disposition," Autie wrote, "I would imagine you had informed him but as I am not and do not care whether you have or not I will not trouble myself about it. So far as I am concerned you write when and where you please." Then, in vintage Armstrong-mixed-message fashion, he added, "The fewer notes or letters of yours, no matter how ordinary, that get into gentlemen's hands the better for your reputation." In truth, he "regretted" learning that she had written Keogh and possibly Cooke as well.[76]

By late spring Libbie was in Monroe where her husband joined her. After "rusticating" awhile, Armstrong returned to New York City.[77] By early July he was again selling mining stock. And once more he threw himself into a busy social scene, escorting Kellogg to various events and traveling by himself to Saratoga for the races. From his room in the "largest" hotel in the world, overlooking "brilliantly lighted" grounds thronged with people, he wrote Libbie, emphasizing how essential she was to his happiness. She may have complained about his socializing with other women, for he now assured her, "I studiously avoid all female society, having conversed with but two ladies since I came. *Her* is the only female that occupys [*sic*] my mind or heart."[78]

During this leave, extended three times and eventually totaling more than seven months, Autie reveled in his new contacts. "Is it not strange to think of me," he noted triumphantly, "meeting to confer with such men as Belmont, Astor, Travers, Barker, Morton and Bliss" They, in turn, introduced him to a host of artists and writers. At one dinner party, Custer was "the only outsider" among a group of newspaper men and literary figures. With Horace Greeley, Bayard Taylor, Whitelaw Reid, and Richard Henry Dana observing, Edmund C. Stedman, poet and journalist, introduced Armstrong as "the beau ideal of the Chevalier Bayard, 'knight sans peur et sans reproche.'" "I repeat this *to you alone*," Autie confided to Libbie, "as I know it will please you."[79] Furthermore, someone else had noted that "no officer holding a commission was so popular with the retired men."[80] This last, as one historian notes, was important since "popularity with the veterans was crucial for a candidate, particularly a Democratic candidate such as Belmont might sponsor."[81] Libbie understood the significance of these accolades, and later in life befriended Edmund Stedman and his family.[82]

At last the extended leave ended, and Armstrong, unable to find more congenial employment, returned to active duty. Although his initial orders sent him to Louisville, Kentucky, after the first of the year, his station would be Elizabethtown, fifty miles to the south. "Personally I should have preferred the Plains," he wrote Libbie, "but for your sake. Duty in the South," he added, perhaps thinking about the implications if he ran for national office, "has a political aspect, which I always seek to avoid."[83]

The Seventh had been sent south to curb the Ku Klux Klan and moonshiners. In addition, Custer oversaw the purchasing of cavalry horses. When Libbie first arrived in Elizabethtown, she found the place depressing. "Imagine yourself your grandmother to get an idea of this place," she wrote Maggie Custer. "Everything is old, particularly the women. . . . The most active inhabitant of the place is a pig."[84]

Given the lack of reasonably priced housing, the couple boarded at the Hill House, where a noisy contraption designed to ward off flies meant they "dine[d] to music."[85] Although Libbie had wanted "a rest after our late excitement," she had never aspired to live in "the stillest, dullest place." Besides being "very poor," the residents were "low and uneducated." Never before had she seen three people riding the same horse, but gazing out her window, she watched as a woman and "two big children just passed, mounted that way."[86]

Eventually the Custers located a moderately priced, four-bedroom, well-furnished house, which they shared with the Smiths. Each week Libbie and Nettie took turns overseeing the household operations. Autie, sensing that Libbie needed some activity to relieve boredom, gave her a sewing machine. Making it "fly," she turned out garments for herself, Armstrong, and Tom. Her brother-in-law, however, proved finicky. While not "finding fault," he preferred lace to ruffles on his nightshirt and wanted his collars sewn flat as in "a dressing gown."[87]

Elizabeth saw that her husband also required something more stimulating than his duties and encouraged him to resume writing. Four years earlier, during his court-martial, the first of Custer's "Nomad" pieces, describing buffalo hunts, had appeared in *Turf, Field and Stream*. Over time this series had established Armstrong's credentials as a "gentleman hunter" on the Great Plains.[88] Now he was at work describing his service on the Plains for *The Galaxy*. Launched as the New York equivalent to the Boston-based *Atlantic*, the magazine gave Armstrong another opportunity to mold his public image. After completing his version of the abortive Hancock campaign, he described his recent success at the Washita, emphasizing his prowess as an Indian fighter.[89]

Kentucky offered Armstrong two temptations difficult to resist—buying horses and betting on races. In addition to these expensive pastimes, he and Libbie were fond of breeding dogs. Their pets were so prolific that they employed Pvt. John Burkman as their "striker" or off-duty servant.

Burkman's thin body and worn visage aroused Libbie's concern. When she discovered that he was recovering from an illness, she ordered her new maid, Mary Adams, to feed him well. Once he regained his strength, his still insatiable appetite and amazing capacity to consume prodigious amounts of food earned him the nickname "Old Neutriment."[90] Though slow of movement and hesitant in speech, the German immigrant shared the Custers' attachment to animals. When he chose a beautiful spot to bury Libbie's favorite horse, Phil Sheridan, he won her affection.[91]

The Custers were so fond of dogs that at one point, according to Burkman, they owned eighty hounds. Allowing for exaggeration, they had too many dogs to control. The canines often roamed loose over the countryside, killing other dogs and cats, and, on one occasion, a neighbor's pig. Rather than troubling Custer about the matter, Burkman reimbursed the angry farmer himself. Years later he explained why. "I figgered that keepin' trouble away from the General was what I was thar fur. He had plenty as 'twas, some o' the officers hatin' him and actin' accordin'." Burkman recalled that despite all the "laughin' and jokin' and cuttin' up pranks" in the Custer household, "they was times when we was alone together I seen a kinda unhappy look in his eyes that worried me considerable."[92]

Burkman loved his commander. Among Custer's admirable qualities, he remembered his pride in the regiment and his ability to inspire his men.[93] Still, Custer often hurt him by accusing him of disobedience, drunkenness, or stealing despite their many years together. As Burkman confided to a friend, years later, "The General and me didn't allus git along."[94]

When he described Libbie, however, the ex-striker had nothing but praise. Although Burkman later fathered a child by Nancy Adams, Mary Adams's sister, none of his relationships with women endured.[95] No one compared to Libbie, his ideal. He saw her as a virtuous and compassionate woman who endured any hardship or inconvenience without complaint, provided she could be with her husband. Moreover, she always intervened when she saw problems developing between him and her husband. Maternally she scolded both for "actin' like a couple o' boys," but in a joking way, "which sorta took the sting out of her words."[96]

Burkman remembered Libbie as being "jist as foolish about the hounds" as her husband, and several always lounged around the house. Elizabeth explained once that she and other women longed to hold "somethin' little and helpless."[97] Lacking children, Libbie may have turned to animals to fill a vacuum in her life. The same was probably true of her husband, who at times devoted large segments of his letters to describing the antics of his dogs.[98] But the animals were not children, and no matter how many the Custers owned, the void remained.

At times the animals burdened Libbie. When Burkman informed her that one of their hounds had killed a neighbor's bird dog, she spared Armstrong the news. Instead Libbie contacted the owner herself, and Burkman watched with amazement as she charmed the angry man. "After she got through talkin' to him and sorta smilin' and lookin' up at him the purty way she had, he want mad no more." To the contrary, the bereaved owner apologized, explaining that had he known the dogs belonged to Custer, he would not have complained. Libbie, nonetheless, commiserated with his loss and insisted that, when their dog Lulu whelped, he would have a puppy.[99]

The most memorable event during the Kentucky years occurred when the grand duke of Russia, Alexis, arrived in the United States in January 1872 as part of a world tour. Since relations between Secretary of State Hamilton Fish and the Russian foreign minister, Constantine Catacazy, had recently deteriorated, President Grant wanted the czar's third son away from Washington and Catacazy's complaints. Thus Sheridan arranged a western buffalo hunt, tapping Custer and scout William F. Cody, better known as Buffalo Bill Cody, to assist in the hunt. The Brulé chief, Spotted Tail, and members of his tribe met the ducal party on the North Platte River, some sixty miles from Fort McPherson.[100] Despite a slow start, Alexis shot nine buffalo the first day and that evening watched entranced as the Indians performed war dances and demonstrated their skill with bow and arrow.[101]

Although the ducal hunt catapulted Custer back into national news, Cody's reputation benefited more. Shortly after, he traveled east and in New York City joined E. Z. C. Judson, better known as Ned Buntline. The author, who had already used Cody as a central figure in his dime novels, now put him on stage in *The Scouts of the Prairies*. Cody was on his way to becoming the nation's most famous western hero.[102]

As the hunting party traveled to and from Denver, towns along the way rivaled one another in celebrating the grand duke's passage. Louisville's city fathers wired Custer, promising the duke a tour of Mammoth Cave and a ball at the Galt House if he visited the city.[103] Alexis agreed, and when he arrived, Libbie joined her husband. One reporter covering the ball described her as "a dark loveliness" at the event.[104] While she waltzed with Alexis, Vice Adm. P. H. Possiet, the dignitary responsible for overseeing the grand duke's tour, hovered over her all evening. Libbie found the night exhausting. Russian dancing consisted of "one gasping breathless rush around the room, dropping the speechless partner at the end of a mad whirl but leaving us only a moment to catch our breath." Nonetheless, whatever her impressions, Alexis liked the Custers so well that he urged them to accompany him to New Orleans as he traveled to the Russian fleet at Pensacola.[105]

Since Alexis enjoyed female companionship, other women were invited, including Colonel Sturgis's daughter. Nina Sturgis, a beautiful young woman, captivated a Memphis plantation owner who entertained the party along the way. When the widower hinted at marriage, Libbie intervened. Armstrong's commanding officer had no desire to lose his daughter so quickly.

Libbie's chaperoning duties paled in comparison to Possiet's responsibilities. Alexis had no interest in the geographical and historical landmarks Possiet constantly pointed out to him, and speeches and ceremonies bored the pleasure-loving twenty-two-year old. Standing six feet four inches tall and puffing on an "eternal" cigarette, his true interest in life was attractive women. Nonetheless, an air of mystery surrounded him. Stories circulated that his father had ordered the grand tour to distract him from an unsuitable love affair, which may have culminated in a secret marriage.[106]

Whatever her concerns for the young women in her care, Libbie enjoyed the change from Elizabethtown. She welcomed coffee and rolls in bed each morning and, since she had never been fond of early rising, heartily approved of breakfast at noon. Unlike her husband, Libbie had never taken the temperance oath and each evening looked forward to lavish dinners served with champagne and three or four wines.[107]

Shortly after the Custers returned to Elizabethtown, they boarded the train for Monroe to attend Maggie's wedding. Since Armstrong had obtained Calhoun's transfer to the Seventh Cavalry and his promotion to first lieutenant, the newlyweds would join the Custers in Kentucky after their honeymoon, to Elizabeth's delight.[108]

By the spring of 1872, Armstrong's earlier dreams of wealth had not materialized. He and his partner in the Stevens Mine, Monroe veteran Darius Hall, had encountered problems raising the $100,000 needed for operations. To begin with, Custer's purported contribution of $35,000 was, in all probability, "a useful fiction." In addition, subscribers had paid only $50 for stock valued at $100. And finally Custer and Hall had tapped some of that money for personal expenses.[109] Mines were risky business, but this undercapitalized venture had virtually no chance of becoming productive.[110]

Moreover, the racehorses Custer had purchased, Blue Grass and Frogtown, were continually "off their time." Adding to his and Libbie's burdens, the couple had recently purchased a Michigan farm jointly with brother Nevin and had to make mortgage payments.[111] The Custers' outlook, if not their balance sheets, brightened, however, when Armstrong's first *Galaxy* article appeared in May, 1872.

Armstrong's duties often called him away to Louisville for long periods. Shortly after Thanksgiving, 1872, Libbie wrote her husband, demanding his prompt return since she found Elizabethtown intolerable without him. Now that winter had arrived, the place was "solitude itself." Elizabeth signed her letter, "Your own loving bunkey," indicating that earlier strains had largely disappeared.[112]

Autie returned, and one day, late in the winter of 1873, began whooping, shouting, and breaking furniture. From experience Libbie knew this meant they would be moving. Suddenly, he approached her, swung his arm around her waist, and hoisted her to the top of a wardrobe. His new orders instructed him to proceed with his regiment to Yankton, Dakota Territory. Construction crews working on the Northern Pacific needed the Seventh's protection from the Sioux.

Glory again beckoned![113]

Libbie at fourteen. Courtesy of the Monroe
County Historical Commission Archives,
Monroe, Michigan.

Top left: Libbie at twenty, when she graduated from the Boyd
Seminary in Monroe, Michigan, and began her courtship with
George Armstrong Custer. Courtesy of the Little Bighorn Battle-
field National Monument.

Bottom left: Libbie dressed in wedding-trip finery at the time
of her marriage. Courtesy of the Monroe County Historical Commission Archives, Monroe, Michigan.

Above: In late winter 1865, Daniel and Rhoda Bacon and
Libbie's cousin, Rebecca Richmond, visited Libbie and Autie
at Winchester, Virginia. Staff and orderlies joined family members for this group picture. Daniel and Rhoda stand behind
Armstrong and Libbie, who are to the left. Rebecca Richmond
sits on the steps directly in front of the couple, and Tom is
seated to the left, holding the dog. Courtesy of the Monroe County Historical Commission Archives, Monroe, Michigan.

Left: Libbie, Autie, and Eliza on April 12, 1865, three days after Appomattox. Libbie wrote a friend that her husband was "thin and worn," which shows in this picture. Note that Libbie has adopted a military style of dress, indicating her identification with her husband and his career. Courtesy of the Little Bighorn Battlefield National Monument.

Above: Libbie, Autie, Tom, Eliza, and Emmanuel Custer (to Eliza's right) pose with members of Custer's staff and their wives on the steps of Custer's headquarters at the Blind Asylum in Austin, Texas, in late 1865. Courtesy of the Little Bighorn Battlefield National Monument.

Left top: Rebecca Richmond, Mary Richmond Kendall, and Charles Kendall stood behind Libbie and Autie when they visited the couple at Fort Leavenworth, shortly after Mary and Charles had married, 1868. Courtesy of the Little Bighorn Battlefield National Monument.

Left bottom: Armstrong thought Libbie might not recognize him, clad in buckskin, in this picture enclosed in his letter of March 1, 1869. "How do you like the beard?" he asked. Courtesy of the Little Bighorn Battlefield National Monument.

Above: Autie, Libbie, and Tom in their "beer garden" alongside Big Creek, near Fort Hays, Kansas. Summer, 1869. Courtesy of the Little Bighorn Battlefield National Monument.

Left top: Agnes Bates sits beside Lt. James Calhoun and Maggie Custer Calhoun. On the next row, Libbie, looking older and matronly, sits beside Autie. The man on the right is Capt. Myles Moylan, and the man sitting in front is Lt. Fred Calhoun. Courtesy of the Little Bighorn Battlefield National Monument.

Left bottom: "Of all our happy days, the happiest had now come to us at Fort Lincoln," Elizabeth wrote years later. The Custers rented a piano from St. Paul, and officers' wives took turns playing. July 1875. Left to right, Boston Custer, Maggie Calhoun, Lt. Winfield S. Edgerly, Libbie (who leans forward pensively), Leonard Swett, Lt. Richard E. Thompson, Nellie Wadsworth, Tom Custer, Armstrong, Emma Watson, and Emily Watson. Courtesy of the Little Bighorn Battlefield National Monument.

Above: Armstrong insisted that Libbie sit beside him while he wrote in his study at Fort Abraham Lincoln. 1875. Courtesy of the Little Bighorn Battlefield National Monument.

Armstrong posed for this
picture in civilian dress in March 1876,
shortly before his death at the Little Bighorn.
Courtesy of the Monroe County Historical
Commission Archives.

Although the lines around Elizabeth's eyes had
deepened, at forty-three she had published *"Boots and
Saddles"* and looked more youthful than she had on the steps
of her home at Fort Lincoln in 1873. Circa 1885. Courtesy
of the Little Bighorn Battlefield National Monument.

Elizabeth usually wore black when she appeared
on the platform or posed for pictures later in life. She was
fifty-eight when this picture was taken in 1900. Courtesy
of the Little Bighorn Battlefield National Monument.

Above: *Custer's Demand*, by Charles Schreyvogel. Frederic Remington called the painting "half baked stuff," but Elizabeth judged it "free from sensationalism" and congratulated the artist on his historical accuracy. From left to right, the Indians are Little Heart, Lone Wolf, Kicking Bird, and Satanta. Others in the picture are a scout, Lieutenant Colonel Custer, Lt. Tom Custer, and Lt. Col. John Schuyler Crosby. Gen. Philip Sheridan and his troops are in the distance. Courtesy of the Thomas Gilcrease Institute of American History and Art, Tulsa, Oklahoma.

Left: Brig. Gen. E. S. Godfrey. As a result of Elizabeth's urging, Godfrey wrote "Custer's Last Battle." It became for decades the most widely accepted version of the Battle of the Little Bighorn. Over time, Godfrey revised the article to make it more pleasing to Elizabeth. President Theodore Roosevelt, however, held Godfrey responsible for the death of women and children at Wounded Knee and impeded his promotion to brigadier general until 1907, shortly before Godfrey's retirement. Courtesy of U.S. Army Military History Institute, Carlisle Barracks, Pennsylvania.

MARCELL
PHOTO CO
DETROIT.

UNVEILING OF
CUSTERS MONUMENT
MONROE MICH. JUNE 4. 10.

Above: Elizabeth could hardly believe "that my dream of so
many years was a reality before me," as she pulled the yellow
ribbon to unveil the Custer statue in Monroe, Michigan, on
June 4, 1910. President William Howard Taft stands behind
her. Courtesy of the Monroe County Historical Commission Archives, Monroe, Michigan.

Right: The Custer Monument in Monroe, Michigan, won
Elizabeth's wholehearted endorsement for it shows no rash
and reckless charger. Instead, the twenty-three-year-old general has just sighted Jeb Stuart's Invincibles on July 3, 1863.
He quickly assesses the scene before winning national glory
at the Battle of Gettysburg. Courtesy of the Monroe County
Historical Commission Archives, Monroe, Michigan.

Elizabeth was sixty-eight when she posed for this picture in
1910 during her trip to Monroe for the Custer Monument unveiling.
She looked more youthful than she had ten years earlier. Courtesy
of the Little Bighorn Battlefield National Monument.

CHAPTER 9

Life in Dakota
Territory

T HE UNITED STATES had signed the Treaty of Fort Laramie with
15,000 Sioux, largely the followers of the Oglala chief, Red Cloud,
and the Brulé chief, Spotted Tail, and their Arapahoe and Cheyenne
allies in the spring of 1868. The government agreed to halt work on the
Bozeman Trail (or Powder River Road), leading into the Montana gold
fields, and to abandon its three military posts along the route. In return the
signatory chiefs consented to live on the Great Sioux reservation in the area
west of the Missouri in present-day South Dakota. The treaty stipulated that
no portion of "their permanent home" could be ceded unless three-fourths
of the adult males gave their consent. It also stated, however, that the United
States government could build roads, including a railroad and "other works
of utility and necessity" across the reservation.[1]

About 3,000 Sioux and 400 Northern Cheyennes disdained reservation
life and never agreed to the treaty. To gain acquiescence from both groups,
federal negotiators granted the Indians a territory "north of the North
Platte River and east of the summits of the Big Horn Mountains." There, in
"unceded Indian territory," they could hunt and roam at will. The treaty
excluded all settlement by outsiders unless the Sioux and their allies gave
permission.[2]

The nontreaty bands, led by chiefs such as Sitting Bull, Crazy Horse, and
Gall, wandered freely in the Powder River region of unceded territory. Their
most respected leader was Sitting Bull of the Hunkpapas, who was also a
medicine man. Over time, he attained such prominence that the nontreaties
became known as Sitting Bull's people. The line between treaty and
nontreaty Sioux remained difficult to draw, for the two groups, bound by
kinship ties, visited back and forth. Many nontreaties joined their relatives

during the winter to receive rations, arms, and ammunition at the various agencies. In summer, recruits from the reservation bands often hunted with the nontreaties in unceded lands.[3]

Four years after the signing of the Fort Laramie Treaty, the Northern Pacific extended as far as Fargo, Dakota Territory. In the summer of 1872, surveying parties for the railroad appeared in the Yellowstone Valley and began working on the south bank of the river. Although the treaty of 1868 left the northern boundary vaguely defined, the Sioux considered this an invasion of their territory. The nontreaties, caring nothing about a treaty they had never signed, were incensed. The arrival of the iron horse in this region threatened their way of life. By the end of summer, skirmishes between Indians and whites had halted the railroad's construction.[4]

Before resuming work the following year, the Northern Pacific sought additional protection. Generals Sherman and Sheridan eagerly complied since both believed nothing would resolve the "Indian problem" on the Northern Plains faster than the completion of a transcontinental line through Sioux lands. The farms, cities, and commerce that inevitably followed would divide buffalo herds, leading to their destruction and eliminating Indian hunting rights in unceded territory. Then, facing starvation, the nontreaties would accept reservation life as their only alternative. Sheridan selected the Seventh, reputedly the army's foremost Indian fighting regiment, as the force to send northward to accompany the Northern Pacific's 1873 Yellowstone Expedition.[5]

The Seventh's camp at Yankton, Dakota Territory, was already established when the Custers arrived on April 10 with bags, dogs, and cages of canaries and mockingbirds. Not all the officers rejoiced over the regiment's reunification. When Armstrong ordered the existing camp torn down and rebuilt, one lieutenant in Captain Yates's company, Charles Larned, grumbled. Custer, he thought, was proving himself "selfishly indifferent to others, and ruthlessly determined to make himself conspicuous at all hazards."[6]

Although the officers's wives had already taken rooms in Yankton's St. Charles Hotel, Libbie stayed in camp with her husband. She rented a flimsy log cabin not far from the laundresses' quarters and sent Mary Adams to town to purchase a stove and supplies. Mary returned empty-handed shortly before the onset of an April blizzard.[7] Custer, in the meantime, had fallen ill and now lay in bed. Other than a few laundresses, whose husbands had been dispatched to find shelter for the horses, the encampment was deserted.[8]

Libbie huddled under blankets, emerging only to administer medicine or investigate strange noises. At one point, she heard a thud and discovered Mary and Ham, a handyman who had remained behind, admitting six soldiers. For the next thirty-six hours, the men, suffering frostbite, groaned in agony.

At last several officers, led by Yankton citizens, appeared with a stove and food. To Libbie's relief none of the soldiers died, although all eventually lost fingers or toes. She also learned, to her amazement, that one of the laundresses had given birth in a tent during the worst night of the blizzard. Remarkably, both mother and child survived.[9]

Armstrong had recovered entirely by the time the territorial governor gave the Seventh an enthusiastic send-off on May 7. Most of the officers' wives and all the laundresses traveled by steamer to the next destination, Fort Rice. Libbie and Maggie Calhoun, leading members of what Lieutenant Larned called the "royal family," accompanied their husbands on a long overland march.[10] Again Libbie was "roughing it," waiting until soldiers had first beaten off rattlesnakes before she rested at campgrounds and sleeping at night on planks laid across a carpenter's horse.[11]

Frequently, she and Autie rode ahead of the column. Once, when another officer accompanied them, Custer bolted away to chase deer. Left behind, Libbie and the officer unexpectedly encountered warriors in the brush. As the Indians reached for their guns, Libbie, obeying her companion's instructions, moved on calmly. When she reached her husband's side, she fainted.[12]

Shortly after, Libbie and Autie unintentionally galloped into a Sioux village. Armstrong calmly greeted the occupants with "How," and Libbie did likewise, "with a salaam so deep that it bent my head down to the pommel of my saddle.!" Afterwards, when Autie suggested she stay with the column for safety, Libbie refused. Whatever the dangers, she found it harder to "be left behind, a prey to all the horrors of imagining what may be happening to one we love. You slowly eat your heart out with anxiety, and to endure such suspense is simply the hardest of all trials that come to the soldier's wife."[13] Besides, her experiences on the march, however unnerving, had heightened her self-confidence. "When a woman has come out of danger," she reflected later, "she is too utterly a coward by nature not to dread enduring the same thing again; but it is something to know that she is equal to it. Even though she may tremble and grow faint in anticipation, having once been through it, she can count on rising to the situation when the hour actually comes."[14]

After six weeks of marching, the Seventh Cavalry finally reached Fort Rice, the assembly point of the expedition. Libbie found the gracious hospitality of the post commander's wife a welcome respite from camping out.[15] The fort itself, however, could not accommodate the Seventh's wives. Until the army constructed new headquarters at Fort Abraham Lincoln, twenty-five miles to the north, the women were ordered out of Dakota Territory. By mid-June, Libbie and Maggie resided in the old Bacon house in Monroe, where Libbie experienced "the summer of my discontent." Once more her days revolved around waiting for the mail on the one o'clock train.[16]

The long column, consisting of companies of the Seventh Cavalry and Seventeenth and Twenty-second infantries, left Fort Rice on June 20 under the command of David S. Stanley, colonel of the Twenty-second Infantry. Two of Custer's friends from West Point, Capt. William Ludlow, chief engineer for Dakota Territory, and Thomas Rosser, division engineer for the Northern Pacific, accompanied the expedition. In the evenings, while Stanley drank and others gambled, Custer and Rosser recalled their wartime exploits in the Shenandoah Valley.[17]

While Stanley's letters to his wife complained of downpours, Armstrong's noted the fine hunting. "I have done some of the most remarkable shooting I ever saw and it is admitted to be such by all," Autie boasted the sixth day out.[18] He also interspersed accounts of Captain Yates's drinking bouts, which augured poorly for Annie Roberts Yates, a bride of sixteen months, and of all-night card games, which Autie assured Libbie he avoided. He had "told Satan to get behind me so far as poker goes."[19] Mostly, however, Armstrong's letters contained statements of love and descriptions of western scenes.

By July 15, when the expedition reached the steamer *Key West* on the Yellowstone, Armstrong had journeyed through a petrified forest, where he had collected mysterious fossils. He had seen magnificent scenery, which "not even a Church or a Bierstadt, could fairly represent," and he wished Libbie were with him.[20] Often prone to respiratory illnesses and sore throats, he had fared well "in this health giving atmosphere."[21]

The president's son, Fred Grant, two years out of West Point, was already a lieutenant colonel on Sheridan's staff, largely because of pressure from his mother, Julia Grant. As young Fred accompanied the troops that summer, he and Armstrong reminisced about the academy and shared pictures of their "sweethearts." By July 22, Grant had left for the east and planned to stop in Monroe to pay Libbie his respects. Armstrong urged his wife to postpone visiting the Barkers so she could meet young Grant at the depot before bringing him home for dinner and possibly a reception. "Have his father's portrait hung in the parlor out of compliment to him."[22]

Armstrong also described the tension between himself and Stanley, which he attributed to the Colonel's frequent inebriation. By July 27 the march had been delayed ten days, and Custer thought, "*Whiskey* alone is the cause."[23] Stanley, in turn, wrote his wife that Custer was an insubordinate officer who came and went as he pleased.[24]

While Armstrong wrote enthusiastically of his adventures that summer, Libbie congratulated herself on escaping life in Monroe. Although old friends were attentive, without her husband she could not "rise above depressing surroundings . . . There are not many joyous people here." The women seemed worn out by "domestic cares, kitchen drudgery," and "leading a monotonous life," while the men lacked "bright women to cheer them up." Recently, she had visited a former schoolmate, now "lingering along with childbirth illness." Mary Dansard, who had borne seven children in the past decade, would gladly have exchanged places with Libbie.[25]

Libbie also felt out of place among civilians who understood few of the problems faced by frontier soldiers and their dependents.[26] Before long, however, even Monroe's most indifferent citizens had heard about Custer's recent skirmishes on the Yellowstone River. On August 4, he had held off Sioux warriors an entire afternoon on the river banks. With the sun fading and ammunition running low, only the fortuitous arrival of reinforcements had saved his two companies from annihilation. Only one soldier was wounded in fighting, but there were three other casualties. The regimental veterinarian, Dr. John Honsinger, and the sutler, Augustus Baliran, with an escort of two soldiers, had strayed from the main body. Sioux warriors intercepted and killed all except for one soldier, who escaped and alerted the troops.[27]

Six days later, Custer again engaged Sioux braves on the banks of the Yellowstone, three miles from the river's source. On the second day, as he renewed his attempt to ford the river, warriors attacked from all sides. In grave danger, he skillfully deployed his troops, holding off the warriors until Stanley's infantry appeared, forcing them to retreat.

In both battles, Custer had proven himself a skilled Indian fighter. But, while he had won fresh laurels, he might have extracted warnings. The Sioux, well-armed with repeating rifles, had not fled as Armstrong expected, but instead fought tenaciously for what they saw as their land.[28]

Associated Press accounts Libbie read left her in turmoil. "Oh Autie who could envy such a day as I have spent. The pride and glory I feel in you is mingled with such thrills of fear and such terrified thoughts at what risks you run to achieve your victory."[29] Worse yet, she faced more of the same until the expedition ended. "It's of no use for me to try to see anything but a world of anxiety and the glory cannot cover the risks you have run."[30] In another letter, Libbie felt "so full of anxiety and care for your safety and so filled with terror at the terrible danger you have been in I cannot regain my cheerfulness — and yet," she added, "do not think me so shortsighted, as not to freely admit how well timed is this victory of yours."[31]

Elizabeth was correct. The Kentucky years, except for the brief hunt with Grand Duke Alexis, had added little to her husband's reputation. Now his fame was again rising. His *Galaxy* articles, describing the Hancock campaign, were still appearing, and Sheldon and Company wanted to turn the series into a book. Recently the *Chicago Post* had extolled Custer as the "Glorious Boy."[32] Libbie saw new possibilities ahead for her husband.

"Autie, your career is something wonderful. Swept along as I am in the current of your eventful life I can still stop to realize that your history is simply marvelous. Every event," she marveled, "seems to fit into every other event like the blocks in a child's puzzle. Does it not seem so strange to you? Can you realize what wonders come constantly to you while other men lead such tame lives?"[33]

Friends and acquaintances noticed too. The Bates family constantly talked about Custer's career, and her old art professor, C. C. Zens, had this advice: "He would wish to see you remain in the army until you are promoted to a real General and then enter another field."[34] What Zens meant became apparent when Libbie added, "Whether I can ever see you go into political [*sic*] without a shudder of fear is a doubtful question. Certainly not as I feel nowadays."[35]

Still she was thinking of a political career for her husband as she reminded him of other Civil War heroes "now almost forgotten. Even those who rushed into politics," she continued, "have had all the honors long ago that any one was willing to spare them and they have hard work to keep their places among men whose life long experiences have taught them the cunning of getting into and keeping office. Oh how thankful I am they did not entrap you. You would not have had the individuality of character or position you now have. I tell you Autie, I have never felt more ambitious for you nor more confident of your success than this summer. I am only a little afraid I can't keep up."[36]

Zens, among others, wanted to write Armstrong's biography. He also wanted to advance Custer's standing with America's German population.[37] Since Libbie's "daily thought" revolved around her husband's "honor & glory," the prospect excited her. "And now if you make no mistakes," she predicted, "you are going on to more honors & greatness than we dreamed of a few years ago."[38]

Such "honor & greatness" included literary as well as military and possibly political fame. Libbie both flattered and pressured her husband, noting that with "this long winter before us you must write up with many an embellishment the stories of this Summer's campaign. Don't let the slightest thing escape you." Autie had become so skillful with words that "my ambition for you in the world of letters almost takes the heart out of my body."[39] In another letter, she extolled his ability to bring characters to life, noting that "unlike your wife," he was able to write speeches as if they had come "from the originator."[40]

In the meantime Monroe grew more depressing each day. Maggie remained "low spirited," and Maria Custer constantly worried about Nevin and his growing family. "But I mention this mostly for one thing," Libbie assured her husband. "It is to tell you how I am perfectly overwhelmed with gratitude when I think what a glorious disposition yours is! I am so buoyed up when I write you. So convinced that everything will turn out for the best. And so indifferent to troubling cares that I feel in your absence, . . . I never realized till now how dependent I am on your grand temperament for my fine spirits, good health, powers of endurance and all the bright glad hours that crowd into my days when I live with you."[41]

Recently, Libbie had seen her former suitor, John Rauch. He was a successful lawyer and an affectionate family man, but "what a humdrum life I had escaped by not marrying him. . . . So monotonous so commonplace and besides I see every day that great ambition I have for you and how I bask daily in the sunshine of your glory."[42] As the chilly nights signaled the onset of autumn, Libbie's thoughts turned towards the approaching winter on the Northern Plains. Her anticipation showed her "over & over again that you are *everything to me*. My 'all in all' in fact."[43]

As usual, Libbie sent Autie poetry. "You know," she wrote, "I have often said . . . I missed you far more than you did me because I immediately settle down to such a quiet and monotonous life while you rush into excitement and danger and new scenes." The following stanzas made her point.

> "There's something in the parting hour
> Will chill the warmest heart—
> Yet kindred, comrades, lovers, friends,
> Are fated all to part:
>
> But this I've seen and many a pang
> Has pressed it on my mind—
> The one who goes is happier
> Than those he leaves behind."[44]

The surveying party had reached its final destination, the explorer William Clark's landmark stone column, Pompey's Pillar, and now headed for Fort Lincoln.[45] Custer traveled a different route back to the post, and having learned taxidermy that summer, brought back animal and bird specimens for his study, his friend Barker, and the Detroit Audubon Society.[46]

More important, he had cemented closer ties with the Northern Pacific. "My little durl never saw people more enthusiastic over the 7th and her dear Bo than are the representatives of the R.R." They knew, Custer boasted, that only his leadership had saved the expedition.[47] In gratitude, the company had agreed to hire his friend Fred Nims at sixty dollars a month, which proved that the West was the fabled land of opportunity after all. If he ever left the army, Armstrong would head westward, "put my shoulder to the wheel," and win advancement.[48]

Increasingly, as he approached Fort Lincoln, Autie's thoughts turned to their new home, under construction at the post. The crew from the supply ship had told him the Custer quarters were "elegant" and "a story higher than the others." The house overlooked the Missouri "for eight miles with a stretch of timber in sight." Other amenities included "large double parlors on the right with *folding* doors, while on the left of the hall are two rooms, my room in the front and the bed room in rear." Not only would their home be superior to others on frontier posts, but it would be insulated through-out with "warm paper." Finally, with six companies of cavalry and four of infantry at Lincoln, Armstrong, now in charge of the Middle District of the Department of Dakota, would command one of the country's largest forts and oversee three other posts as well.[49]

After nine years, the relationship between the Custers had changed. No longer did Autie's letters (the surviving ones anyway) contain frequent references to other women. Instead they were full of praise and flattery for Libbie, along with his usual self-congratulations. Much of the braggadocio sounds like that of an adolescent boy, seeking to draw attention to his accomplishments to prove himself worthy of affection and esteem.

Gone from their marriage too, at least in the extant letters, was much of the early eroticism. During separations there were still references to his "oh so lonely couch" and the longed for "better night" coming, but the ardor was noticeably muted. Instead, Libbie had become less a romantic figure and more a loving mother and adviser to her "bo." Photographs of the 1870s capture this, and one writer notes a "visibly aged Libbie," sitting on the porch steps at Fort Abraham Lincoln.[50]

Yet, while Libbie frequently received forty-page letters from her husband, Autie still chafed under authority, even that of a loving wife. Periodically he resisted anything approaching a demand. When Elizabeth asked why he said nothing about missing her that summer, Armstrong explained: "You recollect the old saying that you can *lead* a horse to water but you cannot *make* him drink. Now I for the time being am the obstinate steed who persistently declined to drink. You have led me to the water and although I am ever so thirsty—almost famished—and intended to drink freely and without limit, yet like Falstaff—on compulsion never. In other words if I devoted line after line and page after page to telling you whether I have missed you or not you would say, and with reason too that I only did so because you had called my attention to it." Surely Libbie knew he always missed her, except for periods when his responsibilities briefly distracted him.[51]

Libbie dealt expertly with such intransigence. Three weeks later Armstrong complained, "I believe I have referred before to other people getting letters when I did not and of a later date when I did." Nor had he received any at Fort Lincoln. Tom had three letters from New York City "of a later date than any I have recd," and while she might argue that Monroe was "such an out of the way place &c &c but unfortunately for this argument Mr. Calhoun has received later dates from that same out of the way place."[52]

Although Libbie withheld her letters, she was so eager to see her husband that she traveled to Toledo to meet him at a reunion of the Army of Tennessee. While shopping downtown, she "felt, rather than saw, a sudden rush from a door, and I was taken off my feet and set dancing in air." When her initial anger subsided, she recognized in the two-toned face before her—part sunburned and part fair, where he had shaved off his beard—her husband.[53]

Soon after, the Custers returned to Dakota Territory with Libbie's friend, Agnes Bates.[54] At the station in Bismarck, the two women knew they were in the "Wild West" when they saw shackled outlaws boarding a train. Afterwards, the travelers braved the strong currents and floating ice of the Missouri River in a rowboat before Libbie climbed into Tom's waiting ambulance. Under her breath she swore, "Here will I live and die, and never go on that river again."[55] As the party drove into Lincoln, Libbie saw before her, not the dark unfurnished house she expected, but instead a brightly illuminated structure. Outside the band played "Home Sweet Home" and "Garry Owen" while inside fireplaces blazed in furnished rooms. On the dining room table, Mary Adams had spread a feast.[56]

On February 6, 1874, a strange acrid odor aroused Libbie from sleep. She awakened her husband, who became alarmed and, bounding upstairs, discovered fire in the attic. Shortly after, an explosion rocked the house, covering Agnes with plaster as she leaped from her bed and fled to the Calhoun residence. Libbie, however, stayed in the burning home until her husband was safely outside. Fortunately, given the lack of water at Fort Lincoln, the absence of wind confined the blaze to the Custer residence.[57]

Next day Libbie and Autie surveyed their losses. They had salvaged all belongings on the lower floor, including Armstrong's clothes and personal effects. Elizabeth's wardrobe, stored on the second floor, was gone. Later, she reminisced that she had lost little of monetary value.[58] Armstrong told his mother a different story, claiming that Libbie had lost twelve dresses, four of which he valued at $150 to $200 each.[59] Libbie felt greater regret over the loss of her wartime scrapbooks and her ballroom wig, made of the curls Autie had clipped before his wedding.[60] Although Armstrong attributed the fire to a defective chimney, the "warm" paper, a coal-tar product used as insulation, had transmitted the blaze throughout the house.[61]

Shortly after the couple had moved into the duplex beside Tom to await completion of a second house on the original site, Armstrong became embroiled in a new dispute. During the previous September, Jay Cooke's Philadelphia banking firm had collapsed, largely because a market no longer existed for its heavily watered Northern Pacific Railroad stocks. The railroad plunged into receivership as the country now entered a severe depression. The transcontinental, however, having received twice the usual amount of land grants, was not without resources. If it attracted additional population to the Northern Plains and, better yet, sold that population its land, the heavier traffic and additional sales might revive its fortunes. Thus Northern Pacific promotional tracts described the land along its route in such glowing terms that Cooke's critics derided it as "Jay Cooke's Banana Belt."[62]

In an article written for the *New York Tribune*, William B. Hazen took issue with the railroad's claims. His two years at Fort Buford in Dakota Territory had convinced him that the land was arid and would never "in our day and generation, sell for one penny an acre, except through fraud and ignorance."[63] Armstrong, alerted to Hazen's statements by his friend, Rosser, rebutted the colonel's views in a letter that appeared in the *Minneapolis Tribune* on April 17. If Hazen was too pessimistic about the region's potentiality, Custer, recalling his summer enthusiasm, was too optimistic. One fact was certain. Custer now served the railroad as valued promoter.[64]

Whatever her husband's disputes, Libbie did her best to create a harmonious environment at Lincoln for officers and post visitors. Throughout the long winters, the Custers hosted frequent dinners and often turned their home over to card games (although Libbie never mastered the pastime). Twice a month they gave hops at which "waltzes . . . were the favorite," along with "lancers, polkas, the gallop and square dances." At other times the officers, their wives, and post visitors attended theatricals produced by the enlisted men.[65] Occasionally Armstrong and Maggie acted in dramas in the Custer quarters. Once Autie played a Sioux chief, and Agnes Bates was his Indian bride. In another tableau, he and Maggie portrayed Quaker Indian agents, while Agnes played the part of the "princess," learning the benefits of white civilization.[66]

Although Armstrong assumed responsibility for planning social events, he sometimes excused himself to work on articles. On those occasions, Libbie entertained their company and periodically joined him in his study. If guests danced in the parlor, she waltzed with her husband in his room. Once, when she failed to appear at the desired interval, Autie sent an orderly with a note: "Do you think I am a confirmed monk?" Their guests, she later recalled, "insisted laughingly upon my going at once to the self-appointed hermit."[67]

Katherine Garret remembered her first meeting with Libbie while visiting her sister, Mollie McIntosh, at Lincoln. As Libbie stood on her porch, "the light breeze lifted her very dark hair slightly as she turned to greet Mollie and Donald." Immediately the post commander's wife, "slim,

[and] girlish looking in a light-colored, out-of-date frock," put Katie at ease, and she found herself gazing into "quiet, intelligent eyes that met one with interest rather than criticism." Libbie's smile, Katie recalled, "warmed one with her friendliness."[68]

When Libbie learned that Lt. Francis Gibson had proposed to Katie, she stole to her tent one night at midnight and shared her own experiences as an army wife. Libbie emphasized the drawbacks—"from the necessity sometimes of associating with uncongenial people, down to living in drab stockade posts." She also noted the poor pay, frequent separations, and dangerous campaigns. In the end, however, "nothing mattered if you loved your man."[69]

Besides, Libbie continued, she and the other wives were "making history, with our men." They were "keeping the home fires burning while the soldiers are guarding the railroad engineers and surveyors against the Indians as, mile by mile, in the face of almost insurmountable obstacles, they are building the railroads straight across the continent until the oceans meet, which will open up the country to civilization."[70]

Then Libbie extolled the future prospects of Dakota Territory. One day, she predicted, "the Western grain and the wheat of Red River Valley, Dakota, said to be the richest in the world, will be conveyed to the Eastern and foreign markets." The mines will yield additional wealth, and "scientific farmers from all over the world will seek this virgin soil. Yes, my dear," she told Katie, "we are the pioneer army women, and we're proud of it."[71]

Although Libbie saw herself and other army wives as "pioneer army women," there were important differences between officers' wives and other women living in western regions. Army wives were relegated largely to western posts, where they had little impact on surrounding communities. They were not permanent settlers. And however much they extolled western potentialities, most would not settle in the West when their husbands' army careers ended. Nonetheless, Katie was so impressed by Libbie's counsel that she decided to marry Lieutenant Gibson when the Seventh returned from its next expedition.[72]

After the long, harsh winter on the Northern Plains, the regiment welcomed the first signs of spring. The early buds, however, signaled new problems. When Sioux raiders stampeded a herd of mules within sight of Lincoln, the Seventh rode off in pursuit. With only one officer at the post, Libbie and the other wives remained frantic until the troops returned.[73]

While Libbie remembered such incidents as frightening, the greater danger lay to the southwest at the more remote Red Cloud and Spotted Tail agencies in northwestern Nebraska. There the "northern Indians," those Sioux and their allies who moved back and forth between reservation and unceded territory, had plunged the agencies into chaos. During the previous winter, they had killed a clerk at the Red Cloud agency, and to the west, another party had taken the lives of an officer and a corporal from Fort Laramie. In response, Sheridan sent troops to the two agencies and ordered the building of forts Robinson and Sheridan. He also called for an additional fort farther north in the Black Hills to afford Nebraska settlements greater protection.[74]

Before selecting a site, the Black Hills in the western part of the Great Sioux reservation had to be explored. Believing that an expedition from the north would meet less resistance, Sheridan assigned the task to the Seventh Cavalry under Custer. Eastern humanitarians objected, charging that the proposed expedition violated the Treaty of Fort Laramie by bringing whites onto the Great Sioux reservation. Army officials countered that the treaty allowed government officials to enter on official business. Besides, the other reservation posts had created no problems.[75]

Behind the debate, however, lay another agenda. The Sioux treasured the Black Hills, wrested from the Kiowas almost a century earlier. Paha Sapa served both as the dwelling place of their gods and a prized hunting ground. For years, however, rumors of gold in the hills had circulated. Given the current depression, "Dakota Promoters," based largely in Yankton and Bismarck, wanted the region thrown open to miners. Thus, Custer invited not only engineers and mapmakers to accompany the expedition, but two "practical miners" to travel with the command. The expedition would look for gold. He also would take with him geologist N. M. Winchell and paleontologist George Grinnell, in addition to Lt. Col. Fred Grant. Unfortunately, the threat of Indian attacks meant that Libbie and Mary Adams had to remain at Lincoln.[76]

William E. Curtis, correspondent for the *Chicago Inter-Ocean* and the *New York World*, arrived at the post. Immediately the twenty-three-year-old fell under the Custers' spell and, perhaps unconsciously, cast wife and husband as models of family life and culture in the West. Libbie struck him as "a charming lady, who has shared marches and victories since early in the war," and he characterized the home she created "as one green spot, if there be no others in the frontier life of the officers of the Seventh." Curtis first met Custer when he was introduced to him in his study. Custer was tutoring two little girls, one black and one white, and both children of Libbie's servants.

He had done this "for several years," Curtis informed his readers, "and all these little people of his household know of written words is what he has taught them."[77]

As the date for departure approached, Armstrong purchased a $5,000 insurance policy naming Libbie his beneficiary.[78] When the various companies and their commanders assembled at Lincoln, Libbie found herself entertaining officers hostile to her husband. She maintained later that Autie never discussed administrative affairs with her, never carried a grudge, and frowned on gossip. Only her female intuition, honed by her love, enabled her to identify Armstrong's enemies.

Or so she claimed. Actually, Armstrong occasionally discussed his animosities in his letters.[79] In that light, it seems unlikely that during the long winter months, when he and Libbie were constantly together, he never discussed personnel matters. Nonetheless, Libbie was correct when she noted that Armstrong did not carry grudges.[80] Others did, however. Frederick Benteen, expert nurturer of resentments, disliked both husband and wife. While most officers and men praised Libbie, whatever they thought of Armstrong, Benteen characterized her as "about as avaricious and parsimonious a woman as you can find in a day's walk."[81]

And Libbie, who had a keen sense of emotional undercurrents, probably had Benteen in mind when she recalled that her husband sometimes found her "not sufficiently cordial" to officers she disliked. As the commanding officer's wife she "belonged to everyone, and . . . should be hospitable upon principle." Nonetheless, Libbie kept her distance until one night, Armstrong presented "a burlesque imitation of my manner. I could not help laughing, even when annoyed, to see him caricature me by advancing coldly, extending the tips of his fingers, and bowing loftily to some imaginary guest." Striving to please her husband, Libbie erred in the other direction, becoming "too demonstrative, and thus giving the impression that I was the best friend of someone I really dreaded."[82]

As the band played "The Girl I Left behind Me," the Black Hills Expedition, consisting of ten companies of the Seventh and two from the Seventeenth and the Twentieth infantries, left Fort Lincoln on July 2, 1874. This time, Armstrong commanded, and in addition to bringing Tom along as a regimental officer, his twenty-five-year-old brother, Boston, was listed on the quartermaster rolls as a "guide."[83]

Once more Libbie endured a summer of separation and worry. She also contended with seasonal plagues. Earlier, hordes of grasshoppers, in one of the most severe infestations ever recorded on the Plains, had destroyed her carefully tended vegetable garden.[84] Now came the mosquitoes. "Fort Lincoln was celebrated as the worst place in the United States for these pests," she later recalled. After the oppressive daily heat the women looked forward to evenings on their porches. To escape the "myriads" of insects, they wore "scarfs and overdresses" over their regular clothes and stuffed newspapers into their shoes. One visiting officer barely suppressed his laughter when Libbie appeared wearing a mosquito net, a "waterproof cloak, buckskin gauntlets, and forgot to hide under my gown the tips of the general's riding boots!" The other women wore equally outlandish regalia as they waved fans and handkerchiefs to stave off their tormentors.[85]

Sometimes Libbie traveled to Bismarck to meet visitors, and occasionally she took the train to St. Paul for shopping. Usually, however, she avoided such outings since they required crossing the Missouri River on a "ram-shackly" boat. The incompetent captain, rather than steering through strong currents, let the craft "shoot down the river at a mad rate," convincing her she headed for Yankton, 500 miles away.[86]

The summer of 1874 also brought drought to the Northern Plains. Water, always scarce, now became a precious commodity. Libbie learned to use it so sparingly that for the rest of her life she never again wasted it.[87] As the landscape turned brown, Libbie and other wives ascended a hill each day to watch for scouts carrying mail. Instead they saw only "floating waves of heated atmosphere," as neither rain nor letters arrived for weeks.[88]

Early one morning Libbie awoke to the sound of hoofbeats. Arikaras were approaching with mailbags marked "Black Hills Express" flung across their saddles.[89] "My darling Sunbeam," began Autie's letter, dated July 15. "We have marched through an exceedingly interesting and beautiful country." Although reporters accompanying the expedition often noted the blistering heat, dust, and alkaline water they had encountered throughout the first 227 miles, Armstrong emphasized the cool forests and running streams of their present location.[90]

While others remembered the sutler's wagon selling liquor and one all-night drinking party, Autie assured his wife, "There has not been a single card party or a drunken officer since we left Lincoln." The long column had halted at a "beautiful" place Armstrong named "Prospect Valley," about twelve miles from Montana Territory. Until the last three days, he had seen no Indians, but he knew they watched the expedition. Still, he expected little trouble from the Sioux. As always he missed his wife.[91]

Armstrong's letters were infrequent that summer, since he spent his spare time writing an article for the *New York World*. By August 2, however, he had exciting news. "We have discovered gold beyond a doubt and probably other valuable metals. For the incidents of the trip you must read the Pioneer and Tribune and wait for the rest until I come home which will be Aug 31st. All are well and have been well."[92]

Shortly before the expedition was due back at Lincoln, Libbie opened a letter postmarked Bear Butte. Inside was a photograph of Armstrong, squatting behind a large felled bear, while to his left was his favorite scout, Bloody Knife. Behind Custer stood Captain Ludlow, and beside him, a private. "I have reached the highest rung on the hunters ladder of fame I have killed my grizzly after a most exciting hunt & combat." (Actually, Ludlow and Bloody Knife had helped bring down the eight-foot bear.) Next year Libbie would see for herself this veritable Eden.[93]

On August 30, the day before Libbie expected Armstrong's return, she heard the strains of "Garry Owen." Elated, she "hid behind the door as the command rode into garrison, ashamed to be seen crying and laughing and dancing up and down with excitement." Forgetting herself, she raced out to greet her husband. Suddenly she heard soldiers cheering, "and the unusual sound, together with the embarrassment into which I had unconsciously plunged myself, made the few steps back to the house seem a mile."[94]

Another onlooker recalled the scene differently. Pt. Theodore Ewert, not an admirer of either Armstrong or Libbie, wrote in his diary, "As we rode past the officers' quarter each would drop out, embrace and kiss his wife, and retire mid welcomes, caresses, etc. Mrs. General Custer came to meet her husband, but just as she came in 'catching' distance she 'fainted?' A very pretty piece of byplay for the men of the command!"[95]

Two days later, Libbie read excerpts from her husband's official report in the *Bismarck Tribune*. Echoing statements printed earlier in Northern Pacific promotional brochures, the report emphasized the availability of water, timber, game, grazing, and, above all, fertile farmland. "I know of no portion of our country where nature has done so much to prepare homes for husbandmen," Custer asserted.[96]

He also reiterated what he had written Libbie earlier and what he had sent his scout, Charley Reynolds, to announce at Fort Laramie. The expedition had discovered gold in the Black Hills. Although the official report was uncharacteristically cautious, the journalist Curtis had wired the *Inter-Ocean* the famous phrase: "From the grass roots down it was 'pay dirt.'"[97]

Not everyone who had accompanied Custer agreed with this assessment. Neither Fred Grant nor geologist Winchell had seen "gold at the roots of the grass."[98] Their statements mattered little. The hope of finding gold during hard times unleashed a frenzy. One prospecting party moved into the Black Hills that autumn and erected a stockade to pass the winter. By now Custer had gone on record, calling for "the extinguishment of the Indian title at the earliest moment."[99]

Regardless of the growing controversy concerning the region, October 1874 found the Custers back east visiting friends, relatives, and attending Fred Grant's marriage in Chicago to Ida Marie Honore. By mid-November the couple had returned to Lincoln with Florence Boyd. The daughter of Libbie's seminary principal now replaced Agnes Bates as Libbie's companion and the Custer quarters' newest attraction. In addition, Armstrong carried a prized possession—a "handsomely bound and attractively embellished" copy of his book, the newly published *My Life on the Plains*.[100]

Winter had already set in on the Northern Plains. The only noteworthy event that season, besides the holidays, concerned Tom Custer and George Yates's courageous trek through bitter cold to Standing Rock Agency. The two captured Rain-in-the-Face, a Sioux warrior who had boasted of killing Honsinger, Baliran, and a trooper on the banks of the Yellowstone in 1873. When they brought him back to Lincoln, Custer imprisoned him pending trial in the white man's court. Three months later, however, Rain-in-the-Face escaped and joined the Sitting Bull bands.[101]

The new commanding officer's house, now complete, was more splendid than the earlier one. Unlike most post dwellings, this included a "billiard hall, reception room and double parlor" thirty-two feet long with a bay window. Mary Adams's sister, Maria Adams, who also served as a maid at Fort Lincoln, remembered the furnishings as "beautiful." Libbie had brought with her two sets of Haviland china and extensive silver settings for her table.[102]

Armstrong's study, befitting a scholarly soldier, was the most important room. There, as they had the previous winter, Autie wrote, and Libbie sat beside him with her basket of sewing. Above their heads mounted antelopes and a black-tailed deer gazed out on the room, while from the mantel, a buffalo observed the owl, sandhill crane, mountain eagle and foxes distributed in various locations. Beside the buffalo, the grizzly looked down at jackrabbits. On the walls, Armstrong had hung pictures of his surrogate fathers—generals McClellan and Sheridan—and his closest friend, Lawrence Barrett. Over his desk he had placed a photograph of his muse—Libbie in her wedding gown.[103]

Other residents of the Custer home included the fox and stag hounds, still numbering about forty. Two or three usually sprawled by the fireplaces, while others lounged throughout the house.[104] When the temperature plunged below zero, Libbie took orphaned puppies to bed with her.[105]

With the less congenial officers stationed elsewhere, Libbie and Autie enjoyed the forty officers and their wives who made up their tightly knit community of friends. Moreover, Tom, Maggie, Boston, and Jimmi Calhoun were on hand to provide the extended family so important to both, but essential to Armstrong. Finally Florence Boyd's fresh face attracted young officers, freshly groomed and paying court to the commanding officer's wife as well. To add to their collective enjoyment, the Custers rented a piano from St. Paul, and the entire group spent many evenings listening while one of the women played. Often everyone exhausted their repertoire of songs from the recent war, their school days, or the spirituals they remembered.[106]

No chapel existed at Fort Lincoln. Most Sundays, except when an occasional itinerant preacher arrived to conduct the service, officers and their wives gathered in the Custer parlor and sang the old standard hymns used by several Protestant denominations.[107] Ministers, such as Samuel Phillips, and writers, such as Catharine Beecher and Harriet Beecher Stowe, encouraged American women to consider their homes alternative places of worship. Libbie was following their advice on a frontier post[108]

"Of all our happy days, the happiest had now come to us at Fort Lincoln," Elizabeth wrote years later. As spring arrived on the Northern Plains, "there was not an hour that we would not have recalled." And yet, while no one ever lived the unbroken idyll free from an hour's depression or a day's sickness Libbie portrayed the Custers were happier than in the past.[109] True, their dreams of wealth were as yet unrealized, but their hopes remained strong.

Husband and wife agreed with Autie's sentiments of the past summer when he had "look[ed] forward with such pleasant anticipations to our future which now seems so brimful of happiness in prospect."[110] Each day at dusk, before the lamps were lit, they watched the firelight in Armstrong's study illuminate "the large glittering eyes of the animals' heads."[111] Together they imagined the bright new possibilities tomorrow would bring and dreamed of the good time coming.

CHAPTER 10

Custer's Luck
Runs Out

L T. COL. Richard Dodge, with 400 soldiers, escorted geologists Walter P. Jenney and Henry Newton as a second Black Hills expedition left Fort Laramie on May 24, 1875. Laramie, closer to the hills than Lincoln, was under the jurisdiction of the Department of the Platte. Its commander, Gen. George Crook, was less likely to take a firm stand against intruding miners than Custer's commander, Gen. Alfred Terry, head of the Department of Dakota.[1] Instead of an exciting summer in the forested regions of the Black Hills, the Custers endured the searing heat at Lincoln.

Armstrong's fame, renewed and heightened by earlier expeditions, brought tourists to Lincoln that summer. At first he welcomed the crowds, but he soon tired of meeting strangers and began hiding. Libbie, acting as his intermediary, greeted visitors and struggled to answer questions about growing wheat in Dakota Territory. When one party insisted on seeing her husband, Elizabeth escorted them through the commanding officer's quarters, including Armstrong's study, but he was nowhere in sight. Later Mary Adams revealed that Autie had almost suffered sunstroke "hidin in the chicken-coop," a building not yet roofed.[2]

Armstrong received another group more willingly. Chief Running Antelope brought his band to Fort Lincoln to complain that corrupt Indian agents had siphoned off his people's rations, and they were destitute. After agreeing to pressure the government for new supplies, Armstrong invited the Sioux to a feast prepared by Mary Adams. Libbie, recalling his hospitality, saw her husband as "a sincere friend of the reservation Indian."[3]

In truth, Armstrong's feelings about Indians mirrored the contradictory attitudes common among his fellow countrymen and women. Dismissing novelist James Fenimore Cooper's "innocent, simple-minded being" as romantic fiction, he characterized the Indian as "a *savage* in every sense of the word; not worse, perhaps, than his white brother would be similarly born and bred, but one whose cruel and ferocious nature far exceeds that of any wild beast of the desert."[4] At the same time, however, he admired the "fearless hunter" and "matchless horseman and warrior of the Plains" and found in Indian life and lore "a book of unceasing interest."[5]

In the end, were he a tribesman, Armstrong would "prefer to cast my lot among those of my people who adhered to the free open plains, rather than submit to the confined limits of a reservation, there to be the recipient of the blessed benefits of civilization, with its vices thrown in without stint or measure."[6] Such sentiments mattered little since he saw their conquest as inevitable. "Destiny," he concluded, "seems to have so willed it, and the world looks on and nods its approval."[7] Unfortunately, Grant's peace policy, based on continued civilian control of Indian affairs, represented the major impediment to achieving this foreordained conclusion as rapidly and thus humanely as possible[8]

The policy's objective, similar to those pursued by earlier administrations, sought to force Indians onto reservations where they would become settled Christian farmers. Its means, however, differed. Given the endemic corruption among Indian agents, unpaid philanthropists now oversaw the dispersal of appropriations. New agents and superintendents, supplied by religious denominations, especially the Society of Friends, staffed many Southern and Central Plains agencies. Finally, the peace policy decreed that Indians on reservations remained subject to the Bureau of Indian Affairs under the Department of the Interior. Off the reservation they fell under the army's jurisdiction, which bore responsibility for policing them.[9]

The peace policy, although well intended, had created new problems. Many Indians, dissatisfied with the grim realities of their new life, used the reservation as a base for raids and then returned to it as a "city of refuge." Thus the task of distinguishing between friendly and hostile Indians, never easy in the past, was now more complicated.[10] Moreover, while ethical standards had improved at some agencies, low salaries encouraged even some denominational representatives to cheat the Indians. Furthermore, the Grant administration itself was riddled with corruption. Recently, Columbus Delano, the secretary of the interior, had added a new element. In 1874, he had rescinded licenses at upper Missouri agencies until traders paid a kickback to the president's younger brother, Orvil Grant.[11]

Custer, like many other officers, saw administration policy as unfair to the military. As long as corruption flourished, many Indians remained sullen and dissatisfied. When conflict arose, however, soldiers, rather than agents or officials, risked their lives in combat. Thus justice dictated, he argued, that the Department of the Interior relinquish the Bureau of Indian Affairs to the War Department.[12] Western frontiersmen and railroad interests agreed. The military, they thought, would respond more swiftly to depredations and bring a quicker end to the "Indian Problem."[13]

That summer, Armstrong became involved in more than hosting Indian chiefs. Although he did not lead the 1875 expedition, he still provided information anonymously to James Gordon Bennett, Jr.'s, *New York Herald*, a leading mouthpiece for the Democratic party.[14] Armstrong also supplied information to Ralph Meeker, the *Herald's* reporter. Masquerading in Bismarck as J. D. Thompson, Meeker investigated graft in the War Department through the sale of post traderships. Armstrong told him, for example, that Robert Seip, the trader at Fort Lincoln, had paid $12,000 to a middleman for his post but recovered his expenses and a hefty profit besides by monopolizing the soldiers' trade and charging them "exorbitant" prices for goods.[15]

Ironically, two army men alleged that Custer himself may have been involved in similar activities. Benteen maintained that between 1867 and 1869, his commander demanded payoffs from sutlers. When they refused, Custer forbade his men to patronize the traders. Those who disobeyed at Fort Hays had "their heads shaved, and [were] trumpeted around camp to tune of 'Rogues' March.'" At Fort McPherson they were immersed in the Platte River.[16] Later, Benteen asserted, Augustus Baliran paid Custer $1,100 as a kickback before his death on the Yellowstone in 1873.[17]

Another officer, Lt. George D. Wallace, had written his father during the Yellowstone Expedition that Custer split additional compensation with the captain of the supply steamboat accompanying the Seventh up the Missouri. Since the boat earned an extra twenty dollars an hour when docked, that "explains why Custer makes such short marches."[18] Later, Benteen stated that, during the Black Hills Expedition, Custer had worked out a "partnership" with sutler John Smith, similar to the one enjoyed earlier with Baliran.[19]

Whatever the truth of the allegations, Custer constantly sought ways to augment his army income. In June 1875, as Darius Hall concluded that the Stevens Mine was about to turn a profit, Custer told him to sell out his share for whatever it would bring.[20] Then, in August, Custer received a letter from an old friend, Rufus Ingalls, now acting quartermaster general of the army. Ingalls and Ben Holladay, the stagecoach magnate and a disreputable businessman even for that era were planning several projects.

"We want to do a big [thing] in the Black Hills." Ingalls confided. "Ben wants to put in Stages and be Sutler to new Posts." Moreover, Holladay had "promise of Interior for Indian trade . . . Now, what think you! Ben counts much on you. . . . Now, what should he do to be in right *place* at right *time*."[21] What Ingalls and Holladay really wanted, in all probability, was Custer's advance knowledge of where in the Black Hills Sheridan planned to build new forts. If Holladay learned that fact, he could acquire the sutlership before bidding by other traders raised the price.[22]

The army also needed a new supply of horseshoes. If a board were created with Custer "as President," it could award contracts to the Goodenough and Elastic companies. Although Ingalls lobbied for these firms, he had no illusions about the quality of their products, "about which I am doubtful more than the half the time."[23] While no evidence, apart from this letter, links Armstrong to either scheme, months later, Holladay cosigned a sizable note for one of Custer's loans.[24]

At the conclusion of their expedition, professors Jenney and Newton reported that gold, existing in the Black Hills in modest quantities, would require costly equipment to extract. Their realistic assessment came too late to prevent a stampede of miners into the region. By midsummer as many as 1,500 miners had encroached on Sioux territory. General Crook ordered them out by August 15 after first allowing them to register their claims.[25] The Grant administration, bowing to the inevitable, now pressured the Sioux to sell their land.[26]

Treaty Indians, angered by the incursions into Paha Sapa, were joined by even more belligerent nontreaties as they met in September with the members of the Allison Commission not far from Red Cloud Agency. After days of increasing rancor, it became clear that few Sioux, let alone three-fourths, would ever agree to sell their land. When negotiations broke down entirely, the Allison Commission returned to Washington, frustrated and angry. Its members now advised the Grant administration to appraise the Black Hills and force the Sioux to sell at a set price.[27]

Early in September, as these events unfolded, Secretary of War William W. Belknap toured the recently established Yellowstone Park. Stopping at Bismarck, he spent two hours at Fort Lincoln. Custer, who saw Belknap as the ultimate profiteer from his department's corruption, told a committee later that he cooly received the secretary's party in his quarters and returned unopened the wine Seip had sent him for the occasion.[28]

Lt. Col. James W. Forsyth, Sheridan's aide and defender of the Grant administration, accompanied Belknap and remembered the incident differently. Armstrong, recovering from dysentery, had left his sick bed to greet Belknap's party in uniform in his quarters before driving them around the post. Libbie, always a gracious hostess, had entreated the party to have lunch with the officers' wives. Unfortunately, to Libbie's "regret," the secretary's busy schedule had necessitated an early departure.[29]

That same month the Custers, including Tom, traveled east. After stopping in Monroe, Libbie stayed with her cousin Rebecca in nearby Grand Rapids before traveling to see relatives in Canandaigua, New York.[30] Armstrong journeyed to New York City, where he met with his publishers, Sheldon and Company. He also visited Bennett of the *New York Herald*, and August Belmont, owner of the *New York World*. Like Bennett, Belmont was a leading figure in the Democratic party. Later at the Lotus Club, a gathering of artists, actors, and writers lauded Armstrong as author and Indian fighter and enthusiastically applauded his extemporaneous remarks.[31]

On November 3, President Grant met with Secretary Belknap; generals Sheridan and Crook; E. P. Smith, the commissioner of Indian affairs; Benjamin Cowen, assistant secretary of the interior; and a new head of the Interior, Zachariah Chandler. The latter had replaced Delano, who had resigned October 1, following disclosures of extensive corruption within his department. Unlike his predecessor, Chandler took a harsh stance towards Indians, which probably accounted for his selection. The Grant administration needed the right man in the right place as it confronted two unattractive prospects.[32] Either it ordered the military to move against the growing number of miners and settlers invading the Black Hills, or it subdued the nontreaties, who had been so vocal a force in the recent uproar attending the Sioux meetings with the Allison Commission.[33]

As the conference concluded, an agreement was reached. While official policy would still preclude miners from the Black Hills, the army would ignore them. The increasing settlement would put additional pressure on the Sioux to cede their land. Finally, all concurred that the days of freedom for the nontreaties were over. They had to be forced onto reservations where they could be controlled. As soon as Sheridan left that meeting, he began planning a winter campaign.[34]

Before then, however, the Grant administration, ever mindful of the Peace party in Congress and eastern humanitarians, had to mount a propaganda campaign. E. C. Watkins, Indian inspector and former "cog in Zachariah Chandler's political machine," was also a personal friend from Civil War days of both Sheridan and Crook. Whether he wrote the report bearing his name or signed one the generals had already prepared, it made no mention of white violations of the Treaty of Fort Laramie. Instead, it emphasized the increase of "wild and hostile" bands in unceded territory and called for their "subjection" to assure public safety.[35] With that report in hand, Chandler now issued an ultimatum. Early in December, runners left the Sioux agencies to tell the Sitting Bull bands that those who failed to report to reservations by January 31, 1876, "would be forced there by the army."[36]

By Christmas, Libbie had joined Armstrong in New York City. She later recalled their pleasure, despite their inability to afford fashionable clothes. Her husband wore an outdated ulster as his overcoat, but such shabbiness bothered him little. "No one so perfectly independent as he was could fail to enjoy everything."[37] Or so she wrote. In reality, Armstrong thought constantly of increasing his income. As the year ended, he contacted his old rival, Wesley Merritt, asking about chances for promotion. Merritt, also a lieutenant colonel, saw little hope since many officers had more seniority than either one.[38]

By now, Armstrong's financial affairs were in chaos. He had become involved in what one historian calls "a wild stock speculation" totaling transactions of $389,983.[39] Without using his own money, Armstrong had instructed Emil Justh, a Wall Street broker, to buy railroad stocks. Had they increased in value, Custer would have pocketed the difference. Unfortunately, he had guessed wrong, and six months of what a court would later call "pretended sale" and "pretended purchasing" had left him owing $8,578. Unable to pay, he signed a six-month -promissory note on February 10, 1876, at 7 percent to Justh and Company. His cosigner was Ben Holladay.[40]

Armstrong always believed in Custer's luck. As he faced this large and troubling debt, a new opportunity arose, which promised the earnings he had long sought. Redpath Lyceum Bureau, a booking agency for lecture tours, offered him five speaking engagements a week for four to five months at $200 each night.[41] Libbie, anxious to help Autie overcome his tendency to talk too fast, had a solution. She would monitor his delivery, and when he lost his audience, "raise an umbrella as a warning to slacken up!"[42]

Whatever their indebtedness, the Custers rented rooms on Fifth Avenue across from the Hotel Brunswick and dined at Delmonico's. Catching up on the cultural activities they missed at a frontier post, they applauded their friend Lawrence Barrett in *Julius Caesar*. They also visited Albert Bierstadt in his studio, where he invited the couple to lunch. Later Armstrong noted with pride that his wife had attracted a host of male admirers at a gathering of the New York Historical Society.[43]

As the Custers savored these eastern pleasures, far to the west, the Sitting Bull bands paid the Grant administration's ultimatum little heed. (Some may not have heard of it until after the January 31 deadline.) Instead, many reservation Sioux, increasingly hostile because of poor rations and the growing number of miners pouring into the Black Hills, looked forward to joining their nontreaty cousins in unceded territory as soon as weather permitted.[44]

On February 1, 1876, Secretary Chandler turned the Sitting Bull bands over to the military. Sheridan now instructed Crook and Terry to prepare for a winter campaign. As he envisioned it, Crook would march northeastward out of Fort Fetterman, Wyoming Territory, while Terry would send an expedition under Custer westward from Fort Lincoln. The two columns would converge on the roaming bands in the Yellowstone River Valley.[45]

Terry, recognizing the dangers and difficulties of supplying and moving troops on the Northern Plains during winter months, expressed serious reservations. Instead, he conferred with Custer at department headquarters in St. Paul on February 15, shortly after Armstrong's leave had ended. Six days later, Terry, who lacked experience fighting Indians, wrote Sheridan of his plans. He proposed to turn his subaltern loose after establishing "a secure base well up on the Yellowstone from which he can operate, at which he can find supplies, and which he can retire at any time the Indians gather in too great numbers for the small force he will have." Custer would leave Fort Lincoln for the Yellowstone on April 6.[46]

Heavy snow had immobilized the Northern Pacific. Officials of the railroad, grateful for Custer's past services, outfitted a special train with three locomotives and two plows for the couple and a few other passengers, including soldiers from the Twentieth Infantry. On March 7, the day after the train left the station, a blizzard struck the Northern Plains. As the snow piled in huge drifts, the train struck a gully sixty-five miles from Bismarck. The Custers were stranded almost a week before a fellow traveler relayed a telegraph message to Fort Lincoln.[47] When Tom learned that the "old lady" was with his brother, he hired a Bismarck stage driver and braved the drifts. After a seemingly interminable ride through a vast plain of snow, the Custers and their surrogate children—three hounds—reached the post on March 13.[48]

The same blizzard had also affected another commander. On March 1, General Crook, with 800 infantry and cavalry, had left Fort Fetterman in severe weather, moving along the old Bozeman Trail. As the snow piled higher and temperatures plummeted, his soldiers' morale and stamina declined. When scouts sighted a village of Northern Cheyennes (with a few Oglalas) on the Powder River, Crook sent Col. J. J. Reynolds ahead with six companies of the Third Cavalry. Although Reynolds attacked the village, and a fierce battle ensued, he failed to hold it. Discouraged, Crook marched back to Fetterman in twenty-below-zero weather.[49]

The battle, nonetheless, had important consequences. The Cheyennes took down their tipis. Despite their casualties, they made the three-day trek through the snow to reach the village of Crazy Horse to the northeast, sustaining additional losses along the way. After they told the Oglala Sioux chief their story, he realized that war was imminent. As the combined bands moved westward across the Powder, Tongue, and Rosebud rivers, they spread the word to other bands, who joined them for mutual defense. Along the way, they also transmitted a heightened sense of pride. Indians had forced the soldiers to retreat.[50]

Two days after arriving at Lincoln, Custer received a telegram from Rep. Heister Clymer, the chairman of the House Committee on Expenditures in the War Department. It summoned him to Washington to testify on corruption in Belknap's War Department. The committee had evidence that Belknap had sold a post tradership at Fort Sill to Caleb P. Marsh, and even though Belknap had resigned on March 2 to avoid impeachment, Clymer had expanded the investigation. Fuller disclosure of similar corruption at other posts could embarrass the Grant administration during an election year.[51] Given the dangers late blizzards still posed to travelers, Libbie remained at Lincoln.[52]

In Washington, Autie described a city where spring had already arrived, where the grass was "green and growing" and ladies were "promenading in front of the hotel, carrying parasols and dressed lightly." By April 1, Armstrong had appeared before the Clymer committee. If the investigation led to impeachment proceedings against Belknap, he doubted they would call him.[53] On April 4, Custer testified again, presenting what Lt. Col. James

Forsyth characterized as "hearsay." Whatever its legal value, Custer's testimony served the Democrats. If they won the national election, key figures might remember his contribution.[54]

On April 8 Autie wrote Libbie, congratulating her on her thirty-fourth birthday. The night before, he had attended a dinner given him by Sen. Thomas Bayard, "whose gentlemanly instincts and manly bearing justify the title Chevalier." Some spoke of Bayard as a possible Democratic presidential nominee, but Armstrong thought it unlikely.[55] The next day, Armstrong dined with Rep. Henry Banning. As the chairman of the Committee on Military Affairs, he had recently given a speech favoring the transfer of the Indian Bureau from the Department of the Interior to the War Department. Banning told Custer, "some of his strongest points" had come from his book, sometimes quoting him "word for word."[56] Armstrong had also learned that General Crook had preferred charges against Colonel Reynolds "for his failure during the recent action against the Sioux, which Crook attributed to cowardice." This showed, Autie noted, "it is not every Tom, Dick and Harry who can conduct a successful campaign against Indians."[57]

Detained longer than expected, Armstrong spent his evenings working on additional articles for *Galaxy*. He also thanked Libbie for the poems she continuously sent him, noting that one woman who had seen them observed, "Your sweetheart sent them. Never your wife." Armstrong had assured her, "Both are one."[58] He also told Libbie of the many compliments he had received on his writing. Sen. Samuel Maxey of Texas maintained, "'No man in the United States Army could wield as powerful a pen as' your dear bo."[59] Later, General Sherman had warned Custer, "You write so well and made such an interesting story that some people are not willing to give you the credit of it but say your wife wrote it." Armstrong responded, "Well Genl in that case they ought to give me credit for exercising both sound judgment and good taste in selecting such a wife."[60]

On April 20, Armstrong, released from the hearings, left Washington. Instead of hurrying to Fort Lincoln, he visited the Centennial Exposition in Philadelphia. April 23 found him in New York City meeting with Belmont. Later he stopped at Sheldon and Company and inquired about sales of *My Life on the Plains*. He also talked with *Galaxy* editors about his Yellowstone series and the beginning installments of his Civil War memoirs, now in print. Then he made plans with Redpath for a fall tour, since both sides agreed that success against the Sioux would bring larger crowds. Armstrong also stopped in the *New York Herald* office to discuss the coming political campaign.[61]

"My Precious Sunbeam—I cannot express my amazement, disappointment. I am stopped, ordered to return to Washington," Libbie read in Autie's letter dated April 25. The day before, the Senate had summoned him to appear at Belknap's impeachment hearing.[62] Very likely either Belknap's supporters or Grant himself stood behind the summons. Custer's testimony against Belknap had implicated not only War Department officials and traders but also Orvil Grant and John Dent, the president's brother-in-law. Thus when Sherman approached the new secretary of war, Alphonso Taft, on April 27 and asked that Custer be released to rejoin his command, Grant intervened. Someone else would lead the Seventh in the coming campaign.[63]

By April 29, the Senate committee granted Armstrong permission to leave Washington, but, on Sherman's advice, he remained behind to see the president. Earlier he had tried twice to pay Grant a courtesy call. On May 1, Custer waited five hours before his friend, Rufus Ingalls, interceded on his behalf. It was no use; Grant would not see him. When Armstrong visited the War Department to confer with Sherman, the general had gone.[64]

Custer, assuming he had received permission from both the Senate committee and Sherman to return to his post, left Washington.[65] In Chicago, as he boarded a train for St. Paul, a porter handed him a copy of General Sherman's telegraph to Sheridan. It stated that Custer should not have left without first seeing Sherman and Grant and, therefore, should be halted.[66] Frantically, Custer telegraphed Sherman several times but to no avail. At last on May 5, he received permission to return to Fort Lincoln. When the Seventh left under Terry he would remain behind.

At Terry's St. Paul departmental headquarters next day, Custer, "with tears in his eyes," pleaded for his superior's help. The kind-hearted general dictated a diplomatic telegraph under Custer's name. It besieged Grant "as a soldier to spare me the humiliation of seeing my regiment march to meet the enemy and I not to share its dangers." Terry, mindful of his lack of experience against Indians, added respectfully, "Lieutenant Colonel Custer's services would be very valuable with his regiment.[67]

Anti-administration papers now charged the president with punishing Custer to deter others who might testify on corruption in his administration. Grant knew that if the Sioux campaign failed, he faced even greater criticism. On May 8, Custer learned he would accompany the Seventh as Terry's subordinate.[68] Elated, Armstrong left Terry's office. Outside department headquarters he met Captain Ludlow, his old friend from West Point and the Yellowstone and Black Hills expeditions. Sharing with him the good news, Custer boasted that he planned to "cut loose" from his commander. After all, he had "got away with Stanley and would be able to swing clear of Terry."[69]

"Although we had seen the men start out on many long campaigns, in those seven years on the plains, we knew that this was different, and we all felt that it might have very serious results," Libbie recalled years later. She and the other women at Lincoln had braced themselves for a long campaign. They had heard "the Indians were giving a great deal of trouble and General Sheridan wanted to crush the uprisings once and for all."[70] While Libbie was anxious, she, nonetheless, had faith in "Custer's luck" and "never really believed anything could happen to my husband." He had escaped death so many times that she thought he lived "a charmed life. No matter what he did or what the odds seemed to be against him, he always came out on top. I naturally began to think that nothing could ever hurt him."[71]

On May 17, after three days of rain had delayed its departure, the Seventh left its encampment near Fort Lincoln, accompanied by two companies of the Seventeenth Infantry, one of the Sixth, and forty Arikara scouts. The column returned to the post to say good-bye and reassure the families by giving them one last look at the size and strength of the troops assembled.

Fog enveloped the fort that morning, but Mary Manley, twelve-year-old daughter of an infantry officer, watched the procession intently. Terry and his staff appeared first, then "a medley of strange and barbaric sounds" signaled the Indian scouts. Behind them came the "Fighting Seventh," led by the band, Custer, and "his beautiful wife." Then followed the cannons and escort, the infantry, and the 150 supply wagons, which "closed the ghostly procession."[72]

Libbie never forgot the Arikara wives "crouched on the ground, too burdened with their trouble to hold up their heads." Others restrained their children, who tried to follow their fathers.[73] The column passed "soap suds row," where the laundresses, "with streaming eyes, held their little ones out at arm's length for one last look at the departing father." Years later Libbie recalled vividly: "The toddlers among the children, unnoticed by their elders, had made a mimic column of their own. With their handkerchiefs tied to stocks in lieu of flags, and beating old tin pans for drums, they strode lustily back and forth in imitation of the advancing soldiers. They were," she noted, "too young to realize why the mothers wailed out their farewells."

Finally as the band played "The Girl I Left behind Me," the officers' wives disappeared into their quarters to weep in private.[74]

As the column wound its way out of the fort through the fog and mist, "the bright sun began to penetrate this veil and dispel the haze, and a scene of wonder and beauty appeared." Ahead Libbie saw a mirage, "which took up about half of the line of cavalry, and thenceforth for a little distance it marched, equally plain to the sight on the earth and in the sky." Later, she interpreted this as an omen. "The future of the heroic band, whose days were even then numbered, seemed to be revealed, and already there seemed a premonition in the supernatural translation as their forms were reflected from the opaque mist of the early dawn."[75]

Afterwards, she recalled the sunlight, which captured "every little bit of burnished steel on the arms and equipments and . . . turned them into glittering flashes of radiating light." Periodically, her husband looked back at his men, urging her to notice "their grand appearance." He also assured her their separation would last no more than a few weeks. She might even accompany the steamer *Far West* when it traveled up the Missouri to the mouth of the Yellowstone to supply the Seventh.[76] Libbie felt comforted. Possibly the expedition was not so dangerous. After all, Armstrong had taken his eighteen-year-old nephew, Autie Reed, as forager.

Libbie and Maggie camped with their husbands the first night, alongside a small river a few miles from Lincoln. The next morning, after the soldiers received their pay, the two women said good-bye and started back with the paymaster. Libbie turned around for one last glance at the column. "It was a splendid picture. The flags and pennons were flying, the men were waving, and even the horses seemed to be arching themselves to show how fine and fit they were. My husband rode to the top of a promontory and turned around, stood up in his stirrups and waved his hat. Then they all started forward again and in a few seconds they had disappeared, horses, flags, men, and ammunition. And we never saw them again."[77]

At Lincoln Elizabeth struggled to master her fears, for "with my husband's departure, my last happy days in the garrison were ended, as a premonition of disaster that I had never known before weighed me down."[78] She spent her days painting and tending a new supply of chickens. Although the days were hot, "the nights," she wrote Autie, "are cool. The lights about hills and valleys are exquisite." Nevertheless, the trumpeter's calls left her "heartsick. I do not wish to be reminded of the Cavalry."[79]

Elizabeth had heard stories of the Washita campaign many times. While she stated that overall strategy made little impression on her, very likely she understood the similarities between that campaign and proposals for defeating the Sitting Bull bands. Plans called for converging columns, so successful against Black Kettle's village in 1868 and later used in the Red River War of 1874–75 against the Kiowas, Comanches, and Southern Cheyennes and Southern Arapahoes.[80] Since no one knew, however, the precise location of the roving bands of nontreaty Sioux and their allies, the coordinated action so effective earlier would be difficult to achieve this time.[81]

Nonetheless, two columns were already in motion. From the west, moving east, Col. John Gibbon, commander of the Seventh Infantry, had left Fort Ellis, Montana Territory, on April 2. With him were about 500 troops composed of his regiment and companies of the Second Cavalry. Presently they patrolled the north bank of the Yellowstone to prevent Sitting Bull's bands from escaping into Canada. Terry and Custer had already moved westward out of Fort Lincoln on May 17, and later that month, General Crook would again move northward out of Fort Fetterman.

These columns planned to converge, not simultaneously, but rather to prevent the Indians from fleeing northward into Canada or southward into the Big Horn Mountains. All campaign planners and participants believed that any one of the three columns could defeat the hostiles. They saw the real problem as catching the Indians, rather than fighting them, although Custer's earlier battles against the Sioux on the Yellowstone had provided ample reason to reconsider that widely held assumption.[82]

While newspapers reported the hostiles might harbor as many as 5,000 warriors, the army, basing its calculations on estimates provided by post traders (with a vested interest in inflating the number of Indians' on reservations), privately fixed the number at 800. Later reports revised this to 1,500.[83] Whether 800 or 1,500, either size, it was thought, could easily be handled. Even if the Indians chose to fight rather than flee, Custer and the other officers believed that the disciplined and well-trained Seventh Cavalry, with a force of about 600 men, could overcome two or three times that number.[84]

Terry's most recent reports convinced him that Sitting Bull's bands were on the Little Missouri River or between it and the Yellowstone. Thus his column marched in that direction, following the Northern Pacific survey line. Four days out, Armstrong wrote Libbie that constant rain and bad roads had slowed their progress, leaving them "only forty-six miles from home."[85] By May 30, he had moved ahead of the column, riding "fifty miles over a rough country, unknown to everybody, and only myself for a guide." Libbie, who always found such statements unnerving, read with relief that reports of many Indians waiting at the Little Missouri were "the merest bosh. None have been here for six months, not even a small hunting-party."[86]

Towards the end of May, the *Far West* docked at Fort Lincoln to take on additional supplies for troops in the field. Libbie and Nettie Smith invited Capt. Grant Marsh to lunch, and afterwards, asked to accompany the steamer to the Yellowstone. Marsh refused, noting the dangers and discomforts of such a trip, although had he brought the *Josephine*, a more comfortable vessel, he might have agreed.[87] Disappointed, Libbie endured her ordeal of waiting, made worse by the fear permeating Lincoln. With few soldiers left at the fort, she and the other wives were afraid Indians might attack.[88]

Elizabeth also found the constant rumors that young Indians were leaving the reservation and joining the Sitting Bull bands frightening. Unfortunately, given the unhappiness treaty Indians felt over the invasion of the Black Hills and the government's ultimatum ordering them out of unceded territory, the rumors were true. She also believed that the Indians were better equipped with weapons than the soldiers. She had seen, she maintained, "a steamer touching at our landing its freight of Springfield rifles piled up on the decks en route for the Indians up the river." The Seventh, by contrast, had "only the short-range carbines that grew foul after the second firing."[89]

During the evenings, officers' wives gathered on porches for comfort and companionship. After conversing awhile, they sang, accompanied by Katie Gibson's guitar. Recently, Katie, acting on a premonition, had insisted that her husband decline Custer's offer to transfer him from Rice to Lincoln. In the present campaign, Lieutenant Gibson remained in Captain Benteen's battalion.[90]

Armstrong's letter to Libbie of June 9 described the column's movement into territory "heretofore unvisited by white men." Even his scout, Charley Reynolds, had "lost his way," but Armstrong had stepped forward and guided the troops "through the worst kind of Bad Lands." He had other news. He had just completed another *Galaxy* article, "which will go out in the next mail; so, you see, I am not entirely idle."[91]

That same day, Terry met Colonel Gibbon aboard the *Far West*. For the first time Terry learned that scouts had sighted the hostiles, not on the Little

Missouri but in the Rosebud Valley. On that basis, Terry planned the rest of the campaign.[92] He ordered Gibbon back to the mouth of the Rosebud. To be certain, however, that the Sioux had not moved east, Terry instructed Major Reno to scout the Powder and Tongue river valleys. "If you will look at the map near my desk you will find the mouth of the Powder River and our present location on the Yellowstone, about due west from Lincoln," Armstrong wrote Libbie on June 11. She found his letter, retrieved from the Yellowstone after a boat had capsized, hard to read. "Follow up the Yellowstone a short distance," she deciphered, "and the first stream you come to is the Tongue River, to which point we will move after resting three or four days." Once Reno returned, he wrote, "I shall then select the nine companies to go with me."[93]

On June 17 the column camped at the mouth of the Tongue. Along the way, they had seen "some very extensive Indian villages — rather the remains of the villages occupied by them last winter," Libbie now read. At one site, Custer had found a skull in the ashes of a fire and nearby a cavalry uniform. He thought the skull belonged to "some poor mortal who had been a prisoner in the hands of the savages, and who doubtless had been tortured to death, probably burned." Turning to a more pleasant subject, he awaited the arrival of the *Josephine* and mail from Libbie, "unless, by good-luck, you should be on board; you might just as well be here as not. . . . I hope," he added, "to begin another *Galaxy* article, if the spirit is favorable."[94]

While Libbie had clamored to accompany the *Far West*, she decided against boarding the *Josephine*. Indians had fired on one steamer.[95] Besides, as she wrote Autie on June 21, if she had gone and missed him, "I would find myself so disappointed, without employment (which is my safety valve you know) and so *public* as I would be on the steamer." Later, she learned that he had started on his scout. She was certain she had not "acted unwisely. But oh it is so hard to think I might have seen you for a few days & missed it."[96]

Their separation had lasted five weeks, and, during that time, Libbie's fear had mounted. "Oh Autie I feel as if it was almost impossible for me to wait your return with patience. I cannot describe my feelings. I have felt so badly for the last few days I have been perfectly unendurable to every one. Most of the time I have spent in my room, feeling my self no addition to any one's society." Nonetheless, the knowledge that Armstrong was "where steamers can reach you" gave her some comfort. "When you get back from *this* scout, if we have no bad news I shall then feel as if the worst of the summer was over."[97]

She had other news as well. "An account of a small *skirmish* Gen Crooks cavalry had with Indians is called a fight. But the Indians were very bad and don't seem one bit afraid."[98] The outcome was worse than Libbie knew. On June 17, Crook's column had halted for mid-morning coffee, when suddenly Sioux warriors, led by Crazy Horse, appeared. Seizing the initiative, they fought in an unusually unified fashion. Although Crook eventually drove the hostiles away, he feared an ambush farther north and retreated with his wounded to his camp on Goose Creek.[99]

Indians were not the only danger threatening Armstrong. Newspapers reported that Belknap's prosecutors wanted Custer to reappear, and the implications frightened Elizabeth. "The radicals have selected such a good man," she noted, referring to Rutherford B. Hayes, the Republican nominee, that "the Democrats stand no show." Armstrong, having served the Democrats perhaps too well, would suffer at the hands of a Hayes administration. "Politicians will try to make something out of *you* and only for their selfish ends."[100]

She had just finished his latest *Galaxy* article. While she liked it, she wished he had not spoken so candidly about McClellan "*for motives of policy alone.*" Moreover, his recent criticism of the Department of the Interior, "finished Mr Chandler as a friend. For that," she noted, "I am sorry for though late years only a passive friend still he can be a very tenacious enemy. I doubt if he ever forgives this last article. I honestly think you would be far better with *some* policy. I do not think," Libbie advised her husband, "you have yet reached that [wood?] on the ladder you are climbing to be able to dare to bid defiance to such powerful enemies." Apologetically, she added, "A cautious wife is a great bore isn't she Autie?"[101]

Elizabeth also noted that her husband's recent dispatches, intended for the *New York World*, had been "partly burned so as to be impossible to decypher them & your letter to the World editor lost."[102] To replace these, "Maggie copied & wrote Jimmi's dispatches as best she could & at her request I wrote a few lines to Mr Hulbert," explaining the situation. "I do hope & trust," she added, "that your communications for the *Herald* & *Galaxy* were all right." As for Autie's recent work, "I think you have done so marvelously well to write a *Galaxy* article. How can I praise you enough?" Wife, trusted confidant, and mother figure, she registered her approval. "To ride as you do, endure all sorts of weather & fatigue and then write for publication is perfectly wonderful. I am delighted."[103]

Ever the moral authority in her husband's life, Libbie sought to improve him further. She warned him "never never play poker on the march again since your literary tastes are even cultivated in the field when most men are idleness itself. You don't need to do as other men do." Self improvement was his task in life, and he must "go on improving under any circumstances. I see that nothing daunts you in your desire for improvement and culture. I wish that your lines had fallen among literary geniuses."[104] Then Libbie closed her letter with a heart-felt plea. "With your bright future and the knowledge that you are positive use to your day and generation, do you not see that your life is precious on that account, and not only because an idolizing wife could not live without you. . . . I shall go to bed and dream of my dear Bo."[105]

Autie never received her letter.

On June 21, the day Libbie wrote the above, Armstrong had news of his own. "Look on my map and you will find our present location on the Yellowstone, about midway between Tongue river and the Big Horn." Reno had returned from scouting, not only the Powder and Tongue river valleys, but the Rosebud River Valley as well. He had seen the remains of a month-old village in the Tongue Valley and its more recent deserted site along the Rosebud. Custer, angry that Reno had not pursued the trail to the next site, about a day and a half away, now planned to "take up the trail where the scouting-party turned back." He had no fear of the hostiles, worrying instead about the "valuable time lost." Still, he looked forward to "accomplishing great results."[106]

Terry was also annoyed with Reno for exceeding his instructions by scouting along the Rosebud. But Reno had discovered important information. Sitting Bull's bands no longer camped on the Rosebud. They could have moved in several directions, but to avoid a collision with their enemies, the Crow, they had probably moved towards the Little Bighorn River.[107] Given that probability, Armstrong now participated in a new plan. The mobile Seventh would strike out after the Indians, and once located, drive them against a less mobile blocking force, Gibbon's infantry.[108] Thus Armstrong's instructions were "to move directly up the valley of the Rosebud," while simultaneously, "General Gibbon's command and General Terry, with steamer, will proceed up the Big Horn as far as the boat can go."[109]

Armstrong was on his own in more ways than one. "I like campaigning with pack-mules much better than with wagons, leaving out the question of luxuries. We take no tents and desire none." Gibbon had given him the Crow Indian scouts, "as they are familiar with the country." Armstrong described them as "magnificent-looking men, so much handsomer and more Indian-like than any we have ever seen." They, in turn, "had heard that I never abandoned a trail; that when my food gave out I ate mule. That was the kind of a man they wanted to fight under; they were willing to eat mule too."[110]

The next day Libbie received an exultant letter from her husband, dated June 22, 11 A.M. "My Darling—I have but a few moments to write as we start at twelve, and I have my hands full of preparations for the scout. Do not be anxious about me," it began. "You will be surprised how closely I obey your instructions about keeping with the column. I hope to have a good report to send you by the next mail. A success will start us all toward Lincoln."[111]

Autie enclosed "an extract from Genl. Terry's official order, knowing how keenly you appreciate words of commendation and confidence in your dear Bo." In it Libbie read: "It is of course impossible to give you any definite instructions in regard to this movement, and, were it not impossible to do so, the Department Commander places too much confidence in your zeal, energy and ability to impose on you precise orders which might hamper your action when nearly in contact with the enemy."[112]

Terry's orders in their entirety were not read by Libbie until later, when they became the source of great controversy. After Autie's excerpt, the commander of the Department of the Dakota had continued: "He [Terry] will, however, indicate to you his views of what your action should be, and he desires that you should conform to them unless you shall see sufficient reason for departing from them." According to Terry's orders,

> You should proceed up the Rosebud until you ascertain definitely the direction in which the trail above spoken of leads. Should it be found (as it appears almost certain that it will be found) to turn towards the Little Horn, he thinks that you should still proceed southward, perhaps as far as the headwaters of the Tongue, and then turn towards the Little Horn, feeling constantly, however, to your left, so as to preclude the possibility of the escape of the Indians to the south or southeast by passing around your left flank.

Terry had placed himself in command of Gibbon's forces, and the rest of the campaign would proceed in this manner:

> The column of Colonel Gibbon is now in motion for the mouth of the Big Horn. As soon as it reaches that point it will cross the Yellowstone and move up at least as far as the forks of the Big and Little Horns. Of

course its future movements must be controlled by circumstances as they arise, but it is hoped that the Indians, if upon the Little Horn, may be so nearly inclosed by the two columns that their escape will be impossible.

As he scouted the Rosebud, Custer was told to "thoroughly examine the upper part of Tullock's Creek, and . . . endeavor to send a scout through to Colonel Gibbon's column with the information of the result of your examination." Gibbon, in turn, would scout lower Tullock's Creek. Finally, Terry planned to send the supply steamer "up the Big Horn as far as the forks if the river is found to be navigable for that distance." Custer was to report to Terry at that place "not later than the expiration of the time for which your troops are rationed, unless in the mean time you receive further orders."[113]

Terry's orders gave Custer the broadest flexibility in unforeseen circumstances. The Seventh's commander carried with him enough rations to last fifteen days, so he could continue his pursuit if the Indians were in flight. At the same time there was a plan subject to changing circumstances. Custer was to follow the Indian trail southward up the Rosebud. If the trail turned west towards the Little Bighorn, his instructions told him to stay on the Rosebud, for the Indians must not be allowed to escape by moving south or east. At the Tongue's headwaters, he was to move down the Little Bighorn from the south.

All this presupposed that time had to be allotted for Gibbon and Terry to march westward and then southward along the Bighorn before arriving on the Little Bighorn. Terry estimated their arrival times as June 26.[114] No one knew that the third element in this campaign—Crook—was no longer on his way northward.

As Custer left that day, he declined Terry's offer to take with him Maj. James Brisbin's battalion of the Second Cavalry and two Gatling guns. Very likely, Custer had no intention of sharing a victory with another regiment. The Gatling guns, moreover, would slow him down given the difficult terrain his regiment faced.[115] Besides, since Reno's scout had discovered 380 lodges, Terry, Custer, and Gibbon estimated the number of warriors they would find at 800, the figure usually given Sitting Bull's bands alone, with no additional agency Indians. But even if the Seventh encountered twice that number, Custer never doubted the outcome. As he had told Capt. William Thompson eight years earlier, "There are not Indians enough in the country to whip the Seventh Cavalry."[116] When Custer's column appeared before Terry at noon, prior to departing, Colonel Gibbon called out, "Don't be greedy now, Custer. Leave some for us." Armstrong replied, in one of his characteristic mixed-message statements, "No, I will not."[117] Then he rode to the head of his column.

On Sunday morning, June 25, the families at Lincoln awoke to an alarm. Twenty-five mounted Indians had been sighted, but to everyone's relief, all had reservation passes.[118] Later that day, Mary Manley remembered Annie Yates playing with her children. The adolescent watched the young mother "run up the hill, bareheaded and laughing, with her abundant black hair, escaping from its fastenings and her husband was to die that day, although she knew it not."[119]

In the afternoon, the wives on post met to sing their usual Sunday hymns. This time, despite their efforts, they found no comfort in the familiar songs. One young wife "threw herself on the carpet and pillowed her head in the lap of a tender friend. Another," Libbie recalled, "sat dejected at the piano and struck soft chords that melted into the notes of their voices." When someone recommended "Nearer, My God, to Thee," another pleaded, "Not that one, dear."[120]

July Fourth came, more festive than ever since the country was celebrating its centennial. Although Libbie had little interest in attending a ball, she went with the sutler's younger brother.[121] The next evening the ladies of the regiment, whose husbands served at Fort Rice, came together on Katie Gibson's porch. Again they sang while Katie accompanied them on her guitar. When they came to "Annie Laurie," popularized by British troops in the Crimean War, all thought of Balaklava and the charge of the light brigade.[122]

Finishing the song, the women, sweltering in the intense heat, lingered on the porch, reluctant to go inside. Just before tattoo, they noticed groups of soldiers congregating and talking excitedly. Suddenly one of the Indian scouts, Horn Toad, ran to them and announced, "Custer killed. Whole command killed." Katie dropped her guitar while others looked on in stunned silence. Finally, Catherine Benteen stepped forward and asked, "How do you know, Horn Toad?" He replied: "Speckled Cock, Indian scout, just come. Rode pony many miles Pony tired. Indian tired. Say Custer shoot himself—at end. Say all dead."[123]

Katie, remembering her husband's admonition not to believe rumors, cried out, "Oh, that's too sweeping, though there may have been a brush." Since Custer's regiment was under Terry's command, it seemed impossible that an entire command could be wiped out. Nonetheless, those without children remained together at Eliza DeRudio's home. After she put her children to bed, she distributed pillows. The women slept fitfully that night on the floor, listening to the chirping of crickets and, in the distance, the howls of coyotes. As Katie Gibson recalled, "The moon cast its silver cover across our impromptu beds, bringing out the pallor of our faces and accentuating our wide, staring eyes."[124]

Libbie spent the same evening in her own quarters with wives whose husbands were stationed at Lincoln. At midnight, the others returned to their homes.[125] About 2 A.M., Capt. William S. McCaskey, Twentieth Infantry, opened a message from General Terry. General Custer and five companies, totaling 261 officers and men, had been killed on June 25 at the Little Bighorn River in a battle with Sioux Indians and their Northern Cheyenne allies.

McCaskey called together the other officers at the post to ask their help in informing the widows. Then, accompanied by J. V. D. Middleton, post surgeon, and Lt. C. L. Gurley, Sixth Infantry, he went to the Custer home. Gurley knocked on the back door and told the maid, Maria Adams, to awaken Mrs. Custer. As he walked through the Custer hallway to admit the other two men, Libbie called out from her bedroom, asking why he was there. Gurley made no response but instead opened the front door and escorted the other men into the parlor.

Soon Libbie, Maggie Calhoun, and Emma Reed joined them. As the captain read his dispatch, the women wept. Elizabeth knew, however, that, as the post commander's wife, she must accompany these men as they told the other widows. Shivering despite the intense heat, she asked for a wrap, placed it on her shoulders, and stepped outside. Suddenly, Maggie ran after them, calling out, "Is there no message for me?" All turned and looked at her. There was no message except, "They had all died fighting."[126]

PART TWO

THE MAKING OF

A MYTH

CHAPTER II

''Prostrated'' Widow

A MERICANS, celebrating their centennial on July 4, 1876, had little intimation that the Seventh, one of the nation's best Indian-fighting regiments, had encountered disaster.[1] Two days later, the *Bismarck Tribune*'s headlines graphically described the outcome at the Little Bighorn, and soon, the entire country knew of the event. The question now became: How had it happened? Over time, Americans pieced together many of the events leading up to the defeat, but the full story would never be known.[2]

Custer's regiment had moved up the Rosebud and on June 23 struck the trail seen earlier by Reno. Following it, the Seventh came upon a large abandoned village, where the troops found a white man's scalp, and the Indian scouts saw indications of a recent Sun Dance. As the regiment pushed on, the trail widened, and pony droppings became fresher. The tracks, now crisscrossing, confused the soldiers, although the Arikara scouts probably knew that immense numbers of Indians had recently come together.[3]

When Crow scouts returned from reconnaissance that night, Custer learned that the Indian trail turned west towards the Little Bighorn. The next morning, taking their sightings from a high ridge known as the Crow's Nest, scouts detected signs of a large Indian encampment on the lower Little Bighorn, about a day's march away.[4] Custer now made a fateful decision. Terry had instructed him to march southward up the Rosebud, orders based on the likelihood the hostiles were located on the upper Little Bighorn. Instead, they were camped directly ahead and, rather than making a detour which might allow them to escape, he decided to follow the trail westward during the night. After resting his command close to the village on June 25, he would attack early on the morning of the 26th, when Terry and Gibbon were within striking distance from the north.[5]

Unfortunately for this plan, Custer received distressing news from Tom. On the morning of the 25th, hardtack had fallen from a mule pack. When soldiers had returned to retrieve it, they encountered several Sioux prying the box open. After exchanging gunfire, the warriors fled. Custer, not knowing that these Indians headed eastward toward their agency, concluded his presence had been detected and the village alerted. Fearing the Indians would flee, he now ordered the entire regiment to advance quickly toward the Little Bighorn Valley.[6]

Upon reaching the headwaters of Ash Creek (later Reno Creek), a stream running to the first ford above the Indian village, Custer assigned one company to the pack mules and divided the regiment into three battalions. He instructed the first three companies under Captain Benteen, some 125 men, to scout to the left to make certain no Indians were on the upper Little Bighorn. Custer assigned three other companies, 140 officers and men, to Major Reno, while five companies remained with him. With the regiment thus organized, Benteen hurried off on his mission, while Custer and Reno marched down opposite sides of the creek.[7]

Arriving at the site of another deserted village, Custer halted and conferred with Reno. As they talked, interpreter Fred Girard shouted from a distance that Indians were fleeing, and dust clouds from the village appeared to confirm his statement. Custer decided to attack immediately. He ordered Reno to cross the Little Bighorn and charge the southern end of the village. As Reno understood, he would "be supported by the whole outfit."[8]

Shortly before 3 P.M., Reno reached the river's west bank and began his charge. As he neared the village, he saw increasing numbers of warriors and no sign of Custer. When the hostiles threatened to turn his left flank, Reno, fearful of being overpowered, halted and formed a defensive position in thick underbrush and trees along the river. As warriors ignited the shrubs and fired heavily from all sides, the rattled major ordered his men out of the timber to the high bluffs across the river. In the din of battle, many never heard the order, which Reno countermanded and then repeated. A disorganized retreat now turned into panic-stricken rout. When Reno reached a vulnerable sanctuary on a high bluff on the Little Bighorn's east bank, his battalion had sustained heavy casualties, including 40 killed, 13 wounded, and others missing.[9]

Custer had turned his battalion to the right and moved along the slope of eastern bluffs until he reached a point that gave him a clear view of the river valley. To his left, he saw Reno's forces then halted in the timber. To his front,

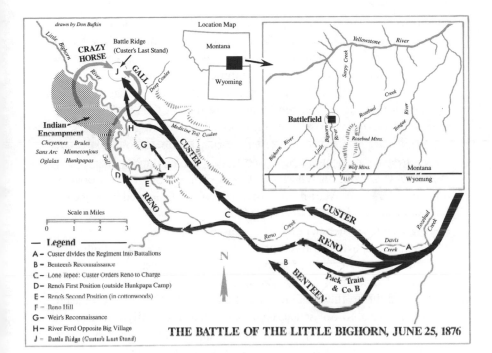

drawn by Don Bufkin

Location Map

Montana

Wyoming

CRAZY HORSE

Battle Ridge (Custer's Last Stand)

Little Bighorn

River

J

GALL

Deep Coulee

Medicine Tail Coulee

CUSTER

H

Indian Encampment

Cheyennes   Brules
Sans Arc   Minneconjous
Oglalas   Hunkpapas

G

D   F

E

Gall

RENO

C

Yellowstone   River

Sarpy Creek

Creek

Battlefield

Rosebud   Mtns.

Bighorn   River

Little   Bighorn   River

Tongue   River

Rosebud Mtns.

Wolf Mtns.

Montana

Wyoming

CUSTER

RENO

Reno   Creek

Davis
Creek

A

Rosebud   Creek

B

Pack Train
& Co. B

BENTEEN

Scale in Miles

0   1   2   3

Legend

A – Custer divides the Regiment into Battalions
B – Benteen's Reconnaissance
C – Lone Tepee: Custer Orders Reno to Charge
D – Reno's First Position (outside Hunkpapa Camp)
E – Reno's Second Position (in cottonwoods)
F – Reno Hill
G – Weir's Reconnaissance
H – River Ford Opposite Big Village
J – Battle Ridge (Custer's Last Stand)

N

THE BATTLE OF THE LITTLE BIGHORN, JUNE 25, 1876

an enormous village stretched for miles along the west bank of the Little Bighorn. It harbored Hunkpapas, Minneconjous, Oglalas, Sans Arcs, Brulés, Blackfeet, Santees, and Yanktonais Sioux, along with Cheyenne and a few Northern Arapahoe allies. The encampment contained 1,500 to 2,000 warriors, and for the first time, Custer must have realized what he faced.[10]

Wasting no time, he ordered Sergeant Kanipe of Company C to find Captain McDougal with the pack train and tell him to bring up the packs. A short time later he dispatched another courier, Trumpeter John Martin, to carry a message to Benteen. Scribbled hastily by Adjutant Cooke it read: "Benteen. Come on. Big Village. Be Quick. Bring packs. W. W. Cooke. P. bring pacs [sic]."[11] As Martin left Custer's battalion, he looked back one last time and saw the soldiers descending Medicine Tail Coulee. "The gray horse troop was in the center and they were galloping."[12]

Benteen, meanwhile, had completed his scout to the left and, finding no sign of Indians, moved toward the main command at a leisurely walk. When he received Cooke's message, he quickened his pace. He found the survivors of Reno's fight on the hill bordering the bluffs and Reno badly shaken. Assuming virtual, if not actual, command, Benteen swiftly established a defense perimeter. With order restored, Captain Weir, later joined by others, led a detachment towards the sound of firing downriver in an attempt to reunite with Custer. Hundreds of warriors appeared, however, and drove them back to Reno Hill.[13]

All day, on June 26, the embattled Reno-Benteen forces fought off Indian assaults, which ended only when darkness fell. As they awaited rescue, some, such as Benteen, concluded that Custer had abandoned them as the captain believed Custer had abandoned Elliott years earlier. Finally, the Indians left their encampment on the morning of June 27, moving south toward the Bighorn Mountains. When Terry and Gibbon arrived later that day, the survivors on Reno Hill learned the whereabouts of Custer's battalion. The bodies of 210 officers and men were scattered along a ridge down the Little Bighorn River some four miles from Reno Hill.[14]

The letters and telegrams of condolences pouring into Fort Lincoln could not dispel the post's bleak mood. The Seventh had suffered a total of 263 officers and men killed, and the *Far West* had brought back 52 wounded. Nelson Miles visited Lincoln and pronounced Elizabeth Custer's despondency an alarming threat to her physical and mental health.[15]

Elizabeth had suffered not only the loss of her husband but in-laws and friends as well. Maggie Custer Calhoun faced the same situation except that her losses included her brothers and a nephew in addition to her husband and friends. The two women drew closer in their common grief as both welcomed brother-in-law David Reed at the post on July 13.[16] When it came to advice, however, Libbie, who had no immediate family save her step-mother Rhoda, turned to the woman who was her dearest friend as well as her closest relative. Cousin Rebecca's letter of July 11 played a critical role in shaping the way Elizabeth adapted to her bereavement.

Rebecca saw Armstrong's death as "like himself—rare, brilliant, startling, heroic! When I think of that my grief is swallowed up in admiration. And the plucky band that shared his fate was worthy of its idolized leader. . . . When I consider that probably not one of those officers would have chosen to be the one left to tell the tale," she continued, "and when I think of the imposing monuments of the event which will be erected by the sculptor, by poet, by painter, and historian; when I consider this I see some reason why the selfish instincts of affection should yield." Then Rebecca counseled Libbie to "bear bravely the trial of a few years separation from our friends for the sake of the far more exceeding weight of glory with which they are thereby crowned. Libbie," she asked, posing a rhetorical question, "how much rather would you be the early widow of such a man than the life-long wife of many another."[17]

As a "good, true, faithful wife to Armstrong," Libbie had given her husband domestic happiness. That, in turn, had helped "make his professional life a success. . . . So, Libbie, your heart's desire in one respect, it seems, was accomplished. His literary reputation was made; his military record was unrivaled. . . . His exit from the stage has been even more unexpected and brilliant than the entrance; it was all in character; I believe he had finished his appointed role."[18]

"When I read in the papers," Rebecca added, "the brief line saying you were in the hospital ministering to the wants of the wounded I thought the mantle of your heroic husband had fallen upon your shoulders. Wear it, Libbie, for his sake!"[19] Elizabeth drew the strength she needed from these words. Later she recalled, "When I heard the news [of Armstrong's death] I wanted to die." Still, she knew she "had to live—a hero's widow—to the end of my appointed time, worthily."[20]

While Libbie and Maggie struggled to endure their grief, Capt. Robert Hughes, from Terry's staff, visited the post. Seeking to comfort the family, he gave Maggie cartridges fired from her husband's gun and drew David Reed a map, showing him where his son Autie had fallen in relation to his uncles. Then, turning to Elizabeth, he described her husband's unmutilated body, pierced by two bullet holes, one in the left temple and the other through the chest. Armstrong and Tom, Hughes assured her, now slept in a grave on a peaceful hillside protected from Indians and beasts.[21]

Libbie also drew comfort from poems and testimonials. Walt Whitman's "A Death Song for Custer" appeared in the *New York Herald* on July 10 and lauded Armstrong as Americans remembered him from earlier days. No longer young and with his thinning hair cut short, Armstrong had not been "thou of the tawny flowing hair" for some time. Nor had he gone into battle with "bright sword in thy hand." But Whitman's stanza, "Now ending well in death the splendid fever of thy deeds," consoled the grieving widow.[22] So too did the people of Will County, Illinois, when they named their new town Custer on July 18. Ten days later, the Texas legislature passed a resolution, citing Custer's "bold and dashing operations against the Indians" and extending its sympathy to Custer's family and "the people of our suffering frontier."[23]

While accolades poured in, Elizabeth, still reeling from her husband's death, discovered with shock and dismay that he was accused of the soldier's gravest sin—disobedience. Inadvertently, his commanding officer set off the controversy. In a confidential report dated July 2 and intended only for Sherman and Sheridan, Terry argued that his original plan had called for cooperation between Gibbon and Custer's columns.

After telling Gibbon to move south along the Bighorn River to the mouth of the Little Bighorn, he had instructed Custer to march up the Rosebud until he came upon the Indian trail struck by Reno earlier. If that trail led to the Little Bighorn Valley, Custers' orders were to march south approximately twenty miles before sweeping north and west to coordinate his column's arrival with Gibbon's.[24] Instead, Custer had followed the trail westward and attacked on June 25, rather than the following day. By contrast: "The movements proposed for Gen'l Gibbon's column were carried out to the letter and had the attack been deferred until it was up I cannot doubt that we should have been successful."[25]

Earlier on June 27, Terry had issued a factual statement describing events at the Little Bighorn and assigning no blame. The scout delivering the report had been delayed while traveling through hostile territory. Thus the eastern press did not receive Terry's first report until July 8. National newspapers carried it the next day. In the meantime an adjutant had forwarded Terry's confidential report to Sheridan at the Philadelphia centennial. Sheridan had passed it on to Sherman, who, anxious to contact the secretary of war immediately, had given it to a reporter posing as a War Department messenger. On the following day, July 7, Terry's second report had appeared in the *Philadelphia Inquirer*.[26]

The publication of Terry's private report two days before newspapers carried his official statement convinced many Custer had defied orders. Reporters rushed to interview officers, and even Sheridan attributed the Seventh's astonishing casualties "to misapprehension and superabundance of courage—the latter being extraordinarily developed in Custer."[27] Those comments hurt Elizabeth, but she found Samuel Sturgis's remarks far more cutting.

Among the dead at the Little Bighorn was twenty-two-year-old James Garland Sturgis, a lieutenant with Company M. Colonel Sturgis now characterized Armstrong as "a brave man, but also a very selfish man," who was "insanely ambitious of glory." Custer had "made his attack recklessly, earlier by thirty-six hours than he should have done, and with men tired out from forced marches." As for Armstrong's "reputation," Sturgis termed it inflated and "to a great extent formed from his writings and newspaper reports." Regarding a monument to the fallen commander, Sturgis had this suggestion. If erected, "for God's sake let them hide it in some dark valley, or veil it, or put it anywhere the bleeding hearts of the widows, orphans, fathers and mothers of the men so uselessly sacrificed to Custer's ambition, can never be wrung at the sight of it."[28]

In death, as in life, Custer generated controversy and few remembered him dispassionately. While some, such as Sturgis, castigated his memory, others, who had loved and admired him, sprang to his defense. McClellan reminded critics that those characterizing Custer as impetuous would have charged cowardice had the Indians fled. Tom Rosser entered the fray, exonerating Custer of rashness and noting that Terry had expected him to attack the hostiles "wherever he found them." He assigned blame, not to Custer, but to Reno, who "took to the hills, and abandoned Custer and his gallant comrades to their fate."[29]

Election-year politics and social and sectional tensions added to the growing controversy. Democrats, viewed by many as the party of treason and disunion, saw a chance to belittle the Republican administration by blaming the tragedy on its Indian policy. "Who Slew Custer? asked the *New York Herald*, as James Gordon Bennett, Jr., began using the fallen hero for political and ideological purposes. "The celebrated peace policy of General

Grant, which feeds, clothes and takes care of their noncombatant force, while the men are killing our troops—that is what killed Custer," was his paper's answer. Closely allied was the "nest of thieves, the Indian Bureau, with its thieving agents and favorites as Indian traders, and its mock humanity and pretense of piety—that is what killed Custer."[30]

While such statements sought to embarrass the current administration, Bennett also wanted his compatriots to draw other lessons from Custer's last stand. Starting with the July 9 issue, the *Herald* had juxtaposed against the heroic figure of George Armstrong Custer, the "savage" Sitting Bull, the figure who, Bennett believed, had brought Custer down. The savage had won, the *Herald* maintained, only because treacherous or misguided whites had assisted him.[31] Earlier, French-Canadian Jesuits had supposedly trained Sitting Bull in the strategy of Napoleon. Later, "outlaws" and Indian Bureau philanthropists had given him material assistance. More important, these figures were metaphors for certain elements in American society.

The *Herald*, by linking priests to Sitting Bull, played on widespread anti-Catholic nativism (a dangerous enterprise for a Democratic newspaper). The "outlaws" signified the "dangerous classes" or the unworthy poor in American cities. The *Herald* saw them as it saw the Sioux. They were inherently and "unredeemably 'savage.'"[32] Finally, the Indian Bureau philanthropists and the denominational agents stood for those misguided idealists who vied with Bennett and other conservatives for political power by championing the rights of labor or the "dangerous classes."[33] In that context Custer's death showed the futility of placating "savages." The imposition of order and discipline, rather than the effecting of reform or social change, provided the real answers to problems, just as the solution to the recalcitrant Indians lay in meting out punishment, not kindness and annuities.[34]

Custer's defeat also provided useful ammunition for those calling for removal of troops from the South. Congressman Samuel S. Cox railed against a government that sent only 2,000 men against the Sioux but kept 3,000 stationed in Florida, Louisiana, and South Carolina. William Rowan, a former Confederate officer, made a similar point when he proposed to lead a regiment of Confederate veterans against the Sitting Bull bands.[35]

Westerners also expressed their outrage. In Montana Territory, newspaper editors begged Congress to disavow the peace policy and strengthen frontier defense.[36] In all sections of the country, however, newspapers often portrayed the hostiles as better armed than white soldiers. The Grant administration had, according to the Little Rock *Daily Arkansas Gazette*, formed its policy to suit rings, who benefited "through traffic with the Indians, which has extended even to supplying them with arms of the most approved style." In a similar vein, an Austin, Texas, newspaper alleged that Indians had received better guns than soldiers: "It is more profitable to sell the good guns to the Indians and give the inferior ones to the army."[37] Such statements reinforced Libbie's preconceptions. She saw the Indian policy that armed aborigines as a major factor in her husband's death.[38]

As widows, Elizabeth and Maggie had no right to army quarters and they now prepared to leave Lincoln. Down came the plants, pictures, and curtains, held back by antlers. Libbie turned most of her household goods over to the post trader to sell to incoming families and shipped east her bedroom set, Autie's desk, and her heirloom china and silver. While she wondered what to do with her foxhounds and staghounds, she wanted her husband's favorite mount, Dandy, for Emmanuel Custer. Officers of the Seventh, eager to ease her pain, were already raising money to purchase the horse.[39] Finally, the evening before her departure, Elizabeth gathered the post children together and gave each a picture of "the General."[40]

On July 30, Libbie, Maggie, and David Reed boarded a special car at Bismarck provided by the Northern Pacific. With them were Nettie Smith, Annie Yates, Annie's three small children, and Annie's brother, Richard Roberts. The latter, a correspondent for the *New York Sun*, had planned to accompany Custer's troops, despite General Sherman's prohibition against reporters. A disabled horse had kept Roberts behind, but the less fortunate Mark Kellogg, representing the *Bismarck Tribune* and the *New York Herald*, had perished on the battlefield.[41]

Large crowds met the train along the way. At some stations, dignitaries greeted the small party with flowers and condolences. In Chicago hotel magnate Potter Palmer sent meals to the widows' cars. Here Libbie announced that she would give her dogs to anyone willing to pay their transportation and give them a good home.[42]

On August 4, Libbie, Maggie, and Annie arrived in Monroe, leaving Nettie Smith to travel alone to her parents' home in Herkimer, New York. As Libbie alighted from the train, she saw her old principal waiting for her at the station. Uttering "a shriek of anguish," she collapsed in Erasmus Boyd's arms.[43] When she regained her composure, Boyd took the three widows to the old homestead, where they secluded themselves. Local reporters, who sought an interview, learned that Mrs. Custer was "very greatly prostrated, not being able to go out at all."[44]

Whatever her physical and emotional condition, Elizabeth was already applying her acute intelligence to a new and exacting role—functioning as the widow of George Armstrong Custer. In August 1876, she threw herself into her new vocation as she planned, with Reverend Mattoon, her husband's service at the Monroe memorial for its fallen heroes.

Armstrong had been Elizabeth's "other self," her alter ego.[45] He had achieved the public stature and fame that she, as a conventional woman, could never attain on her own. Now that he was gone, Libbie could no longer "bask daily" in her husband's "glory" unless he lived on in public memory as a hero.[46] Then, as his widow, clothed in his "mantle," she might derive some compensation for her terrible loss. In addition, Elizabeth's character predisposed her to begin the process of mythologizing her late husband. From courtship on, she had viewed Armstrong in the light of literary themes, as she had "read him in all [her] books."[47] Later, as a wife, she had told her husband that "every event" in his life "seems to fit into every other event like the blocks in a child's puzzle."[48]

Now the recent articles, speeches, and editorials appearing in the press reinforced her underlying views. In addition to using Custer's death for political and ideological purposes, newspapers drew historical and biblical analogies. The *New York Herald* on July 7 had led the way by comparing the Little Bighorn to the Charge of the Light Brigade. The newspaper had also equated the Custer family to the "Curiatii from Roman history and the Maccabees from the Hebrew."[49] Eight days later, Ohio Rep. James Garfield had likened Custer to Leonidas at Thermopolae.[50]

Americans would have interpreted the Battle of the Little Bighorn in light of older familiar stories from their cultural heritage had Elizabeth Custer never lived. The vision of a small band of men fighting against insurmountable odds atop a lonely hill conjured up not only the Greeks at Thermopolae but Saul and the Israelites on Mount Gilboa and Roland and his men at Roncesvalles.[51] The drawing of parallels and analogies was inevitable.

In the centennial year of 1876, Elizabeth Custer's compatriots had a stronger need than usual for heroes and heroic events. Although they displayed with pride the newest technology, including the dynamo and Alexander Graham Bell's recently invented telephone at Philadelphia, and although politicians gave speeches on the nation's glorious destiny, their celebration masked deep uncertainties. Only recently, the failure of their political institutions to resolve the divisive question of slavery had plunged the United States into civil war. When peace came after four years of bloodletting, few Americans had expected the hero of Appomattox to preside over unprecedented corruption.[52]

Equally as disturbing, the United States in 1876 was in the throes of depression, inaugurated by the bankruptcy of that engine of progress and civilization, the Northern Pacific Railroad. And now to the west, where Americans believed, as Armstrong had, they could escape hard times and achieve success if they "put shoulder to the wheel," the unthinkable had happened. The aborigines had defeated one of the nation's best-known fighting forces.[53]

Mitigating the last was the sense that a heroic little band had met the savage foe and had gone down fighting to the last man for God and country. Americans eagerly embraced the fallen Custer and his men. Many saw in them self-sacrificing patriotism and an affirmation of the individual. How comforting to know these still counted in an age of increasingly crowded cities, growing impersonality in human and social relations, and a rising sense, springing from the theory of evolution, that change and flux, rather than order, described the universe.[54] While no one had survived to tell the story, Custer's compatriots believed that this band of men and their leader had met death with gallantry, defiant courage, and true nobility. They believed it because, by accepting the heroic version as true, they could fit Custer's last stand into a larger pattern and extract from it solace, meaning, and, most important, a message for future generations.[55]

These national needs coincided with the personal needs of Elizabeth Bacon Custer. While the process of mythologizing Custer had already begun, the widow would reinforce and sustain it. And since many of Custer's contemporaries had admired him fervently, Elizabeth would enlist their assistance and draw on their praise of her dead spouse to validate her "wish-related knowledge" about what manner of man her husband had been and what his life and death had meant.[56]

On August 13, a stifling Sunday afternoon, Monroe citizens crowded into the Methodist Church to hear eulogies and prayers in honor of the six fallen men. The service started with a roll call of the dead—the three Custer brothers, George Armstrong, Thomas Ward, and Boston; their nephew, Harry Armstrong Reed; Maggie's husband, James Calhoun; and Annie's husband, George Yates. Much of the ceremony, however, glorified Armstrong, whose photograph, encircled with evergreens, the symbol of life everlasting, stood on the altar.[57]

Reverend Mattoon recalled Custer as the temperate and pure Christian soldier. Despite his national acclaim, Armstrong had always taken "pleasure in being a boy again and sitting at the feet of his venerated mother."[58] The minister noted, in words reminiscent of letters Libbie had written her husband, that Custer was "never idle. When he laid down the sword he took up his pen. More years and leisure would have given him distinction as an author."[59]

After lauding Custer's character, the clergyman turned to frontier service and final days. Like so many since, Mattoon imagined Custer as the last to die. Surely, Armstrong's final thoughts had been of his wife, "who had shared with him the hard fate of the soldiers' tent, buckled on his armor, bid him to be brave and true, and often followed him to the very verge of battleground, and with him chased the wild bison over the plains—with her who once said when she received the parting benediction, 'He's gone and all the world has gone with him.'"[60]

Then, after placing Custer in the pantheon of ancient and modern heroes, including Caleb, Leonidas, Horatio Nelson, Oliver Hazard Perry, Stephen Decatur, and Thomas MacDonough, Mattoon dismissed allegations of rashness. One had only to read of Armstrong's preparation for the Washita in *My Life on the Plains* to know the charge was false.[61] Brave men, however, always attracted envious and ignoble detractors. "The great Teacher and Founder of our religion was no exception to the rule."[62] In the end, despite persecution from Grant's administration, Armstrong had done his duty as "a citizen of this Republic; and be assured . . . his countrymen will vindicate his honor. They will build a monument to the memory of so brave a son."[63]

Mattoon also extracted other meanings from the tragedy. No longer should the government allow the aborigines to live as tribesmen. Instead they must become individuals, "accountable to the laws of the land," and their only annuities "seeds, clothing and implements of husbandry—not guns and implements of warfare, to make war on any nation." For God had ordained the land for "civilization and christianity, and what right have a few heathen and barbarous Indians to set up their authority and stay the tide of progress."[64]

The political capital that Democrats extracted from Custer's last stand and Belknap's impeachment trial that summer led the Grant administration to react defensively. In September, Libbie read in anger the president's statement to a *New York Herald* reporter. "I regard Custer's massacre as a sacrifice of troops brought on by Custer himself, that was wholly unnecessary . . . He was not to have made the attack before effecting the junction with Terry and Gibbon." Custer had been "notified," Grant continued, "to meet them on the 26th, but instead of marching slowly, as his orders required, in order to effect the junction on the 26th, he enters upon a forced march of eighty-three miles in twenty-four hours, and thus has to meet the Indians alone on the 25th."[65] Elizabeth, possessing part of Terry's orders from Armstrong's last letter, viewed that interpretation as unwarranted. The earlier antagonism she had felt towards Grant for depriving her husband of command of the Sioux campaign now became enmity.[66]

Other jolts awaited Elizabeth. Shortly after Grant voiced his opinions on the Little Bighorn, she received a disturbing letter from Emil Justh. Armstrong's note for $8,500 at 7 percent was due, and he wanted payment. The amount must have frightened her as she learned the extent of Armstrong's indebtedness.[67]

On August 9, an initial inventory of Custer's estate had assessed the value of his personal property at $2,140. In addition, Libbie and her husband owned a farm in partnership with brother Nevin. Eventually, as Autie's heir, Elizabeth planned to sell her equity in that property, subject to the $2,000 mortgage she owed. Even so, as she totaled her projected assets against indebtedness, the balance sheet was grim.

Altogether, including the Justh note, the claims against Custer's estate exceeded $13,000.[68] Elizabeth's assets, including her insurance, would amount to $8,000 at most. Moreover, an earlier attempt by Congressman A. S. Williams to raise her pension from $30 to $50 a month and award Armstrong's parents $80 a month was stalled in the Senate.[69] Adding to her troubles, the Equitable Assurance Company notified her in October that the $3,000 policy Autie had carried on his parents had lapsed for nonpayment of the June premium.

Elizabeth responded immediately. Her husband had assured her before leaving on the expedition that all policies were "paid up." She had received no notice to the contrary. Since the general, "a devoted son," had supported his parents throughout his army career, they now became her responsibility. "It is with the most intense regret that I find myself so situated financially that I cannot provide for them as I would wish. They are very old and poor and the mother is a confirmed invalid."[70]

While Libbie awaited word on the disposition of Armstrong's policy, other groups sought to relieve the plight of the Seventh's widows. Soon after learning of the disaster on the Little Bighorn, the *New York Herald* set aside

$1,000 towards a Custer monument and invited additional contributions. On July 13, a retired army officer wrote the newspaper, describing Libbie as "reduced to beggary. . . . Do you not think, " he asked, "that if Custer himself could speak he would prefer bread for his widow to a stone for himself?"[71] Others disagreed, noting that Custer had carried insurance, and Libbie's father had bequeathed her, they thought, a large estate. Nonetheless, when proposed legislation to relieve the distress of the Little Bighorn widows languished in the Senate Committee on Invalid Pensions, the *Army and Navy Journal* called on the military to care for its own.[72]

Palmer Potter sent $250, and the entire garrison at Fort Lyon in Colorado gave to the fund. Most donations, however, were small. One contributor, a ninety-year-old veteran, harked back to the Black Hawk War. Charles Braden, a Seventh Cavalry veteran, disabled on the Yellowstone in 1873, sent $5.[73] By mid-September the *Army and Navy Journal* fund totaled more than $5,000.

The September 16 issue noted that an officer's wife, writing for two others besides herself, expressed the group's "appreciation of your remembrance of us." However, "we particularly desire that our share of the fund so generously raised be given to the widows and children of the enlisted men." Very likely this letter came from Monroe, Michigan, and represented the feelings of Libbie, Maggie, and Annie Yates.[74] These women, while experiencing financial difficulties, would soon receive their insurance.

Early in November, the *Journal* announced that the fund, now totaling, $13,800, would be distributed according to rank and pension guidelines. Libbie received $900, while Maggie's share, calculated on her pension of $20 a month, netted her $510. Annie Yates, entitled to an additional $5 a month per child, gratefully accepted her $1,050. The wives of enlisted men divided $6,300 among themselves, a welcome boon since their pension amounted to $8 a month and $2 per child.[75]

In November the three Monroe widows received their checks from the New York Life Company. For Elizabeth this amounted to $4,750, and she paid off the $1,500 mortgage she and Armstrong had taken out on her father's homestead.[76] Shortly after, the Equitable Life Assurance Company sent Armstrong's parents $3,000, and the Widow Custer breathed easier.[77] True, Justh's claim troubled her, but settlement lay in the future. For now, she turned towards commemorating her husband with a newly discovered ally.

Frederick Whittaker, British expatriate and dime novelist, had met Custer at Sheldon and Company. In September 1876, Whittaker's *Galaxy* article had presented Custer as a brave man, overwhelmed by superior numbers at the Little Bighorn. If blame were warranted, Whittaker faulted Terry for sending out separate columns without adequate means of communication. Certainly Custer could not have known the army had underestimated Indian strength. Nor could he have imagined that Sitting Bull's strategical abilities matched Napoleon's, as the chief had masterfully deployed his forces, first against Crook and then against Custer. As for Reno, Whittaker thought the major had lacked "sufficient force" to carry out his orders but "managed to escape after a severe mauling."[78]

The article indicated Whittaker's interest in the subject and initially his impartiality. While he saw Custer as a "bright meteor flashing from the multitude" and the "incarnation of courage," he also discerned a "natural recklessness" and "vanity" in the American Leonidas. Whittaker's article, nonetheless, suggested that while Custer had told part of his story in *My Life on the Plains*, his "comrades [should] take up the tale" before memories faded.[79]

Whether he approached Elizabeth or she contacted him is unknown, but this much is certain. Whittaker came under Libbie's spell. Before long he was at work on a full-length biography of Custer. While he relied heavily upon *My Life on the Plains*, Elizabeth provided him with Armstrong's personal correspondence with family and friends.[80] Rhoda, who worried about her stepdaughter's depression, observed her participation in this project with concern. "[W]hat a labour & tryal [*sic*] to gather all the material by looking over all the papers for the General's life," she wrote in mid-November. Whittaker had finished the book, however, and Rhoda hoped Elizabeth "nervous system will gradually strengthen now since you have completed the painful task of writing and arranging those papers. How much more revolution [*sic*] you have had," she observed, "than I had when my husband Mr. Pitts dyed [*sic*]. When D. D. Tompson had asked her to supply material for a biography, "I could not even look over his letters."[81]

In the process of completing his work, Whittaker had come to new conclusions about the boy general. Custer had never been the "reckless" charger his jealous enemies maintained but instead "a remarkably quiet, thoughtful man . . . who never became flurried and excited in the hottest battle."[82] Thus the onus for the defeat at the Little Bighorn lay on the shoulders of others. If Reno had continued his charge courageously, and if Benteen had obeyed the order to "come quick," then the battle might have been *"Custer's last and greatest Indian victory."*[83] Even earlier, if the president had not removed Custer from command of his column because of his desire for "private revenge," the soldier *would be alive to-day and the Indian war settled*." The nation's "best Indian-fighter" would have collaborated successfully with Colonel Gibbon, an experienced frontier soldier. Finally, neither Reno nor Benteen would have "dreamed of disobeying their chief, had they not known he was out of favor at court."[84]

Whittaker's book was more than a biography. It was a polemic, designed to shift blame from Custer and instigate an investigation. As the author wrote Libbie, if a court of inquiry found sufficient evidence to order a court-martial, then slurs against Armstrong would cease entirely. As publication day drew near, Whittaker shared with Elizabeth their mutual hopes and concerns. "In some respects the unsettled condition of the country will hurt us," he confided, referring to the disputed election between Rutherford B. Hayes and Democrat Samuel Tilden. Nonetheless, although Tilden seemed likely to prevail, should Hayes win, "investigations will be in order anyway, as soon as Congress meets, our own among the number."[85]

Whittaker had asked officers of the Seventh to provide statements criticizing Reno's actions at the Little Bighorn.[86] All except Weir had refused outright. Still, he gave Whittaker no statement and instead had written Libbie in October, "I have so much to tell you that I will tell you nothing now. . . . *I am coming to Monroe to see you all*."[87] A month later, after his transfer to New York City, Weir again promised to visit and assured Libbie it was his "life business to vindicate my friends of that day."[88]

Weir, in all probability, had no secret to divulge. More likely, he faced an impossible situation. As his friend, Charles Braden, later disclosed, the Captain found Whittaker so troublesome that he could not discuss the writer without resorting to profanity.[89] At the same time, however, Weir knew that Whittaker was acting on behalf of himself and the Widow Custer. And Weir, who was drawn to Elizabeth (and may have been in love with her), would have done nothing to hurt her.[90]

Throughout the years, despite the occasion when Custer had "tackled" him at Fort Harker, Weir had remained a close and trusted confidant of Libbie, Maggie, and Annie. He revealed as much in his November letter. "I know if we were all of us alone in the parlor, at night," he noted, harking back to past occasions, "the curtains all down and everybody else asleep, one or the other of you would make me tell you everything I know." Still, if he could come to Monroe, he could "say something to you all that would make you feel glad for a little while at least."

Very likely, Weir's message concerned his own actions. At the Little Bighorn, he had not waited for Reno's permission when he had attempted to aid Custer's battalion by moving towards the sound of fire. Before the hostiles had driven him back, his subaltern, Lt. Winfield S. Edgerly, had joined him, and others had followed.[91]

Weir never arrived in Monroe. Nor did he answer Whittaker's letters. Instead, the writer unexpectedly appeared at his Hudson Street apartment. The captain, while cordial, refused to sign an affidavit. As Weir explained, he had quarreled with Reno on the bluffs. Thus his statements would be viewed as coming "from Reno's personal enemies." Still, Whittaker believed Weir "will speak out when the fight begins."[92]

Unfortunately, the captain was ill. Although his doctor characterized his malady as "melancholia," he suffered, as Whittaker's letter of November 28 hinted, from the advanced stages of alcoholism. "He spoke out, as freely as I could wish, to me, but I was very sorry to see him as he was, for he cannot live long if he goes on at that rate. But, clouded as he was . . . he was quite clear in his head, clearer than I expected."[93] Three weeks later, on December 9, Weir died.[94]

Whittaker's *The Complete Life of Gen. George A. Custer* appeared on store shelves by late November. In addition to extolling Custer, it excoriated Reno, Benteen, and President Grant. Custer appeared not as a fallible man but, as one scholar has noted, a composite American hero and an ideal "American boy." To achieve this, Whittaker had applied common literary conventions to different stages of Custer's life.[95]

First, on the basis perhaps of Custer family legend or, more likely, his own fertile imagination, he presented Armstrong as the descendant of a Revolutionary War Hessian soldier. Then he argued that, as a child, Armstrong had shown signs of becoming a frontier hero by demonstrating senses "as sharp of those of an Indian even then." Later, Armstrong's intuitive wisdom had enabled him to easily outwit "constituted authorities at school, with ingenious evasion."[96] While physically strong and attracted to martial arts from early days, Custer was to his beloved mother and sister, Lydia Ann, "the most docile of boys." Moreover, while he grew to become a "brilliant warrior"—shades of Mattoon's August eulogy—his family always saw him as "the exemplary son and brother, who never omitted a duty, never abated in his love." And yet, Whittaker maintained, Custer's education had taught this future "knight" little about "medieval lore, and less of European history. . . . He was then, and remained to the last, a thorough American, a Western boy at that."[97]

The relations between Elizabeth and Armstrong played a critical role in the book. Whittaker wrote that their meeting and Custer's determination to make her his wife dated back to adolescence. Custer, he maintained, had been about fourteen when he had passed the Bacon mansion one day. Libbie (who would have been twelve at the time, although Whittaker described her as eight) called out, "Hello! you Custer boy!" Then, fearful of appearing unladylike, she fled inside the house.

Although Marguerite Merington later wrote that Elizabeth disputed the story, Whittaker emphasized its importance. "The sweet arch face of that little girl was the first revelation to the wild young savage, whose whole idea of life was that of physical exercise, war, and the chase, of something else, of another side of life. It was, to him," the biographer continued, "love at first sight, and he then and there recorded an inward vow, that some day that little girl should be his wife. He kept the vow through many obstacles."[98] Once married, Libbie continued uplifting her husband. "Finding him good, she left him perfect, and her sweet and gracious influence can be traced on all his after life."[99]

The appearance of Whittaker's biography, with its various allegations against Reno, Benteen, and Grant, unleashed a storm. Many objected to the author's assertions, and some readers questioned his methods and obvious bias. On December 23, the reviewer for the *Army and Navy Journal* noted that Whittaker's book displayed little critical analysis. "To indiscriminately laud your hero is undoubtedly the easiest way of writing a biography, and there is much excuse for it in the case of a work hastily rushed into print, to catch the fleeting tide of popular interest."[100] Another critic disparaged Whittaker for relying upon the "conflicting and unreliable newspaper reports published at the time." Moreover, he had assumed the "self-appointed task of apotheosizing [Custer] at the expense of every one else, living or dead, and therefore" had lost all objectivity.[101] To answer his critics, Whittaker cited his sources. He had visited Monroe, and despite their grief, "the surviving members of the Custer family [felt] that they had no right to withhold information as to Custer's career from the nation whose trusted and honored servant he was."[102]

The controversy surrounding the Whittaker biography, like the controversy surrounding the Battle of the Little Bighorn, deepened Elizabeth's depression. Whittaker, now her confidant, encouraged her to correspond with him freely, "no matter how gloomy you may feel, nay even when you feel most gloomy and despondent. I know from the long ago experience of a not very happy life how much the heart is relieved by such an outlet when the waters seem to close darkest overhead."[103]

He also advised her to complete her own memoir of life with Custer. The work would prove beneficial for "by bringing your mind to nothing but thoughts of the *happy past*, it will insensibly lead you to think of the *happier future* that is coming to you as surely as Death and Almighty God can bring it. . . . The work will help to bridge over the time, before you and your husband meet again."[104]

Elizabeth had more immediate concerns than recalling happier days or awaiting her death. Since she expected to live awhile, she needed employment because liens against Armstrong's estate threatened to deplete her resources. She also worried about Armstrong's parents, who had lost all their sons save Nevin and Emmanuel's son by his first marriage, Brice W. Custer, a bridge inspector who lived in Cleveland, Ohio.[105]

The Civil War, more than a decade earlier, had claimed the lives of over 620,000 men and had left countless others incapacitated. Many women, as a result, had never married, and others, deprived of the support of husbands or fathers, had been compelled to enter the paid labor force. The percentage of women working for wages had increased by almost 50 percent since 1860, but the alternatives available to women and especially middle-class women were still severely limited.[106]

Elizabeth could perhaps become a teacher, but her previous Sunday school experience had left her unenthusiastic about that possibility. Besides, teaching paid poorly, especially for female teachers, who often received one half of what their male counterparts earned.[107] Elizabeth had another idea. She recalled seeing female clerks in Washington during the Civil War, hurrying home from their government jobs. In correspondence with Frank E. Howe, agent for the United States Pension Office, she learned that female clerks working in government positions earned as much as $900 a year. She also discovered that he had given her letter to President Grant.

"It touched him very much although there was a little reflection in it on him. He promptly said something must be done for you at once, and has treated the whole matter in the most tender manner." Grant had directed Zachariah Chandler and Postmaster James Tyner to look into the possibility of making Libbie postmistress of Monroe, an occupation many women had entered in recent years.[108]

Although such a position sounded attractive since it would enable her to stay close to Armstrong's parents and employ Maggie as assistant, Elizabeth perceived serious drawbacks. First, she could accept no favor from Grant or his administration for "reasons," she explained to Howe, "you will readily understand."[109] Second, both her father's close friend Frazy Winans (who left a sick bed to register his objection) and, more important, Rebecca counseled her against entering government employment. "Armstrong loved you at first for your fresh, unsullied modesty," Rebecca wrote, "and he would ever have shielded you from such contact with the business world as would have endangered those peculiar characteristics."[110]

Faced with these attitudes and restrictions Elizabeth's options were painfully limited. By late spring, 1877, she wanted out of her hometown, a place she had for years found constricting. Now an agricultural crossroads of 5,000 between Toledo and Detroit, it offered little to a woman who had socialized with European royalty, members of the British Parliament, and leading generals and politicians. Moreover, Whittaker's biography still drew harsh comments. Many took issue with his various statements, often to the detriment of Armstrong's reputation.[111] If Libbie wanted to counter such aspersions effectively, she needed to be closer to the seat of power and influence.[112]

Rebecca, who still hoped Elizabeth did not really have to "have a paid position to support yourself comfortably," now advised her to move to New York City. There she could put "pen and pencil" to work and gain "desirable luxuries," including money for trips. If she wanted more, then she could find genteel employment with other women working towards charity or benevolence.[113] There was no limit, Rebecca thought, to what a persevering woman could accomplish in Gotham. A recently widowed friend was "making a very nice living" doing what Elizabeth had longed to do as a child. She worked "as correspondent for several newspapers, does copying; and other occupations."[114]

Reflecting on Rebecca's advice and remembering her excitement as a thirteen-year-old at the thought of one day becoming a writer and journalist like Grace Greenwood, Libbie made up her mind. At thirty-five, the widow of a western hero packed her belongings and boarded a train. East, not West, was the land where she would "put shoulder to the wheel" and strive for success. Elizabeth Custer was starting over.

CHAPTER 12

The Wrong Monument

E LIZABETH had left Monroe so quickly that even Rebecca was astonished. "All right! We like your energy and decision!" As Armstrong used to say: "'Be sure you are right and then go ahead,'" and that was good advice. Besides, Libbie would find New York City "the one place in my small world where women who are rightly disposed and who know what they are about, can enjoy a great degree of the sweet freedom and independence which in other places is accorded only to men."[1]

During her first weeks in the metropolis, Elizabeth rented a room from the William Russells, in Newark, New Jersey.[2] This was the same family she had visited in 1864 when Armstrong had arrived unexpectedly following the Battle of Cedar Creek. While there, she volunteered for charitable work at New York hospitals to escape the sadness of such memories.

Briefly she also considered enrolling in Bellevue Hospital's two-year nursing program. While the Civil War had brought middle-class women into the field, they had been generally over thirty and, for the most part, motivated by their altruistic desire to serve the Union cause. Afterwards, many of them had left nursing.[3] Despite Bellevue's standing as the first school to meet the Englishwoman Florence Nightingale's standards, most Americans still considered the work domestic rather than medical.[4] Moreover, Elizabeth would have to live at the hospital and endure twelve-hour days. Rebecca dissuaded her cousin, arguing that the conditions were "too confining and exposing" from the standpoint of health and possibly too depressing given Libbie's emotional state.[5]

Elizabeth's benevolent activities, nonetheless, brought her into contact with such prominent women as Louisa Lee Schuyler and Elizabeth C.

Hobson. While making hospital rounds, Libbie learned that a newly formed organization, the Society of Decorative Arts, needed a part-time secretary. Immediately, she scheduled an interview with its founder, Candace Wheeler.[6]

Wife of engineer and surveyor Thomas Wheeler, Candace Thurber Wheeler had established the organization following the death of her daughter, Candace Wheeler Stimson. The forty-nine-year-old woman had been immersed in her grief until an "exquisitely worked scroll" over the doorway of the Royal School of Art and Needlework Pavilion at the Philadelphia centennial had captured her attention. Inside, a "superb collection of . . . embroidery and needlework" completed by impoverished women had left her entranced. The Kensington School of England had trained these women to produce artistically beautiful and marketable work. And now these "decayed gentlewomen" earned money without leaving the sanctuary of their home.[7]

Wheeler thought that American women, well-trained in traditional crafts, could do likewise, and, in the current depression, many needed that opportunity. Shortly after Wheeler founded her organization, she expanded its program to include classes in decorating china, slate, porcelain, pottery, and ecclesiastical vestments and tapestries. She also established "auxiliary committees" to develop similar programs elsewhere. Overall, Wheeler aspired to create "breaches in the invisible wall of prejudice and custom," which kept "well-bred women" from earning a living.[8]

Mrs. David Lane, who had gained experience in the New York Sanitary Commission during the Civil War, supplied the administrative talent to coordinate these activities.[9] To assure success, she and Wheeler enlisted a well-chosen board. Among its members were Mrs. John Jacob Astor; Mrs. Levi P. Morton; Caroline Belmont, the wife of August Belmont; Mrs. J. W. Pinchot; and Julia Bryant, the daughter of William Cullen Bryant, poet and editor of the *New York Evening Post*.[10] Given its ambitious goals, the society needed someone to work three days a week keeping abreast of correspondence.[11] Elizabeth, who loved art and had some training, believed her background would serve the organization well. More important, she would benefit from the contacts it offered.

When Mrs. Lane first mentioned Elizabeth Custer's interview, Candace Wheeler was annoyed. "Oh, don't," she replied. "I am as sorry for her as I can be, but we must have a business-like and useful secretary." Later, Wheeler remembered Elizabeth's arrival. "She came, the pathetic figure in widow's weeds, which seemed to hold the shadow of a heart-rending tragedy." Elizabeth was "so modest in her estimate of herself, so earnest in her desire to do something for our enterprise, and so fixed in her determination to do something practical for her own needs!" In spite of misgivings, "my jealous love for the cause of the society melted in a sense that this one lone woman was an integral part of the great cause."[12]

The salary was small, but over time Elizabeth and Candace Wheeler forged a close relationship that grew stronger with the passing years. The older woman, moreover, knew many people in a variety of fields. In time she also introduced Elizabeth to influential writers and journalists. Libbie, in turn, more than satisfied the fastidious Mrs. Wheeler. "The letters of explanation and instruction and encouragement to our army of luckless contributors became a flood," Wheeler recalled, but Libbie never fell behind.[13]

Although Elizabeth worked only three days a week, the long hours and confinement to a basement room proved difficult. She soon tired of the additional burden of commuting from Newark to New York City and found furnished rooms at 122 Madison Avenue, not far from her office at 67 Madison Avenue. A few months later, restless and lonely, she rented a room at the Glenham Hotel on Fifth Avenue.[14] During this time of adjustment to wage earning and life in the large city, Elizabeth learned that she could give her husband a West Point burial. Shortly after, she wrote Gen. John Schofield, West Point superintendent, asking him to select a site and set the day for the funeral.[15]

The move east was turning out well, but old concerns and unresolved matters in Michigan still burdened the widow. Armstrong's estate remained unsettled, and his family was hard pressed financially. Moreover, Elizabeth feared for Maggie, who saw no reason for living. With Jimmi gone, the young woman felt like a "a nonidentity," for he, at least, had considered her "necessary to his happiness."[16] Maggie's headaches, always a problem, now left her so debilitated that she despaired of accompanying Annie Yates to the reburial ceremony for their husbands and Tom at Fort Leavenworth. Nor, Maggie wrote, was Maria Custer reconciled to Libbie's departure. "She feels very badly to think you have left home for good as it were—excepting visits—and that you are out in the world *alone*."[17]

As the first anniversary of the Little Bighorn approached, Elizabeth steeled herself, but newspaper accounts made the ordeal worse than expected. When Col. Michael Sheridan arrived on the battlefield to collect the officers' remains, he found horse and human bones strewn about. Photographers, unfortunately, captured the scene for the nation's newspapers.[18] The original burial had been perfunctory since neither Reno's men nor Gibbon's had possessed proper tools. Moreover, they had left the battlefield quickly to obtain medical attention for Reno's wounded. Although soldiers had buried Armstrong and Thomas with care, a year later animals and birds of prey had uncovered some of the bodies. Many now questioned whether any of the remains could be properly identified.[19]

Joseph Tilford, a major in the Seventh Cavalry, relieved Elizabeth about her husband. He had, he assured her, "personally superintended the transfer of the remains from the box in which they came from the battlefield to the casket which conveys them to West Point." Tilford also included a lock of Armstrong's hair in his letter, after keeping some himself. Custer, he confided, had been his "beau ideal of a soldier and honorable Gentleman."[20] Finally, Michael Sheridan dispelled any further doubts when he wrote Elizabeth that he had easily located the stakes driven into the ground over the officers' graves. Beneath were cartridges with names, which permitted him to identify "the body of *every* officer I brought in without the slightest difficulty."[21]

When Elizabeth discovered that her husband's remains headed eastward faster than expected, she saw a new danger. Schofield had warned her that if Armstrong were buried in the summer, few persons would be present at West Point, and his interment would receive little notice. She immediately rescheduled Armstrong's reburial in October or November, when "a full corps of cadets and officers" would be on hand and Schofield could "pay the honor he wishes to the heroic dead." Until then, she directed Sheridan to deposit the "sacred dust" in a Poughkeepsie vault, owned by Philip Hamilton, whose son, Capt. Louis Hamilton, had died at the Washita.[22] Elizabeth's mental state improved further when she learned that Maggie had found the strength to accompany Annie to the reburial service for their husbands and Tom at Leavenworth on August 3.[23] Later, the remains of Boston and Autie Reed were returned to Monroe and buried in the family plot.

As summer gave way to fall, Elizabeth traveled to Monroe to settle the claims against Armstrong's estate. Debts still stood at $13,291.10, including the amount owed Justh, and assets were still assessed at $2,140.[24] Frogtown's sale brought $220. When Libbie auctioned her portion of the farm she and Autie had owned jointly with Nevin Custer, Nevin's bid of $775 gave him ownership of 114 acres of contiguous land along the River Raisin. After the probate court retotaled holdings and subtracted the $1,000 Libbie had withdrawn over fifteen months of widowhood, she had $1,447.74 left.

When Elizabeth discharged her husband's debts at ten cents on the dollar and paid court costs and attorney fees, her husband's estate was depleted.[25] She was left with her pension and some income from the army and navy fund and the insurance money left over after paying off the mortgage she and Autie had taken out on the Bacon homestead. Although she was not destitute, her funds were limited, and Emmanuel and Maria still needed help. Her attorney, John Rauch, found her situation so distressing that he filed a claim to recover the $3,000 the federal government had seized from Daniel Bacon's estate in 1869.[26]

With Armstrong's estate settled, Elizabeth returned to New York for his funeral. On October 10, as the morning fog lifted, crowds lined the Hudson River to watch the bunting-draped *Mary Powell*, with flags at half-mast, bring Custer's remains from Poughkeepsie to West Point. The coffin, draped with Captain Hamilton's flag and adorned with two stars made of tuberoses against a shoulder strap of geraniums, lay in state at the academy until the funeral began.[27]

Shortly before 2 P.M., Libbie arrived at the chapel accompanied by General Schofield. Behind her came Emmanuel, Maggie, and more distant relatives and friends. Inside, Dr. John Forsyth, the West Point chaplain, intoned the Episcopal funeral service, while the widow gazed at the altar through a blur of tears. As the last notes from the comforting Nineteenth Psalm, "Lord, thou has been our dwelling place in all generations," died away, cadets carried the coffin outside to the waiting caisson. The riderless horse, with boots turned backwards, followed as the funeral cortege wound its way to the cemetery north of the post.

By the grave site, Forsyth concluded the prayers and then sprinkled dust on the lowered coffin, a signal for the firing of three volleys. "The echoes reverberated from side to side of the river, flung back from cliff to cliff, and died mournfully away," a journalist reported. Elizabeth left the academy grounds with Nettie Smith, Mrs. Gibbs, and Cora Bean.[28] Although the occasion was sad, she was satisfied she had kept her word. On this bright October afternoon, heavy with the scent of autumn leaves, she had given her husband a hero's funeral and buried him at West Point, his best-loved place on earth.

Returning to New York City, Libbie resumed her duties at the Society for Decorative Arts and derived comfort and companionship from her fellow workers. Despite her grief, she had followed the Sioux campaign and noted that neither Crook nor Terry had driven the hostiles onto reservations. Only when Miles had outfitted his Fifth Infantry in buffalo overcoats and relentlessly pursued the Indians through snowstorms and bitter cold had the nontreaty Sioux and their allies been defeated.

By spring 1877, almost all the bands had surrendered. On May 6, Crazy Horse had given himself up at the Red Cloud Agency. Sitting Bull's followers, who had fled to Canada, were the only nontreaties still at large. But each year more buffalo disappeared, and this remnant barely staved off starvation.

Earlier, in September and October 1876, in the aftermath of the Little Bighorn, commissioners had arrived at the Sioux agencies. Dispensing with the requirement that they obtain the consent of three-fourths of the Sioux adult males, they forced chiefs to sign away their people's right to unceded territory and the Black Hills by threatening to withhold rations. Soon after, the United States had seized additional land and closed the two Nebraska agencies, Red Cloud and Spotted Tail. Red Cloud's Oglalas and 500 Northern Cheyennes resided at Pine Ridge Agency, while Spotted Tail's Brulés were relocated at Rosebud Agency. Not only had the Sioux lost the freedom to roam between reservation and unceded territory, but the federal government, spurred on by eastern reformers, urged them to become farmers. The Sioux, whose culture glorified the warrior and the hunter, felt tremendous pressure as they faced a new way of life on the Northern Plains.[29]

Elizabeth treasured a letter from Miles, stating that his winter campaigning had increased his respect for Armstrong. More than ever, he understood that her husband's accomplishments had not been based on luck. Rather, "patient study, sleepless vigilance, laborious toil and iron nerve," applied by a dedicated professional, along with "great energy and persistency," explained Custer's successes.[30]

Nor did Miles believe Custer guilty of inadequate reconnaissance for his last battle. "As far as possible he made himself familiar with the character of the country and the strength and condition of his enemy." Defeat had occurred because Armstrong had "met overwhelming numbers, better armed for close fighting, and in a position where it was most difficult for him to handle his command." Moreover, interviews with Indians had persuaded Miles that Custer had fought against overwhelming odds, but "on that field he at least won the respect of his savage enemies."[31]

In June 1878, Miles again visited the Little Bighorn battlefield. His continuing conversations with those who had fought against Custer led him to the same conclusion others had reached earlier. Subordinates had failed, not Armstrong. Miles wrote in later memoirs that the Indians *would have fled if Reno's troops had not retreated, for the troops could not have been dislodged."* Furthermore, once Benteen had arrived at Reno Hill, the seven companies should have gone on the attack and pursued the Indians. That would have placed the hostiles *"between two fires,"* forcing them *"to retreat."*[32]

While Miles formed his opinions, others also asked questions, chiefly, Whittaker. Although some officers saw Whittaker's attacks as part of a plot to fan controversy and revive sagging book sales, he was obsessed with proving Reno's culpability.[33] On June 13, 1878, he explained to Elizabeth his latest actions.[34] Working through W. W. Corlett, congressional delegate from Wyoming Territory, Whittaker had contacted Chairman Banning of the House Committee on Military Affairs. In his letter, he had argued that "statements of an officer since deceased" warranted an investigation into Reno's actions at the Little Bighorn.[35] Certain now that the long-sought court of inquiry would materialize, Whittaker believed it would "clear the General of the charge of rashness and leave him with his laurels unstained by the shadow of a slur. That is my object," he wrote Elizabeth, "and it will be accomplished in God's good time. I am glad, all things considered, that you knew nothing of all this till the papers informed you."[36]

Major Reno was already in trouble. Recently Emiline Bell, the wife of Capt. James Bell, had rebuffed his advances. In retaliation, Reno, as post commander at Fort Abercrombie in Dakota Territory, had not only imposed irritating restrictions on her in her husband's absence but he had sullied her name. Upon his return, Bell had filed charges. Reno's defense that Emiline's alleged reputation for loose behavior represented extenuating circumstances carried no weight. The major received a two-year suspension from rank, pay, and duty.[37]

Now, finding himself faced with defamatory comments in Congress, Reno requested a court of inquiry. Late in November 1878, President Rutherford B. Hayes authorized the investigation. Although it was not a court-martial, it would determine if further action were warranted. If not, Reno expected to clear his name of the charge of cowardice.[38]

The Reno court of inquiry met for a month, beginning January 13, 1879, at Chicago's Palmer House. The examining committee consisted of Lt. Col. W. B. Royall, Third Cavalry, and Custer's old Civil War rival, Wesley Merritt, now colonel, Fifth Cavalry. John H. King, colonel, Ninth Infantry, served as presiding officer, while Lt. Jesse M. Lee, Ninth Infantry, was appointed recorder. Lyman D. Gilbert, Pennsylvania's assistant attorney general, defended Reno.[39]

Libbie found the suspense almost unendurable. To bolster her spirits, Cousin Rebecca, Aunt Loraine, and Maggie moved in with her for the proceeding's duration. The household combed the newspapers each day to keep abreast of developments.[40] Early on, the court summoned Whittaker. The writer had told the press about an affidavit he possessed signed by the late Thomas Weir and blaming Reno and Benteen for the annihilation of Custer's battalion. Pressed by the court, Whittaker admitted no such document existed and offered a statement based on alleged conversations with the dead man.[41]

Capt. Charles Braden was present, and while he did not present formal testimony, he provided information. The disabled veteran disclosed that, while residing in the same building as Weir during his last days, he had heard the captain frequently complain about Whittaker's constant entreaties. Braden also noted that Weir had no intention of signing Whittaker's statement because he disagreed with the author. He did not believe that Reno, by failing to come to Custer's aid, was responsible for his defeat. Following that revelation, Whittaker announced that, based on conversations with trumpeter Martin, bearer of the famous last message, he now absolved Benteen of disobedience. It mattered not; his testimony was inadmissable.[42]

To add to Whittaker's problems, the only officer who criticized Reno even mildly was Capt. Godfrey, who accused him of "nervous timidity." Some endorsed Reno's actions, although testimony indicated that Benteen had emerged the true commander on the bluffs. Civilian witnesses, however, were more critical. Dr. Henry Porter and interpreter Fred Girard accused the major of mishandling the retreat from the valley to the bluffs. Among the packers who testified, B. F. Churchill and John Frett accused Reno of drunkenness on the evening of June 25.[43]

None of the officers supported that charge. Reno, in his own defense, argued that Custer had never shared his battle plan.[44] Moreover, the major characterized his ill-managed rout as a "charge." Some who never heard the order had been left behind and rejoined the survivors on the bluff after dark. Reno, nonetheless, argued that the whole battalion could not have remained in place unless they "stayed forever," once Sioux warriors began turning his left flank. While those present accepted his judgment, the debate over Reno's actions would continue for decades.[45]

After twenty-six days, the court of inquiry presented its findings. "The conduct of the officers throughout was excellent and while subordinates in some instances did more for the safety of the command by brilliant displays of courage than did Major Reno," it concluded, "there was nothing in his conduct which requires animadversion from this Court." Thus "no further proceedings are necessary."[46]

The result left Elizabeth despondent, but she made no public statement. Whittaker, however, wrote the *New York Sun*, characterizing the proceedings as a "Mockery of Justice." The court had exonerated Reno, he maintained, because the major had "sneer[ed] at Custer for his Civil War record, an appeal to the old rivalry between Custer and Merritt, now one of the court." Beyond that, Whittaker charged "whitewash," convinced that officers had drawn together to protect the army against outside criticism. Merritt, he alleged, had been "afterward closeted with the Recorder alone for several hours, and, it is understood, did most of the work of the decision, the Recorder having no voice save to present the case on trial."[47]

Seeking to console herself, Elizabeth investigated the possibility of commissioning a bronze or marble bust from a model that sculptor Vinnie Ream had cast of Armstrong shortly before his death.[48] Congress, however, had neither raised her pension nor reimbursed her for the $3,000 taken from her father's estate. Given her financial circumstances, Elizabeth put aside her hope of obtaining the bust until an event occurred that left her at first dumbfounded and then incensed.

Shortly after the Reno court of inquiry, Elizabeth learned that a committee had been formed to erect a monument to her husband at West Point. Chaired by journalist Thurlow Weed, it included among its members generals Hancock and Schofield, New York Congressman Algernon S. Sullivan, and businessman Thomas Le Clear. Not only had she never been consulted, she had been ignored.

Elizabeth was not one to challenge male dominance in politics, government, or business. As she sought heroic stature for her late husband, however, she undoubtedly expected respect for her domestic role as widow. After all, in the middle-class society in which she lived and within the officer corps as well, with its code of chivalry, female roles within the family were usually accorded public reverence whatever the private reality.[49] Elizabeth Custer was discovering a bitter truth. Her domestic role, although ideologically inflated by Americans at large, did not necessarily translate into actual power.[50]

The committee of the Custer Statue Fund was the culmination of two separate drives. The *New York Herald*'s early fundraising attempt had lost momentum when the contested election of 1876 had diverted national attention from the Little Bighorn. In Monroe, meanwhile, John Bulkley, Armstrong's former classmate and a groomsman at the Bacon-Custer wedding (and Elizabeth's former suitor), had spearheaded a second drive. Even with General Sheridan as honorary president, the Monroe organization had raised only $1,000.[51]

Custer's West Point funeral, however, had revived interest in these projects. The *Herald*, with slightly more than $4,000 from its earlier effort, now solicited additional contributions. In November 1877, actress Clara Morris's benefit performance in *Jane Eyre* raised almost $1,800. John Jacob Astor and William Libby donated $500 each, while Theodore Roosevelt and James A. Roosevelt each gave $100. Albert Bierstadt sent $50 to August Belmont, treasurer of the fund-raising effort.[52]

Late in 1877, the Monroe association had completed 5,000 handwritten letters asking for contributions. Suddenly it discovered that Elizabeth Custer "preferred" a monument at West Point "or in New York." Shortly after, it sent its $1,000 to the *New York Herald* fund and disbanded its organization.[53] For now, Emmanuel Custer, riding Dandy in parades, and Maggie and Annie, two black-draped figures walking daily along the river, remained Monroe's most vivid reminders of her famous son.[54]

With funds from two separate drives, the *Herald* had collected less than $10,000. That precluded an equestrian statue, and only two artists bothered to submit designs. The committee selected J. Wilson MacDonald. A "self-taught sculptor" known for his busts of Thomas Hart Benton and Central Park's Fitz-Green Halleck, his reputation proved unsatisfactory to Custer's protective widow.[55] By now, however, Auguste Rodin's selection would not have placated her. The West Point statue was, from its inception, anathema to Elizabeth.

The committee had its first intimation of trouble when it received August Belmont's forwarded letter from the widow, along with his answer. How, Elizabeth wondered, had the artist and model been chosen? Belmont's reply listed the prestigious members of the monument committee. At the same time, the work had progressed so far that MacDonald had already received part of his commission.[56]

John Bulkley, as the liaison between Monroe and New York, remained in close contact with General Hancock as the statue neared completion. He wrote Elizabeth that MacDonald's model, unveiled earlier in August 1878, had been "very much admired by all who had seen it." Besides: "The statue is completed, the stone for the pedestal on the ground, and everything in readiness to place the statue." The committee had only to fix the date, and he planned to attend the ceremony.[57]

Not Elizabeth Bacon Custer. In the crowd of 3,000 that gathered on August 30, 1879, to unveil the statue, the widow was notably absent. Neither was her husband's best friend, Lawrence Barrett, nor his wife in the audience. Among the prominent speakers who participated that afternoon, Rep. Algernon Sullivan presented the statue on the committee's behalf. He struck a keynote theme Elizabeth would have applauded had she been present. "It is the good fortune of some soldiers, that with their death stroke they are swept along at once into the land of legend, and their names are enveloped in the purple mist of song."[58]

John Bulkley remembered years later that the crowd held its breath as the sculptor stepped forward, pulled the ribbon, and nothing happened. Several times he tugged, and finally in exasperation he called for a ladder, climbed it, and untied the threads. As the flags fell away, the band struck up "Garry Owen." The cheering crowd now beheld an eight-foot Custer with long hair and full-dress uniform. In his right hand he carried a saber, and in his left, a cocked pistol, flung against his chest. Beneath his feet stood a marble pedestal, six feet high, with four panels. The front showed Custer on horseback, while buffalo heads adorned the sides. On the back, an inscription gave Custer's name, rank (including actual and brevet), and the facts of his death.[59] Nonetheless, it was not an auspicious beginning.

After the last strains of "Garry Owen" and the reverberations of a thirteen-gun salute had died away, General Schofield accepted the statue, noting its appropriateness for West Point. Custer's monument would "remind young soldiers that all they have on earth, save their honor, may at any time be required of them as a sacrifice for the security and welfare of their countrymen."[60] Then Nathaniel Banks, a major general during the Civil War, served as the day's orator. Echoing Whittaker, he praised Custer as a fine example of the splendid soldiers produced by those of Hessian ancestry.[61] After the poem, "Custer's Last Charge," delivered by the tragedian John McCullogh, the West Point choir sang "Hail! And Farewell to Custer," composed especially for the occasion. The chaplain's benediction and another thirteen-gun salute concluded the ceremony.[62]

Despite some awkwardness, the service had placed Custer in a heroic mold, but Libbie was not reconciled. Even journalistic praise such as the

New York Herald's description of the statue as "An Art Treasure!" meant nothing to the widow. She hated the statue without seeing it, and her antipathy increased when the *Detroit Free Press* reported the comments of some army men. "Several of them sneered at the statue and said it was a ridiculous one. That no soldier ever held a sword and a pistol in that way and that Custer did not die with his colonel's uniform on as represented, and that he certainly would not fight in such a coat. One prominent officer," the report continued, "thought Custer was a hero made by the newspapers and that military men did not look on him as did the general public."[63] Apparently no one objected to the inaccuracy of Custer's long hair or noted that he had carried no sword at the Little Bighorn.

The year 1879, which had brought Reno's escape from censure and the monstrous statue, had not been good to Elizabeth. Once more she resumed her correspondence with Vinnie Ream, now married to Lt. Richard Hoxie. "I was never consulted and did not even know about it until it was done. The bitter disappointment I feel is such a cross for me to bear it seems to me I cannot endure it. I shall not," Elizabeth vowed, "see the statue until I can do something to counteract the effect that such a face as Mr. McDonald [*sic*] has modelled, must surely produce."[64]

Elizabeth had been so enraged that she had gone to church to pray for guidance. While there an inspiration had come to her. "It was that I might in time buy the bust that you have modelled and put in the library at West Point to let the world see what General Custer's face and head really can be when copied so truthfully from life as you have done." Vinnie's bust would remain in place "until divine Providence points out the way for me to see a better statue of my husband than the one that now disfigures the spot he so loved." Friends, noting that MacDonald's statue had the face of "a man sixty years old," had warned Elizabeth to stay "away from West Point and not see what would throw me into despair."[65]

Such correspondence raised Vinnie's hopes. Her standing in the art world was higher than ever since she had recently won the coveted Farragut Monument commission. Given Elizabeth's anger, she had no doubt that the days of the West Point monument were numbered. Next time Elizabeth would undoubtedly choose the sculptor, and Vinnie wanted that assignment. In the meantime, she had distressing news. Rep. John B. Clark of Missouri had recently introduced a bill requesting funds to duplicate MacDonald's statue in Washington, D.C. If Libbie, however, visited immediately, the two could head off its duplication.[66]

Elizabeth was aghast. "My blood boils at the thought of that wretched statue being repeated. Years of life in public and efforts at suppression have failed to quell my temperament and I get frantic," she related, "at the very thought of this last act." Nonetheless, while she appreciated Vinnie's advice, she felt drained and humiliated. As she explained, "a wounded thing must hide and I cannot go to Washington and stay as I should do among General Custer's old friends, . . . and," she lamented, "I cannot think the statue else than a great insult to Autie's memory."[67]

Although Elizabeth did not appear in the capital city that year, she mounted a campaign against the West Point statue's duplication. She contacted Edward Whitaker, Custer's chief of staff during the Civil War and the head of the Washington Monument Committee. Shortly after, he voiced his objections to representing Custer except on horseback. Then Elizabeth and Vinnie alerted others, including the Barretts. Soon Monument Committee members, congressmen, and senators learned that numerous people considered MacDonald's statue ludicrous. Elizabeth herself critiqued it unmercifully. No cavalry officer ever wore "full dress coat and the top boots that only belong to undress uniform. The whole costume is incongruous and incorrect." Even worse, her husband was "armed like a desperado in both hands—while some of General Custer's most brilliant charges were made without a firearm about him."[68]

The bill, requesting $12,000 in funds to reproduce the West Point statue, encountered heated debate in the House of Representatives. On March 1, 1880, Rollin Daggett of Nevada read a bitter letter from Elizabeth, characterizing the statue as a "bronze lie" and chronicling its many defects.[69] Others opposed it for different reasons. Citizens from Detroit, Michigan, and Rochester, New York, protested because of Custer's "alleged departure from the rules of organized warfare," probably a reference to his actions at the Washita. A small but vehement group, their objections, combined with those registered by Elizabeth and her friends, assured the bill's defeat when Daggett's committee reported on it unfavorably.[70]

Other commemorative efforts, more pleasing to Elizabeth, were now under way. As Colonel Sheridan's men had retrieved the officers' bodies from the Little Bighorn battlefield in 1877, the *New York Herald* had called for a monument "in the lonely valley." Both Custer and "the humblest trooper in his command" merited honor.[71] Twenty-seven months later, on August 1, 1879, Headquarters of the Army issued General Orders No. 78, establishing Custer Battlefield National Cemetery on the site. The burial of soldiers in a common grave, grouped around a monument, would alleviate the earlier distress over scattered bones.[72]

Following Custer's defeat at the Little Bighorn, Congress had authorized new forts in unceded territory. Colonel Miles's cantonment on the bank of the Yellowstone River, at the source of the Tongue, became Fort Keogh. The second post, Fort Custer, was erected at the confluence of the Bighorn and Little Bighorn rivers.[73] Soldiers stationed there cared for the battlefield cemetery, eleven miles away, until the War Department appointed a superintendent in 1893. He was needed, for beginning in the late 1880s, the men who had died in the Fort Fetterman massacre were transferred to the site. Later the remains of Indian fighters from forts Smith, Rice, Buford, Sisseton, Pembina, and Assinniboine joined them.[74]

Massachusetts sculptor Alexander McDonald designed the monument shortly after the national cemetery's establishment. In 1881, three sections of granite, weighing eighteen tons, arrived by water at Duluth, Minnesota. After they were transferred to Bismarck by rail, a steamer towed them to the mouth of the Bighorn River. From there, mule-driven sleds hauled the immense segments over the snow to the building site. One served as a base, and the other two formed a pyramid around which the enlisted men's skeletons were interred.[75]

Although Elizabeth Custer never visited the place where her husband had died, she watched these events unfold with great interest. Over the years she would monitor the maintenance of the Custer Battlefield National Cemetery and campaign for upgrading its status. Eventually she would call for a museum on the site.[76]

In fall, 1881, that lay in the future. Libbie was earning extra money "entertaining a querulous old lady every evening after working all day" in order to buy Vinnie's bust. "I need not tell you," she confided to the sculptor, "what hard work is, or what it is for a woman to struggle for what she needs." If only she were not concerned about Armstrong's family, "I would not be so anxious about the financial part of the question."[77] Nonetheless, while she still lacked the funds for a marble or bronze bust, Elizabeth's life had become more peaceful, even if happiness eluded her. "I have a little dot of a flat with a widowed friend who is working also & we enjoy this haven more than we can express."[78]

Early in 1882, Vinnie Ream Hoxie gave Libbie a plaster cast of her Custer bust. As Libbie had requested, Armstrong was depicted, not in buckskin, which had become so commercialized, but in a major general's undress uniform. "My little home is indeed a home now owing to your kindness," she assured her friend. "Just above my desk, that grand face looks up as if ready to face any future! I thank you with all my heart." All she needed were instructions for "painting the plaster."[79]

Elizabeth had enjoyed visiting the Hoxies over the holidays, but their happiness had intensified her own sense of loss. "My dear Mrs. Hoxie you know, without my telling you what a paradise is yours, to love and be loved as you are! The world is so empty, so unsatisfactory and life is not worth living, to a loving woman without such love!"[80] But while Libbie envied her friend, Vinnie was paying a heavy price. Lt. Richard Hoxie insisted that her career was over now that she was married. Thus, even though Elizabeth had saved enough for a bronze or marble bust, Vinnie refused her commission. She could no longer sell her work.[81]

Libbie felt other deprivations in her life besides the absence of marital love. The Senate had ruled "adversely" on Elizabeth's petition to recover the money taken from her father's estate.[82] Thus Libbie had left the Hoxie residence hurriedly to seek General Sherman's help in raising her pension from thirty to fifty dollars a month, the amount paid generals' widows. Once seated across from his desk, however, Elizabeth was unable to broach the subject of finances. Instead their conversation ended on a pleasant but unsatisfactory note. Returning to New York, she immediately wrote Sherman, asking his assistance and referring to herself as "desolate me."[83]

Others also helped. A friend, using the initials "LL" wrote the *New York Herald* on February 5, 1882, describing Elizabeth Custer's situation. Characterizing her pension as "a mere pittance," LL noted that her only other income was "the salary paid her by the Society of Decorative Art, which is about equal to a day laborer's pay." Although Elizabeth would have lived well had her husband survived, his death, "in the discharge of his duty as a soldier," had left her in debt. And "although not legally bound to do so," the writer thought she had "applied every dollar" of his insurance "to the settlement of claims on the estate." While LL found it "painful" to discuss the widow Custer's "personal affairs," it was "still more painful to see so estimable a lady . . . living in straitened circumstances."[84]

Two days later, the *Herald* carried a lengthy article on the subject. Elizabeth Custer was, the newspaper maintained, entitled to the pension paid a general's widow. After all, her husband had held that rank throughout much of the war and afterwards had commanded a division in Texas. Perhaps the true reason she received less than her due arose from anti-Custer sentiment in Congress. "If . . . political enmity has been carried to such an extreme as to deny to his widow the pension which has been given to the widows of other officers of the same rank," the *Herald* maintained, "the people should know it, so that the action of their servants in Congress shall at least be placed in its true light."[85]

Such efforts bore fruit. In July 1882, a bill introduced two months earlier by Rep. Thomas Ferry passed Congress, awarding her fifty dollars a month, the pension paid a general's widow.[86] Shortly after, Elizabeth retired as secretary from the Society of Decorative Arts, a position she had held for five and a half years.

Throughout these years, her correspondence with officers' wives, such as Katie Gibson, had kept Elizabeth informed about events in the Seventh Cavalry. The *Army and Navy Journal* and newspapers also reported on the careers of military men. Recently, Libbie had learned, Reno had been dismissed from the army. Now living in Washington, the major's appeals for reinstatement always died in the House Military Affairs Committee.

Less than a year after the court of inquiry, Reno had been confined at Fort Meade in the Black Hills for brawling and destroying property while intoxicated. On the night of November 10, 1879, Ella Sturgis, the twenty-one-year-old daughter of Colonel Sturgis, had caught him looking in her window. This time, even Sherman's appeal could not prevent his discharge following another court-martial. According to Benteen, Lucy Hayes had convinced her husband, President Hayes, that Reno was "deficient in that respect to the female sex which is so essential."[87]

When Benteen tried to pay his respects to Elizabeth, she refused to see him. She did learn, however, that Edward Godfrey, who had been promoted to captain following Weir's death, had given a talk at West Point complimenting her husband. This was encouraging, and in the future her relations with him and his wife became increasingly cordial.[88]

Elizabeth's association with Whittaker had, on the other hand, largely ended. She had found his book poorly written, and his misrepresentation about the purported affidavit from Weir had embarrassed her. Worse yet, John Bulkley had cautioned her that the writer was exploiting Custer's "sacred memory for his own enrichment."[89] Still, Whittaker's work had benefitted Elizabeth Custer. By 1882, most Americans saw her husband as Whittaker had presented him, although most had never read his book.

That was because Whittaker's heroic Custer, based at least in part on information and interpretations Elizabeth had supplied, had, in turn, influenced a host of other writers. J. W. Buel's 1881 *Heroes of the Plains* was only one of many popular books depicting George Armstrong Custer as an idealized, larger-than-life figure. A model for American youth, the soldier had died "with the glory of accomplished duty in his conscience and the benediction of a grateful country on his head."[90]

That same year, John Mulvaney completed his painting entitled *Custer's Last Rally*." Clothed in uniform rather than buckskin and holding both a saber and pistol, Custer dominated the picture. His courage, undaunted despite the immense odds he faced, represented for the Irish-born artist the virtues worth emulating in his adopted land. Elizabeth tried twice to view the painting in Chicago but each time recoiled from its realism. Still she appreciated the tribute to her husband. Walt Whitman, who studied the oil canvas long and hard, declared, "Nothing in the books like it, nothing in Homer, nothing in Shakespeare; more grim and sublime than either, all native, all our own, and all a fact."[91]

In the summer of 1882, six years after the Little Bighorn, Elizabeth was formulating new plans. With Alfred Gibbs's widow, she was going to England and France with free passes from an English firm, Irwin, Irwin & Company. One of the partners, identified only as Mr. Graves, remembered fondly his hunting days with the Custers on the Kansas plains.[92]

When Elizabeth returned she was thinking of writing a book describing her last years with Autie. She recalled Whittaker's earlier advice. "*You* can vindicate and justify his *private character* and the general tenor of his life as no one else can. . . . Remember that you are the centre of interest to a great proportion of our nation and that every one is anxious to hear what Custer's wife can tell them of the inner life of their pet and hero."[93] When she had expressed concern about her ability to write well enough for publication, Whittaker had counseled her to "talk on paper as you talk viva voce, and you conquer all mankind."[94] Still, one other consideration gave her pause. As a woman, she did not want others to see her "with the thought that I was an author."[95] On the other hand, only her book could bring Armstrong "before his people in his private life—as a Son—a brother a husband."[96]

One other matter weighed on the widow's mind. The West Point monument must come down, or she would know no peace. During the past summer the *New York Times* had carried an article, "West Point in Danger," poking fun at the statue with its "dandified coat" and its "mass of hair done up in an invisible net." No soldier, the newspaper maintained, ever wore the "costume of a rope dancer" and engaged in "melodramatic antics" while facing death.[97]

To eliminate the atrocity, Elizabeth needed a powerful ally. After careful thought, she chose her target. Sherman, the commanding general of the United States Army, had always been cordial and sympathetic and since Armstrong's death even more so.[98] In part, he was responding to her bereavement, but Elizabeth still had the power to engage others. Now in her forties, photographs suggest that she was more attractive than she had been at thirty-four. Despite the lines etched around her eyes, she seemed more youthful than the heavy-set, matronly figure on the steps of the Fort Lincoln residence.

As Elizabeth sat in her office and pondered her plans—a trip to Europe, removal of the hated statue, and possibly the writing of a book—she looked up at the bust of her husband. Her recollections, dimmed by time, focused on his many endearing qualities. As Whittaker had written in his biography of Custer, "Finding him good, she left him perfect."[99] That was exactly what Elizabeth was accomplishing as she gazed at her plaster saint. Certainly, as the perfect husband, he deserved better than the monstrosity at his old alma mater. Powerful men had put up the West Point statue, but the Widow Custer would bring it down.

CHAPTER 13

A Fitting
"Custer Memorial"

SHERMAN, amazed that the committee of the Custer Statue Fund had not consulted Elizabeth about the West Point monument, advised her to contact Robert Lincoln, secretary of war. Lincoln, however, turned the matter over to Gen. O. O. Howard, the superintendent of West Point, who, in turn, bequeathed the problem to his successor, Wesley Merritt.[1] Exasperated, Elizabeth again wrote the commanding general. When all else failed, she reminded others of her bereavement. "I have little hope. But what hope I now have," she confided, "rests in you, the kindest and truest of friends to me, when I so need all that they can do to make my sad life endurable."[2] Why, she wondered, could Lincoln not simply order the statue removed as she desired?

Moreover, Elizabeth had little hope of obtaining Merritt's help, "unless you ask him to do it, dear General Sherman. A wife's love sharpens her eyes and quickens her instinct, and years ago I knew (not from my husband) that General Merritt was his enemy." Later, during a visit on the Plains, Merritt seemed to have overcome the "enmity and jealousy that was so bitter in the Army of the Potomac." The Reno court of inquiry, unfortunately, had dispelled her illusions. Without Sherman's prodding the "audacious and conspicuous representation" would remain in place.[3]

The kind general, moved by Elizabeth's pleas, advised her to take courage. Even Lincoln "has in his heart a warm place for you, who have been so brave, so true to Custer and his memory, that every man who is a man must respond to your appeal." At the same time, however, the secretary of war faced a delicate situation. MacDonald saw the statue as "the heroic creation of his genius," and it was "backed by the subscribers." Lincoln might be embarrassed were it removed.

Nonetheless, Sherman advised Elizabeth to draw up a provisional contract for an obelisk or shaft as replacement, along with a "short strong letter demanding as the widow of Custer, the *sole* and *exclusive* right to mark the grave of your husband." He would forward these to Lincoln, with the recommendation that, as Custer's widow, Elizabeth had the "natural, unqualified Right" to demand the monument's removal. As for Merritt, her fears were unfounded. If "jealous of Custer living, he cannot but admire his plucky widow." Still, Elizabeth could always confide in Sherman with "absolute frankness for I sympathize with every pulsation of your wounded heart." In the meantime, he suggested that she add Italy and southern Austria to England and France as touring places when she went abroad.[4]

Shortly before Elizabeth returned from Europe in August 1883, an embarrassing report appeared in the *Army and Navy Journal*. Justh, unhappy over receiving ten cents on the dollar from Custer's estate, had brought suit against Ben Holladay, cosigner of Armstrong's note. Although the stockbroker had won in a lower court, the Supreme Court of the District of Columbia ruled on appeal that the amount owed was a gambling debt. He could not legally demand repayment.[5]

Furthermore, the court added, Justh had known the circumstances, since Custer could never have paid for almost $400,000 worth of transactions. "The disparity between the pecuniary ability of Custer and the immense amount of purchases and sales within half a year's time, would certainly be regarded by business men as a circumstance in contradiction of the idea that he intended to make actual contracts so much beyond his means of payment."[6] If any doubt remained, Custer's letters to Justh enjoining secrecy reinforced the court's belief "that they refer to an illicit business, with which Custer was rather ashamed to be connected." The soldier had used the language "men use when speaking of their so-called 'debts of honor,' and not of their legitimate, ordinary money transactions."[7]

Elizabeth never responded publicly to this unfavorable publicity. Any threat to her beloved's reputation, however, only increased her determination to remove the hated statue. Despite Sherman's earlier reassurances, neither Lincoln nor Merritt had taken action against the West Point monument. When Sherman retired as commanding general in November 1883, the dreaded figure still stood on the bluff below headquarters, immediately visible to visitors arriving by train or boat.[8] To Elizabeth, enough was enough.

Revitalized from nine months abroad, she found a new ally in Leonard Swett of Chicago. He remembered fondly Elizabeth's gracious hospitality when he had visited Fort Lincoln in 1875. Moreover, as one of Abraham Lincoln's friends from circuit-riding days, his letters to the late president's son were guaranteed a careful reading. By the spring of 1884, Swett was enclosing Libbie's letters inside his correspondence to Robert Lincoln. Feeling increasingly pressured, the secretary pleaded that had the government erected the statue, he could remove it. But given the "prominent citizens, who presumably take great pride in it, and with whom it would be difficult to consult," Lincoln remained cautious. Still, as Chester Arthur's administration drew to a close and Lincoln prepared to leave the War Department, he thought that "a gradual removal might be begun which would result in making it difficult to find the statue."[9]

In November 1884, Lincoln wrote Swett that, given Elizabeth's most recent "urgent application," Merritt had removed the statue, which was now "securely boxed and stored at the Post."[10] Later in life, Elizabeth insisted that she had "literally cried it off its pedestal." True, but as one scholar notes, "The tears had to be applied in the right places—and persistently."[11]

During this period Elizabeth had not contented herself with simply working behind the scenes to take down a hated monument. Desiring to drown out negative publicity from the Justh matter and offset the hated representation of her husband, she had thrown herself wholeheartedly into completing her book, describing her years in Dakota Territory with Autie. Swett had not only helped her remove the hated statue, he had put to rest her lingering doubts about the propriety of stepping forward in the public role of author. Emphatically he had told her she "had no right to bear the [Custer] name" unless she described Armstrong's domestic life.[12]

The mechanics had given Elizabeth little trouble, given her natural facility with words, but the work had proved more arduous than expected. As she reread old letters to extract information on the Little Bighorn and excerpts for her appendix, a flood of buried memories resurfaced. For years, Elizabeth had dealt with her pain by keeping so busy that "my own personal affairs had no part." Now she found herself "always looking back in my waking hour and dreaming the saddest most unsatisfactory dreams of my beloved one at night."[13] During this time, Elizabeth called on her deepest reserves as she found herself "strained to the utmost with excessive exhaustive emotion." Worse, she feared she could not "so frame a little story of his home life that any one would be willing to read." Any "thread of my own sorrow," she later confided to a friend, would repel Americans, an "anxious, overtaxed, nervous people."[14]

After Elizabeth sent her completed manuscript to Harper & Brothers, she went to bed, physically exhausted and mentally depressed. Maggie, whose mother had died in January 1882, moved in with her at her apartment at Third Avenue and 18th Street while she regained her strength.[15] One morning, the two women awoke to the sound of a maid crying "fire," as flames shot out of a heating shaft. The three hurriedly left the Stuyvesant Apartment Building after warning the other residents. Soon after, when Libbie and Maggie returned to retrieve letters and mementoes, firemen held them back until they extinguished the blaze. When the women finally reentered their home they found money and treasured items missing. Nonetheless, amidst the wreckage, Elizabeth discovered that her husband's letters, stored in an iron safe, had survived. So too had Vinnie Ream's head of Autie along with another less treasured bust.[16] These were good omens despite the other losses.

In March 1885, *"Boots and Saddles"* appeared in the bookstores. Elizabeth had dedicated the small volume to "My Husband: The Echo of Whose Voice Has Been My Inspiration." The title, referring to a cavalry call for a march, was an appropriate choice for a woman who prided herself on being "the only officer's wife who always followed the regiment."[17] Willingly she had accompanied her spouse anywhere, whether "Lapland" or its equivalent, Dakota Territory.[18] Given her depiction of the man she lovingly called "my husband," her readers knew why.

In the flesh, the heroic soldier had been "the most agile, active man I ever knew, and so very strong and in perfect physical condition that he rarely knew even an hour's indisposition."[19] Equally impressive was his character. As regimental commander, Custer had been solicitous of his enlisted men and impartial towards his officers. By temperament he had eschewed gossip and grudge-holding, and had risen above petty jealousy. In addition, the knight of the Plains had been a man of letters, widely read and deeply appreciative of literature and poetry.[20]

But it was the family man, the loving son so devoted to his mother that he wept when he left her, the comrade brother and considerate husband, who emerged most clearly[21] If home life both made and reflected character, then by implication, this soldier would never have jeopardized his cavalrymen's lives for the mere chance of winning glory through victory. While Elizabeth covered events leading up to the Little Bighorn in a brief but moving fashion, she never mentioned the controversies that had dogged Armstrong's career. Nothing critical of her husband appeared in her text. Instead corruption among Indian agents, superior arms among Indians, and inferior arms among soldiers explained the Little Bighorn.[22]

Elizabeth wrote in a disarming fashion. In the introduction she noted that few people knew about the domestic life of the cavalry at frontier outposts, and she would be dealing in some instances with minutiae. Modestly, as became a female, she apologized. Actually, by escorting the reader into her home and discussing the commonplace, she made that person her confidante. She also wrote in a witty and self-deprecating fashion, with a flair for the telling detail or anecdote. Thus her book exudes her personal charm. It was the same charm—based on "simplicity and originality"—that had worked so well during her Boyd Seminary commencement speech in June 1862. And it was the same charm—based on her "lively and unversed and talkative" manner—that had won her numerous suitors in Monroe.[23]

Accordingly, Elizabeth extolled her late husband while she silenced his critics. An unidentified but "prominent officer" had belittled Custer's record in conversation with a *Detroit Free Press* reporter during the unveiling of the West Point statue. How could he and others like him publicly challenge her statements? What officer or enemy of Custer would have had the temerity or callousness to disagree openly with a bereaved and loving spouse? Which one of them would have shown such disrespect for a widow's fidelity? And, most telling of all, how could a man not fundamentally superior to ordinary men inspire such devotion in a woman seen by politicians and journalists as an ideal wife?[24] In short, by publishing her well-written book on her private life with "my husband," Elizabeth expanded her personal influence and infused her domestic role with public power. For five years Elizabeth Custer had fought to remove a statue erected by others. Victorious, she now replaced it with her own monument. "This entertaining book, by the widow of the late General Custer, ought to be called the 'Custer memorial,' for this it practically is," wrote one discerning reviewer.[25]

But Elizabeth's book was more. Subtitled *Life in Dakota with General Custer*, it was also a domestic treatise. In its pages, she told the story of a marriage in which humor and a minimum of complaint enabled affection to survive separations, dangers, the primitive hardships of frontier posts, and even death itself. Set in the "separate . . . world" of the frontier, it appealed to a broader audience than a similar story, located North or South, given the memories of the family quarrel that had ended at Appomattox two decades earlier.[26]

In 1858, Teresa Vielé, the wife of Lt. Egbert L. Vielé, had published *Following the Drum*, depicting army life in Texas. Ten years later, Margaret Carrington's *Ab-sa-ra-ka* had appeared, portraying her army life with Col. Henry Carrington.[27] Like these two women before her and the other military wives whose works appeared later, Elizabeth described with wit and unfailing humor the difficulties middle-class women faced when they tried to create a proper home in the male-dominated world of the United States frontier army.

Regulations took no account of them, classifying them as "camp followers." Nonetheless, in Elizabeth Custer's view, the officers were so appreciative of the willingness of their wives to live on the frontier that they poured their bath water and buttoned their shoes. Their chivalry transformed these women into "queens," who ruled in the realm of affections.[28] And rightly so, for implicitly these queens were agents of civilization and played a key role in staving off threats of barbarism.

On one side loomed the aborigines, whom Elizabeth viewed as savages. She conveyed her message by unobtrusively stressing differences between Indian and Anglo-American home life. Indian families produced warriors, and mothers encouraged their male children, even as infants, to strike a blow for the honor of counting coup. Indian women, Elizabeth argued, were beasts of burden, not mistresses of the hearth.[29] Therefore, whatever nobility these primitive people possessed (and she, like her husband, accorded them nobility), fate ordained their removal in the face of a genteel, progressive, and Christian civilization.[30]

The primitive foe was not the only danger threatening frontier posts. Equally grave was the possibility that officers, away from the influence of their families and homes and sentenced to rigorous and boring duty far from Eastern amenities, would succumb to temptation. On the other side of the river, as Libbie explained in "Breaking Up of the Missouri," were the shanties or the "canvas-covered cabin," bearing names such as "My Lady's Bower" or "Dew Drop Inn," where liquor dealers and prostitutes beckoned. Nonetheless, in the creation of a home, based on a loving marriage, lay the antidote to "hog-ranches." Elizabeth considered the wife's role so important that Maggie found her over-zealous. When young officers arrived from West Point, Libbie often greeted them, her sister-in-law claimed, with the statement, "I'm very glad to see you; I hope that you are engaged."[31]

Reviewers praised *"Boots and Saddles,"* approving of both subject matter and the "charm of the narrative," which lay in "its simplicity." The *San Francisco Weekly Bulletin* characterized Libbie as "a hero worshipper" but accepted her veracity, since "the story is told with a degree of candor which makes it a trustworthy biography."[32] The *New York Independent* observed: "To his wife, General Custer is a hero *sans peur et sans reproche*," but it too recommended her book. Composed "in the most natural strain . . . the tone is so genial and sympathetic that the reader becomes attached to the author, her gallant husband, the servants, the soldiers, and indeed, to nearly every character in the volume."[33]

Two publications expressed reservations. The *Nation* cautioned young readers to remember that Elizabeth Custer had "less to tell about lieutenants than lieutenant-colonels."[34] *The Academy* (London) offered the most critical evaluation. "The Indians had out-generalled the general, and meted out to him the fate he had prepared for them. The book is, therefore, not one to be judged too severely, even did it require any consideration beyond what its merits deserve." Elizabeth Custer's subject was her "hero. Every act of his life is to her of greater importance than such trivialities can be to one less intimately concerned with his career. . . . But, we are not bound to take our opinion of him from his widow," the reviewer continued. "His tragic end was due to a lack of caution, and it is still affirmed by those who ought to know, that Black Kettle, whom he defeated and killed in 1868, had always been a friend to the whites, and on this very occasion was not on the warpath, but on an expedition to receive his annuity."[35]

Such caveats or criticisms were the exception. On the whole the reception of *"Boots and Saddles"* pleased Elizabeth. One reviewer satisfied her entirely. Norman Fox, in an essay entitled "Christianity and Manliness," recommended her book as required reading for Sunday schools. Husband and wife, he argued, embodied "noble Christian manhood and womanhood." For young boys, the "dashing fighter" emerged as "a man of pure and noble personal character, hilariously fun-loving, but tender, gentle and kind," not only to humans but animals. Boys learned "that a man may be a gallant soldier and yet pure of life, delicate in speech, gentle in act, and a Christian." As for young women, Elizabeth's example showed that domestic happiness followed when "the heroic coexisted with womanly timidity."[36]

As a widow, Elizabeth reminded one reviewer of Queen Victoria. The monarch had commended herself to British and Americans alike by her devotion to family and her long period of mourning for her late husband, Prince Albert. The *Philadelphia Inquirer* spelled out the parallels between the two: "The volume should be of as much personal interest to Americans as Queen Victoria's personal narratives were to Englishmen."[37]

In mid-April 1885, journalist Jeannette Gilder interviewed Libbie. The editor of the *Critic*, a small but influential biweekly newspaper that celebrated American writing and offered literary criticism interspersed with gossip, Gilder praised *"Boots and Saddles."* It would become, she predicted, "the favorite 'juvenile' of many years to come and will hold its own with works, such as Richard Henry Dana's 'Three Years Before the Mast.'"[38]

Turning to Elizabeth's personal life, Gilder described her "little flat in a house in East Eighteenth Street" as a place where "aestheticsm and comfort in furnishing are admirably combined." Although Elizabeth's pension freed her from wage-earning, it afforded few luxuries. Nonetheless, she required no sympathy. Her "poverty" bothered her friends more than herself, and they constantly invited her on trips "anywhere from Mexico to England." As Elizabeth explained, "My friends are kindness itself and seem to feel that I am their special care."[39]

Armstrong's reputation had opened doors for the widow, but her own efforts were bringing her important new contacts. Among the patrons who supported Jeannette Gilder's magazine was Andrew Carnegie. Eventually, he and his wife Louise befriended Elizabeth.[40] More important, Jeannette was the sister of Richard Gilder, former editor for *Scribner's Monthly* and now chief editor of *Century Monthly Magazine*.[41] Before long, she introduced Elizabeth to her brother.[42]

The publication of her book also gave Elizabeth the chance to augment her income by writing newspaper columns. Her essays were distributed to various publications, including the *Worcester Sunday Telegram*, the *New York World*, and the *Chicago Tribune*.[43] In the summer of 1885, Elizabeth covered New York City's funeral parade for Ulysses S. Grant, who had died of throat cancer in July. She described the black-draped statues and mannequins in stores in honor of "a departed president." Grant—her enemy's name—never appeared in her column.[44]

Early in September, Elizabeth received a message etched on birchbark from Candace Wheeler: "Lotus Land, Careaway Cottage, Catskills—Come up and rest, little woman, We all want you." As New York City temperatures hovered in the nineties, Libbie caught the West Shore Railroad. By mid-afternoon she had joined her friends on Candace Wheeler's porch in the mountains, where the thermometer registered fifty degrees. Inside, a fire crackled.[45]

Elizabeth felt immediately at home in the rustic cabin, outfitted with unpainted furniture and decorated with denim table cloths, rag rugs, and bean jars filled with wildflowers. Gazing out the widow, she saw the surrounding mountains, covered with evergreens, birches, and the deciduous trees whose leaves were turning yellow, brown, and red. Although she was not among the "bonanzas" and "belong[ed] to what might be called the supernumerary women of the world—the old maids and widows," she wanted her own mountain cabin someday.[46]

She had arrived at Candace Wheeler's Onteora, two miles above Tannersville, New York. While the setting was beautiful, its attraction lay in the artists and writers drawn to the colony. That afternoon, Elizabeth met Samuel Clemens and his wife, Olivia; Adam Badeau, who had completed his first work on the late President Grant; the philanthropist Henry Sage and his wife; and the Thurbers. Francis Thurber, Candace Wheeler's brother, was a wholesale merchant. His wife Jeannette had been the driving force behind the establishment of the New York-based American School of Opera.[47]

While Elizabeth's modest circumstances were improving, Michigan veterans had read Gilder's description of her "poverty." When they nominated her for an opening in the Detroit Pension Agency, she expressed interest on behalf of Maggie. The last few years had not been kind to her sister-in-law. In addition to losing Maria almost four years earlier, Maggie had suffered the disruption of her romance with Stephen Baker, captain in the Seventh Infantry.[48] Currently, Maggie resided with her brother-in-law Fred Calhoun and his family at Vancouver Barracks, Wyoming.[49] Since the life of a widowed aunt hardly satisfied a vivacious woman in her thirties, Elizabeth hoped Maggie could return to Michigan and live independently. Government employment would make that possible.

When Elizabeth arrived in Washington to plead her sister-in-law's case, she endured humiliation. Neither the commissioner of pensions nor the senator, who had invited her to the capital, would see her. She took her seat in the anterooms among the throngs of Democratic petitioners who had arrived in Washington, seeking a position now that their party had captured the White House for the first time in twenty-four years. After finding herself directed to assistants, Elizabeth demanded a meeting with L. Q. C. Lamar, secretary of the interior. He ushered her into his office, but when he sat on his sofa, rather than behind his desk, Elizabeth knew that no business would be conducted. After a brief exchange of pleasantries and kind words for Armstrong, he showed her the door.[50]

Shortly after, Elizabeth read in a newspaper that the president "does not consider it consistent with the dignity of true womanhood to come here to seek appointments." Angered, she responded in the *Chicago Tribune*.[51] Only her desire "to honor the family of a soldier" had brought her to the capital, certainly not a desire to meddle in the male domain of politics. A woman, "chameleon-like," only reflected "the opinions of the man, be he brother, husband, or father, who had most to do in shaping her character."[52] Nonetheless, her unhappy experience convinced her: "If any woman contemplates coming, there is just one word I would like to appropriate that Lord Chesterfield quotes from *Punch* in reply to his son appealing to him for advice about getting married—'Don't.'"[53] For the present, she could give Maggie no help.

Nevertheless, Elizabeth wrote Gov. Russell A. Alger, thanking her fellow Michigan citizens. While she would have welcomed a government salary, "I felt that my duty and my greatest privilege lay in working to commemorate my husband. I feel my life set apart for that purpose. As soon as I can get the nerve (for writing of him taxes every breath) I am going to write a boy's book that I may implant my husband in the minds of the coming generation." *"Boots and Saddles"* had already sold 15,000 copies, which meant that at least 30,000 had read it. She hoped to bring Armstrong before the public again "while the interest is reawakened."[54]

Despite strong sales, however, Elizabeth had realized little profit from royalties. If her native state wished to help her, someone should buy her Monroe home.[55] The governor, who had served with Custer's brigade in the Civil War, suggested that Michigan citizens purchase her homestead on a subscription basis. He pledged $500, for "Mrs. Gen. Custer seems to be in pressing need of money."[56] Nothing came of Alger's suggestion, and the property remained unsold until 1890, when Elizabeth's attorney John Rauch bought it for his family.[57]

Elizabeth continued augmenting her income by writing brief pieces for newspapers. She described her travels, including her "pilgrimage" to Mount Vernon and her fall, 1885, trip to Boston—the seat, she thought, of national learning. Even more enjoyable, her work gave her the opportunity to explore her own city's varied offerings. One Sunday morning she heard her friend Moncure Conway, former abolitionist and noted freethinker, lecture on the common origins of the world's religions.[58] Soon after, she attended Lilli Lehmann's debut in the Karl Goldmark opera *The Queen of Sheba*. Two days later Elizabeth reported on the Japanese village on display in Madison Square Garden.[59] Much of the improvement in the city's offerings had come, Elizabeth thought, from women. While earlier they had been "confined to the narrow limits of the home or their own society circle," their influence now pervaded Gotham. Recently several matrons, using stereopticon views of sculpture and painting, had inaugurated free history and mythology classes for children at Cooper Union.[60]

But if New York City provided a host of stimulating activities, it also had its darker side. Middle-class Americans, such as Elizabeth, read about the political corruption on one hand and the frightening scenes of violence on the other, especially between workers and employers as labor became more militant. Moreover, the city was changing too quickly. Since her arrival in 1877, Elizabeth had watched Gotham become increasingly polyglot as greater numbers of immigrants arrived from eastern and central Europe. More and more New Yorkers were themselves either immigrants or the children of immigrants, and persons of Elizabeth's background were increasingly the minority.[61] Her essays reflected her concerns about these changes. She characterized the neighborhood around St. Stanislas Polish curch as "vile," and once let slip a reference to the "refuse population of foreign lands" on New York streets.[62]

When Elizabeth needed comfort in the face of such tumultuous change, she sometimes visited Plymouth Church in Brooklyn to listen to America's most celebrated clergyman. By December 1885, Henry Ward Beecher was showing his age, but his sermons were still bracing. Whatever the nation's disorders, he assured his congregation, the old principles of right and wrong, emanating from an orderly universe, prevailed. Despite their upheavals, Americans remained a chosen people.[63] Those who maintained their faith in the eternal verities would have no problem facing death. For Elizabeth his sermon "was as if a clarion note of joy had sounded. No lugubrious willows and prostrate forms came to our vision," for which she was grateful—"rather a glorious army of men and women whose dying had been like their living, and whose song of rejoicing sounded above the sighs and wails."[64]

During the 1885–86 holiday season Elizabeth heard the song "Across the Sands of Dee." New York judge-advocate, Gen. Horatio King, had set the words to music from a poem by the late British clergyman and novelist Charles Kingsley.[65] As the tune floated in and out of Elizabeth's consciousness, she opened a letter one day early in 1886. Her correspondent was Frances Kingsley, Charles Kingsley's widow, a woman known to her friends as Fanny.[66]

Charles Kingsley, who had served briefly as Victoria's chaplain, had special meaning for Libbie. While many of his writings had dealt with social problems, and although he had campaigned untiringly for sanitary reform, he had loved military history. In two of his novels, *Westward Ho!* and *Two Years Ago*, he had presented warfare as potentially ennobling, for individuals and for nations. During the Crimean War Kingsley had published a tract (anonymously at first) entitled *Brave Words for Brave Soldiers and Sailors*. "The Lord Jesus Christ is not only the *Prince of Peace*; He is the *Prince of War* too."[67] And, finally, Kingsley, like many Victorians, had advocated the chronicling of heroic lives as a way of inspiring future generations.[68]

Kingsley had died in 1875, and shortly after, his widow, listing herself simply as "His Wife," had penned her own memorial, *Charles Kingsley: His Letters and Memories of His Life*. The two-volume work, published in 1877, included edited portions of her husband's letters and excerpts from his writings, tied together with biographical narrative. Fanny Kingsley's work had depicted her husband both as an intellectual responding to the currents and questions of his time and as loving husband and father within his home.[69]

Elizabeth poured out her fears, hopes, and experiences to the woman with whom she felt such affinity. She described her turbulence while writing *"Boots and Saddles"* and her physical and emotional collapse afterwards. "But you see our Heavenly Father was not through with me and I rose from the bed inspired to live to keep his memory fresh and make him new friends." Once the book appeared, her life had changed for the better.[70]

The complimentary reviews and warm letters had told Elizabeth she remained "the beloved of my people because I was his chosen wife." Moreover, the widow who had no parents, children, or siblings drew comfort from the public's "possession of me which is very dear to me, alone as I am." Armstrong had been the people's "Bayard," but "now they tell me they love him anew because he was such a son, brother, husband, friend. . . . I am so thankful to have been the instrument in God's hands of having in a measure mirrored my husband to his people" that she would endure the pain of writing all over again "for the privilege of speaking to his land of him I love."[71] Although the exertion had, she claimed, almost taken her life, God had spared her "to do further honor to a man sacrificed by his country. For dear Mrs. Kingsley, the Indian Policy of our government has spilled some of its best blood without its being necessary."[72]

Elizabeth then described the details of her existence, including her "tiny flat" and the friend's mother she had "borrowed" to share her home. "We live very simply but it is an independent life for me." While newspaper writing added to her income, equally important was her volunteer work, which she planned to continue all her life. As the youngest board member of the Bellevue Training School of Nurses, the institution she had almost entered earlier, Elizabeth supervised training in one of the wards. In addition, she served as a trustee for Elizabeth Blackwell's New York Infirmary for Women and Children, a major school for women physicians.[73]

But the important work lay ahead, "for my whole soul is fixed in putting my husband in the hearts of the boys who will be the men of the day soon."[74] Years ago, Elizabeth had read Fanny Kingsley's "tribute" to her husband, and "it was due to *you* that I prayed and struggled to do my work. Is it not strange that *you* having had such unconscious influence over me should be moved to write me so tenderly?" Elizabeth enclosed pictures of herself and Armstrong.[75]

Fanny Kingsley's response arrived quickly, complete with photographs of herself and her husband, along with the message that she expected to die soon. Pondering the pictures and the "trembling lines," Elizabeth confided to her new-found friend that she considered her the ideal wife. "The [pathetic?] patient look in your soulful face tells me worlds about you and makes it clear to me why your loved husband was able to make his impress on the hearts of all feeling people. A man, be he ever so noble," Elizabeth continued, "cannot develop into the broad, large hearted creature God intended him to be and reach out far stretching hands of sympathy all over the world unless he has, as his background, a woman who loves, encourages, inspires. If you only knew," she added, "what your life is to women, what an influence it was as his wife, what gratitude we women feel to point to such fidelity and how proudly we speak always of you as you have made me feel as his *wife* and never as a widow." Already the Kingsleys' photographs hung in Elizabeth's bedroom, where they would remain "for the rest of my life as my example and my inspiration."[76]

Other letters arrived daily, telling Elizabeth that her book had "made my country feel that I belong to them and made even the humblest persons feel certain that they can say what they like to 'Elizabeth' for so they call me in their letters." Although she planned to visit Mexico or California in the spring, when she returned, she would begin another book. "Your words complete the inspiration necessary."[77]

In August 1886, Rhoda died while visiting relatives in New Bedford, Massachusetts.[78] Elizabeth now inherited $5,000 set aside earlier as her stepmother's life estate. This windfall, combined with her pension, enabled her to give up most of her columns and devote more time to her second book.

Shortly after Rhoda's funeral in Tecumseh, Michigan, Elizabeth received a letter from Buffalo Bill Cody. Libbie had followed his career since the days he had hunted buffalo with Armstrong, Sheridan, and Grand Duke Alexis in 1872. After her husband's death, she had read that Cody had interrupted his performing briefly to resume scouting, serving as guide for the Fifth Cavalry. Riding ahead of the troops in July 1876, he had encountered a Cheyenne Indian, Hay-o-wei, whose name another scout translated as "Yellow-Hand." At a place called War Bonnet Creek, Cody had killed the warrior and returned with the "First Scalp for Custer."[79]

Cody's show, known as Buffalo Bill's Wild West, had toured the country since 1883. The production offered exhibitions of shooting and riding with Annie Oakley, the female sharpshooter, as a major attraction. With uncanny accuracy, she hit glass balls, clay pigeons, and three-by-five cards bearing her picture and a heart, which she then tossed to the roaring crowd.[80]

In 1885, Sitting Bull had been among the featured performers. Only four year earlier, he and his band had surrendered to American soldiers at Fort Buford. After two years confinement at Fort Randall, Sitting Bull had arrived at Standing Rock reservation in 1883. A year later, after watching Annie Oakley's exhibition at St. Paul, he had joined Cody's Wild West show to watch "Little Sure Shot" perform daily. But although Canadian crowds received him warmly, United States audiences, holding him responsible for Custer's death, often hissed and booed. After one season, Sitting Bull left the company.[81]

After his departure, Cody, still anxious to attract crowds, had inaugurated *The Drama of Civilization*. He staged a series of vignettes, including Indians attacking an emigrant train, residents of a settler's cabin fighting off another Indian attack, and a cyclone destroying the mining town of Deadwood. With all this excitement, interspersed with displays of sharpshooting, Buffalo Bill needed an even more spectacular grand finale. Nothing could surpass Custer's last stand.[82]

Most of Elizabeth Custer's compatriots now understood, after events surrounding the West Point statue, that no person or organization used George Armstrong Custer's name or incidents from his life without first consulting her. Even those wishing to establish a George A. Custer chapter of the Grand Army of the Republic usually requested her permission.[83] In September, Cody wrote Elizabeth, asking her "sanction" for his plan. He promised to "spare no expense to do credit to our exhibition and deepen the lustre of your glorious husband's reputation as a soldier and a man." The act, moreover, would transcend show business and educate those unacquainted with "the valor and heroism of the men who have made civilization possible on this continent." Finally, if Elizabeth attended opening night, her presence would "attract the attention of all the good women in America who would share your pride and my triumph."[84]

Elizabeth was there, and despite the pain associated with the Little Bighorn, enjoyed the show. Later she characterized it as the "most realistic and faithful representation of a western life that has ceased to be, with advancing civilization."[85] She returned many times, always visiting the cast afterwards. Before long she became acquainted with Annie Oakley, in private life Mrs. Phoebe Ann Moses Butler, a prim young woman who embroidered between acts. That winter Elizabeth and Phoebe, despite almost twenty years difference in ages, passed many hours together. As the snow fell softly on the city outside, they exchanged confidences in one another's apartments. In time "Little Sure Shot" came to know Custer, not as the soldier who "stood like a sheaf of corn with all the ears fallen around him," as Sitting Bull described him. Rather she knew him as the gallant husband of her friend Elizabeth.[86]

Later that year Eliza arrived in New York City. Now married to a southern Ohio lawyer and approaching fifty, Eliza Brown Denison had come to help Elizabeth recall events of the period following the Civil War. Libbie toured New York with her, taking her to the Fifth Avenue Hotel, where Eliza had stayed with the Custers. Elizabeth also showed her the changes technology had wrought in the metropolis. The two women rode the elevated train with its thrilling curves and crossed Brooklyn Bridge, open to traffic for three years and already attracting suicides. They also viewed the Statue of Liberty in New York harbor.[87]

What enthralled Eliza more than any other outing, however, was the Wild West show. Afterwards, Elizabeth sent her backstage with a card introducing her to the cast as the Custers' Eliza. The physical resemblance between Armstrong and William F. Cody struck Eliza immediately. Undoubtedly Cody was pleased when she blurted out, "Mr. Buffalo Bill, when you cum up to the stand and wheeled around, I said to myself, 'Well, if he ain't the 'spress image of Ginnel Custer in battle, I never seed any one that was.'"[88]

After Eliza left, Elizabeth, deluged by old memories, gave herself over completely to her second manuscript. Instead of sending it to Harper &

Brothers, however, she accepted a contract with C. L. Webster & Company. Headed by Samuel Clemens, the firm marketed her book on a subscription basis. Simultaneously it also arranged for publication in London by Sampson, Low, Marston, Searles & Rivington.[89]

By Christmas, Elizabeth's *Tenting in the Plains* was in the stores. The two-volume work began with a brief biography of Armstrong, then covered the conclusion of the war, the events in Louisiana and Texas, Custer's entry into the Seventh Cavalry, and the Hancock campaign. It concluded with Armstrong's unexpected appearance at Fort Riley and "the one long, perfect day" that followed. Libbie said nothing of the later charges and court-martial that ended in her husband's suspension from rank, pay, and service for a year.

Finally, Eliza emerged as a prominent figure in this work. Early in the narrative, Elizabeth introduced her and described her 1886 visit to New York. Since nothing is accidental in Libbie's seemingly discursive books, this digression made important points. Elizabeth presented Eliza as "a good war historian, a modest chronicler of a really self-denying and courageous life," and the person who mothered her during the Civil War. She also gave her former servant full credit for freeing herself instead of depending on others for liberation. Asked why she had left the known world of her relatives and plantation to take her chances on the fortunes of war, Eliza responded, "I didn't set down to wait to have 'em all free *me*." I helped to free myself."[90]

Although Eliza joined the army, she came through the war with her virtue intact. As she noted, "There's many folks says that a woman can't follow the army without throwing themselves away, but I know better. I went in, and I cum out with the respect of the men and the officers."[91] Elizabeth's character sketch transcended racial and class distinctions long enough to give her reader the most salient facts about Eliza as a person. Moreover, Libbie clearly admired her former servant for her self reliance and bravery. One of the sketches in the book shows "Eliza, cooking under fire," while the accompanying text indicates that the brave servant grumbled when exploding shells impeded her work.[92]

After presenting her many admirable human qualities, Elizabeth noted the improvement in Eliza's dress and speech. No longer, except for occasional lapses (which Libbie found "charming"), did she speak "like field-hands," and use "whar and thar." At Eliza's insistence, Elizabeth explained that, despite the drawing, "she don't wear them rags now." Truly, Eliza's life had been one of upward mobility, from slave to servant to wife of a small-town lawyer.[93] Although Elizabeth had given a remarkable woman her due, the overall impact of her description of the 1886 tour of New York City and her comments on Eliza's mobility strongly suggest that Elizabeth saw herself as her former servant's uplifter. Elizabeth was the teacher who enjoyed introducing an awestruck woman to civilization's newest engineering feats.[94]

And in the end, despite shared memories and their common womanhood, race and class separated them. "Miss Libbie, you don't take notice, when me and yo's walking on a-lookin' into shop-window, and a-gazin' at the new things I never seen before, how the folks does stare at us. But I see 'em a-gazin'," Eliza noted, "and I can see 'em a-ponderin' and sayin' to theirsel's, 'Well, I do declar'! that's a lady, there ain't no manner of doubt. She's one of the bongtong; but whatever she's a-doin' with that old scrub nigger, I can't make out."[95]

Again reviews were favorable as Elizabeth presented her late husband as a noble man and a dashing soldier. While the first book had subtly deflected criticism regarding Armstrong's actions at the Little Bighorn by blaming federal Indian policy and poor weapons, this book answered other critics. Elizabeth knew that veterans of volunteer forces had published works decrying Armstrong's activities in Louisiana and Texas. Now she subtly and unobtrusively countered them.[96] She covered the insubordination of western troops in Louisiana but blamed the soldiers, their officers, and the conflicting demands placed on a twenty-five-year-old as he dealt with a conquered people.[97]

The book also covered her husband's entry into the Seventh Cavalry and his attempts to build the regiment a cohesive fighting force. Finally, in covering the Hancock campaign, Elizabeth relied heavily upon Armstrong's correspondence. She also reiterated his statement that the appearance of cholera and the nonappearance of supplies (in addition to her terror) explained his sudden appearance at Fort Riley.[98]

Once more, Elizabeth's good friend Jeannette Gilder assured her readers that admittedly a "devoted wife" would show her husband at his best. At the same time, she often saw him "at his worst which make the very fact of her being devoted and enthusiastic a guarantee of her good judgement as well as her love."[99] Whatever one's judgment, however, the book's real charm lay in the portrait Elizabeth had drawn of herself. "Anything more free from egotism than these pages it would be impossible to imagine." The *Chicago Dial* echoed that sentiment: "Not the least acceptable thing in this book is the unconscious revelation of her own character as a heroic woman and the perfection of a wife."[100]

In her brief sketch of Armstrong's life, Elizabeth presented a poor boy who rose to prominence through his family's sacrifices and his own efforts. She also depicted him as a man of great strength and unsurpassed agility. This time, she left the reader with an unforgettable scene that Sigmund Freud might have enjoyed immensely. Frederic Remington drew a sketch of Autie lifting her from her saddle and holding her suspended in space as the couple rode furiously over the plains. The reviewer for the London *Saturday Review* displayed shrewd insight when he noted that no other western hero, including Buffalo Bill, had performed this feat.[101]

The same critic judged it "a pity that a writer like Mrs. Custer, who possesses a natural energy and descriptive art quite unusual, does not find a new topic or a new way of using her topic." The two volumes were "less interesting and a good deal longer than was *Boots and Saddles*, that vivid account of the life and death of a modern equestrian Boone." Overall, the book needed editing. Others agreed, and in 1893 Webster, her publisher, issued an abridged version.[102]

By midsummer Elizabeth was in Europe, a trip made possible by "a nice Boston girl," as she explained to Vinnie Ream Hoxie in a hurried note.[103] While in London, Libbie toured the People's Palace and interviewed Walter Besant, whose 1882 novel, *All Sorts and Conditions of Men*, had inspired its construction. A large complex, the palace provided both recreation and training to the poorer classes. It served, Elizabeth thought, as a model for New Yorkers, faced with increasing numbers of impoverished immigrants. More important, the complex directed most of its effort towards salvaging children of the Whitechapel District, an approach Elizabeth approved. It was as futile, she thought (perhaps unconsciously echoing past *New York Herald* editorials) "to work over depravity in an adult in our cities as it is to try to make a civilized, peaceful citizen out of an old Sioux brave."[104]

Nonetheless, Elizabeth noted that most of the facilities, including the gymnasium and training courses, were designed for men and boys. Girls as young as ten often cared for younger siblings since many of their mothers were wage earners or drank heavily. Elizabeth thought the complex should offer child care, and surely young girls should have access to the swimming pool more than one out of seven days. "As a rule," she observed, the girls "get anything the boys may chance to leave. If one is going to have the misfortune to be born in England, there can be, but one prayer—that one might be born a boy."[105]

Elizabeth's visit to Fanny Kingsley's home, Bishop's Tachbrook, near Leamington represented the high point of this trip to England. After returning to New York, Libbie wrote her friend, thanking her for the treasured memory of "that hallowed room, with your books, your sacred relics, [and] your rose blooming window." Never would she forget "the warm and tender manner in which you took me in your arms."[106]

While Elizabeth was abroad, Philip Sheridan died at fifty-seven of heart disease. His departure heightened her awareness that an era in American history was drawing to a close. Earlier, she had begun soliciting recollections and judgments regarding her husband and his military career from various officers. In addition, she now used Henry Romeike's Bureau of Press Cuttings, a clipping service that sent her copies of reviews of her book and any newspaper or magazine article that mentioned Armstrong.[107]

As Sherman approached seventy, Elizabeth asked his evaluation of her husband's contribution to the settlement of the West. The retired general responded graciously, assuring her that Armstrong's activities in the late 1860s "in the valley of the Platte were more valuable in the great cause of civilization than his more appreciated and brilliant actions" in the last year of the war. Sherman considered the transcontinental worth more "than a hundred Richmonds."[108]

During the Little Bighorn, Custer's "natural impetuosity had led him to divide his command, and repeat the tactics which had proved so successful at the Washita." Unfortunately, Sherman noted, instead of meeting 800, he had encountered 2,200 "and was himself overwhelmed." Nonetheless, his sacrifice had brought about "the end of the Sioux nation. . . . They are now corralled; the buffalo and large game have disappeared, and the Sioux must work, or sell their diminished reservation to the emigrants, who are pressing them from every quarter."[109]

Although fur traders, miners, farmers, and railroads had contributed to the westward movement, all had depended on the army, "whose officers and men have been the advance guard in this battle of civilization. Their victory," Sherman thought, "is now as complete as that of Yorktown, and far more rich in its results."[110] His letter was reprinted in the Boston Cyclorama Company's program when it took "Gen. Custer's Last Fight Against Sioux Indians" on tour. Although invited to the opening in Detroit, Elizabeth declined, "unable to summon the courage."[111]

Elizabeth learned in the spring of 1889, that Marcus Reno had died of throat cancer. Among his personal effects friends and relatives found an unfinished manuscript on the Little Bighorn. Years afterwards, "the harrowing sight of those mutilated and decomposing bodies crowning the heights on which poor Custer fell" still haunted him. To the end he attributed Custer's defeat to failure to follow Terry's orders, division of the regiment without adequate reconnaissance, and finally, the soldiers' fatigue from forced marching.[112]

Shortly after, Frederick Whittaker died. Following the Reno court of inquiry, he had become more eccentric. During the last two years of his life, he had embraced spiritualism so fiercely that he alienated even family members. Bitter quarrels resulted, and, increasingly suspicious, he armed himself with a revolver. One day, while hurrying upstairs, Whittaker caught his cane in the banister, tripped, and fell. His gun discharged, and a half hour later, he died.[113]

The detractor, Reno, and the defender, Whittaker, were gone, but Libbie remained poised to challenge new defamers or acknowledge new defenders. By now, many accepted her portrait of Custer, for who knew him better?[114] More important, if he had been less than she claimed, how could he have inspired such devotion in so noble a woman?

An 1889 lithograph, completed by the Chicago firm of Kurz and Allison and entitled "Battle of the Big Horn" captured much of the popular perception. It showed an even more heroic Custer than Mulvaney's earlier commander. Larger than the soldiers around him, this Custer fought amidst clouds. Only three Indians were shown in combat; the others rode by. The artists did not see the famous battle as a conflict between Custer and the aborigines. Instead pygmy white men, fighting among themselves, had endangered the hero, who existed on a higher plane.[115]

Elizabeth was now working on another book, *Following the Guidon*, which covered Custer's active service after the lifting of his court-martial sentence. The text never mentioned the trial and instead directed readers' attention to the Battle of the Washita and the campaign to drive Southern Plains Indians onto their reservations. As she had done earlier, Elizabeth incorporated Armstrong's correspondence. In the process she edited many letters to cast her husband in a more flattering light.[116]

By stressing Armstrong's success in rescuing white women from Cheyenne captivity, Elizabeth deflected critics who viewed Custer's attack on Black Kettle's village as the killing of peaceful Indians. The captives, she emphasized, had been subjected to "terrible insults . . . too dreadful to be chronicled here."[117] As before, Elizabeth presented Indian women as beasts of burden, exploited by their husbands, the braves. By contrast, officers were romantic, chivalrous, and affectionate towards their wives and sweethearts.[118] This time, Elizabeth's sentimentality carried her away. Soldiers had such respect for motherhood, she maintained, that following General Custer's example, they spared buffalo cows when hunting and detoured around birds' nests while marching.[119]

If Elizabeth knew of the gossip concerning her husband and Monahsetah, she countered it brilliantly. Straightforwardly she incorporated the young woman into her narrative, transforming her into a supporting character as Armstrong had done earlier in *My Life on the Plains*. Like Marina with Hernan Cortés and Pocahontas with John Smith, Monahsetah became one more Indian woman of high birth who used her skills and lore to assist the white hero. In Elizabeth's version, the "sweet face[d]" woman called "Sallie Ann" seems an unlikely candidate for the affections of the man referred to, not as "my husband," as in earlier books, but rather as "General Custer."[120]

Elizabeth devoted extensive portions of *Following the Guidon* to descriptions of buffalo and buffalo hunting. As justification for the "fearful destruction" of the great herds, she cited Theodore Roosevelt's opinion that "nothing has done more to settle the Indian question." Although regrettable, it had been a necessary repetition of the principles of total war practiced by Union forces in the fall of 1864. "It was a grief to lay waste the beautiful valley of the Shenandoah and destroy that garden of the South, thus cutting off the source of fruitful supplies for General Lee's army, and yet, here again, it shortened our war and saved thousands of valiant men."[121] At the same time, Elizabeth noted that Miles still believed that, in the end, the army had defeated the Indians. Unsubdued, the general argued, they would have hunted cattle once the buffalo had vanished.[122]

Finally, Elizabeth found ways to tie herself and her husband into the rich vein of western lore Americans now treasured. *Following the Guidon* described violent frontier towns such as Hays City and Ellsworth, Kansas, where gunfights constantly claimed new victims for the nearby "boot hills."[123] She also included in her cast of characters James Butler Hickok, better known as Wild Bill. At one time he had scouted for the army. Since Elizabeth appreciated attractive men, she extolled his "physical perfection," noting that he reminded her of a "thorough-bred horse."[124]

Unfortunately, a violent encounter had forced Hickok to leave Hays City. Although Jack McCall ended his life abruptly in July 1876 (shortly after

Armstrong's death), Elizabeth claimed that in the intervening years, this kindred spirit had "sent friendly messages by many a roundabout route."[125] As for scouts in general, Elizabeth devoted a chapter to these colorful characters. This work, like her husband's earlier book, however, never mentioned Ben Clark, chief of scouts during the Battle of the Washita.

Webster's marketing of *Tenting on the Plains* had disappointed Elizabeth. Despite Samuel Clemens' plea for another chance, she sent her third manuscript to Harper & Brothers.[126] Unfortunately, as she explained to Fanny Kingsley, her efforts to make it into a boy's book had failed. Nonetheless, since she often visited children's homes, she had written it with their questions in mind.[127]

Once more Elizabeth poured out her life to the woman who inspired her. By 1889, she passed her summers in a cabin on the Pocono River near Stroudsburg, Pennsylvania. Although nearby townspeople were friendly, Libbie saw few persons save an "adopted aunt," her maid, and two widowed friends who lived with her. By writing outside, close to woods and acres of rhododendron, and by sleeping at night in a tent, her work progressed more rapidly. She enjoyed the outdoor life so much that she dreaded her return to her flat at 41 East Tenth Street on November 1.[128]

Recently Elizabeth had sent her first attempt at writing fiction, "To the Victor Belongs the Spoils," to *The Home-maker*. Presently she was working on a story for boys. Without destroying the frontier's romance, she hoped to present a more realistic view of the West. The novels about Buffalo Bill and the popularity of his show, "truly an historical one—has set the boys crazy about the life," and many had run away to become cowboys. Moreover, Capt. Charles King, a disabled veteran, sold a western novel every few months. Elizabeth thought she might appeal to the same market and, more important, perform a service. "Our people have awakened to the knowledge that the frontier has gone and scarcely anyone to chronicle it."[129]

Harpers published *Following the Guidon* in late summer, 1890. As Elizabeth awaited reviews and the letters that inevitably followed, the Redpath Lyceum Bureau invited her to participate in the Melrose Lecture Course. She would begin by speaking to a crowd of 400 in Concord, Massachusetts.[130] The chance to relate her husband's story and tell of the contribution of the frontier army in the settlement of the West had long since merged in her mind as one and the same cause. Despite her reservations about the propriety of women speaking in public, she accepted the offer.[131]

It was a challenge, but at forty-eight, Elizabeth, inveterate traveler, woman of means, and established writer in her own right, was ready to try new ventures. Shortly before the disaster on the Little Bighorn, Redpath had asked Armstrong to participate in its speaker circuit. Now, fourteen years later, his widow, clothed in his "mantle," would appear instead.

First, however, she had some sightseeing of her own to do. After all, the frontier was closing, and Elizabeth wanted to revisit it before it disappeared forever.

CHAPTER 14

"My Husband as He Should Be Known"

W HILE VISITING northern Idaho's Fort Sherman in July 1890, Elizabeth recorded her impressions about the changes occurring in the military. She applauded the sutler's replacement with the canteen and its fresh baked goods. She also approved of the more humane discipline since soldiers no longer carried logs, hung by thumbs, or walked repetitive beats for hours. After fourteen years of civilian life, however, protocol struck her "like some play being acted," as did the "salaams and obsequience" enlisted men gave officers. She felt relieved that "nothing is required of me as wife of the commanding officer. It used to be oppressive sometimes."[1]

If some ritual seemed absurd, new ceremonies involving the flag thrilled Elizabeth. While some at Fort Sherman worried that too much flag-waving was making Old Glory a "common place feature of military life," all agreed they saw "fresh enthusiasm for the U.S. flag all over the country." William Carlin, colonel of the Fourth Infantry, thought "the anarchists might have driven people, law abiding people to realize how necessary with the influx of foreigners that the Americans be infused with love for the flag and that the children be made to love it in contradistinction to the red flags of the labor movements."[2]

That summer and fall, Elizabeth traveled extensively throughout the Northwest. The high point of her journey was her meeting with Ranald MacDonald, the half-blood son of a Scottish fur trader. Now in his sixties, MacDonald lived a secluded life. Nonetheless, he knew of George Armstrong Custer and was delighted to meet his widow. He regaled her with stories of the days when the Hudson Bay Company, his father's employer, had sent out its fur-trading brigades. He also told her of his adventures as one of the first Americans to enter Japan. On her way home, Elizabeth visited Yellowstone Park, but she avoided the Little Bighorn Battlefield.[3] In a later essay, describing her trip, she counseled fellow countrymen and women to see the West before developers made it "tame and commonplace" like the "beaten paths" back east.[4]

When Elizabeth returned home, she found in her mail a letter from D. F. Barry. A photographer of western scenes and Indians, he had interviewed Rain-in-the-Face at Standing Rock. Elizabeth had devoted one chapter in *"Boots and Saddles"* to Tom's capture of the warrior and the Indian's later escape. Afterwards, she wrote, the Hunkpapa had sent word from unceded territory vowing "revenge for his imprisonment." The "incarnate fiend" had his chance when soldiers discovered "on the battlefield that he had cut out the brave heart of the gallant, loyal, and lovable man, our brother, Tom."[5]

No one had torn the heart out of Tom's mutilated body. In the smoke, din, and confusion of battle, the Indians, unaware they were fighting Custer's regiment, had not searched for individual officers. Shortly after, however, the well-known poet Henry Wadsworth Longfellow had composed "Revenge of Rain-in-the-Face," naming Armstrong as the purported victim. Later, Elizabeth's version, identifying Tom as the prey, had given the tale greater credence.[6]

When Barry had shown Rain-in-the-Face Armstrong and Tom's photographs, the Hunkpapa had gazed at both before averting his eyes. Barry doubted that the Indian, now his friend and "a great admirer" of Custer, had killed either man. Rain-in-the-Face, however, asked about Custer's widow and learned with surprise that she remained single. It struck him as incongruous that "white women didn't get married when their husbands died." Barry explained that often they did not, and as they parted, the Hunkpapa expressed two wishes. He wanted an education and he desired a picture of Elizabeth.[7] This was the first, but not the last, kind message the widow received from those who had fought her husband.

Other items in Libbie's mail were more disturbing. Her clippings from Romeike's indicated that excerpts from an August 1890 article in *Harper's New Monthly Magazine* had been reprinted around the country.[8] The author, Charles King, had praised *Tenting on the Plains*, and Elizabeth had considered him her friend.[9] Now she felt betrayed as she read in "Custer's Last Battle" that King assigned major responsibility for defeat at the Little Bighorn to her husband. Terry's plan for coordinated action against the Indians would have worked, King claimed, except "Custer disappointed him in an unusual way." By force-marching his command to win a victory unshared by any other regiment, Custer had arrived in the Little Bighorn valley a day early. "Men and horses were wellnigh used up," so that when Terry appeared, "it was all over with Custer and his pet troops (companies) of the regiment."[10]

Apologetically King assured Elizabeth that the article, written seven years earlier, did not reflect his current thinking. Nor, Elizabeth noted, did it incorporate the testimony Captain Godfrey had obtained from Indian witnesses at the tenth anniversary meeting held at the Little Bighorn Battlefield. She found it incomprehensible that *Harper's Monthly* had published the essay "without a word to me from the editors."[11]

In an effort to counter King's allegations, Elizabeth asked Miles, now a major general, to write an article defending her husband. When Miles refused, noting that he could not state his views in an essay, Elizabeth approached Godfrey. The captain's argument, attributing her husband's defeat to the surprising number of Indians concentrated in one place, Reno's failure to sustain his charge, and the soldiers' reliance on weapons that jammed when fired, won her enthusiastic endorsement.[12] Godfrey's plea that he was too fatigued availed him nothing. Instead Elizabeth wrote the assistant editor of *Century Magazine*, C. C. Buel, in November advising him that the captain "may be quite well now" and should soon submit his essay.[13]

Meanwhile, Elizabeth wrote Theodore Roosevelt, now a member of the United States Civil Service Commission, thanking him for his recent praise of her husband. Roosevelt assured her, "It was written from the heart. I need not tell you that General Custer has always been a favorite of mine."[14]

By December 1890, Elizabeth was in Washington, D.C., where niggardly congressmen, chiefly Joseph Cheadle, obstructed efforts to raise her pension to $100 a month. The Indiana politician believed military widows, whatever their deceased husbands' rank, deserved no more than the $8 a month awarded a private's widow. A reporter observed Elizabeth "lobbying in the interest of her bill, and of course she made a dead set at Cheadle." Since she was both "pretty" and "tactful" and could "arouse sympathy," the outcome was predictable. "She made short work of Cheadle, for she captured him in five minutes talk, and lo, when the bill came up Mr. Cheadle not only did not object, but he actually voted yea."[15]

As the year ended, western events again made headlines. Many Sioux, demoralized by the loss of their old way of life and dispossessed of much of their remaining land, had met little success as farmers on the drought-stricken Northern Plains. Adding to their suffering, the government had cut their rations, and weakened by hunger and plagued by disease, they had yielded to the messianic visions of Wovoka. The Paiute prophet promised his followers that if they followed his teachings and practiced the Ghost Dance, a slow, trance-inducing shuffle around sacred trees, the buffalo would return. More important, white domination would end.[16]

Although Wovoka preached a blend of Christian and Indian beliefs, the Sioux added other elements. Leaders, such as Kicking Bear, believed that confrontation with the white man would hasten the arrival of the Sioux millennium. Moreover, by donning a special "Ghost shirt," the Sioux would become impervious to the white man's bullets. Such assertions and the spectacle of hundreds of frenzied ghost dancers alarmed Indian agents, who called for the deployment of troops. The army positioned cavalry, infantry, and artillery units near and on reservations and planned to push bands regarded as dangerous onto agency grounds at Pine Ridge, South Dakota. Authorities hoped to avoid armed conflict.[17]

Among Kicking Bear's followers was Sitting Bull. Given his influence, Nelson Miles and James McLaughlin, agent at Standing Rock, ordered the chief arrested. As Indian police under Lt. Bull Head escorted Sitting Bull from his lodge, warriors appeared. In the ensuing fight, the chief and many of his followers were killed. The police also sustained heavy casualties, and the struggle ended only when artillery fire from the supporting cavalry scattered the warriors. Observers remembered afterwards the reaction of Sitting Bull's "old gray circus horse," a gift from Buffalo Bill. As the Sioux chieftain died in a hail of bullets, gunfire caused the animal to perform his tricks. Despite the lead flying in all directions, the stallion escaped harm.[18]

Miniconjou followers of Big Foot, joined by remnants attached to the late Sitting Bull, were on their way to Pine Ridge when Seventh Cavalry soldiers ordered them to encamp at Wounded Knee Creek. The next morning, as Col. James Forsyth and eight companies of the Seventh tried to disarm these Indians, a deadly close-quarter fight broke out. As the outnumbered Indians fled, artillery fire shredded their camp. When the fighting ceased, 150 Indians, including many women and children, lay dead, and 50 others were wounded, some mortally. Forsyth's loss was 25 killed and 39 wounded.[19]

Godfrey, as captain of Troop D, led a small detachment in search of Miniconjous who had fled the battle scene. Learning that soldiers had sighted Indians along the banks of a stream, he called out warnings.

Obtaining no response, Godfrey ordered the firing of a volley into the brush. It killed a woman, two children, and a boy, variously described as eight to fourteen.[20]

A brief spate of resistance followed. At Drexel Mission, warriors trapped a Seventh Cavalry battalion, exacting some revenge before black troopers from the Ninth Cavalry arrived and drove them off. By mid-January 1891, however, Sioux opposition had ended entirely. Gone was the Indian frontier, an area, according to one scholar, characterized by ethnic interaction between whites and Indians.[21] Instead the white domination, viewed as inexorable by George Armstrong Custer years earlier in *My Life on the Plains*, was now a reality.[22]

Once more there was controversy. While some newspapers presented the Seventh's actions as the triumph of righteous soldiers over insurgent Indians, others accused the regiment of deliberately murdering women and children in retaliation for the Little Bighorn. The criticism leveled against Godfrey cast a long shadow over his army career and eventually delayed his rise to brigadier.[23] Despite the controversy, however, he submitted the promised article to *Century Magazine* in February 1891.

At the same time, Elizabeth learned of the views of James B. Fry. Maggie's relative by marriage, the colonel (brevet major general) exonerated her husband for the defeat at the Little Bighorn. When Elizabeth asked that his commentary accompany Godfrey's article, the magazine acceded. Earlier, Fry had helped assistant editors, C. C. Buel and Robert Underwood Johnson, in the compilation of *Century's* four-volume work, *Battles and Leaders of the Civil War.*[24]

After Elizabeth had ordered photographs from D. F. Barry for the forthcoming articles she packed for Europe. Before leaving, however, she learned that, in December, while events had unfolded at Wounded Knee, Terry had died. T. T. Munger, a well-known Congregational minister, had eulogized the "Hero of Fort Fisher" during his funeral service as a man of unsung virtue. Among his kind acts, Terry had gone to his grave without telling the full story of the Little Bighorn to avoid "subject[ing] a brave but indiscreet subordinate to a charge of disobedience."[25] Dismayed and angry, Elizabeth now asked Fry to refute Munger's comments. His military arguments and Godfrey's narrative, by "an actor in the drama," would carry "far more weight with the public" than statements from a wife.[26]

By early summer, Elizabeth had ended her visit with the Carnegies at Cluny Castle in Inverness Shire in Scotland. As she headed home aboard a luxury liner, the RMS *Germanic*, she thanked the head of "the firm" for his parting bouquet of heather and his kind comments about Autie. She also expressed gratitude to Louise Carnegie, since she saw herself "on the outside of everybody's windows now . . ." enjoying "the fire light on other people's hearths when some tender woman takes me in as you have."[27]

By October, Elizabeth eagerly awaited the January issue of *Century Magazine*. At last Godfrey and Fry's brilliance would disarm her husband's detractors, leaving them forever discredited. Fervently Libbie shared with C. C. Buel her expectations. "This is an hour that I have waited for, for fifteen years . . . and you know that my earnestness is great in my anxiety to have every fact brought to light." Two days later, she confided, "Oh if you knew how I think & think & plan at night in the still hours, ways to have the world see my husband as he should be known."[28]

By Thanksgiving, Elizabeth's euphoria was gone. She had learned that Godfrey's article included a quotation attributed to Capt. Myles Moylan questioning Armstrong's judgment. Shortly after Benteen's battalion had returned from its scout to the left, a group of officers had congregated "on the edge of the bluff overlooking the valley and were discussing the situation." Then followed the words that horrified Elizabeth. "Among our number was Captain Moylan, a veteran soldier, and a good one too, watching intently the scene below. Moylan remarked, quite emphatically: 'Gentlemen, in my opinion General Custer has made the biggest mistake of his life, by not taking the whole regiment in at once in the first attack.'"[29]

Elizabeth protested vehemently. "Did Captain Godfrey finally listen to your suggestion that the mistake in dividing forces rested with the planners of the campaign who had sent out three great columns without any means of communication with each other," she wrote Buel in exasperation. That "rather than . . . the dividing of the small portion of the command with which my husband had to fight the battle, was the cause of the disaster." If Moylan's comment remained in the article, Godfrey's argument was no longer "logical. . . . It would set my heart at peace so," she entreated Buel, "if I knew that you had convinced him [of his error] and that you had edited that portion."[30]

Whether Elizabeth's request came too late or whether Godfrey refused to comply, the quotation remained when the article appeared early in January 1892. Although disappointed, Elizabeth did not despair. Perhaps one day Godfrey would see his error. Meanwhile, Fry's "Comment" echoed her conclusions.

The defeat at the Little Bighorn had arisen from poor strategy on the part of the campaign planners rather than Custer's disobedience.[31] In fact, Fry argued, the original plan "had neither the force nor importance which it subsequently acquired in Terry's mind." Obviously Terry had thought the Seventh strong enough to defeat any Indians it met. "Otherwise isolated forces would not have been sent to 'operate blindly,' without means of mutual support, against an enemy in the interior of an almost unknown region." No one, moreover, had known the hostiles would exceed 500 to 800 warriors. Thus, if Terry had considered Custer's forces sufficient to continue up the Rosebud to await an Indian assault, then both he and Custer had believed the Seventh powerful enough to attack the Indians.

Finally, the only orders Custer had received had instructed him to march up the Rosebud River. "Surely he did not disobey that. Everything else was left to his discretion." Nor had Terry told Custer what to do when he came "in contact with the enemy." Finally, once Benteen had rejoined Reno after the scout to the left, the "come quick" orders applied to their combined battalions. And since Godfrey had heard the sound of firing for "a long time" from the direction of Custer's battalion, Reno's movement in that direction "might have enabled Custer to extricate the command." Unfortunately, "when he did move out it was too late; Custer's men had been killed, and the enemy was able to oppose Reno with his whole force and drive him back and invest him in his place of refuge." Those factors collectively, rather than Custer's purported disobedience, accounted for the disastrous events at the Little Bighorn.[32]

Fry also disclosed that Col. Robert Hughes, Terry's son-in-law and for years one of the general's aides, had given Munger the "defamatory" information for the eulogy. Hughes had stated that Custer had disobeyed both written and verbal orders. Fry, however, having characterized Terry's June 22, 1876, statements to Custer as largely directives, now argued that Hughes had failed to make his case. These were not orders, and Terry had not given another set of orders since no other copies had gone to superiors from this careful soldier. As Elizabeth read all this, she undoubtedly remembered Hughes as the captain who had appeared at Fort Lincoln seeking to comfort her by assuring her that Custer's body had not been mutilated.[33] It mattered not; from this point on Elizabeth considered Hughes her enemy.

Despite the widow's hopes that the Godfrey-Fry essays would exonerate Custer once and for all, the debate reopened. Col. Henry Carrington, whose own career had been tarnished by the Fetterman massacre while commanding Fort Phil Kearny, faulted the reasoning of both Godfrey and Fry. Neither had mentioned Terry's instructions telling Custer to "make a wide sweep, so as to give Gibbon ample time to co-operate with him against the Indians in the Big Horn Valley." Custer's failure to comply had led to "the premature attack."[34]

Finding himself part of a national dispute, Hughes now submitted his own article to *Century Magazine*. The editors sent it back, instructing him to confine his remarks to the same number of pages allotted Fry's "Comments." Hughes declined. Fry's commentary stemmed naturally from Godfrey's preceding article, but he had constructed a different argument entirely. Moreover, he needed adequate space to counter "errors of fact in both productions."[35] His arguments went unheeded with the magazine editors, Gilder, Buel, and Johnson, all of whom knew Elizabeth well. Frustrated, Hughes put his essay aside until he knew the impact of Godfrey and Fry on public opinion.

In 1892, Charles King was greatly relieved when Elizabeth allowed him to honor her in his newest story. The dedication to "A Soldier's Secret" read: "To Elizabeth Bacon Custer, whose devotion as wife, whose desolation as widow, and whose bravery and patience through long years 'In the Shadow' have touched all hearts, this story is *inscribed*."[36] A year later, when Lippincott reprinted it as part of a bound volume, the dedication reappeared.

During these years, while Elizabeth monitored articles and urged others to defend her husband, she also toured the country. Throughout the Northeast and Midwest, she spoke on "Garrison Life on the Plains" and "Buffalo Hunting." As she explained to Louise Carnegie, she addressed "women's clubs, girls' schools, missionary societies and philanthropies that need money" in halls, churches, and private homes.[37] One newspaper noted that Elizabeth avoided "mixed audiences" (meaning those open to both sexes). Instead she addressed "women's clubs or audiences of men and women invited by such clubs, before schools and church societies."[38]

Elizabeth's belief that her appearances publicized her late husband's contribution to western settlement overcame her lingering aversion to appearing in public—that and her desire for a permanent home. For most of her life, she had moved constantly, and although she owned one small rental house, she was aging. She wanted a permanent place that satisfied her aesthetically and represented a good real estate investment.[39] She had found the answer in Lawrence Park, a section of Bronxville, a Westchester County suburb of New York City.

Libbie's old friend Sarah Bates, the sister of Agnes Bates, had married William Van Duzer Lawrence, a "Gilded Age millionaire." He had developed Bronxville, according to one authority, as "an exclusive preserve for the very prosperous and very artistic." Instead of the gridiron, his streets followed cowpaths and left in place many of the trees, rocks, and natural foliage. Lawrence also mandated architectural diversity, and the result was a beautiful suburb, "endlessly copied and never matched."[40] By 1892, Libbie planned to build her own home among the Gothic, Italian, and Roman-esque-revival dwellings.[41]

Elizabeth discovered to her delight that lecturing paid better than writing. After one Chicago speaking engagement in May 1892 brought her $388, she rejoiced, "The cupola on the house will be lifted some day."[42] And little wonder, for the small figure, dressed in black save for "snowy lawn bands at her neck and wrists" attracted large and receptive audiences.[43]

Although Elizabeth frequently worried that someone might classify her as a "platform woman," one of those "who always has grievances and seeks perpetually to reconstruct something," her concerns proved groundless.[44] A newspaper reporter noted, early in 1892, that Elizabeth's predominant characteristic was the "happy faculty of taking things just as they are in the world." Thus it was not surprising that she was "not actively engaged with any of the great reforms of the day, and belongs to none of the organizations of women devoted to either political, social or dress agitation." Rather, "her chief ambition in life is to honor her husband's memory through her books and lectures." As Elizabeth explained, she lived "a reflected life."[45]

Elizabeth, "perpetually troubled about coming out in such a public way," derived further assurance she remained "absolutely feminine" when one young woman, "deeply interested in every cause for the good" of her sex, urged her to continue lecturing. Elizabeth's demeanor and her manner of speaking "might prove to other women that it was possible to tell their story or plead their cause in a quiet unobtrusive way and without awakening the criticism of those who dread the typical platform woman."[46] And finally a Detroit clergyman alleviated her fears when he characterized her as a woman who came before the public "bravely struggling for a home, such a laudable purpose and so worthy the brave wife of a hero to whom her life had been devoted."[47]

Whatever her early misgivings about appearing before an audience, Elizabeth soon discovered that she enjoyed the limelight. In a journal she analyzed her performance in order to improve her skills and effectiveness.

Always nervous at first, she breathed deeply to steady herself before beginning. As a way of projecting her voice, she spoke to a listener in the back row. Elizabeth never mentioned her husband's death and instead covered frontier army life in a light and humorous vein. Still, her famous bereavement was, as Mr. and Mrs. Charles Dudley Warner explained, "always there unconsciously to me" and to everyone else.[48]

Over time Elizabeth became more accomplished, in part because she willingly accepted criticism. When a professor corrected her pronunciation and warned her against gasping, she wrote, "I was honestly indebted to him and he believed me when I told him so." When he suggested, however, that she attend Boston's Emerson School of Oratory, she dismissed his advice. She had no interest in becoming studied and unnatural, preferring instead to lecture in the same conversational way she spoke and wrote.[49]

While she usually met a warm reception, some audiences proved more formidable than others. Standing behind the lectern in Cambridge, Massachusetts, to address the Woman's Alliance, Elizabeth felt skepticism permeating the hall. Wondering what "audaciousness" had possessed her "in venturing on such classic ground so near the hub," she threw away caution. She told her listeners that she wondered if any of them "when they addressed their clubs or read their reports in their hospitals had the same time swallowing their heart" that she was experiencing. When hers returned "to its proper place," she would begin reading. Her disclosure won them over, and she watched as Mrs. Charles Eliot, the wife of Harvard's president, nodded her satisfaction.[50]

If approbation from "the hub" delighted Elizabeth, rapt attention from children exhilarated her. They were the future, and she wanted boys to adopt Autie as their model. She smiled when one youngster blurted out, "Isn't it interesting Mother." And she beamed when another woman introduced her long-haired son, explaining that General Custer was "his hero." Yet another mother had taken her child from algebra and Latin since Elizabeth's talk held more valuable lessons.[51]

At times, when she stood before an audience surrounded by her husband's pictures or flags and bunting, Elizabeth experienced genuine happiness. One Detroit home had so many national symbols, including red, white, and blue lampshades, that her hostess confessed that even the dog, Ko-Ko, was "a compulsory patriot."[52] For the moment at least, Elizabeth, having no immediate family, gained a sense of belonging. She loved hearing the audience murmur that she came from Michigan. And she warmed inside when one Detroit friend characterized her as "my little girl." She was "so proud to feel myself owned by anyone."[53]

Albert Barnitz introduced her to an audience at Cleveland. Fondly he recalled her husband's service in the Union Army and the first time that he, as a soldier in the Third Division, had seen the boy general's lovely young bride. Elizabeth did not know that, given Barnitz's later disenchantment with Custer on the Kansas plains, his compliments said more about his respect for her than her deceased husband.[54]

Although Elizabeth found lecturing satisfying and remunerative, she also found it exhausting. Some days lasted eighteen hours, and at times accidents or snowdrifts delayed her trains. Public transportation, moreover, often left her blocks away from "where I am [speaking and] so tired that holding up my dress and my heavy m[anu]s[cript] is an exertion."[55] Elizabeth always felt the stress in addition to the exhilaration of performance. After her talks, she found it hard to while away late hours with hosts who expected stories of her life and scintillating conversation, when she longed to sleep. Once, after a rigorous schedule, she experienced a "dismal time getting home in the chill and fog. There was a wreck in our train out on the Jersey flats."[56]

Despite the balmy days when the young girls sat before her in their pastel dresses and showered her with smiles and later roses, carnations, or chrysanthemums, Elizabeth grew tired. For a while, the meetings with old veterans, who hung back until the crowd around her had thinned and then grasped her hand with tears in their eyes, gave her the strength to continue. She enjoyed the income, the compliments, the assurances she scarcely looked her age, and the unexpected reunions. Still, "There is no royal way to earn one's living and the way of the 'show woman' is not easy."[57] By the mid-1890s, she had reduced her speaking schedule.[58]

Libbie now resided at 6 Chester Avenue—a stone and brown-shingled dwelling in Lawrence Park. Nearby lived the Lawrences, and not far away was Agnes Bates, now married to architect William Wellington.[59]

Beginning in 1894, Elizabeth spent her summers with Candace Wheeler and other artists and writers at Onteora in the Catskills. At first she stayed in the Bear and Fox Inn, built by Candace's son, the architect Dunham Wheeler. But after 1898, Libbie's cabin, "The Flags," took its place alongside Jeannette Gilder's "Cloud Cabin," Samuel Clemens's "The Balsam," and naturalist John Burrough's "Slabsides."[60] At Onteora, Elizabeth also became acquainted with the writer Frank Stockton and Carr Van Anda, the managing editor of the *New York Times*. Her best friend among the men, however, remained Burroughs, who, finding her "a bright charming woman," sought her company at dinner parties[61]

More important to Elizabeth were the women of Onteora. In addition to Wheeler and Gilder, she formed close ties with Mary Mapes Dodge and Ruth McEnery Stuart. Both wrote fiction, and Dodge, moreover, had won international renown for "Hans Brinker and the Silver Skates" and the high quality of her children's magazine, *St. Nicholas*.[62] These women provided Elizabeth with professional support, understanding, and camaraderie. By 1896 all were widows, except Gilder, who had never married. Thus they knew firsthand the difficulties talented females faced making a living in a male-dominated society. Wheeler later recalled that Elizabeth once looked around the room and blurted out, "Why we are all working women; *not a lady among us!*"[63]

Although Libbie had little patience with women who sought "reconstruction" of existing relations between the sexes, she recognized the inequities women faced. Earlier she had noted the scant attention girls received at the People's Palace in East London. If planners of social programs often gave females slight consideration, however, so too did writers. Elizabeth undoubtedly told her Onteora friends about her conversation with Robert Louis Stevenson one evening at Saranac Lake in the Adirondacks.

Stevenson had attended the dinner with Edward Trudeau, the physician who treated him for tuberculosis. "Now why is it, Mr. Stevenson," Elizabeth had asked, "that you never put a real woman in your stories?" Startled, the author had replied, "Madame I have little knowledge of Greek." "But," she insisted, "you have some knowledge of women, surely! Why, you have been a married man these seven years." To this, Stevenson responded, "With the result, Mrs. Custer, that I have forgotten all the Greek I ever knew."[64]

Elizabeth persisted. "But the public expects it of you, and the feminine portion demands it. Come! When are we to be introduced to the Stevenson woman in fiction?" Turning serious, Stevenson promised her "a woman in my next book." Afterwards, his host, Stephen Chalmers, saw steady improvement in the writer's female characters. Eventually Stevenson produced Catriona, a complex and believable woman in *David Balfour*, a development Chalmers attributed to the charming but tenacious Elizabeth Custer.[65]

At Onteora, Libbie met another important woman in her life. Marguerite Merington, a young playwright and author of children's books, came to the artists' colony in 1894 and dined with Elizabeth and Maggie that summer. Since Merington suffered frequently from insomnia, she often slept through breakfast. When that happened, Libbie always brought a meal to her room. The friendship forged that summer endured until Elizabeth's death.[66]

When Elizabeth and Candace Wheeler tired of the Catskills colony, they repaired to Wheeler's home near Thomasville, Georgia. Soon Libbie constructed her own retreat among the "Georgia pines," which she named Caddice Case, (after a fly's hiding place). Here, in what one reporter characterized as a "romantic military post built of logs," she placed Armstrong's desk and other memorabilia. Nearby she kept a tent for sleeping outside as in army days.[67] When autumn arrived, Libbie returned to the city, reinvigorated for her occasional speech or essay and her intermittent work on memoirs of the Civil War.

In Bronxville, Elizabeth maintained other valuable contacts. *Century's* assistant editor, Robert Underwood Johnson, found her an engaging dinner guest whose conversational wit and storytelling ability guaranteed an enjoyable evening. Once he invited guests to a dinner in honor of Rudyard Kipling, then a Vermont resident. When Kipling became ill with typhoid fever, Elizabeth's cancellation failed to arrive in the mail. She appeared at the Johnson home in "her best gown and smile, radiant with expectation of an enchanting evening with the prince of story tellers." At her host's insistence she stayed for dinner and later regaled those present with "a chronicle of cowboy life that made us think that West indeed was East." Afterwards Johnson reflected that, while Kipling made a place as little known as India interesting, he, in turn, had "missed a delightful evening" listening to Elizabeth's frontier stories.[68]

In 1895 *Scribner's Magazine* began publishing E. Benjamin Andrews's "A History of the Last Quarter-Century in the United States." The author, then president of Brown University, accepted the Godfrey-Fry interpretation of the Battle of the Little Bighorn. Although Terry's friends had accused Custer of disobeying orders, such allegations, Andrews claimed, were now "disproved."[69] Incensed by this statement, Colonel Hughes decided "the authentic facts should be placed where they may be accessible to the historian writing of this period." In January 1896, the *Journal of the Military Service Institution of the United States* published the article rejected by *Century* earlier.[70]

Hughes argued that Terry had ordered Custer to march up the Rosebud, past the point of Reno's earlier scout, and then continue almost to that river's source before turning westward toward the Little Bighorn. Had Custer followed these instructions, he maintained, both the Seventh and Gibbons's infantry would have "simultaneously reached their point of combined work and simultaneously advanced against the Indians." Then, who could deny that "one of the most brilliant victories over the Indians would have been won?"[71]

Furthermore, Hughes contended, Terry had issued his orders believing that the Indians, numbering more than "500 to 800 warriors," were located on the Little Bighorn. Since events bore him out, then no matter how politely he had phrased his directives, they remained orders, and Custer had not met sufficient reason to depart from them.[72] Although the kind Terry had shown "complete abnegation of self" to protect "a dead man from the public blame," after his death, Hughes could not remain silent. He had to "expose facts enough to meet the case." In truth, he believed that Custer had planned "willful disobedience." As evidence he cited Custer's statement to Captain Ludlow in St. Paul. He had "got away with Stanley and would be able to swing clear of Terry."[73]

Hughes's article, published in a military journal, received neither the attention nor the circulation given Godfrey's earlier essay. Nevertheless, when Andrews's essays appeared in book form a year later, he dismissed the colonel's argument, stating that Hughes had failed "to justify his views." Elizabeth, nevertheless, was not content. She now searched for someone to refute Hughes's statement.[74]

Recently she had derived encouragement from Nelson Miles's strong support of her husband in his 1896 memoirs. Now the commanding general of the army, Miles's conclusion that Custer's plan would have worked if Reno had sustained his attack carried weight with military men and the public alike. Moreover, since everyone with Custer had perished, no one would ever know the conditions governing his decisions. "I have no patience," Miles protested, "with those who would kick a dead lion." Instead, he wondered why the military had been so ignorant and misinformed about "the number and character of the Indians then opposed to the United States forces."[75]

Then Miles announced that he possessed an affidavit concerning Terry's words to Custer on the evening before the Seventh's departure. After the conference on the *Far West* on the night of June 21, Terry had remarked, "Custer, I don't know what to say for the last." To this the lieutenant colonel had responded, "Say whatever you want to say." Terry then replied, "Use your own judgment and do what you think best if you strike the trail; and whatever you do, Custer, hold on to your wounded."[76] If this document existed, and if it were valid, then the charge of disobedience leveled against Custer evaporated. Miles's failure to say where the affidavit came from or who had signed it, however, assured the controversy's continuation.

Whatever the dispute among military men, in the popular press and in literary works Custer was a hero. Ella Wilcox, whose lack of literary talent proved no impediment to fame, published *Custer and Other Poems* in 1896. In the long title piece, she tied the "noble soldier, nobler man" to biblical and Homeric figures and threw in Elizabeth for romantic inspiration. "Greece her Archilles claimed, immortal Custer, we." As for his battalion: "Like gods they battled and like gods they died."[77] The long-winded tome also referred to an imaginary event, accepted as true by many Americans. The Crow scout, Curley, had arrived at the *Far West* on June 28 and, in an interview translated by George Morgan, the husband of a Crow Indian, had described his observations of the Battle of the Little Bighorn from his hiding place in a ravine.[78]

Whittaker's biography had embellished Curley's original narrative by inserting a scene in which the scout had purportedly shown Custer an escape route.[79] Now Wilcox, like others, repeated the story. She described Curley telling Custer: "Death lies before, dear life remains behind / Mount thy sure-footed steed, and hasten with the wind." When Custer refused because of his allegiance to "God and Elizabeth," and instead decided "to join that fated few who stood at bay," Wilcox celebrated this imaginary event's significance: "Ah! deeds like that the Christ in man reveal / Let Fame descend her throne at Custer's shrine to kneel."[80]

Given such praise, many now viewed Custer more favorably than they had in the past. Gen. Jesse M. Lee, former recorder at the Reno court of inquiry, numbered among the recent converts. In June 1897, he wrote Elizabeth, informing her that he was no longer "influenced by the prejudicial opinions of those whose motives I did not understand, and whose sources of information I then had no means of testing."[81]

That same month, Elizabeth privately printed a pamphlet for distribution to friends and allies entitled "Mrs. Custer's Letter: Quoting an Unnamed Officer's Reply to Col. R. P. Hughes' Charge that Custer Had Disobeyed Orders." She hoped, she maintained in her introduction, to avoid an "unprofitable and inconclusive discussion of many matters." The remainder of her pamphlet contained the opinion of an unnamed officer, "who held the closest personal and official relations with General Custer during the Civil War."[82]

The writer, reissuing an earlier challenge put forth by the now deceased Fry, called on Hughes to produce a set of orders actually violated by Custer. Indirectly, however, he also countered allegations by the late James Brisbin, a Second Cavalry major in Gibbon's command during the Sioux campaign. Brisbin had written Godfrey in 1892, shortly after the publication of his *Century* article, charging him with deleting a concluding sentence from Terry's orders. Brisbin's version ended with the statement, "It is desired that you conform as nearly as possible to these instructions and that you do not depart from them unless you shall see *absolute necessity for doing* so." Shortly afterwards the major had died. No one ever found his version of Terry's orders.[83]

The unnamed officer, without citing Brisbin but obviously referring to those allegations, maintained that the only orders in existence were those Terry had written on June 22, 1876. That matter disposed of, he then restated Fry's earlier arguments. Terry had sent out "against an enemy of unknown numbers and in an uncertain location a column of troops which for a time must be entirely self-sufficient and liable to come in hostile contact before support could be had. General Terry himself," the anonymous writer noted, "was to be out of reach for instructions in any emergency."[84]

After praising Custer's military skills and professional ability, the writer noted that Terry had expressed his "entire confidence" in Custer's judgment in the orders cited by Godfrey. Moreover, Terry had not wanted to limit Custer's options in unforseen circumstances, especially since he believed Custer possessed sufficient force to meet any contingency. Thus, the only order Custer had received was to march up the Rosebud, which he had not violated. How then, the writer asked, had Custer disobeyed? Or, would his detractors maintain he had disobeyed "when he came nearly in such contact [and] all things were at his discretion, and unless he failed to play the soldier and the man at that moment there is no longer a question of disobedience of orders."[85]

While Elizabeth engaged military men or veterans to put forth her arguments, she also continued her own writing. In 1900, she published "Where the Heart Is: A Sketch of Woman's Life on the Frontier" in February's *Lippincott Magazine* and "Home-Making in the American Army" in the September 22 issue of *Harper's Bazaar*. Both essays again told her readers how amiably self-sacrificing officers' wives had created homes under primitive and trying conditions in the frontier army. The second article also gave her a chance to relate once more the boyish antics of her husband. That September, *St. Nicholas* carried her short story, "The Kid."[86]

Elizabeth's tale concerned young Alfred McKee, who, by growing up on an army post, represented the ideal son Armstrong would have raised had he been a father. In one scene, the commanding general (an older Armstrong) incited the infant's rage by bouncing him towards the animal heads on the wall. His brother (obviously Tom) added to the pandemonium by blowing on a hunting horn. Elizabeth informed her reader: "Naturally, any child if it was in its nature would soon develop enthusiasm, courage, and coolness, when reared in such a school."[87]

As young Alf grew into boyhood, his father nurtured him on stories of his revolutionary war grandfather. Before long the young boy mastered horseback riding. Since, he was both mischievous and devious (shades of Whittaker's all-American boy), he easily eluded teachers and caretakers to join Indian children at play. After learning Indian sign language and native lore, his frontier skills eventually permitted him to save the post from unexpected attack.[88]

Elizabeth wanted to reach children, but this effort proved no more successful than her adult story, the rambling, disconnected "To the Victor, Belongs the Spoils," published a decade earlier. Wisely, she gave up writing fiction for juveniles or adults. She also decided that someone else should complete a boy's book of Custer. Elizabeth turned that assignment over to a woman she had met at Onteora. Mary E. Burt, a friend of John Burroughs and author of children's books, edited a condensed version of Libbie's three books in her 1901 *The Boy General.*[89]

Published as a volume in its Series of School Reading, the work was promoted by Scribner as "a valuable accessory in teaching history and geography." More important, it would teach children "fortitude, self-sacrifice, temperance, self-control, tenderness, a patriotism that cannot be bribed, and a resistance of temptation to dishonorable wealth—lessons in manliness that mean more than dates and statistics."[90] As an endorsement from the *School Journal* noted, "The lessons in manliness will prove to be worth far more than any formal instruction in good conduct."[91] Equally gratifying, school books interpreted Custer's defeat at the Little Bighorn in heroic and inspirational terms. William H. Mace's *A School History of the United States*, a popular text, charged the Sioux with having "murdered settlers," thereby necessitating the sending of troops against them in 1876.

Unfortunately Custer and his men were "suddenly surrounded by ten times their number of wild Sioux horsemen." Nonetheless, all died bravely.[92]

In spring, 1902, promoters of Custer, Colorado, invited Elizabeth Custer and Buffalo Bill Cody to an unveiling of a Custer statue to mark the town's opening. Promotional brochures described the region as rich in mineral ores and the location as "one of the most picturesque in Colorado." When the Denver and Rio Grande Railroad arrived, it would inevitably become the next Cripple Creek.[93]

On dedication day, June 10, former governor Alva Adams, the initiator of legislation creating Custer County in 1877, presided over the ceremonies. After the current governor, James Orman, prophesied the town's glowing future, residents celebrated with athletic games ending in fireworks.[94] Elizabeth, realizing some might construe her appearance as endorsement of the founders' claims, and uncertain of their validity, was not present.[95] Her instincts were sure. The town was part of a real estate and mining stock scheme. When the shafts produced no ore and the Denver and Rio Grande bypassed Custer City, the original forty buildings fell into disrepair, and the population left. Custer City became a ghost town, and its statue, like the one at West Point, disappeared. Very likely this cavalryman became a source of badly needed bronze during World War I.[96]

Early in 1903, Charles Schreyvogel's *Custer's Demand* created a stir at the Knoedler Art Galleries in New York City At the painting's center is a long-haired Custer astride a horse. The scene depicts his December 1868 meeting with Kiowa chiefs Satanta, Kicking Bird, Lone Wolf, and Little Heart. Custer is shown demanding their surrender and ordering them to lead their people onto the reservation. Others portrayed include scout and interpreter Amos Grover (not actually present), Lt. Tom Custer, and Lt. Col. John Schuyler Crosby, General Sheridan's aide. In the background, Little Phil commands the combined Seventh Cavalry and Nineteenth Kansas Volunteer forces.[97] The *New York Herald* had followed Schreyvogel's career since the appearance of *My Bunkie*, two years earlier. On April 19, 1903, it praised the Hoboken, New Jersey, artist as the "Painter of the Western Frontier."[98]

Nine days later a letter from Frederic Remington appeared in th newspaper "While I do not want to interfere with Mr. Schreyvogel's hallucinations, I do object to his half baked stuff being considered seriously as history." Remington then criticized the young artist's depiction of weapons, cartridge belts, Indian regalia, and army uniforms. Among the numerous inaccuracies were Crosby's pants, which should have been rendered in "cerulean type." In conclusion Remington noted, "Now the picture as a whole is very good for a man who knows only what Schreyvogel does know about such matters, but as for history—my comments will speak for themselves." Remington had thrown down the gauntlet, and the *Herald* waited to see "who knows the West best."[99]

The soft-spoken Schreyvogel remained silent at first since he considered Remington "the greatest of us all." When the assertions continued, however, the younger painter gave the *Herald* a letter he had received on April 24, four days before the appearance of Remington's challenge. In it, Elizabeth Custer praised Schreyvogel's work, finding the "likenesses excellent, the composition of the picture and harmony of color admirable." More important: "It all shows how familiar the plains and frontier life are to you."[100] Elizabeth applauded the informal campaign uniforms and the boots. She also congratulated the painter on "the fidelity of the likeness and the costume of the Indians." She thought the entire painting "free from sensationalism, and yet so spirited, that I want to commend your skill." In closing, she promised to visit the artist and his wife Lulu soon.[101]

Remington had known Libbie from the days he had illustrated *Tenting on the Plains*. He now accused Schreyvogel of fleeing "to the protecting folds of Mrs. General Custer's skirts, whereat his position will be impregnable as far as I am concerned." Determined to prove himself correct, Remington enclosed a check for $100. The *Herald* could donate it to any charity if Colonel Crosby agreed that army men wore those trousers on duty in 1869.[102]

Delighted by the controversy, the *Herald* located Crosby. The retired soldier found Remington's remarks about the painting and Mrs. Custer offensive. Despite his reticence, he decided "to put [Remington] out of his pain—always presupposing that his fellow artist and Mrs. Custer's reputation and indorsement have not already done so." Then, inserting the stiletto, Crosby indicated that the younger artist had painted the picture "after the facts, meaning it to be a historical one, and not after a nice sense of the proprieties derived from misleading dates." Point by point, he dismissed Remington's criticisms, excluding only the trousers, which admittedly "were not the shade of blue depicted in the picture." However, "they were blue, but not that shade." Thus, Remington should decide how much to deduct from the $100 he owed the *Herald*. Actually, Schreyvogel had based the trousers on an old pair taken from Crosby's trunk.[103]

"I don't mind your 'wooling' me," Remington wrote Crosby in a letter marked "Personal." He was, however, "awfully put out to discover that Mrs.

Custer had an interest in that picture. If I had dreamed that, I should have never said a word. I venerate the memory of General Custer and wouldn't offend Mrs. C on my life. That's why I pulled in my horse because I despise Schreyvogel. I have been getting for years [*sic*] to try at General Custer and I want to ask you some questions."[104]

Unfortunately for Remington, Crosby sent his letter to Elizabeth with a notation: "Further Schreyvogel information—should keep confidential. . . . JSC." Elizabeth, no more inclined to confidentiality than Crosby, forwarded it to Schreyvogel.[105] Before the year ended, the Schreyvogels welcomed their first child, a daughter whom they named Ruth Elizabeth. Libbie, delighted with her namesake, called her "Little Elizabeth."[106]

As for Remington, he had lost the public debate with the younger man. That same year, however, *Collier's* agreed to pay him $12,000 annually—an unheard of amount—for a series illustrating the frontier period in American life. Whatever Schreyvogel's success, Remington remained the "master illustrator of the Old West."[107]

Elizabeth had more pressing concerns in 1903 than the Schreyvogel-Remington debate. That summer she hosted her sister-in-law's wedding at Onteora when Maggie married John Halbert Maugham. In the late 1880s, Maggie had toured as an elocutionist before serving as state librarian for Michigan. Emmanuel's death in 1892 had set her back emotionally, but recently her physical and mental well being had improved greatly. Following the wedding, the couple left for their honeymoon in Mexico.[108]

By late October, Elizabeth, still adventurous at sixty-one, was aboard the PMSS *Siberia*, bound for Egypt, Turkey, China, and Japan. She had visited the land of pyramids in 1898, but she and her party, composed mainly of other widows, were among the earliest western tourists allowed into Japan. Their guide escorted them through Tokyo, Kyoto, and Osaka's temples and gardens before taking them to Mount Fuji. Elizabeth recorded, "The day we gazed upon it," was "really one of the days of my life." She concurred with a friend's statement, "Once let me see Fugiami [*sic*] and Southern Cross, the Taj. Mahal and I'll Say 'Lord now let thy servant depart in peace.'" Libbie and her companions also tried to replicate the silent tea ceremony they had witnessed. "Straight fronts, narrow skirts and the buttons of our walking shoes burrowing into our ankles" proved too distracting.[109]

As for the Japanese, Elizabeth viewed them as "small" and their industry as "primitive." She applauded the country's efforts to modernize but agreed with a companion's statement. "The Japanese takes himself very seriously and we do not dare smile when there is something doing that some one's great grandfather did and that is not quite up to the 20th Century."[110]

Summer, 1905, found Elizabeth touring Germany with her friend, Agnes Bates Wellington. Her pleasure ended when she discovered in her forwarded mail an article in *Pearson's Magazine*, written by Cyrus T. Brady, an Episcopalian bishop. In it, he raised again the question of Custer's compliance with Terry's orders.[111]

Recently, Gen. George Forsyth, famous for withstanding an eight-day siege at Beecher's Island in 1868, had defended Custer's actions at the Little Bighorn. Forsyth's autobiography admitted that Terry's plan had envisioned the Seventh moving up the Rosebud farther south before turning westward towards the Little Bighorn. Nonetheless, the Indian Bureau had estimated the hostiles at no more than 1,000. Moreover, Custer, thinking they had sighted him and fearing their flight, had acted correctly. Moreover, Terry's orders had given him the necessary "latitude" to use his judgment when "nearly in contact with the enemy."[112] When Elizabeth added Forsyth to Miles, Godfrey, Fry, and Andrews and weighed their opinions against Hughes's writings in an obscure journal and Carrington's earlier letter, she considered the controversy settled in her husband's favor.

Now Brady had reopened it in an article that forecast a coming book. When Elizabeth voiced her objections, the bishop offered to publish her views in an appendix, where experts would argue the question. Andrews, Miles, and Godfrey would champion Custer, while Hughes and Carrington would oppose his actions. Charles Woodruff, formerly a lieutenant with Colonel Gibbon's infantry and now a general, would present an impartial view. "I think this is a just distribution—at least I so intend it to be," he explained.[113]

Elizabeth, as her husband's wife, had no intention of entering into a public debate on military matters. Moreover any statement she made might heighten interest in Brady's book; the fewer sales it enjoyed and the less publicity it attracted, the better. She did, however, persuade her old friend, Jacob Greene, to enter the arena on her behalf.[114]

When Brady's *Indian Fights and Fighters* appeared later that year, much of the argument in the appendix turned on the question of Miles's affidavit. The famous Indian fighter had ignored Brady's three requests to produce the document.[115] Hughes, in turn, denied its existence, since Terry would never have insulted Custer by telling him something so "elementary" as "hold on to your wounded."[116] Finally, General Woodruff dismissed the whole matter as nonsense and, rather than remaining impartial, as Brady had promised, stated unequivocally that Custer had disobeyed orders. Either that or, "I do not see how it is possible for the charge of disobedience of orders to hold against any man, under any circumstances, when away from his superior." Woodruff also faulted Custer for not scouting Tullock's Creek and sending someone through to Gibbon.[117]

Jacob Greene, ignoring the affidavit, added a new element, based on information Elizabeth had sent him. Given the rumors circulating at Lincoln regarding Custer's reluctance to serve under Terry, Armstrong had summoned his wife to a private meeting with the general. When the three were closeted together, Elizabeth had heard her husband say that a man usually "means what he says" in his wife's presence. Whatever the gossip, Armstrong wanted Terry to know he was happy to "serve under you," adding, "not only that I value you as a soldier, but as a friend and a man." Elizabeth, believing her husband sincere, saw no reason for disobedience.[118]

By November the widow was incensed. She had seen a *New York Times* advertisement stating Brady's appendix would prove "that Custer himself was responsible for [the defeat] by ignoring to a certain degree orders." She wrote the *Times* book review editor, noting again that Terry's order had given Custer "such latitude" since he had trusted his "judgment so entirely." What she resented most, although she stated it unclearly, was not Brady's appendix so much as Brady's assertion within his text that Custer had intentionally disobeyed orders.

Brady's conclusions echoed those advanced earlier by Hughes. Gibbon's recollection of telling Custer, "Don't be greedy, but wait for us," and Custer's response, "No, I will not," weighed heavily with the bishop. So too did Ludlow's remembrance of Custer's statement that he planned to "swing clear of Terry."[119] In the end, Brady maintained, it had been Custer's disobedience that had brought him "practically in contact with the enemy" on June 25. Then, with no order to guide him, Custer "was thrown on his own resources—just what he wanted, and what he had schemed and planned for."[120]

Brady's analysis left Elizabeth embittered and depressed since "[a]mong the enemies of my husband none has ever made such a terrible accusation. It remains for him to say that Gen. Custer deliberately planned disobedience."[121] Her obvious distress moved R. W. Barkley, who remembering Brady from Annapolis, wrote her advising her not to take the Bishop seriously. "He is not a deep water sailor. He is not always accurate, even where his knowledge is first hand."[122]

But until Brady was refuted, Elizabeth would not be mollified. In the meantime, she derived comfort from the granite shaft she placed on the pedestal of her husband's grave in 1905. A year later, she learned she could face death with greater equanimity. In response to her earlier request, Albert L. Mills, superintendent at West Point, had ordered the head and shoulders carved from the hated MacDonald statue. Obviously Elizabeth no longer found the face offensive, for she asked Mills to display the bust in a suitable location. Despite assurances he would comply as soon as he found "an appropriate place," the bust was never displayed.[123]

Shortly after, Elizabeth received more good news. Two rival organizations, the Lansing-based Michigan Cavalry Brigade Association and the Michigan Custer Memorial Association, formed in Monroe, sought state funding for a Custer monument in the 1907 legislative session. Despite his Ohio birth, the cavalry veterans argued that the boy general had transformed Michigan regiments into the North's best-known cavalry brigade.[124]

The Monroe-based organization led by businessman Charles Greening and Libbie's old friends, Frederick Nims and John Bulkley, among others, sent out 3,000 letters. They asked clergymen, Grand Army of the Republic posts, and prominent persons to indicate support for the monument. Among the respondents was President Theodore Roosevelt. Custer, he noted, "has become, in a peculiar sense, the typical representative of the American regular officer who fought for the extension of our frontier, and it is eminently fitting that such a memorial as is proposed should be raised to him."[125]

Early in February, Monroe's willingness to donate a site persuaded Gov. Fred Warner to support that town as the statue's location rather than the state capital, Lansing. No one, however, knew what the Elizabeth wanted. When a telegram reached her at her cabin in the Catskills, she braved a blizzard to telephone her answer. Her choice of Monroe decided the matter, and the two Michigan organizations joined to pressure the state legislature for $50,000.[126]

The legislature's $25,000 appropriation in June 1907, while disappointing, sufficed for an equestrian statue. Governor Warner appointed a monument commission including William O. Lee, the head of the Michigan Cavalry Brigade Association; James Kidd, colonel of the Sixth Michigan Cavalry; and Fred Nims. George Briggs, who had played an important role in the design of the Michigan Cavalry Monument, dedicated at Gettysburg in 1889, chaired the commission.[127] Although Elizabeth was not officially a member, no one wanted to repeat the West Point debacle. As Nims explained, "Your wishes are to be our guide from the begining [*sic*] to the end," and members would take no action without her approval.[128]

Vinnie Ream Hoxie, learning of the appropriation, contacted Elizabeth. After Vinnie had suffered a heart attack in 1905, her husband, fearing for her life, had allowed her to resume her profession. Immediately, she had received commissions, including Cornell University's statue of its founder, Ezra Cornell. Vinnie, however, wanted the Custer commission. "I feel that no one can reproduce him in bronze . . . more faithfully than I can. Will you write . . . and ask them to allow me to make the statue?"[129]

Elizabeth's noncommittal response proved disappointing. For years, Vinnie had remembered her "as the warm hearted loving wife who wrote me so lovingly and enthusiasticly [*sic*] about the bust of Genl Custer. . . . I have always carefully preserved the letters which were more precious to me than gold." Now Libbie's answer, "so conventional, so unsympathetic, with no kind word even or mention of my likeness of the brave Genl Custer," left her "hurt." Although she continued to plead her case, Vinnie received no consideration. She had never completed an equestrian statue.[130]

As the committee began its search for an artist, Elizabeth joined about 300 veterans from nineteen of the twenty-one regiments Armstrong had commanded during the Civil War. Four veterans from the Seventh Cavalry, including John Martin, the trumpeter who had carried the "Come Quick" message to Benteen, were also present at the August 1907 meeting at Canandaigua, New York. While Elizabeth found the praise for her husband gratifying, the constant handshaking grew painful. The struggle to remember faces and names after many years left her so "unnerved that I did not get over it for months, tho' Dr. Bode gave me hydropathy, osteopathy, and Kneipe herbs for six weeks."[131]

Weary, Elizabeth postponed a visit to India; the Taj Majal could wait. As questions arose on the statue, she conferred with other members of the Custer family. Maggie wanted Autie depicted at the "age and period when *he* represented Michigan." When the inevitable question of hair arose, Maggie objected to an "extreme" length but wanted it "long enough to justify the description always associated with his personal appearance."[132]

The commission agreed. Chairman Briggs noted that members hoped to cast in bronze "a faithful representation of Gen. Custer as he appeared in actual warfare, mounted upon a splendid specimen of a horse, and where both horse and rider are alive to the important and dangerous duty in which they are engaged." If the artist succeeded, "future generations" would be inspired to "turn to history to learn the record of his splendid achievements."[133]

While Briggs reminded Elizabeth that any artist had to win "the approval of the commission as well as yourself," he encouraged her to investigate on her own. When she found someone acceptable, her views would have "a deciding influence with the Committee."[134] Working together, Elizabeth and the commission considered Solon Borglum, Alexander Proctor, Henry Shrady, and Henry Brush-Brown.

Edward Potter's request to examine the site so impressed the widow, however, that she gravitated towards him, as did Chairman Briggs. After previewing models, the other commission members agreed. Late in February 1908, Potter, famous for his equestrian statues of Gen. Charles Devens at Worcester, Massachusetts; Hernando de Soto at Saint Louis; and "Mad Anthony" Wayne at Valley Forge, received the contract.[135]

By early March Elizabeth learned that, among the five models submitted by Potter, one depicted Custer as having suddenly halted his horse at Rummel's barn. He had just seen Jeb Stuart's forces on the third day of the Battle of Gettysburg. "This because it shows the General to better advantage is more original and dramatic," wrote Briggs, "and the horse is less conspicuous than the one with heads up. I feel that the controlling and central idea of our statue should be 'General Custer.' That which detracts from such an idea should be eliminated."[136]

Elizabeth's agreement settled the matter. The statue would show a twenty-three-year-old Custer in a quick moment of reflection—exactly the way the widow wanted her husband depicted. Potter would portray no rash, unthinking charger but instead would immortalize in bronze an intelligent surveyor taking in the entire scene in one glance before moving on to glory. All that remained was for Potter to complete his work.

Soon after, Elizabeth boarded the S.S. *Oceanic* for Europe where she planned to visit France, Germany, and Russia. Despite earlier threats to her husband's reputation from Hughes and Brady, recently she had encountered only good news. John Philip Sousa had changed the name of Gustave Luder's "A Cavalry Charge" to "Custer's Last Charge." And Gifford Pinchot, chief of the Forestry Service, had notified her that Otter Forest in Montana would soon become Custer Forest.[137]

Given these honors, questions about Armstrong's judgment or possible disobedience receded. The past winter Buffalo Bill had written Elizabeth from his home in Cody, Wyoming, close to the Little Bighorn Battlefield. At least once a month he spoke on Custer and his last stand, and he had no patience with those who charged insubordination. "For General Terry told me himself," he maintained, "that General Custer did not disobey any order he gave him."[138]

As Elizabeth surrendered to the pleasures of an ocean voyage, she confided to her journal, "When there's a widow there's a way—when there's a *will* there's a widow."[139] At last she would see a fitting monument to Armstrong unveiled in her home town. Never mind that she had played a disruptive role earlier. Now she heartily approved of a statue that would show the world her "husband as he should be known." Relaxing in her deck chair and enjoying the sea breezes, Elizabeth concluded, it was about time!

CHAPTER 15

"Tradition and History Will Be So Mingled"

WHEN ELIZABETH learned that the monument would be unveiled on June 4, 1910, she purchased "very 'glad rags'" for her moment in the "lime light." Remembering that veterans had told her at Canandaigua three years earlier, "You aint so young as you once was," she bought a veil to "conceal the wrinkles and gray locks" from peering eyes. And noting that recent photographs of Anna Howard Shaw, that "fine honest suffragist whom I know," showed her bridgework, Elizabeth reminded herself not to smile too broadly.[1] One event, however, dampened her elation. When Maggie discovered she had cancer, as a convert to Christian Science, she relied on the prayers of healer Wentworth Bryan Winslow. For a while she seemed to improve, and then, unexpectedly, on March 22, Maggie died.[2]

As Elizabeth struggled to adapt to one more loss, citizens in her home town worked frantically throughout April and May. They planted flowers, purchased flags and buntings, and decorated graves. Catching the spirit, the Water Department painted fire hydrants red to match the neckties worn by brigade veterans, and city crews erected four large electric arcs around Loranger Square, the monument's home. In mid-May the Gorham factory in Providence, Rhode Island, shipped the 7,500-pound bronze statue. Monroe hoped to shine, but late May brought nothing but downpours and cold winds off Lake Erie.[3]

Elizabeth left New York, accompanied by Mary Logan. As the widow of John Logan, Civil War general, congressman, and senator, Mary Logan had played vital roles in the dedication of her husband's statues in Chicago and Washington, D.C. Thus she was a source of valuable advice for her friend.[4] Arriving in Monroe on June 2, the two women went immediately to the home of Armstrong's niece, Clara Custer Vivian. Despite *"such* a rain," nine former schoolmates from the Boyd Seminary visited Elizabeth. Several were "very frail," but all, having "braved the cold and wind," wondered why their friend had stayed away so long. Libbie explained, "When I was tired with work and my nerves exhausted from constant endeavor to perpetuate my husband's memory, I have gone to the other side." There she met "people and sights that had nothing to do with my past" and returned revitalized to resume her life's work.[5]

Early the next day a white-haired man of seventy appeared at the Vivian residence. John Burkman had come from Billings, Montana, on borrowed money. As he and Elizabeth exchanged memories after thirty-four years apart, a reporter from the *Detroit Free Press* arrived, requesting an interview. Elizabeth refused until she saw that the journalist was a female. She knew first hand that "for a sensitive delicate woman" making a living was a "hard ordeal. That is why," she confided, "it is in my heart to build as a memorial to the general a home for girls."[6]

Catching the reporter by surprise, Elizabeth elaborated. "You see, the general always felt that girls, no matter how brave they were, needed so much help and protection, and since I have lived in New York, I have seen much of the suffering of poor girls, living in hall bedrooms, subsisting on tea and crackers and going out to work—proud, noble-hearted girls, so many of them, who never wince or cry aloud." Elizabeth had selected the site and set aside the money for "Custer's Club, and I know," she added, "that no memorial I could build to him would please him half as much."[7]

The interviewer may have thought a girls' home a strange memorial for a general, but Elizabeth knew of other homes for working women. In 1891, Jane Addams had founded the Jane Club in Chicago as a cooperative boarding house to help young working women weather dismissals and strikes.[8] Closer to home in New York City, both Grace Hoadley Dodge (whose mother, Sarah Hoadley Dodge, had worked with Elizabeth as a member of the Bellevue Hospital visiting committee) and Mary White Ovington had established working girls' clubs.[9] There middle- and upper-class women befriended female factory workers and taught them domestic, economic, and social skills and "character building."[10] By emulating these examples, Elizabeth hoped to do for her sex what she thought *The "Boy General"* was accomplishing for boys.

Elizabeth was also working on her Civil War memoirs, "a human document of the general's life and mine." Although it would "throw the true light on [Armstrong's] lovable, noble character," it would remain un-published "until after my death, and as we have no children, I need feel no hesitation on that score."[11]

Other journalists also arrived, and all were as interested in Elizabeth's appearance as in her plans. Her first interviewer described her dress in detail, lingering over the "flowing morning gown of black and white, with the bit of Irish lace at the throat and the soft white shawl thrown over her shoulders," as if she were a renowned actress or visiting royalty. Another thought her uncommonly youthful in her appearance. None mentioned her age, since Elizabeth believed ladies never disclosed that fact. Burkman, however, constantly nudged her and muttered under his breath, "how old be you?"[12]

While reporters praised her "compelling charm," the "musical modulation," of her voice, and her "warmth" and "dignity," the female journalist discerned in Elizabeth something else. She greeted some guests, "never letting down the barriers, but incapable of the shadow of offense." Yet another interviewer noted her "unique" career among the remarkable women of America. She has lived for Gen. Custer." He was "manifestly the one grand subject," and her conversation indicated "this is not a cool, settled pride, but an ever fresh enthusiasm."[13]

Elizabeth talked at length about honors paid her husband, not only in Monroe, but throughout the country. Even people "who never knew us, and young boys," she announced, "seem to regard him as a hero, as he was. Some schools have a 'Custer day,' and schools ask for pictures." For that reason, she added, "I regret that Cyrus Townsend Brady has blamed the general for disobeying orders at the Little Big Horn."[14] Asked if her success in commemorating her husband had made her happy, Elizabeth replied that her life had lost "the best and dearest it possessed." Still, she was "content, and that is a great deal."[15]

Inevitably, she resurrected the most common charges against Custer in order to demolish them. He had chosen his peculiar costume during the Civil War, not out of vanity but to remain visible to his men even in the thick of battle. He had never been rash. Instead, as Potter depicted him, he had made "a quick survey of the field," and, after comprehending it in a glance, "he might order a charge. If he did, he would pull his hat down on his head and dash away. In the statue," Elizabeth explained, "he is alert, tense, his hat in hand."[16]

On Friday night before the dedication, Elizabeth was the guest of honor at the Michigan brigade banquet. The speakers praised her for keeping the general before the public through her writings and lectures. When one of the veterans declared, "We loved him but we adore her," the crowd roared its approval. As Elizabeth basked in the accolades, she felt "inwardly conscious of my shortcomings, of my rooted belief that another woman would have done so much more for her husband's memory." Still, those assembled had "comforted my soul by saying that I *have* done much for A. and that the Statue (for which I never worked knowingly) is greatly due to what I have written and the vigilance I have tried to observe." Gazing at the veterans, their wives, children, and grandchildren, she concluded that whatever charges her husband's critics had hurled, they meant nothing to "the young [and], the unbiased admirers." Instead, "he is on a pedestal with them and always will be."[17]

Among the songs that evening a woman sang a lengthy ballad of the Battle of the Little Bighorn, followed by "Then You'll Remember Me." Since it was the first piano music Autie had given Libbie during courtship, it brought back a flood of memories, leaving her emotionally drained.[18] Afterwards, she ignored the buckskin-clad man who claimed to be a scout she had met in Cheyenne, a city she had never visited. Instead she shook the "horny, knuckled, rheumatic" hands of the veterans. When they whispered "God bless you! . . . I told them how I needed such words, and it was a sincere rejoinder," she noted, perhaps thinking of Maggie, her most recent loss, as well as Armstrong. "For the inevitable result of those who try always to go smiling through life, and put up a bluff of perpetual content," she noted later, "[is] that only a few—the nearest, dearest or the most discerning and sympathetic ever know that the hours that one sees people and keeps up the farce of perpetual happiness are few compared with the never ending hours when one is alone with the past, and all those who were nearest have 'gone to the country from which no traveller returns.'"[19]

Elizabeth awoke next morning to see sunshine streaming through the window. Outside farm wagons and interurbans brought people pouring onto the main streets, while on the sidewalks, hawkers sold souvenirs. By 8:30, the crowd, estimated at 15,000 to 25,000, stirred restively waiting for President William Howard Taft's arrival.

When the executive train belatedly reached the station, a cavalcade of cars rushed him to Saint Mary's Academy, where flag-waving schoolgirls in white dresses serenaded him with patriotic songs. Afterwards an automobile carried him to a place opposite the old Bacon homestead, where he reviewed parading veterans from the Michigan brigade, the Third Division, and the Seventh Cavalry. Across the street Libbie watched the same event, standing on the porch where she had played as a child.

As Elizabeth ascended the steps to the grandstand in nearby Loranger Square, she felt a sense of momentary "fright." The crowd, realizing that the woman dressed in black and wearing a large hat and feather boa was Mrs. Custer, erupted in cheers. Taft's statement that he had enjoyed her books alleviated her nervousness somewhat, but in her floundering responses, "I did not cover myself with glory."[20]

Taking her seat, Elizabeth noted to the left the church where she had married and to her right the courthouse where her father had served as judge. Amidst the huge trees along the square, "the sun poured down on this circle as if it were hallowed ground." She scanned the faces before her, searching for Custer family members and Godfrey, now a retired brigadier, who was there with his daughter. Even Curley, the Crow scout, was somewhere in the crowd.[21]

As reporters jostled one another, vying for camera angles and furiously snapping pictures, a telegraph operator on stage relayed the ceremony throughout the United States.[22] After the invocation and commission report, Potter spoke briefly, explaining that the monument faced southward to avoid shading Custer's face. More important, since it showed Custer sighting the enemy on July 3, 1863, it followed Gettysburg Battlefield practices, where statues faced the enemy. "I think it is very appropriate that the statue of Custer should face south." As the crowd applauded, he added, "For whoever heard of Custer showing the tail of his horse to a Southerner?"[23] Whatever the reason, the choice was unconsciously brilliant. By facing a northern general southward (especially one who had maintained warm relations with former West Point comrades on the Confederate side), the monument symbolized the national reconciliation that had occurred in the decades since Appomattox.

The moment arrived for the unveiling. As the crowd rose, Elizabeth stepped forward. finding herself in front of the president, she became momentarily flustered and offered to defer to Taft. The genial man responded, "We are all here to pay honor to you and yours." Recalling that the flags had failed to fall from the West Point statue, Elizabeth asked, "Do I have to pull very hard?" She also expressed delight that the ribbons were "yellow, the cavalry colors. I wanted it to be in the cavalry colors."[24]

At the first tug, the two flags fell away, revealing the heroic-sized statue with its large letters stating simply "CUSTER." As "a great shout" came from the crowd, Elizabeth concluded that "never was anything more life-like and beautiful than that golden image of the hero of the day." The bronze surface sparkled in the sun as the band struck up the National Anthem and a seventeen-gun salute reverberated in the distance. Elizabeth could hardly believe "that my dream of so many years was a reality before me."[25]

Sen. William A. Smith, the day's orator, used the occasion to warn of dangers threatening the republic. Given the recent tide of immigration, he feared "we make citizens too easily in America. The honest aliens I welcome," he assured his audience, "but such men as Custer did not give up their lives and women of whom Mrs. Custer is so conspicuous an example did not give up all they had and have not suffered all these years that our country should be turned over to anarchists. Our heroes," he continued, "have taught us the lessons of high ideals, and the ignorant and vicious of other lands cannot stop the march of American patriotism."[26]

Smith extracted other lessons from Custer's life. Echoing themes found in Whittaker's biography and Elizabeth's books, the senator described the boy general as an incorruptible, self-made man. Born into "poverty and distress," Custer, a "special messenger of God at Gettysburg and Appomattox," had joined the pantheon of national heroes through his courageous acts. Despite his fame, however, Custer had remained "tender and affectionate in his home, loving and dutiful as a son, loyal and devoted to the girl-wife."[27]

Through his contributions, Old Glory shone brighter over a more prosperous nation. Today, "singing spindles, happy hearts from ocean to ocean declaim his marvelous prowess." Custer's chief importance, however, lay not in his deeds, but in his character: "Clean and manly in his private life he exemplified the highest soldierly attainment." Smith's hero, furthermore, was no swarthy immigrant. Instead he could be either Teutonic or Anglo-Saxon, for he was "flaxen-haired, blue-eyed, lithe in figure, straight as an arrow, his long hair setting off a countenance, upon which the god of nature, must have pondered as she set it upon a man."[28] One veteran turned to his friend and announced, "If Custer was here and heard some of that, he'd be glad he was dead." After pondering that sentence, his perplexed companion asked, "What part of Ireland were you from?"[29]

Taft, while noting Custer's Civil War contributions, preferred to remember him as a western hero. By doing so, he underscored the soldier's appeal to the entire country, for all Americans celebrated their common pioneering heritage in the trans-Mississippi West.[30] Custer had been, the president told his audience, "one of the small band of twenty-five thousand men constituting the regular army of the United States, without whose service, whose exposure to danger, whose loss of life and whose hardships and trials, it would not have been possible for us to have settled the great west."[31]

Gov. Fred Warner, speaking for the state, presented the statue, not to Monroe, but "to the world." The monument would serve as "a sacred inspiration to generations yet unborn." Nations must honor their heroes, he warned, so that young people learned "the people are not ungrateful, but rather hold in fond and lasting remembrance and reverence those who strive and sacrifice for the betterment of humanity and the preservation of the nation." In this way "are our youth inspired to lives of rectitude and honorable service to mankind."[32]

The ceremony ended with the placing of wreaths on the statue and the singing of "The Old Brigade" and "America." Almost imperceptibly the president's train had nudged carefully through the crowd. Soon Taft waved good-bye from the platform as he and his entourage of Secret Service men headed towards Jackson, Michigan, for a rally in one of the Republican party's birthplaces.[33]

That afternoon Elizabeth greeted guests at a Park Hotel reception hosted by Monroe's Civic Improvement Association. One reporter noted the "continuous stream of visitors who came to touch the hand and figuratively speaking [were] content to 'kiss the hem of the garment' of the hero's widow." Despite the "hundreds, perhaps thousands of people" the reporter observed, all left feeling she had appreciated their presence. The sixty-eight-year-old woman show no "trace of fatigue" when she greeted the last visitor as enthusiastically as the first.[34]

Compliments on the statue had reinvigorated Elizabeth as the day wore on. Veterans proclaimed every detail perfect from the cavalry grip of the single rein in Custer's hands to the horseshoes. They also assured her that they had forgiven her for choosing Monroe over Lansing.

Elizabeth had never doubted her decision. "It was right to place it where there was a foundation of personal love and admiration to pass down to the younger generation." Eventually it would "mean much more to the people of the future because of the personal element which will not die out but rather grow with time until the day will come when tradition and history will be so mingled that no one will be able to separate them, and he will pass into *history* as a man without faults and only heroic virtues—a hero as he really was, 'sans peur et sans reproche.'"[35]

After delivering a speech the following evening on the Oberammergau passion play, Elizabeth left to visit the Farnham Lyons in Saginaw, Michigan. The recent excitement and strain of traveling and appearing in public had exhausted her. Monroe citizens soon read that a "completely worn out" Mrs. Custer remained in bed until strong enough to return to New York.[36]

Mid-July found Elizabeth back at work, writing thank-you letters and expressing appreciation that Monroe had demonstrated its "ownership in me as well as my husband."[37] Although she had promised friends and in-laws she would return more frequently now that she could see her boy in bronze, she did not keep her word. She missed the first four anniversaries of the monument dedication and appeared only for Nevin Custer's funeral in February 1915. Afterwards she gave speeches describing recent trips abroad and discussing events in Europe, now in the throes of war.[38]

The fall of 1911 had found her aboard the F.M.S. *Dunottar Castle* bound for Marseilles, Port Said, Suez, Bombay, Calcutta, Rangoon, and Madras. Elizabeth's good friend, *Century* editor Robert Underwood Johnson, told a story about this voyage. After stopping in London, Elizabeth learned that a transport would take British officers and their families to the Durbar, the coronation of King George the Fifth and his queen as emperor and empress of India. Libbie visited the War Department and asked if she could accompany the group. The authorities, noting she was an American, turned her away. As she was leaving, the officer at the desk noticed the name on her calling card. He asked if she was related to Gen. George Armstrong Custer, the "famous Indian-fighter." Discovering she was his widow, he relayed her request to his superiors, who bounded out of their offices to shake her hand. When the British transport departed for Delhi, Elizabeth was aboard.[39]

The summer of 1914 had found her motoring through Germany with four other American women. While staying at a hotel in Manheim, the group heard of the assassination at Sarajevo, Serbia, of Franz Ferdinand, heir to the Austrian throne. When the women reached Freiberg on July 28, they read of Austria's ultimatum. A newspaper account of Serbia's "very conciliatory" reply convinced Elizabeth all danger had passed, but that day Austria declared war.[40]

Elizabeth and her party traveled to Lucerne, Switzerland, where they discovered the true situation and learned that Russia and Germany had entered the war. Unable to exchange money or buy gasoline since the Swiss government had requisitioned supplies, they waited for word from their government. At last, on August 8, American dollars arrived in Swiss banks as Elizabeth learned that France had entered the conflict. As she read "these appalling bulletins," she wrote in her journal: "The few days seem like months, and really, it is to us as if the end of the world was coming."[41] Several days later, to her great relief, the party managed to book passage home.

In many ways, the world as Elizabeth and her generation knew it was coming to an end, but in 1916, many, including Libbie's friend Godfrey, looked to the past. Assisted by George B. Grinnell and western photographer I. A. Huffman, the retired brigadier coordinated ceremonies to mark the fortieth anniversary of the Little Bighorn. His contingent of horsemen retraced the Seventh Cavalry's route to the battlefield, where they met Two Moon, the first Cheyenne to have given an interview on the battle in 1898.[42]

Godfrey recalled in a breaking voice the discovery of the dead, their burial, the destruction of the deserted Indian camp, and the exhuming and reburial of bodies a year later. After former scout White Man Runs Him spoke for the Crows, Two Moon, now blind, came forward. After a long silence, he began. "Forty years ago we had a fight here with Custer. I came to fight Custer. We wiped him from the face of the earth. But, now we are brothers under the same flag."[43] Godfrey then delivered a message from Elizabeth Custer. Mexicans under Pancho Villa raided along the southwest border of the United States. Unless Americans supported the military, she feared "another sacrifice as there was of Custer."[44] Afterwards the firing of three volleys concluded the ceremony as Godfrey's contingent and the Indians shook hands while a Crow band played "Garry Owen." The ceremony pleased the participants, and they hoped to hold a more impressive commemoration in the near future.[45]

In New York, Elizabeth wrestled with her book on the Civil War. "Reminiscences play 'by by' with me—I can barely catch the incident I want—half in time to [jot] it down—will of the wisp memory," she wrote in her journal.[46] But while her own memory failed, support came from unexpected places. Charles Woodruff had written an article praising the heroic band of men at the last stand and castigating Indian policy. When Elizabeth thanked him, he responded from a California veteran's home. "It pleases me to know that words of mine, in reference to your gallant husband and his sterling regiment, gave you satisfaction."[47]

Brady too had capitulated. In his 1914 novel, *Britton of the Seventh*, he presented a heroic Custer. Moreover, his preface acknowledged that in the past, "possibly I was unduly severe, perhaps just a little harsh. Those who loved this brave man, this gallant gentleman, this ideal swordsman and cavalry leader may perhaps accept this as some *amende*." In the novel he attributed defeat to Reno's incompetence. Elizabeth, refusing to be placated, informed Godfrey, "I cannot forgive Cyrus Townsend Brady for his article on the battle—inspired by Captain Hughes."[48]

Another author, Frederick Dellenbaugh, pleased Libbie in 1917 by writing a biography for juveniles entitled *George Armstrong Custer*. He drew heavily on Elizabeth's books and Whittaker's work, and she, in turn, composed an introduction for the small volume. The Custer who appears in these pages—compassionate, uncomplaining, bold, brave, and never "rash"— deserves both emulation and canonization. Elizabeth scrutinized the manuscript and praised the author. "Such a gift Mr. Dellenbaugh," she observed, "to usher your hero into the present so dramatically so [concisely?] so truthfully. The first sentence will capture your reader."[49]

Others also worked to keep "the General" before the American public. David Hollingsworth, congressman from John Bingham's Eighteenth District in Ohio, tried repeatedly to obtain appropriations to build a Custer monument in the nation's capital or Custer's birthplace in New Rumley, Ohio. At one point he suggested raising funds "through small collections by the school children of the country." His efforts had failed, however, because of what he termed "quiet, not open, opposition." Now that the United States had entered World War I, no money would be available until the peace arrived.[50]

As Hollingsworth's proposed legislation languished in committee, Elizabeth sought a home for the cast of Potter's statue. Years earlier Candace Wheeler's grandson, Henry Stimson, then Taft's secretary of war, had told her there was no place at West Point sufficient "to hold a heroic size statue of General Custer."[51] Now, seven years later, friends for the indefatigable widow explored the possibility of housing the mounted cavalryman in Columbus, Ohio, at a park or on the Ohio State University campus. During these negotiations, however, the Gorham Manufacturing Company informed Elizabeth that "owing to war activities," they had moved many models and some had been "ruined," among them, her husband's.[52]

Despite that setback, 1920 brought encouraging developments. The Detroit Board of Education named an elementary school after George A. Custer, and a few months later Congress created the Custer State Park Game Sanctuary in the Black Hills (present-day Harney National Forest).[53] That same year a national highway beginning at Omaha, Nebraska, and ending at Glacier National Park became the Custer Battlefield Highway.

An offshoot of the good roads movement, its promoters formed themselves into the Custer Battlefield Hiway Association. Diligently, they sought funds for paving and marking the 1,475 miles of highway, which eventually tied Omaha, Nebraska, to Glacier National Park. In 1921, the association's representative, White Eagle, a Sioux from Gillette, Wyoming, rode his pony, Red Bird, from Hardin, Montana, to Omaha. At various stops, he distributed pamphlets, encouraging Americans, most of whom now lived in cities, to escape urban congestion by vacationing in the West.

A year later White Eagle arrived in New York City, where Elizabeth greeted him hospitably at her latest residence, 71 East 87th Street. With the automobile's growing popularity, he informed her, more families were using the scenic highway to camp in national parks and visit historic sites.[54] Elizabeth, overjoyed at these developments, wrote the association. "In the silent night I waken to see in my mind's eye, the long stretches of country across the continent carrying my husband's name."[55]

That same year, Hardin, Montana, marked the forty-fifth anniversary of the Little Bighorn by unveiling a Custer statue. Civic leaders planned the dedication ceremonies in collaboration with the battlefield program. Among the events, the Pathe Company filmed a motion picture of the mock battle between Indians from the nearby Crow Agency and whites from the Hardin American Legion. While Elizabeth did not attend, she gave Hardin's Carnegie-built library a framed picture of her husband and the buckskin attire he had worn on campaigns.[56]

At her request, *Century Magazine* printed and distributed 1,000 copies of Godfrey's "Custer's Last Battle." In 1908, following the controversy generated by Brady's book, Godfrey had revised his article. Among the changes, he had deleted Myles Moylan's quotation, which had offended Elizabeth earlier. He no longer included the statement, "Gentlemen, in my opinion General Custer has made the biggest mistake in his life, by not taking the whole regiment in at once in the first attack."[57] Instead, he argued that "division of the command was not in itself faulty." What had worked at the Washita might well have worked at the Little Bighorn if Reno had at least maintained "a bold front."[58]

Godfrey maintained that his studies over the years had altered his views of the famous battle. More likely, his long friendship with the Widow Custer had persuaded him to accept Fry's more partisan arguments. Terry had given the Seventh's commander "practically a *free hand*," and his orders had said nothing about bringing the two commands together on June 26.

Finally: "It was an absurdity to think that two commands, of 700 and 400, separated by from fifty to one hundred miles, could co-ordinate their movements in that open country and hold the Hostiles for a co-operative attack."[59]

Originally Elizabeth had planned to include an additional essay she attributed to retired Gen. Winfield S. Edgerly. When *Century* sent the former lieutenant in Benteen's battalion page proofs, he returned them uncorrected. He had not written the essay, which blamed the disaster largely on Terry's original deployment. Nor did he "agree with all of its statements and conclusions."[60] The embarrassed editor noted that Libbie had expressed some confusion herself about the article. In later years, Custer scholar William Graham concluded that the essay's most likely author was Nelson Miles. If so, Miles never claimed authorship.[61]

Although Elizabeth could not use the second article, nothing prevented her from including her own preface. She had made the reprints available because after forty-five years she still sought "to set at rest some of the fictions that were spread broadcast . . . by the enemies of General Custer, or by friends of General Terry, who thought the latter needed protection from blame or censure." Equally as important, the "story of courage and sacrifice should be re-told . . . to the present generation."[62]

As the dedication of another Custer statue drew near, one person more than any other comprehended Elizabeth's success. Rebecca Richmond, now frail and almost blind, wrote her cousin: "You certainly have accomplished your heart's desire, and kept the memorial fires burning down to the third generation, and I congratulate your persistence and devotion. They have placed in our National History a tragically romantic figure which can never be duplicated on account of changed conditions. Bravo!"[63]

The forty-fifth anniversary ceremony attracted between 3,500 and 5,000 people, among them Charlie Russell, the western artist, and photographer D. F. Barry. Godfrey had contacted the dwindling numbers of Little Bighorn veterans and worked with Crow, Sioux, and Cheyenne Indians to plan the program. He had also arranged for the Seventh Cavalry's participation. In nearby Hardin, Montana's Gov. Joseph M. Dixon delivered the address at the dedication of the newest Custer statue. Bronson Case of Kansas City, representing his cousin, Elizabeth Custer, told the audience, "No woman is her peer in American History."[64] Undoubtedly many in the audience agreed, since Americans admired her unflagging loyalty to her dead husband.

If Elizabeth showed signs of growing infirmity by her confusion over the article she mistakenly ascribed to General Edgerly, her promotional instincts for publicizing Armstrong remained sharp. After learning that the Hardin monument included a bronze marker delineating Custer's military record, she suggested that Monroe place a similar inscription on the Michigan statue. After all, present-day youth, several generations removed from "the General," needed this inspiring information. On the day that the Montana town unveiled its cavalryman, a judge, congressman, and scouting organizations witnessed the dedication of a bronze marker in Monroe.[65]

These events consoled Elizabeth, who faced her eightieth birthday more alone than ever. In 1914, her close friend Annie Yates had died two hours after she had either fallen or been thrown in front of a train in the 14th Street subway shortly before Christmas. Three years later, despite attempts by Elizabeth and Olivia Clemens to raise money for medical treatment, Ruth McEnery Stuart, their companion from Onteora, had died of bronchial pneumonia. Most recently, in 1921, Elizabeth had lost her good friend, John Burroughs.[66]

Elizabeth's own strength was declining. She caught bronchitis more easily and in 1922 began spending part her winters in Florida to escape the cold. Christmas found her at Daytona Beach's Osceola Gramatan Hotel. a southern offshoot of the Gramatan Inn, built by her friends, Sarah Bates Lawrence and William Van Duzer Lawrence in Bronxville. While Elizabeth enjoyed the warm sunshine and scent of orange blossoms, once settled into the hotel, she began "sighing already for that enticing old city by the sea!"[67]

Peter Thompson, a former private in Reno's battalion at the Little Bighorn, lived in Daytona and worked as a musician at the Ormond Hotel. He called on Elizabeth and afterwards contacted several Volusia County musicians who were also veterans of the Seventh Cavalry's regimental band. They arranged a stirring rendition of "Garry Owen" in her honor at a local concert.[68] Elizabeth also visited the nearby village of Cassadega, a community of spiritualists. She wrote a relative, "A Dr. Howard here tells me that a medium nearby has spoken to the General and that he said to tell me not to grieve and that he is near me constantly because of the several brave survivors of the Seventh who have played for me here in Florida."[69]

While Thompson and others provided Libbie with a comforting connection with the past, her world was changing in troubling ways. In 1923, she learned to her distress of a plan to move the Custer statue in Monroe from Loranger Square to a park on the Toledo road. Recently an automobile had collided with the cavalryman, and with more cars competing for space on narrow streets, the monument obstructed traffic. Others argued that vibration from nearby trains would loosen the statue's foundation.[70]

Elizabeth immediately telegramed her home town, calling attention to the statue's "present excellent location" and noting she would "feel very great regret if the change is made." Despite her opposition, the Monroe City Commission moved the general to Riverside Park, now renamed Soldiers and Sailors Memorial Park. The state of Michigan's appropriation of $3,000 for the statue's "repairs and removal" left the widow depressed.[71] Rough drafts of a letter to Armstrong's niece, May Custer Elmer, show that Elizabeth thought of borrowing money to buy land if necessary so she could place the statue in a more prominent location.[72]

Constantly she pondered ways of commemorating Armstrong. When Elizabeth saw the movie *The Covered Wagon,* she noted the genuine artifacts from the pioneering era and conceived of a new plan. If a filming company could locate such articles, why not build a pioneering museum for similar items at the Montana battlefield? "I have in mind some sort of a memorial hall on the Battlefield of the Little Big Horn to commemorate the frontiersmen as well as our Soldiers," she wrote the filmmakers.[73]

Briefly Elizabeth worked with Sen. Thomas B. Walsh. When she discovered, however, that his bill sought only $15,000 for construction at the Little Bighorn, she turned against it. That was barely enough to house a custodian and provide public rest rooms. Nelson Miles, coming to her aid, urged Congress to allocate at least $40,000 to build a "commodious Memorial Building that would store the trophies . . . [and] be a fitting tribute" to soldiers of the Indian Wars buried there. Although the bill failed to pass, Elizabeth, attributing its failure to congressional preoccupation with the Teapot Dome scandal, remained optimistic. One day, she believed, the museum would be built.[74]

Despite her disappointments, Elizabeth's private life had settled into a comfortable routine. After moving constantly, she resided contentedly on the ninth floor of a cooperative apartment at 71 Park Avenue. Her maid, Margaret Flood, lived with her, as did Margaret's husband, a furniture delivery man for a department store. Patrick Flood, as Elizabeth described him to John Burkman, was "more like one of our 7th Cavalry men than any one that I have met so far."[75]

Every Thursday, Margaret walked Elizabeth to the nearby Cosmopolitan Club, where she spent the day. Elizabeth noted proudly that she had been "taken in the club in 33rd st at its *very beginning*."[76] She considered the women's club movement one of the "greatest blessings of the day" and "a consolation to the widow and the old maid."[77] At times Elizabeth gave talks to club members on her Civil War or frontier experiences. In 1927, the Board of Governors honored her with a reception, during which they showed *The Pottery Maker*. In the brief movie, directed by the well-known actress Maude Adams and filmed at the Metropolitan Museum of Art, Elizabeth played "Grandma."[78]

Although she was now in her eighties, the widow still attracted admirers. Col. Charles Bates, a Michigan veteran of the Spanish American War, was her neighbor in Bronxville, where she owned property and voted. As Westchester County built its integrated park and boulevard system, Bates campaigned for the creation of a bridle path from "Mrs. Custer's long-time home to General Custer's final resting place" at West Point. If residents developed their equestrian skills, they would age as well as Elizabeth had. During one of her three trips around the world, the widow, then in her seventies, had traveled from Afghanistan to India through the Khyber Pass on horseback.[79]

Bates's plans for commemorating Custer were ambitious, for he envisioned an impressive opening ceremony and the unveiling of a national monument where the trail began. In 1876, the sacrifice of Custer and his men had revealed to his compatriots the need to stop arming Indians and end the corruption in government. Peace had come shortly after. Today, however, new threats confronted the country. Echoing the recent "Red Scare" and a continuing fear of immigrants in cities, Bates argued, "There could be no more effective Americanization at the gateway of New York City than such a ceremony. It would give direct notice to those not familiar with our history who are striving in a subtle way to undermine our patriotism and nullify the laws of the land to beware of the indignation of an aroused America."[80]

Although his plans never materialized, Bates undertook his own study of the Little Bighorn. For the most part, he restated the arguments of Miles, Godfrey, and Fry. More than the others, however, he portrayed Custer's besieged battalion, waiting in vain and hoping against hope, as the longed-for aid from Reno never arrived. In 1926, shortly before the fiftieth anniversary of the Little Bighorn, his version of the battle, one entirely satisfactory to Elizabeth, appeared in the *New York Times*.[81]

The widow also relied on Godfrey's continuing loyalty. When Col. William A. Graham completed *The Story of the Little Big Horn* in 1925, the retired brigadier refused to supply a foreword unless the author altered his manuscript.[82] Graham, who had tried to be objective, was disappointed. Like Godfrey and Elizabeth, he identified the large number of well-armed Indians and corrupt Indian policy as factors in Custer's defeat. He did not, however, indict Reno. Moreover, he believed that by dividing his command, Custer had contributed to the disaster. Godfrey rejected these arguments, and retired Brigadier Edgerly wrote the foreword instead.[83]

In his book, Graham also dismissed the affidavit, signed by Mary Adams, as "worthless." In 1924, Godfrey, Edgerly, and Col. Charles Varnum had assured him that Custer's maid had "neither accompanied the troops nor was present at any time during the campaign."[84] After many years, Godfrey and the others had forgotten that Armstrong had brought Mary Adams along. Separate letters written by Tom Custer and Autie Reed to their families indicate that she had been with the regiment until it began its march up the Rosebud on June 22. Thus she may have overheard the conversation between Terry and Custer, which the affidavit described.[85]

As Godfrey and others planned the fiftieth anniversary commemoration of the Little Bighorn, they learned of a movement to dedicate a monument to Major Reno during the ceremonies. Immediately Godfrey protested to J. A. Shoemaker, coordinator of events. Reno's "cowardly panic retreat from the valley" had cost the lives of twenty-nine soldiers, and when Benteen returned, he had "practically abdicat[ed]." Moreover, Godfrey believed that only Benteen's refusal had prevented Reno from stealing away from the bluffs the night of June 25 and leaving the wounded to perish at the hands of the Sioux.[86]

Elizabeth, who had seen Godfrey's letter, entreated Shoemaker "not to permit any memorial of any kind to be placed on that sacred battlefield to so great a coward as Col. Reno." Never before had she committed her feelings to paper, but now she asked him to use his "influence" against "so unworthy a man. . . . The battle of the Little Big Horn was his first battle and he seemed not to *try* to hide his cowardice." As she wrote, Elizabeth sensed her "husband's hand taking the pen away from me," for he had never wanted her to interfere in military matters. She asked Shoemaker to keep her letter "confidential," although he could say she was "opposed and have *unquestionable reasons* for opposition. . . . I *long*," she added, "for a memorial to our heroes on the battlefield of the Little Big Horn but not to *single out* for honor, the one coward of the regiment."[87]

Shoemaker and others planning the fiftieth anniversary acceded to Elizabeth and Godfrey. Instead of a monument to Reno, they arranged a reenactment of Reno's retreat to the bluffs on June 24 to honor his battalion. Three years later, on August 14, 1929, a marker was dedicated to the companies that had held off Indian attackers for two days. No names appeared on the inscription.[88]

An aviator flying overhead at the Little Bighorn Battlefield on June 25 calculated that 14,000 automobiles had brought more than 60,000 persons. Others estimated the number at 35,000. As visitors arrived, they climbed the steep hills, and many never saw the actual ceremonies. Instead they took pictures of the Sioux, Cheyenne, and Crow Indians in ceremonial regalia and the Seventh Cavalry and Indian War veterans in uniform.[89]

George Grinnell, now unquestionably the foremost expert on the Cheyennes, watched the proceedings with his wife. Not far away, E. A. Brininstool furiously took notes. Author of *A Trooper with Custer*, Brininstool was becoming increasingly critical of Custer and more sympathetic to Reno.[90] Mary Roberts Rinehart, a novelist and passionate advocate for the Blackfeet Indians, had helped plan the ceremonies and busily compiled her report for the *Saturday Evening Post*.[91] Also present were the western film star William S. Hart and his friend Chief Standing Bear. The day before, the Sioux had made Hart an honorary chief, giving him the name Crazy Horse.[92]

Elizabeth had considered attending until she realized she could not "suppress the emotions that the *day*, the *ceremonies*, the *place*, would surely call forth."[93] Recent events had depressed her. The previous year had opened with Rebecca's death on January 10, 1925. Although her cousin had "grown morbid" during her last years and stopped corresponding, Elizabeth had never forgotten that this "noble woman" had motivated her "to do something with my wrecked life." A few months later, as she struggled to adjust to the loss of her last close relative, the news arrived that Burkman would be missing from the ceremonies.[94] At eighty-six, the former striker, despondent over his inability to enter an old-age home for veterans, had shot himself.[95] In one respect, however, his life had ended long ago. Although he had served in Company L, part of Custer's battalion, he had been detached to Captain McDougall's pack train to look after Dandy. Thus Burkman had escaped with his life, but afterwards, he had never forgiven himself for not sharing his commander's fate.[96]

Elizabeth listened to a radio narration of events, sitting in the sun parlor of a nearby hotel.[97] As a funeral march played in the background, she heard the announcement that the Seventh Cavalry approached from the southeast. At the marker, where her husband's body had been found, Col. Fitzhugh

Lee, accompanied by Godfrey, halted his five companies. There he awaited the Sioux and Cheyenne, who approached from the west led by White Bull, Sitting Bull's nephew and a participant in the famous battle.

As White Bull signaled peace, seventy-one-year-old White Man Runs Him, sole survivor of Custer's Crow scouts, offered a peace pipe. In turn, Godfrey sheathed his sword. He and White Bull shook hands and traded a flag for a blanket. Then, after the placing of wreaths at the Custer marker and the firing of three volleys, a lone bugler played "Taps" over the graves. As the notes died away, each soldier joined an Indian, and two by two, these "brothers in arms" left the field, following the American flag.[98] Marguerite Merington was with Libbie that afternoon as she listened to the broadcast. When the program ended, Merington saw that her friend had been transported into another world. Wisely, she declined Elizabeth's dinner invitation, leaving her to savor her memories alone.[99]

The publicity given the fiftieth anniversary ceremonies renewed interest in Custer's widow. One reporter remarked in 1926 that when Elizabeth spoke of the past, her "blue eyes sparkled and her gentle face, in its frame of soft white curls, flushed with pleasure at the thought of the praise coming to her hero husband. One sees," he observed, that after half a century "he is still her hero." Summarizing her life, he added, "The last fifty years have offered her nothing so precious as her memories."[100] True, but Elizabeth had transformed her memories into an inspirational force for others. Proudly she noted, "Throughout the whole country schoolboys made of General Custer a symbol of courage which has helped to mold the soul of an entire generation."[101]

Elizabeth, who had always enjoyed a sense of humor, needed it when a letter arrived shortly after the semi-centennial celebration. Written by a "survivor" of the Battle of the Little Bighorn, it owed more to a famous picture, hanging in numerous saloons and bars throughout the United States, than actual fact.[102] Perhaps no illustration in American life contributed so much to mythology as the F. Otto Becker lithograph, based on an earlier painting completed by Cassilly Adams in 1886. While artistically superior to the original work, Becker's lithograph perpetuated the image of a long-haired Custer, brandishing a sword, while others around him had fallen.

When the Anheuser-Busch Company distributed over 150,000 prints to saloons across the country, the work became one of the most frequently viewed pieces in American history.[103] Although Elizabeth never visited such establishments, she undoubtedly concluded that her correspondent had gained his information from long nights in barrooms. Willard J. Carlyle assured the widow that he had watched the battle from a nearby hill, where he had seen Custer "left with his comrades dead around him. One sweep of his saber and an Indians head was split in two, one flash of his revolver, his last shot, and a red-skin got the bullet between the eyes, then he fell with a bullet in the breast, the last of that brave band. I saw him," he informed her, "within 15 minutes after he was shot, and there was still a smile on his face. Perhaps he was thinking of his home, his beloved wife or Mother. Who can tell."[104]

Carlyle, as one of many "survivors," received no more attention than the rest. At this stage of her life, Elizabeth had two concerns. She wanted her husband's heroic stature firmly established so she could die peacefully, and she worried about disposing of her estate. At some point, she had decided her resources were insufficient to build a Custer Club for working women. She still wished, however, to do something for less fortunate members of her sex. In 1926 she drew up a will, leaving the bulk of her estate to the "General George Armstrong Custer and Elizabeth Bacon Custer Scholarship Fund for Daughters of Army Officers" at Vassar College. Most of her mementoes, trophies, and memorabilia—the relics of her husband—were assigned to the future museum at the Little Bighorn Battlefield or other museums if it never materialized.[105]

In 1927, an article appeared on Elizabeth in *Collier's*. The writer, John B. Kennedy, had interviewed her in her apartment surrounded by "pictures of the past." Although she appeared "serene," and "the gray curls that frame her face are flattering measurement of her years," she seemed like someone from a Victorian novel. Nonetheless, she talked easily. When he asked her to name her greatest disappointments, she noted her husband's death and the absence of a "son to bear his honored name."[106]

Then, twisting her wedding band, Elizabeth turned reflective. "The widow of a national hero has responsibilities. In my case it has required heroism to face the curious just as it required my husband's heroism to face the cruel." Nonetheless, she had no regrets. "I see my country prosperous, strong and sure of its destiny, and I know, as the wife of every hero knows, that in some small measure my life has contributed to that." Thankfully, she had lived long enough to hear the late President Theodore Roosevelt say, "General Custer's name was a shining light to all the youth of America."[107]

While Elizabeth was at peace, she showed confusion. She referred to Rep. John Bingham as "Congressman Ballinger" and told of accompanying the general "to Fisher's Hill, Winchester, Yellow Tavern, Five Forks and Appomattox."[108] She had been with her husband only at Winchester. And yet the little old lady in lavender remained open to new ideas on topics other than her husband's heroism. Over time she had even softened her attitude towards Indians.

As the 1920s wore on, and largely because of her friendship with Charles Bates, Elizabeth became more aware of the wrongs Indians had sustained. Others who also helped broaden her views included the photographer D. F. Barry, the ethnologist Joseph K. Dixon, and the poet Julia Taft-Bayne, a woman who used Indian traditions as a source of inspiration. Additionally, White Eagle's visit and his promotional work for the Custer National Highway had pleased Libbie. She remembered too that Indians had fought with whites in World War I against a common foe.[109]

In this context the widow in 1927 composed a brief introduction to an article Bates had written stressing the wrongs whites had perpetrated against the Sioux.[110] After examining briefly the background of the Treaty of Fort Laramie, he maintained, "The ink was scarcely dry . . . when it was broken in 1869 through a military order." Elsewhere, he charged, "Five times the Sioux were promised land 'as long as water runs and grass grows,' but each time they were ordered on under the thin pretense of a cancellation of a treaty. The truth was," he continued, "there was no place for them to go, no place the white man did not want—except the Bad Lands, into which they might at last be hurled like Napoleon's cavalry and forgotten by all the world."[111] Bates never criticized the Seventh's commander. Rather, he argued that Custer, by befriending the Indians and speaking out against their mistreatment by corrupt agents, had himself become a victim.[112]

Elizabeth in *"Boots and Saddles"* had presented her husband as "a sincere friend of the reservation Indian." She meant that he had accepted the Indian who knew his place—the one assigned him by the white man—and stayed there.[113] Later, in rough drafts of unpublished manuscripts Elizabeth had argued that Indians prospered from the allotment system resulting from the Dawes Severalty Act of 1887.[114] She had no awareness that, under this measure, Indians had lost the bulk of their land and faced, in many cases, dire poverty.[115]

Nonetheless, by 1927 Elizabeth had arrived at some understanding of why the Sioux had resisted. "The Indians deeply cherished the Black Hills. The country was so different," she wrote, "from the dry plains and the Bad Lands because there was timber there and water and wonderful hunting. The chiefs said their people would fight to keep the land which had been promised them." Although she made no mention of the 1874 Black Hills

Expedition, which had brought miners stampeding onto Sioux land, she had changed her sentiments. "There was a time after the battle of the Little Big Horn when I could not have said this, but as the years have passed I have become convinced that the Indians were deeply wronged."[116]

When the anniversary of the Little Bighorn drew near in 1929, journalist and biographer Ishbel Ross interviewed Elizabeth. At eighty-seven, Mrs. Custer still worked hard, maintaining a large correspondence with veterans and others interested in her husband. Otherwise, her "New England conscience," instilled by her mother, permitted no rest.[117]

Ross asked Elizabeth what she thought about modern women who wore "short skirts, suntan backs" and exhibited other "extremes of youth." The eighty-seven-year-old, self-described "antique" waved her black fan against the summer heat, "lifting her tendril curls, which still are worn in the manner of the '80s." Sitting upright in her high-backed chair, she replied, "You know, I keep my sense of the ludicrous."[118] Then, displaying her pride in the life she had made for herself, Elizabeth changed the subject. "It's really rather suspicious of me to be living on Park Avenue, don't you think?" At any rate, she loved her apartment with its view of the East River, off in the distance, and its quiet in the midst of the city. She had lived in places earlier where the elevated trains had rattled the walls.

Asked about recent developments that gave her hope, Elizabeth grew thoughtful. While she loved theater and movies, she avoided dramas that dealt with war. In a brief reference to the Kellogg-Briand Pact, signed the summer before, she expressed hope "that the world is slowly moving towards the ideal of peace. I have been greatly interested in the signing of the peace treaty and the gathering together of the representatives of all the nations."[119]

In the aftermath of World War I, disillusionment with war and military heroes had been growing among some groups in American society. Many women's organizations, reformers, religious groups, and intellectuals were questioning the efficacy of war as an instrument of national policy. The peace advocates were minorities, to be sure, but they were articulate minorities. Although their voices elicited a powerful backlash during the conservative 1920s, they had some influence, as the Washington Naval Conferences of 1921, the flourishing peace societies on college campuses, and most recently, the Kellogg-Briand Pact disclosed.[120]

The 1920s was also a period in which iconoclastic biographies appeared. Lytton Strachey of England had led the way, and the process of "debunking" was cheered on by H. L. Mencken and other journalists and historians in the United States.[121] In that context the question of Custer's responsibility for the Little Bighorn should have been raised again. One factor, however, had prevented many from speaking out for decades. Many men refused to offend Custer's widow.

In 1898, one observer had perceived Elizabeth as "so beloved in the army of that day that by a sort of common consent . . . [Custer's] misdeeds were not given much publicity."[122] A few years later, in 1915, Katie Gibson's husband, Francis M. Gibson, had written George L. Yates, Annie Yates's son, concerning the Battle of the Little Bighorn. "You know, George, the survivors have been accused of everything in the calendar, but they have been silent, on account of their high regard and admiration for General Custer, and their fondness and affection for Mrs. Custer, so they have not even attempted an excuse for being alive."[123]

Some had planned to speak out after Elizabeth's death. As she lived on, however, those who might have made statements in her absence were less likely to say anything that might offend her in her old age. Luther Hare adhered to this chivalrous code. Originally Godfrey's subaltern, he had served with the Indian scouts at the Little Bighorn. In 1893, he told Colonel Hughes that the scouts had warned Custer he faced an extraordinary number of warriors ahead.[124]

Later, Colonel Graham discussed Hare with W. M. Camp. The railroad engineer had conducted extensive interviews with officers and scouts for his projected history of the Little Bighorn. Graham learned that Hare had been "unwilling, so long as Mrs. Custer was alive, to talk for publication about the battle of the Little Big Horn; and he did not want Camp to make use of anything he said." Nonetheless, Hare believed *"General Custer was to blame for the entire disaster*, but because of the great regard he held for Mrs. Custer, he would not permit himself to be quoted to that effect."[125]

Theodore Goldin, a veteran who had served as an enlisted man at the Little Bighorn, corresponded with Albert W. Johnson in the late 1920s and early 1930s on Custer's last campaign. Goldin described Mrs. Custer as "a loyal, loving wife" and remembered "every man's heart bled for her." That fact, "alone," he explained, was "responsible for the suppression of a lot of matters that may throw a clearer light on that campaign." Unfortunately, while "her loving loyalty to the General was respected," some soldiers thought "she was worshipping an image of clay."[126]

Two years later, Robert Bruce, a contributor to military history, wrote R. G. Carter, a retired army officer and author of *On the Border with MacKenzie or Winning West Texas from the Comanches*. Bruce wanted to reprint one of Carter's essays, but he hesitated to include two paragraphs contrasting the Indian-fighting abilities of Custer and Ranald Mackenzie. As long as Elizabeth Custer was alive "someone might send her copies (in fact she has at times asked me for them direct), and would think I might be printing something she might not like to see in print." Bruce had no "intentions of 'covering up' anything," but his "admiration for Mrs. Custer in holding tenaciously to the well-known memories of her husband, is so great that I would not want to do anything to disturb her at this time of her life."[127]

By 1931 Frederic Van de Water was researching his book on Custer. He wrote Godfrey, noting that he found Custer's character "strange," indeed almost unfathomable. That left him wondering "how much of true historical importance has been omitted by those who have written of him, out of consideration for his widow. This is only surmise, of course," Van de Water added, "but otherwise it is hard to explain the inconsistencies and reticences that two years of reading, off and on, leave still unexplained."[128]

That same year, I. D. O'Donnell, a friend of the late John Burkman, arrived at Elizabeth's apartment door. Margaret Flood refused to admit him until he instructed her to tell her mistress, "I am John Burkman's friend." When she ushered him upstairs he met "a little, white-haired old lady," who struggled to rise from her chair. "Save for the undaunted glow of youth in the bright eyes there was nothing," he noted, "about this frail, stooped, pain-twisted little figure to remind one of the gay, laughing Miss Libby" of other days. Now she was "bent almost double and leaned heavily on the stout cane that tap-tapped across the polished floor." Nonetheless, after their conversation, she told O'Donnell that, had Burkman been alive, he would have asked: "How old you be, Miss Libby." And she would have told him "that last month Miss Libby was eighty-nine years old."[129]

To the end, despite her infirmities and her confusions, Elizabeth retained her consuming interest in all projects regarding the general and the West. The semi-centennial celebration had renewed interest in creating her long-sought museum at the Little Bighorn Battlefield. By 1931, however, the only progress had been the government's purchase of land from the Crow Indians.[130] With the Great Depression deepening across the land, further improvements were unlikely.

Instead, Elizabeth discovered that the federal government planned to close old forts to save money. Tears welled in her eyes when she spoke to a reporter on the fifty-fifth anniversary of the Little Bighorn. "We ought not to allow every vestige of that period to die. After all, this country has very little history, considering how big it is, and we should preserve what we have." Whatever her "beautiful sentiments," the forts had to go.[131] Saving money had become more important than preserving the past.

With General Godfrey's death on April 1, 1932, Elizabeth lost her last contact with her husband's Seventh Cavalry. In her personal life, she relied more heavily than ever on Marguerite Merington. She also enjoyed occasional visits from George Yates and his wife, Suzanne, and May Custer Elmer and her husband, Charles. On Sundays, when weather permitted, Elizabeth hobbled with her cane the three blocks to the Cosmopolitan Club, where she dined with friends.[132]

That spring Ohio dedicated a statue to Custer in New Rumley. Completed under the direction of the Ohio State Archaeological and Historical Society, the $15,000 appropriation from the General Assembly represented a significant bequest, given the state's depression-wracked cities. The New Rumley monument showed Custer as he appeared during the Civil War, clad in a broad-rimmed hat, flowing tie, and sailor collar. His hand held a sword, but there was no money for a horse. Elizabeth, too frail to attend, sent the Elmers to represent her at the dedication ceremony.[133]

Increasingly Elizabeth thought about her coming death. In 1929, she had revised her will, withdrawing most of her bequest (except for a trust fund) to Vassar College and leaving the bulk of her estate to May Elmer and Agnes Bates Wellington.[134] Through her good friend, H. P. Silver, formerly the West Point chaplain, Elizabeth also learned the comforting news that wives could be buried beside their husbands at the academy.

On Sunday, April 2, 1933, Libbie suffered a heart attack. May Elmer and another niece, Lulu Custer, were with her when she died on Tuesday, just four days short of her ninety-first birthday.[135] Friends held a brief service in her apartment on Wednesday. The following Saturday, a small group of friends and members of the Custer family gathered to bury Elizabeth beside her husband. On her left hand was the gold band, worn thin after seventy years, during which she had never removed this symbol of her fidelity.[136] Her grave was simply marked by a flat stone with the words, "Elizabeth Bacon, wife of George Armstrong Custer" carved on it. Beside her husband's obelisk, it is easily overlooked. In death, as in life, the man whose reputation she worked so hard to protect overshadowed her.

Her ambition had been to see the day "when tradition and history will be so mingled that no one will be able to separate them." By devoting fifty-seven years of her life to shaping her husband's image, defending his honor, and keeping his name alive, she had gained her heart's desire. Her achievement was both stunning and tragic. A journalist had noted, fifty years after the Little Bighorn, that nothing had been "so precious as her memories."

And nothing had exacted so high a cost.

Epilogue

ELIZABETH Bacon Custer left an estate valued at $113,581. The Appomattox table went to the Smithsonian Institution, along with Armstrong's sword and scabbard. Her executors stored most of her mementoes at West Point, awaiting the building of a museum at the Little Bighorn Battlefield or their dispersal elsewhere.[1] Almost $5,000 in a trust fund became the basis for the George A. Custer and Elizabeth B. Custer Scholarship Fund for Daughters of Army Officers at Vassar College. Today it still provides scholarships.[2]

In 1934, one year after Elizabeth's death, Bobbs-Merrill published Frederic Van de Water's *Glory-Hunter: A Life of General Custer*.[3] In the first iconoclastic biography of the boy general, the author portrayed the major figure as a perpetual adolescent, addicted to fame and responsible for defeat at the Little Bighorn. Unable to reconcile his subject's contradictions, Van de Water incorporated them into his story. Custer, a man either loved or hated by his contemporaries, "seems in his brief time to have been many men." He was "paradox; the word made flesh."[4] Regarding Custer's family life and marriage, Van de Water softened his judgment. Elizabeth's books and her fifty-seven years of loyalty convinced him: "The love his wife bore him and he bore her may be George Armstrong Custer's most intrinsically sound fame."[5]

In the 1930s, E. A. Brininstool continued his investigation of the Little Bighorn. Increasingly he decried Custer and defended Reno, and, in 1935, published *Major Reno Vindicated*.[6] Four years later, Brininstool's friend, Fred Dustin of Saginaw, Michigan, produced *The Custer Tragedy*, which portrayed Custer as "one of the most over-rated men on the stage of American life."[7] Moreover, Dustin also believed that Reno had been maligned, in part because of the writings and influence of Elizabeth Custer. Her "personality, charm, and literary ability," he asserted, "have had a powerful influence in preventing writers from telling the cold truth."[8]

The work of revision, under way among historians, soon spread to novelists. In the next two decades, Harry Sinclair Drago's *Montana Road*, Ernest Haycox's *Bugles in the Afternoon*, Will Henry's *No Survivors*, and Clay Fisher's *Yellow Hair*, among others, interpreted Custer in light of Van de Water, rather than Whittaker.[9]

While Custer's historical reputation was undergoing reevaluation, the first steps towards building a battlefield museum were taken. With the depression easing, two Little Bighorn enthusiasts, Cols. Edward S. Luce and Eugene D. Hart, worked with Brininstool and Burton K. Wheeler, senator from Montana, to win passage of Senate Bill 28. When the House reduced the original request of $75,000 to $25,000, the amended bill passed Congress and became law on August 10, 1939.[10]

A year later, the Custer Battlefield National Cemetery was transferred to the National Park Service under the Department of the Interior. United States entry into World War II prevented further action until President Harry Truman signed legislation making the National Cemetery a National Monument in 1946. Finally in 1952, the museum was opened to the public, and Elizabeth Custer's mementoes had a permanent home. One item, however, had gone elsewhere. A year earlier, in a simple ceremony, Edward S. Luce, the National Monument's first superintendent, had given the white towel used as a Confederate flag of surrender to Appomattox Courthouse.[11]

Although historians, journalists, and novelists were revising their view of Custer, his image in motion pictures changed more slowly. Americans emerged from the Great Depression more critical of businessmen and corporations. Thus Raoul Walsh's Custer, who challenged corruption among railroads and the Indian Bureau, was an attractive and timely hero in the 1941 film *They Died with Their Boots On*. The movie, moreover, appeared in theaters as Americans entered World War II and sustained reverses at Guam, Wake Island, and in the Philippines. Understandably they felt a need to celebrate military heroism[12] Nonetheless, Errol Flynn's heroic Custer could not stem the scholarly reevaluation underway.

The reformulation of American Indian policy reinforced this process. In 1934, John Collier, Bureau of Indian Affairs commissioner, had won passage of the Indian Reorganization Act. By ending allotments and encouraging the re-establishment of tribal governments and courts, it reversed the Dawes

Act, which Elizabeth Custer had seen as beneficial to Indians. Although the constitutions adopted by tribes often originated in the Bureau of Indian Affairs, the consequences were, nonetheless, profound. Many American Indians experienced a renewed sense of pride as they rediscovered their heritage and culture and gained a greater degree of political autonomy. Simultaneously, this era also laid the basis for a pan-Indian movement. Finally, by 1946, the creation of an Indian Claims Commission gave American Indians another means by which they could seek some restitution for past injustices.[13]

By now writers and historians were already reevaluating the westward movement. Some no longer viewed it simply as the inexorable march of progress, civilization, and Christianity, as Elizabeth and most of her contemporaries had seen it. Historians such as Angie Debo and Mari Sandoz narrated the taking of land and resources from Indians by chicanery and force.[14]

Fiction and later films depicted these changing attitudes. Again, Frederic Van de Water had led the way. One year before the appearance of *Glory Hunter*, he had published the novel, *Thunder Shield*. In it, his major character, young Hiram Shaw, chose to die with the Cheyennes at the Little Bighorn rather than live with white men.[15] Thirty-one years later, Thomas Berger's *Little Big Man* again depicted the Cheyenne way of life as preferable to Anglo-European civilization.

In this 1964 work, Custer emerged as a complex and flawed figure who, nonetheless, proved heroic in his dying and won a grudging respect from Jack Crabb, the major character. By contrast, Arthur Penn's 1970 film of the same name presented a foolishly arrogant and evil Custer. Richard Mulligan played the Seventh's commander as "a cruel megalomaniac bent on sending the Indians the way of the buffalo, winking at the murder of their women, and ordering the slaughter of their ponies."[16]

If the handsome and charismatic Errol Flynn had been the prevailing version of Custer for many Americans in 1941, others today remain convinced that Mulligan's insane figure is an accurate depiction. Neither is correct. As Paul Hutton has noted, the only consistency in the way Americans have viewed Custer, from decade to decade, has been "a remarkable disregard for historical fact."[17]

Other concerns Elizabeth dealt with resurfaced after her death. Although she had never finished her book on the Civil War, in 1950 her friend Marguerite Merington published *The Custer Story: The Intimate Letters of*

General George A. Custer and His Wife Elizabeth. Scholars who have worked in the New York Public Library archives have discovered from the few surviving originals that Merington not only edited letters, but altered and expurgated many. In the process, she heightened the couple's attractiveness. But she only followed the example Elizabeth had set earlier when she had altered letters appearing in *Following the Guidon.* Since much information on the Custers exists only in these sources, "tradition and history" have become even more "mingled," and the task of the historian and biographer more arduous.

In this same decade, John Byers, a young cadet at West Point, became interested in the Custer statue he saw in old schoolbooks. Despite his diligent search for the surviving bust through warehouses and storage areas, he found no trace of "Garry Owen's wandering cavalryman."[18] It had disappeared entirely.

Had Elizabeth been alive in 1955, she would have applauded her home town's decision to move her bronze boy to the southwest corner of Monroe and Elm street in the heart of the city. She would, however, have bitterly resisted another step taken twelve years later. At the request of Marcus Reno's great-nephew Charles Reno and the American Legion, the Army Board for Corrections of Military Records reviewed the major's suspension from the service. Taking into account his personal tragedies, including the loss of his wife, the hardships of the frontier army, and events of the Little Bighorn, the board recommended his honorable discharge from the Army as of April 1, 1880. After Reno's remains were moved from an unmarked grave in Glenwood Cemetery in Washington, D.C., he was reburied, with full military honors, at the Custer Battlefield National Cemetery.[19]

Based on her 1927 essay, "General Custer and the Indian Chiefs," Elizabeth would have been sympathetic to a 1980 decision in which eight tribes of Missouri Sioux received an award of $105 million. The Supreme Court in *United States v. Sioux Nation* upheld an earlier Court of Claims decision. It also ruled that Congress had violated the Fifth Amendment rights of the Sioux in 1877 by taking the Black Hills from them without adequate compensation.[20]

It is unlikely that Elizabeth would have approved of another development. She herself referred to the battlefield where her husband died as the "battlefield of the Little Big Horn" when she willed her mementoes to its future museum.[21] Given her unflagging efforts to glorify Armstrong, however, it is hard to imagine that she would have supported the movement to change the name of the Custer Battlefield National Monument to the Little Bighorn Battlefield National Monument. Nonetheless, legislation introduced by Colorado Congressman Ben Nighthorse Campbell, whose ancestor had fought Custer, was signed into law in 1991.[22]

This last development reveals that almost sixty years after Elizabeth's death, much of her work has been eroded. Not only have historians uncovered a flawed and contradictory individual beneath her attractive boy general, but many Americans have now come to appreciate the negative connotations the old name—Custer Battlefield National Monument—has long held for Indians. In that light, as one historian has noted, it was time "to embrace the more neutral, and the more accepted usage in naming battlefields, of Little Bighorn Battlefield National Monument." Custer's name, however, remains on the Battlefield National Cemetery created in 1879.[23]

Now that Elizabeth Custer's glorification of her husband has been in large measure undone, how should her life and work be evaluated? Surely her loyalty to her spouse and her perseverance and diligence in memorializing him demand respect, whatever one thinks of the man she married. There is also much to admire in the manner in which she met adversity following her husband's death.

Then too, as a "professional widow," she built for herself a successful career. Her books sold well, and she was in demand on the lecture circuit. In her private life, moreover, she fashioned fast friendships that lasted a lifetime, and she satisfied her hunger for adventure and travel many times over. Starting off with indebtedness, she achieved prosperity for herself through hard work and shrewd investments, and she died on Park Avenue.

But while her life was interesting, rich, and rewarding, it was also based on the perpetuation of an idealized version of the past. If one values the ability of individuals to live honestly and confront the truth, then one finds little to celebrate in the Widow Custer's achievements.

We know enough about Elizabeth, however, to understand that she would not have evaluated herself in these terms. Like many nineteenth-century women, she never saw herself primarily as an individual. Instead, she viewed herself first and foremost as the member of a family. Her responsibility to that family—in this case her husband—took precedence over her responsibility to herself. In this way, the domestic ideology she had internalized from her earliest years gave her life meaning while it also shaped her responses to critical events.[24] As a young woman not yet twenty, she had dreamed of herself as a future wife, facing grave dangers and experiencing "many perils all of which I was willing to do for my spouse."[25] And although the dream had left her "terribly agitated," since she had killed someone in self defense, it had revealed her future. In light of what she valued most highly—her life as a wife and later widow—Elizabeth had been faithful to her ideals.

In the end, too, Elizabeth, a woman without parents, siblings, or children, had done her best to transform her dead husband into the ideal spouse and family man of the ideal family she never had. "Dear *Father*," she had written after the Battle of Cold Harbor, as she sent Armstrong her drawing of their imaginary children and a paternal Autie, "do you think you will look that way?"[26] Later she was proud that her husband, "as he should be known," became a figure who "helped to mold the soul of an entire generation."[27] Even an enemy understood and approved of such efforts. Capt. Frederick Benteen wrote in 1879, "Cadets for ages to come will bow in humility at the Custer shrine at West Point, and—if it makes better soldiers and men of them, why the necessity of knocking the paste eye out of their idol?"[28]

And yet, even in her own terms, Elizabeth paid a high price. In addition to putting her husband's reputation ahead of all other considerations, her life was full of loneliness. For it was the long years, spanning more than half a century of widowhood, that provided the best testimony to her depiction of Custer's character. Her contemporaries (and many since) believed that only a true hero could have motivated such loyalty. Her decision to live a "reflected life," moreover, exacted from her a cost that would not have been expected of her spouse had their deaths been reversed. There is no guarantee that a second marriage or even a close relationship with another man would have materialized for Elizabeth had she opened herself to that prospect. Nonetheless, by devoting her whole widowhood to memorializing Armstrong, she closed herself off from that source of human happiness.

Elizabeth revealed something of the cost on the eve of her greatest triumph, the unveiling of her bronze hero. In her recollections for her friends, she noted, "The hours that one sees people and keeps up the farce of perpetual happiness are few compared with the never ending hours when one is alone with the past, and all those who were nearest have 'gone to the country from which no traveller returns.'"[29]

Perhaps in the end it was worth it to her. The next day she pulled the yellow ribbons, and the flags fell away. Afterwards, she recorded, "A great shout rose from the thousands on the stand and packed about us far, far down the street. The light color of the metal takes the sun so readily, it glowed all over the burnished surface and was so splendid, so alive. . . . It seemed impossible for me to realize that my dream of so many years was a reality before me."[30]

Over time, the bronze statue has darkened and no longer catches and reflects as much of the sunlight. So, too, has the figure of George Armstrong Custer darkened, now that Elizabeth no longer stands guard to repair and polish his image. The dreamer has gone, and her dream is no longer our only reality. Nonetheless, Elizabeth Bacon Custer wrote her works so well and lived with such fidelity that, even today, there are those who still cherish and venerate Libbie's General Custer.

Abbreviations

AGO	Adjutant General's Office
BCWCC	Brice C. W. Custer Collection, a private collection
BLCU	Butler Library, Columbia University Library
BSS	*"Boots and Saddles"* Scrapbook, Custer Collection, Monroe County Historical Commission Archives
CAC	Carnegie Autograph Collection, New York Public Library
CC	Custer Collection, Monroe County Historical Commission Archives
CCP	Century Company Papers, New York Public Library
CM	Walter S. Camp Manuscript, Lilly Library, Indiana University, Bloomington, Indiana
CP	Walter S. Camp Papers, Harold B. Lee Library, Brigham Young University, Provo, Utah
CS	Marguerite Merington, *The Custer Story: The Life and Intimate Letters of General George A. Custer and His Wife Elizabeth*
EBCC	Elizabeth Bacon Custer Collection, Little Bighorn Battlefield National Monument
EBCJ	Elizabeth Bacon Custer's Journal, Custer Collection, Monroe County Historical Commission Archives
EBCM	Elizabeth B. Custer Manuscript Collection, Western Americana Collection, Beinecke Rare Book and Manuscript Library, Yale University
ECBJ	Elizabeth Clift Bacon Journal, 1852–1860, Elizabeth B. Custer Manuscript, Western Americana Collection, Beinecke Rare Book and Manuscript Library, Yale University
FCC	Lawrence A. Frost Collection of Custeriana, Monroe County Historical Commission Archives

GACC	George Armstrong Custer Collection, Monroe County Library System, Monroe, Michigan
GACM	George A. Custer Manuscript Collection, Western Americana Collection, Beinecke Rare Book and Manuscript Library, Yale University
GFP	Godfrey Family Papers, United States Army Military History Institute, Carlisle Barracks, Pennsylvania
GP	Grierson Papers, Edward Ayers Collection, Newberry Library, Chicago, Illinois
LBJ	Libbie Bacon's Journal, Brice C. W. Custer Collection
LC	Library of Congress
MCHCA	Monroe County Historical Commission Archives
MMP	Marguerite Merington Papers, New York Public Library, New York City
NA	National Archives
NS	Newspaper Scrapbook, Custer Collection, Monroe County Historical Commission Archives
NYPL	New York Public Library
PHSP	Philip H. Sheridan Papers, Library of Congress
PMF	Provost Marshal's File
RG	Record Group
TPS	*Tenting on the Plains* Scrapbook, Custer Collection, Monroe County Historical Commission Archives
VRP	Vinnie Ream (Hoxie) Papers, Library of Congress
WD	War Department
WTSP	William T. Sherman Papers, Library of Congress

Notes

1. *New York Times*, 5 April 1933.

2. *New York Herald Tribune*, 5 April 1933.

3. Frazier Hunt, "The Life of General Custer," "New York Life Radio Hour," Tuesday, 27 October 1931, Custer Collection, Monroe County Historical Commission Archives, Monroe, Michigan. Hereafter referred to as CC, MCHCA.

4. John B. Kennedy, "A Soldier's Widow," *Collier's*, 29 January 1927, 10.

5. Henry Nash Smith, *Virgin Land: The American West as Symbol and Myth*, v.

6. Brian Dippie, *Custer's Last Stand: The Anatomy of an American Myth*, 2.

7. Rhys Isaac, "The Enlightenment and the Problems of Systematizing the Plantation," speech delivered at the conference entitled "Re-creating the World of the Virginia Plantation, 1750–1820," Charlottesville, Virginia, 1 June 1990.

8. Dippie, *Custer's Last Stand*, 7–10; Richard Slotkin, *Fatal Environment*, 3–9.

9. Richard Slotkin's comments on this point, although applying to more recent works, hold true for the earlier debate. "' . . . & *Then* the Mare will Go!' An 1875 Black Hills Scheme by Custer, Holladay, and Buford," *Journal of the West* 15 (July 1976): 60.

10. See Marguerite Merington, *The Custer Story: The Life and Intimate Letters of General George A. Custer and His Wife Elizabeth*, 38 Hereafter referred to as CS.

11. Historians have identified this ideology as the "cult of true womanhood" or "separate spheres." See Barbara Welter, "The Cult of True Womanhood: 1820–1860, *American Quarterly* 18 (Summer 1966): 151–74. In recent years, many avoid the word "cult," and others find that "separate spheres" lacks precision. Metaphorically it can mean "an ideology *imposed on* women, a culture *created by* women, a set of boundaries *expected to be observed* by women." Linda Kerber, "Separate Spheres, Female Worlds, Woman's Place: The Rhetoric of Women's History" *Journal of American History*, 75 (June 1988): 17–18. Robert L. Griswold sees domestic ideology as a "cultural system" rather than a dogmatic set of principles women slavishly adhered to throughout their lifetimes. Robert L. Griswold, "Anglo Women and Domestic Ideology in the American West in the Nineteenth and Early Twentieth Centuries," in *Western Women: Their Land, Their Lives*, ed. Lilian Schlissel, Vicki L. Ruiz, and Janice Monk, 15. See also Julie Roy Jeffrey's commentary in *Western Women*, 39–41. Jeffrey, in her pi-

oneering work, *Frontier Women: The Trans-Mississippi West, 1840–1880*, xiv, 178, finds evidence that this ideology had permeated women of lower-class economic origins as well.

12. Griswold, "Anglo Women and Domestic Ideology in the American West in the Nineteenth and Early Twentieth Centuries," 15.

13. Libbie to Autie, 30 October 1864, Lawrence A. Frost, *General Custer's Libbie*, 121.

14. Quoted by Merington, CS 327.

15. I thank Glenda Riley for reminding me of the similarities between Elizabeth Custer and other "professional widows," notably Sarah Josepha Hale. Like Custer, Hale idealized her husband. See Ruth E. Finley, *The Lady of Godey's: Sarah Josepha Hale*, 36–37. See also Angela Marie Howard Zophy, "For the Improvement of My Sex: Sarah Josepha Hale's Editorship of *Godey's Lady's Book, 1837–1877*."

16. Cyrus T. Brady, *Britton of the Seventh: A Romance of Custer and the Great Northwest*, viii–ix.

17. Stephen Ambrose, noting Elizabeth Custer's abilities, states, "What a waste!" *Crazy Horse and Custer: The Parallel Lives of Two American Warriors*, 168–69.

18. Libbie to Autie, undated. Many of the Custer letters are undated. In those cases, I have put brackets around the most probable date, based on internal evidence. [March 1866], Brice C. W. Custer Collection. A private collection. Hereafter referred to as BCWCC. Libbie to Autie, July 1864, Merington, CS, 112.

19. W. T. Sherman to Mrs. Custer, 17 October 1882, BCWCC; Griswold notes that domestic ideals bound men as well. "Anglo Women and Domestic Ideology," 26–28.

20. See Kerber, "Separate Spheres," 38–39; Joan Kelly, "The Doubled Vision of

Feminist Theory: A Postscript to the 'Women and Power' Conference," *Feminist Studies* 5 (Spring 1979): 220–23; Michelle Zimbalist Rosaldo, "The Use and Abuse of Anthropology: Reflections on Feminism and Cross-cultural Understanding," *Signs* 5 (Spring 1980): 409, 416–17; Marilyn Strathern, *The Gender of the Gift: Problems with Women and Problems with Society in Melanesia* 32–34.

21. Stanley Weintraub, *Victoria: An Intimate Biography*, 308. Douglas McChristian notes "the Victorian obsession for memorializing the dead." "In Search of Custer Battlefield," *Montana: The Magazine of Western History* 42 (Winter 1992): 76.

22. Walter E. Houghton, *The Victorian Frame of Mind, 1830–1870*, 417–18. The second quote is from Edwin P. Hood, *The Uses of Biography: Romantic, Philosophic, and Didactic*, 195. Houghton cites J.B. Brown and Charles Kingsley as other Victorians who emphasized the value of inspirational biographies.

23. Hood, *The Uses of Biography*, 124, 195, 203–204; Houghton, *Victorian Frame of Mind*, 417–20.

CHAPTER I

1. Daniel Bacon to Dear Sister, 5 September 1862, Lawrence A. Frost Collection of Custeriana, MCHCA. Hereafter referred to as FCC, MCHCA. Joshua V. H. Clark, *Onondaga; or Reminiscences of Earlier and Later Times*, 2:134; Frost, *Custer's Libbie*, 14–15; Merington, CS, 14–15.

2. W. Elliot Brownlee, *Dynamics of Ascent: A History of the American Economy*, 196.

3. Certificate from the Onondaga County, New York, school inspectors, 12 March 1819, BCWCC; Merington, CS, 14–15.

4. Merington, CS, 14–15.

5. Monroe County Historical Society, "River Raisin Massacre and Battles of the War of 1812 in Historic Monroe," MCHCA; Talcott E. Wing, *History of Monroe County, Michigan*, 59.

6. Alec R. Gilpin, *Territory of Michigan, 1805–1837*, 135–36; Frost, *Custer's Libbie*, 14.

7. Daniel Bacon to Parents, November 1822, Merington, CS, 15.

8. Merington, CS, 16.

9. Ibid., 18; Frost, *Custer's Libbie*, 15–17; John T. Blois, *Gazetteer of the State of Michigan, in Three Parts*, 407.

10. Paul R. Peck, *Landsmen of Monroe County. An Atlas and Plat of First Landowners of Monroe County, Michigan*, 63, 203.

11. Frost, *Custer's Libbie*, 15–16; Merington, CS, 18. See also Steven Mintz and Susan Kellogg, *Domestic Revolutions: A Social History of American Family Life*, 57–58. For cultural characteristics of Michigan's early Whigs, see Ronald P. Formisano, *The Birth of Mass Political Parties, Michigan, 1827–1861*, 44–45.

12. Merington, CS, 18–19.

13. Ibid., 20–21.

14. Such legislation flourished in Jacksonian America. See Bray Hammond, *Banks and Politics in America: From the Revolution to the Civil War*, 600–604.

15. John Bulkley, *History of Monroe County, Michigan* 1:346–49. Merchants and Mechanics Bank Folder, Box 4, Monroe County Industries Collection, MCHCA. See also Alpheus Felch, *Report of the Pioneer Society of the State of Michigan*, 1:III–25; Frost, *Custer's Libbie*, 16.

16. Merington, CS, 21.

17. Ibid., 21–22.

18. Copy of notations from family bible of Judge Daniel S. Bacon, made by Carrie L. Boyd of Monroe, Michigan, May 1945, CC, MCHCA; Bulkley, *Monroe County*, 1:349. Judgments totalled over $9,000. The Circuit Court for the County of

Monroe, "Judgment of the Same Received against Levi J. Humphrey and Daniel S. Bacon, on behalf of Wedworth Wadsworth, Jr.," 29 November 1841, FCC, MCHCA. For changing views on bankruptcy see Thomas C. Cochran, *Frontiers of Change: Early Industrialization in America*, 25.

19. Beth Charles, "Bacon House," 1–2; Boyd, Bacon family bible, CC, MCHCA.

20. F. Clever Bald, *Michigan in Four Centuries*, 165; John T. Blois, *Gazetteer of the State of Michigan, in Three Parts*, 328.

21. Boyd, Bacon family bible, CC, MCHCA.

22. Daniel Bacon to Leonard Bacon, undated, Daniel Bacon to Sophia Bacon, undated, Merington, CS, 22.

23. Boyd, Bacon family bible, CC, MCHCA; Merington, CS, 22.

24. Eleanor Sophia Bacon's obituary, *Monroe Commercial*, 17 August 1854. The Sunday school movement represented Northern evangelism. See Anne M. Boylan, *Sunday School: The Formation of an American Institution, 1790–1880*, 166–70.

25. Merington, CS, 23. Maria Adams Dutriueille, formerly a maid at Fort Abraham Lincoln, noted Libbie's "wonderful disposition." See "Mrs. Maria [Adams] Dutriueille," *Great Falls Yesterday: Comprising a Collection of Biographies and Reminiscences of Early Settlers*, 377.

26. Philip Greven, *The Protestant Temperament: Patterns of Child-Rearing, Religious Experience, and the Self in Early America*, 35.

27. Merington, CS, 23; Mary Ryan discusses these new methods of child-rearing in *Cradle of the Middle Class: The Family in Oneida County, New York, 1790–1865*, 160–61.

28. Elizabeth Clift Bacon Journal, 8 April 1852 to 31 December 1860. Gift of Marguerite Merington to Western Americana Collection, Beinecke Rare Book and

Manuscript Library, Yale University, New Haven, Connecticut. Hereafter referred to as ECBJ.

29. ECBJ, 9 April 1852, 10 April 1852, 11 April 1852, 12 April 1852, 18 April 1852.

30. Ibid., 16 April 1852, 19 April 1852. See also Frost, *Custer's Libbie*, 22.

31. ECBJ, 5 August 1852, 20 August 1852.

32. Ibid., 8 September 1852.

33. Ibid., 3 September 1852, 10 September 1852; Elizabeth B. Custer, *Tenting on the Plains; or, General Custer in Kansas and Texas*, 66.

34. ECBJ, 4 September 1852, 5 September 1852, 11 September 1852.

35. Walter F. Peterson, "Christmas on the Plains," *American West* 1 (Fall 1964): 53–57.

36. ECBJ, 14 March 1853, 24 April 1853, 19 September 1852.

37. Ibid., 5 January 1854, 25 January 1854, 27 January 1854, 22 February 1854.

38. Ibid., 14 March 1854. Libbie noted that Bacon was reading the *Narrative of the Proceedings of the Monthly Meeting of New-York . . . in the case of Isaac T. Hopper*. For information on the impact of *Mothers' Magazine*, see Richard A. Meckel, "Educating a Ministry of Mothers: Evangelical Maternal Associations, 1815–1860," *Journal of the Early Republic* 2 (Winter 1982): 403–23

39. ECBJ, 27 August 1854.

40. Merington, CS, 38.

41. ECBJ, 12 November 1854.

42. *Thirteenth Annual Catalogue of the Officers and Pupils of the Young Ladies' Seminary and Collegiate Institute at Monroe City, Michigan*, 20–21, Boyd Seminary Collection, MCHCA.

43. Ibid.

44. Ibid.

45. For insights into early female academies and seminaries, see Katherine Kish Sklar, *Catharine Beecher: A Study in Amer-*

ican Domesticity, 90–101. Background on Sarah Boyd is presented in Wing, *Monroe County, Michigan*, 501.

46. ECBJ, 12 November 1854.

47. Merington, CS, 38.

48. ECBJ, 24 April 1855, 25 April 1855, 26 April 1855, 27 September 1855.

49. EB Custer, *Tenting*, 342, 620; Libbie to Parents, 28 March 1864, Merington, CS, 89.

50. ECBJ, 25 December 1855.

51. Ibid., 1 January 1856.

52. Ibid. Grace Greenwood (Sara Lippincott) published *History of My Pets* and *Merrie England* for children in 1851. See Barbara Welter, "Sara Jane Clarke Lippincott," *Notable American Women 1607–1950* 2:408, ed. Edward T. James, Janet James, Paul Boyer.

53. Both were published in Auburn, New York, by Miller, Orton & Mulligan. Sara Parton also published *Little Ferns for Fanny's Little Friends* the same year, but Libbie made it clear that she had read two volumes of *Fern Leaves*.

54. For information on Fanny Fern, see Elizabeth B. Schlesinger, "Sara Willis Parton," *Notable American Women* 3:24–25. I am indebted to Ann Wood's excellent analysis of Fanny Fern's writings. "The 'Scribbling Women' and Fanny Fern: Why Women Wrote," *American Quarterly* 23 (1971): 3, 18–19. For examples of contrasting messages, see Fern, *Fern Leaves from Fanny's Portfolio*, 30–31, 146, 324, 326, 331, 362–63.

55. Fanny Fern, *Rose Clark*, 283.

56. Fanny Fern, *Fresh Leaves*, 78–79.

57. Lippincott was fearless in her personal life and took a strong and costly stand against slavery. Welter, "Sara Lippincott," *Notable American Women* 2:408–9.

58. Grace Greenwood (Sara Lippincott), *Greenwood Leaves: A Collection of Sketches and Letters*. In this work, see

"Sophie Norton's Way of Heading a Conspiracy," 1–10, and "The Society of Four," 23–27.

59. Wood, "'Scribbling Women'" 6–11. Mary P. Ryan's, *The Empire of the Mother: American Writing about Domesticity, 1830–1860*, 97–114, discusses the strains increasingly evident in this literature.

60. Greenwood, *Greenwood Leaves*, 310–11.

61. Ibid., 311.

62. ECBJ, 2 January 1856, 3 January 1856, 4 January 1856, 9 January 1858.

63. Ibid., 5 January 1856.

64. See John L. Hammond, *The Politics of Benevolence: Revival Religion and American Voting Behavior*, 41–42; Greven, *Protestant Temperament*, 64–65.

65. ECBJ, 9 January 1858.

66. Ibid., 13 January 1858, 14 January 1858, 15 January 1858.

67. Ibid., 10 January 1858, 12 January 1858.

68. Ibid., 15 January 1858.

69. Years later, while editing the letters between Elizabeth and George A. Custer, Marguerite Merington saw the Brownes as the source of Libbie's intense adolescent guilt. Either Merington misunderstood Libbie, or Libbie herself had forgotten the nature of her experience at Auburn. Merington, CS, 39. For information on the Auburn Young Ladies Institute, see Henry Hall, *History of Auburn*, 289–91. Julie Roy Jeffrey sees Auburn, the home of the Auburn Theological Seminary, as a center of revivalism in the 1820s. *Converting the West: A Biography of Narcissa Whitman*, 25. Undoubtedly revivalism was still strong in the city's life in the 1850s.

70. Libbie to Daniel Bacon, 8 January 1859, Frost, *Custer's Libbie*, 31.

71. For information on Finney, see Keith J. Hardman, *Charles Grandison Finney, 1792–1875*. On New York City missions, see Carroll Smith-Rosenberg, *Religion and the Rise of the American City Mission Movement, 1812-1870*, 64–69.

72. Obituary in *Tecumseh [Michigan] News*, 19 August 1886.

73. Frost, *Custer's Libbie*, 32.

74. ECBJ, 18 May 1859.

75. Ibid.

CHAPTER 2

1. ECBJ, 2 October 1860; Daniel Bacon to Sister, 1861, Merington, CS, 41–42.

2. Wing, *Monroe County*, 314; Merington, CS, 49; Libbie (Elizabeth Clift) Bacon's journal, 1861–1863, BCWCC, 15 February 1862, 2 April 1863. Hereafter cited as LBJ.

3. LBJ, 1 January 1861, 3 January 1861, 18 January 1861.

4. Ibid., 4 January 1861.

5. Ibid., 19 January 1861, [no day] February 1861, 17 June 1861.

6. Ibid., Sunday [early], February 1861; James McPherson, *Battle Cry of Freedom: The Civil War Era*, 246–50.

7. LBJ, 8 April 1861; McPherson, *Battle Cry*, 272–74; Wing, *Monroe County*, 527–29.

8. LBJ, 17 June 1861, 18 June 1861, 23 June 1861, [no day] February 1861.

9. Bruce Catton, *The Civil War*, 39–49.

10. Daniel Bacon to Dear Sister, 5 September 1861, FCC, MCHCA.

11. Merington, CS, 48–49.

12. LBJ, 1 January 1862.

13. Ibid., 10 January 1862.

14. Ibid.

15. Ibid., [26] January 1862, 31 January 1862, 24 February 1862.

16. Wing, *Monroe County*, 564–569.

17. McPherson, *Battle Cry*, 396–400; LBJ, 24 February 1862.

18. LBJ, 28 February 1862.

19. Ibid., 30 March 1862, 13 April 1862.

20. *Detroit Free Press*, 20 June 1862; LBJ, 25 June 1862; Rebecca Richmond to Parents June 1862, Merington, CS, 43–44; Libbie to Eliza Sabin, June 1862, Merington, CS, 44.

21. LBJ, 25 June 1862; *Detroit Free Press*, 20 June 1862.

22. LBJ, 19 October 1862, 20 October 1862; Merington, CS, 44.

23. LBJ, 19 October 1862, 20 October 1862, 18 June 1861.

24. Merington, CS, 46–47. Although Libbie maintained in *"Boots and Saddles"; or, Life in Dakota with General Custer*, 86, that her husband was "nearly six feet in height," West Point records show he was five feet eight and one-eighth inches tall at seventeen. See Norman Maclean, "Custer's Last Fight as Ritual Drama," *Chicago Westerners Brand Book*, 15 (October 1958): 58. See also Kent Steckmesser, *The Western Hero in History and Legend*, 202.

25. Robert Utley, *Cavalier in Buckskin: George Armstrong Custer and the Western Military Frontier*, 13–14; Charles B. Wallace, *Custer's Ohio Boyhood*, 12–26.

26. Utley, *Cavalier*, 15.

27. Wallace, *Custer's Ohio Boyhood*, 23–24; Jay Monaghan, *Custer: The Life of General George Armstrong Custer*, 10–11. See also Erving E. Beauregard, "The General and the Politician," *Blue and Gray Magazine* 6 (October 1988): 33–35.

28. Utley, *Cavalier*, 15.

29. Ibid., 17–18; Stephen Z. Starr, *The Union Cavalry in the Civil War. Volume 1: From Fort Sumter to Gettysburg, 1861–1863*, 59–61.

30. Utley, *Cavalier*, 18; George Armstrong Custer, chapter four of war memoirs, *Galaxy Magazine*, June 1876, reprinted in *Custer in the Civil War: His Unfinished Memoirs*, comp. and ed. John M. Carroll, 114–17.

31. Monaghan, *Custer*, 61.

32. D. V. N., "The Late General Custer," *Army and Navy Journal*, 22 July 1876.

33. Stephen W. Sears, *Landscape Turned Red: The Battle of Antietam*, 336–45; Richard Slotkin, *Fatal Environment: The Myth of the Frontier in the Age of Industrialization, 1800–1890*, 378, 382.

34. Merington, CS, 47; LBJ, 17 December 1862.

35. LBJ, 17 December 1862.

36. Ibid.

37. Ibid., 29 December 1862.

38. Ibid., 1 January 1863.

39. Merington, CS, 49; LBJ, [15] January 1863.

40. Monaghan, *Custer*, 112; LBJ, Sunday, Monday [no dates], February 1863.

41. Libbie to Daniel Bacon, [February 1863], quoted in Merington, CS, 50–51.

42. LBJ, Sunday, Monday [no dates], February 1863.

43. Ibid.

44. Ibid., 5 April 1863.

45. Ibid., 7 April 1863.

46. Ibid.

47. Ibid., 18 April 1863; Slotkin, *Fatal Environment*, 382.

48. LBJ, 26 April 1863.

49. Ibid., 18 April 1863, 26 April 1863.

50. Ibid., 26 April 1863.

51. Utley, *Cavalier*, 20–21.

52. Starr, *Union Cavalry* 1:337–38.

53. R. Ernest Dupuy and Trevor N. Dupuy, *Military Heritage of America*, 265.

54. R. Ernest Dupuy and Trevor N. Dupuy, *The Compact History of the Civil War*, 211; Don E. Alberts, *Brandy Station to Manila Bay: A Biography of General Wesley Merritt*, 46–47.

55. LBJ, 15 June 1863.

56. Ibid., 15 June 1863, 21 April 1863.

57. Ibid., 15 June 1863; Elizabeth B. Custer's "Notes on Stevensburg," 1864, EBCC, Roll 4, Frames 4008–4009. Elizabeth left behind rough draft material worked on at

various times. I have used titles of the Little Bighorn Battlefield National Monument's microfilm catalogue and frame numbers.

58. LBJ, 22 June 1863.

59. Libbie to Autie, July 1873, Merington, CS, 251, Maggie Custer Calhoun to Libbie, 3 September 1877, FCC, MCHCA.

60. Utley, *Cavalier*, 21–22.

61. Ibid. Unfortunately, E.J. Farnsworth died shortly after at the Battle of Gettysburg.

62. Ibid., 22–24; *Battles and Leaders of the Civil War* 3:397–403.

63. Utley, *Cavalier*, 22–23; James McPherson, *Ordeal by Fire: The Civil War and Reconstruction*, 330.

64. Stephen E. Ambrose, "Custer's Civil War," *TimeLine* 7 (August, September 1990): 28.

65. LBJ, 6 July 1863.

66. Ibid.

67. Ibid.

68. Ibid.

69. Ibid.

70. George A. Custer to Annette Humphrey, 19 July 1863, Merington, CS, 62.

71. George A. Custer to Lydia Ann Reed, 27 May 1863, 26 July 1863, EBCC, Roll 1.

72. McPherson discusses the pros and cons of Mead's actions. McPherson, *Battle Cry*, 664–67.

73. Utley, *Cavalier*, 24–25.

74. Annette Humphrey to George A. Custer, 24 August 1863, Frost, *Custer's Libbie*, 69.

75. LBJ, 3 October 1863.

76. Ibid., 18 October 1863, 31 October 1863.

77. Ibid., 25 October, 1863.

78. Ibid., 18 October 1863.

79. Merington, CS, 64.

80. Daniel Bacon to Libbie Bacon Custer, 11 April 1865, Merington, CS, 163.

81. See Charles K. Hofling on this point. *Custer and the Little Big Horn: A Psychobiographical Inquiry*, 76.

CHAPTER 3

1. Daniel Bacon to George A. Custer, 22 October 1863, FCC, MCHCA.

2. George A. Custer to Judge Bacon, October 1863, Merington, CS, 67.

3. Libbie to Autie, [November] 1863, Merington, CS, 73.

4. Jacob Greene to George A. Custer, 19 October 1863, Frost, *Custer's Libbie*, 78; LBJ, 19 October 1863.

5. LBJ, 15 November 1863.

6. Ibid.

7. Libbie to Autie, [November] 1863, January 1864, Merington, CS, 74, 80. Monaghan sees Libbie as "coy" in *Custer*, 1/3. Nineteenth-century women, aware of their loss of legal identities and property rights and knowledgeable about the dangers of childbearing, often approached marriage with fear. Motz, *True Sisterhood*, 17–18.

8. Weddings had been simple earlier. Now they were becoming complicated. Ellen Rothman, *Hands and Hearts: A History of Courtship in America*, 170–72. Libbie to Autie, [November] 1863, Merington, CS, 73–74.

9. Autie to Libbie, 22 November 1863, 17 December 1863, FCC, MCHCA.

10. Libbie to Autie, January 1864, Merington, CS, 79.

11. Libbie to Autie, January, 1864, Merington, CS, 80.

12. Libbie to Autie, Winter, 1863, Merington, CS, 75.

13. Daniel Bacon to Autie, 12 December 1863, FCC, MCHCA.

14. Ibid.

15. Libbie to Autie, [November] 1863, Merington, CS, 73–74.

16. Libbie to Autie, [26] December 1863, 1 January 1864, Merington, CS, 76–77.

17. For a discussion on the role of wives in uplifting their husbands in the nineteenth century, see Carl Degler, *At Odds: Women and the Family in America: From the Revolution to the Present*, 30–32; Libbie to Autie, 1 January 1864, Merington, CS, 78.

18. Libbie to Autie, [26] December 1863, Merington, CS, 76–77.

19. Autie to Libbie, 22 November 1863, BCWCC.

20. Libbie to Autie, [26] December 1863, Ibid. 76–77; Wing, *Monroe County*, 314.

21. Libbie to Autie, January 1864, Merington, CS, 79; Frost, *Custer's Libbie*, 92.

22. Autie to Daniel Bacon, 19 January 1864, Marguerite Merington Papers, Rare Books and Manuscript Division, New York Public Library, Astor, Lenox, and Tilden Foundations, New York City. Hereafter referred to as MMP. See Merington, CS, 80, for an altered version. McPherson discusses the term "copperhead" in *Battle Cry*, 493–94. Gregory J. W. Urwin discusses Austin Blair's objections to Custer in *Custer Victorious: The Civil War Battles of General George Armstrong Custer*, 51. See also Slotkin, *Fatal Environment*, 381–82; James Harrison Wilson, *Under Two Flags* 1:125; Frederick Whittaker, *The Complete Life of Gen. George A. Custer*, 132–33; G. A. Custer to Honorable J. M. Howard, 4 January 1864, 19 January 1864, reprinted in Hamilton G. Howard, *Civil War Echoes: Character Sketches and State Secrets*, 304–13, especially 312–13.

23. Frost, *Custer's Libbie*, 151.

24. Libbie to Autie, 23 December 1863, January 1864; Rebecca Richmond to Mary Richmond, February 1864, Merington, CS, 76, 79–80, 81–82.

25. Rebecca Richmond to Mary Richmond, February 1864, Merington, CS, 81–

82; Rothman, *Hands and Hearts: A History of Courtship in America*, 171.

26. Daniel Bacon to Charity, 11 February 1864, Merington, CS, 81; Rothman, *Hands and Hearts*, 173.

27. Daniel Bacon to Rebecca and Mary Richmond February, 1864, Merington, CS, 85.

28. Monaghan, *Custer*, 179.

29. Rothman, *Hearts and Hands*, 175.

30. Rebecca Richmond to Mary Richmond, February 1864; Daniel Bacon to Rebecca and Mary Richmond, February 1864, Merington, CS, 81–85.

31. Libbie to Daniel Bacon, February 1864, Merington, CS, 84.

32. Merington, CS, 84–85.

33. Libbie wrote years later: "Though I lived through a blaze of sunshine for 12 years there were many silent seasons which I learned to." Then her notes became unintelligible. E. B. Custer, "Writings of West Point," EBCC, Roll 5, Frame 5128. See similar comments on Frame 5139.

34. Ibid, Frame 5128.

35. Zachariah Chandler, quoted by Frost, *Custer's Libbie*, 94.

36. E. B. Custer, *Tenting*, 12.

37. E. B. Custer, "Stevensburg," EBCC, Roll 5, Frame 4460; Frost, *Custer's Libbie*, 95.

38. Ibid. Eliza's age is estimated. Libbie wrote in *Tenting* 39, that Eliza in 1886 was not quite fifty. Thus I estimate she was born in 1837.

39. E. B. Custer, *Tenting*, 40–42.

40. E. B. Custer, "Stevensburg," EBCC, Roll 5, Frame 4326. Elizabeth was not totally ignorant of housework since the Boyd Seminary had trained young women in some domestic chores.

41. E. B. Custer, *"Boots and Saddles,"* 102–4.

42. E. B. Custer, rough draft notes, Frost, *Custer's Libbie*, 96.

43. E. B. Custer, "Manuscript with some Corrections," EBCC, Roll 5, Frame 4174; Libbie to Parents, 20 March 1864, MMP.

44. Libbie to Parents, spring 1864, Merington, CS, 86–87.

45. *Battles and Leaders* 4:93–94; Dupuy and Dupuy, *Compact History*, 279–80.

46. E. B. Custer, "Stevensburg," EBCC, Roll 5, Frames 4456–57.

47. *Battles and Leaders* 4:94.

48. Alfred Pleasonton to Elizabeth B. Custer, Frost, *Custer's Libbie*, 100.

49. See Autie to Libbie, 16 April 1864, 20 April 1864, MMP. The first appears in Merington, CS, 89 in expurgated form.

50. Frost, *Custer's Libbie*, 102.

51. E. B. Custer, "Stevensburg," EBCC, Roll 5, Frame 4460.

52. Anna Jones, "Statement," Provost Marshal's File, War Department, Record Group 107, National Archives, Washington, D. C. Hereafter referred to as PMF, WD, RG 107, NA.

53. "Statement of George Armstrong Custer," PMF, WD, RG 107, NA. Eventually through the intercession of Lincoln and Congressman Fernando Wood, Annie Jones was released in July from the Boston House of Corrections. Honorable Fernando Wood to Honorable E. A. Stanton, 8 July 1864, PMF, WD, RG 107, NA.

54. Libbie to Parents, 20 March 1864, MMP.

55. William S. McFeely, *Grant: A Biography*, 151–52; Libbie to Parents, 28 March 1864, Merington, CS, 87–88.

56. Libbie to Parents, 28 March 1864, Merington, CS, 87–88. Many observers found Grant quiet. McFeely, *Grant*, 154.

57. *Harper's Weekly*, 19 March 1864, 26 March 1864, cited by Frost, *Custer's Libbie*, 103.

58. Libbie to Parents, 28 March 1864, Merington, CS, 87–89.

59. Libbie to Parents, 3 April 1864, MMP.

60. Paul Andrew Hutton, *Phil Sheridan and His Army*, 14; Monaghan, *Custer*, 187–88.

61. Autie to Daniel Bacon, 23 April 1864, EBCC, Roll 1. Gregg commanded the Second Cavalry Division.

62. Libbie to Parents, April 1864, April 1864, Merington, CS, 87–89, 90–91.

63. Autie to Libbie, 23 April 1864, Merington, CS, 92–94; Libbie to Autie, July 1864, Merington, CS, 112–13.

64. Monaghan, *Custer*, 8; Frost, *Custer's Libbie*, 299; Slotkin, *Fatal Environment*, 376.

65. For acute observations on Custer's image-making abilities, see Brian W. Dippie, "George Armstrong Custer," *Soldiers West*, 101.

66. Libbie to Parents, April 1864, Merington, CS 90–92.

67. Autie to Libbie, 23 April 1864, Merington, CS, 92–93.

68. Rep. F. W. Kellogg to George A. Custer, 17 April 1864, EBCC, Roll 2.

69. Autie to Libbie, 23 April 1864, Merington, CS, 92.

70. Libbie to Autie, 6 September 1864, Merington, CS, 115–16.

71. Autie to Libbie, 23 April 1864, Merington, CS, 92. Col. Benjamin Grierson voiced similar sentiments to his wife, Alice, during the Civil War. See William H. Leckie and Shirley A. Leckie, *Unlikely Warriors: General Benjamin H. Grierson and His Family*, 28–29. See also William W. Hassler, *The General to His Lady: The Civil War Letters of William Dorsey Pender to Fanny Pender*, 57–58.

72. Autie to Libbie, 1 May 1864, Merington CS, 95. Welter notes that Americans of that era considered piety "the core of woman's virtue." "The Cult of True Womanhood," 152.

73. Autie to Libbie, 1 May 1864, Merington, CS, 95.

74. Libbie to Parents, 1 May 1864, Merington, CS, 94.

75. McPherson, *Ordeal by Fire*, 410–24.

76. Autie to Libbie, 4 May 1864, Merington, CS, 95.

77. McPherson, *Battle Cry*, 724–28.

78. Ibid., 728–38.

79. Hutton, *Phil Sheridan*, 14; Stephen Z. Starr, *The Union Cavalry in the Civil War*, vol 2, *The War in the East from Gettysburg to Appomattox, 1863-1865*, 103–7.

80. Philip H. Sheridan and Michael V. Sheridan, *Personal Memoirs of Philip Henry Sheridan, General, United States Army* 1:378–79; Emory M. Thomas, *Bold Dragoon: The Life of J. E. B. Stuart*, 292–93.

81. Autie to Libbie, 14 May 1864, Merington, CS, 97.

82. Autie to Libbie, 16 May 1864, Merington, CS, 97–98.

83. Autie to Libbie, 17 May 1864, MMP.

84. Autie to Libbie, 21 June 1864, Merington, CS, 103–5; McPherson, *Battle Cry*, 739; Urwin, *Custer Victorious*, 158–64. Ambrose notes that Custer's brigade suffered losses of 45 percent in the May 1864 Campaign of the Wilderness. Out of 1,700 men in his brigade, 98 were killed, 330 were wounded, and 348 were missing in action. See Ambrose, "Custer's Civil War," 29.

85. McPherson, *Battle Cry*, 739.

86. Autie to Libbie, 21 June 1864, Merington, CS, 103–105.

87. Libbie to Autie, June 1864, Merington, CS, 105–6.

88. Daniel Bacon to Libbie, June 1864, Merington, CS, 103.

89. Libbie to Autie, 10 June 1864, Merington, CS, 102. Armstrong's treatment for venereal disease at West Point may have affected his ability to father children. See Brian Pohanka, "In Hospital at West Point: Medical Records of Cadets Who Later Served with the Seventh Cavalry," *Newsletter, Little Big Horn Associates* 23 (July 1989): 5. Pohanka notes the need for more research.

90. Libbie to Autie, June 1864, Merington, CS, 100–101.

91. Isaac P. Christiancy served intermittently in the 1850s and 1870s as an associate justice on the Michigan Supreme Court and as United States senator from 1875 to 1879. Wing, *Monroe County*, 247, and Formisano, *Birth of Mass Political Parties*, 214, 253.

92. Libbie to Autie, early June 1864, Merington, CS, 100–101.

93. Libbie to Autie, early June 1864, Merington, CS, 101.

94. Autie to Libbie, June 1864, Merington, CS, 101–102.

95. Libbie to Autie, early June, 1864, Merington, CS, 101.

96. Ibid.

97. Autie to Libbie, 21 June 1864, Merington, CS, 103–105.

98. Libbie to Parents, June 1864, Merington, CS, 108–109; Margaret Leech, *Reveille in Washington, 1860-1865*, 326.

99. Leech, *Reveille in Washington*, 326–27; Libbie to Aunt Eliza, 3 July 1864, EBCC, Roll 1.

100. E. B. Custer, "Notes on Stevensburg," EBCC, Roll 4, Frames 3960–62.

101. Libbie to Autie, July 1864, Merington, CS, 112–13.

102. Libbie to Laura Noble, 18 August 1864, Merington, CS, 113–14.

103. McPherson, *Battle Cry*, 742–43.

104. Starr, *Union Cavalry* 2:234–35; *Battles and Leaders* 4:492–99; Dupuy and Dupuy, *Compact History of the Civil War*, 345–46; McPherson, *Ordeal by Fire*, 428–29. Wallace is remembered for the novel *Ben Hur* rather than his ability as a soldier.

CHAPTER 4

1. Libbie to Laura Noble, 18 August 1864, Merington, CS, 113–14.

2. *Battles and Leaders* 4:498–99; McPherson, *Battle Cry*, 756–57.

3. Libbie to Laura Noble, 18 August 1864, Merington, CS, 114; Frost, *Custer's Libbie*, 112.

4. Libbie to Autie, 6 September 1864, Merington, CS, 116–17.

5. Throughout the book, a word followed by a question mark and enclosed in brackets represents the author's best attempt at deciphering a word that is illegible in the original text.

6. E. B. Custer, "Civil War," EBCC, Roll 5, Frames 5007–8. Few women held clerical positions before the war. Mary Massey, *Bonnet Brigades*, 9. Cindy S. Aron covers the entry of women into government clerking. "'To Barter Their Souls for Gold': Female Clerks in Federal Government Offices, 1862–1890," *Journal of American History* 67 (March 1981): 835–53.

7. Elizabeth B. Custer, "Libbie's Personal Recollections," Lawrence Frost, *The Boy General in Bronze: Michigan's Hero on Horseback*, 129; McPherson, *Battle Cry*, 760.

8. E. B. Custer, "Stevensburg," EBCC, Roll 5, Frame 4935.

9. McPherson, *Battle Cry*, 756, 758; Catton, *Civil War*, 213–14; E. B. Custer, "Civil War," EBCC, Roll 5, Frames 4130–31.

10. McPherson, *Battle Cry*, 757–58, 755–56.

11. Ibid., 758–60, 742.

12. Ibid. 778.

13. Ibid., 758, 777; *Battles and Leaders* 4:500–1; Alberts, *Brandy Station*, 98–99; Sheridan, *Personal Memoirs* 1:471–72, 484–85.

14. Autie to Libbie, mid-August 1864, Merington, CS 114; Frost, *Custer's Libbie*,

114. See also Gerald Linderman, *Embattled Courage: The Experience of Combat in the American Civil War*, 9.

15. Autie to Libbie, 21 August 1864, Merington, CS, 115.

16. McPherson, *Battle Cry*, 771.

17. Libbie to Parents, September 1864, Merington, CS, 118.

18. McPherson, *Battle Cry*, 771; Catton, *Civil War*, 217; Libbie to Autie, Fall, 1864, Merington, CS, 118.

19. McPherson, *Battle Cry*, 774–75; Libbie to Parents, September 1864, Merington, CS, 118.

20. Sheridan, *Personal Memoirs* 1:467–77; Frost, *Custer's Libbie*, 112.

21. Autie to Daniel Bacon, 2 September 1864, Autie to Lydia Ann Reed, 17 September 1864, EBCC, Roll 1.

22. Frost, *Custer's Libbie*, 113; *Webster's New Twentieth Century Dictionary of the English Language*, 1347.

23. Autie to Libbie, 11 September 1864, Merington, CS, 119; McPherson, *Ordeal by Fire*, 190.

24. Starr, *Union Cavalry* 2:269–77; *Battles and Leaders* 4:506–9, 523–24.

25. Monaghan, *Custer*, 207–10; Alberts, *Brandy Station*, 114–15.

26. *New York Times*, 27 October 1864.

27. Newspaper report originally appearing in *New York Tribune* and reprinted in *Monroe Monitor*, 31 August 1864, quoted by Frost, *Custer's Libbie*, 114

28. Alberts, *Brandy Station*, 114–15.

29. Starr, *Union Cavalry* 2:279–80; Autie to Libbie, 30 September 1864, Merington, CS, 119; Sheridan, *Personal Memoirs* 2:31.

30. Autie to Libbie, 30 September 1864, Merington, CS, 120.

31. James K. Richards, "Come On, You Wolverines!" *Timeline* 7 (August–September 1990): 24.

32. Autie to Libbie, 30 September 1864, Merington, CS, 119–20.

33. McPherson, *Battle Cry*, 778.

34. Sheridan, *Personal Memoirs* 2:55–56; *Battles and Leaders* 4:512–13.

35. Libbie to Parents, October 1864, Merington, CS, 120.

36. Autie to Libbie, 10 October 1864, Merington, CS, 122; Monaghan, *Custer*, 212. See also Sheridan, *Memoirs* 2:56–59.

37. Autie to Libbie, 15 October 1864, Merington, CS, 123.

38. Libbie to Autie, July 1864, Merington, CS, 112. See Hofling's insights on this point, *Custer and the Little Big Horn*, 78.

39. Catharine Beecher's highly influential *Domestic Treatise*, 27–29, quoted from Alexis de Tocqueville's *Democracy in America*, which extolled American women for submitting to their "yoke" with pride. Furthermore, Libbie's evangelical upbringing stressed submission to God's will, and for women, that meant submission to husbands. Greven, *Protestant Temperament*, 125; Welter, "The Cult of True Womanhood," 161–62.

40. Libbie to Autie, October 1864, Merington, CS, 121. Regarding wedlock, Greenwood warned against a union or "altar of sacrifice," which required a woman to give up her identity. Such a marriage would demand "that . . . almost my very identity, must not mingle with, but be *lost* in his." See *Greenwood Leaves*, 41.

41. Although Libbie acknowledged her husband as her "superior," her mixed feelings about submissiveness probably reflected changing standards among Americans. The ideology of the "true woman" was not frozen in time. Many now celebrated the "capable" woman who managed crises and disasters. See Glenda Riley, *Women and Indians on the Frontier*, 27–30.

42. Libbie to Autie, October 1864, Merington, CS, 121.

43. Libbie to Parents, October 1864, Merington, CS, 122.

44. Libbie to Autie, October 1864, Merington, CS, 122–23. Chandler detested McClellan. Mary Karl George, *Zachariah Chandler: A Political Biography*, 63–67.

45. *Battles and Leaders* 4:516–18.

46. Ibid., 518–20; Starr, *Union Cavalry* 2:315–18.

47. Rhoda to Libbie, October 1864; Libbie to Autie, October 1864, Merington, CS, 120–21, 124.

48. Libbie to Parents, 25 October 1864, Merington, CS, 126.

49. Ibid.

50. Merington, CS, 127.

51. Monaghan, *Custer*, 218–19; Libbie to Parents, October 1864, Merington, CS, 127–28.

52. Libbie to Autie, 30 October 1864, Frost, *Custer's Libbie*, 121.

53. Libbie to Autie, Fall 1864, Merington, CS, 128.

54. Libbie to Autie, 30 October 1864, Frost, *Custer's Libbie*, 121.

55. Autie to Libbie, 28 October 1864; Libbie to Autie, October 1864, Merington, CS, 129; Monaghan, *Custer*, 219.

56. Libbie to Parents, 6 November 1864, Merington, CS, 131. Much of northern Virginia was "known as Mosby's Confederacy." McPherson, *Battle Cry*, 737–38.

57. Autie to Daniel Bacon, 2 September 1864; "Orders Sent," War Department, AGO, 10 October 1864, EBCC, Roll 1; Monaghan, *Custer*, 220; Francis Heitman, *Historical Record and Dictionary of the United States Army*, 2:881.

58. Libbie to Rebecca Richmond, 15 November 1864; Libbie to Parents, 6 November 1864, Merington, CS, 131–33.

59. Libbie to Parents, 13 November 1864, Merington, CS, 131–32.

60. E. B. Custer, "Stevensburg Series," EBCC, Roll 5, Frames 4030–34. See also Frost, *Custer's Libbie*, 123.

61. Libbie to Parents, Merington, CS, 135–36.

62. George A. Custer to Rev. D. C. Mattoon, 19 February 1865, Frost, *General Custer's Libbie*, 124. See also John Bulkley, "The Impressive Ceremonies of Unveiling the Statue at Monroe, Michigan," *The Christian Work and Evangelist*, 18 June 1910, 827-28.

63. Daniel Bacon to Autie, 8 February 1865, FCC, MCHCA.

64. Libbie to Autie, 8 March 1865, Merington, CS 136; Roy Basler, *Collected Works of Abraham Lincoln* 8:33

65. Libbie to Autie, 8 March 1865, Merington, CS, 136–37.

66. Starr, *Union Cavalry* 2:372–73; Monaghan, *Custer*, 226–27.

67. Merington, CS 137; Monaghan, *Custer*, 228; Frost, *Custer's Libbie*, 125.

68. Autie to Libbie, 11 March 1865, Merington, CS, 140.

69. Sheridan, *Personal Memoirs* 2:134–35.

70. Autie to Libbie, 11 March 1865, Merington, CS, 140–41.

71. Libbie to Autie, 13 March 1865, Merington, CS, 142.

72. Autie to Libbie, 16 March 1865, Merington, CS, 141.

73. Autie to Libbie, 20 March 1865, Merington, CS, 142.

74. Theodore J. Holmes, chaplain, First Connecticut Cavalry, to Gen. G. A. Custer, 21 March 1865, Merington, CS, 143. The eastern theater was experiencing "a 'pentecostal season' of unsurpassed magnitude" in 1865. Gardiner H. Shattuck, Jr., *A Shield and Hiding Place: The Religious Life of the Civil War Armies*, 89.

75. Emmanuel Custer to Libbie, March 1865, Merington, CS, 143–44.

76. Libbie to Autie, March 1865, Merington, CS, 144.

77. Ibid.

78. Ibid.

79. Libbie to Autie, 26 March 1865, Merington, CS, 145.

80. Ibid.

81. Autie to Libbie, 24 March 1865, Merington, CS, 146.

82. Autie to Libbie, 30 March 1865, MMP. Altered version appears in Merington, CS, 146–47.

83. Ibid.

84. Autie to Libbie, fragment of undated letter, MMP. Merington interjects this into her edited letter of 30 March 1865, Merington, CS 147.

85. Libbie to Parents, 2 April 1865, Peter Boehm to Elizabeth Custer, 15 September 1910, Merington, CS, 147–48.

86. Urwin, *Custer Victorious*, 236–38; Alberts, *Brandy Station*, 147; Starr, *Union Cavalry* 11:438–40; Merington, CS, 148.

87. *Battles and Leaders* 4:725; Alberts, *Brandy Station*, 150–51; Urwin, *Custer Victorious*, 238–244; Starr, *Union Cavalry* 2:447–50; Sheridan, *Memoirs* 2:164 65.

88. Disputes arose concerning Custer's claim that he captured fifteen pieces of artillery. See Douglas Southall Freeman, *Lee's Lieutenants: A Study in Command* 3:706,n. 38. See also Starr, *Union Cavalry* 2:470–72; *Battles and Leaders* 4:720–22; Dupuy and Dupuy, *Compact History*, 413.

89. Autie to Daniel Bacon, 1865, Merington, CS, 150–51; Monaghan, *Custer*, 238.

90. Dupuy and Dupuy, *Compact History*, 413–14; *Battles and Leaders* 4:724; Sheridan, *Personal Memoirs* 2:190; McPherson, *Battle Cry*, 848.

91. Freeman, *Lee's Lieutenants* 4:733–37.

92. Michael Sheridan to Libbie, undated, Merington, CS, 156–57.

93. McPherson, *Battle Cry*, 849.

94. Merington, CS, 158; Elizabeth B. Custer, "Where Grant Wrote Peace," *Harper's Weekly*, 24 June 1911, 6–7.

95. P. Sheridan to Libbie, 10 April 1865, Custer, "Where Grant Wrote," 7.

96. Libbie to Daniel Bacon, 11 April 1865, Merington, CS, 163.

97. Libbie to Laura Noble, April 1865, Merington, CS, 163–64; E. B. Custer, "Cosmopolitan Club Talk Notes—Richmond," EBCC, Roll 5, Frames 4381–82.

98. Autie to Daniel Bacon, 20 April 1865, Merington, CS, 165.

99. Sheridan, *Personal Memoirs* 2:205–6.

100. Ibid: *Battles and Leaders* 4:766

101. Custis Lee was George Washington Custis Lee. For information on his role at Five Forks, see *Battles and Leaders* 4:721–22.

102. Libbie to Parents, April 1865, Merington, CS 165.

103. Paddy Griffith, *Battle Tactics of the Civil War*, 33–40.

104. Sheridan, *Personal Memoirs* 2:208–10.

105. Merington, CS, 166–67; Slotkin, *Fatal Environment*, 387; Utley, *Cavalier*, 35.

106. Merington, CS, 167, 160-61.

107. Daniel Bacon to Libbie, 10 April 1865, 11 April 1865, Merington, CS, 162–63.

108. Griffith, *Battle Tactics*, 40–48; William T. Sherman, *Memoirs of General William T. Sherman* 2:377–78; McPherson, *Ordeal by Fire*, 486.

CHAPTER 5

1. E. B. Custer, *Tenting*, 31.

2. Ibid 63–67; Frost, *Custer's Libbie*, 136.

3. E. B. Custer, *Tenting*, 66–67; Libbie to Rebecca Richmond, 29 June 1865, EBCC, Roll 1.

4. E. B. Custer, *Tenting*, 74–75 Libbie to Parents, July 1865, Merington, CS, 168–69.

5. E. B. Custer, *Tenting*, 73–74.

6. Utley, *Cavalier*, 36; Minnie Dubbs Millbrook, "The Boy General and How He Grew: George Armstrong Custer after Appomattox," *Montana The Magazine of Western History* 23 (April 1973): 34–36.

7. "General Orders No. 2," 24 June 1865, quoted by Charles W. Lothrop, *History of First Regiment Iowa Cavalry*, 218–19. See also John M. Carroll, *Custer in Texas: An Interrupted Narrative*, 30.

8. Millbrook, "Boy General," 38; Millbrook, "Custer's March to Texas," *The Prairie Scout* 1:34–35.

9. Millbrook, "Boy General," 36–39.

10. Millbrook, "Custer's March," 35–36 E. B. Custer, *Tenting*, 94–95; Frost, *Custer's Libbie*, 137–38.

11. Millbrook, "Boy General," 39–40. See also Utley, *Cavalier*, 37.

12. Ibid.

13. Millbrook, "Boy General," 40–43; Monaghan, *Custer*, 258; E. B. Custer, *Tenting*, 104–105; Carroll, *Custer in Texas*, 50–51.

14. E. B. Custer, *Tenting*, 102.

15. Millbrook, "Boy General," 41.

16. Ibid.

17. E. B. Custer, *Tenting*, 112.

18. Daniel Bacon to Libbie, 14 May 1865, BCWCC.

19. Autie to Daniel Bacon, July 1865, Merington, CS, 167–68.

20. Hutton, *Phil Sheridan*, 20–21.

21. Albert D. Richardson, *Personal History of Ulysses S. Grant*, 503.

22. Thomas M. Browne, "Diary," Thomas S. Cogley, *History of the Seventh Indiana Cavalry Volunteers*, 167.

23. Millbrook, "Custer's March to Texas," 36; Carroll, *Custer in Texas*, 62.

24. "General Order No. 15," 7 August 1865, Headquarters Second Cavalry Division, Military Division of the Gulf, EBCC, Roll 1.

25. Millbrook, "Custer's March," 37–39.

26. Ibid., 41–42. See also Lothrop, *First Iowa Cavalry*, 250-51.

27. Libbie to Eliza Sabin, 3 September 1865, MMP.

28. Cogley, *Seventh Indiana Cavalry*, 165. See also William L. Richter, "'A Better Time Is in Store for Us': An Analysis of the Reconstruction Attitudes of George Armstrong Custer," *Military History of Texas and the Southwest* 11 (1973):32.

29. E. B. Custer, *Tenting*, 146–48; Cogley, *Seventh Indiana Cavalry*, 165.

30. E. B. Custer, *Tenting*, 139–40, 129–30; William Richter, *The Army in Texas During Reconstruction, 1865-1870*, 19.

31. E. B. Custer, *Tenting*, 126–29, 133–34.

32. Ibid., 141–44; Millbrook, "Custer's March," 44; Lothrup, *First Iowa Cavalry*, 225–26.

33. Libbie to Eliza Sabin, 3 September 1865, MMP; E. B. Custer, *Tenting*, 120–21.

34. Libbie to Eliza Sabin, 3 September 1865, MMP; E. B. Custer, *Tenting*, 150–51.

35. George W. Stover to Mrs. C. H. Lothrop, 29 August 1890, reprinted in Lothrop, *First Iowa Cavalry*, 290–91.

36. Millbrook, "Custer's March," 49–50; Libbie to Aunt Eliza, 3 September 1869, MMP; E. B. Custer, *Tenting*, 151–52.

37. E. B. Custer, *Tenting*, 152–53; Monaghan, *Custer*, 262.

38. E. B. Custer, *Tenting*, 179–80.

39. Ibid. 152–60; Millbrook, "Custer's March," 49–50.

40. E. B. Custer, *Tenting*, 114.

41. Quoted from the (Warsaw) *Indianian*, 6 August 1868, Millbrook, "Custer's March," 50–51. The officer was not identified.

42. "Co. G, Second Wisconsin, Returns for July and August, 1865," NA, quoted by Millbrook, "Custer's March," 51–52.

43. Lothrop, *First Iowa Cavalry*, 290–91. See also Carroll, *Custer in Texas*, 232-33.

44. G. W. Stover to Mrs. Lothrop, 29 August 1890, Lothrop, *First Iowa Cavalry*, 291. See also Millbrook, "Custer's March," 52–55.

45. Millbrook, "Custer's March to Texas," 55–56; Richter, "'A Better Time Is

in Store for Us,'" 32–33; Merington, CS, 192.

46. Philip Sheridan to George Armstrong Custer, 13 November 1865, quoted by Millbrook, "Custer's March to Texas," 61.

47. Philip Sheridan to Ulysses S. Grant, 15 December 1865, quoted by Millbrook, "Custer's March to Texas," 61.

48. E. B. Custer, *Tenting*, 110.

49. Ibid 114.

50. Ibid. 155–64.; Libbie to Parents, 22 October 1865, Merington, CS, 171; Frost, *Custer's Libbie*, 142–43.

51. Autie to Mr. and Mrs. Bacon, 5 October 1865, MMP. See also Merington, CS, 174–76, for edited version. Armstrong and Tom heard a Confederate supporter call his wife "the old lady," and thinking it humorous, applied it to Libbie. E. B. Custer, *"Boots and Saddles"*, 184–85. Stephen Ambrose, in a perceptive essay, sees Libbie's mastery of equestrian skills as indicative of her competence while accepting gender role restrictions. "Sidesaddle Soldier: Libbie Custer's Partnership in Glory," *Timeline* 3 (April–May 1986): 3–12.

52. Daniel Bacon to Libbie, July [31] 1865, BCWCC; Daniel Bacon to Eliza Sabin, 10 October 1865, Daniel Bacon to Libbie, 10 October 1865, FCC, MCHCA.

53. E. B. Custer, *Tenting*, 201.

54. Ibid., 207–8.

55. Ibid., 220–21; Libbie to Rebecca Richmond, 17 November 1865, EBCC, Roll 1; Carroll, *Custer in Texas*, 162.

56. E. B. Custer, *Tenting*, 190–92, 226–27, 211–20. Officers' wives often "shrewdly assessed" economic potential of new regions. Sandra Myres, "Romance and Reality on the American Frontier: Views of Army Wives," *Western Historical Quarterly* 13 (October 1982): 411.

57. E. B. Custer, *Tenting*, 218–19. For background information, see Robert Wal-

ter Shook, "Federal Occupation and Administration of Texas, 1865-1870," Ph.D. dissertation, North Texas State University, 1970, 43–48.

58. E. B. Custer, *Tenting*, 237–57, especially 243; Autie to Lydia Ann Reed, 12 January 1866, EBCC, Roll 1; A. C. Greene, "The Durable Society: Austin in Reconstruction," *Southwestern Historical Quarterly* 82 (April 1969): 495; Lothrop, *First Iowa Cavalry*, 272–73.

59. E. B. Custer, *Tenting*, 220–21, 264–66.

60. Libbie to Rebecca Richmond, 17 November 1865, EBCC, Roll 1.

61. Autie to Daniel Bacon, July 1865, Merington, CS, 167–68; Libbie to Parents, 22 October 1865, Merington, CS, 169–70; Frost, *Custer's Libbie*, 143–44.

62. Merington, CS, 176.

63. Grant wrote Sheridan on December 1, 1865: "There is great complaint of cruelty against General Custer. If there are grounds for these complaints relieve him from duty." Quoted by Shook, "Federal Occupation and Administration of Texas," 71, n. 50.

64. Autie to Daniel Bacon, July 1865, Merington, CS 167–68.

65. Autie to Mr. and Mrs. Bacon, 5 October 1865, Merington, CS, 175. See also Richter, "'A Better Time Is in Store for Us,'" 31–50.

66. Autie to Mr. and Mrs. Bacon, 5 October 1865, Merington, CS, 175.

67. Ibid.

68. Libbie to Parents, 22 October 1865, Merington, CS, 171; E. B. Custer, *Tenting*, 263.

69. E. B. Custer, *Tenting*, 267–305; Monaghan, *Custer*, 266; Frost, *Custer's Libbie*, 146.

70. Maj. Gen. George A. Custer, "Report to House of Representatives Joint Committee on Reconstruction," 39th Cong., 1st sess, pt. 4, 72–78. Reprinted in

Carroll, *Custer in Texas*, 272–78. See Richter's analysis in "'A Better Time Is in Store for Us,'" 35–39.

71. Autie to Libbie, 12 March 1866, Merington, CS, 178.

72. Ibid.; Eric Foner, *Reconstruction: America's Unfinished Revolution, 1863-1877*, 250–51.

73. Autie to Libbie, 23 March 1866, BCWCC.

74. Libbie to Autie [March 1866], BCWCC. See also E. B. Custer, *Tenting*, 307–8.

75. Autie to Libbie, 29 March 1866, BCWCC.

76. Ibid.; Pat M. Ryan, "Maggie Mitchell," *Notable American Women* 2:551–52.

77. Autie to Libbie, 29 March 1866, 1 April 1866, 3 April 1866, Merington, CS, 180–181; Autie to Libbie, 8 April 1866, BCWCC.

78. Autie to Libbie, 30 March 1866, BCWCC; 3 April 1866, Merington, CS, 181.

79. Autie to Libbie, April, 1866, Merington, CS, 181. (Incorrect date in Merington.) "Bal Masque," *Harper's*, 14 April 1866, 232–234. For information on Clara Louise Kellogg, see *Memoirs of an American Prima Donna*. Brief reference to Custer is on 57–58.

80. E. B. Custer, *Tenting*, 304; Autie to Libbie, 20 April 1866, Frost, *Custer's Libbie*, 148.

81. Quoted by Monaghan, *Custer*, 11.

82. Autie to Mollie (Mary) Holland, 1 January 1859, George Armstrong Custer Manuscript, Western Americana Collection, Beinecke Rare Book and Manuscript Library, Yale University, New Haven, Connecticut. Hereafter referred to as GACM. In all probability, Custer was signing his name, "your true and devoted H[usban]d GAC."

83. Thirty-five-year-old Brice William Custer, the sole surviving child from Em-

manuel's first marriage, had left his father's home in 1850. Wallace, *Custer's Ohio Boyhood*, 8–22, 47, n. 17.

84. Autie to Libbie, 22 April 1866, BCWCC.

85. Autie to Libbie, 21 April 1866, BCWCC.

86. Ibid.

87. Philip Sheridan to Edwin Stanton, 6 April 1866, EBCC, Roll 2.

88. Autie to Libbie, Saturday, [14] April 1866, BCWCC.

89. Autie to Libbie, 20 April 1866, Frost, *Custer's Libbie*, 148, Autie to Libbie, 23 April 1866, BCWCC.

90. Autie to Libbie, 16 March 1866, Merington, CS, 178; Libbie to Eliza Sabin, May 1866, Merington, CS, 182.

91. Libbie to Eliza Sabin, May 1866, Merington, CS, 182; E. B. Custer, *Tenting*, 312.

92. Although Frost gives Bacon's death as March 18, 1866, the March should read May. Daniel Bacon's obituary, *Monroe Monitor*, 23 May 1866. Libbie to Eliza Sabin, May 1865, Merington, CS, 182. Libbie later implied that Autie was in Detroit when her father died. See *Tenting*, 322.

93. E. B. Custer, *Tenting*, 208.

CHAPTER 6

1. "In the Matter of the Estate of Daniel S. Bacon," 22 May 1866, File No. 1545, Monroe County, Michigan, Probate Court.

2. Libbie to Eliza Sabin, May 1866, Merington, CS, 183; E. B. Custer, *Tenting*, 308–9.

3. Monaghan, *Custer*, 268.

4. Ibid. 269; Slotkin, *Fatal Environment*, 389–90. Custer insisted on commanding whites. Otherwise he might have been the colonel of the Ninth or Tenth Cavalry. Philip Sheridan to Edwin Stanton, 6 April 1866, Andrew Johnson Papers,

LC, cited by Richter, "'A Better Time Is in Store for Us,'" 41, 49, n. 32.

5. Foner, *Reconstruction*, 64-65.

6. Monaghan, *Custer*, 269–71; Slotkin, *Fatal Environment*, 389–90.

7. *Monroe Commercial*, 26 July 1866, 20 September 1866; Frost, *Custer's Libbie*, 154–55.

8. Libbie to Rebecca Richmond, 29 August 1866, EBCC, Roll 1.

9. Ibid.

10. Monaghan, *Custer*, 275–76.

11. Undated excerpt from Libbie's diary, Merington, CS, 188–89.

12. Erving E. Beauregard, "The General and the Politician: Custer and Bingham," *Blue and Gray Magazine* 6 (October 1988): 33–35; *Cleveland Plain Dealer*, 6 December 1931.

13. Autie to Libbie, 22 September 1866, BCWCC; Monaghan, *Custer*, 278–79.

14. Autie to Libbie, 22 September 1866, BCWCC.

15. E. B. Custer, *Tenting*, 339–40; *Monroe Commercial*, 2 August 1866; Frost, *Custer's Libbie*, 155.

16. Minnie Dubbs Millbrook, "Mrs. General Custer at Fort Riley, 1866," *Kansas Historical Quarterly* 40 (Spring 1974): 65, n. 11; Libbie to Rebecca Richmond, 6 December 1866, EBCC, Roll 1.

17. E. B. Custer, *Tenting*, 343–47; Libbie to Rebecca Richmond, 6 December 1866, EBCC, Roll 1.

18. E. B. Custer, *Tenting*, 366–68; Millbrook, "Mrs. General Custer, 1866," 63. See also U.S. War Department, Surgeon General's Office, *Circular No. 4: A Report on Barracks and Hospitals with Descriptions of Military Posts*, 287–89. Hereafter referred to as *Circular No. 4*.

19. E. B. Custer, *Tenting*, 368–69.

20. Minnie Dubbs Millbrook, "The West Breaks in General Custer," *Kansas Historical Quarterly* 36 (Summer 1970): 113–14; Slotkin, *Fatal Environment*, 390–91;

Hofling, *Custer and the Little Big Horn*, 92–93.

21. E. B. Custer, *Tenting*, 368–71.

22. Ibid., 371–74; *Circular No. 4*, 288–89; Utley, *Frontier Regulars*, 82.

23. E. B. Custer, *Tenting*, 435–38; Utley, *Cavalier*, 45.

24. Utley, *Cavalier*, 45; Frederick Van de Water, *Glory-Hunter: A Life of General Custer*, 152–53.

25. Utley, *Cavalier*, 46; E. B. Custer, *Tenting*, 427–31; Monaghan, *Custer*, 281-82; Robert Utley, *Life in Custer's Cavalry: Diaries and Letters of Albert and Jennie Barnitz, 1867–1868*, 6.

26. Charles K. Mills, *Harvest of Barren Regrets: The Army Career of Frederick William Benteen*, 129.

27. E. B. Custer, *Tenting*, 429–31; Libbie to Rebecca Richmond, 6 December 1866, EBCC, Roll 1; Frost, *Custer's Libbie*, 158; Merington, CS, 194.

28. E. B. Custer, *Tenting*, 433; Utley, *Cavalier*, 44–45.

29. Utley, *Frontier Regulars*, 22–24.

30. Ibid., 18–22. For the comments of one army wife on brevet ranks, see Frances Roe, *Army Letters from an Officer's Wife, 1871–1877*, 5.

31. E. B. Custer, *Tenting*, 433–36.

32. Van de Water, *Glory-Hunter*, 18; Utley, *Cavalier*, 13.

33. E. B. Custer, *Tenting*, 433–35; Monaghan, *Custer*, 282–83.

34. E. B. Custer, *Tenting*, 433.

35. Libbie to Rebecca Richmond, 6 December 1866, EBCC, Roll 1; E. B. Custer, *Tenting*, 411–12, 388–89.

36. Minnie Dubbs Millbrook, "West Breaks," 114; Melbourne C. Chandler, *Of Garryowen in Glory: The History of the Seventh United States Cavalry*, 2; Utley, *Cavalier*, 41-42.

37. William H. Leckie, *The Military Conquest of the Southern Plains*, 10–12;

Utley, *Cavalier*, 43–44; Utley, *Frontier Regulars*, 3–4.

38. Utley, *Cavalier*, 47; Leckie, *Military Conquest*, 28–33.

39. Leckie, *Military Conquest*, 31–32; Robert M. Utley, *The Indian Frontier of the American West, 1846–1890*, 112.

40. E. B. Custer, *Tenting*, 484.

41. Utley, *Cavalier*, 47; Libbie to Autie, 5 April 1867, E. B. Custer, *Tenting*, 521–22, 535–36.

42. Autie to Libbie, 10 April 1867, E. B. Custer, *Tenting*, 526; Leckie, *Military Conquest*, 37–39; Slotkin, *Fatal Environment*, 392.

43. Autie to Libbie, 10 April 1867, E. B. Custer, *Tenting*, 552–53.

44. Leckie, *Military Conquest*, 40–41; Minnie Dubbs Millbrook, "Custer's First Scout in the West," *Kansas Historical Quarterly* 39 (Summer 1973): 78; Autie to Libbie, 14 April 1867, E. B. Custer, *Tenting*, 559–60; George Armstrong Custer, *My Life on the Plains, or, Personal Experiences with Indians*, 32; Henry M. Stanley, *Early Travels and Adventures in America and Asia* 1:26.

45. Autie to Libbie, 15 April 1867, E. B. Custer, *Tenting*, 560–61; Millbrook, "Custer's First Scout," 83–84.

46. Autie to Libbie, 20 April 1867, E. B. Custer, *Tenting*, 564–68; G. A. Custer, *My Life*, 49–52.

47. Libbie to Autie, 23 April 1867, E. B. Custer, *Tenting*, 541–43.

48. Autie to Libbie, 20 April 1867, E. B. Custer, *Tenting*, 570.

49. Autie to Libbie, 22 April 1867, E. B. Custer, *Tenting*, 570–71.

50. Leckie, *Military Conquest*, 42–45; Millbrook, "Custer's First Scout," 89–92.

51. The Thirty-eighth Infantry was one of four black infantries made up largely of veterans of the Civil War. The others were the Thirty-ninth, Fortieth, and Forty-first.

In 1869, Congress consolidated the four regiments into the Twenty-fourth and Twenty-fifth Infantries. Arlen L. Fowler, *The Black Infantry in the West, 1869–1891*, 15, n. 30.

52. E. B. Custer, *Tenting*, 504–12.

53. Ibid., 512. Few officers or their wives were without prejudice and fear. Erwin N. Thompson, "The Negro Soldier on the Frontier: A Fort Davis Case Study," *Journal of the West* 7 (April 1968): 231–32. Alice Grierson, wife of Benjamin H. Grierson, colonel of the Tenth Cavalry, an all-black unit, was relatively unbiased. See Shirley A. Leckie, *The Colonel's Lady on the Western Frontier: The Correspondence of Alice Kirk Grierson*, 22–24.

54. Autie to Libbie, 22 April 1867, E. B. Custer, *Tenting*, 570–71; Millbrook, "Custer's First Scout," 94–95.

55. Libbie to Autie, 26 April 1867, E. B. Custer, *Tenting*, 543–44.

56. Autie to Libbie, 4 May 1867, E. B. Custer, *Tenting*, 580.

57. Autie to Libbie, 6 May 1867, Merington, CS, 202.

58. Autie to Libbie, 25 April 1867, E. B. Custer, *Tenting*, 574.

59. Autie to Libbie, 10 May 1867, BCWCC.

60. Autie to Libbie, 9 May 1867, BCWCC.

61. Autie to Libbie, 10 May 1867, Merington, CS, 204.

62. Autie to Libbie, 10 May 1867, BCWCC.

63. Ibid.

64. Ibid.

65. Autie to Libbie, 12 May 1867, BCWCC.

66. Theodore Davis, "With General in Their Camp Homes: General George A. Custer," *Westerners Brand Book*, 118–19. See also Utley, *Cavalier*, 50.

67. Albert Barnitz to Jennie Barnitz, 15 May 1867, Utley, *Life in Custer's Cavalry*, 50.

68. Utley, *Cavalier*, 50.

69. Libbie to Autie, 18 April 1867, E. B. Custer, *Tenting*, 537; E. B. Custer, *Tenting*, 600–9.

70. Albert Barnitz to Jennie Barnitz, 18 May 1867, Utley, *Life in Custer's Cavalry*, 52–53.

71. Monaghan, *Custer*, 291.

72. Utley, *Cavalier*, 50, G. A. Custer, *My Life*, 66.

73. Theodore Davis, "A Summer on the Plains," *Harper's Monthly Magazine*, February 1868, 301; George Armstrong Custer, "Notes," 8 June 1867, Merington, CS, 204–205. Some of the officers blamed Custer, stating that he had ordered the surgeon to deny Cooper alcohol while he suffered from delirium tremens. See also Mills, *Harvest of Barren Regrets*, 143–44.

74. Leckie, *Military Conquest*, 49–50; Autie to Libbie, 15 June 1867, Lawrence A. Frost, *The Court-Martial of General George Armstrong Custer*, 46–47.

75. W. T. Sherman to G. A. Custer, 17 June 1867, GACM; Millbrook, "West Breaks," 123; Utley, *Cavalier*, 51.

76. Autie to Libbie, 17 June 1867, E. B. Custer, *Tenting*, 581–82; Jennie Barnitz's Journal, 17 June 1867, Utley, *Life in Custer's Cavalry*, 58.

77. E. B. Custer, *Tenting*, 619–22; Jennie Barnitz's Journal, 5 June 1867, Utley, *Life in Custer's Cavalry*, 56.

78. E. B. Custer, *Tenting*, 636–37. See also Jennie Barnitz's Journal, 7 June 1867, Utley, *Life in Custer's Cavalry*, 56–57. Eastern women were often caught off guard by the torrential rains and rapid flooding on the Plains. Glenda Riley, *The Female Frontier: A Comparative View of Women on the Prairie and the Plains*, 77.

79. E. B. Custer, *Tenting*, 640–44; Jennie Barnitz's Journal, 7 June 1867, Utley, *Life in Custer's Cavalry*, 56–57.

80. E. B. Custer, *Tenting*, 645–54.

81. Ibid. 664–67; Jennie Barnitz's Journal, 17 June 1867, 19 June 1867, Utley, *Life in Custer's Cavalry*, 58–59.

82. Utley, *Life in Custer's Cavalry*, 59.

83. G. A. Custer, *My Life*, 77–78; Millbrook, "West Breaks," 123–25.

84. G. A. Custer, *My Life*, 79–87; Davis, "With Generals in Their Camp Homes," 124–25; Millbrook, "West Breaks," 125–26.

85. G. A. Custer, *My Life*, 88–98; Millbrook, "West Breaks," 126–28.

86. Libbie to Autie, 27 June 1867, E. B. Custer, *Tenting*, 547–49. Libbie later wrote that Lieutenants Robbins and Cooke had arrived at camp to take her to Wallace, but Hancock intervened. *Tenting*, 625–27. This is impossible since Jennie Barnitz's diary entry of June 17, indicates that Libbie left Big Creek on June 17, the same day that Custer instructed her to go to Wallace. Utley, *Life in Custer's Cavalry*, 58. See also Millbrook, "West Breaks," 127, n.53.

87. Ibid.

88. Millbrook, "West Breaks," 128; Utley, *Cavalier*, 52.

89. Millbrook, "West Breaks," 129; Monaghan, *Custer*, 295.

90. Monaghan, *Custer*, 295–96.

91. Millbrook, "West Breaks," 133; testimony of Dr. I. T. Coates, Frost, *Court-Martial*, 165–72.

92. G. A. Custer, *My Life*, 109–12; Millbrook, "West Breaks," 133–34.

93. Frost in *Court-Martial*, 54, interprets Armstrong's comments, written on June 22, as arising from anxiety about cholera at Fort Riley. While the first of two cases at Riley was diagnosed that day, Custer could not have heard of it that day. When he wrote his wife, "I never was so anxious in my life," his anxiety arose from his intense desire to have her with him. See Autie to Libbie, 22 June 1867, E. B. Custer, *Tenting*, 582–83.

Millbrook studied cholera's arrival in Kansas, using "Epidemic Cholera," *Report of Surgeon General's Office*, 10 June 1868, *Circular No. 1*. Hereafter referred to as *Circular No. 1*. Millbrook concluded that cholera was not yet a problem at Kansas posts on June 22. See "West Breaks," 137. On page 138, she notes: "Mrs. Custer was at Fort Riley where there was no cholera." However, *Circular No. 1*, viii, 27–28, indicates one case of cholera at Fort Riley on June 22 and another on July 11.

94. G. A. Custer, *My Life*, 114; E. B. Custer, *Tenting*, 695–97, 700–1.

95. Millbrook, "West Breaks," 135. On July 31, Captain Keogh reported one incident of Indian fighting the past month and one soldier wounded. He added, "Since then stages have travelled without being molested." "Fort Wallace Post Returns, 1866–1882, Fort Wallace, Kansas." Kansas State Historical Society, Topeka, Kansas.

96. Keogh had written in his report of July 8 that rations "will last only until the 15th of August and until then only in case no more troops come here needing them." Capt. Myles Keogh to Acting Assistant Adjutant Weir, 8 July 1867; see also Capt. Keogh to Capt. W. G. Mitchell, 16 July 1867, "Letters Sent," Fort Wallace Records. Cited by Millbrook, "West Breaks," 135, n. 90.

97. See *Circular No. 1*, xii, 54–55. Given the "debilitated" condition of the soldiers after the Platte River expedition, cholera took its toll on the Seventh camped near Wallace. The garrison escaped cholera.

98. Millbrook, "West Breaks," 136–37; Utley, *Cavalier*, 52.

99. G. A. Custer, *My Life*, 114; E. B. Custer, *Tenting*, 700–1.

100. John M. Carroll, "Custer: From the Civil War to the Big Horn," 7.

101. Col. E. G. Mathey, interviewed by Walter M. Camp, 19 October 1910, Box 6,

Folder 5. Walter M. Camp Papers, Harold B. Lee Library, Brigham Young University, Provo, Utah. Hereafter referred to as CP.

102. Jennie Barnitz's journal entries, 8 June 1867, 17 June 1867, Utley, *Life in Custer's Cavalry*, 56–59.

103. See Roe, *Army Letters from an Officer's Wife*, 143, 188; Katherine Gibson Fougera, *With Custer's Cavalry: From the Memoirs of the Late Katherine Gibson, Widow of Captain Francis M. Gibson of the Seventh Cavalry, U.S.A. (Retired)*, 134. See also Libbie's remarks in *"Boots and Saddles,"* 105. Duane M. Greene also comments on flirtations in *Ladies and Officers of the United States Army; or, American Aristocracy. A Sketch of the Social Life and Character of the Army*, 75–77. See also Oliver Knight, *Life and Manners in the Frontier Army*, 42–44.

104. See Utley's comments in *Cavalier*, 107.

105. E. B. Custer, *Tenting*, 671, Millbrook, "West Breaks," 136–38.

106. Sgt. James Connelly's testimony, Frost, *Court-Martial*, 139–40. See also Capt. Louis Hamilton's testimony, Frost, *Court-Martial*, 107–9.

107. Louis Hamilton, Testimony and response to "Cross Examination," Frost, *Court-Martial*, 107–13. The references to "demoralized" are found on 107 and 112.

108. G. A. Custer, "Official Report," Frost, *Court-Martial*, 176–77. See also Millbrook, "West Breaks," 139–40.

109. G. A. Custer, *My Life*, 117.

110. Libbie disclosed that Custer found none of her letters at Wallace. They "met him at Forts Hays and Harker." E. B. Custer, *Tenting*, 701. See also Millbrook, "West Breaks," 136, n. 91.

111. Millbrook, "West Breaks," 140–41; Frost, *Court-Martial*, 126–28.

112. Millbrook, "West Breaks," 141–42; T. B. Weir's testimony, Frost, *Court-Mar-*

tial, 128–30; Carroll, "Custer: From the Civil War to the Little Big Horn," 7; Mathey, interviewed by Camp, 19 October 1910, CP. According to Camp, "Mathey says it was reported that when Custer met Weir a scene was enacted and Weir 'got down on his knees to Custer.'"

113. Col. A. J. Smith's testimony, Frost, *Court-Martial*, 150.

114. E. B. Custer, *Tenting*, 699.

115. Ibid. 700–2.

116. Millbrook, "West Breaks," 142–43.

117. E. B. Custer, *Tenting*, 702.

CHAPTER 7

1. Frost, *Court-Martial*, 99–102; Millbrook, "West Breaks," 144–45.

2. Libbie to Rebecca Richmond, 13 October 1867, September 1867, Merington, CS, 214, 212.

3. T. B. Weir to G. A. Custer, 14 August 1867, Frost, *Court-Martial*, 89–91.

4. See Weir's testimony, Frost, *Court-Martial*, 123–25, 214–15.

5. Frost, *Court-Martial*, 245–46; Millbrook, "West Breaks," 144–46.

6. Monaghan, *Custer*, 303.

7. Libbie to Rebecca Richmond, 13 October 1867, Merington, CS, 213.

8. Custer attributed this view to Sheridan, and later actions bear it out. Custer to Mr. Walker, September 1867, Merington, CS, 211–12. See also Philip Sheridan to George Armstrong Custer, 12 December 1867, Frost, *Court-Martial*, 256. Many historians believe Custer was a scapegoat. See Frost, *Custer's Libbie*, 169–70; Hutton, *Phil Sheridan*, 33; Slotkin, *Fatal Environment*, 394.

9. Millbrook, "West Breaks," 146–47; Stan Hoig, *The Battle of the Washita: The Sheridan-Custer Indian Campaign of 1867–69*, 19–20.

10. Libbie to Rebecca Richmond, 20 November 1867, Merington, CS, 214. See also Jennie Barnitz to Mother, 13 December 1867, Utley, *Life in Custer's Cavalry*, 130.

11. (Sandusky, Ohio) *Daily Register*, 28 December 1867, cited by Frost, *Court-Martial*, 257–260; *Army and Navy Journal*, 4 January 1868, cited by Millbrook, "West Breaks," 146–47, n. 128. See also *New York Times*, 28 December 1867.

12. (Leavenworth) *Daily Conservative*, 19 January 1868, cited by Minnie Dubbs Millbrook, "Rebecca Richmond's Diary," *Kansas Historical Quarterly* 42 (Winter 1976): 374, n. 16.

13. Leckie, *Military Conquest*, 58–62; Paul Prucha, *American Indian Policy in Crisis: Christian Reformers and the Indian, 1865–1900*, 20; Albert Barnitz's Journal, 28 October 1867, Utley, *Life in Custer's Cavalry*, 115. Douglas C. Jones notes the changes Indians insisted on and argues they understood more than Major Elliott thought. *The Treaty of Medicine Lodge*, 200–201.

14. Millbrook, "Rebecca Richmond's Diary," 370–77; See also Elizabeth B. Custer, *Following the Guidon*, 131–46. The Custers and several other officers kept so many dogs that an order went out stating that any animals "running loose" after April 20 would be summarily shot. Frost, *Custer's Libbie*, 173.

15. Frost, *Custer's Libbie*, 173; Autie to Libbie, 27 August 1868, BCWCC.

16. Utley, *Indian Frontier*, 122–23; Leckie, *Military Conquest*, 68–71.

17. Leckie, *Military Conquest*, 80–83; Hutton, *Phil Sheridan*, 48–49; Utley, *Cavalier*, 60.

18. Hutton, *Phil Sheridan*, 51; Utley, *Cavalier*, 60.

19. G. A. Custer, *My Life*, 183.

20. Ibid.

21. Leckie, *Military Conquest*, 88–89; Utley, *Cavalier*, 60.

22. Autie to Libbie, 4 October 1868, E. B. Custer, *Guidon*, 11–12.

23. Hutton, *Phil Sheridan*, 54.

24. Autie to Libbie, 24 October 1868, EBCC, Roll 4.

25. Autie to Libbie, 28 October 1868, EBCC, Roll 4.

26. Autie to Libbie, 27 August 1867, BCWCC. Autie wrote from Detroit.

27. Autie to Libbie, 26 October 1868, 28 October 1868, Frost, *Custer's Libbie*, 177; Autie to Libbie, 5 November 1868, BCWCC.

28. Autie to Libbie, 28 October 1868, Frost, *Custer's Libbie*, 177–78.

29. Autie to Libbie, 31 October 1868, Frost, *Custer's Libbie*, 178.

30. John B. Kennedy, "A Soldier's Widow," *Collier's*, 29 January 1927, 10; Hofling, *Custer and the Little Big Horn*, 83.

31. Autie to Libbie, 28 October 1868, EBCC, Roll 4.

32. Autie to Libbie, 5 November 1868, BCWCC. Edward S. Godfrey, "Some Reminiscences, Including the Washita Battle, November 29, 1868," *Cavalry Journal* 37 (October 1928): 483; Monaghan, *Custer*, 309; Robert C. Carriker, *Fort Supply, Indian Territory: Frontier Outpost on the Plains*, 16–17.

33. Autie to Libbie, 21 November 1868, EBCC, Roll 4; Godfrey, "Some Reminiscences," 487.

34. Autie to Libbie, 22 November 1868, EBCC, Roll 4; Hoig, *Washita*, 82.

35. Autie to Libbie, 22 November 1868, EBCC, Roll 4.

36. Autie to Libbie, November 1868, Merington, CS, 219; Godfrey, "Some Reminiscences," 489.

37. Godfrey, "Some Reminiscences," 489; Autie to Libbie, November 1868, Merington, CS, 220.

38. Autie to Libbie, November 1868, Merington, CS, 220; Godfrey, "Some Reminiscences," 491.

39. G. A. Custer, *My Life*, 233; Merington, CS, 220.

40. Monaghan, *Custer*, 316; Utley, *Cavalier*, 65.

41. Merington, CS, 220–21; Custer, *My Life*, 238–39; Utley, *Cavalier*, 67.

42. Hoig, *Washita*, 127–34; Utley, *Cavalier*, 67–68.

43. Godfrey, "Some Reminiscences," 493–95. Godfrey joined the Seventh after West Point in 1867. Utley, *Life in Custer's Cavalry*, 260–61.

44. Godfrey, "Some Reminiscences," 495–96; Hoig, *Washita*, 141–42.

45. G. A. Custer, *My Life*, 258–59; Ben Clark, according to one author, suggested this feint. Kevin Thomas, "Ben Clark: The Scout Who Defied Custer," *Oldtimers Wild West*, February 1980, 48–49. See also Slotkin, *Fatal Environment*, 399.

46. Philip H. Sheridan to Elizabeth B. Custer, 29 November 1868, EBCC, Roll 2.

47. Autie to Libbie, 6 December 1868, EBCC, Roll 4.

48. Ibid; Utley, *Cavalier*, 71.

49. Autie to Libbie, 19 December 1868, EBCC, Roll 4. Edited version without numbers is in E. B. Custer, *Guidon*, 46. Donald Berthrong, *The Southern Cheyennes*, 327–28; Utley, *Cavalier*, 70–71. Benjamin H. Grierson, colonel, Tenth Cavalry, estimated the number of braves killed as eighteen. Benjamin H. Grierson to John Kirk, 6 April 1869, letters and documents, Grierson Papers, Manuscript 343 A, Edward Ayer Collection, Newberry Library, Chicago, Illinois. Hereafter referred to as GP.

50. Autie to Libbie, 19 December 1868, EBCC, Roll 4. Clara Blinn is described in Lonnie J. White, "White Women Captives of Southern Plains Indians, 1866–1875," *Journal of the West* 8 (July 1869): 338–39.

51. White, "White Women Captives," 335–38. E. A. Brininstool, *Campaigning*

with *Custer and the Nineteenth Kansas Volunteer Cavalry on the Washita Campaign, 1868–69 by David L. Spotts*, 207–15. Slotkin suggests that the Indians may have taken hostages to exact concessions. See Slotkin, *Fatal Environment*, 398–99.

52. Hutton, *Phil Sheridan*, 83–84.

53. Ibid. 85–86.

54. Autie to Libbie, 19 December 1868, EBCC, Roll 4; Utley, *Cavalier*, 72.

55. Autie to Libbie, 26 December 1868, 1 January 1869, EBCC, Roll 4.

56. Autie to Libbie, 19 December 1869, EBCC, Roll 4.

57. Utley, *Frontier Regulars*, 152; Berthrong, *Southern Cheyennes*, 331–32.

58. Stan Hoig, *The Peace Chiefs of the Cheyennes*, 119–21. Hoig notes that while Black Kettle could not control his hotheads, neither could whites control their analogous group. For varying nineteenth-century views on Black Kettle, see Berthrong, *Southern Cheyennes*, 329, 331–32; Hutton, *Phil Sheridan*, 97–98.

59. Utley, *Cavalier*, 78. Historians disagree. Monaghan describes a Cheyenne woman disemboweling a white child in front of the startled soldiers. *Custer*, 318. Hoig depicts the same incident as a Cheyenne mother, killing her light-skinned child in suicidal desperation. See *Washita*, 134.

60. Dippie, "George A. Custer," *Soldiers West*, 104; Utley, *Cavalier*, 77–78; Slotkin, *Fatal Environment*, 399–402.

61. Libbie to Eliza Sabin, undated letter from Fort Hays, Merington, CS, 284.

62. Autie to Libbie, 2 January 1869, EBCC, Roll 4.

63. Autie to Libbie, 26 December 1868, EBCC, Roll 4.

64. E. B. Custer, *Guidon*, 252–54.

65. Autie to Libbie, 8 January 1869, MMP (edited and misdated version appears in Merington, CS, 225); Wilbur S. Nye, *Carbine and Lance: The Story of Old Fort*

Sill, 89–93. Soldiers hoped to name it Fort Elliott, but Sheridan named it Fort Sill to honor Joshua Sill, killed at the battle of Stone Ridge. Benjamin Grierson to John Grierson, 23 July 1869, GP.

66. Autie to Libbie, 14 January 1869, E. B. Custer, *Guidon*, 49.

67. Ibid.

68. Utley, *Cavalier*, 107.

69. Autie to Libbie, 8 January 1869, MMP. Edited version in Merington, CS, 225, 226–27. Merington divided the letter and misdated it because of Armstrong's confusion over his anniversary.

70. Autie to Libbie, 31 October 1868, Frost, *Custer's Libbie*, 178.

71. Autie to Libbie, 8 January 1869, MMP.

72. Anna to Dear Gen., 27 January 1869, BCWCC.

73. Benteen linked Custer and Lieutenant Cooke with one of Libbie's companions. See Frederick Benteen to Theodore Goldin, 17 February 1896, John Carroll, *The Benteen-Goldin Letters on Custer and His Last Battle*, 261–62. Anna Darrah was involved with Cooke. Frost, *Custer's Libbie*, 186; Autie to Libbie, 14 December 1869, BCWCC.

74. Hattie Mitchell to Maj. Gen. G. A. Custer, 29 August 1866, BCWCC.

75. Anna to Dear Gen., 27 January 1869, BCWCC.

76. Autie to Libbie, 8 February 1869, E. B. Custer, *Guidon*, 49–50.

77. Utley, *Cavalier*, 73; Berthrong, *Southern Cheyennes*, 333–34.

78. Libbie to Autie, 1 March 1869, E. B. Custer, *Guidon*, 55.

79. Ibid.

80. Custer, *My Life*, 282, 350–51, 359, 365–66.

81. Frederick Benteen to Theodore Goldin, 14 February 1896, 17 February 1896, Carroll, *Benteen-Goldin Lettes*, 258, 271.

82. Ben Clark, interviewed by W. M. Camp, Ben Clark Field Notes, Box 2, Folder F. Walter Camp Manuscript, Lilly Library, Indiana University, Bloomington, Indiana. Hereafter, Ben Clark Field Notes, CM. See also Utley, *Cavalier*, 107; Hutton, *Phil Sheridan*, 389–90, n. 45. Clark and Custer encountered problems, as Thomas indicates in his article, "Ben Clark: The Scout Who Defied Custer," 48. Clark did not name the Indian woman, but Sheridan called him "the most reliable and accomplished man of his class on the plains." Quoted by Hutton, *Phil Sheridan*, 301.

83. See Thomas B. Marquis, *Custer on the Little Bighorn*, 35, 43; Mari Sandoz, *Cheyenne Autumn*, xvii, xix, 21, 32, 215; Charles J. Brill, *Conquest of the Southern Plains: Uncensored Narrative of the Battle of the Washita and Custer's Southern Campaign*, 22, 45–46; David Humphreys Miller, *Custer's Fall: The Indian Side of the Story*, 67–68. There are inconsistencies in these narratives, and the dates given for the birth of Monahsetah's second child vary. Sandoz states that the child was born "in the fall," while Brill's information, based on the testimony of the Cheyennes, Little Beaver, and his mother, Red Dress, moved the birth to the summer of 1869. This latter date is impossible.

Many historians doubt the story. See Frost, *Custer's Libbie*, 182; Slotkin, *Fatal Environment*, 402–403; Ambrose, *Crazy Horse and Custer*, 298; Monaghan, *Custer*, 328–29; Blaine Burkey, *Custer, Come At Once!: The Fort Hays Years of George and Elizabeth Custer, 1867–1870*, 64–68. On the other hand, Edgar Stewart states that historians can neither prove nor disprove the allegations. He notes, too, "When subjected to the same tenets of historical criticism, there is no reason for not accepting the testimony of the Indians since it is

equally as reliable as the testimony of any-
one else." See Stewart's introduction to the
University of Oklahoma Press's reprint of
G. A. Custer, *My Life*, xx. Paul Hutton in
Phil Sheridan, 389–90, n. 45 makes reference to "the Cheyenne oral tradition as *independently reported* [italics added] by
Thomas Marquis, Mari Sandoz, Charles
Brill, and David Miller," which is an important point. Finally, Utley, *Cavalier in
Buckskin*, 107, refers to the story "that she
[Monahsetah] bore Custer's child" and
adds: "She may have. She had three
months with him after the birth of the 'little papoose,' and tradition hints of another infant late in 1869."

84. Ben Clark identified the scout Ro-
mero as the procurer. See Ben Clark field
notes, CM; see also Frederick Benteen to
Theodore Goldin, 17 February 1896, Carroll, *Benteen-Goldin Letters*, 271.

85. Brill, *Conquest of the Southern Plains*,
22; Sandoz, *Cheyenne Autumn*, 21. See
Slotkin's incisive comments in *Fatal Environment*, 403.

86. Utley, *Cavalier*, 74; Autie to Libbie,
24 March 1869, E. B. Custer, *Guidon*, 56–
57, see also 57–60.

87. Hutton, *Phil Sheridan*, 80; unidentified Seventh Cavalry officer (Frederick Benteen) to "My Dear Friend"
(William J. DeGress), 22 December 1868,
Missouri Democrat, 8 February 1869, quoted by Mills, *Harvest of Bitter Regrets*, 181–
83. See also *New York Times*, 14 February
1869. Custer called his officers together
and threatened to horsewhip the author.
Benteen stepped forward, adjusting his
gun in his holster. Custer dropped the
matter. Mills, *Harvest of Bitter Regrets*, 184.

88. Utley, *Cavalier*, 75–77; Slotkin, *Fatal
Environment*, 400.

89. W. S. Harvey Diary, 7 April 1869,
cited by Blaine Burkey, *Custer, Come at
Once!*, 47.

90. Slotkin, *Fatal Environment*, 394,
400–401.

CHAPTER 8

1. E. B. Custer, *Guidon*, 80, 190–91.
Miles had emerged from the Civil War
a brevet major general of volunteers.
His marriage to Mary Hoyt Sherman
probably retarded rather than advanced
his career. See Utley, "Nelson Miles,"
Soldiers West, 215–16; Minnie Millbrook,
"Big Game Hunting with the Custers,
1869–1870," *Kansas Historical Quarterly*
41 (Winter 1975): 434–35, n. 18. For
information on buffalo hunting with the
Miles, see E. B. Custer, *Guidon*,
192–212.

2. E. B. Custer, *Guidon*, 71–75.

3. Ibid., 75–76; Glenda Riley sees Cooper's *The Prairie* and *The Last of the Moh-
icans* as highly influential. *Women and Indians on the Frontier*, 21–23.

4. E. B. Custer, *Guidon*, 83–89.

5. Ibid., 91–92. Artist George Catlin and
Thomas McKenney, among others, had
popularized this common view. Katherine
M. Weist, "Beasts of Burden and Menial
Slaves: Nineteenth Century Observations
of Northern Plains Indian Women," *The
Hidden Half: Studies of Plains Indian
Women*, 29–52. Sherry Smith believes that
many officers' wives saw Indian women as
degraded because that view inflated their
"place and purpose on the western frontier." *The View from Officers' Row: Army
Perceptions of Western Indians*, 62–64. See
also 56–57, 201, n. 4. Smith also notes that
officers such as John Bourke, Joseph
Sladen, Randolph Marcy, and Philippe
Regis de Trobriand, recognized the personal freedom, physical skills, and property rights accorded women in many tribes.
Smith, *View from Officers' Row*, 59–62. See

also George B. Grinnell, *Cheyenne Indians*, 1:127.

Sandra Myres notes that frontierswomen did not hold monolithic views on Indians. Nor does she see them as more prejudiced than men. Moreover, contact with Indians often destroyed some of their prejudices. See *Westering Women and the Frontier Experience, 1800–1915*, 38–39, 53–56; "Romance and Reality," 413–14. See also Riley, *Women and Indians*, 151–53. Riley notes that different tribes elicited different responses, a factor often not taken into account.

6. E. B. Custer, *Guidon*, 90. See also Smith, *View from Officers' Row*, 57.

7. E. B. Custer, *Guidon*, 91–92, 95.

8. G. A. Custer, *My Lif*, 282.

9. E. B. Custer, *Guidon*, 95.

10. Ibid., 94–95.

11. Ibid., 95–97.

12. Ibid., 99.

13. Ibid., 110; G. A. Custer, *My Life on the Plains*, 378. See also Burkey, *Custer, Come at Once!*, 72–73.

14. Sturgis replaced A. J. Smith in May 1869. Heitman, *Historical Register* 2:934; Utley, *Cavalier*, 105–6. Upton assumed his position in 1870. *Register of Graduates and Former Cadets of the United States Military Academy, 1980: Cullum Memorial Edition*, 8.

15. E. B. Custer, *Guidon*, 113–14, 120, 126–27.

16. Millbrook, "Big Game Hunting," 431.

17. Ibid.; Libbie to Laura Noble Stoddard, 19 September 1869, EBCC, Roll 1. One member of the House of Lords was Lord Berkeley Paget. The other may have been Henry A. Cavendish. Burkey, *Custer, Come at Once!*, 83–85, n. 30.

18. Libbie to Laura Noble Stoddard, 19 September 1869, EBCC, Roll 1; E. B. Custer, *Guidon*, 191–93.

19. Miss (no first name given) Talmadge, quoted by Frank Tallmadge, "Buf-

falo Hunting with Custer," *Cavalry Journal* 33 (January 1924): 10; Millbrook, "Big Game Hunting," 435–36; Utley, *Cavalier*, 105–6.

20. Richard Bartlett, *The New Country: A Social History of the American Frontier*, 33–35.

21. Libbie to Laura Noble Stoddard, 19 September 1869, EBCC, Roll 1. See also Millbrook, "Big Game Hunting," 430.

22. E. B. Custer, *Guidon*, 238.

23. Libbie to Laura Noble, 19 September 1869, EBCC, Roll 1; Manion, "Custer's Cooks and Maids," 156.

24. Anne E. Bingham, "Sixteen Years on a Kansas Farm," *Kansas Historical Collections* 15 (1919–1922): 501–506.

25. Autie to Libbie, 27 November 1869, MMP.

26. Autie to Libbie, 2 May 1867, Merington, CS, 199–200.

27. "A Bill for the Relief of Elizabeth B. Custer," H.R. 3120, 45th Cong., 2d sess., 8 February 1878, BCWCC. See also Frost, *Custer's Libbie*, 248.

28. Autie to Libbie, 25 November 1869, BCWCC.

29. Autie to Libbie, 11 December 1869, BCWCC.

30. Bingham, "Sixteen Years," 503.

31. Millbrook, "Diary of Rebecca Richmond," 396–99.

32. Questionnaire dated 3 April 1870, from Topeka, from Frank Mericante, Grand Rapids, Michigan. Typescript copy found in Elizabeth B. Custer File in George Armstrong Custer Collection of the Monroe Country Library System, Ellis Reference and Information Center, Monroe, Michigan. Hereafter referred to as GACC.

33. Hutton, *Phil Sheridan*, III.

34. Elizabeth Bacon Custer, "Kansas and Buffalo Ann," EBCC, Roll 4, cited by Millbrook, "Big Game Hunting," 446–47.

35. Ibid. See also E. B. Custer, *Guidon*, 243; Sidney E. Whitman, *The Trooper: An Informal History of the Plains Cavalry*, 146–47. For information on the soldier's activities, see Millbrook, "Big Game Hunting," 450–451.

36. Libbie to Rebecca Richmond, 6 November 1870, EBCC, Roll 1.

37. Brian Pohanka, *A Summer on the Plains, 1870: From the Diary of Annie Gibson Roberts*, 16–18.

38. E. B. Custer, "Kansas and Buffalo Ann," EBCC, Roll 4, cited by Millbrook, "Big Game Hunting," 449.

39. Annie Roberts Yates, "General Custer As I Knew Him," unpublished manuscript in EBCC, Roll 6, Frame 5814. See also Frost, *Custer's Libbie*, 320.

40. E. B. Custer, *"Boots and Saddles"*, 184; Pohanka, *A Summer on the Plains, 1870*, 62–63, n. 61.

41. P. T. Barnum, *Struggles and Triumphs, or Forty Years Recollections of P. T. Barnum*, 855. See also *Topeka Record*, 26 October 1870, cited by Millbrook, "Big Game Hunting," 447–48; P. T. Barnum to General Custer, 29 November 1875, EBCC, Roll 1.

42. Millbrook, "Big Game Hunting," 447, n. 52; Libbie to Rebecca Richmond, 6 November [1870], EBCC, Roll 1.

43. Libbie to Rebecca, 16 October [1870], EBCC, Roll 1.

44. Millbrook, "Big Game Hunting," 453. See (Topeka) *Commonwealth*, 12 November 1870, quoted by Millbrook.

45. Libbie to Rebecca Richmond, 16 October [1870], EBCC, Roll 1. Benzine boards are covered by Utley, *Frontier Regulars*, 15; J. W. Hall to George Armstrong Custer, 29 November 1870. EBCC, Roll 2.

46. Autie to Libbie [December 1870]. Two portions of this letter came from the MMP, and another comes from GACM. This portion is found in MMP. A highly edited fragment appears in Merington, CS, 321.

47. Mills, *Harvest of Barren Regrets*, 130.

48. Autie to Libbie [December 1870]. This portion comes from GACM.

49. Ibid. This second fragment from the same letter comes from GACM.

50. Ibid. This portion comes from MMP.

51. Ibid.

52. Ibid. The statement from a letter to Mollie (Mary) Holland is quoted by Monaghan, *Custer*, 11.

53. There is no other testimony to support Benteen's allegations, other than Armstrong's letter, which points to grave difficulties in the Custer marriage.

54. See comments on this point in Utley, *Cavalier*, 107. Hattie Mitchell in her letter to Armstrong indicated her regret that she had agreed to write him under a pseudonym and emphasized that he was "a *married* man." Hattie Mitchell to Maj. Gen. G. A. Custer, 29 August 1866, BCWCC. There is also the letter from Anna to Dear Gen., 27 January 1869, BCWCC. Neither letter convicts Armstrong of infidelity, but both raise serious questions.

55. Frederick Benteen to Theodore Goldin, 17 February 1896, Carroll, *Benteen-Goldin Letters*, 262.

56. Autie to Libbie, 24 November 1869, 25 November 1869, BCWCC.

57. Autie to Libbie, 19 December 1870, BCWCC.

58. Howard, *Civil-War Echoes*, 241.

59. Autie to Libbie, 20 December 1870, BCWCC.

60. Autie to Libbie, 27 December 1870, BCWCC.

61. LBJ, 19 October 1863.

62. Chandler, *Of Garry Owen*, 35; Utley, *Cavalier*, 109.

63. Autie to Libbie, 31 March 1871, BCWCC; see also Frost, *Custer's Libbie*, 191.

64. Frank Dibbon and Jarius W. Hall to Drake Brothers, June 1871, BCWCC; Slotkin, *Fatal Environment*, 405; Utley, *Cavalier*, 109. In 1871 the Custers mortgaged the Bacon homestead to Mary A. Smith for $1,500. See Charles, "Bacon House," typescript manuscript, MCHCA.

65. Autie to Libbie, 7 April 1871, 8 April 1871, BCWCC.

66. Autie to Libbie, 8 April 1871, BCWCC.

67. Autie to Libbie, 31 March 1871, 7 April 1871, BCWCC; Autie to Libbie, May 1871, MMP; Autie to Libbie, May 1871, Frost, *Custer's Libbie*, 194; Merington, CS, 238.

68. Autie to Libbie, 7 April 1871, BCWCC; Autie to Libbie, undated, Merington, CS, 232, 234, 235, 236, 237. See also Autie to Libbie, May, 1871, Frost, *Custer's Libbie*, 194.

69. Autie to Libbie, 1871, Merington, CS, 233–35.

70. Ibid.

71. Autie to Libbie, 1871, Merington, CS, 237.

72. Autie to Libbie, 1871, Merington, CS, 238.

73. Ibid.

74. Autie to Libbie, May 1871, Frost, *Custer's Libbie*, 193–94.

75. Ibid.

76. Autie to Libbie, May 1871, Frost, *Custer's Libbie*, 192–93.

77. *Monroe Commercial*, 8 June 1871, cited by Frost, *Custer's Libbie*, 194.

78. Autie to Libbie, 15 July 1871, BCWCC.

79. Autie to Libbie, 1871, Merington, CS, 239.

80. Ibid.

81. Slotkin, *Fatal Environment*, 406.

82. Correspondence from Elizabeth B. Custer to various members of the Stedman family, beginning in the late 1880s and extending into the 1900s, exists in the Sted-

man Manuscript Collection, Butler Library, Columbia University Library, New York. Edmund Clarence Stedman served as Libbie's literary agent as well as her friend. See Elizabeth B. Custer to Edmund Clarence Stedman, 22 January [1900].

83. Autie to Libbie, 1871, Merington, CS, 239. See Slotkin's perceptive reading of this correspondence in *Fatal Environment*, 406.

84. Libbie to Maggie Custer, 1871, Merington, CS, 240–41. Merington calls Maggie "Mrs. Calhoun," but Maggie did not marry until March 1872. See also Theodore Crackel, "Custer's Kentucky: General George Armstrong Custer and Elizabethtown, Kentucky, 1871–1873," *Filson Club Historical Quarterly* 48 (April 1974): 151–52.

85. Libbie to Maggie Custer, 1871, Merington, CS, 240–41.

86. Libbie to Eliza Sabin, 1871, Merington, CS, 241.

87. Frost, *Custer's Libbie*, 197; Tom Custer to Libbie, 1871, Merington, CS, 242–43.

88. George Armstrong Custer [Nomad], *Nomad: George Armstrong Custer in Turf, Field and Farm*, ed. Brian Dippie, 7–12; Slotkin, *Fatal Environment*, 395. See also Dippie's comments, *Nomad*, xiv-xvi.

89. Slotkin *Fatal Environment*, 407.

90. Ibid.; E. B. Custer, *"Boots and Saddles,"* 51–52.

91. Glendolin Damon Wagner, *Old Neutriment*, 105.

92. Ibid., 63–64.

93. Ibid., 49–50.

94. Ibid., 39–42.

95. Manion, "Custer's Cooks and Maids," 170–73; Wagner, *Old Neutriment*, 42–43.

96. Wagner, *Old Neutriment*, 42.

97. Ibid., 64.

98. Autie to Libbie, 10 October 1868, 18 October 1868, 4 November 1868, EBCC, Roll 4. See also Ambrose, "Sidesaddle Soldier," 10.

99. Wagner, *Old Neutriment*, 61–62.

100. Hutton, *Phil Sheridan*, 212–14.

101. Ibid.; telegram from Autie to Libbie, 1 February 1872, BCWCC; Elizabeth B. Custer and John S. Manion, "Custer, Cody and the Grand Duke Alexis," *Research Review: The Journal of the Little Big Horn Associates* 4 (January 1990): 2–14, 31–32. John Manion edited and annotated Libbie's unfinished manuscript. The original is in EBCC, Roll 4, Frames 3242–59, 3265–66, 3287–91 and 3760–3816.

102. Hutton, *Phil Sheridan*, 214–15; Slotkin, *Fatal Environment*, 407–8. The *Scouts of the Plains* came later. Don Russell, *Life and Legend of Buffalo Bill*, 205.

103. Crackel, "Custer's Kentucky," 148–49.

104. Monaghan, *Custer*, 337.

105. E. B. Custer Diary, 5 February 1872, Merington, CS, 246–47; E. B. Custer and Manion, "Custer, Cody and the Grand Duke Alexis," 11–12.

106. Ambrose, *Custer and Crazy Horse*, 319; E. B. Custer Diary, 5 February 1872, Merington, CS, 246–47; E. B. Custer and Manion, "Custer, Cody and the Grand Duke Alexis," 7, 12, 31–32, n. 14.

107. E. B. Custer diary, 5 February 1872, Merington, CS, 246–47; Wagner, *Old Neutriment*, 47–48.

108. Frost, *Custer's Libbie*, 200.

109. Slotkin, *Fatal Environment*, 405.

110. Ibid; Utley, *Cavalier*, 109–10.

111. Monaghan, *Custer*, 338; Frost, *Custer's Libbie*, 239.

112. Libbie to Autie, undated [late November], 1872, EBCC, Roll 1.

113. E. B. Custer, *"Boots and Saddles"*, 5.

CHAPTER 9

1. Edward Lazarus, *Black Hills/White Justice: The Sioux Nation Versus the United States, 1775 to the Present*, 433–49; George Hyde, *Red Cloud's Folk: A History of the Oglala Sioux Indians*, 162–63; Virginia Cole Trenholm, *The Arapahoes, Our People*, 221; Utley, *Cavalier*, 112–14; Robert Utley, *Custer and the Great Controversy: The Origin and Development of a Legend*, 18–19; Stanley Vestal, *Sitting Bull: Champion of the Sioux*, 109–10; Edgar Stewart, *Custer's Luck*, 49–51.

2. Utley, *Cavalier*, 113; Angie Debo, *A History of the Indians of the United States*, 202–203; Stewart, *Custer's Luck*, 49–50.

3. Utley, *Cavalier*, 113; Vestal, *Sitting Bull*, 113–131; Debo, *History of the Indians*, 203.

4. Debo, *History of the Indians*, 203; Lazarus, *Black Hills*, 68; Hyde, *Red Cloud's Folk*, 200; Utley, *Cavalier*, 114.

5. Utley, *Cavalier*, 112–14.

6. E. B. Custer, *"Boots and Saddles"*, 6–9; Charles Larned, quoted by Roger Darling, *Custer's Seventh Cavalry Comes to Dakota: New Discoveries Reveal Custer's Tribulations Enroute to the Yellowstone Expedition*, 62–63, 94.

7. Darling, *Custer's Seventh*, 62; E. B. Custer, *"Boots and Saddles"*, 10–12.

8. Darling, *Custer's Seventh*, 71–72; E. B. Custer, *"Boots and Saddles"*, 12.

9. Darling, *Custer's Seventh*, 73–77; E. B. Custer, *"Boots and Saddles"*, 13–16.

10. Utley, *Cavalier*, 115.

11. E. B. Custer, *"Boots and Saddles"*, 26–35.

12. Ibid., 56–58.

13. Ibid., 60.

14. Ibid.

15. Ibid., 68–69.

16. Ibid., 70–71; Libbie to Autie, July, 1873 Merington, CS, 250.

17. Monaghan, *Custer*, 340–44; Utley, *Cavalier*, 117–18.

18. Autie to Libbie, 26 June 1873, MMP. Edited version, Merington, CS, 248–50.

19. Autie to Libbie, [June 1873], MMP. See an edited portion of this letter, as part of another letter, in Merington, CS, 248.

20. Autie to Libbie, 19 July 1873, MMP. Edited version, Merington, CS, 253–59.

21. Autie to Libbie, 22 July addendum to letter of 19 July 1873, MMP. Edited version, Merington, CS, 259.

22. Autie to Libbie, 22 July 1873, MMP. Edited version, Merington, CS, 258; Utley, *Cavalier*, 118.

23. Autie to Libbie, 27 July 1873, MMP.

24. D. S. Stanley, *Personal Memoirs of Major-General D. S. Stanley, U.S.A.*, 239–40. See also Monaghan, *Custer*, 342–43.

25. Libbie to Autie, July 1873, Merington, CS, 250–51.

26. Libbie to Autie [August 1873], BCWCC.

27. Utley, *Cavalier*, 120–21.

28. Ibid., 122–23.

29. Libbie to Autie, Thursday, [14] August, 1873, BCWCC.

30. Libbie to Autie, August 1873, BCWCC.

31. Libbie to Autie, [26] August 1873, BCWCC.

32. Autie to Libbie, undated letter [August 1873], GACM.

33. Libbie to Autie, [26] August 1873, BCWCC.

34. Libbie to Autie, August 1873, BCWCC.

35. Ibid.

36. Libbie to Autie, August 1873, BCWCC.

37. Ibid.

38. Libbie to Autie, August 1873, BCWCC.

39. Libbie to Autie, August 1873, BCWCC.

40. Libbie to Autie, [September] 1873, BCWCC.

41. Libbie to Autie, August or September 1873, BCWCC.

42. Libbie to Autie, [31] August 1873, BCWCC.

43. Ibid.

44. Libbie to Autie, August or September 1873, BCWCC. Elizabeth used these stanzas in her second book. E. B. Custer, *Tenting*, 486.

45. Don Rickey, *History of Custer Battlefield*, 6–7; Utley, *Cavalier*, 123.

46. George Armstrong Custer to Dear Friend [K. C. Barker], 6 September 1873, MMP.

47. Autie to Libbie, 10 September 1873, MMP.

48. Autie to Libbie, July or August 1873, GACM. Edited version, Merington, CS, 254–59.

49. Autie to Libbie, 10 September 1873, 6 September 1873, MMP.

50. By contrast, see the letters between Captain Benteen and his wife, Catherine, after fifteen years of wedlock. John Carroll, *Camp Talk*, xx–xxii, 102–4, 109–11. Utley notes that Libbie became "surrogate mother and confidant." *Cavalier*, 108. For the comment on the "visibly aged Libbie," see David Nevin, *The Soldiers*, 191.

51. Autie to Libbie, 6 September 1873, MMP.

52. Autie to Libbie, 28 September 1873, MMP.

53. E. B. Custer, *"Boots and Saddles"*, 74.

54. Frost, *Custer's Libbie*, 206.

55. Ibid.; E. B. Custer, *"Boots and Saddles"*, 75–77.

56. E. B. Custer, *"Boots and Saddles"*, 77–78.

57. Ibid. 93–94.

58. Ibid.

59. George Armstrong Custer to Maria Custer, 9 February 1874, Frost, *Custer's Libbie*, 210, n. 45.

60. E. B. Custer, *"Boots and Saddles"*, 93.

61. George Armstrong Custer to Lt. Col. William P. Carlin, 6 February 1874, MMP. Investigation determined that the fire was caused "by combustion of coal gas fumes emitted from the coal-tar paper insulation." See Patricia Jessen, "Fort Abraham Lincoln, Commanding Officer's Residence," 15.

62. Slotkin, *Fatal Environment*, 288.

63. Ibid., 413–14; Utley, *Cavalier*, 125.

64. Thomas Rosser to George Armstrong Custer, 16 February 1874, cited by Slotkin, *Fatal Environmet*, 413–14; *New York Tribune*, 7 February 1874.

65. E. B. Custer, *"Boots and Saddles"*, 104, 182, 181; "Mrs. Maria [Adams] Dutriuelle," *Great Falls Yesterday: Comprising a Collection of Biographies and Reminiscences of Early Settlers*, 377.

66. See photographs from Little Bighorn Battlefield National Monument Collection reproduced in Lawrence A. Frost, *Custer Album: A Pictorial Biography of General George A. Custer*, 144.

67. E. B. Custer, *"Boots and Saddles"*, 118.

68. Katherine Gibson Fougera, *With Custer's Cavalry*, 85.

69. Ibid., 137.

70. Ibid.

71. Ibid.

72. Ibid. See the comments by Myres, "Romance and Reality," 424–26.

73. E. B. Custer, *"Boots and Saddles"*, 130–36.

74. Utley, *Cavalier*, 132–33; Robert W. Frazer, *Forts of the West: Military Forts and Presidios and Posts Commonly Called Forts West of the Mississippi River to 1898*, 90; Hutton, *Phil Sheridan*, 290.

75. Utley, *Cavalier*, 133; Hutton, *Phil Sheridan*, 290–91.

76. Utley, *Cavalier*, 134–35; E. B. Custer, *"Boots and Saddles"*, 150–51.

77. *Chicago Inter-Ocean*, 9 July 1874, cited by Slotkin, *Fatal Environment*, 247. See also E. B. Custer, *"Boots and Saddles"*, 117.

78. Photostatic copy of Policy No. 106.707. Effective date 11 June 1874. Copyright 1960. New York Life Insurance Company, CC, Folder 1, MCHCA.

79. Personnel problems were discussed in Autie to Libbie, 24 October 1868, EBCC, Roll 4 (edited version appears in E. B. Custer, *Guidon*, 13–14). Gossip appears in Autie to Libbie, 26 October 1868, *Custer's Libbie*, 177, and in Autie to Libbie, 5 November 1868, BCWCC.

80. E. B. Custer, *"Boots and Saddles"*, 123–24; Autie to Libbie, 24 October 1868, EBCC, Roll 4. Armstrong's statements about Robert West do not appear in edited version in E. B. Custer, *Guidon*, 13–14. Note that despite hostility between the two, Custer described West as an able Indian fighter in *My Life*, 88.

81. Frederick Benteen to D. F. Barry, 29 March 1897, John M. Carroll, *The D. F. Barry Correspondence at the Custer Battlefield: The Juiciest Ones Being from Capt. Benteen*, 46.

82. E. B. Custer, *"Boots and Saddles"*, 114-15.

83. Utley, *Cavalier*, 135–37; Monaghan, *Custer*, 354.

84. E. B. Custer, *"Boots and Saddles"*, 139–40. See also Riley, *Female Frontier*, 78; Max E. Gerber, "The Custer Expedition of 1874: A New Look," *North Dakota History* 40 (Winter 1973): 9.

85. E. B. Custer, *"Boots and Saddles"*, 152–53.

86. Ibid., 154–55.

87. Dorothy Johnson, *Some Went West*, 120.

88. E. B. Custer, *"Boots and Saddles"*, 156–57.

89. Ibid., 157–58.

90. Autie to Libbie, 15 July 1874, MMP; edited version, Merington, CS, 272–74.

91. Autie to Libbie, 15 July 1874, MMP; Gerber, "Custer Expedition of 1874," 10, n.33.

92. Autie to Libbie, 2 [August] 1874, MMP.

93. Autie to Libbie, 15 August 1874, MMP; edited version, Merington, CS, 274–75; Utley, *Cavalier*, 137. See George B. Grinnell's comments on Custer's boasting. See also John F. Reiger, *The Passing of the Great West: Selected Papers of George Bird Grinnell*, 105.

94. E. B. Custer, *"Boots and Saddles"*, 158–59.

95. John M. Carroll and Lawrence A. Frost, *Private Theodore Ewert's Diary of the Black Hills Expedition of 1874*, 82.

96. *Bismarck Tribune*, 2 September 1874. Slotkin points out the similarities between Custer's Official Report and the Northern Pacific promotional literature. See *Fatal Environment*, 417.

97. Slotkin, *Fatal Environment*, 417; Utley, *Cavalier*, 140.

98. Slotkin, *Fatal Environment*, 418; Utley, *Cavalier*, 141.

99. Slotkin, *Fatal Environment*, 418–19.

100. Frost, *Custer's Libbie*, 214; *Monroe Commercial*, 5 November 1874, cited by Frost, *Custer's Libbie*, 214, 219, n. 33.

101. E. B. Custer, *"Boots and Saddles"*, 169–78.

102. "Mrs. Maria [Adams] Dutriueille," *Great Falls Yesterday*, 377; see also E. B. Custer, *"Boots and Saddles"*, 143; Sandy Barnard, *Shovels and Speculation: Archeology Hunts Custer*, 32–36. By contrast, Col. B. H. Grierson remembered the commanding officer's quarters at Fort Concho in Texas as "an old rat trap." Leckie and Leckie, *Unlikely Warriors*, 252.

103. E. B. Custer, *"Boots and Saddles"*, 144–46.

104. Wagner, *Old Neutriment*, 59.

105. Ibid.

106. E. B. Custer, *"Boots and Saddles"*, 179–80.

107. Ibid. 205–6, 179.

108. Catharine Beecher and Harriet Beecher Stowe's *The American Woman's Home*, 456–57, included suggestions for transforming a parlor into a home church. See also Maxine Van de Wetering, "The Popular Concept of 'Home' in Nineteenth-Century America," *Journal of American Studies* 18 (April 1984): 5–28; Colleen McDannell, *The Christian Home in Victorian America, 1840–1900*, xiii–xvii, 48–51; Louise L. Stevenson, *Victorian Homefront: American Thought and Culture 1860–1880*, 8–11.

109. E. B. Custer, *"Boots and Saddles"*, 192–93, 86. Custer had been ill at Yankton. Moreover, Autie's letter of July 19, 1873, MMP, indicates he suffered upper respiratory infections. Later in her rough drafts on her early marriage, Libbie noted Autie's periods of silence. See "Writings of West Point," EBCC, Roll 5, Frame 5132. See also Frame 5139. Burkman noted Custer's periods of unhappiness in Wagner, *Old Neutriment*, 63–64.

110. Autie to Libbie, 15 July 1874, MMP.

111. E. B. Custer, *"Boots and Saddles"*, 149.

CHAPTER 10

1. Watson Parker, *Gold in the Black Hills*, 63; Utley, *Cavalier*, 142–43. Slotkin, *Fatal Environment*, 419.

2. E. B. Custer, *"Boots and Saddles"*, 201–2.

3. Ibid., 186–87.

4. G. A. Custer, *My Life*, 13.

5. Ibid., 21, 19.

6. Ibid. 22.

7. Ibid., 23.

8. Ibid., 123, 172–81.

9. Utley, *Frontier Regulars*, 190–92.

10. Utley, *Indian Frontier*, 164–65.

11. Robert Utley, "The Celebrated Peace Policy of General Grant," *The American Indian: Past and Present*, 166–68; Utley, *Cavalier*, 152.

12. G. A. Custer, *My Life*, 164–81. Custer's views were common in the army. See Smith, *View from Officers' Row*, 92–112.

13. Utley, *Frontier Regulars*, 112–13. Eastern humanitarians and an occasional army officer, such as Col. Benjamin H. Grierson, saw strict adherence to treaty terms and prompt payment of promised annuities as the solution and supported the peace policy. See Leckie and Leckie, *Unlikely Warriors*, 169, 171, 178–79, 180.

14. James Bennett, Jr., to George Armstrong Custer, 1 April 1875, EBCC, Roll 2.

15. Utley, *Cavalier*, 152; John S. Gray, *Centennial Campaign: The Sioux War of 1876*, 60; John M. Carroll, *A Custer Chrestomathy*, 48–49.

16. Carroll, "Custer: From the Civil War to the Little Big Horn," 3. See also Albert Barnitz to Jennie Barnitz, Utley, *Life in Custer's Cavalry*, 51.

17. Frederick Benteen to Theodore Goldin, 12 February 1896, Carroll, *Benteen-Goldin Letters*, 255–56; Utley, *Cavalier*, 153.

18. Utley, *Cavalier*, 153.

19. Frederick Benteen to Theodore Goldin, 12 February 1896, Carroll, *Benteen-Goldin Letters*, 256. Benteen's source was John Smith. See also Utley, *Cavalier*, 153. Brian Dippie sees Custer's concerns in 1875–76 as those of the "aspiring capitalist." "George Armstrong Custer," 107.

20. J. W. Hall to George A. Custer, 17 April 1875, 3 June 1875, EBCC, Roll 2. See also Slotkin, *Fatal Environment*, 405–6. Slotkin, "'And Then the Mare Will Go!,'" 71.

21. Slotkin, "'And Then the Mare Will Go!,'" 62. See also Slotkin, *Fatal Environment*, 422–23; Utley, *Cavalier*, 154.

22. Slotkin, "'And Then the Mare Will Go!,'" 62, 70.

23. Ibid., 62.

24. *Emil Justh v. Benjamin Holliday* [sic], 7 May 1873, *1906 Decennial Edition of the American Digest: A Complete Table of American Cases from 1658 to 1906*, G-L 23:346.

25. Parker, *Gold in the Black Hills*, 54; John S. Gray, *Centennial Campaign. The Sioux War of 1876*, 20.

26. Utley, *Cavalier*, 143, John Gray, *Custer's Last Campaign: Mitch Boyer and the Little Bighorn Reconstructed*, 123–24.

27. Gray, *Custer's Last Campaign*, 124; Utley, *Cavalier*, 143.

28. Gray, *Centennial Campaign* 60; Earl K. Brigham, "Custer's Meeting with Secretary of War Belknap at Fort Abraham Lincoln," *North Dakota History* 9 (August 1952): 129–30; Edgar I. Stewart, *Custer's Luck*, 127.

29. Brigham, "Custer's Meeting with Secretary of War Belknap," 130–31.

30. Frost, *Custer's Libbie*, 216–17.

31. Autie to Libbie, 3 October 1875, BCWCC.

32. Gray, *Centennial Campaign*, 24–25.

33. Ibid.; Stewart, *Custer's Luck*, 69–70.

34. Stewart, *Custer's Luck*, 69–71; Hutton, *Phil Sheridan*, 299–300. Stewart views the war as culminating from long-standing and unresolved tension between the Grant administration and the nontreaties. Force seemed an easy solution since no one thought the army would meet more than a few hundred warriors.

35. Gray, *Centennial Campaign*, 28; Utley, *Cavalier*, 146.

36. Utley, *Cavalier*, 146; Stewart, *Custer's Luck*, 69; Gray, *Centennial Campaign*, 27–30; Hutton, *Phil Sheridan*, 300.

37. E. B. Custer, *"Boots and Saddles"*, 207–8.

38. Wesley Merritt, 27 December 1875, MMP. Shortly after, Merritt became colo-

nel of the Fifth Cavalry. Alberts, *Brandy Station*, 226.

39. *Justh v. Holliday* [*sic*], 7 May 1883, *1906 American Digest* 23:346–47. The quotation is from Slotkin, *Fatal Environment*, 424.

40. *Justh v. Holliday* [*sic*], 7 May 1883, *1906 American Digest* 23:346–47. See also *Army and Navy Journal*, 21 July 1883; Utley, *Cavalier*, 155.

41. Autie to Tom, January 1876, Merington, CS, 277; J. R. [Poncil] to George Armstrong Custer, 6 February 1876, MMP.

42. E. B. Custer, *"Boots and Saddles"*, 121.

43. Libbie to Tom Custer, December 1875; Autie to Tom Custer, January 1876, Merington, CS, 276–77.

44. Don Rickey, "Myth to Monument: The Establishment of Custer Battlefield National Monument," *Journal of the West* 7 (April 1968): 205.

45. Gray, *Custer's Last Campaign*, 125.

46. Ibid.; Utley, *Cavalier*, 156–57.

47. Utley, *Cavalier*, 157; E. B. Custer, *"Boots and Saddles"*, 210–13.

48. E. B. Custer, *"Boots and Saddles"*, 213–15; Utley, *Cavalier*, 157.

49. Joseph Porter, *Paper Medicine Man: John Gregory Bourke and His American West*, 30–36.

50. Ibid., 36; Utley, *Cavalier*, 157, 170; Stewart, *Custer's Luck*, 96.

51. Utley, *Cavalier*, 158–59; Slotkin, *Fatal Environment*, 425. Belknap's deceased wife, Carrie Belknap, and afterwards her sister, Amanda, the next Mrs. Belknap, had worked out the initial arrangement with Marsh. McFeely, *Grant*, 428–29.

52. Merington, CS, 79; Frost, *Custer's Libbie*, 219.

53. Autie to Libbie, 1 April 1876, MMP. Edited version in Merington, CS, 281–82.

54. Utley, *Cavalier*, 159; Slotkin, *Fatal Environment*, 425–26.

55. Autie to Libbie, 8 April 1876, MMP, typescript and incomplete copy. See also

Merington, CS, 283–84. Some scholars have argued that Democratic leaders, such as James Gordon Bennett, Jr., may have been interested in nominating Custer. See Ambrose, *Crazy Horse and Custer*, 368–69, 373–74; Ambrose "Sidesaddle Soldier," 11. If so, there is no mention of that possibility in the extant correspondence between Libbie and Autie. Moreover, one of Libbie's earlier letters indicated that she believed her husband must first become a "real General" before entering politics. Libbie to Autie, August 1873, BCWCC. See also Utley, *Cavalier*, 164.

56. Autie to Libbie, 10 April 1876, MMP.

57. Ibid. See also Porter, *Paper Medicine Man*, 36.

58. Autie to Libbie, 17 April 1876, Merington, CS, 290. Merington has dropped a portion of the April 10th letter into this letter, but the original is not in MMP.

59. Autie to Libbie, 10 April 1876, MMP.

60. Ibid.

61. Slotkin, *Fatal Environment*, 425. See Carroll, *Custer in the Civil War: His Unfinished Memoirs*.

62. Autie to Libbie, 25 April 1876, Merington, CS, 292.

63. McFeely, *Grant*, 437; Ambrose, *Crazy Horse and Custer*, 369; Utley, *Cavalier*, 160–61.

64. Utley, *Cavalier*, 161; Ambrose, *Crazy Horse and Custer*, 371.

65. Frost, citing the *Monroe Commercial*, 4 May 1876, maintains that Custer left by way of Monroe and stopped overnight to see his parents. When he boarded the train he took with him his relatives, Autie and Emma Reed. See *Custer's Libbie*, 222.

66. General William T. Sherman to Gen. Philip S. Sheridan, 2 May 1876, NA. Quoted by Frost, *Custer's Libbie*, 222. See also Monaghan, *Custer*, 368, 434 n. 23.

67. Utley, *Cavalier*, 162–63; Ambrose, *Crazy Horse and Custer*, 372–73.

68. Utley, *Cavalier*, 163; Ambrose, *Crazy Horse and Custer*, 371–72.

69. Stewart, *Custer's Luck*, 138; Utley, *Cavalier*, 163; Ambrose, *Crazy Horse and Custer*, 373.

70. Undated interview with Elizabeth B. Custer, reprinted in *Monroe Evening News*, 7 April 1933.

71. Ibid.

72. Mary Manley Parmelee, "A Child's Recollections of the Summer of '76," *The Tepee Book* 1 (June 1915): 124–25. Mary Manley's 18 May 1876 letter to *St. Nicholas* appeared in August 1876. She later added commentary as Mrs. Parmelee.

73. E. B. Custer, *"Boots and Saddles"*, 216–17.

74. Ibid., 218.

75. Ibid.

76. Ibid., 218–19; undated E. B. Custer interview, *Monroe Evening News*, 7 April 1933.

77. Undated E. B. Custer interview, *Monroe Evening News*, 7 April 1933.

78. E. B. Custer, *"Boots and Saddles"*, 220.

79. Libbie to Autie, May 1876, Merington, CS, 299–300.

80. E. B. Custer, *Guidon*, 38. On the Red River War, see Leckie, *Military Conquest*, 185–235.

81. Utley, *Cavalier*, 169–70.

82. As Sheridan wrote Sherman on May 29, "I have given no instructions to Generals Crook or Terry, as I think it would be unwise to make any combinations in such country as they will have to operate in. Each column will be able to take care of itself, chastising the Indians should it have the opportunity." Quoted by Utley, *Cavalier*, 169–70.

83. Slotkin, *Fatal Environment*, 429. For a discussion on the army's information on the number of possible hostiles, see Stewart, *Custer's Luck*, 139, 309–12; John Gray, *The Centennial Campaign*, 355–57.

84. Utley, *Cavalier*, 196-97.

85. Stewart, *Custer's Luck*, 139; Slotkin, *Fatal Environment*, 430; Autie to Libbie, 20 May 1876, E. B. Custer, *"Boots and Saddles"*, 266.

86. Autie to Libbie, 30 May 1876, E. B. Custer, *"Boots and Saddles"*, 267–68.

87. Joseph M. Hanson, *The Conquest of the Missouri: Being the Story of the Life and Exploits of Grant Marsh*, 239–41.

88. E. B. Custer, *"Boots and Saddles"*, 221.

89. Ibid., 220. The Seventh was equipped with the single-shot breech loading Springfield of .45/70 caliber, which often jammed when subjected to rapid firing. Larry Koller, *The Fireside Book of Guns*, 111.

90. Fougera, *With Custer's Cavalry*, 250–54, 261.

91. Autie to Libbie, 9 June 1876, E. B. Custer, *"Boots and Saddles"*, 270–71. Terry rebuked Custer for moving ahead. Gray, *Centennial Campaign*, 101.

92. Utley, *Cavalier*, 172. See John Gibbon, "Last Summer's Expedition against the Sioux and Its Great Catastrophe," *American Catholic Quarterly Review*, April 1877, reprinted in *Gibbon on the Sioux Campaign*, 19–20.

93. Utley, *Cavalier*, 172; Autie to Libbie, 11 June 1876, E. B. Custer, *"Boots and Saddles"*, 272.

94. Autie to Libbie, 17 June 1876, E. B. Custer, *"Boots and Saddles"*, 273–74.

95. E. B. Custer, *"Boots and Saddles"*, 221.

96. Libbie to Autie, 21 June 1876, MMP.

97. Ibid.

98. Ibid.

99. For an overview, see Jerome A. Greene, "George Crook," *Soldiers West*, 123–24. A more complete account is found in Porter, *Paper Medicine Man*, 41–46.

100. Libbie to Autie, 21 June 1876, MMP.

101. Ibid.

102. Ibid. See also Slotkin, *Fatal Environment*, 415.

103. Libbie to Autie, 21 June 1876, MMP.

104. Ibid. This is all that is left of this letter in the Merington collection. An edited and enlarged version appears in Merington, CS, 303–304, but the comments regarding the *New York World* are eliminated.

105. This is the remainder of the letter, dated June 21, 1876, which is reprinted in Merington, CS, 304, but which is missing from the MMP letter.

106. Autie to Libbie, 21 June 1876, E. B. Custer, *"Boots and Saddles"*, 274–75; Utley, *Cavalier*, 174.

107. Gibbon, "Last Summer's Expedition against the Sioux," 21–22; Utley, *Cavalier*, 174–75.

108. Utley, *Cavalier*, 175; Gray, *Centennial Campaign*, 147; Gray, *Custer's Last Campaign*, 203.

109. Autie to Libbie, 21 June 1876, E. B. Custer, *"Boots and Saddles"*, 274–75.

110. Ibid.

111. Autie to Libbie, 22 June 1876, Merington, CS, 307–308.

112. Ibid.

113. E. W. Smith, captain, acting assistant adjutant-general to George Armstrong Custer, reprinted in Utley, *Great Controversy*, 23–24. The region was largely unknown, and military authorities used the terms Little Horn and Big Horn instead of Little Bighorn and Bighorn rivers.

114. Utley, *Cavalier*, 175–76. Gray concludes that Terry expected Custer "to strike the village, probably while still unsupported, and from a direction that would drive it northward." Terry's force would act as the block. See *Custer's Last Campaign*, 203.

115. Utley, *Cavalier*, 176.

116. Ibid., 176, 65.

117. Gibbon, "Last Summer's Expedition," 23.

118. Parmelee, "Child's Recollection," 126.

119. Ibid.

120. E. B. Custer, *"Boots and Saddles"*, 221–22; Merington, CS, 321.

121. Merington, CS, 321.

122. Fougera, *With Custer's Cavalry*, 263.

123. Ibid., 264. Parmelee maintained that no one suspected the disaster until word arrived the morning of July 6. See "Child's Recollection," 128–29.

124. Fougera, *With Custer's Cavalry*, 264–65.

125. Hanson, *Conquest of the Missouri*, 312–13; Frost, *Custer's Libbie*, 227.

126. Capt. John McCluskey to Libbie, 2 October 1876, MMP; Merington, CS, 323.

CHAPTER II

1. Brief accounts had surfaced in the *Bozeman Times*, 3 July 1876; *Helena Herald*, 4 July 1876 (evening edition); and the *Salt Lake Tribune*, 5 July 1876. Sheridan and Sherman dismissed the story as unfounded. W. A. Graham, *The Custer Myth: A Source Book of Custeriana*, 349–51; Utley, *Great Controversy*, 34–36; Hutton, *Phil Sheridan*, 315.

2. Recent studies disclose much. See Douglas D. Scott and Richard Fox, with Dick Harmon, *Archaeological Insights in the Custer Battle: An Assessment of the 1984 Field Season*; John Gray's evaluation of Indian testimony, especially Crow scout Curley's; and distance and time analysis in *Custer's Last Campaign*, 333–72.

3. Gray, *Custer's Last Campaign*, 215; Stewart, *Custer's Luck*, 262; Utley, *Cavalier*, 177–78.

4. Gray, *Centennial Campaign*, 166–67; Monaghan, *Custer*, 381. Later, Custer

looked from the Crow's Nest, but haze obscured his vision. Stewart, *Custer's Luck*, 275.

5. Utley, *Cavalier*, 180–81; Gray, *Centennial Campaign*, 163–64.

6. W. A. Graham, *The Story of the Little Big Horn: Custer's Last Fight*, 21–22; Edward S. Godfrey, "Custer's Last Battle," *Century* 43 (January 1892): 368; Utley, *Cavalier*, 181; Gray, *Centennial Campaign*, 170–71.

7. Gray, *Custer's Last Campaign*, 215; Utley, *Cavalier*, 182.

8. Major Reno's testimony, *The Reno Court of Inquiry: The Chicago Times Account*, 212; Stewart, *Custer's Luck*, 326; Gray, *Custer's Last Campaign*, 275.

9. M. A. Reno, "Official Report," *Army and Navy Journal*, 5 August 1876; Gray, *Centennial Campaign*, 287–90; Utley, *Cavalier*, 188.

10. Gray, *Custer's Last Campaign*, 340–46; Gray, *Centennial Campaign*, 176–77.

11. Gray, *Centennial Campaign*, 177; Stewart, *Custer's Luck*, 341. See also W. A. Graham, "The Lost Is Found—Custer's Last Message Comes to Light," Graham, *Custer Myth*, 296–300.

12. Utley, *Cavalier*, 186.

13. Godfrey, "Custer's Last Battle," 372–75; *The Reno Court of Inquiry*, 135–42; Gray, *Custer's Last Campaign*, 319–26.

14. Godfrey, "Custer's Last Battle," 375–77. See especially 375. See also Kenneth Hammer, *Custer in 76: Walter Camp's Notes on the Custer Fight*, 249. Gray, *Centennial Campaign*, 294.

15. Virginia W. Johnson, *The Unregimented General: A Biography of Nelson A. Miles*, 87.

16. *Monroe Commercial*, 10 August 1876; Frost, *Custer's Libbie*, 231–32.

17. Rebecca Richmond to Elizabeth B. Custer, 11 July 1876, Frost, *Custer's Libbie*, 233–34.

18. Ibid.

19. Ibid.

20. Libbie to Marguerite Merington, quoted in *Monroe Evening News*, 25 June 1976.

21. *Monroe Evening News*, 25 June 1976; *Monroe Commercial*, 10 August 1876.

22. Whitman renamed his poem "From Far Dakota's Cañons." See also Slotkin, *Fatal Environment*, 10–11.

23. *New York Times*, 18 July 1876; *Resolution of Condolence of the Legislature of Texas*, 28 July 1876, cited by Brian Dippie, "What Will Congress Do About It: The Congressional Reaction of the Little Bighorn Disaster." *North Dakota History* 37 (Summer 1970): 167.

24. Graham, *Custer Myth*, 279; Utley, *Great Controversy*, 42.

25. Graham, *Custer Myth*, 279; Utley, *Great Controversy*, 42.

26. Utley, *Great Controversy*, 32–36, 42–43.

27. Hutton, *Phil Sheridan*, 318.

28. *New York Times*, 17 July 1876. See also Minnie Dubbs Millbrook, "A Monument to Custer," *Montana The Magazine of Western History* 24 (Spring 1974): 22; Utley, *Great Controversy*, 45–46; John M. Carroll and Byron Price, *Roll Call on the Little Big Horn*, 28 June 1876, 101.

29. Monaghan, *Custer*, 394; Thomas Rosser quoted by Utley, *Great Controversy*, 47. See Reno's response, 20 July 1876, *Army and Navy Journal*, 12 August 1876.

30. *New York Herald*, 16 July 1876; see also Utley, *Great Controversy*, 39–40; Slotkin, *Fatal Environment*, 453–463.

31. Slotkin, *Fatal Environment*, 459–61. Slotkin notes that the *Herald* began using Sitting Bull as a metaphor for "savage" elements in American society on July 9, and he characterizes it as "one of the longest and most elaborately presented stories published by the *Herald* in the whole 1873–76 period."

32. Ibid., 459–60.

33. Ibid., 461–62.

34. Ibid., 462–63. See also 451.

35. Brian Dippie, "What Will Congress Do," 163–64, and "Southern Response to Custer's Last Stand," *Montana The Magazine of Western History* 21 (April 1971): 22–23, 30; Monaghan, *Custer*, 394–95.

36. Rex C. Myers, "Montana Editors and the Custer Battle," *Montana The Magazine of Western History*, 26 (April 1976): 24.

37. *Daily Arkansas Gazette*, 11 July 1876; *Daily State Gazette*, 29 July 1876, quoted by Dippie, "Southern Response," 21.

38. E. B. Custer, *"Boots and Saddles"*, 220; Elizabeth B. Custer to Mrs. (Frances) Kingsley, 6 January [1886], Elizabeth B. Custer Manuscript Collection, Western Americana Collection, Beinecke Rare Book and Manuscript Library, Yale University. Hereafter referred to as EBCM. The Custer letters are often in fragments, and on the microfilm, two letters have been put together incorrectly. Elizabeth dated this letter at the end as January 6, and internal evidence indicates it was written in 1886.

39. William E. Curtis, *Chicago Inter-Ocean*, 9 July 1876, 8 July 1876, cited by Slotkin, *Fatal Environment*, 347, 470–71; "Memorandum of Articles received from Mrs. General Custer for disposal," Frost, *Custer's Libbie*, 231, 234, n. 25.

40. Parmelee, "Child's Recollection," 129.

41. *Monroe Commercial*, 10 August 1876. Roberts was also listed as a herder. See Frost, *Custer's Libbie*, 232.

42. *St. Louis Globe Democrat*, 7 August 1876, cited by D. Alexander Brown, *Year of the Century: 1876*, 178–79.

43. F. Y. Commagere, Toledo *Journal*, 5 August 1876, cited by Frost, *Custer's Libbie*, 232.

44. *Monroe Commercial*, 10 August 1876.

45. Libbie had indicated her desire not to be separated from her "other self," in "Questionnaire dated 3 April 1870, from Topeka, from Frank Mericante, Grand Rapids, Michigan, "typescript copy in Elizabeth B. Custer File, GACC.

46. Libbie to Autie, August or September 1873, BCWCC.

47. Libbie Bacon's Journal, 18 October, 1863, BCWCC.

48. Libbie to Autie, [26] August 1873, BCWCC.

49. *New York Herald*, 7 July 1876.

50. Brian Dippie, "What Will Congress Do?" 166–67.

51. See Bruce Rosenberg, *Custer and the Epic of Defeat*, 157–60, 177–79, for similarities between the Little Bighorn and other last stands. Rhys Isaac speaks of the "mythic story," which is "unconsciously recognizable" and thus strikes a chord. "The Enlightenment and the Problems of Systematizing the Plantation."

52. Brian Dippie, *Custer's Last Stand: The Anatomy of an American Myth*, 7–10. Slotkin, *Fatal Environment*, 3–9.

53. Dippie, *Custer's Last Stand*, 9–10; Slotkin, *Fatal Environment*, 7–9; Autie to Libbie, [August or September] 1873, GACM.

54. Slotkin, *Fatal Environment*, 10–12; Dippie, *Custer's Last Stand*, 9–10. Dippie argues that many concluded that the old values of "sense of duty, love of country, courage, self-sacrificing heroism" were still alive, and he points out how important these were in the "post-Darwinian world."

55. See Dippie's comments on myth in *Custer's Last Stand*, 2; Slotkin, *Fatal Environment*, 13–32.

56. As noted earlier, myth as "wish-related knowledge" is a term used by Isaac, "The Enlightenment and the Problems of Systematizing the Plantation."

57. *Monroe Commercial*, 17 August 1876; *Monroe Evening News*, 25 June 1976.

58. *Monroe Commercial*, 17 August 1876.

59. Ibid., Libbie to Autie, August 1873, BCWCC; Libbie to Autie, 21 June 1876, MMP.

60. *Monroe Commerical*, 17 August 1876. See Libbie's comments on the ideal military wife, buckling on her husband's sword. Custer, *"Boots and Saddles"*, 208.

61. *Monroe Commerciul*, 17 August 1876.

62. Ibid.

63. Ibid.

64. Ibid.

65. *New York Herald*, 2 September 1876.

66. T. E. Howe to Elizabeth B. Custer, 15 January 1877, Frost, *Custer's Libbie*, 238. According to Brice C. W. Custer, his Aunt Elizabeth stated she would "sooner eat corn with the hogs" than take anything from Grant. "Aunt Elizabeth As I Knew Her," typescript essay, 8 February 1968, BCWCC.

67. Emil Justh to Elizabeth B. Custer, 21 September 1876, Frost, *Custer's Libbie*, 239.

68. The Estate of George Armstrong Custer, File No. 2458, Monroe County Probate Court, Monroe, Michigan. The exact amount was $13,291.06. See also *Army and Navy Journal*, 21 July 1883; Frost, *Custer's Libbie*, 239.

69. 15 July 1876, *Congressional Record*, 44 Cong., 1st sess., 15 July 1876, 4627–29, cited by Michael Tate, "Girl He Left Behind: Elizabeth Custer and the Making of a Legend," *Red River Valley Historical Review* 5 (Winter 1980): 9.

70. Elizabeth B. Custer to the Equitable Assurance Company, 18 October 1876, BCWCC.

71. *New York Herald*, 13 July 1876, cited by Millbrook, "Monument," 22.

72. Millbrook, "Monument," 22; *Army and Navy Journal*, 29 July 1876, cited by Edgar Stewart, "The Custer Battle and Widow's Weeds," *Montana The Magazine of Western History* 22 (January 1972): 54; Tate, "Girl He Left Behind," 8.

73. *Army and Navy Journal*, 5 August 1876, 12 August 1876, 26 August 1876, cited by Stewart, "Widow's Weeds," 54–56; Tate, "Girl He Left Behind," 8.

74. *Army and Navy Journal*, 16 September 1876, quoted by Tate, "Girl He Left Behind," 9; Stewart, "Widow's Weeds," 54–55.

75. Stewart, "Widow's Weeds," 56–57; Tate, "Girl He Left Behind," 9. Elizabeth Custer wrote of twenty-six widows in *"Boots and Saddles"*, 222. F. S. Godfrey cited thirty-nine. Graham, *Custer Myth*, 148.

76. Policy No. 106.707, New York Life Insurance Company, CC, Folder 1, MCHCA. Frost believes 5 percent was deducted for wartime risks. *Custer's Libbie*, 236. Elizabeth discharged her mortgage on 26 November 1876. *Monroe Evening News*, 22 July 1965, cited by Charles, "Bacon House," CC, MCHCA.

77. Rhoda Pitts Bacon to Libbie, 13 November 1876, FCC, MCHCA.

78. Albert Johannsen, *The House of Beadle and Adams, and Its Dime and Nickel Novels: The Story of a Vanished Literature* 1:301. Frederick Whittaker, "General George A. Custer," *The Galaxy*, September 1876, 362–371. Whittaker's assesses blame on 370–71.

79. Whittaker, "General George A. Custer," 365–71. See especially 368.

80. Scholars disagree on whether Elizabeth Custer collaborated with Whittaker. Utley views Whittaker's book as "permeated with the influence of Mrs. Custer." *Great Controversy*, 52; Tate in "Girl He Left Behind" argues that the "new material" in Whittaker's biography "bore the unmistakable influence of Mrs. Custer," 11. Frost in *Custer's Libbie*, 237, sees her as too devastated following Armstrong's death. Eliz-

abeth gave Whittaker her husband's correspondence with Lydia Ann Reed, Annette Humphrey, Daniel Bacon, and other miscellaneous material. I interpret this as evidence of collaboration. Frederick Whittaker to Elizabeth B. Custer, 18 November 1876, BCWCC.

81. Rhoda Pitts Bacon to Libbie, 13 November 1876, FCC, MCHCA.

82. Whittaker, *Gen. George A. Custer*, 609–10.

83. Ibid., 606.

84. Ibid., 607–08.

85. Ibid., 608. Frederick Whittaker to Elizabeth B. Custer, 18 November 1876, BCWCC.

86. Utley, *Great Controversy*, 53.

87. Thomas Weir to Elizabeth B. Custer, 11 October 1876, Frost, *Custer's Libbie*, 236.

88. Thomas Weir to Elizabeth B. Custer, 15 November 1876, Frost, *Custer's Libbie*, 236.

89. Robert Newton Price, letter to *Philadelphia Times*, 13 March 1879; W. A. Graham, *The Custer Myth: A Source Book of Custeriana*, 330.

90. Carroll, "From the Civil War to the Big Horn," 7; Mathey, interviewed by Camp, 19 October 1910, CP.

91. Thomas Weir to Elizabeth B. Custer, 15 November 1876, Frost, *Custer's Libbie*, 236; Gray, *Custer's Last Campaign*, 319–26.

92. Frederick Whittaker to Elizabeth B. Custer, 28 November 1876, BCWCC.

93. Frederick Whittaker to Elizabeth B. Custer, 28 November 1876, BCWCC.

94. Mills, *Harvest of Barren Regrets*, 287; Frost, *Custer's Libbie*, 236.

95. Slotkin, *Fatal Environment*, 504–5.

96. Whittaker, *Gen. George A. Custer*, 3, 5–6, 8; Autie to Libbie, 23 April 1876, CS, 291.

97. Whittaker, *Gen. George A. Custer*, 10.

98. Ibid., II, 47; Merington, CS, 46.

99. Whittaker, *Gen. George A. Custer*, 218.

100. *Army and Navy Journal*, 23 December 1876.

101. James Joseph Talbot, "Custer's Last Battle," *Penn Monthly* 8 (September 1877), quoted by Utley, *Great Controversy*, 55–56.

102. Frederick Whittaker to Editor, *Army and Navy Journal*, 6 January 1877.

103. Frederick Whittaker to Elizabeth B. Custer, [January] 1877, BCWCC.

104. Ibid.

105. Whittaker, *George A. Custer*, 4; Wallace, *Custer's Boyhood*, 47.

106. The percentage of women in the paid labor force rose from 9.7 in 1860 to 14.7 in 1880. U.S. Bureau of the Census, *Historical Statistics of the U.S.: Colonial Times to 1970* 1:129–30, 134; Nell Irvin Painter offers a good overview of women's limited choices in this era. *Standing at Armageddon: The United States, 1877–1919*, 235, 242-43.

107. As Sklar notes, by 1888, females made up almost two-thirds of American teachers since Americans viewed the profession as an extension of maternal duties and because women worked for much less than men. *Catharine Beecher*, 180–81. See also Mary Elizabeth Massey, *Bonnet Brigades*, 130.

108. Frank E. Howe, undated. Frost, *Custer's Libbie*, 238. Paulina Wright Davis noted in 1870 that 1,460 females were postmistresses in the United States. Most had been hired since 1868. *A History of the National Woman's Rights Movement for Twenty Years, from 1850 to 1870*, 26.

109. Elizabeth Custer to Frank E. Howe, no date, Frost, *Custer's Libbie*, 238. Cindy Aron notes that women often used the "rhetoric of domesticity" to justify taking such positions. *Ladies and Gentlemen of the Civil Service: Middle-Class Workers in Victorian America*, 61.

110. F. Winans to Elizabeth B. Custer, 22 January 1877, Frost, *Custer's Libbie*, 238; Rebecca Richmond to Libbie, 7 March 1877, FCC, MCHCA. Winans's and Rebecca's attitudes were common even though increasing numbers of middle-class women entered such positions each year. See Aron, *Ladies and Gentlemen*, 185.

111. *Army and Navy Journal*, 10 March 1877; J. G. Barnard to Editor, *Army and Navy Journal*, 23 June 1877; Frederick Whittaker's response, *Army and Navy Journal*, 30 June 1877.

112. Tate, "Girl He Left Behind," 10.

113. Rebecca to Libbie, 5 April 1877, FCC, MCHCA.

114. Ibid.

CHAPTER 12

1. Rebecca Richmond to Libbie, 7 May 1877, Frost, *Custer's Libbie*, 240.

2. W. N. Russell to Libbie, 28 March 1877, BCWCC.

3. Jane E. Schultz, "The Inhospitable Hospital: Gender and Professionalism in Civil War Medicine," *Signs: Journal of Women in Culture and Society* 17 (Winter 1992): 389–91. See also Barbara Melosh, *"The Physician's Hand": Work Culture and Conflict in American Nursing*, 3–4, 29–34; Lori D. Ginzberg, *Women and the Work of Benevolence: Morality, Politics, and Class in the Nineteenth-Century United States*, 193–95.

4. Robert D. Cross, "Louisa Lee Schuyler," *Notable American Women* 3:245. Melosh notes that of 13,000 "practical nurses" in 1880, only 560 had graduated from the new schools. *Physician's Hand*, 30. The census still listed nurses under domestics at the turn of the century. Nancy Woloch, *Women and the American Experience*, 285. See also Massey, *Bonnet Brigades*, 63–64.

5. Woloch, *Women and the American Experience*, 224; Rebecca Richmond to Libbie, 22 April 1877, FCC, MCHCA.

6. Laura Oremieulx to Libbie, 23 May 1877, Frost, *Custer's Libbie*, 241.

7. Madeline Stern, *We the Women: Career Firsts of Nineteenth-Century America*, 273.

8. Madeline Stern, "Candace Thurber Wheeler," *Notable American Women* 3:575; Candace Wheeler, quoted by Stern, *We the Women*, 277–78.

9. Candace Wheeler, *Yesterdays in a Busy Life*, 216–17; Stern, "Candace Thurber Wheeler," *Notable American Women* 3:575. Mrs. David Lane may have been Caroline Lane, identified by Ginzberg in *Women and the Work of Benevolence*, 142. If Caroline Lane was her maiden name, however, Mrs. David Lane was someone else.

10. Wheeler, *Yesterdays*, 216. Other prominent New Yorkers who played a role in the organization were Mrs. Hamilton Fish, Mrs. Louis C. Tiffany, Mrs. A. S. Hewitt, and Mrs. Cyrus W. Field. Stern, *We the Women*, 279.

11. Wheeler, *Yesterdays*, 217–18.

12. Ibid., 218–19.

13. Ibid.

14. Frost, *Custer's Libbie*, 248.

15. Libbie to Gen. John Schofield, undated [late spring or early summer], 1877, EBCC, Roll 1.

16. Maggie to Libbie, 18 June 1877, FCC, MCHCA.

17. Maggie to Libbie, 24 June 1877, FCC, MCHCA.

18. See the photograph by Stanley J. Morrow taken in summer, 1877, and reproduced in Millbrook, "Monument," 21.

19. Fred Dustin, "Some Aftermath of the Little Big Horn Fight in 1876: The Burial of the Dead," in Graham, *The Custer Myth*, 362–67; Don Rickey, Jr., "Myth to Monument: The Establishment of Cus-

ter Battlefield National Monument," *Journal of the West* 7 (April 1968): 210–11.

20. Maj. Joseph G. Tilford to Elizabeth B. Custer, 28 July 1877, Frost, *Custer's Libbie*, 241–42.

21. Michael V. Sheridan to Elizabeth B. Custer, 8 August 1877, Frost, *Custer's Libbie*, 242. See also "Colonel Sheridan's Report," Graham, *The Custer Myth*, 373–75.

22. Elizabeth B. Custer to Michael Sheridan, 18 July 1877, 20 July 1877, 27 July, 1877, Philip H. Sheridan Papers, LC; Millbrook, "Monument," 24.

23. Maggie to Libbie, 11 August 1877, Frost, *Custer's Libbie*, 242; plans for the ceremony were described in *Army and Navy Journal*, 9 June 1877.

24. The Estate of George Armstrong Custer, File No. 2458, Monroe County Probate Court Records, Monroe, Michigan.

25. Ibid., 1 October 1877. See also Frost, *Custer's Libbie*, 239. Emil Justh unsuccessfully petitioned the court on February 1, 1878, to negate the sale of the farm land. He offered at least $1,000 more than Nevin Custer paid. His action is part of the George Armstrong Custer Estate File No. 2458 in Monroe County Probate Court Records.

26. "A Bill for the Relief of Elizabeth B. Custer," H. R. 3120, 45th Cong, 2d sess., 8 February 1878, 2; 22 March 1878, 1990; 25 March 1878, 1993. See also Frost, *Custer's Libbie*, 248.

27. "The Funeral of General Custer," *Harper's Weekly*, 27 October 1877; *New York Times*, 11 October 1877.

28. "The Funeral of General Custer," *Harper's Weekly*, 27 October 1877; *New York Times*, 11 October 1877.

29. Utley, *Indian Frontier*, 184–89; Stanley Vestal, *Sitting Bull: Champion of the Sioux*, 181–207; Angie Debo, *History of the Indians of the United States*, 207–9; Utley, *Frontier Regulars*, 272; Robert Utley, *The Last Days of the Sioux Nation*, 20–23. Other agencies included Crow Creek, Cheyenne River, Lower Brulé, and Standing Rock.

30. Col. Nelson Miles to Elizabeth B. Custer, 16 March 1877, CBNM, Roll 2.

31. Ibid.

32. Nelson Miles, *Serving the Republic: Memoirs of the Civil and Military Life of Nelson A. Miles*, 191.

33. Robert Price to the *Philadelphia Times*, 13 March 1879, reprinted in Graham, *The Custer Myth*, 329–32; Frederick Whittaker to Elizabeth B. Custer, 18 November 1876, 28 November 1876, [January or February], 1877, BCWCC.

34. Frederick Whittaker to Elizabeth B. Custer, 13 June 1878, BCWCC.

35. Ibid. See also Utley, *Great Controversy*, 56–57; *Reno Court of Inquiry*, 5–7.

36. Frederick Whittaker to Elizabeth B. Custer, 13 June 1878, BCWCC.

37. Patricia Stallard, *Glittering Misery: Dependents of the Indian Fighting Army*, 113–17; Mills, *Harvest of Barren Regrets*, 287–91.

38. Monaghan, *Custer*, 399; Utley, *Great Controversy*, 57.

39. *Reno Court of Inquiry*, 1; Utley, *Great Controversy*, 57–58.

40. Monaghan, *Custer*, 399. Reporters were barred from taking notes until the army relented after they devised a relay system based on memorization. Utley, *Great Controversy*, 58.

41. Price, *Philadelphia Times*, 13 March 1879, Graham, *Custer Myth*, 330–31.

42. Ibid.

43. Utley, *Great Controversy*, 59–61. For Godfrey's statement, see *Reno Court of Inquiry*, 184–85. The packers' testimony is on 172–73, 186–87. See also Graham, *Custer Myth*, 331.

44. *Reno Court of Inquiry*, 211–29. Monaghan argues Reno should have known Custer "charged in on the flank." *Custer*, 400.

45. *Reno Court of Inquiry,* 213–15. For the ongoing debate, see Graham, *Custer Myth,* 302–5; Stewart, *Custer Luck,* 364–66.

46. *Reno Court of Inquiry,* 266; Utley, *Great Controversy,* 61; Graham, *Little Big Horn,* 157–58.

47. Frederick Whittaker to *New York Sun,* 26 February 1879, Graham, *Custer Myth,* 326–29; Utley, *Great Controversy,* 61–62. See also Elizabeth B. Custer to Gen. William T. Sherman, [15] October 1882, WTSP, LC.

48. Monaghan, *Custer,* 401.

49. William T. Sherman agreed. Sherman to Libbie, 17 October 1882, BCWCC. During the Civil War, Sherman had refused to intervene when officers complained that nurse Mother (Mary Ann) Bickerdyke ignored regulations. Sherman responded she "ranks me," meaning that when she functioned in her maternal role, she superseded him. Gen. Benjamin Butler responded the same way to similar complaints against Clara Barton. See Ann Douglas Wood, "The War within a War: Women Nurses in the Union Army," *Civil War History* 18 (September 1972): 208–9.

50. Peggy Pascoe notes that female reformers in the West sometimes discovered that their "moral influence" did not necessarily translate into "social power." See *Relations of Rescue: The Search for Female Moral Authority in the American West, 1874–1939,* xvi–xvii.

51. *Monroe Commercial,* 20 July 1876; Millbrook, "Monument," 20–23.

52. Millbrook, "Monument," 25; Frost, *Custer's Libbie,* 250.

53. John Bulkley, *Detroit Post and Tribune,* 1 September 1879, quoted by Millbrook, "Monument," 23.

54. Millbrook, "Monument," 23; on Emmanuel and Dandy, see E. B. Custer, *Guidon,* 336–41.

55. Millbrook, "Monument," 25–26.

56. August Belmont to Elizabeth B. Custer, 3 April 1879, EBCC, Roll 2.

57. John Bulkley to Elizabeth B. Custer, 28 July 1879, EBCC, Roll 2.

58. *New York Times,* 31 August 1879.

59. Ibid.; *Detroit Free Press,* 31 August 1879; Millbrook, "Monument," 27. John Bulkley told Libbie of the embarrassing disruption of the West Point ceremonies in 1910. See E. B. Custer, "Libbie's Personal Recollection," Frost, *Boy General,* 145.

60. *New York Times,* 31 August 1879.

61. Ibid. See Whittaker, *Gen. George A. Custer,* 5.

62. *New York Times,* 31 August 1879; Millbrook, "Monument," 28.

63. *Detroit Free Press,* 31 August 1879.

64. Elizabeth Custer to Vinnie Ream (Hoxie), 29 September 1879, Vinnie Ream Papers, LC. Hereafter referred to as VRP, LC.

65. Ibid.

66. Vinnie Ream (Hoxie) to Elizabeth B. Custer, 5 June 1880, FCC, MCHCA; Elizabeth B. Custer to Vinnie Ream (Hoxie), 15 March [1880], VRP, LC; Millbrook, "Monument," 29; Frost, *Custer's Libbie,* 252.

67. Elizabeth B. Custer to Vinnie Ream (Hoxie), 15 March [1880], VRP, LC.

68. Elizabeth B. Custer to Lawrence Barrett, no date, quoted by Millbrook, "Monument," 29.

69. H.R. 4841, *Congressional Record,* 46th Cong., 2d sess., 1 March 1880, 1231; letter from Elizabeth Bacon Custer to Representative Daggett, *Congressional Record,* 46th Cong., 2d sess., 21 April 1880, 2629; see also Francis Phelps Wiesenburger, *Idol of the West: The Fabulous Career of Rollin Mallory Daggett,* 64–65.

70. *Congressional Record,* 46th Cong., 2d sess., 11 May 1880, 3264. See also Millbrook, "Monument," 29; Tate, "Girl He Left Behind," 14–15. A second bill was introduced in December 1881 but died in

committee. *Congressional Record*, 47th Cong., 1st sess., 16 December 1881, 179. The Rochester and Detroit citizens accused Custer of mistreating Piegan Indians, a nonsensical charge.

71. *New York Herald*, 30 May 1877, cited by Don E. Rickey, "Myth to Monument: The Establishment of Custer Battlefield National Monument," *Journal of the West* 7 (April 1968): 210.

72. Don Rickey, *History of the Custer Battlefield*, 29–30.

73. Sheridan had called for building these forts in unceded territory in 1875. Utley, *Cavalier*, 145, 204.

74. Rickey, *Custer Battlefield*, 46, 51–52. Rickey gives the date as 1888, but Douglas McChristian gives the date as 1886. "In Search of Custer Battlefield," *Montana The Magazine of Western History* 42 (Winter 1992): 76.

75. Rickey, *Custer Battlefield*, 60–63.

76. Ibid., 31; Tate, "Girl He Left Behind," 19–20.

77. Elizabeth B. Custer to Vinnie Ream (Hoxie), 16 September [1881], VRP, LC.

78. Ibid. Libbie never stated who her widowed friend was. She may have been Almira Wells, widow of Rhoda Pitts Bacon's nephew. Mrs. Wells had moved to Paterson, New Jersey, after her husband's death in 1875. See Frost, *Custer's Libbie*, 248.

79. Elizabeth B. Custer to Vinnie Ream (Hoxie), 15 March 1880, 2 January 1882, VRP, LC.

80. Ibid.

81. Ibid; Gordon Hall, *Vinnie Ream*, 123–24, 129–30; Thurman Wilkins, "Vinnie Ream," *Notable American Women* 3:122–23. See the photograph of Vinnie Ream Hoxie's bust in *Cosmopolitan Magazine*, July 1891, 301, in Frost, *Custer's Libbie*, 252.

82. Senate Bill 459 for Relief of Elizabeth B. Custer, 46th Congress., 2d sess.,

12 March 1880, 1496. The bill was "reported adversely" and "indefinitely postponed" after favorable action by the House.

83. Monaghan, *Custer*, 403–4.

84. *New York Herald*, 6 February 1882. It is unlikely that Elizabeth applied "every dollar" of her insurance to Armstrong's debts.

85. *New York Herald*, 8 February 1882.

86. Frost, *Custer's Libbie*, 253.

87. Stallard, *Glittering Misery*, 116–17; Sherman suggested suspension and close confinement on post for one year, along with reduction by "five files" among cavalry majors. Mills, *Harvest of Barren Regrets*, 325–26.

88. Mills, *Harvest of Barren Regrets*, 217–18; Monaghan, *Custer*, 402.

89. Monaghan, *Custer*, 396; John Bulkley to Elizabeth B. Custer, 28 July 1879, EBCC, Roll 2.

90. J. W. Buel, *Heroes of the Plains, or Lives and Wonderful Adventures*, 391. See also Utley, *Great Controversy*, 124. Utley provides an overview of "Branches from the Whittaker Trunk" on pages 155–58. Among these he lists John H. Beadle, *Western Wilds and the Men Who Redeem Them*, 1881; E. G. Cattermole, *Famous Frontiersmen, Pioneers and Scouts*, first published in 1884; and W. F. Cody, *Story of the Wild West and Camp-fire Chats*, 1889.

91. See Harrison Lane, "Brush-Palette and the Little Big Horn," *Montana: The Magazine of Western History* 23 (Summer 1973): 69–70 and Don Russell, *Custer's Last*, 28; Frost, *Custer's Libbie*, 256; Dippie, *Custer's Last Stand*, 49.

92. Elizabeth B. Custer to Mrs. (Frances) Kingsley, 13 February 1886, ECBM.

93. Frederick Whittaker to Elizabeth B. Custer, undated letter [late January or early February 1877], BCWCC.

94. Frederick Whittaker to Elizabeth B. Custer, 31 March 1877, Frost, *Custer's Libbie*, 240.

95. This is what Elizabeth wrote as late as June 1926. She explained that she had written her "little book" only to honor her husband's name. Elizabeth B. Custer to J. A. Shoemaker, 1 June 1926, EBCC, Roll 1.

96. Ibid.

97. *New York Times*, 22 July 1882.

98. Merington, CS, 327.

99. Whittaker, *Complete Life of Gen. George A. Custer*, 214.

CHAPTER 13

1. Merington, CS, 327; Frost, *Custer's Libbie*, 253; Millbrook, "Monument to Custer," 29–30.

2. Elizabeth B. Custer to General William T. Sherman, [15] October 1882, WTSP, LC.

3. Ibid.

4. W. T. Sherman to Mrs. Custer, 17 October 1882, BCWCC.

5. *Justh v. Holliday* [sic] 7 May 1883, *1906 American Digest* 23:346–60. See also *Army and Navy Journal*, 21 July 1883; Slotkin, *Fatal Environment*, 423–24.

6. *Justh v. Holliday* [sic] 23:359; *Army and Navy Journal*, 21 July 1883.

7. *Justh v. Holliday*, [sic] 23:355–56; *Army and Navy Journal*, 21 July 1883.

8. Millbrook, "Monument," 31.

9. Robert Lincoln to Leonard Swett, 24 April 1884, EBCC, Roll 2. See also Frost, *Custer's Libbie*, 254–55.

10. Robert Lincoln to Leonard Swett, 28 November 1884, EBCC, Roll 2; Frost, *Custer's Libbie*, 255; Millbrook, "Monument," 31.

11. Millbrook, "Monument," 29.

12. Elizabeth B. Custer to J. A. Shoemaker, 1 June 1926, EBCC, Roll 1.

13. Elizabeth B. Custer to Mrs. (Frances) Kingsley, 6 January [1886], EBCM.

14. Ibid.

15. Ibid.; *Monroe Commercial*, 20 January 1882; *Monroe Democrat*, 11 September 1884, cited by Frost, *Custer's Libbie*, 256.

16. Frost, *Custer's Libbie*, 256.

17. E. B. Custer, *"Boots and Saddles,"* 4. Elizabeth had expressed herself as always ready to follow her husband when "Boots and Saddles" sounded in 1876. Lizzie Champney, "Custer's Family in Camp," *Army and Navy Journal*, 16 September 1876.

18. E. B. Custer, *"Boots and Saddles"*, 4–5.

19. Ibid., 86.

20. Ibid., 81–82, 97–99, 113–15, 122–25.

21. Ibid., 75–76, 77–78, 101–2.

22. Ibid., 186–89, 220–21.

23. Ibid., xxix; Libbie Bacon's Journal, 25 June 1862, 15 June 1863, BCWCC.

24. See, for example, Howard, *Sketches and State Secrets*, 241; W. Curtis, *Chicago Inter-Ocean*, 9 July 1874; Champney, *Army and Navy Journal*, 16 September 1876.

25. Unidentified and undated clipping from *"Boots and Saddles"* Scrapbook, Box 7, CC, MCHCA. Hereafter referred to as BSS, Box 7, CC, MCHCA.

26. On page 35 of *"Boots and Saddles"*, Libbie used a march to emphasize the growth of her character as she learned not to complain. See also the description of her devotion to her sick husband in the chapter entitled "The Blizzard." For examples of officers' consideration for their wives, see pages 95, 101–106. Regarding the "separate . . . world" of the frontier, in her preface, Elizabeth wrote: "Our life, therefore, was often as separate from the rest of the world as if we had been living on an island in the ocean." See page xxix.

27. Teresa G. Viele, *"Following the Drum": A Glimpse of Frontier Life*; Margaret Carrington, *Ab-sa-ra-ka: Home of the Crows, Being the Experiences of an Officer's Wife on the Plains*.

28. E. B. Custer, *"Boots and Saddles,"* 101–6. See also Elizabeth's comments on page 180 on the officers' appreciation of any skill or talent their wives possessed.

29. Ibid., 109, 196–97.

30. See Elizabeth's description of Running Antelope's visit. The chief was of "lordly mein" but lacked table manners. *"Boots and Saddles"*, 186–88.

31. E. B. Custer, *"Boots and Saddles,"* 190–92, 181–82.

32. *Boston Gazette*, 4 April 1855; *San Francisco Bulletin*, April 1885, BSS, Box 7, CC, MCHCA.

33. *New York Independent*, 7 May 1885, BSS, Box 7, CC, MCHCA.

34. *The Nation*, 30 April 1885, BSS, Box 7, CC, MCHCA.

35. London *Academy*, 16 May 1885, BSS, Box 7, CC, MCHCA.

36. Unidentified newspaper clipping with no date, BSS, Box 7, CC, MCHCA.

37. *Philadelphia Inquirer*, 10 April 1885, BSS, Box 7, CC, MCHCA.

38. Herbert W. Smith, "Jeannette Gilder," *Notable American Women* 1:33; untitled newspaper review (The Critic?), BSS, Box 7, CC, MCHCA.

39. Untitled newspaper review, (*The Critic?*) 30 April 1885, BSS, Box 7, CC, MCHCA.

40. Smith, "Jeannette Gilder," *Notable American Women* 2:33. See collection of letters from Elizabeth Custer to Mrs. Andrew Carnegie, from 1890 to about 1910, in Carnegie Autograph Collection, NYPL. Hereafter referred to as CAC.

41. Gilder's conformist views endeared him to the powerful according to Burton Raffel. *Politicians, Poets, and Con Men: Emotional History in Late Victorian America*, 116–20.

42. Elizabeth B. Custer to R. W. Gilder, 22 October 1890, R. W. Gilder Papers, Astor, Tilden, and Lenox Foundation, NYPL.

43. See the scrapbook of newspaper clippings in Box 7, CC, MCHCA. Most of these clippings do not indicate the newspaper, and often the year must be derived from internal evidence. The majority were written in 1885–86. Hereafter referred to as NS, Box 7, CC, MCHCA.

44. Unidentified newspaper clipping, dated 13 August 1885, NS, Box 7, CC, MCHCA.

45. Unidentified newspaper clipping, dated 19 September [1885], NS, Box 7, CC, MCHCA.

46. Ibid.

47. Ibid.; Dena J. Epstein, "Jeannette Meyers Thurber," *Notable American Women* 3:458–59. Jeannette Thurber brought Anton Dvořák to the United States as head of the National Conservatory of Music between 1892 and 1895.

48. *Monroe Commercial*, 4 August 1882, had noted Maggie's engagement to Captain Baker.

49. Frost, *Custer's Libbie*, 259.

50. Elizabeth B. Custer, "Office Seeking As It Is," *Chicago Tribune*, 15 November 1885.

51. Ibid.

52. Ibid.

53. Ibid.

54. *Detroit Tribune*, 21 November 1885.

55. Ibid. Elizabeth received 10 percent of the sales after the first 500 copies and thus, in her first year, made $217.50. See Archives of Harper & Brothers, 1817–1914, Reel No. 2, Contract Books 5:17, Butler Library, Columbia University Library. Hereafter referred to as BLCU.

56. *Detroit Tribune*, 21 November 1885.

57. *Monroe Evening News*, 5 April 1933; Beth Charles, "The Bacon House," CC, MCHCA.

58. "Mrs. Custer's Letter," *Worcester Sunday Telegram*, 29 November 1885, uni-

dentified newspaper articles written by Elizabeth B. Custer, dated 30 November 1885, 26 December 1885, NS, Box 7, CC, MCHCA; "Mrs. Custer's Letter," *Worcester Sunday Telegram*, 20 December 1885.

59. Unidentified newspaper article written by Elizabeth B. Custer, 17 December 1885, NS, Box 7, CC, MCHCA; "Mrs. Custer's Letter," *Worcester Sunday Telegram*, 20 December 1885.

60. Elizabeth B. Custer, "Up in the Cock Lift," written 17 December 1885, unidentified newspaper, NS, Box 7, CC, MCHCA.

61. Painter, *Standing at Armageddon*, 36–53. Painter cites Ida Tarbell's statement, "The eighties dripped with blood," on page 72. By 1890, 80 percent of New York City's population was foreign born or the children of foreign born. See U.S. Bureau of the Census, *Eleventh Census 1890*, vol. 1, pt. 1, 17.

62. "Mrs. Custer's Letter," *Worcester Sunday Telegram*, 3 January 1886; Elizabeth B. Custer, "In Darkest London. Mrs. Gen. Custer Visits the Whitechapel District," [*New York World*], [1888], undated, NS, Box 7, CC, MCHCA.

63. Clifford E. Clark, Jr., *Henry Ward Beecher: Spokesman for a Middle-Class America*, 275.

64. Ibid., 275; "Mrs. Custer's Letter," *Worcester Sunday Telegram*, 27 December 1885.

65. "Mrs. Custer's Letter," *Worcester Sunday Telegram*, 27 December 1885.

66. Elizabeth B. Custer to Mrs. (Frances) Kingsley, 6 January [1886], EBCM; Larry Uffelman, *Charles Kingsley*, 16.

67. Una Pope-Hennessy, *Canon: Charles Kingsley: A Biography*, 137–45, 286–87; Elspeth Huxley, *The Kingsleys: A Biographical Anthology*, 76–77.

68. Walter Houghton notes Kingsley's work in this area and cites especially *The*

Heroes; or, Greek Fairy Tales for My Children, published in 1856. Houghton observes that in telling his wife to look for God in "His dealings in History" and "in all good men—great good men," Kingsley "might just as well have written, 'His dealings in myth'" and "His image in legendary heroes." *Victorian Frame of Mind*, 315.

69. The work was published in London by Henry J. King & Company.

70. Elizabeth B. Custer to Mrs. (Frances) Kingsley, 6 January [1886], EBCM. Again, as noted earlier, two letters on microfilm have been pieced together incorrectly. On microfilm, the letter, dated at the end, January 6, was attached to another letter. I have rearranged the two letters correctly.

71. Ibid.

72. Ibid.

73. For information on the New York Infirmary, see Dorothy Clarke Wilson, *Lone Woman: The Story of Elizabeth Blackwell, the First Woman Doctor*, 397–98, 415–18.

74. Elizabeth B. Custer to Mrs. (Frances) Kingsley, 6 January [1886], ECBM.

75. Ibid.

76. Elizabeth Custer to Mrs. (Frances) Kingsley, 13 February 1886, EBCM.

77. Ibid.

78. *Monroe Democrat*, 12 August 1886; *Tecumseh News*, 19 August 1886.

79. The Indian's name was probably "Yellow Hair," and the place more correctly, Hat Creek, near present-day Montrose, Nebraska. Russell, *Buffalo Bill*, 214–15; Paul L. Hedren, *First Scalp for Custer: The Skirmish at Warbonnet Creek, Nebraska, July 17, 1876*, 34.

80. Johannsen, *The House of Beadle and Adams 1:4*; Don Russell, *The Wild West, or A History of the Wild West Shows*, 22; Shirl Kasper, *Annie Oakley*, 35–40.

81. Vestal, *Sitting Bull*, 231–34, 250–51; Kasper, *Annie Oakley*, 25; Russell, *Buffalo Bill*, 316–17.

82. Russell, *Buffalo Bill*, 322–23; Russell, *Wild West*, 22; Sarah J. Blackstone, *Buckskins, Bullets, and Business: A History of Buffalo Bill's Wild West*, 19–20.

83. Tate, "Girl He Left Behind," 16–17.

84. Russell, *Buffalo Bill*, 332–33; W.[illiam] F. Cody to Mrs. Geo. A. Custer, 13 August 1886, BCWCC.

85. E. B. Custer, *Tenting*, 46.

86. Walter Havinghurst, *Annie Oakley of the Wild West*, 98. For Sitting Bull's 1877 comments on Custer, which were "told to me," see *New York Herald*, 16 November 1877, Graham, *Custer Myth*, 73.

87. E. B. Custer, *Tenting*, 44–46.

88. Ibid., 47.

89. Jane Stewart, "Introduction," University of Oklahoma Press reprint of *Tenting on the Plains*, x. For information on Charles Webster and Company, see Justin Kaplan, *Mr. Clemens and Mark Twain*, 289–92. The British firm may have been the contact given Elizabeth by Fanny Kingsley. Elizabeth B. Custer to Mrs. (Frances) Kingsley, 13 February 1886, EBCM.

90. Custer, *Tenting*, 42.

91. Ibid.

92. Ibid.

93. Ibid., 44.

94. Ibid., 45.

95. Ibid., 47–48.

96. See Cogley, *History of the Seventh Indiana Cavalry Volunteers* (1876); Nathaniel B. Baker, *Report of the Adjutant General to the Honorable William M. Stone, Governor of Iowa* (1867), Carroll, *Custer in Texas*, 93–96. Marguerite Merington's inclusion of responses to these reports indicates that the charges volunteer soldiers leveled against her husband disturbed Elizabeth. See Merington, CS, 172–74.

97. E. B. Custer, *Tenting*, 93–112.

98. Ibid., 670–75, 696–702.

99. *The Critic*, 19 May 1888, *Tenting on the Plains* Scrapbook, Box 7, CC, MCHCA. Hereafter referred to as TPS, Box 7, CC, MCHCA.

100. *The Critic*, 19 May 1888; *Chicago Dial*, May 1888, TPS, Box 7, CC, MCHCA.

101. E. B. Custer, *Tenting*, 1–3, 387; London *Saturday Review*, 16 June 1888, Box 7, CC, MCHCA.

102. London *Saturday Review*, 16 June 1888, Box 7, CC, MCHCA; Jane Stewart, "Introduction," *Tenting*, x.

103. Libbie to Vinnie Ream (Hoxie), 5 June 1888, VRP, LC.

104. E. B. Custer, "In Darkest London," [New York] *World*, [1888], undated and untitled newspaper report, Box 7, CC, MCHCA.

105. Ibid.

106. Elizabeth B. Custer to Mrs. (Frances) Kingsley, 7 September 1889, EBCM.

107. Hutton, *Phil Sheridan*, 370–72; B. J. D. Irwin to Elizabeth B. Custer, 4 June 1887; Edward R. Wright to Elizabeth B. Custer, 30 April 1888, EBCC, Roll 2; Elizabeth B. Custer to Gen. (Edward R.) Wright, 13 May 1888, ECBM. Some newspaper articles in the BCWCC were sent to Libbie by Henry Romeike's Bureau of Press Cuttings at 110 Fifth Ave., New York. He advertised himself as "inventor of this System."

108. William T. Sherman to Elizabeth B. Custer, 24 January 1889, EBCC, Roll 3.

109. Ibid.

110. Ibid.

111. Elizabeth B. Custer to Proprietors of the Boston Cyclorama Co., 25 January 1889, in "Cyclorama of Gen. Custer's Last Fight Against Sioux Indians," EBCC, Roll 7. E. Pierpont and staff completed the painting. Russell, *Custer's Last Stand*, 37.

112. Utley, *Great Controversy*, 63–64.

113. Ibid.; 64 Johannsen, *House of Beadle and Adams* 1:301–302.

114. Utley notes Elizabeth's persuasiveness in spreading her views, *Great Controversy*, 122–23. Millbrook states, "Of all the image makers, she turned out to be the most successful." "Monument," 23.

115. Lane, "Brush-Palette and the Little Big Horn," 71.

116. Elizabeth did note on page 21 that arrests and court-martials were commonplace and did not carry the same significance as civilian arrests and trials. For Elizabeth's editing of letters, see, for example, Autie to Libbie, 24 October 1868, 28 October 1868, 4 November 1868, 9 November 1868, 22 November 1868 in EBCC, Roll 4. These should be compared to Elizabeth's versions in *Guidon*, 13–17. Elizabeth deleted, among other materials, most of the comments concerning Armstrong's feud with Captain West. Armstrong's letter, 19 December 1868, EBCC, Roll 4, contains the estimate of 133 warriors killed. Libbie's edited version in *Guidon*, page 46, excludes that comment and other material.

117. For references to Indian atrocities against white women, see E. B. Custer, *Guidon*, 2, 58–62. Quotation is on page 60. Riley discusses the fascination captivity narratives held for Americans for two centuries in *Women and Indians*, 17–19. See also, Riley, *Female Frontier*, 9–10.

118. E. B. Custer, *Guidon*. For descriptions of officers as "lovers," see pages 67–68, 187–90. Descriptions of the role and status of Indian women are found on 85–88, 91–93.

119. Ibid., 187–88. Ralph K. Andrist calls Elizabeth's writing here "purest moonshine." *The Long Death: The Last Days of the Plains Indians*, 178–79.

120. Custer, *My Life*, 350–51, 359, 365–66; E. B. Custer, *Guidon*, 91, 95–97, 110. See also Slotkin, *Fatal Environment*, 101.

121. E. B. Custer, *Guidon*, 179–80.

122. Ibid., 180.

123. Ibid., 153–54.

124. Ibid., 161–62.

125. Ibid., 162–65. See also Dippie, *Custer's Last Stand*, 103–104.

126. Elizabeth B. Custer to Mrs. (Frances) Kingsley, 7 September 1889, ECBM.

127. Ibid.

128. Ibid.

129. Ibid. *Homemaker Magazine* published "To the Victor Belongs the Spoils" in installments in January 1890, 277–87; February 1890, 375–81; March 1890, 160–64; April 1890, 30–34.

130. Elizabeth B. Custer to Redpath Lyceum Bureau, 10 August 1890, Lisle Reedstrom Collection, cited by Frost, *Custer's Libbie*, 264.

131. Ibid. As a touring lecturer, Elizabeth harbored concerns about remaining "womanly" and not being mistaken for a "platform woman." Elizabeth B. Custer, journal beginning 10 May 1892 and ending 7 June [1893], Box 7, CC, MCHCA. [20 October 1893], 82, [10 October 1892], 26. Elizabeth made her entries in this journal out of sequence in several places. Since journal pages are numbered, I have included the page numbers as well as the actual or probable date. Hereafter referred to as EBCJ, 1892-[93].

CHAPTER 14

1. Elizabeth B. Custer Journal, 1890, 16 July 1890, Box 7, CC, MCHCA. Hereafter referred to as EBCJ, 1890.

2. Ibid.

3. Elizabeth B. Custer, "An Out of the Way 'Outing,'" *Harper's Weekly*, 18 July 1891, 534–35; *New York Mail and Express*, 9 October 1890; *Chicago Tribune*, 7 October 1890; *New York Star*, 15 October 1890, cited

by Rickey, *History of Custer Battlefield*, 40, 137, n. 74.

4. Custer, "An Out of the Way 'Outing,'" 534.

5. D. F. Barry to Elizabeth B. Custer, 15 July 1890, EBCC, Roll 1; E. B. Custer, *"Boots and Saddles"*, 169–78. Quotation is on 178.

6. Both Benteen and Dr. H. P. Porter examined Tom's body. Utley, *Great Controversy*, 127–29. See also Kill Eagle's statement. Graham, *Custer Myth*, 55.

7. D. F. Barry to Elizabeth B. Custer, 15 July 1890, EBCC, Roll 1. John Greenleaf Whittier had campaigned unsuccessfully for Rain-in-the-Face's admittance to Hampton Industrial School through a poem, "On the Big Horn." *Atlantic Monthly*, April 1887, 433. In 1894, plied with liquor, Rain-in-the-Face told reporters that he had in fact cut out Tom Custer's heart. Utley, *Great Controversy*, 129; Hutton, "Little Bighorn to Little Big Man," 26.

8. Elizabeth B. Custer to C. C. Buel, 13 November 1890, Century Company Papers, NYPL, Astor, Lenox and Tilden Foundations, NYPL. Hereafter referred to as CCP.

9. Charles King to Elizabeth B. Custer, 1 July 1888, BCWCC.

10. Charles King, "Custer's Last Battle," *Harper's New Monthly Magazine*, August 1890, 381–82.

11. Elizabeth B. Custer to C. C. Buel, 13 November, 1890, CCP. W. A. Graham presents excerpts from important Sioux testimony in *The Custer Myth: A Source Book of Custeriana*, 45–100. The Cheyennes had not given their testimony in 1890.

12. Godfrey, "Custer's Last Battle," 383–84.

13. Elizabeth B. Custer to C. C. Buel, 13 November 1890, CCP.

14. Theodore Roosevelt to Elizabeth B. Custer, 22 August 1890, BCWCC.

15. Unidentified and undated newspaper clipping on Elizabeth B. Custer's Pension, BCWCC. See also "Elizabeth B. Custer." Report No. 3328 to Accompany H.R. 12242, 51st Cong., 2d sess, 20 December 1890, 1–4, BCWCC; Frost, *Custer's Libbie*, 267.

16. Robert M. Utley, *Last Days of the Sioux Nation*, 40–83; Debo, *Indians of the United States*, 242–43; Utley, *Indian Frontier*, 227–51.

17. Utley, *Sioux Nation*, 84–145.

18. Ibid., 145–66; James McLaughlin, *My Friend the Indian*, 201–21; Utley, *Indian Frontier*, 255; Vestal, *Sitting Bull*, 300–301.

19. Utley, *Sioux Nation*, 200–28.

20. Ibid., 217–18, 223–24.

21. Ibid., 238–41; Utley, *Indian Frontier*, 257–61.

22. G. A. Custer, *My Life*, 22–23.

23. Utley, *Sioux Nation*, 229–30; Utley, *Life in Custer's Cavalry*, 261.

24. EBCJ, 1890, 23 February 1890; Libbie to C. C. Buel, 28 November 1890, 26 February 1891, CCP; *Battles and Leaders* 1:x.

25. Elizabeth B. Custer to C. C. Buel, 22 April 1891, CCP; James Grant Wilson, "Two Modern Knight Errants," *Cosmopolitan Magazine*, July 1891, 302; Utley, *Great Controversy*, 64–65. See also James Fry, "Comments by General Fry on Godfrey's Narrative," *Century Magazine* 43 (January 1892): 386.

26. Elizabeth B. Custer to C. C. Buel, 22 April 1891, 27 April 1891, CCP.

27. Elizabeth B. Custer to Mrs. (Louise) Carnegie, 15 June [1891], 16 June [1891], 8 July [1891], Carnegie Autograph Collection, NYPL, Astor, Lenox and Tilden Foundations. Hereafter cited as CAC. For information on Carnegie's Cluny, see Burton J. Hendrick, *The Life of Andrew Carnegie* 1:314–29.

28. Elizabeth B. Custer to C. C. Buel, 21 October 1891, 23 October 1891, CCP.

29. Godfrey, "Custer's Last Battle," 373.

30. Elizabeth B. Custer to C. C. Buel, Thanksgiving Day, 1891, CCP.

31. Fry, "Comments," 386–87.

32. Ibid., 385–87.

33. Ibid.; *Monroe Commercial*, 10 August 1876.

34. Henry Carrington to T. T. Munger, 12 January 1892, reprinted in *Boston Daily Traveller*, 15 January 1892.

35. Robert P. Hughes, "The Campaign Against the Sioux in 1876," *Journal of the Military Service Institution of the United States* 79 (January 1896): 1–44. Reprinted as appendix in Graham, *Little Big Horn*. See 1-2.

36. Charles King to Elizabeth B. Custer, 7 January 1892, CBNM, Roll 1. In 1893 Lippincott published *A Soldier's Secret: A Story of the Sioux War of 1890; and An Army Portia. Two Novels.*

37. EBCJ, 1892–[93]. Elizabeth B. Custer to Mrs. (Louise) Carnegie, 27 November 1891, CAC.

38. *New York Sun*, 30 January 1892.

39. Elizabeth B. Custer to Mrs. (Louise) Carnegie, 27 November 1891, CAC; Frost, *Custer's Libbie*, 283.

40. Kenneth T. Jackson, *Crabgrass Frontier: The Suburbanization of the United States*, 95–96.

41. At some point Elizabeth also lived at 20 Park Avenue in Bronxville. Frost, *Custer's Libbie*, 283–84.

42. Elizabeth B. Custer to Mrs. (Louise) Carnegie, 27 November 1891, CAC; EBCJ, 1892-[93], [10] May 1892, 5.

43. *New York Sun*, 30 January 1892.

44. EBCJ, 1892-[93], 11 March [1893], 81.

45. *New York Sun*, 30 January 1892.

46. EBCJ, 1892-[93], [20 December 1892], 41–42.

47. Ibid., 16 January [1893], 50.

48. Ibid., 21 November [1892], 29, 19 February [1893], 62, 29 October [1892], 20.

49. Ibid., 29 October [1892], 21–22; *New York Sun*, 30 January 1892.

50. EBCJ, 1892-[93], 22 February [1893], 64–65.

51. Ibid., 21 November [1892], 29–30, 6 May [1893], 79, 10 May 1892, 4, 4 April [1893], 83–84.

52. Ibid., 15 October [1892], 13, 20 May 1892, 8.

53. Ibid., 9 May 1892, 3–4.

54. Albert Barnitz, "Remarks of Introduction," 3 June 1892, Frost, *Custer's Libbie*, 276. See Barnitz's disillusioned comments on Custer in Utley, *Life in Custer's Cavalry*, 46, 50–53, 92, 205.

55. EBCJ, 1892-[93], 19 February [1893], 61, 24 February [1893], 68–69.

56. Ibid., [7] November [1892], 26, 23 February [1893], 17, 21 November [1892], 28.

57. Ibid. 16 February [1892], 10–11, 9 May 1892, 2–3, [20 April 1893], 94, 29 October [1892], 21, [15 November 1892], 28.

58. Elizabeth still toured, as manuscript notes at the EBCC indicate. In February 1896, she spoke at Wellesley College. See Roll 5, Frame 4241.

59. Frost, *Custer's Libbie*, 283–84.

60. Stern, *We the Women*, 301.

61. Frost, *Custer's Libbie* 279; Clara Barrus, *The Life and Letters of John Burroughs* 1:10, 294, 304, 106.

62. Lewis P. Simpson, "Ruth McEnery Stuart," *Notable American Women* 3:407–8; Henry Steele Commanger, "Mary Elizabeth Mapes Dodge," *Notable American Women* 1:495–96.

63. Wheeler, *Yesterdays in a Busy Life*, 422.

64. Steven Chalmers, *The Penny Piper of Saranac*, 41.

65. Ibid., 42–46.

66. *Monroe Evening News*, 11 February 1950, cited by Frost, *Custer's Libbie*, 279. Dodd, Mead & Company compiled Merington's plays into two volumes entitled

Holiday Plays and *Festival Plays. Monroe Evening News*, 14 March 1942.

67. Stern, "Candace Wheeler," *Notable American Women* 3:576; *Chicago Times-Herald*, 7 August 1898.

68. Robert Underwood Johnson, *Remembered Yesterdays*, 398.

69. E. Benjamin Andrews, "A History of the Last Quarter-Century in the United States," *Scribner's Magazine*, June 1895, 732–33, cited by Utley, *Great Controversy*, 68.

70. Hughes, "Campaign against the Sioux," 2.

71. Ibid., 38–42. Quotation is on 42.

72. Ibid., 16–18, 22–27.

73. Ibid., 43, 14, 32.

74. E. Benjamin Andrews, *The History of the Last Quarter-Century of the United States, 1870–1895* 1:191.

75. Utley, "Nelson A. Miles," *Soldiers West*, 225; Miles, *Personal Recollections*, 198–99.

76. Miles, *Personal Recollections*, 204–205.

77. Ella Wilcox, *Custer and Other Poems*, 93–134.

78. Graham dismissed Curley's testimony because his interpreter stated he had disguised himself in a blanket, a statement Graham found absurd Utley, *Great Controversy*, 137–38. While historians in the past discounted his testimony, a more recent study concludes Curley's account was more accurate than originally perceived. See Gray, *Custer's Last Campaign*, 374–82.

79. Whittaker, *Life of General Custer*, 599–600.

80. Ella Wilcox, *Custer and Other Poems*, 133–34.

81. J. M. Lee to Elizabeth B. Custer, 27 June 1897, EBCC, Roll 3.

82. "Mrs. Custer's Letter: Quoting an Unnamed Officer's Reply to Col. R. P. Hughes' Charge that Custer Had Disobeyed Orders," Elizabeth B. Custer to Dear Sir, 21 June 1897, MMP, hereafter cited as "Mrs. Custer's Letter."

83. Graham, *Custer Myth*, 155–56. See also "Additional Notes By Colonel Godfrey," in Appendix, Cyrus T. Brady, *Indian Fights and Fighters*, 377–78. Given the friendship between Godfrey and Elizabeth, she undoubtedly knew about Brisbin's statement soon after Godfrey received the letter in 1892.

84. "Mrs. Custer's Letter."

85. Ibid.

86. "'Where the Heart Is': A Sketch of Woman's Life on the Frontier," *Lippincott Magazine*, February 1900, 305–12; "Home-Making in the American Army," *Harper's Bazaar*, 22 September 1900, 1309–13; "The Kid," *St. Nicholas*, September 1900, 964–79.

87. E. B. Custer, "The Kid," 964–65.

88. Ibid., 965–79.

89. Mary E. Burt, *The Boy General: Story of the Life of Major-General George A. Custer*, as told by Elizabeth B. Custer; Barrus, *John Burroughs* 1:294.

90. "Opinions of the Press on *The Boy General*," advertising pamphlet put out by Scribner Series of School Reading, BCWCC.

91. Ibid.

92. William H. Mace, *A School History of the United States*, 425–26.

93. George A. Weston to Libbie, 15 May 1902, EBCC, Roll 3; "The Custer Mining and Realty Company," EBCC, Roll 7; Weston and Company Investment Securities, "Report on the Custer Mining and Realty Company," EBCC, Roll 7; Perry Eberhart, *Guide to Colorado Ghost Towns and Mining Camps*, 439–40.

94. Eberhart, *Guide*, 449; *Pueblo Chieftain*, 11 June 1902.

95. Frost, *Custer's Libbie*, 285–86. Tate believes that Elizabeth did not want to be involved in any activity that brought dis-

honor to her husband's name. "Girl He Left Behind," 18.

96. Eberhart, *Guide*, 449; Robert Brown, *Ghost Towns of the Colorado Rockies*, 116–17; Frost, *Custer's Libbie*, 285–86.

97. The painting is located at the Thomas Gilcrease Institute of American History and Art, Tulsa, Oklahoma. William H. Goetzmann and William N. Goetzmann, *West of the Imagination*, 214; Paul Hutton, *Phil Sheridan*, 86.

98. *New York Herald*, 19 April 1903; James D. Horan, *The Life and Art of Charles Schreyvogel: Painter-Historian of the Indian-Fighting Army of the American West*, 35–36.

99. *New York Herald*, 28 April 1903; Horan, *Schreyvogel*, 36.

100. Elizabeth B. Custer to Charles Schreyvogel, 24 April 1903, *New York Herald*, 30 April 1903.

101. Ibid.

102. *New York Herald*, 30 April 1903; Frost, *Custer's Libbie*, 288; Horan, *Schreyvogel*, 37.

103. *New York Herald*, 2 May 1903. See also Horan, *Schreyvogel*, 37–38; Goetzmann and Goetzmann, *West of the Imagination*, 214–15.

104. Frederic Remington to John Schuyler Crosby, 6 May 1903, National Cowboy Hall of Fame and Western Heritage Center, quoted by Frost, *Custer's Libbie*, 288. See also Horan, *Schreyvogel*, 38–39.

105. Horan, *Schreyvogel*, 39.

106. Ibid., 40.

107. Goetzmann and Goetzmann, *West of the Imagination*, 254. For poignant insights into Remington's later personal life, see G. Edward White, *The Eastern Establishment and the Western Experience*, 201.

108. Frost, *Custer's Libbie*, 262–63, 286; Margaret Custer Calhoun to Nevin Custer, 13 December 1892, FCC, MCHCA.

109. *Chicago-Times Herald*, 7 August 1898; passenger list, PMSS *Siberia*, Voyage No. 4, sailing from San Francisco . . . Friday, October 23, 1903; BCWCC; Susan Wabuda, "Elizabeth Bacon Custer in Japan, 1903," *Manuscripts* 35 (Winter 1983): 14–16.

110. Wabuda, "Custer in Japan," 16.

111. Cyrus T. Brady to Elizabeth B. Custer, 14 August 1904, care of Agnes Wellington, Manheim Germany, EBCC, Roll 3.

112. George A. Forsyth, *The Story of a Soldier*, 328–29.

113. Cyrus T. Brady to Elizabeth B. Custer, 15 August 1904, EBCC, Roll 3.

114. Jacob Greene to Libbie, 16 August 1904, 19 August 1904, Jacob Greene to Cyrus T. Brady, 1 September 1904, EBCC, Roll 3.

115. Cyrus T. Brady, *Indian Fights and Fighters*, 361–66, 397.

116. Robert Hughes to Cyrus T. Brady, 18 November 1903, *Indian Fights and Fighters*, 366–70, especially 368.

117. C. A. Woodruff to Cyrus T. Brady, 3 May 1904, *Indian Fights and Fighters*, 380–85. The quotation is on 381.

118. Jacob Greene to Cyrus T. Brady, 1 September 1904, *Indian Fights and Fighters*, 393.

119. Ibid., 223–24. See also Hughes's letter to Brady, 18 November 1903, 367.

120. Ibid., 231.

121. Elizabeth B. Custer to *New York Times*, 10 December 1904.

122. R. W. Barkley to Elizabeth B. Custer, 12 December 1904, EBCC, Roll 3.

123. Elizabeth B. Custer to A. Mills, June 1906, West Point Museum Archives, cited by Frost, *Custer's Libbie*, 291; A. Mills to Elizabeth B. Custer, 20 June 1906, EBCC, Roll 3.

124. George G. Briggs to Elizabeth B. Custer, 2 July 1906, Frost, *Custer's Libbie*, 291–92; Michigan Custer Memorial Association Minutes, November 1906, Decem-

ber 1906, January 1907, cited by Frost, *Custer's Libbie*, 291–92.

125. Theodore Roosevelt to Honorable H. A. Conant, 16 January 1907, Michigan Custer Memorial Association Minutes, quoted by Frost, *Custer's Libbie*, 292.

126. Frost, *Custer's Libbie*, 292–93; Tate, "Girl He Left Behind," 17; E. B. Custer, "Libbie's Personal Recollections," Frost, *Boy General*, 139; Frederic A. Nims to Libbie, 24 March 1907, FCC, MCHCA.

127. Frederick Nims to Libbie, 19 June 1907, 15 July 1907, FCC, MCHCA; James A. Kidd to Elizabeth B. Custer, 26 July 1907, BCWCC; Frost, *Custer's Libbie*, 262, 294.

128. Fred Nims to Libbie, 15 August 1907, FCC, MCHCA.

129. Vinnie Ream (Hoxie) to Elizabeth B. Custer, 12 July 1907, FCC, MCHCA.

130. Vinnie Ream (Hoxie) to Elizabeth B. Custer, 25 July 1907, 25 November 1907, FCC, MCHCA.

131. E. B. Custer, "Libbie's Recollections," Frost, *Boy General*, 127.

132. Margaret Custer Calhoun Maughan to Libbie, 20 September 1907, Frost, *Custer's Libbie*, 295.

133. George Briggs to Elizabeth B. Custer, [27 September] 1907, FCC, MCHCA.

134. Ibid.

135. George Briggs to Elizabeth B. Custer, 2 December 1907, Frederic Nims to Libbie, 23 February 1908, George Briggs to Elizabeth B. Custer, 24 February 1908, Frost, *Custer's Libbie*, 296.

136. George Briggs to Elizabeth B. Custer, 2 March 1908, Frost, *Custer's Libbie*, 297.

137. John Philip Sousa to Elizabeth B. Custer, 11 July 1907, EBCC, Roll 3; Gifford Pinchot to Elizabeth B. Custer, 19 December 1907, FCC, MCHCA.

138. William F. Cody to Elizabeth B. Custer, 5 January 1908, EBCC, Roll 3.

139. Elizabeth B. Custer, unpublished manuscript entitled "My Ocean Voyage," Frost, *Custer's Libbie*, 297.

CHAPTER 15

1. *Monroe Evening News*, 24 June 1983; E. B. Custer, "Libbie's Personal Recollections," Frost, *Boy General*, 133, 140. Libbie did not know Shaw too well, since she called her "Dr. Mary Anna Shaw."

2. *New York Times*, 23 March 1910; *Monroe Democrat*, 1 April 1910; Monaghan, *Custer*, 409; Frost, *Custer's Libbie*, 298.

3. *Monroe Democrat*, 20 May 1910; *Detroit News Tribune*, 5 June 1910.

4. *Toledo Blade*, 28 May 1910, cited by Frost, *Custer's Libbie*, 298; George Worthington Adams, "Introduction" and "Postlude," Mary Logan, *Reminiscences of the Civil War and Reconstruction*, x, 292; Louise M. Young, "Mary Simmerson Cunningham Logan," *Notable American Women* 2:421–22.

5. E. B. Custer, "Libbie's Recollections," Frost, *Boy General*, 126.

6. Ibid., 126–27; *Detroit Free Press*, 3 June 1910.

7. *Detroit Free Press*, 3 June 1910.

8. Jane Addams, *Twenty Years at Hull-House: with Autobiographical Notes*, 136–37.

9. Robert D. Cross, "Grace Hoadley Dodge," *Notable American Women* 1:490; Ginzberg, *Women and the Work of Benevolence*, 199; Alice Kessler-Harris, *Out to Work: A History of Wage-Earning Women in the United States*, 93–95.

10. Harris, *Out to Work*, 93–94.

11. *Detroit Free Press*, 3 June 1910.

12. Ibid.; *Monroe Democrat*, 4 June 1910; Wagner, *Old Neutriment*, 124.

13. *Detroit Free Press*, 3 June 1910, *Detroit Journal*, [5] June 1910, EBCC, Roll 6, Frame 6326.

14. *Detroit Journal*, [5] June 1910, EBCC, Roll 6, Frame 6326.

15. *Detroit Free Press*, 3 June 1910.

16. *Detroit Journal*, [5] June 1910, EBCC, Roll 6, Frame 6326.

17. E. B. Custer, "Personal Recollections," Frost, *Boy General*, 129–30.

18. Ibid., 128–30; *Detroit Free Press*, 3 June 1910.

19. E. B. Custer, "Personal Recollections," Frost, *Boy General*, 131–32.

20. *Detroit News Tribune*, 5 June 1910; E. B. Custer, "Libbie's Personal Recollections," Frost, *Boy General*, 138–141.

21. E. B. Custer, "Libbie's Personal Recollections," Frost, *Boy General*, 138; *Toledo Blade*, 4 June 1910; *Detroit Free Press*, 5 June 1910; *San Francisco Call*, [5] June 1910, EBCC, Roll 6, Frame 6331.

22. *Detroit News Tribune*, 5 June 1910; E. B. Custer, "Libbie's Personal Recollections," Frost, *Boy General*, 141–42.

23. Quoted by Frost, *Custer's Libbie*, 303.

24. "Ceremonies attending the unveiling of the Equestrian Statue of Major General Gorge Armstrong Custer," typescript account of proceedings. FCC, MCHCA.

25. E. B. Custer, "Libbie's Personal Recollections," Frost, *Boy General*, 146.

26. *Detroit Free Press*, 5 June 1910, *Grand Rapids Sunday Herald*, 5 June 1910.

27. *Detroit Free Press*, 5 June 1910, *Grand Rapids Sunday Herald*, 5 June 1910.

28. *Grand Rapids Sunday Herald*, 5 June 1910. Smith's use of Custer as a Teutonic or Anglo-Saxon hero should be placed in the context of the time. See Bronwen J. Cohen, "Nativism and Western Myth: The Influence of Nativist Ideas on the American Self-Image," *Journal of American Studies* 8 (1974):25–26. Cohen points out that Anglo-Saxons were perceived as "the noblest branch of the Teutonic family." He

also notes that, as many nativists rejected immigrants, they turned to the American West and its heroes to define themselves as different from the newcomers. Robert Athearn in *The Mythic West in Twentieth-Century America*, 165, states that Owen Wister's Virginian was "impeccably Anglo-Saxon at a time when immigrants from southern and eastern Europe were flooding into the country." See also Leslie Fiedler's comments on the hero in a western novel as a WASP "in the wilderness." *The Return of the Vanishing American*, 24.

29. *Detroit News Tribune*, 5 June 1910.

30. Athearn, *Mythic West*, 165.

31. Bulkley, *Monroe County* 1:241.

32. *Detroit Free Press*, 5 June 1910.

33. *Toledo Blade*, 4 June 1910.

34. *Monroe Democrat*, 10 June 1910.

35. E. B. Custer, "Libbie's Personal Recollections," Frost, *Boy General*, 153.

36. *Monroe Record-Commercial*, 16 June 1910.

37. Elizabeth B. Custer to "My Friends in Monroe and in Michigan," undated letter of appreciation, FCC, Folder 42, MCHCA.

38. Frost, *Custer's Libbie*, 307–9.

39. Johnson, *Remembered Yesterdays*, 498–99.

40. Unpublished manuscript kept as a journal by Libbie in 1914, Frost, *Custer's Libbie*, 308.

41. Ibid.

42. Hamlin Garland, "General Custer's Last Fight as Seen by Two Moon," *McClure's*, September 1898, 446–48, Graham, *Custer Myth*, 101–3.

43. *Billings Gazette*, 27 May 1961.

44. Elizabeth B. Custer to E. H. Thompson, *The Tepee Book* 1 (June 1916): 23.

45. Edward Tabor Linenthal, *Sacred Ground: Americans and Their Battlefields*, 134; Don Rickey, Jr., *The History of Custer Battlefield*, 77–78.

46. Elizabeth B. Custer's Notebook, 18 May 1917, Box 7, CC, MCHCA.

47. C. A. Woodruff to Elizabeth B. Custer, 17 October 1910, EBCC, Roll 3.

48. Brady, *Britton of the Seventh*, viii-ix, 305–6, 309–10; Elizabeth B. Custer to E. S. Godfrey, 1 June [1916], Godfrey Family Papers, United States Army Military History Institute, Carlisle Barracks, Pennsylvania. Hereafter referred to as GFP.

49. Frederick Dellenbaugh, *George Armstrong Custer*, 4–5. Libbie's comments on Dellenbaugh's book are in EBCC, Roll 5, Frames 4097–4100.

50. H.R. 11000, 61st Cong., 1st sess., 31 July 1909, EBCC, Roll 3; D. A. Hollingsworth to Libbie, 25 August 1909, EBCC, Roll 3; H.R. 4006, 65th Cong., 1st sess., 1 May 1917, EBCC, Roll 3; D. A. Hollingsworth to Libbie, 25 May 1918, EBCC, Roll 3.

51. Henry Stimson to Elizabeth B. Custer, 19 February 1912, EBCC, Roll 3.

52. James H. Barry to Arthur I. Vorys, 12 August 1919; T. H. Connell to H. A. Conant, 25 August 1919; Joseph T. Harrison to Park Commissioners, Columbus, Ohio, 3 September 1919; William A. Day (Gorham Manufacturing Company), 13 August 1919, EBCC, Roll 3.

53. H. S. Reeves to Elizabeth B. Custer, 22 April 1920; H.R. 11398, 66th Cong., 2d sess., "An Act for the Creation of the Custer State Park Game Sanctuary, in the State of South Dakota and for Other Purposes," 5 June 1920, EBCC, Roll 3.

54. *Custer Battlefield Hiway News*, 15 March 1921, 1; Glacier National Park was especially popular among tourists. Earl Pomeroy, *In Search of the Golden West: The Tourist in Western America*, 150–51; Brice C. W. Custer, "Aunt Elizabeth As I Knew Her," BCWCC.

55. Elizabeth B. Custer to W. D. Fisher, 27 July 1920, *Custer Battlefield Hiway News*, 15 August 1920.

56. Frost, *Custer's Libbie*, 313; Edmund Lawton to Elizabeth B. Custer, 23 May 1921, EBCC, Roll 3; Elizabeth B. Custer to E. Fearis, 31 May 1921, EBCC, Roll 1.

57. Godfrey's 1908 revision is found in *Contributions of the Historical Society of Montana* 9:144–212. Most of this revision is reprinted in Graham, *Custer Myth*, 125–49. Graham cites the deleted quotation in a footnote on page 141.

58. Graham includes this portion. See *Custer Myth*, 146–47. See also the 1921 edition from the *Historical Society of Montana* 9:204–206. .

59. Utley, *Great Controversy*, 151; Graham, *Custer Myth*, 148–49; see also 1921 revision from *Historical Society of Montana* 9:209.

60. William Fayal Clarke to Elizabeth B. Custer, 14 June 1921, EBCC, Roll 3; Graham, *Custer Myth*, 217.

61. Graham, *Custer Myth*, 217.

62. Elizabeth B. Custer, "Preface" to "Custer's Last Battle," *Historical Society of Montana* 9:142.

63. Rebecca Richmond to Libbie, 10 June 1921, EBCC, Roll 3.

64. *Billings Gazette*, 25 June 1921, 26 June 1921, quoted by Frost, *Custer's Libbie*, 313.

65. Monroe *Evening News*, 27 June 1921, Frost, *Custer's Libbie*, 313.

66. Pohanka, *A Summer on the Plains*, 73–74; Elizabeth B. Custer to [Mr.] Rossiter, 12 April 1917, 13 April 1917, Alfred W. Anthony Collection, NYPL, Astor, Lenox and Tilden Foundations; Simpson, "Ruth McEnery Stuart," *Notable American Women* 3:407.

67. Libbie to Frances Elmer, 30 December [1923], FCC, MCHCA.

68. *Daytona* [Florida] *News and Observer*, 18 March 1984. Peter Thompson, "C" Company, was one of five soldiers whose horses gave out. Attacked by Sioux

warriors, he, nonetheless, survived. Graham, *Custer Myth*, 44.

69. Quoted by Michael Quigley and Diane Quigley, "Gen. Custer and the Irish Connection," *Daytona News and Observer*, 18 March 1984.

70. Frost, *Custer's Libbie*, 314.

71. *Monroe Evening News*, 11 June 1923, 13 June 1923, 23 June 1923, 16 June 1923, cited by Frost, *Custer's Libbie*, 314–15.

72. Libbie to [May Custer Elmer], undated mid-to-late 1920s, EBCC, Roll 4, Frames 3170–71. See also "The Observer's" interview with Marguerite Merington, *Monroe Evening News*, 14 March 1942. While the removal of the statue angered Elizabeth, that was not the reason she stayed away from Monroe, according to Merington.

73. Elizabeth B. Custer to David Helger, 2 May [1923], EBCC, Roll 1.

74. Rickey, *History of Custer Battlefield*, 31–33, 35–36; Senate Bill No. 323, 68th Cong., 1st sess., 6 December 1923, 87; Nelson A. Miles to the Honorable Senators and Members of Congress, 19 December 1923, EBCC, Roll 3.

75. Frost noted she moved twenty times between 1877 and 1902. *General Custer's Libbie*, 306. Libbie to John Burkman, 16 January [1924], reprinted in Glendolin Wagner, *Old Neutriment*, 11–12; Monroe *Evening News*, 11 February 1950.

76. Elizabeth B. Custer, rough draft notes on herself, EBCC, Roll 5, Frame 4198.

77. Ishbel Ross, "Mrs. Custer Turns Pages of the Past," *New York Herald Tribune*, 25 June 1929.

78. Communication from Mrs. William H. Griggs, archivist for the Cosmopolitan Club, to Lawrence Frost, 16 June 1968, cited by Frost, *Custer's Libbie*, 306–307, 311, n. 12.

79. Charles F. Bates, "The Westchester Horse and the 'Custer Trail,'" *Cavalry Journal* 33 (July 1924): 312.

80. Ibid., 317–18, 323.

81. Charles F. Bates, "Lost and Won: Custer's Last Battle," *New York Times*, 20 June 1926.

82. Graham, *Custer Myth*, 217; Charles King wrote the "Introduction," *The Story of the Little Big Horn*, xiii–xxxiii.

83. Graham, *Little Big Horn*, 95–99; W. S. Edgerly, "Forward," xxxv–xxxvii.

84. Graham, *Little Big Horn*, 176–77.

85. Tom Custer to Emma Reed, 5 June 1876, cited by Lawrence Frost, *Custer Legends*, 200–201; Autie Reed to Ann and David Reed, 21 June 1986, Frost, *Custer's Libbie*, 270. Captain Custer had written, "Today we found a sage hen's nest and caught about a dozen young ones, and Mary [Adams] has them and is going to try and raise them." Autie Reed wrote his mother and father: "Mary [Adams] is staying on the boat [*Far West*]."

William Falconer, a Bismarck citizen, told Graham that Mary Adams was at Fort Lincoln with Libbie. Her sister, Maria, was there instead, but Falconer thought they were the same person. John Manion has established through canceled checks, located at the Little Bighorn Battlefield National Museum, that Mary and Maria were sisters. John S. Manion, *Last Statement to Custer*, 35–40.

86. E. S. Godfrey to J. A. Shoemaker, 2 March 1926, EBCC, Roll 4.

87. Elizabeth B. Custer to J. A. Shoemaker, 19 March 1926, GFP.

88. Rickey, *History of Custer Battlefield*, 64; Frost, *Custer's Libbie*, 321.

89. Maj. A. J. Ostrander, "The Custer Semi-Centennial," *The Custer Semi-Centennial Ceremonies*, 17; R. S. Ellison, "Hasty Notes on the Semi-Centennial of the Little Big Horn or Custer Fight near Crow Indian Agency, Montana," 33–34, EBCC, Roll 7.

90. Ostrander, "The Custer Semi-Centennial," 7–8, 18; Graham, *Custer Myth*, 301.

91. Ellison, "Hasty Notes on the Semi-Centennial," 32–33; Mary Roberts Rinehart, "To Wyoming," *Saturday Evening Post*, 2 October 1926, 16–17, 161–62, 165–66, 169. Rinehart concluded Custer had been told to scout, but the Hancock campaign had taught him how swiftly Indians could evade whites.

92. Ellison, "Hasty Notes on the Semi-Centennial," 34.

93. Libbie to J. A. Shoemaker, 19 December 1925, EBCC, Roll 1.

94. Frost, *Custer's Libbie*, 317; Merington, CS, 44; Elizabeth B. Custer to Frances Elmer, 18 January [1924], FCC, MCHCA; Elizabeth B. Custer to Mrs. (Frances) Kingsley, 6 January 1886, ECBM.

95. C. O. Marcyes to E. S. Godfrey, 15 November 1925, EBCC, Roll 3.

96. Wagner, *Old Neutriment*, 181–82.

97. Possibly this was the Doral Hotel, across the street from her apartment.

98. *Monroe Evening News*, 11 February 1950; Ostrander, "The Custer Semi-Centennial, 15–17.

99. *Monroe Evening News*, 11 February 1950. See also Frost, *Custer's Libbie*, 13.

100. *New York Herald*, 25 June 1926.

101. Ibid.

102. Willard J. Carlyle to Libbie, 4 July 1926, EBCC, Roll 4.

103. Lane, "Brush, Palette, and the Little Big Horn," 68–69; Don Russell, *Custer's Last*, 31–35; Dippie, *Custer's Last Stand*, 51–52.

104. Willard J. Carlyle to Libbie, 4 July 1926, EBCC, Roll 4.

105. Elizabeth B. Custer's Last Will and Testament, 18 November 1926, Clerk of the Surrogate's Court, County and City of New York, New York.

106. John B. Kennedy, "A Soldier's Widow," *Collier's*, 29 January 1927, 10, 41.

107. Ibid., 41.

108. Ibid.

109. D. F. Barry to Elizabeth B. Custer, 15 July 1890, EBCC, Roll 1; Joseph K. Dixon to Elizabeth B. Custer, 1 December 1910, Julia Taft-Bayne to Elizabeth B. Custer, 13 July 1916, EBCC, Roll 3; *Custer Battlefield Hiway News*, 15 May 1921; Red Tomahawk's Remarks, M. E. Hawkins, "The Burial of the Hatchet," *Semi-Centennial Ceremonies*, 43–44, EBCC, Roll 7.

110. Elizabeth B. Custer, "General Custer and the Indian Chiefs," introduction to Charles Francis Bates, "The Red Man and the Black Hills," *Outlook Magazine*, 27 July 1927, 408.

111. Bates, "The Red Man and the Black Hills," 409.

112. Ibid., 410–11.

113. E. B. Custer, *"Boots and Saddles"*, 187.

114. Elizabeth B. Custer, "The Indians at Peace," unpublished manuscript in EBCC, Roll 4, Frames 3621–24.

115. Sharon O'Brien, "Federal Indian Policies and the International Protection of Human Rights," Vine Deloria, Jr., *American Indian Policy in the Twentieth Century*, 43. Utley notes that by 1934, the Indians had lost 60 percent of their land. *Indian Frontier*, 269.

116. E. B. Custer, "General Custer and the Indian Chiefs," 408.

117. Ishbel Ross, "Mrs. Custer Turns Pages of the Past," *New York Herald Tribune*, 25 June 1929.

118. Ibid.

119. Ibid.

120. Charles DeBenedetti, *Origins of the Modern American Peace Movement, 1915–1929*, 82–119.

121. Dippie, *Custer's Last Stand*, 68; Paul Hutton, "From Little Bighorn to Little Big Man: The Changing Image of a Western Hero in Popular Culture," *Western Historical Quarterly* 7 (January 1976): 33.

122. "Billings Man Gives New Version of Custer Battle," (Billings) *Herald*, 28 June 1951, clipping in the Billings Public Library, Folder M, Custer Battle—1941 to date. Statement attributed to Fred Huntington and quoted by Dippie, *Custer's Last Stand*, 68.

123. F. M. Gibson to George L. Yates, 28 April 1915, EBCC, Roll 3.

124. Ray Meketa, "A Letter from Luther Hare," *Custer and His Times: Book Three*, ed. Gregory Urwin, 209–10.

125. Graham to Capt. R. G. Carter, 20 March 1925, reprinted in Graham, *The Custer Myth*, 312. See also Theodore Goldin to Albert W. Johnson, 11 September 1930, Carroll, *Benteen-Goldin Letters*, 30. W. M. Camp died before his book was completed. Kenneth Hammer, *Custer in '76: Walter Camp's Notes on the Custer Fight*, 3.

126. Theodore W. Goldin to Albert W. Johnson, 28 July 1928, Carroll, *Benteen-Goldin Letters*, 14.

127. Robert Bruce to R. G. Carter, 22 March 1930, 25 March 1930, John S. du-Mont, "A Debate of Authors on the Custer Fight—1," *The Westerners Brand Book*, 2.

128. Frederic F. Van de Water to E. S. Godfrey, 26 May 1931, William Ghent Papers, Container 22, LC.

129. Wagner, *Old Neutriment*, 218–20.

130. Rickey, "Myth to Monument," 212–13.

131. [*New York Sun*], 4 July 1931. See also *Monroe Evening News*, 25 June 1931.

132. Utley, *Life in Custer's Cavalry*, 261; Frost, *Custer's Libbie*, 323–24.

133. *Cadiz Republican*, 23 June 1932, cited by Frost, *Custer's Libbie*, 326, n. 36; Millbrook, "Monument," 33.

134. Elizabeth B. Custer's Last Will and Testament, codicil, dated 23 August 1929, Surrogates Court, County and City of New York, New York. William Van Duzer

Lawrence had opened Sarah Lawrence College for Women in Bronxville in honor of Agnes's sister in 1928. Nonetheless, there is no record of a bequest to Sarah Lawrence from Elizabeth Custer. Susan Gleason, archivist, Sarah Lawrence College, to Shirley A. Leckie, 7 February 1992.

135. *Monroe Democrat*, 6 April 1933, *New York Times*, 5 April 1933.

136. Brice C. W. Custer, "Aunt Elizabeth As I Knew Her."

EPILOGUE

1. *Monroe Evening News*, 2 March 1934. After probating, the estate was valued at $101,492.

2. Ibid. Elizabeth B. Custer's Last Will and Testament, codicil dated 23 August 1929, Surrogates Court, County and City of New York, New York; Delma Vander Veer, director of principal gifts, Vassar College, Poughkeepsie, New York, to Shirley Leckie, 11 June 1991.

3. Frederic Van de Water, *Glory-Hunter: A Life of General Custer*.

4. Ibid., 17–19.

5. Ibid., 123.

6. The book was privately published by the author in Hollywood, California.

7. Fred Dustin, *The Custer Tragedy: Events Leading up to and Following the Little Big Horn Campaign of 1876*, xiii.

8. Ibid., xv.

9. Drago' *Montana Road* was published by William Morrow in 1935, and the others were published by Little, Brown; Random House; and Houghton Mifflin in 1944, 1950, and 1954, respectively.

10. Rickey, *History of Custer Battlefield*, 34–36.

11. Ibid., 88–94.

12. Hutton, "Little Bighorn to Little Big Man," 36; Paul Hutton, "Celluloid

Custer," *Red River Valley Historical Review* 4 (Fall 1979): 31.

13. Graham D. Taylor, *The New Deal and American Indian Tribalism: The Administration of the Indian Reorganization Act, 1934–45*, 97–100, 144–50; Paul Prucha, *The Indians in American Society*, 66–69; O'Brien, "Federal Indian Policy and Human Rights," 43–44.

14. Angie Debo, "Preface," *And Still the Waters Run: The Betrayal of the Five Civilized Tribes*, ix-xi; Mari Sandoz, "Preface," *Cheyenne Autumn*, v–vi. Others had championed the cause of Indians earlier. See Helen Hunt Jackson, *Century of Dishonor*, which was published in 1881. Joseph Porter, in *Paper Medicine Man*, 301, notes that John Bourke' advocacy of Indians (and Crook) left him a captain at the end of his career.

15. Bobbs-Merrrill also published this work.

16. "Richard Mulligan Portrays Custer as Legend Never Saw the General," *Little Big Man* Cinema Center Films Pressbook, 1971, 3, quoted by Hutton, "The Celluloid Custer," 43.

17. Hutton, "Little Big Horn to Little Big Man," 45.

18. Millbrook, "Monument," 31–32.

19. *Monroe Evening News*, 27 July 1967; Hutton, "Little Bighorn to Little Big Man," 38.

20. *Monroe Evening News*, 1 July 1980; *New York Times*, 1 July 1980; Lazarus, *Black Hills/White Justice*, 374–75, 401–28. Lazarus notes that the Sioux have left their award in the United States Treasury since many argue that "the Black Hills are not for sale."

21. E. B. Custer, "Last Will and Testament," 18 November 1926. See also Mc-

Christian, "In Search of Custer Battlefield," 76.

22. *Dallas Morning News*, 23 June 1991; Robert Utley, "Whose Shrine Is It?: The Ideological Struggle for Custer Battlefield," *Montana The Magazine of Western History* 42 (Winter 1992):70; McChristian, "In Search of Custer Battlefield," 76. The legislation, which had passed the House of Representatives earlier, passed the Senate on November 25, 1991. See "Editor' Note," *Montana The Magazine of Western History* 42 (Winter 1991): 70.

23. Millbrook, "Monument," 33; Utley, "Whose Shrine Is It?" 72–73; McChristian, "In Search of Custer Battlefield," 75–76.

24. Gerda Lerner sees the "true history of women" as "the history of their ongoing functioning in that male-defined world *on their own terms*." *The Majority Finds Its Past: Placing Women in History*, 148. Ideology as a means of enabling individuals to make sense of their lives while also often predetermining their responses to events is discussed by Clifford Geertz in "Ideology As a Cultural System," *The Interpretation of Culture Selected Essays*, 193–233. See especially 214–15 and 219–20. See also Griswold, "Anglo Women and Domestic Ideology in the American West," 16.

25. LBJ, 28 February 1862.

26. Libbie to Autie, 10 June 1864, Merington, CS, 102.

27. *New York Herald*, 25 June 1926.

28. Frederick Benteen to Robert N. Price, 6 March 1879, Graham, *Custer Myth*, 325.

29. E. B. Custer, "Libbie' Personal Recollections," Frost, *Boy General*, 131–32.

30. Ibid., 146.

Bibliography

MANUSCRIPT MATERIALS

Brice C. W. Custer Collection, A Private Collection
    Elizabeth Clift Bacon Journal, 1860–1863.
    Correspondence and Miscellaneous.
Columbia University, Rare Book and Manuscript Collection, Butler Library, New York, New York
    Stedman Family Papers.
Kansas State Historical Society, Topeka, Kansas
    Fort Wallace Post Returns, 1866–1882, Fort Wallace, Kansas.
Harold B. Lee Library, Bringham Young University, Provo, Utah
    Walter M. Camp Papers.
Library of Congress, Washington, D.C.
    William Ghent Papers.
    Vinnie Ream Papers.
    William T. Sherman Papers.
    Philip H. Sheridan Papers
Lilly Library, Indiana University, Bloomington, Indiana
    William M. Camp Manuscripts.
Little Bighorn Battlefield National Monument, Crow Agency, Montana
    Elizabeth B. Custer Correspondence.
    Elizabeth B. Custer Library and Manuscript Notes.
    George A. Custer Correspondence, Orders, and Miscellaneous Documents
        and Others.
Monroe County Historical Commission Archives, Monroe County Historical Museum, Monroe, Michigan
    The Custer Collection.
    The Lawrence A. Frost Collection of Custeriana.
Monroe County Library System, Ellis Reference and Information Center, Monroe, Michigan
    George Armstrong Custer Collection.

National Archives and Records Service, Washington, D.C.
    Records of the War Department, Provost Marshal's Office.
    Record Group 109.
Newberry Library, Chicago, Illinois
    Edward Ayer Collection.
New York Public Library, Manuscript Division, New York, New York
    Carnegie Papers.
    Century Collection.
    Marguerite Merington Collection.
U.S. Army Military History Institute, Carlisle Barracks, Archives Branch, Carlisle, Pennsylvania
    The Godfrey Family Papers.
Yale University, Beinecke Rare Book and Manuscript Library, Western Americana Collection, New Haven, Connecticut
    Elizabeth B. Custer Manuscript Collection.
    George A. Custer Manuscript Collection.

GOVERNMENT PUBLICATIONS

Heitman, Francis E. *Historical Register and Dictionary of the United States Army.* 2 vols. Washington, D.C.: Government Printing Office, 1899.

United States Congress, House of Representatives. H.R. No. 30, 39th Cong., 1 sess., 1866, Report of the Joint Committee on Reconstruction.

United States Congress, House of Representatives. Report No. 3328s. 51st Cong., 2d sess., 1890, Elizabeth B. Custer Report to Accompany H.R. 12242.

United States Department of Commerce. *Historical Statistics of the United States: Colonial Times to 1890.* 2 vols. Washington, D.C.: Government Printing Office, 1975.

United States War Department. Surgeon General's Office. *Circular No. 4: A Report on Barracks and Hospitals with Descriptions of Military Posts.* Washington, D.C.: Government Printing Office, 1870.

United States War Department. Surgeon-General's Office. *Report on Epidemic Cholera and Yellow Fever in the Army of the United States, during the Year 1867.* Washington, D.C.: Government Printing Office, 1868.

ARTICLES

Aron, Cindy S. "'To Barter Their Souls for Gold': Female Clerks in Federal Government Offices, 1862–1890." *Journal of American History* 67 (March 1981): 835–53.

Bibliography

Ambrose, Stephen E. "Custer's Civil War." *Timeline* 7 (August–September 1990): 16–23, 27–31.

———. "Sidesaddle Soldier: Libbie Custer's Partnership in Glory." *Timeline* 3 (April–May 1986): 3–12.

Bates, Charles Francis. "The Red Man and the Black Hills." *Outlook Magazine*, 27 July 1927, 408–11.

———. "The Westchester Horse at the 'Custer Trail.'" *Cavalry Journal* 33 (July 1924): 312–18, 323.

Beauregard, Ewing E. "The General and the Politician: Custer and Bingham." *Blue and Gray Magazine* 6 (October 1988): 33–35.

Bingham, Anne E. "Sixteen Years on a Kansas Farm." *Kansas Historical Collection* 15 (1919–1922): 501–31.

Brigham, Eric. "Custer's Meeting with Secretary of War Belknap at Fort Abraham Lincoln." *North Dakota History* 9 (August 1952): 129–31.

Bulkley, John M. "The Impressive Ceremonies of Unveiling the Statue at Monroe, Michigan." *Christian Work and Evangelist*, 21 June 1910, 827–28.

Carroll, John M., ed., "Custer: From the Civil War to the Big Horn." Manuscript, photocopied in fifty copies of Frederick Benteen's marginal notes on a copy of *Wild Life on the Plains and Horrors of Indian Warfare*. Bryan, Texas: John M. Carroll, 1981.

Cohen, Bronwen J. "Nativism and Western Myth: The Influence of Nativist Ideas on the American Self-Image." *Journal of American Studies* 8(1974):23–39.

Crackel, Theodore J. "Custer's Kentucky: General George Armstrong Custer and Elizabethtown, Kentucky, 1871–1873." *Filson Club Historical Quarterly* 48 (April 1974): 144–55.

"Custer Buried at West Point." *Harper's Weekly*, 27 October 1877, 839–42.

Custer, Elizabeth Bacon. "Custer's Favorite Photo of Himself." *Tepee Book* 1 (July 1916): 4–5.

———. "The General Custer Statue." *Michigan Historical Commission Historical Collection* 39 (1915): 291–93.

———. "General Custer and the Indian Chiefs." *Outlook Magazine*, July 1927, 408.

———. "Home Making in the American Army." *Harper's Bazaar*, 22 September 1900, 1309–13.

———. "The Kid." *St. Nicholas Magazine*, September 1900, 964–79.

———. "An Out-of-the Way 'Outing.'" *Harper's Weekly*, 18 July 1891, 534–35.

———. "To the Victor Belongs the Spoils." *Home-Maker Magazine*, January 1890, 277–83; February 1890, 375–81; March 1890, 460–64; April 1890, 30–34.

———. "Where Grant Wrote Peace." *Harper's Weekly*, 24 June 1911, 6–7.

———. "'Where The Heart Is': A Sketch of Women's Life on the Frontier." *Lippincot Magazine*, February 1900, 305–12.

Davis, Theodore R. "General Custer's Command." *Harper's Weekly*, 3 August 1867, 481, 484.

———. "A Summer on the Plains." *Harper's New Monthly Magazine*, February 1868, 292–307.

———. "With Generals in Their Homes." *Chicago Brand Book* (1945–46): 115–30.

Dippie, Brian W. "Southern Response to Custer's Last Stand." *Montana The Magazine of Western History* 26 (April 1971): 18–31.

———. "'What Will Congress Do About It?': The Congressional Reaction to the Little Big Horn Disaster." *North Dakota History* 37 (Summer 1970): 161–89.

duMont, John S. "A Debate of Authors on the Custer Fight." *Westerners Brand Book, Chicago Corral* 30 (July 1973): 1–40.

Gerber, Max E. "The Custer Expedition of 1874: A New Look." *North Dakota History: Journal of the Northern Plains* 40 (Winter 1973): 4–23.

Godfrey, Edward S. "Custer's Last Battle." *Century Illustrated Monthly Magazine* 43 (January 1892): 358–84.

———. "Custer's Last Battle." Revised in 1908 with a 1921 postscript. *Contributions to the Historical Society of Montana* 9:142–212.

———. "Some Reminiscences, Including the Washita Battle, November 29, 1868." *Cavalry Journal* 37 (October 1928): 481–500.

Green, A. C. "The Durable Society: Austin in Reconstruction." *Southwestern Historical Quarterly* 82 (April 1969): 492–506.

Griswold, Robert L. "Anglo Women and Domestic Ideology in the American West." *Western Women*, edited by Lillian Schlissel, Vicki L. Ruiz, and Janice Monk. Albuquerque: University of New Mexico Press, 1988.

Hazen, William. "The Great Middle Region of the United States and Its Limited Space of Public Land." *North American Review* 120 (January 1875): 1–34.

Hofling, Charles K., M.D. "George Armstrong Custer: A Psychoanalytic Approach." *Montana The Magazine of Western History* 22 (Spring 1971): 32–43.

Hughes, Robert P. "The Campaign against the Sioux in 1876." *Journal of the Military Service Institution of the United States* 79 (January 1896): 1–44.

Hutton, Paul A. "The Celluloid Custer." *Red River Historical Review* 4 (Fall 1979): 20–43.

———. "From Little Bighorn to Little Big Man: The Changing Image of a Western Hero in Popular Culture." *Western Historical Quarterly* 7 (January 1976): 19–45.

Kelly, Joan. "The Doubled Vision of Feminist Theory: A Postscript to the 'Women and Power' Conference." *Feminist Studies* 5 (Spring 1979): 216–27.

Kennedy, John B. "A Soldier's Widow." *Collier's*, 29 January 1927, 10, 41.

Kerber, Linda K. "Separate Spheres, Female Worlds, Woman's Place: The Rhetoric of Women's History." *Journal of American History* 75 (June 1988): 9–39.

King, Charles. "Custer's Last Battle." *Harper's New Monthly Magazine*, August 1890, 378–87.

Lane, Harrison. "Brush-Palette and the Little Big Horn." *Montana The Magazine of Western History* 23 (Summer 1973): 67–80.

Maclean, Norman. "Custer's Last Fight as Ritual Drama." *Westerners Brand Book. The Chicago Corral.* 15 (October 1958): 57–64.

McChristian, Douglas C. "In Search of Custer Battlefield." *Montana The Magazine of Western History* 42 (Winter 1992): 75–76.

McMurtry, R. G. "The Two-Year Residence of General George A. Custer in Kentucky." *Kentucky Progress Magazine* 5 (Summer 1933): 32–33, 50.

Manion, John, and Elizabeth B. Custer. "Custer, Cody and the Grand Duke Alexis." *Research Review: The Journal of the Little Big Horn Associates* 4 (January 1990): 2–14, 31–32.

Manion, John. "Custer's Cooks and Maids." *Custer and His Times. Book Two*, edited by John M. Carroll. Fort Worth, Texas: Little Big Horn Associates, 1984, 150–206.

Meckel, Richard A. "Educating a Ministry of Mothers: Evangelical Maternal Associations, 1815–1860." *Journal of the Early Republic* 2 (Winter 1982): 403–23.

Millbrook, Minnie Dubbs. "Big Game Hunting with the Custers, 1869–1870." *Kansas Historical Quarterly* 41 (Winter 1975): 429–53.

———. "The Boy General and How He Grew: George Custer After Appomattox." *Montana The Magazine of Western History* 23 (Spring 1973): 34–43.

———. "Custer's First Scout in the West." *Kansas Historical Quarterly* 39 (Summer 1973): 75–95.

———. "Custer's March to Texas." *Prairie Scout*, 1973, 31–69.

———. "A Monument to Custer." *Montana The Magazine of Western History* 24 (Spring 1974): 18–33.

———. "Mrs. General Custer at Fort Riley, 1866." *Kansas Historical Quarterly* 40 (Spring 1974): 63–71.

———. "Rebecca Visits Kansas and the Custers: The Diary of Rebecca Richmond." *Kansas Historical Quarterly* 42 (Winter 1976): 366–402.

———. "The West Breaks in General Custer." *Kansas Historical Quarterly* 36 (Summer 1970): 113–48.

Myers, Rex C. "Montana Editors and the Custer Battle." *Montana The Magazine of Western History* 26 (April 1976): 18–31.

Myres, Sandra L. "Frontier Historians, Women, and the 'New' Military History." *Military History of the Southwest* 19 (Spring 1989): 27–37.

———. "Romance and Reality on the American Frontier: Views of Army Wives." *Western Historical Quarterly* 13 (October 1982): 409–27.

Parmelee, Mary Manley. "A Child's Recollection of the Summer of '76." *Teepee Book* 1 (June 1915): 122–30.

Peterson, Walter F. "Christmas on the Plains." *American West* 1 (Fall 1964): 53–57.

Richards, James K. "Come On, You Wolverines!" *Timelines* 7 (August-September 1990): 24–25.

Richter, William L. "A Better Time Is in Store for Us: An Analysis of the Reconstruction Attitudes of George Armstrong Custer." *Military History of Texas and the Southwest* 11 (1973): 31–50.

Rickey, Don, Jr. "Myth to Monument: The Establishment of Custer Battlefield National Monument." *Journal of the West* 7 (April 1968): 209–16.

Rinehart, Mary Roberts. "To Wyoming." *Saturday Evening Post*, 2 October 1926, 16–17, 161–62, 165–66, 169.

Rosaldo, M. Z. "The Use and Abuse of Anthropology: Reflections on Feminism and Cross-Cultural Understanding." *Signs: Journal of Women in Culture and Society* 5 (Spring 1980): 389–417.

Schlesinger, Elizabeth B. "Parton, Sara (Willis)." *Notable American Women 1607–1950: A Biographical Dictionary*, vol. 3, edited by Edward T. James, Janet Wilson James, and Paul S. Boyer. Cambridge, Massachusetts: Harvard University Press, 1971, 24–25.

Schultz, Jane E. "The Inhospitable Hospital: Gender and Professionalism in Civil War Medicine." *Signs: Journal of Women in Culture and Society* 17 (Winter 1992): 363–92.

Slotkin, Richard. "'. . . & Then the Mare Will Go!': An 1875 Black Hills Scheme by Custer, Holladay and Buford." *Journal of the West* 15 (July 1976): 60–77.

Smith, Herbert F. "Jeannette Gilder." *Notable American Women 1607–1950: A Biographical Dictionary*, vol. 2, edited by Edward T. James, Janet Wilson James, and Paul S. Boyer. Cambridge, Massachusetts: Harvard University Press, 1971, 32–34.

Stewart, Edgar I. "The Custer Battle and Widow's Weeds." *Montana The Magazine of Western History* 22 (January 1972): 52–59.

Tallmadge, Frank. "Buffalo Hunting with Custer." *Cavalry Journal* 33 (January 1924): 6–10.

Tate, Michael. "'The Girl He Left Behind': Elizabeth Custer and the Making of a Legend." *Red River Valley Historical Review* 5 (Winter 1980): 5–22.

Thomas, Kevin. "Ben Clark: The Scout Who Defied Custer." *Oldtimers Wild West*, February 1980, 22–29, 48–50.

Thompson, Erwin N., "The Negro Soldier on the Frontier: A Fort Davis Case Study." *Journal of the West* 7 (April 1968): 217–35.

Utley, Robert. "The Celebrated Peace Policy of General Grant." *North Dakota History* 20 (July 1953): 121–42.

Utley, Robert. "Whose Shrine Is It? The Ideological Struggle for Custer Battlefield." *Montana The Magazine of Western History* 42 (Winter 1992): 70–74.

Van de Wetering, Maxine. "The Popular Concept of 'Home' in Nineteenth-Century America." *Journal of American Studies* 18 (1984): 5–28.

Wabuda, Susan. "Elizabeth Bacon Custer in Japan: 1903." *Manuscripts Magazine* 35 (Winter 1983): 12–18.

Weist, Katherine M. "Beasts of Burden and Menial Slaves: Nineteenth Century Observations of Northern Plains Indian Women." *The Hidden Half: Studies of Plains Indian Women*, edited by Patricia Albers and Beatrice Medicine. Lanham, Maryland: University Press of America, 1983, 29–52.

Welter, Barbara. "The Cult of True Womanhood: 1820–1860." *American Quarterly* 18 (Summer 1966): 151–74.

———. "Sara Jane Clarke Lippincott." *Notable American Women 1607–1950: A Biographical Dictionary*, vol. 2, edited by Edward T. James, Janet James, and Paul Boyer. Cambridge, Massachusetts: Harvard University Press, 1971, 407–9.

White, Lonnie J. "White Women Captives of Southern Plains Indians, 1866–1875." *Journal of the West* 8 (July 1869): 327–54.

White, Richard. "The Winning of the West: The Expansion of the Western Sioux in the Eighteenth and Nineteenth Centuries." *Journal of American History* 65 (September 1978): 319–43.

Whittaker, Frederick. "General George A. Custer." *Galaxy Magazine*, September 1876, 362–71.

Wilson, Gen. James G. "Two Modern Knights Errant." *Cosmopolitan Magazine*, July 1891, 294–302.

Wood, Ann D. "'The Scribbling Women' and Fanny Fern: Why Women Wrote." *American Quarterly* 23 (1971): 3–23.

BOOKS

Addams, Jane. *Twenty Years at Hull-House*. New York: Macmillan, 1910.

Alberts, Don E. *Brandy Station to Manila Bay*. Austin: Presidial Press, 1980.

Ambrose, Stephen. *Crazy Horse and Custer: The Parallel Lives of Two American Warriors*. Garden City, New York: Doubleday, 1975.

American Digest System. *1906 Decennial Edition of the American Digest: A Complete Table of American Cases From 1658 to 1906. G-L.* Vol. 23. St. Paul: West Publishing, 1912.

Andrews, E. Benjamin. *The History of the Last Quarter-Century in the United States, 1870–1895.* 2 vols. New York: Charles Scribner's Sons, 1896.

Andrist, Ralph K. *The Long Death: The Last Days of the Plains Indians*. New York: Macmillan, 1964.

Aron, Cindy Sondik. *Ladies and Gentlemen of the Civil Service: Middle-Class Workers in Victorian America.* New York: Oxford University Press, 1987.

Asay, Karol. *Gray Head and Long Hair: The Benteen-Custer Relationship*. New York: J. M. Carroll, 1983.

Athearn, Robert G. *Forts of the Upper Missouri*. Englewood Cliffs, New Jersey: Prentice-Hall, 1967.

———. *The Mythic West in Twentieth Century America*. Foreword by Elliott West. Lawrence: University Presses of Kansas, 1986.

———. *William Tecumseh Sherman and the Settlement of the West*. Norman: University of Oklahoma Press, 1956.

Bald, Clever F. *Michigan in Four Centuries* New York: Harper & Row, 1961.

Barnard, Sandy. *Shovels and Speculation: Archeology Hunts Custer*. Terre Haute, Indiana: AST Press, 1990.

Barnum, P. T. *Struggles and Triumphs, or Forty Years' Recollections of P. T. Barnum.* Buffalo: Warren, Johnson, 1872.

Barrus, Clara. *The Life and Letters of John Burroughs.* 2 vols. Boston: Houghton Mifflin, 1925.

Battles and Leaders of the Civil War. 4 vols. Edited by Robert Underwood, Johnson, and Clarence Clough Buel. Secaucus, New Jersey: Castle, 1982.

Beecher, Catharine E. *A Treatise on Domestic Economy, for the Use of Young Ladies at Home, and at School.* Rev. ed. New York: Harper & Brothers, 1846.

Beecher, Catharine E., and Harriet Beecher Stowe. *The American Woman's Home, or Principles of Domestic Science*. New York: J. B. Ford, 1869.

Berthrong, Donald. *The Southern Cheyennes*. Norman: University of Oklahoma Press, 1963.

Besant, Walter. *All Sorts and Conditions of Men: An Impossible Story*. New York and London: Harper & Brothers Publisher, 1899; original publication 1882.

Blackstone, Sarah J. *Buckskins, Bullets, and Business: A History of Buffalo Bill's Wild West*. New York: Greenwood Press, 1986.

Bibliography

Blois, John T. *Gazetteer of the State of Michigan, in Three Parts*. Detroit: Sydney L. Rood, 1838.

Boyd, Lois A., and R. Douglas Brackenridge. *Presbyterian Women in America: Two Centuries of a Quest for Status*. Westport, Connecticut: Greenwood Press, 1983.

Boylan, Anne M. *Sunday School: The Formation of An American Institution, 1790–1880*. New Haven: Yale University Press, 1988.

Brady, Cyrus T. *Britton of the Seventh: A Romance of Custer and the Great Northwest*. Chicago: A. C. McClurg, 1914.

———. *Indian Fights and Fighters: The Soldier and the Sioux*. New York: McClure, Phillips, 1904.

Brill, Charles J. *Conquest of the Southern Plains*. Oklahoma City: Golden Saga Publishers, 1938.

Brininstool, E. A. *Major Reno Vindicated*. Hollywood: Privately printed, 1935.

———. *A Trooper with Custer*. Columbus: Hunter-Trader-Trapper, 1926.

Brininstool, E. A., ed. *Campaigning with Custer and the Nineteenth Kansas Volunteer Cavalry on the Washita Campaign, 1868–69*, by David L. Spotts. Los Angeles: Wetzel Publishing, 1928. Reprint. Lincoln: University of Nebraska Press, 1988.

Brown, D. Alexander. *Bury My Heart at Wounded Knee: An Indian History of the American West*. New York: Holt, Rinehart & Winston, 1973.

———. *The Gentle Tamers: Women of the Old Wild West*. New York: Putnam, 1958.

———. *The Year of the Century: 1876*. New York: Charles Scribner's Sons, 1966.

Brown, Robert L. *Ghost Towns of the Colorado Rockies*. Caldwell, Idaho: Caxton Printers, 1968.

Brownlee, W. Elliot. *Dynamics of Ascent: A History of the American Economy*. 2d ed. New York: Alfred A. Knopf, 1979.

Buel, J. W. *Heroes of the Plains*. San Francisco: A. L. Bancroft, 1881.

Bulkley, John McClelland. *History of Monroe County, Michigan*. 2 vols. Chicago: Lewis Publishing, 1913.

Burkey, Blaine. *Custer, Come at Once! The Fort Hays Years of George and Elizabeth Custer, 1876–1870*. Fort Hays, Kansas: Thomas More Prep, 1976.

Burt, Mary E., ed., as told by Elizabeth B. Custer. *The Boy General: Story of the Life of Major-General George A. Custer*. New York: Charles Scribner's Sons, 1901.

Carriker, Robert C. *Fort Supply, Indian Territory: Frontier Outpost on the Plains*. Norman: University of Oklahoma Press, 1970.

Carrington, Margaret I. *Ab-sa-ra-ka, Home of the Crows: Being the Experiences of an Officer's Wife on the Plains*. Philadelphia: Lippincott, 1868.

Carroll, John M., ed. *The Benteen-Goldin Letters on Custer and His Last Battle*. New York: Liveright, 1974.

———. *Camp Talk: The Very Private Letters of Frederick W. Benteen of the 7th U.S. Cavalry to His Wife, 1871 to 1888*. Mattituck, New York, and Bryan, Texas: J. M. Carroll, 1983.

———. *A Custer Chrestomathy*. Bryan, Texas: John M. Carroll, 1981.

———. *The D. F. Barry Correspondence at the Custer Battlefield (the Juiciest Ones Being from Captain Benteen)*. Bryan, Texas: Privately printed, 1980.

———. *I. Varnum*. Glendale, California: Arthur H. Clark, 1982.

Carroll, John M., comp. *Custer of the Civil War: His Unfinished Memoirs*. San Rafael, California: Presidio Press, 1977.

———. *Custer in Texas: An Interrupted Narrative*. New York: Sol Lewis/Liveright, 1975.

Carroll, John M. and Byron Price. *Roll Call on the Little Big Horn*. Fort Collins, Colorado: Old Army Press, 1974.

Cavalry Scraps: The Writings of Frederick W. Benteen. Edited by John M. Carroll. Guidon Press, 1979.

Catton, Bruce. *The Civil War*. New York: Fairfax Press, 1980. Reprint. American Heritage, 1960.

Chalmers, Steven. *The Penny Piper of Saranac*. Boston: Houghton Mifflin, 1916.

Chandler, Melbourne C. *Of Garry Owen in Glory: The History of the Seventh United States Cavalry Regiment*. Annandale, Virginia: Turnpike Press, 1960.

Clark, Clifford E., Jr. *Henry Ward Beecher*. Urbana: University of Illinois Press, 1978.

Clark, Joshua. *Onondaga, or Reminiscences of Earlier and Later Times*. 2 vols. Syracuse, New York: Stoddard and Babcock, 1849.

Coffman, Edward. *The Old Army: A Portrait of the American Army in Peacetime, 1784–1898*. New York: Oxford University Press, 1986.

Cogley, Thomas. *History of the Seventh Indiana Cavalry Volunteers*. Laporte, Indiana: Herald Company Steam Printers, 1876.

Cochran, Thomas C. *Frontiers of Change: Early Industrialization in America*. Oxford: Oxford University Press, 1981.

Custer, Elizabeth B. *"Boots and Saddles"; or, Life in Dakota with General Custer*. New York: Harper & Brothers, 1885. Reprint. Norman: University of Oklahoma Press, Western Frontier Library, 1961.

———. *Following the Guidon*. New York: Harper & Brothers, 1890. Reprint, with introduction by Jane R. Stewart. Norman: University of Oklahoma Press, Western Frontier Library, 1966.

———. *Tenting on the Plains; or, General Custer in Kansas and Texas*. New York:

Charles L. Webster, 1887. Reprint. Norman: University of Oklahoma Press, Western Frontier Library, 1971.

Custer and His Times. Book Two. Edited by John Carroll. Fort Worth, Texas: Little Big Horn Associates, 1984.

Custer and His Times. Book Three. Edited by Gregory Urwin. Conway, Arkansas: Little Big Horn Associates/University of Central Arkansas Press, 1987.

Custer in '76: Walter Camp's Notes on the Custer Fight. Edited by Kenneth Hammer. Norman: University of Oklahoma Press, 1988.

Custer, George Armstrong |Nomad|. *Nomad: George Armstrong Custer in Turf, Field and Farm.* Edited by Brian Dippie. Austin: University of Texas Press, 1980.

———. *My Life on the Plain; or, Personal Experiences with Indians.* New York: Sheldon, 1875.

Darling, Roger. *Custer's Seventh Cavalry Comes to Dakota: New Discoveries Reveal Custer's Tribulations Enroute to the Yellowstone Expedition.* Vienna, Virginia: Potomac-Western Press, 1988.

Davis, Paulina Wright. *A History of the National Woman's Rights Movement for Twenty Years, from 1850 to 1870.* New York: Journeymen Printers' Cooperative Association, 1871.

DeBenedetti, Charles. *Origins of the Modern American Peace Movement, 1915–1929.* Millwood, New York: KTO Press, 1978.

Debo, Angie. *And Still the Waters Run: The Betrayal of the Five Civilized Tribes.* Princeton, New Jersey: Princeton University Press, 1940. Reprint. Norman: University of Oklahoma Press, 1984.

———. *A History of the Indians of the United States.* Norman: University of Oklahoma Press, 1970.

Dellenbaugh, Frederick S. *George Armstrong Custer.* New York: Macmillan, 1917.

Degler, Carl. *At Odds: Women and the Family in America, from the Revolution to the Present.* Oxford: Oxford University Press, 1980.

Dippie, Brian W. *Custer's Last Stand: The Anatomy of an American Myth.* Missoula: University of Montana, 1976.

———. *The Vanishing Americans: White Attitudes and U.S. Indian Policy.* Middleton, Connecticut: Wesleyan University Press, 1982.

Douglas, Ann. *The Feminization of American Culture.* New York: Alfred A. Knopf, 1977.

Dupuy, R. Ernest, and Trevor N. Dupuy. *The Compact History of the Civil War.* New York: Hawthorn Books, 1960.

———. *Military Heritage of America.* New York: McGraw-Hill, 1956.

Dustin, Fred. *The Custer Tragedy: Events Leading up to and Following the Little Big Horn Campaign of 1876.* Ann Arbor: Edwards Brothers, 1939.

Eberhart, Perry. *Guide to the Colorado Ghost Towns and Mining Camps.* 4th rev. ed. Athens, Ohio: Swallow Press, n.d.

Felch, Alpheus. *Report of the Pioneer Society of the State of Michigan.* 2 vols. Lansing: Robert Smith Printing Co., 1901.

Fern, Fanny (Sara Parton). *Fern Leaves from Fanny's Portfolio.* Auburn, New York: Miller, Orton & Mulligan, 1854.

———. *Fern Leaves . . . Second Series.* Auburn, New York: Miller, Orton & Mulligan, 1854.

———. *Fresh Leaves.* New York: Mason Brothers, 1857.

———. *Rose Clark.* New York: Mason Brothers, 1856.

Fiedler, Leslie. *The Return of the Vanishing American.* New York: Stein & Day, 1968.

Finley, Ruth E. *The Lady of Godey's: Sarah Josepha Hale.* Philadelphia: J. B. Lippincott, 1931. Reprint. New York: Arno Press, 1974.

Foner, Eric. *Reconstruction: America's Unfinished Revolution, 1863–1877.* New York: Harper & Row, 1988.

Formisano, Ronald P. *The Birth of Mass Political Parties, Michigan, 1827–1861.* Princeton, New Jersey: Princeton University Press, 1971.

Forsyth, George A. *The Story of a Soldier.* New York: Appleton and Company, 1909. Originally published in 1900.

Fougera, Katherine Gibson, ed. *With Custer's Cavalry: From the Memoirs of the Late Katherine Gibson, Widow of Captain Francis M. Gibson of the Seventh Cavalry U.S.A.* Caldwell, Idaho: Caxton, 1940. Reprint. Lincoln: University of Nebraska Press, 1986.

Fowler, Arlen L. *The Black Infantry in the West, 1869–1891.* Westport, Connecticut: Greenwood Publishing Corporation, 1971.

Frazer, Robert. *Forts of the West: Military Forts and Presidios and Posts Commonly Called Forts West of the Mississippi River to 1898.* Norman: University of Oklahoma Press, 1972.

Freeman, Douglas Southall. *Lee's Lieutenants: A Study in Command.* 4 vols. New York: Charles Scribner's Sons, 1944–46.

Frost, Lawrence A. *Boy General in Bronze: Custer, Michigan's Hero on Horseback.* Glendale, California: Arthur H. Clark, 1985.

———. *The Court-Martial of General George Armstrong Custer.* Norman: University of Oklahoma Press, 1968.

———. *The Custer Album: A Pictorial Biography of General George A. Custer.*

Seattle: Superior Publishing Company. Reprint. Norman: University of Oklahoma Press, 1990.

——. *General Custer's Libbie.* Seattle: Superior Publishing Company, 1975.

Frost, Lawrence A., ed. *With Custer in '74: James Calhoun's Diary of the Black Hills Expedition.* Provo: Brigham Young University Press, 1979.

Furman, Emma. *A Child's Parent Dies: Studies in Childhood Bereavement.* New Haven: Yale University Press, 1974.

Geertz, Clifford. *The Interpretation of Culture: Selected Essays.* New York: Basic Books, 1973

George, Mary Karl. *Zachariah Chandler: A Political Biography.* East Lansing: Michigan State University Press, 1969.

Gibbon, John. *Gibbon on the Sioux Campaign of 1876.* Bellevue, Nebraska: Old Army Press, 1970.

Gilpin, Alec R. *Territory of Michigan, 1805–1837.* East Lansing: Michigan State University Press, 1971.

Goetzmann, William H. *Exploration and Empire: The Explorer and the Scientist in the Winning of the American West.* New York: Alfred A. Knopf, 1966.

Goetzmann, William H., and William N. Goetzmann. *West of the Imagination.* New York: W. W. Norton, 1986.

Graham, W. A. *The Custer Myth: A Sourcebook of Custeriana.* New York: Bonanza Books, 1963.

——. *The Story of the Little Big Horn: Custer's Last Fight.* Harrisburg, Pennsylvania.: Stackpole, 1959.

Gray, John S. *Centennial Campaign: The Sioux War of 1876.* Fort Collins, Colorado: The Old Army Press, 1976.

——. *Custer's Last Campaign: Mitch Boyer and the Little Big Horn Reconstructed.* Lincoln: University of Nebraska Press, 1991.

Great Falls Yesterday: Comprising a Collection of Biographies and Reminiscences of Early Settlers. Great Falls, Montana: Works Progress Administration, 1939.

Great Sioux War 1876–77: The Best from Montana The Magazine of Western History. Edited by Paul L. Hedren. Helena: Montana Historical Society Press, 1991.

Greene, Duane M. *Ladies and Officers of the United States Army; or American Aristocracy, a Sketch of the Social Life and Character of the Army.* Chicago: Central Publishing Company, 1880.

Greenwood, Grace (Sara Lippincott). *Greenwood Leaves: A Collection of Sketches and Letters.* 2d ed. Boston: Ticknor, Reed, and Fields, 1850.

——. *History of My Pets.* Boston: Ticknor, Reed, and Fields, 1851.

————. *Merrie England.* Boston: Ticknor and Fields, 1855.

Greven, Philip. *The Protestant Temperament: Patterns in Child-Rearing, Religious Experience, and the Self in Early America.* New York: Alfred A. Knopf, 1977.

Grierson, Alice K. *The Colonel's Lady on the Western Frontier: The Correspondence of Alice Kirk Grierson.* Edited by Shirley A. Leckie. Lincoln: University of Nebraska Press, 1989.

Griffith, Paddy. *Battle Tactics of the Civil War* New Haven: Yale University Press, 1989. Reprint. United Kingdom: Crowood Press, 1987, under the title, *Rally Once Again.*

Grinnell, George B. *The Cheyenne Indians.* 2 vols. New Haven: Yale University Press, 1923.

Hall, Gordon Langley. *Vinnie Ream: The Story of the Girl Who Sculptured Lincoln.* New York: Holt, Rinehart & Winston, 1963.

Hall, Henry. *History of Auburn.* Auburn: Dennis Bro's, 1869.

Hammond, Bray. *Banks and Politics in America: From the Revolution to the Civil War.* Princeton, New Jersey: Princeton University Press, 1957.

Hammond, John L. *The Politics of Benevolence: Revival Religion and American Voting Behavior.* Norwood, New Jersey: Ablex Publishing Corporation, 1979.

Hanson, Joseph Mills. *The Conquest of the Missouri: Being the Story of the Life and Exploits of Grant Marsh.* New York: Murray Hills Books, 1946.

Hardman, Keith J. *Charles Grandison Finney, 1792–1875: Revivalist and Reformer.* Syracuse, New York: Syracuse University Press, 1987.

Haskell, Louise Porter. *Alexander Cheves Haskell: The Portrait of a Man.* Norwood, Massachusetts: Privately printed at the Plimpton Press, 1934.

Hassler, William W., ed. *The General to His Lady: The Civil War Letters of William Dorsey Pender to Fanny Pender.* Chapel Hill: University of North Carolina Press, 1966.

Havighurst, Walter. *Annie Oakley of the Wild West.* New York: Macmillan, 1954.

Hedren, Paul L. *First Scalp for Custer: The Skirmish at Warbonnet Creek, Nebraska, July 17, 1876, with a Short History of the Warbonnet Battlefield.* Glendale, California: Arthur H. Clarke, 1980.

Hellerstein, Erna O., Leslie P. Hume, and Karen M. Offen, eds. *Victorian Woman: A Documentary Account of Women's Lives in Nineteenth-Century England, France, and the United States.* Stanford, California: Stanford University Press, 1981.

Hodgson, Godfrey. *The Colonel: The Life and Wars of Henry Stimson, 1867–1950.* New York: Alfred A. Knopf, 1990.

Hofling, Charles. *Custer and the Little Big Horn—A Psychobiographical Inquiry.* Detroit: Wayne State University Press, 1981.

Hoig, Stan. *The Battle of the Washita: The Sheridan-Custer Indian Campaign of 1867–69.* Garden City, New York: Doubleday, 1976.

———. *The Peace Chiefs of the Cheyennes.* Norman: University of Oklahoma Press, 1980.

Hood, Edwin Paxton. *The Uses of Biography: Romantic, Philosophic, and Didactic.* London: Partridge and Oakey, 1852.

Horan, James D. *The Life and Art of Charles Schreyvogel: Painter-Historian of the Indian-Fighting Army of the American West.* New York: Crown Publishers, 1969.

Houghton, Walter E. *The Victorian Frame of Mind, 1830–1870.* New Haven: Yale University Press, 1957.

Howard, Hamilton Gay. *Civil-War Echoes: Character Sketches and State Secrets.* Washington, D.C.: Howard Publishing Company, 1907.

Hunt, Frazier. *Custer: The Last of the Cavaliers.* New York: Cosmopolitan Book Corporation, 1928.

Hutton, Paul A. *Phil Sheridan and His Army.* Lincoln: University of Nebraska Press, 1985.

Hutton, Paul Andrew, ed. *The Custer Reader.* Lincoln: University of Nebraska Press, 1992.

———. *Soldiers West: Biographies from the Military Frontier.* Lincoln: University of Nebraska Press.

Hyde, George. *Red Cloud's Folk: A History of the Oglala Sioux Indians.* Norman: University of Oklahoma Press, 1937.

Jackson, Donald. *Custer's Gold: The United States Cavalry Expedition of 1874.* New Haven: Yale University Press, 1966.

Jackson, Kenneth T. *Crabgrass Frontier: The Suburbanization of the United States.* New York: Oxford University Press, 1985.

James, Edward T., Janet Wilson James, and Paul S. Boyer, eds. *Notable American Women 1607–1950: A Biographical Dictionary.* 3 vols. Cambridge, Massachusetts: Harvard University Press, 1971.

Jeffrey, Julie Roy. *Converting the West: A Biography of Narcissa Whitman.* Norman: University of Oklahoma Press, 1991.

———. *Frontier Women: The Trans-Mississippi West, 1840–1880.* New York: Hill and Wang, 1979.

Johannsen, Albert. *The House of Beadle and Adams and Its Dime and Nickel Novels.* 3 vols. Norman: University of Oklahoma Press, 1950–1952.

Johnson, Dorothy M. *Some Went West.* New York: Dodd, Mead, 1965.

Johnson, Robert U. *Remembered Yesterdays.* Boston: Little, Brown, 1923.

Johnson, Virginia Weisel. *The Unregimented General: A Biography of Nelson A. Miles.* Boston: Houghton Mifflin, 1962.

Jones, Douglas C. *The Treaty of Medicine Lodge.* Norman: University of Oklahoma Press, 1966.

Kaplan, Justin. *Mr. Clemens and Mark Twain.* New York: Simon and Schuster, 1966.

Kasper, Shirl. *Annie Oakley.* Norman: University of Oklahoma Press, 1992.

Kelley, Mary. *Private Woman, Public Stage: Literary Domesticity in Nineteenth-Century America.* New York: Oxford University Press, 1984.

Kellogg, Clara Louise. *Memoirs of an American Prima Donna.* New York: G. P. Putnam's Sons, 1913.

Kessler-Harris, Alice. *Out to Work: A History of Wage-Earning Women in the United States.* New York: Oxford University Press, 1982.

Kidd, James H. *Personal Recollections of a Cavalryman.* Ionia: Sentinel Printing, 1908.

King, Charles. *A Soldier's Secret: A Story of the Sioux War of 1890; and An Army Portia.* Philadelphia: Lippincott, 1893.

Kingsley, Charles. *His Letters and Memoirs of His Life.* Edited by his wife. 2 vols. London: Henry J. King, 1877.

The Kingsleys: A Biographical Anthology. Compiled by Elspeth Huxley. London: George Allen & Unwin, 1973.

Knight, Oliver. *Life and Manners in the Frontier Army.* Norman: University of Oklahoma Press, 1978.

Koller, Larry. *The Fireside Book of Guns.* New York: Simon and Schuster, 1959.

Kuhlman, Charles. *Did Custer Disobey Orders at the Battle of the Little Big Horn?* Harrisburg, Pennsylvania: Stackpole, 1957.

———. *Legend into History: The Custer Mystery.* Harrisburg, Pennsylvania: Stackpole, 1952.

Lazarus, Edward. *Black Hills/White Justice: The Sioux Nation Versus the United States, 1775 to the Present.* New York: Harper Collins, 1991.

Leech, Margaret. *Reveille in Washington, 1860–1865.* New York: Harper's, 1941.

Leckie, William H. *The Military Conquest of the Southern Plains.* Norman: University of Oklahoma Press, 1963.

Leckie, William H., and Shirley A. Leckie. *Unlikely Warriors: General Benjamin H. Grierson and His Family.* Norman: University of Oklahoma Press, 1984.

Leonard, Thomas C. *Above the Battle: War-Making in America from Appomattox to Versailles.* New York: Oxford University Press, 1978.

Lerner, Gerda. *The Majority Finds Its Past: Placing Women in History.* New York: Oxford University Press, 1979.

Linenthal, Edward Tabor. *Sacred Ground: Americans and Their Battlefields.* Urbana: University of Illinois Press, 1991.

Linderman, Gerald. *Embattled Courage: The Experience of Combat in the American Civil War.* New York: Free Press, 1987.

The Little Big Horn, 1876: The Official Communications, Documents and Reports. Compiled by Lloyd J. Overfield II. Lincoln: University of Nebraska Press, 1990.

Logan, Mary. *Reminiscences of the Civil War and Reconstruction.* Edited with an introduction by George Worthington Adams. Carbondale and Edwardville, Illinois: Southern Illinois University Press, 1970.

Longstreet, James. *From Manassas to Appomattox, Memoirs of the Civil War in America.* Philadelphia: J. B. Lippincott, 1896.

Lystra, Karen. *Searching the Heart: Women, Men, and Romantic Love in Nineteenth Century America.* New York: Oxford University Press, 1989.

McDannell, Colleen. *The Christian Home in Victorian America.* Bloomington: Indiana University Press, 1986.

McFeeley, William S. *Grant: A Biography.* New York: W. W. Norton, 1981.

McLaughlin, James. *My Friend the Indian.* Houghton Mifflin, 1910. Reprint, with introduction by Robert M. Utley. Lincoln: University of Nebraska Press, 1989.

McPherson, James. *Battle Cry of Freedom: The Civil War Era.* New York: Oxford University Press, 1988.

———. *Ordeal by Fire: The Civil War and Reconstruction.* New York: Alfred A. Knopf, 1982.

Mace, William H. *A School History of the United States.* Chicago: Rand, McNally, 1919.

Manion, John S. *Last Statement to Custer.* Monroe, Michigan: Monroe County Library System, 1983.

Marquis, Thomas B. *Custer on the Little Bighorn.* Lodi, California: End-Kian Publishing Co., 1969.

———. *Keep the Last Bullet for Yourself: The True Story of Custer's Last Stand.* New York: Reference Publications, 1976.

Massey, Mary Elizabeth. *Bonnet Brigades.* New York: Alfred A. Knopf, 1966.

Matthews, Jill Julius. *Good and Mad Women: The Historical Construction of Femininity in Twentieth Century Australia.* Sydney: George Allen and Unwin, 1984.

Mays, Victor. *Pathways to a Village.* Bronxville: Nebko Press, 1904.

Melosh, Barbara. *"The Physician's Hand": Work, Culture and Conflict in American Nursing.* Philadelphia: Temple University Press, 1982.

Merington, Marguerite, ed. *The Custer Story: The Life and Intimate Letters of*

General George A. Custer and His Wife Elizabeth. New York: Devon-Adair, 1950. Reprint. Lincoln: University of Nebraska Press, Bison Books, 1987.

Miles, Nelson A. *Personal Recollections and Observations of General Nelson A. Miles.* New York: Da Capo Press, 1969.

Miles, Nelson. *Serving the Republic: Memoirs of the Civil and Military Life of Nelson A. Miles.* New York: Harper & Brothers, 1911.

Miller, David Humphreys. *Custer's Fall: The Indian Side of the Story.* New York: Duell, Sloan and Pearce, 1957. Reprint. Lincoln: University of Nebraska Press, Bison Books, 1985.

Mills, Charles K. *Harvest of Barren Regrets: The Army Career of Frederick William Benteen, 1834–1898.* Glendale, California: Arthur H. Clark, 1985.

Monaghan, Jay. *Custer: The Life of General George Armstrong Custer.* Boston: Little, Brown, 1957. Reprint. Lincoln: University of Nebraska Press, Bison Books, 1971.

Motz, Marilyn Ferris. *True Sisterhood: Michigan Women and Their Kin, 1820–1920.* Albany: State University of New York Press, 1983.

Myres, Sandra L., ed. *Cavalry Wife: The Diary of Eveline M. Alexander, 1866–1867.* College Station: Texas A&M University Press, 1977.

Myres, Sandra L. *Westering Women and the Frontier Experience, 1800–1915.* Albuquerque: University of New Mexico Press, 1982.

Nevin, David. *The Soldiers.* New York: Time–Life Books, Old West Series, 1973.

Painter, Nell Irvin. *Standing at Armageddon: The United States, 1877–1919.* New York: W. W. Norton, 1987.

Parker, Watson. *Gold in the Black Hills.* Norman: University of Oklahoma Press, 1966.

Pascoe, Peggy. *Relations of Rescue: The Search for Female Moral Authority in the American West, 1874–1939.* New York: Oxford University Press, 1990.

Passing of the Great West: Papers of George Bird Grinnell. Edited by John R. Reiger. Norman: University of Oklahoma Press, 1985.

Peck, Paul R. *Landsmen of Monroe County: An Atlas and Plat of First Landowners of Monroe County, Michigan.* Liberty Town Press: Paul R. Peck, 1984.

Pioneer Collections: Report of the Pioneer Society of the State of Michigan. 2 vols. 2d ed. Lansing: Robert Smith Printing Co., 1901.

Pohanka, Brian. *A Summer on the Plains, 1870: From the Diary of Annie Gibson Roberts.* Mattituck, New Jersey: J. M. Carroll, 1983.

Pomeroy, Earl. *In Search of the Golden West: The Tourist in Western America.* New York: Alfred A. Knopf, 1957.

Pope-Hennessy, Una. *Canon Charles Kingsley: A Biography.* New York: Macmillan, 1949.

Porter, Joseph C. *Paper Medicine Man: John Gregory Bourke and His American West.* Norman: University of Oklahoma Press, 1986.

Powell, Peter J. *Secret Medicine.* 2 vols. Norman: University of Oklahoma Press, 1969.

Pratt, Fletcher. *Ordeal by Fire: A Short History of the Civil War.* 1948. Reprint. New York: W. Morrow in association with Harper & Row, 1966.

Private Theodore Ewert's Diary of the Black Hills Expedition of 1824. Edited by John M. Carroll and Dr. Lawrence A. Frost. Piscataway, New Jersey: CRI Books, 1976.

Prucha, Francis Paul. *Indian Policy in the United States: Historical Essays.* Lincoln: University of Nebraska Press, 1981.

———. *American Indian Policy in Crisis: Christian Reformers and the Indian, 1865–1900.* Norman: University of Oklahoma Press, 1976.

———. *The Indians in American Society: From the Revolutionary War to the Present.* Berkeley: University of California Press, 1985.

Raffell, Burton. *Politicians, Poets, and Con Men: Emotional History in Late Victorian America.* Hamden, Connecticut: Archon Books, 1986.

Randell, William Pierce. *Centennial: American Life in 1876.* Philadelphia: Chilton Book Company, 1969.

Reid, Whitelaw. *Ohio in the War: Her Statesmen, Generals, and Soldiers.* 2 vols. New York: Moore, Wilstach & Baldwin, 1868.

The Reno Court of Inquiry: The Chicago Times Account. Fort Collins, Colorado: Old Army Press, 1983.

Richardson, Albert D. *A Personal History of Ulysses S. Grant.* Hartford, Connecticut: American Publishing, 1902.

Riley, Glenda. *The Female Frontier: A Comparative View of Women on the Prairie and the Plains.* Lawrence: University Press of Kansas, 1988.

———. *Women and Indians on the Frontier, 1825–1915.* Albuquerque: University of New Mexico Press, 1984.

Richter, William L. *The Army in Texas during Reconstruction, 1865–1870.* College Station: Texas A&M University Press, Military History Series, 1987.

Roe, Frances M. A. *Army Letters from an Officer's Wife, 1871–1914.* New York: Appleton, 1909. Reprint, with introduction by Sandra L. Myres. Lincoln: University of Nebraska Press, Bison Books, 1981.

Roll Call on the Little Big Horn, 28 June 1876. Compiled by John M. Carroll and Byron Price. Fort Collins, Colorado: Old Army Press, 1974.

Rosenberg, Bruce A. *Custer and the Epic of Defeat.* University Park: Pennsylvania State University Press, 1974.

Rothman, Ellen K. *Hearts and Hands: A History of Courtship in America.* New York: Basic Books, 1984.

Russell, Don. *Custer's Last.* Fort Worth: Amon Carter Museum of Western Art, 1968.

———. *The Lives and Legend of Buffalo Bill.* Norman: University of Oklahoma Press, 1973.

———. *The Wild West; or, a History of the Wild West Shows.* Fort Worth: Amon Carter Museum of Art, 1970.

Ryan, Mary. *Cradle of the Middle Class: The Family in Oneida County, New York, 1790–1865.* Cambridge: Cambridge University Press, 1981.

———. *The Empire of the Mother: American Writing about Domesticity, 1830–1860.* New York: Haworth Press, 1982.

Sandoz, Mari. *Cheyenne Autumn.* New York: McGraw-Hill, 1953.

Scott, Douglas D., and Richard A. Fox, Jr., with contributions by Dick Harmon. *Archaeological Insights in the Custer Battle: An Assessment of the 1984 Field Season.* Norman: University of Oklahoma Press, 1987.

Sears, Stephen W. *Landscape Turned Red: The Battle of Antietam.* New Haven: Ticknor & Fields, 1983.

Shattuck, Gardiner H., Jr. *A Shield and Hiding Place: The Religious Life of the Civil War Armies.* Macon, Georgia: Mercer University Press, 1987.

Sheridan, Philip H. *Personal Memoirs of P. H. Sheridan, General United States Army.* 2 vols. New York: Charles Webster, 1888.

Sherman, William T. *Memoirs of Gen. W. T. Sherman, Written by Himself.* 2 vols. New York: D. Appleton, 1875.

Sklar, Kathryn Kish. *Catharine Beecher: A Study in American Domesticity.* New Haven: Yale University Press, 1973.

Slotkin, Richard. *The Fatal Environment: The Myth of the Frontier in the Age of Industrialization, 1800–1890.* New York: Atheneum, 1985.

Smith, Henry Nash. *The Virgin Land: The American West as Symbol and Myth.* New York: Vintage Books, 1950.

Smith, Sherry L. *The View from Officers' Row: Army Perceptions of Western Indians.* Tucson: University of Arizona Press, 1990.

Smith-Rosenberg, Carroll. *Religion and the Rise of the American City: The New York City Mission Movement, 1812–1870.* Ithaca: Cornell University Press, 1971.

Stanley, D. L. *Personal Memoirs of Major-General D.L. Stanley, U.S.A.* Cambridge, Massachusetts: Harvard University Press, 1917.

Stanley, Henry M. *My Early Travels and Adventures in America and Asia.* 2 vols. New York: Charles Scribner's Sons, 1905.

Stallard, Patricia Y. *Glittering Misery: Dependents of the Indian Fighting Army.* Fort Collins, Colorado: Old Army Press, Presidio Press, 1978.

Starr, Stephen Z. *The Union Cavalry in the Civil War.* Vol. 1, *From Fort Sumter to Gettysburg, 1861–1863,* and Vol. 2, *The War in the East: From Gettysburg to Appomattox, 1863–1865.* Baton Rouge: Louisiana State University Press, 1979 and 1981.

Steckmesser, Kent L. *The Western Hero in History and Legend.* Norman: University of Oklahoma Press, 1965.

Stern, Madeleine R. *We the Women: Career Firsts of Nineteenth-Century American Women.* New York: Schulte Publishing Company, 1963.

Stevenson, Louise L. *The Victorian Homefront: American Thought and Culture, 1860–1880.* New York: Twayne Publishers, 1991.

Stewart, Edgar I. *Custer's Luck.* Norman: University of Oklahoma Press, 1955.

———. *Penny-an-Acre Empire in the West.* Norman: University of Oklahoma Press, 1968.

Strathern, Marilyn. *The Gender of the Gift: Problems with Women and Problems with Society in Melanesia.* Berkeley: University of California Press, 1988.

Taylor, Graham D. *The New Deal and American Indian Tribalism: The Administration of the Indian Reorganization Act, 1834–45.* Lincoln: University of Nebraska Press, 1980.

Thirteenth Annual Catalogue of the Officers and Pupils of the Young Ladies' Seminary and Collegiate Institute of Monroe City, Michigan. Monroe: N. P. Hampton, Printer, 1863.

Thomas, Emory M. *Bold Dragoon: The Life of J. E. B. Stuart.* New York: Harper & Row, 1986.

Thorp, Margaret F. *Charles Kingsley, 1819–1875.* New York: Octagon Books, 1969.

Trenholm, Virginia Cole. *The Arapahoes, Our People.* Norman: University of Oklahoma Press, 1973.

Uffelman, Larry K. *Charles Kingsley.* Boston: Twayne Publishers, a division of G. K. Hall, 1979.

Urwin, Gregory W. *Custer Victorious: The Civil War Battles of General George Armstrong Custer.* East Brunswick, New Jersey: Associated University Presses, 1983.

Utley, Robert M. *Cavalier in Buckskin: George Armstrong Custer and the Western Military Frontier.* Norman: University of Oklahoma Press, Oklahoma Western Biographies, 1988.

———. *Custer and the Great Controversy: The Origin and Development of a Legend.* Pasadena, California: Westernlore Press, 1980.

———. *Frontier Regulars: The United States Army and the Indian, 1866–1891.* New York: Macmillan, Wars of the United States, 1973.

———. *The Indian Frontier of the American West, 1846–1890*. Albuquerque: University of New Mexico Press, 1985.

———. *The Last Days of the Sioux Nation*. New Haven: Yale University Press, 1963.

Utley, Robert M., ed. *Life in Custer's Cavalry: Diaries and Letters of Albert and Jennie Barnitz, 1867–1868*. New Haven: Yale University Press, 1977.

Van de Water, Frederic F. *Glory-Hunter: A Life of General Custer*. Indianapolis: Bobbs-Merrill, 1934.

Vestal, Stanley. (Walter Campbell). *Sitting Bull: Champion of the Sioux*. New York: Houghton Mifflin, 1932. Reprint. Norman: University of Oklahoma Press, 1957.

Vielé, Teresa Griffin. *"Following the Drum": A Glimpse of Frontier Life*. Lincoln: University of Nebraska Press, 1984.

Wagner, Glendolin Damon. *Old Neutriment*. Boston: Ruth Hill, 1934. Reprint. Lincoln: University of Nebraska Press, Bison Books, 1989.

Wallace, Charles B. *Custer's Ohio Boyhood*. Freeport, Ohio: Freeport Press, 1978.

Weintraub, Stanley. *Victoria: An Intimate Biography*. New York: Truman Talley Books/E. P. Dutton, 1987.

Westbrook, Perry. *John Burroughs*. New York: Twayne Publishers, n.d.

Wheeler, Candace. *Yesterdays in a Busy Life*. New York: Harper and Brothers, 1918.

White, G. Edward. *The Eastern Establishment and the Western Experience: The West of Frederic Remington, Theodore Roosevelt and Owen Wister*. New Haven: Yale University Press, 1968. Reprint. Austin: University of Texas Press, 1989.

Whittaker, Frederick. *The Complete Life of Gen. George A. Custer*. New York: Sheldon & Company, 1876.

Wiesenburger, Francis Phelps. *Idol of the West: The Fabulous Career of Rollin Mallory Daggett*. Syracuse, New York: Syracuse University Press, 1965.

Wilcox, Ella. *Custer and Other Poems*. Chicago: W. B. Conkey, 1986.

Williams, E. Gray, and Ethel W. Williams. *First Land Owners of Monroe County, Michigan*. Kalamzoo, Michigan, 1968.

Wilson, Dorothy Clarke. *Lone Woman: The Story of Elizabeth Blackwell, the First Woman Doctor*. Boston: Little, Brown, 1970.

Wilson, James Harrison. *Under the Old Flag*. 2 vols. New York: D. Appleton and Company, 1912.

Wing, Talcott E., ed. *History of Monroe County Michigan*. New York: Munsell and Company, 1890.

Wisenburger, Francis Phelps. *Idol of the West: The Fabulous Career of Rollin Mallory Daggett*. Syracuse, New York: Syracuse University Press, 1965.

With Custer in '74: James Calhoun's Diary of the Black Hills Expedition. Edited by Lawrence A. Frost. Provo, Utah: Brigham Young University Press, 1979.

Bibliography

Woloch, Nancy. *Women and the American Experience.* New York: Alfred A. Knopf, 1984.

Woolf, Virginia. *A Room of One's Own.* New York: Harcourt Brace Jovanovich, 1957.

Wooster, Robert. *The Military and United States Indian Policy, 1865–1903.* New Haven: Yale University Press, 1988.

Works Projects Administration. *New York: A Guide to the Empire State.* New York: Oxford University Press, 1940.

NEWSPAPERS AND MAGAZINES

Army and Navy Journal

Billings Gazette

Blue and Gray Magazine

Boston Daily Traveler

Boston Gazette

Cadiz Republican

Century Magazine

Cheyenne Daily Leader

Chicago Dial

Chicago Inter-Ocean

Chicago Sunday Times Herald

Chicago Tribune

Collier's

Cosmopolitan Magazine

Dallas Morning News

Daytona News and Observer

Denver Rocky Mountain News

Detroit Free Press

Detroit Journal

Detroit News Tribune

Detroit Post and Tribune

Detroit Tribune

Harper's Bazaar

Harper's Monthly Magazine

Harper's Weekly

Helena Daily Herald

Iowa State Register

Lippincott's Monthly Magazine

(London) *Academy*

(London) *Saturday Review*

(Monroe) *Commercial Advertiser*

Monroe Democrat

London Spectator

McClure

Monroe Commercial

Monroe Evening News

Monroe Monitor

The Nation

New York Herald

New York Herald Tribune

New York Sun

New York Independent

New York Times

New York Tribune

New York World

North American Review

Outlook Magazine

Philadelphia Times

Philadelphia Inquirer

Pueblo Chieftain

Record-Commercial

Rocky Mountain News

(Saint Louis) *Globe Democrat*

San Francisco Bulletin

Saturday Evening Post

Scribner's Magazine

St. Paul's Pioneer Press   *Toledo Journal*
St. Nicholas   *Topeka Commonwealth*
Tecumseh [Michigan] *News*   *Weekly Iowa State Register*
Toledo Blade   *Worcester Sunday Telegram*

UNPUBLISHED MATERIALS

Isaac, Rhys. "The Enlightenment and the Problems of Systematizing the Plantation." Re-creating the World of the Virginia Plantation conference held at
Charlottesville, Virginia, May 31–June 2, 1990.

Jessen, Patricia M. "Fort Abraham Lincoln, Commanding Officer's Residence."
Historic Structure Report. Prepared for the Fort Abraham Lincoln Foundation. 10 August 1987.

Shook, Robert W. "Federal Occupation and Administration of Texas, 1865–1870."
Unpublished Ph.D. diss., North Texas State University, 1970.

Zophy, Angela Marie Howard. "For the Improvement of My Sex: Sarah Josepha
Hale's Editorship of *Godey's Lady's Book*, 1837–1877." Unpublished Ph.D. diss.,
Ohio State University, 1978.

Index